*lonely planet*

# Eastern Europe

Mark Baker, Greg Bloom, Marc Di Duca, Peter Dragicevich, Anita Isalska, Tom Masters, Hugh McNaughtan, Lorna Parkes, Leonid Ragozin, Tim Richards, Simon Richmond, Tamara Sheward

## PLAN YOUR TRIP

## ON THE ROAD

LAKE BALATON REGION (P193), HUNGARY

PRAGUE (P136), CZECH REPUBLIC

PGABORPHOTOS / SHUTTERSTOCK ©

SORIN COLAC / SHUTTERSTOCK ©

EMI CRISTEA / SHUTTERSTOCK ©

# Contents

DUBROVNIK (P126),
CROATIA

# ON THE ROAD

LMSPENCER / SHUTTERSTOCK ©

SOFIA (P88), BULGARIA

# Contents

BAY OF KOTOR (P272), MONTENEGRO

## SURVIVAL GUIDE

# Welcome to Eastern Europe

*From soaring mountains to golden sands, Eastern Europe reveals a tapestry of quaint and contemporary cultures – always with enough rough edges to keep you intrigued.*

## Cultural Explosion

Eastern Europe is a warehouse of culture, whether your preference is fine arts or folk singing. Cities such as Prague, St Petersburg and Budapest are effortlessly elegant, housing remarkable art collections in palatial surrounds. Some locations are akin to open-air museums, like Moscow's vast Red Square and the art nouveau architecture across Rīga. For every age-old powerhouse of classical music and opera, you'll also discover a plucky up-and-comer, building a reputation for avant-garde nightlife (Belgrade) or gritty galleries (Cluj-Napoca).

## Spectacular Scenery

Sandy beaches, windswept plains, rugged mountain ranges – Eastern Europe has it all. Glide down the Danube River, bob across Macedonia's Lake Ohrid or splash around in Hungary's Lake Balaton. Gulp down fresh air and solitude in Albania's Accursed Mountains, Transylvania's crisscrossing ranges, or the High Tatras, which rumble along the Poland–Slovakia border. Test the white-water in Slovenia's Triglav National Park, or explore canyons and caverns in Montenegro or Bosnia and Hercegovina. You can be exhilarated or lulled into contentment exploring Eastern Europe's great outdoors.

## Historic Overload

History surrounds you in Eastern Europe. Gaze at St Basil's Cathedral on Moscow's Red Square, a legacy of Ivan the Terrible's brutal reign; cross the bridge where Archduke Ferdinand was assassinated in Sarajevo; feel the echo of the Romanian Revolution on Bucharest's Revolution Square or more recent tragic events on Kyiv's Maydan Nezalezhnosti. Stroll even further back in time through the remains of Diocletian's Palace in Split, Croatia; or through Sofia and Plovdiv in Bulgaria, where ancient ruins continue to be unearthed.

## Folklore & Festivals

Eastern Europe is the heartland of Orthodox Christianity: the religion's rites permeate many aspects of cultural life, particularly in Russia and Ukraine. Roman Catholic, Muslim and Jewish communities add their own influences, while whiffs of pagan tradition can be felt in the Baltics. Baltica International Folklore Festivals, Slovakia's Východná and Bulgaria's Rose Festival are captivating events, full of insight into age-old Europe. Traditional woodcarvers still hunch over workbenches in Slovakia, while glass icons continue to be painted in Romania, allowing travellers to take home a piece of Eastern European craft.

# Why I Love Eastern Europe

By Anita Isalska, Writer

Eastern Europe is peppered with the unexpected. Gothic spires and Lego-block buildings share the same streets. Eerie communist-era wrecks glower over beaches and walking trails. I'm fascinated by how this region incorporates a bloody, border-shifting past into the spirited present – often with dry humour. Soviet-themed cafes from Moscow to Chişinău balance irony with nostalgia, and Budapest's crumbling buildings have morphed into ruin bars. Eastern Europe revives not only dilapidated neighbourhoods, but raises entire cities from rubble. When proud, irrepressible Eastern Europe gets under your skin, it's impossible to resist exploring.

**For more about our writers, see p480**

Above: State Hermitage Museum (p351), St Petersburg, Russia

# Eastern Europe

0 ———— 250 miles
0 ———— 500 km

**St Petersburg, Russia**
Imperial palaces packed with art (p347)

**Rīga, Latvia**
Art-nouveau architecture and charming streets (p214)

**Moscow, Russia**
Stand at Russia's beating, brutal heart – Red Square (p336)

**Prague, Czech Republic**
Experience dawn on the Charles Bridge (p136)

NORWAY
Oslo

SWEDEN
Stockholm

FINLAND
Helsinki
Narva
Tallinn
ESTONIA
Hiiumaa
Pärnu
Tartu
Saaremaa

St Petersburg
Lake Ladoga
Gulf of Finland 60°N

RUSSIA
Moscow
Volga
Don

DENMARK
Copenhagen

GERMANY
Berlin

Gulf of Bothnia
Åland
Gotland
Öland
Gulf of Riga
LATVIA
Rīga
Ventspils
Liepāja
Rēzekne
Daugavpils
Šiauliai
Vitsebsk
Mahilieu
Minsk
BELARUS
Homel

BALTIC SEA
Bornholm
Klaipėda
Curonian Spit
Kaliningrad
RUSSIA
Suwałki
Olsztyn
Kaunas
Vilnius
LITHUANIA
Nemunas
Hrodna
Brest
Kovel

Rügen
Koszalin
Szczecin
Gdańsk
Białystok
Warsaw
POLAND
Lublin
Zamość
Chernihiv
Sumy

Zielona Góra
Poznań
Łódź
Kielce
Vistula

Wrocław
Odra

Ústi Nad Labem
Plzeň
Elbe

Skagerrak
Kattegak
Lake Vänern

15°E
20°E
10°E
55°N

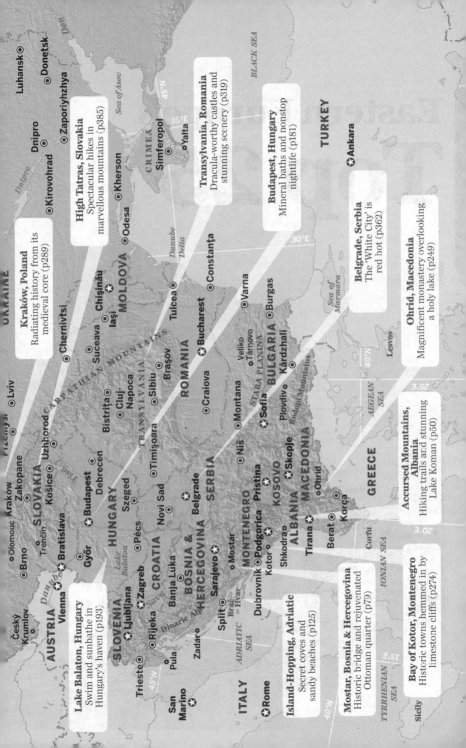

# Eastern Europe's
# Top 25

**1**

## Budapest, Hungary

**1** Straddling the romantic Danube River, with the Buda Hills to the west and the start of the Great Plain to the east, Budapest (p181) is one of Europe's most beautiful cities. Its famous thermal baths huff steam, the stately architecture is second to none, while museums and churches brim with treasures. Its active cultural life unfolds to a backdrop of verdant parks and pleasure boats gliding up and down the Danube Bend. Meanwhile, a diverse social scene, with coffee houses, intimate wine spots and rambunctious 'ruin bars', throbs until dawn.

## Island-Hopping, Adriatic, Croatia

**2** Board a boat and zoom past some of Croatia's 1244 islands, strung like jewels along the Adriatic coast. Drop anchor for golden shores, glide past rocky coves, and look out for a beach of your own (only 50 islands are inhabited), such as one of the Pakleni Islands (p125). Travelling by sea is the most thrilling way to experience the Adriatic, whether it's a short jaunt from Dubrovnik or overnight rides along the length of the coast. If you have cash to splash, take it up a couple of notches and charter a sailboat to island-hop in style.

## Prague, Czech Republic

**3** The Czech capital (p136) is a near-perfectly preserved museum of European architecture through the ages. From the Old Town Square, across the Charles Bridge (pictured) and up to Prague Castle, it's almost as if a 14th-century metropolis has been transported in time and plunked down in the heart of modern Europe. After you've meandered the alleyways, neck sore from craning to spy the statues and gargoyles, retire to a local pub for some Czech beer – the country's pride and joy.

## Castles & Mountains of Transylvania, Romania

**4** Fiends from both fiction and history enjoy eternal repose in this Romanian region (p319). Castles nested in the Carpathian Mountains inspired writer Bram Stoker to set his *Dracula* novel in Transylvania. The region was also a stomping ground for the historical Dracula, aka Vlad the Impaler. Bran Castle (pictured), south of Braşov, is suitably vampiric, but our favourite haunt is 13th-century Râşnov fortress. If (unlike the count) you don't shrink from sunlight, Transylvania is also ideal for hiking, biking and skiing.

## Bay of Kotor, Montenegro

**5** There's a sense of secrecy and mystery to the Bay of Kotor (p272). Grey mountains rise steeply from steely-blue waters, protectively hugging the inner bay. Here, ancient stone settlements cling to the shoreline, with the old alleyways of Kotor concealed in its innermost reaches behind hefty stone walls. It's a majestic, timeless view: a fusion of fjord-like cliffs dropping to cobalt water, and the warm-hued stone of medieval streets and Venetian palaces. And life here is exuberantly Mediterranean, lived full of passion on these time-worn streets.

## Walking the Old City Walls, Dubrovnik, Croatia

**6** History is unfurled from the battlements of Dubrovnik's spectacular city walls (p126). No visit is complete without a leisurely stroll along these ramparts, the finest in the world and Dubrovnik's main claim to fame. Built between the 9th and 16th centuries, the walls are still remarkably intact. Vistas over terracotta rooftops and the Adriatic Sea are sublime, especially at sunset. The views may even look a little familiar, thanks to Dubrovnik's starring role in the fantasy TV series *Game of Thrones*.

## Hiking the High Tatras, Slovakia

**7** The rocky peaks of the High Tatras (p386) are the highest in the Carpathians, soaring over 2500m. But hiking this impressive little range doesn't necessarily demand Olympian effort. From Starý Smokovec you can ride a funicular to Hrebienok, the starting point for many mid-elevation trails among thick forest and yawning valleys. Stop at a log-cabin hikers' hut, drink in a cold beer along with the views, and you can still trundle down to another of the Tatras' dinky resort towns in time for dinner.

## Art Nouveau Architecture, Rīga, Latvia

**8** In between cobblestones and Gothic spires, Latvia's capital, Rīga (p214), dazzles visitors with art nouveau architecture. Over 750 buildings (more than any other city in Europe) boast this style – a menagerie of mythical beasts, twisting flora, goddesses and goblins, often set to vibrant colours and layer-cake roofs. Rīga's compelling jigsaw puzzle of buildings propels you between elaborate mansions, weathered apartments, and steaming coffee houses tucked behind pastel-painted facades.

7

PGABORPHOTOS / SHUTTERSTOCK ©

ALEX ALEKSEEV / SHUTTERSTOCK ©

## Lake Balaton, Hungary

**9** Hungary's 'sea' (and central Europe's largest freshwater lake) is where the populace comes in summertime to sun, swim and try stand-up paddleboarding. The quieter side of Lake Balaton (p193) mixes sizzling beaches and oodles of fun on the water with historic waterside towns such as Keszthely and Balatonfüred. Tihany, a protected peninsula jutting 4km into the lake, is home to a stunning abbey church, and Hévíz boasts a thermal length where you can bathe even when it's snowing.

## Moscow's Red Square, Russia

**10** With the gravitational pull of a black hole, Red Square (p337) sucks in every visitor to Russia's capital, leaving them slack-jawed with wonder. Standing on the rectangular cobblestoned expanse – surrounded by the candy-coloured swirls of the cupolas atop St Basil's Cathedral (pictured), the red-star-tipped towers of the Kremlin, Lenin's squat granite mausoleum, the handsome red-brick facade of the State History Museum, and GUM, a grand emporium of consumption – you are literally at the centre of Russia's modern history.

## State Hermitage Museum, St Petersburg, Russia

**11** Little can prepare you for the scale of the exhibits, nor for their quality at Russia's most famous museum (p351). Within lies an almost-unrivalled history of Western art, including a staggering number of Rembrandts, Rubens, Picassos and Matisses. In addition, there are superb antiquities, sculptures and jewellery on display. If so much finery overloads your senses, content yourself with wandering through the Winter Palace (pictured), home of the Romanovs until 1917.

## Mostar, Bosnia & Hercegovina

**12** If the 1993 bombardment of the iconic 16th-century stone bridge (pictured) in Mostar (p79) underlined the heartbreaking pointlessness of Yugoslavia's brutal civil war, its reconstruction has proved symbolic of a peaceful post-conflict era. The Ottoman quarter has been convincingly rebuilt and is once again a delight to explore. Though occasional bombed-out buildings interrupt Mostar's enchanting atmosphere, many of these damaged husks now feel like an organic part of the townscape.

## Belgrade Nightlife, Serbia

**13** Brassy Belgrade (p362) may seem a million light years away from hedonistic hot spots like Barcelona and Berlin. But somehow, the sociable Serbian spirit, carpe-diem attitude and numerous nightspots have propelled this gritty city to fame as one of the top party destinations in the world. Belgrade by night (and well past dawn) pulsates to the beat of countless clubs, bars and *splavovi* (floating pleasure pontoons). Ask locals for their favourite haunts, follow the crowds or, better yet, time your visit for a gig or festival.

## Kraków, Poland

**14** As popular as it is, Poland's former royal capital (p289) never disappoints. An aura of history radiates from the sloping stone buttresses of medieval buildings in the Old Town. The enormous main square (pictured) is enlivened by flower sellers, a bustling market hall, and the clippety-clop of horses and carriages, which ferry enraptured tourists beneath the spires. Throw in the extremes of a castle complex with remarkable art and subterranean chambers, plus the low-key chic of revived Jewish quarter Kazimierz, and it's a city you'll want to seriously get to know.

## Ohrid, Macedonia

**15** Whether you come to sublime, hilly Ohrid (p249) for its sturdy medieval castle, to wander the stone laneways of its Old Town or to gaze at Plaošnik, its restored multidome basilica, every visitor pauses at the Church of Sveti Jovan (pictured) at Kaneo, set high on a bluff overlooking Lake Ohrid and its popular beaches. It's the prime spot for absorbing the town's beautiful architecture, idling sunbathers and distant fishing skiffs – all framed by the rippling green of Mt Galičica to the southeast and the endless expanse of lake.

TOMAS LABURDA / SHUTTERSTOCK ©

### Hiking, Accursed Mountains, Albania

**16** Albania's natural landscape is its greatest drawcard. It's best experienced in the country's north, where the Accursed Mountains (p50) offer superb hiking and traditional villages that still look like they're living in the 19th century, plus there's a ferry ride across stunning Lake Koman. The most popular hike is the day trek from Valbona to Theth, which shouldn't be missed. For long-distance trekkers, the Peaks of the Balkans Trail winds through not only Albania but the mountains of Kosovo and Montenegro.

### Cycling the Curonian Spit, Lithuania

**17** Allegedly created by the giantess Neringa, the fragile sliver of land forming the Curonian Spit (p237) juts out into the Baltic Sea. Its celestial origins infuse it with other-worldly ambience, heightened by folkloric wood carvings and the giant sand dunes that earned it the nickname 'Lithuania's Sahara'. The best way to explore is by bicycle, riding through dense pine forest from one cheerful village to the next, stopping to sample freshly smoked fish, or – if you're lucky – to glimpse elusive wildlife: elk, deer and wild boar.

### Wine Tasting, Moldova

**18** Only dedicated oenophiles are aware of Eastern Europe's greatest wine secret: little-touristed Moldova has the ideal conditions for growing grapes, and offers some of the region's best wines. Whites include chardonnay, riesling and the local Fetească Albă, while cabernet sauvignon, merlot and Fetească Neagră are all popular for reds. The most renowned wineries are Cricova and Mileştii Mici (pictured; p265), with underground cellars that stretch for hundreds of kilometres. Tour them by car, or better yet linger in their chandeliered chambers for a tasting session.

## Tallinn, Estonia

**19** The Estonian capital (p164) is rightly famous for its Old Town, a maze of intertwining alleys, picturesque courtyards and red-rooftop views from medieval turrets. But be sure to step outside its walls and experience the other treasures of Tallinn. No visit is complete without sampling the city's stylish restaurants, its buzzing Scandinavian-influenced design community, and its ever growing number of galleries. Contemporary architecture and venerable domed churches form an enthralling contrast in this city perched by the Baltic Sea.

## Black Sea Beaches, Bulgaria

**20** Bulgaria has almost 400km of sparkling Black Sea coastline (p102), dotted with resorts for every taste (and a fair few hidden beaches, too). Sunning yourself along the so-called Bulgarian Riviera is easy on the wallet and there is a stretch of sand to suit every taste. Party-hard playgrounds like Sunny Beach attract international tourists keen on water sports and nightlife, cosmopolitan Varna offers long, white-sand beaches and parks, while the heritage-rich harbours of Nesebâr (pictured) and Sozopol dish up culture by the spadeful.

19

20

## Minsk, Belarus

**21** Minsk (p60) is no typical Eastern European capital. Almost totally destroyed in WWII, the ancient city underwent a Stalinist rebirth in the 1950s and is now a masterpiece of socialist architecture. Minsk is a riveting starting point to explore the Soviet time capsule that is modern Belarus. While its initial appearance is severe and austere, a few days in Minsk allows you to feel the city's pulse: lofty lookouts gazing across a bizarre and compelling urban skyline, green spaces galore, and plenty of burst-at-the-seams Belarusian cuisine. National Library of Belarus

## Český Krumlov, Czech Republic

**22** Showcasing a magnificent Old Town, Český Krumlov (p150) is the most popular day trip from Prague. But a rushed few hours navigating the town's meandering lanes and audacious clifftop castle sells short the CK experience. Stay at least one night to lose yourself in the Old Town's shape-shifting after-dark shadows and get cosy in riverside cafes and pubs. The following morning raft or canoe on the Vltava River, explore surrounding meadows by horse or mountain bike, or tour neighbouring towns.

## Mt Triglav & Vršič Pass, Slovenia

**23** For such a small country, Slovenia's got it all: quaint towns, epic lakes, great wines, a Venetian-inspired seashore and, most of all, mountains. The highest, Mt Triglav (p403) stands, at 2864m, particularly tall in local lore. Indeed, the saying goes that you're not really Slovene until you've climbed to the top of this triple-peaked mountain. If time is an issue and you're driving, head for the Vršič Pass: the highest road in Slovenia, it ducks and dives across the Julian Alps in one hair-raising, spine-tingling hour.

## Prizren, Kosovo

**24** Kosovo's most charming town is Prizren (p209), nestled in the valley of the Bistrica River and dominated by minarets and church towers. Despite the dark legacy of war, Prizren today is a progressive and upbeat sort of place, with one of Eastern Europe's best documentary film festivals, Dokufest, bringing a splash of international sophistication every summer. The rest of the year you can explore the town's rich heritage in the form of its hilltop fortress, grand mosques and ancient churches.

## Lviv, Ukraine

**25** Elegant and idyllic, Lviv (p419) is an island of sophistication in a post-Soviet sea. Ukraine's great hope for tourism is this moody city of arabica-scented coffee houses, verdant old parks, trundling trams and Austro-Hungarian manners. Tourists are beginning to wise up to Lviv, though it remains a haven, untouched by the crowds of Prague or Kraków. Melodiously accented Ukrainian provides the soundtrack while incense billows through medieval churches that miraculously avoided their dates with Soviet dynamite, and violin-toting schoolchildren compete for seats on buses with smiling nuns.

# Need to Know

**For more information, see Survival Guide (p425)**

## Currency

Euro (€) in Estonia, Kosovo, Latvia, Lithuania, Montenegro, Slovakia and Slovenia, local currency elsewhere.

## Language

Apart from national languages, Russian, German and English are also widely understood.

## Visas

EU, US, Canadian, Australian and NZ passport holders do not require a visa to visit most of the region. Visas are needed by all for Russia.

## Money

ATMS are common, credit and debit cards are accepted in cities and major towns. Always carry cash though.

## Mobile Phones

The GSM 900 network is used in the region. Coming from outside Europe it's usually worth buying a prepaid local SIM.

## Time

GMT/UTC plus one, two or three hours, depending on country.

## When to Go

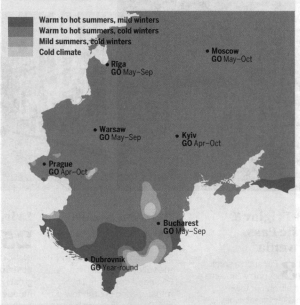

Warm to hot summers, mild winters
Warm to hot summers, cold winters
Mild summers, cold winters
Cold climate

Moscow
GO May–Oct

Rīga
GO May–Sep

Warsaw
GO May–Sep

Kyiv
GO Apr–Oct

Prague
GO Apr–Oct

Bucharest
GO May–Sep

Dubrovnik
GO Year-round

### High Season
(Jul–Aug)

➡ Expect high temperatures and long evenings.

➡ Hotels prices rise by up to 30% and you'll need to reserve in advance.

➡ Big draws such as Prague, Budapest and Kraków will be crowded, as will some hiking trails.

### Shoulder
(May–Jun, Sep–Oct)

➡ Crowds and prices drop off but weather remains pleasant.

➡ Spring, music and wine festivals unfold.

➡ Overall the best time to travel in Eastern Europe.

### Low Season
(Nov–Apr)

➡ Hotel prices drop to their lowest, except in ski zones.

➡ Days are short and weather is cold – in some places brutally so.

➡ Summer resorts are like ghost towns, while winter-sports areas fill to the brim.

## Useful Websites

**Lonely Planet** (www.lonely planet.com/europe) Destination information, hotel bookings, traveller forum and more.

**Deutsche Bahn** (www.bahn.de) The best online train timetable for the region.

**Like a Local** (www.likealocal guide.com) Free online guides to cities across the region, written by locals.

**Atlas Obscura** (www.atlas obscura.com) Crowd-sourced travel guide to offbeat attractions around the world; plenty on Eastern Europe.

**VisitEurope** (www.visiteurope. com) Info and inspiration for travel in 36 European countries.

**Spotted by Locals** (www.spot tedbylocals.com) Insider tips for cities across Europe.

## What to Take

**Flip-flops (thongs)** for overnight trains, hostel bathrooms and beaches

**Hiking boots** for treks and cobbled streets

**Earplugs and eyeshades** for hostels and overnight trains

**European plug adaptors**

**Unlocked mobile phone** to use local SIM cards

**Spork or cutlery** for hikes, markets and train picnics

## Exchange Rates

| AU | A$1 | €0.69 | R44 |
| --- | --- | --- | --- |
| CAN | C$1 | €0.71 | R45 |
| JPN | ¥100 | €0.81 | R52 |
| NZ | NZ$1 | €0.66 | R42 |
| UK | UK£1 | €1.18 | R75 |
| US | US$1 | €0.96 | R61 |

For current exchange rates, see www.xe.com

## Daily Costs

**Budget:
Less than €40**

➡ Hostel beds €10–25

➡ Admission to museums €1–15

➡ Canteen meals €3–6

➡ Beer €1.50–4

**Midrange:
€40–150**

➡ Midrange hotel €40

➡ Main meal in a decent restaurant from €10

➡ Inner-city taxi trip €10–15

➡ Half-day activity like horseriding or rafting €30–50

**Top End:
More than €150**

➡ Top-end hotel rooms per night from €100

➡ Swanky, big-city restaurant meal from €20

➡ Hire cars per day, around €30

➡ Private hiking or tour guide per day €75–150

## Accommodation

**Hotels** From Soviet-era behemoths to palatial five-star places.

**Guesthouses and pensions** Small, family-run, and generally good value.

**Hostels** From bare bones to hipster chic.

**Homestays and Farmstays** Find out how locals live.

**Camping grounds** Cheap, though quality is variable. Wild camping is usually forbidden.

**Mountain huts** Mattresses on floors or private rooms in no-frills lodges. They will always find room for hikers.

## Arriving in Eastern Europe

**Václav Havel Airport Prague** (p160; Prague) Airport Express buses cost 60Kč and run from 5am to 10pm, every 30 minutes, taking 35 minutes. Taxis cost from 500Kč to 650Kč.

**Domodedovo** and **Sheremetyevo airports** (p357; Moscow) Trains (R340–400) run from 5.30am to 12.30am, every 30 minutes, and take 40 minutes. Taxis cost R2000 to R2200 (R1500 to R1800 if booked in advance).

**Ferenc Liszt International Airport** (p190; Budapest) Minibuses, buses and trains to central Budapest run from 4am to midnight (350Ft to 3200Ft); taxis cost from 6500Ft.

## Getting Around

**Train** Connects nearly all major cities, but not all countries have straightforward train links to neighbours.

**Bus** Covers almost all of Eastern Europe; particularly useful for reaching remote areas.

**Car** Drive on the right. Main roads are generally good. Many car-rental companies limit which countries their vehicles can be taken to.

**Ferry** International sea services connect Baltic countries with Russia, while Danube ferries travel between Hungary and Slovakia.

**Plane** International flights connect most capitals to neighbouring countries and Western European hubs.

**Bicycle** Cycling infrastructure varies by country. Where bike-hire schemes exist, it's a great way to explore.

For much more on **getting around**, see p436

# If You Like...

## Old Towns

**Kraków, Poland** Arguably Eastern Europe's finest Old Town; the incredible Rynek Główny (Main Sq) shouldn't be missed. (p289)

**Prague, Czech Republic** Fall instantly in love with the spiky spires and narrow lanes of the incredibly preserved Staré Město. (p136)

**Dubrovnik, Croatia** Prowl the city's fantastical defensive walls before strolling marble-paved Stradun down below. (p126)

**Vilnius, Lithuania** One of Europe's largest old towns offers cobbled streets, artists' workshops and countless church steeples. (p227)

**Tallinn, Estonia** As fairytale as they come, conical watchtowers guard the historic heart of Estonia's capital. (p164)

**Plovdiv, Bulgaria** A visual feast of cobbled lanes, Bulgarian National Revival–era mansions, boutique galleries and quirky bars. (p96)

**Lviv, Ukraine** Bookish coffee houses and well-worn shop fronts cluster beneath bell towers within this cosmopolitan city. (p419)

**Berat, Albania** White Ottoman houses on a rugged mountainside in this 'town of a thousand windows'. (p52)

## Coasts & Beaches

**Hvar Island, Croatia** This sun-dappled and herb-scented Adriatic isle is a jumping-off point for the Pakleni Islands. (p124)

**Curonian Spit, Lithuania** World Heritage sand dunes slide into bracing Baltic waters along this enchanting sliver of land. (p237)

**The Riviera, Albania** Gorgeous sandy beaches on Albania's fast-disappearing undeveloped coastline; enjoy it undisturbed outside high summer. (p54)

**Black Sea Coast, Bulgaria** The best beaches on the Black Sea, from Varna's big resorts to less hectic Sozopol. (p102)

**Jūrmala, Latvia** Dip into the spa scene at Soviet-era sanatoriums along the Baltic Riviera. (p221)

**Odesa, Ukraine** Stroll dishevelled promenades and join the tanning and party fest on a Black Sea beach. (p421)

## Castles & Palaces

**Bran Castle, Romania** This Transylvanian beauty looks straight out of a horror movie even if it has little to do with Dracula himself. (p322)

**Malbork Castle, Poland** Live out medieval fantasies at this whopping brick castle, founded by 13th-century Teutonic knights. (p307)

**Catherine Palace, Russia** Marvel at this glittering baroque palace, restored to tsarist splendour after destruction in WWII. (p353)

**Karlštejn Castle, Czech Republic** An apparition of fairy-tale Gothic, this Bohemian beauty near Prague makes for a great day trip. (p147)

**Ljubljana Castle, Slovenia** Amazing views from the watchtower and gourmet food in one of the city's top restaurants. (p398)

**Mir Castle, Belarus** A stocky castle painstakingly restored to 16th-century splendour, from gilded interiors to manicured grounds. (p66)

## Mountains & Hiking

**Slovenský Raj National Park, Slovakia** Waterfalls, gorges and thick forests decorate Slovakia's outstanding national park. (p390)

**Bulgaria's mountains** Don't miss the trails around stunning Rila Monastery or the beautiful Rodopi Mountains. (p95)

**Carpathian Mountains, Poland** Use Zakopane as a base for long walks, including to emerald-green Lake Morskie Oko. (p297)

**Tatras Mountains, Slovakia**
These snow-streaked Alpine peaks are bisected by one of Europe's loveliest long-distance hikes. (p385)

**Zlatibor, Serbia** Rolling hills and expansive views in this corner of western Serbia are ideal for gentle hikes and skiing. (p373)

**Apuseni Nature Park, Romania** Hike and clamber to cliffs and caves squirrelled beneath the forest-furred Apuseni Mountains. (p325)

## Historical Sites

**Diocletian's Palace, Croatia** Imposing Roman ruin in the beating heart of Split, encompassing 220 ancient buildings. (p120)

**Rila Monastery, Bulgaria** Heavenly, Unesco-listed monastery, dating back over 1000 years and an enduring stronghold of Bulgarian culture. (p95)

**Kremlin, Russia** The seat of power to medieval tsars and modern presidents alike is packed with incredible sights. (p336)

**Butrint, Albania** Ruins of an ancient Greek fortified city in a tranquil national-park location. (p53)

**Kalemegdan, Serbia** Destroyed over 40 times, this fortress was once squeezed between the Ottoman and Austro-Hungarian Empires. (p362)

**Pula Roman Amphitheatre, Croatia** Enormous limestone arena from the 1st century AD, which once seated 20,000 baying spectators. (p117)

PLAN YOUR TRIP IF YOU LIKE...

**Top:** Tatras Mountains (p385), Slovakia
**Bottom:** Inside the Catherine Palace (p353), Russia

## Spectacular Scenery

**Lake Koman Ferry, Albania** Witness the majesty of Albania's remote, mountainous north on this stunning ferry ride. (p50)

**Triglav National Park, Slovenia** A three-headed mountain presides over a swath of turquoise river gorges and placid meadows. (p407)

**Danube Delta, Romania** Wild, reedy wetlands teeming with birds where the Danube flows into the Black Sea. (p326)

**Hortobágy National Park, Hungary** Windswept grasslands speckled with long-horned cattle and occasional *csikósok* (cowboys). (p198)

## Food & Drink

**Hungarian cuisine** Savour the national dish, goulash, with gulps of blood-red wine in this gastronomically inclined country. (p201)

**Istrian delights, Croatia** Truffles, wild asparagus and fresh seafood are on the menu in Istria; there's also a superb local wine scene. (p115)

**Slow food, Macedonia** Homespun cooking, from paprika-tinged sausages to foraged mushrooms, is putting Macedonia firmly on the menu. (p254)

**Nordic cuisine, Estonia** Dip into cutting-edge Nordic cuisine at Ö and seasonal game at Rataskaevu 16. (p169)

**Wine tasting, Moldova** Sip a lesser-known vintage in plucky little Moldova, producer of world-class wines. (p265)

## Nightlife

**Belgrade, Serbia** One of the most exciting, vibrant – not to mention affordable – places to party until daybreak. (p362)

**Budapest, Hungary** Pop-up clubs in abandoned buildings have put the Hungarian capital's nightlife on par with Berlin. (p181)

**Moscow, Russia** Evolving into an essential stop on the clubber's world map, with bars and clubs aplenty. (p336)

**Cluj-Napoca, Romania** Cluj's historic backstreets house perhaps the friendliest bunch of student party animals in Europe. (p325)

**Plovdiv, Bulgaria** Hipster haunts and cocktail bars spill into the cobbled lanes of Kapana artistic quarter. (p96)

## Art Collections

**Hermitage, St Petersburg, Russia** One of the world's greatest art collections, stuffed full of treasures from mummies to Picassos. (p351)

**Danubiana Meulensteen Art Museum, Slovakia** Sculptures as special as the wind-blown setting at this inspiring out-of-town gallery on the Danube. (p384)

**State Tretyakov Gallery, Moscow, Russia** This fabulous repository of Russian culture covers it all from religious icons to contemporary sculpture. (p337)

**Mucha Museum, Prague, Czech Republic** Be seduced by sensuous art-nouveau posters, paintings and decorative panels of Alfons Mucha. (p139)

**Art Museum Rīga Bourse, Rīga, Latvia** The old stock exchange is a worthy showcase for the city's art treasures. (p214)

**Kumu, Tallinn, Estonia** An ark of copper and glass housing a lavish collection of Estonian art. (p168)

**Fabrica de Pensule, Cluj-Napoca, Romania** The grungy, avant-garde 'Paintbrush Factory' is a workspace for up-and-coming artists. (p326)

## Folk & Traditional Culture

**Spa culture, Budapest** Luxuriate in Czech spa spot Karlovy Vary or Russia's *bani* (saunas), but Budapest's baths are best. (p181)

**Trubači, Serbia** Ragtag *trubači* (brass bands) wander the streets of many Serbian cities and villages year-round. (p360)

**Valley of the Roses, Bulgaria** Petal-processing methods have barely changed in Bulgaria's florid valleys such as Kazanlâk, producing rose liqueurs, soaps and oils. (p99)

**Hill of Crosses, Lithuania** Thousands of crosses are amassed at this site north of Šiauliai, including folk-art masterpieces. (p235)

## Relics of Communism

**Lenin's Mausoleum, Moscow, Russia** A waxy Lenin continues to lie in state on impressive Red Square. (p337)

**Minsk, Belarus** Rebuilt in the 1950s in Stalinist style after WWII destruction, Minsk has barely changed since. (p60)

Széchenyi Baths (p185) in Budapest, Hungary

**Transdniestr, Moldova** This still-communist slice of Moldova is a self-proclaimed country and living relic of Soviet history. (p266)

**Grūtas Park, Druskininkai, Lithuania** Hundreds of communist-era statues set in grounds designed to resemble a Siberian labour camp. (p233)

**Maršal Tito's Grave, Belgrade, Serbia** Gigantic marble mausoleum, also displaying hundreds of kitsch birthday batons presented by young 'Pioneers'. (p362)

**Bunk'Art, Tirana, Albania** Fantastic conversion of a massive Cold War bunker into a history and contemporary-art museum. (p44)

**Memento Park, Budapest, Hungary** Once-imposing statues look forlorn assembled at this haphazard graveyard of Hungary's past. (p182)

## Contemporary Architecture

**Museum of Contemporary Art, Zagreb, Croatia** Sleek stunner designed by Igor Franić, and a stellar example of clever use of light and space. (p109)

**Kumu, Tallinn, Estonia** A world-class, concrete-and-glass building that holds an excellent art collection. (p168)

**Bratislava, Slovakia** Its zany skyline includes the seemingly upside-down Slovak Radio Building and a UFO-topped bridge. (p377)

**Garage Museum of Contemporary Art, Moscow, Russia** In Moscow's revitalised Gorky Park, this museum occupies a 1960s pavilion redesigned by Rem Koolhaas. (p344)

## Outdoor Activities

**Water-sports, Bovec, Slovenia** An unrivalled location for high-adrenalin water-sports, offering everything from canyoning to hydrospeeding. (p407)

**Technical-assist hikes, Slovenský Raj, Slovakia** Scramble up ladders, balance on walkways and don't look down over gorges in thrilling Slovenský Raj. (p390)

**Swimming and paddleboading, Lake Balaton, Hungary** From sunbathing to stand-up paddleboarding, all activity levels are possible at this scenic lake. (p193)

**Belavezhskaya Pushcha National Park, Belarus** Cycle or hike around Europe's oldest wildlife refuge, home to 300-odd European bison. (p68)

# Month by Month

## January

January is an enchanting time to experience countryside blanketed with snow and Old Towns dusted with frost. Most towns are relatively tourist-free and hotel prices are at rock-bottom, though ski resorts are lively.

### ☆ Küstendorf Film & Music Festival, Serbia

Created and curated by Serbian director Emir Kusturica, this international indie-fest (http://kustendorf-filmandmusicfestival.org) in the town of Drvengrad, near Zlatibor in Serbia, eschews traditional red-carpet glitz for oddball inclusions vying for the 'Golden Egg' prize.

## February

Still cold, but with longer days, February is when colourful carnivals are held across the region, while skiers and snowboarders enjoy more sunshine. Low hotel prices and the off-season feel continue.

### ✨ Kurentovanje, Slovenia

A procession of hairy masks, bell-ringing and the occasional wry slap form the dramatic rites of spring in Ptuj for Kurentovanje (www.kurentovanje.net), Slovenia's most distinctive Mardi Gras festival.

### 🍷 Golden Grapes Festival, Bulgaria

Melnik and other Bulgarian winemaking towns have their vines blessed by a priest before lavishly toasting the patron saint of wine. It's celebrated on the first and/or 14th day of the month. (p95)

### ✨ Rijeka Carnival, Croatia

A kaleidoscope of costume and colour unfolds in Rijeka, host to Croatia's most dazzling pre-Lent celebrations. Other events kick off in Zadar, Split and Dubrovnik too.

## March

Spring arrives in southern regions, northerly countries remain in winter's slushy grip, and skiers continue to make merry in the mountains. Days can be bright and sunny, though hiking trails are perilous with melting snow.

### ✨ Drowning of Marzanna, Poland

Head to Poland in March for the rite of the Drowning of Marzanna, a surviving pagan ritual in which an effigy of the goddess of winter is immersed in water at the advent of spring.

### ☆ Ski-Jumping World Cup, Slovenia

Held on the third weekend in March, this international competition (www.planica.si) in Planica is the place to marvel at world-record-making ski jumps.

### ☆ Vitranc Cup, Slovenia

Slovenia's major downhill skiing event, held annually in early March in Kranjska Gora, will elicit gasps from both dedicated snowheads and casual observers.

## ✘ Maslenitsa (Pancake Week), Russia

There is no such thing as too many pancakes at this Shrovetide festival. Maslenitsa celebrates the end of winter and encourages pre-Lenten pancake guzzling. Folk dancing and pancake stalls can be enjoyed across Russia.

## ☆ Easter Festival of Sacred Music, Czech Republic

Choral and orchestral concerts (www.mhf-brno.cz) take place in the oldest churches in Brno, including the beautiful Cathedral of Sts Peter & Paul, during the two weeks following Palm Sunday.

# April

Spring kicks off in April, though the winter-sports season sometimes lingers and lofty mountain passes may still be treacherous. Days are getting warmer and sunnier, and outside the Easter holidays, hotel prices remain low.

## ☆ Budapest Spring Festival, Hungary

One of Europe's top classical music events is this two-week festival in mid-April. Concerts are held in a number of beautiful venues including several stunning churches, the Hungarian State Opera House and the National Theatre.

## ☆ Music Biennale Zagreb, Croatia

Held during odd-numbered years since the 1960s, Croatia's lauded live-music highlight features modern-day classical concerts across a multitude of venues.

# May

An excellent time to visit Eastern Europe, May is sunny and warm and full of things to do, but never too hot or crowded. Big destinations feel busy, though hiking areas and villages remain quiet.

## ⚒ International Labour Day, Russia

Bigger than Christmas back in communist times, International Labour Day (1 May) may have dropped in status since the fall of the Berlin Wall, but it's still a national holiday in Russia and several other former Soviet republics. You'll find fireworks, concerts and even military parades.

## 🍺 Czech Beer Festival, Czech Republic·

An event most travellers won't want to miss is the Czech Beer Festival (www.ceskypivnifestival.cz), where lots of food, music and – most importantly – over 150 beers from around the country are on offer in Prague from mid- to late May.

## ☆ Prague Spring & Fringe, Czech Republic

Three-week international music festival Prague Spring is the most prestigious event in the Czech capital's cultural calendar, with concerts held in an array of venues. Meanwhile, the Prague Fringe Festival (www.praguefringe.com) is a more irreverent line-up of theatre, comedy and music. (p142)

# June

Shoulder season is well under way – it's already summer in southeastern Europe and the sun barely sets in the Baltic as the solstice approaches. One of the best times to travel, if not the cheapest.

## ⚒ St John's Eve & St John's Day, Baltic Countries

The Baltic region's biggest annual night out is a celebration of midsummer on 23 and 24 June. It's best experienced out in the country, where huge bonfires flare for all-night revellers who sing, dance and leap over fires.

## ☆ White Nights, Russia

The barely setting sun across the Baltic encourages locals to party through the night. The best place to join the fun is in the imperial Russian capital, St Petersburg, where classical concerts, an international music festival (http://wnfestival.ru) and other summer events keep spirits high.

## ⚒ Rose Festival, Bulgaria

Join Bulgaria's celebration of its most fragrant export as the Valley of the Roses bursts into bloom. Kazanlâk's main square holds the main event on the first weekend in June, but smaller villages have their own rituals, from folk dancing to sipping rose liqueur. (p98)

## ✵ Mikser Festival, Serbia

Creative thinking is at the heart of Belgrade's Mikser Festival, which hosts thought-provoking art exhibitions, cultural forums and cutting-edge design around the edgy Savamala district.

## ☆ Moscow International Film Festival, Russia

Russia's premier film festival runs for 10 days at the end of the month and includes retrospective and documentary film programs as well as the usual awards.

## ✵ Jewish Culture Festival, Poland

Kraków rediscovers its Jewish heritage during a packed week of music, art exhibitions and lectures (www.jewishfestival.pl) in late June/early July. Poland's festival is the biggest and most exciting Jewish festival in the region.

## July

The middle of summer sees Eastern Europe packed with both people and things to do. Temperatures and prices soar by the end of July, but hotel room rates remain reasonable early in the month.

### Východná, Slovakia

Slovakia's top folk festival is held over the first weekend of July each year in the tiny Tatras Mountain village of Východná. Over a thousand performers descend here to celebrate traditional music, dance, arts and crafts. (p385)

## Ivana Kupala, Ukraine

Fern wreaths, leaping over bonfires and late-night dancing are the mystical hallmarks of this suggestive fertility festival, held on the night of 6 or 7 July to purify participants in time for midsummer.

## ☆ EXIT Festival, Serbia

Eastern Europe's most talked-about music festival takes place each July within the walls of the Petrovaradin Citadel in Serbia's second city, Novi Sad. Book early for tickets as big international headlining acts attract music lovers from all over the continent. (p372)

## ☆ Karlovy Vary International Film Festival, Czech Republic

Held in one of the most beautiful spa towns in the Czech Republic, the region's own Cannes (www.kviff.com) is a far smaller affair than its French cousin, but it still shows hundreds of movies in its packed program.

## ☆ Bazant Pohoda Festival, Slovakia

Slovakia's largest music and arts festival, held in Trenčín, represents all genres of music, from rock to orchestral, over multiple stages.

## ✵ Festival of Medieval Arts & Crafts, Romania

During July the beautiful Romanian city of Sighişoara hosts open-air concerts, parades and

ceremonies, all glorifying medieval Transylvania and taking the town back to its fascinating 12th-century origins.

## ☆ Ohrid Summer Festival, Macedonia

The month-long Ohrid Summer Festival comprises a wealth of performances from classical, opera and rock acts to theatre and literature, all celebrating Macedonian culture. (p249)

## ☆ Slavyansky Bazaar, Belarus

Held in the old Russian city of Vitsebsk (in modern Belarus), this festival is one of the biggest cultural events in the former Soviet Union, featuring theatrical performances, music concerts and exhibits from all over the Slavic world.

## ☆ Ultra Europe, Croatia

Now one of the largest electronic music festivals in the world, Ultra Europe lights up the city of Split before continuing the action in Bol, Hvar and Vis.

## ☆ Belgrade Summer Festival, Serbia

BELEF, a dynamic sampling of innovative music, dance, theatre and visual-arts displays, takes over the Serbian capital for a month from mid-July.

## ☆ International Music Festival, Czech Republic

Thousands of music lovers congregate in Český Krumlov for classical concerts, as well as jazz, rock and folk music, at this impressive month-long festival (www.festivalkrumlov.cz), which runs from mid-July to mid-August.

### ☆ Dubrovnik Summer Festival, Croatia

From mid-July to late August, Croatia's most prestigious summer festival presents a program of theatre, opera, concerts and dance on open-air stages throughout the city.

### ☆ Baltica International Folklore Festival, Baltic Countries

This rotating festival (www.cioff.org) of traditional Baltic folk music and dance will be hosted in Lithuania in 2017 and Estonia in 2019.

### ☆ Electric Castle, Romania

An extravaganza of pop and rock music sets Romania's Bánffy Castle, near Cluj-Napoca, vibrating. The four-day festival showcases international electronica, house, metal and reggae live acts.

## August

It's easy enough to escape crowds and expense, even at summer's height. There's a huge amount to see and do in August, and the weather – from the Baltic coast to the Adriatic – is sizzlingly hot.

### ☆ Sarajevo Film Festival, Bosnia & Hercegovina

This globally acclaimed festival that grew out of the ruins of the '90s civil war

screens commercial and art-house movies side by side in the Bosnian capital. (p75)

### ☆ Kaliningrad City Jazz, Russia

This jazz event in Kaliningrad attracts performers from across Europe. It's held over three days around the city, with nightclub jams, big concerts and even free open-air sessions.

### ☆ Sziget Festival, Hungary

A week-long music festival held all over Budapest, Sziget features bands from around the world representing a dizzying array of genres, from hypnotic trance to the blackest heavy metal. (p185)

### ☆ Guča Festival, Serbia

Much more than old brass, Guča's trumpet festival is one of the most exciting and bizarre events in Eastern Europe. Thousands of revellers descend on the small Serbian town of Guča to damage their eardrums, livers and sanity over four cacophonous days. (p360)

### ☆ Nišville International Jazz Festival, Serbia

The sprawling Niš Fortress hosts this jazz festival each August with acts from around the world on the program. (p374)

## September

Summer crowds have dropped off and prices are no longer sky high, but great weather lingers across the region.

September is a fantastic month to head to Eastern Europe, particular for hiking and outdoor activities.

### ☆ Cow's Ball, Slovenia

This Slovenian mid-September weekend of folk dancing, music, eating and drinking in Bohinj marks the return of the cows from their high pastures to the valleys in typically ebullient Balkan style.

### ☆ Dvořák Autumn, Czech Republic

This classical-music festival honours the work of the Czech Republic's favourite composer, Antonín Dvořák. The event is held over three weeks in the spa town of Karlovy Vary (www.kso.cz).

### ☐ Coffee Festival, Ukraine

Eastern European coffee culture thrives in Lviv, even more so during the annual coffee festival. Taste coffees from all over the world and channel the buzz into bike rides, film screenings and other events.

### ☆ Apollonia Arts Festival, Bulgaria

Seaside Sozopol hosts a vast festival of music, drama and dance for the first week of September (www.apollonia.bg).

## October

October remains mild in the south but gets chilly in the north. Prices stay low and crowds lessen with each passing day. Some hiking and biking trails are off limits. Summer resorts may start hibernating.

## 🍷 Wine Festival, Moldova

Winemakers, wine tasting, wine buying and wine-enriched folkloric performances in and around Chişinău draw buyers and more casual oenophiles to this wine festival. (p265)

## ☆ Tirana International Film Festival, Albania

From the last week of October to the first week of November Tirana holds a short- and feature-film festival (www.tiranafilmfest. com), the only one of its kind in tiny Albania. It's a great way to take stock of Eastern European film-making.

# November

Eastern Europe's in-between days: after hikers shuffle home and before snow brings winter-sports fans. Days are short, weather is cold, but you'll have most of Eastern Europe's attractions to yourself and accommodation is cheap.

## ☆ Jazz Festival, Bosnia & Hercegovina

Held in Sarajevo in early November, this festival showcases the sultry sounds of local and international jazz musicians.

---

### ORTHODOX CHRISTMAS & EASTER

Orthodox Christianity uses the Julian calendar for its religious festivals and events, not the Gregorian calendar as is the case for the West. Hence Christmas Day falls on 7 January. On Christmas Eve (6 January) special Masses are held in churches at midnight and believers fast from morning to nightfall. Russians then have a feast that includes roast duck and porridge.

Easter begins with midnight services on Easter Sunday. Afterwards, Russians have a tradition of eating *kulich* (traditional dome-shaped bread) and *paskha* (cheesecake), and painted wooden Easter eggs are used as decorations from homes to guesthouses and restaurants.

---

## 🍷 Martinje in Zagreb, Croatia

The Feast of St Martin is an annual wine festival held in Zagreb to celebrate the end of the grape harvest as Croatian wineries begin the crushing process. Expect sampling of new wines, complementary nibbles and an upbeat mood.

# December

Christmas decorations brighten dark streets and, despite the cold across much of the region, as long as you avoid Christmas and New Year's Eve, prices remain surprisingly low. Ski season starts towards the month's end.

## 🔒 Christmas Markets

Throughout December Eastern Europe heaves with German-style Christmas markets. You'll find these in many cities in the region, though we recommend Bratislava for its charm and beautiful setting.

## ✨ Christmas

Most countries celebrate on Christmas Eve (24 December) with an evening meal and midnight Mass. However, in Russia, Ukraine, Belarus, Moldova, Serbia, Montenegro and Macedonia, Christmas falls in January.

## ✨ New Year's Eve

Even back when communist officials frowned on Christmas, New Year's Eve remained a big holiday in Eastern Europe. Join the party wherever you are and see in the new year with locals.

# Itineraries

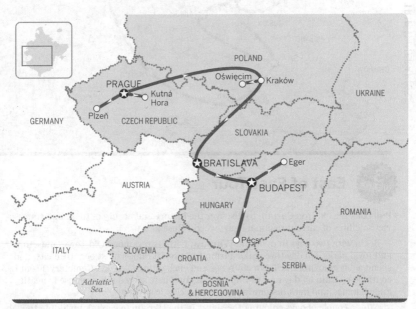

## 2 WEEKS Essential Eastern Europe

Combine highlights of the Czech Republic, Poland, Slovakia and Hungary for a quintessential introduction to Eastern Europe's charms.

Start in **Prague**, spending two days absorbing the Old Town, Malá Strana and Prague Castle. Day-trip to **Kutná Hora**, to peep at its eerie ossuary and medieval silver-mining history, and take a beer pilgrimage to **Plzeň**.

On day five head by train into Poland to reach regal **Kraków**, with its gob-smacking Old Town and vast Rynek Główny (Main Sq). Over three days, ramble Wawel Castle, the off-beat Kazimierz district, and take a trip to harrowing **Oświęcim** (Auschwitz).

On day eight head south to Slovakia, passing through the magnificent High Tatras before reaching **Bratislava**, with its grand castle and Danube views. Spend the evening in wine bars and beer halls; the next morning enjoy a lazy Old Town brunch and take a half day excursion to crumbling Devín Castle.

On day 10 take a boat down the Danube to **Budapest**. Spend a couple of days simmering in outdoor baths, exploring coffee houses and ruin bars, and admiring dazzling architecture. From here bolt to the baroque city of **Eger**, and finish with a day trip to **Pécs**, full of relics from the Turkish occupation.

## 3 WEEKS East of East Tour

Pull back the old Iron Curtain to discover the history and beauty of these one-time Soviet satellites of current regional heavyweight Russia.

Begin with two days in dynamic **Warsaw**, with its revamped Old Town, museums and royal parks. On day three take a train to **Lviv**, Ukraine's most beautiful city, and spend a day enjoying Old Town churches and enchanting Lychakiv Cemetery. From Lviv, continue by train on day four to imposing **Kyiv**, where sacred relics repose beneath gilded domes, and dark history mingles with eclectic street art.

After a couple of days enjoying the sights in the Ukrainian capital, including the labyrinthine Pecherska Lavra complex and perhaps a guided tour of Chornobyl's exclusion zone, on day six take the sleeper train to **Moscow**, a place of striking extremes, dazzling wealth and gridlocked traffic. Drink in the history of the Kremlin, see Lenin's Mausoleum, St Basil's Cathedral and Red Square, and sample the nightlife and fashion.

On day nine leave Moscow and visit picturesque **Veliky Novgorod** en route to the beautiful baroque and neoclassical architecture of **St Petersburg**. You can easily spend three days in the city itself, although there are abundant sights outside it as well, such as the tsarist palace Tsarskoe Selo.

On day 13 take the train to Estonia's magical capital, **Tallinn**, where you can soak up the medieval Old Town. Head south on day 15 and relax on the golden-sand beaches of **Pärnu** before continuing to the Latvian capital **Rīga** which boasts Europe's finest collection of art-nouveau architecture. Latvia has plenty of other highlights: squeeze in day trips to the caves and medieval castles of **Sigulda**, and the breathtaking Baltic coastline around **Ventspils**.

Cross into Lithuania on day 18, where a night or two in charming **Vilnius** will reveal the Baltic's most underrated capital. From Vilnius make a trip to the huge sand dunes and fragile ecological environment of the **Curonian Spit**. If you've arranged a double-entry visa for Russia, cross over into **Kaliningrad**. Alternatively, if you've sorted a Belarus visa, take the train to this isolated republic with its Stalinist-style, but surprisingly pleasant capital **Minsk** before re-entering Poland and heading back to Warsaw.

## 3 WEEKS Breezing through the Balkans

Taking its name from the Balkan Mountains, this is a fascinating region of Eastern Europe lapped by several different seas, with enigmatic fortresses and intriguing towns along the way.

Begin in lively little Slovenia, where the capital **Ljubljana** is a pedestrian delight. Indulge in superb scenery and adrenaline-rush sports in the **Julian Alps** before heading south to Croatia and working your way through the beaches along the **Dalmatian Coast**. Stop in **Dubrovnik** to explore the Old Town and the surrounding islands.

Detour into Bosnia – first visit **Mostar** to see the legendary bridge and the multi-ethnic community that has enjoyed rejuvenation since the Balkan Wars, then a night or two in the bustling capital of **Sarajevo**. Head back south to the coast and east into Montenegro: visit the walled city of **Kotor**, see the impressive coastline and surrounding mountains, and enjoy some of the country's top beaches around the fortified island village of **Sveti Stefan** before pressing south into Albania.

After exploring **Tirana**, a mountain-shrouded ramshackle capital on the rise, make an excursion to the Unesco-listed town of **Berat**, before taking a bus through the mountains into Macedonia, ending up in sublime **Ohrid**. Spend at least two days here, enjoying the ancient churches and swimming in the eponymous lake. Make your way to **Skopje**, Macedonia's fun capital where an abundance of gleaming modern Italianate structures are redefining the city for the 21st century. Take the train to **Pristina**, Kosovo's dainty though cosmopolitan capital, from where it's an easy hop to **Prizren**, a charming mosque-filled old town.

To reach Serbia's capital **Belgrade**, you'll need to backtrack to Skopje and board the international train. Don't miss the city's ancient Kalemegdan Citadel and the hip restaurant and clubbing scene. Take a detour to laid-back **Novi Sad** with its fine neoclassical buildings, outdoor cafes and Danube fortress views.

Another cross-border train will take you into Bulgaria. Head east to **Veliko Târnovo**, the ancient capital and a university town with a dramatic setting. From here it's an easy bus to **Varna** by the Black Sea, complete with beaches, Roman ruins and open-air nightclubs.

## On The Edge

**3 WEEKS**

Covering the easternmost edge of the region (before Russia), this itinerary balances pretty old towns and fortresses with the forbidding architecture of time-trapped Belarus and border anomaly Transdniestr.

Start in one of Romania's underrated westerly cities: either museum-packed **Timişoara**, which broods with its history of anti-Ceauşescu revolt, or edgy **Cluj-Napoca**, harbouring avant-garde nightlife and coffee spots within its Gothic-modern mash-up. On day three, head east to elegant, Saxon-tinged **Sibiu**, before pressing on to **Braşov** on day four. Allow three days to traipse Braşov's forested hills, meander medieval laneways and day-trip to bear country or dramatic **Bran Castle**.

Start week two by bidding goodbye to the beaten track and entering lost-in-time Moldova. Spend a day or two exploring gritty but green capital **Chişinău**: excellent local wine is plentiful and cheap, and stately monuments jostle alongside decaying Soviet relics. Allow one day to visit the stunning cave monastery at **Orheiul Vechi**, and another to time-travel into Transdniestr, a country that doesn't officially exist. In the fascinating 'capital' **Tiraspol** little appears to have changed since the Soviet era of the mid-'80s.

Entering Ukraine on day 11, make a beeline for **Kyiv**, which demands around four days' attention. An ancient seat of Slavic and Orthodox culture, today Kyiv is a modern and pleasant metropolis. Don't miss the Pecherska Lavra complex and St Sophia's Cathedral, as well as ousted ex-president Viktor Yanukovych's opulent mansion Mezhyhirya. For a complete contrast, detour to the western edge of the country where Unesco World Heritage–listed **Lviv** is a town of quaint cobbles, aromatic coffeehouses and rattling trams; its Parisian vibe feels a continent away from the war-torn badlands of Ukraine's east.

The final stops on this tour of the region's lesser discovered highlights take you to Belarus, Europe's so-called 'last dictatorship'. Around day 17, have a blast in monolithic **Minsk**, a city dominated by huge Stalinist avenues and Soviet memorials. Heading southwest, stop at **Brest** on the border and visit the fortress. Use Brest as a base to visit **Belavezhskaya Pushcha National Park**, where you'll be able to see Europe's largest mammal, the European bison, as well as a host of other wild beauties before crossing back into the EU.

Top: Bran Castle
(p322), Romania

Right: *Courage*,
sculpture in Brest
Fortress (p67), Belarus

UDMURD / SHUTTERSTOCK ©

 **4 WEEKS** ## The Ionian to the Baltic

This eight-country odyssey extends from the Ionian to Baltic Seas, darting between sea-facing fortresses, mountainous vistas and some of Eastern Europe's undiscovered old towns.

Arrive in Albania by ferry from Corfu at the busy port of **Saranda**, and head to the ancient ruins in **Butrint** near the Greek border. Continue up through Albania to Unesco-listed **Gjirokastra**, whose stone-and-slate old town on a hillside is Albania's loveliest. Press on to Albanian capital **Tirana**, for a couple of days of colourful cityscapes and inventive museums before journeying on to Montenegro.

Base yourself in ancient, walled **Kotor**, soaking up its coastal setting. Move on to **Budva** to dally in the atmospheric Old Town and beaches. Head north to the cliff-face-hugging **Ostrog Monastery**, and on to **Durmitor National Park**, a great place for hiking, rafting and canyoning.

From Montenegro's capital Podgorica catch an overnight train to vibrant Serbian capital **Belgrade**. Spend a couple of days here, then continue north to convivial **Novi Sad** and explore the serene **Fruška Gora** monasteries and vineyards nearby.

Cross into Hungary at verdant, culture-crammed **Szeged** and head for **Lake Balaton** for sublime swimming. Keep surging north into Slovakia, aiming for plucky **Bratislava**, to spend a few days hopping between cute cafes, mighty castles and perhaps a trip out to the inspiring Danubiana Meulensteen Art Museum. Venture onward to chilly gorges and cascades in high-octane **Slovenský Raj National Park**.

Crossing the Tatra Mountains into Poland, travel to **Wrocław**, spending a few days admiring street art and edgy galleries before dropping in on pastel-coloured **Poznań**. From here, head for the Baltic coast: **Gdańsk** is a thriving port city. From here, make day trips to beaches and to **Malbork**, famed for Europe's biggest Gothic castle.

Next up is the intriguing Russian exclave of **Kaliningrad** which combines elements of old Prussia, the USSR and modern Russia. Return to the coast to travel through **Kursh-skaya Kosa National Park** and cross into the Lithuanian section of birch tree-forested Curonian Spit, aiming for **Klaipėda**, Lithuania's main port with a merry, beer-loving nightlife. End your trip in baroque **Vilnius**, Lithuania's many-steepled capital.

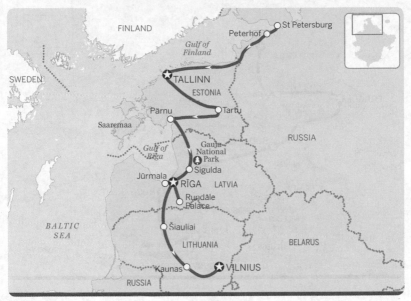

 **Baltic Blast**

This trip weaves through four very different countries: skirting the Baltic coast, plunging through thick forests, and taking in treasured art. In the space of a fortnight you'll see rolling countryside, discover three capital cities – Tallinn, Rīga and Vilnius – along with timeless St Petersburg and quirky Baltic towns.

Set aside three nights for the heart-stoppingly beautiful city of **St Petersburg** to see the Hermitage, vast Nevsky Prospekt's mansions, and the amazing Church on the Spilled Blood. Head out of town to the reconstructed palaces and manicured gardens of **Peterhof**, which belonged to Peter the Great.

Take a bus or train to the Estonian capital **Tallinn** for two days. Wander the chocolate-box streets and stone towers of the 14th- and 15th-century Old Town before heading to the university town of **Tartu**, packed with interesting museums, parks and handsome wooden buildings. Duck west to the Baltic coast where you'll find the inviting Estonian beach resort of **Pärnu**. Rest here for a day to indulge in all the pleasures of Eastern European summer holiday-making: mud baths, Bacchanalian nightlife and golden-sand beaches.

At the beginning of week two, continue south into Latvia, stopping off in cheerful, castle-rich **Sigulda**. Spend a day walking in the tranquil landscapes and dense forests of **Gauja National Park**. On day 10, continue on to **Rīga**, Latvia's delightful capital, where you can soak up fantastic art-nouveau architecture, plus bleak history and a constrastingly friendly Old Town, over two days. On one of the days, take an excursion to the opulent **Rundāle Palace** to see how 18th-century aristocrats lived. On day 12, day-trip to the lovely beaches and wooden villas of **Jūrmala**.

Lithuania is next, and it greets you with the astounding Hill of Crosses in **Šiauliai**, an icon of Lithuanian identity (even if there's no reason to dawdle in the town). Spirited university town **Kaunas** boasts a leafy old centre and bookish cafes, as well as being just a short distance away from the chilling history of war and deportation at Ninth Fort. End your journey in beautiful **Vilnius**, the country's crowning glory, which clasps an artistic quarter, weathered watchtowers and an alluring Old Town within its bounds.

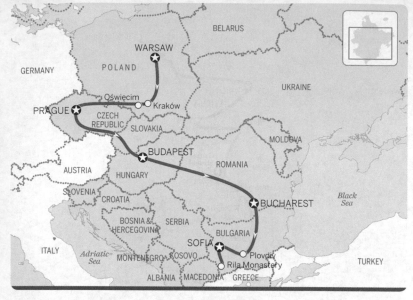

## Eastern Europe 101

**2 WEEKS**

Looking to cram history, culture and nightlife into a zippy fortnight-long trip? This itinerary knits together highlights from five Eastern European countries.

Start off by flying to the Polish capital **Warsaw** for one night, seeing the beautifully restored Old Town and eating delicious *pierogi* (dumplings) before taking the train south to **Kraków**. Staying for two nights gives you time to see the Old Town, Wawel Castle and Kazimierz, and do a day trip to **Oświęcim** (Auschwitz) before taking the overnight train to **Prague**. Spend another two days on intensive sightseeing – Prague Castle, Charles Bridge, wandering the Malá Strana and the Old Town and tasting genuine Czech beer in a local brewery.

At the end of day five, take another overnight train to **Budapest** for two nights in Hungary. Soak in the city's glorious Gellért Baths, take a cruise on the Danube, see the magnificent Hungarian Parliament building and wander Castle Hill before yet another overnight train (at the end of day seven) to Romania's underrated capital, **Bucharest**. With a one-night stay you can cover the main sights, including the amazing Palace of Parliament, wander the small historic centre and pick up a sense of the city's energy in its bars and clubs.

On day nine, continue by train to **Plovdiv** in Bulgaria, equally rich in Roman ruins, creaky Bulgarian Revival-era mansions, inventive galleries and bars. Stay two nights here, allowing time to amble through the Old Town, pose in the Roman Amphitheatre, and take a half-day trip to vertiginous Asen's Fortress. On day 11, take the train to **Sofia** for two nights exploring the grit and glamour of the Bulgarian capital, in particular the golden-domed Aleksander Nevski Cathedral and the Ancient Serdica Complex.

On your last day, take a day trip from Sofia through the Rila Mountains to the country's spiritual nucleus. Thousand-year-old **Rila Monastery** is Bulgaria's holiest site and one of the most important monasteries in Eastern Europe, in a mountain setting as spine-tingling as its apocalyptic frescoes. From here you can fly out of Sofia or continue to bigger air hubs such as nearby Athens or İstanbul to get a flight home.

# On the Road

# Albania

## Best Places to Eat

➡ Boutique de l'Artiste (p47)

➡ Uka Farm (p48)

➡ Mullixhiu (p47)

➡ Mare Nostrum (p53)

## Best Places to Stay

➡ Stone City Hostel (p55)

➡ Tradita G&T (p49)

➡ Trip'n'Hostel (p45)

➡ Hotel Mangalemi (p52)

## Why Go?

Albania has natural beauty in such abundance that you might wonder why it took 20 years for the country to take off as a tourist destination since the end of a particularly brutal strain of communism in 1991. So backward was Albania when it emerged blinking into the bright light of freedom that it needed two decades just to catch up with the rest of Eastern Europe. Now that it has arguably done so, Albania offers a remarkable array of unique attractions, not least due to this very isolation: ancient mountain codes of behaviour, forgotten archaeological sites and villages where time seems to have stood still are all on the menu. With its stunning mountain scenery, a thriving capital in Tirana and beaches to rival any elsewhere in the Mediterranean, Albania has become the sleeper hit of the Balkans. But hurry here, as word is well and truly out.

## When to Go
### Tirana

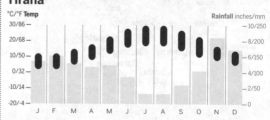

**Jun** Enjoy the perfect Mediterranean climate and deserted beaches.

**Jul–Aug** Albania's beaches may be packed, but this is a great time to explore the mountains.

**Dec** See features and shorts at the Tirana Film Festival, while the intrepid can snowshoe to Theth.

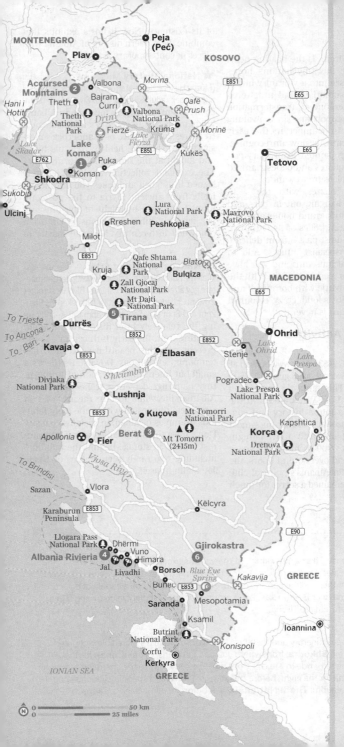

**Albania Highlights**

**① Lake Koman Ferry** (p50) Join the hardy locals on this magical boat ride through stunning mountain scenery across an immense man-made lake.

**② Accursed Mountains** (p50) Do the wonderful day trek between the isolated mountain villages of Valbona and Theth and experience some of Albania's best scenery.

**③ Berat** (p52) Explore this Unesco World Heritage–listed museum town, known as the 'city of a thousand windows'.

**④ Albania Riviera** (p54) Catch some sun at one of the many gorgeous beaches and coves on Albania's Ionian coast.

**⑤ Tirana** (p44) Feast your eyes on the wild colour schemes and experience Blloku cafe culture in the plucky Albanian capital.

**⑥ Gjirokastra** (p54) Take a trip to this traditional Albanian mountain town, with its spectacular Ottoman-era mansions and impressive hilltop fortress.

# TIRANA

📷 04 / POP 835,000

Lively, colourful Tirana is the beating heart of Albania, where this tiny nation's hopes and dreams coalesce into a vibrant whirl of traffic, brash consumerism and unfettered fun. Having undergone a transformation of extraordinary proportions since awaking from its communist slumber in the early 1990s, Tirana's centre is now unrecognisable, with buildings painted in primary colours, and public squares and pedestrianised streets that are a pleasure to wander.

Trendy Blloku buzzes with the well-heeled and flush hanging out in bars and cafes, while the city's grand boulevards are lined with fascinating relics of its Ottoman, Italian and communist past – from delicate minarets to loud socialist murals. Add to this some excellent museums and you have a compelling list of reasons to visit. With the traffic doing daily battle with both itself and pedestrians, the city is loud, crazy, colourful and dusty, but Tirana is never dull.

## ⊙ Sights & Activities

### ★ Bunk'Art                                    MUSEUM

(📷 067 2072 905, 068 4834 444; www.bunkart.al; Rr Fadil Deliu; with/without audio guide 700/500 lekë; ⊘ 9am-5pm) This fantastic conversion – from a massive Cold War bunker on the outskirts of Tirana into a history and contemporary art museum – is Albania's most exciting new sight and easily a Tirana highlight. With almost 3000 sq metres of space underground spread over several floors, the bunker was built for Albania's political elite in the 1970s and remained a secret for much of its existence. Now it hosts exhibits that combine the modern history of Albania with pieces of contemporary art.

### ★ National History Museum           MUSEUM

(Muzeu Historik Kombëtar; www.mhk.gov.al; Sheshi Skënderbej; adult/student 200/80 lekë; ⊘ 9am-2pm & 4-7pm) The largest museum in Albania holds many of the country's archaeological treasures and a replica of Skanderbeg's massive sword (how he held it, rode his horse and fought at the same time is a mystery). The excellent collection is almost entirely signed in English and takes you chronologically from ancient Illyria to the postcommunist era. One highlight of the museum is a terrific exhibition of icons by Onufri, a renowned 16th-century Albanian master of colour.

### ★ National Gallery of Arts           GALLERY

(Galeria Kombëtare e Arteve; www.galeriakombetare.gov.al/en/home/index.shtml; Blvd Dëshmorët e Kombit; adult/student 200/100 lekë; ⊘ 9am-2pm & 5-8pm May-Sep, 10am-8pm Oct-Apr) Tracing the relatively brief history of Albanian painting from the early 19th century to the present day, this beautiful space also has temporary exhibitions. Downstairs there's a small but interesting collection of 19th-century paintings depicting scenes from daily Albanian life, while upstairs the art takes on a political dimension with some truly fabulous examples of Albanian socialist realism. Don't miss the small collection of communist statues in storage behind the building, including two rarely seen statues of Uncle Joe Stalin himself.

---

## ITINERARIES

### One Week

Spend a day in busy **Tirana**, checking out the various excellent museums as well as the Blloku bars and cafes. On day two, make the three-hour trip to the Ottoman-era town of **Berat**. Overnight there before continuing down the coast to spend a couple of days on the beach in **Himara** or **Drymades**. Loop around for one last night in charming **Gjirokastra** before returning to Tirana.

### Two Weeks

Follow the first week itinerary and then head north into Albania's incredible 'Accursed Mountains'. Start in **Shkodra**, from where you can get transport to **Koman** for the stunning morning ferry ride to **Fierzë**. Continue the same day to the charming mountain village of **Valbona** for the night, before trekking to **Theth** and spending your last couple of nights in the beautiful **Theth National Park** before heading back to Tirana.

## BUNKER LOVE

On the hillsides, beaches and generally most surfaces in Albania, you will notice small concrete domes (often in groups of three) with rectangular slits. Meet the bunkers: Enver Hoxha's concrete legacy, built from 1950 to 1985. Weighing in at 5 tonnes of concrete and iron, these little mushrooms are almost impossible to destroy. They were built to repel an invasion and can resist full tank assault – a fact proved by their chief engineer, who vouched for his creation's strength by standing inside one while it was bombarded by a tank. The shell-shocked engineer emerged unscathed and tens of thousands were built. Today, some are creatively painted, one houses a tattoo artist and some even house makeshift hostels.

Two enormous bunkers, the scale of which do not compare to these tiny sniper installations, can be found in Tirana and Gjirokastra. In Tirana, Bunk'Art (p44) is the city's most fascinating site, a history museum housed inside a vast government bunker. In Gjirokastra, the Cold War Tunnel (p55), in fact a similarly massive government bunker, can also be visited, though minus the history museum and art display.

### Sheshi Skënderbej
SQUARE

(Skanderbeg Sq) Sheshi Skënderbej is the best place to start witnessing Tirana's daily goings-on. Until it was pulled down by an angry mob in 1991, a 10m-high bronze statue of Enver Hoxha stood here, watching over a mainly car-free square. Now only the **equestrian statue of Skanderbeg** remains, and the 'square' – once Tirana's most popular meeting point in the decades where 99% of people were forced to get around on foot – is now a huge traffic roundabout.

### Et'hem Bey Mosque
MOSQUE

(Sheshi Skënderbej; ⊙ 8am-11am) To one side of Sheshi Skënderbej, the 1789–1823 Et'hem Bey Mosque was spared destruction during the atheism campaign of the late 1960s because of its status as a cultural monument. Small and elegant, it's one of the oldest buildings left in the city. Take your shoes off to look inside at the beautifully painted dome.

### Mt Dajti National Park
NATIONAL PARK

Just 25km east of Tirana is Mt Dajti National Park (1611m). It is the most accessible mountain in the country and many Tiranans go there to escape the city rush and have a spit-roast lamb lunch. A sky-high, Austrian-made cable car, **Dajti Express** (✆ 04 2379 111; www.dajtiekspres.com; return 800 lekë; ⊙ 9am-10pm Wed-Mon, to 7pm Oct-Apr), takes 15 minutes to make the scenic trip to (almost) the top. Once there, you can avoid all the touts and their minibuses and take the opportunity to stroll through lovely, shady beech and pine forests.

## Tours

### Tirana Free Tour
TOURS

(✆ 069 6315 858; www.tiranafreetour.com) This enterprising tour agency has made its name by offering a free daily tour of Tirana that leaves at 10am year-round. In July, August and September a second tour is offered at 6pm. Tours meet outside the National History Museum on Sheshi Skënderbej. Tips are appreciated if you enjoy the two-hour tour, and further (paid) tours are available.

## Sleeping

### ★ Trip'n'Hostel
HOSTEL €

(✆ 068 2055 540, 068 3048 905; www.tripnhostel. com; Rr Musa Maci 1; dm/d from €10/30; 🛜) Tirana's coolest hostel is on a small side street, housed in a design-conscious, self-contained house with a leafy garden out the back, a bar, a kitchen and a cellar-like chill-out lounge downstairs. Dorms have handmade fixtures, curtains between beds for privacy and private lockable drawers, while there's also a roof terrace strewn with hammocks.

### ★ Tirana Backpacker Hostel
HOSTEL €

(✆ 068 4682 353, 068 3133 451; www.tiranahostel. com; Rr e Bogdaneve 3; dm €10-13, d €35, cabin per person €14; 🗶 @ 🛜) Albania's first-ever hostel goes from strength to strength and remains one of the best-value and most enthusiastically run places in the country. Housed in a charmingly decorated house, with a garden, in which there are several cute cabins for those wanting more than a dorm room, the place is stylishly designed, excellently located and superfriendly.

# Tirana

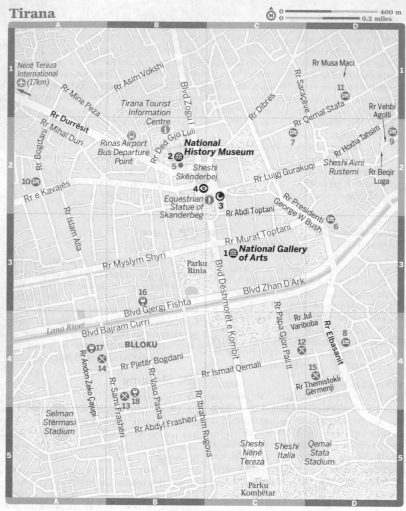

0          400 m
0          0.2 miles

Nënë Tereza International (17km)

Rr Mine Peza

Rr Asim Vokshi

Rr Musa Maci

Rr Durrësit

Rr Mihal Duri

Blvd Zogu I

Rr Dibrës

Rr Saraçeve

Rr Qemal Stafa

Rr Vehbi Agolli

Tirana Tourist Information Centre

Rinas Airport Bus Departure Point

Rr Ded Gjo Luli

**National History Museum**

Sheshi Skënderbej

Rr Luigj Gurakuqi

Sheshi Avni Rustemi

Rr Beqir Luga

Rr Hoxha Tahsim

Rr e Kavajës

Rr Bogdani

Equestrian Statue of Skanderbeg

Rr Abdi Toptani

Rr Presidenti George W Bush

Rr Islam Alla

Rr Murat Toptani

**National Gallery of Arts**

Rr Myslym Shyri

Parku Rinia

Blvd Deshmorët e Kombit

Blvd Zhan D'Ark

Blvd Gjergj Fishta

Lana River

Blvd Bajram Curri

Rr Jul Variboba

Rr Papa Gjon Pali II

Rr Elbasanit

**BLLOKU**

Rr Andon Zako Çajupi

Rr Pjetër Bogdani

Rr Ismail Qemali

Rr Themistokli Germenji

Rr Sami Frashëri

Rr Vaso Pasha

Rr Ibrahim Rugova

Rr Abdyl Frashëri

Selman Stërmasi Stadium

Sheshi Nënë Tereza

Sheshi Italia

Qemal Stafa Stadium

Parku Kombëtar

---

## Destil Hostel
HOSTEL €

( ☎ 069 8852 388; www.destil.al; Rr Qamil Guranjaku; dm €8-12; ❄ 🛜) If you seek a rather cool place to lay your head and aren't concerned about a cultivated hostel vibe, then Destil may just be the antihostel for you. The four minimal yet stylish rooms are all dorms, but each has its own bathroom. There's no kitchen, but instead there's a fantastic restaurant/cafe/bar/chill-out area downstairs where guests can mingle with the city's creative classes.

## Milingona Hostel
HOSTEL €

( ☎ 067 6748 779; www.milingonahostel.com; Rr Vehbi Agolli 5; dm €8-10, d €28; @ 🛜) This superchilled villa in a side street in the middle of Tirana's old town is a friendly place with small four- and six-person dorms, though the basement's 10-bed dorm is the coolest spot in summer. There's a communal kitchen, plus an outside bar with hammocks slung between trees and lots of space for socialising. Extras include free yoga in summer, individual lockable boxes under each bed and free use of computers.

# Tirana

ALBANIA TIRANA

**Capital Tirana Hotel**                     HOTEL €€
(☑ 069 2080 931, 04 2258 575; www.capitaltirana-hotel.com; Rr Qemal Stafa; s/d incl breakfast from €35/55; P ❄ 🛜) This thoroughly modern 29-room hotel just a stone's throw from Sheshi Skënderbej is very good value given its centrality. It may be a little sterile and business-like, but the rooms are of good quality with flat-screen TVs and minibars, staff are very helpful and the busy shopping street outside is great for local atmosphere.

⭐ **Brilant Antik Hotel**        BOUTIQUE HOTEL €€€
(☑ 04 2251 166; www.hotelbrilant.com; Rr Jeronim de Rada 79; s/d incl breakfast €60/90; ❄ 🛜) Easily one of Tirana's best midrange offerings, this charming house-cum-hotel has plenty of character, a central location and welcoming English-speaking staff to ease you into Tirana life. Rooms are spacious, decently furnished with the odd antique, and breakfast downstairs is a veritable feast each morning.

## ❌ Eating

**New York Tirana Bagels**                    CAFE €
(☑ 069 540 7583; http://newyorktiranabagels.com/; Rr Themistokli Gërmenji; bagels & sandwiches 80-300 lekë; ⊙ 7.30am - 9.30pm; 🛜 🅿) Believe it or not, Tirana is home to the Balkans' best bagels. Pick up one for breakfast from the aptly named New York Tirana Bagels, a cafe and social enterprise whose profits go towards supporting people in need.

**Era**                          ALBANIAN, ITALIAN €€
(☑ 04 225 7805; www.era.al; Rr Ismail Qemali; mains 400-900 lekë; ⊙ 11am-midnight; 🅿) This local institution serves traditional Albanian and Italian fare in the heart of Blloku. The

inventive menu includes oven-baked veal and eggs, stuffed eggplant, pizza and pilau with chicken and pine nuts. Be warned: it's sometimes quite hard to get a seat as it's fearsomely popular. There's a second branch near the Stadium.

**Juvenilja**                            ALBANIAN €€
(Rr Sami Frashëri; mains 200-950 lekë; ⊙ 10am-11.30pm; 🛜) This fairly unassuming Blloku establishment actually has a range of excellent traditional Albanian dishes on the menu, including veal escalope with wine and lemon, and piglet ribs with broad beans. There's an English menu and superhelpful, liveried staff.

⭐ **Mullixhiu**                          ALBANIAN €€€
(☑ 069 666 0444; Shëtitore Parku i Madh; mains 1000-2000 lekë; ⊙ noon-4pm & 6-11pm; 🛜 🅿) Around the corner from the chic cafes of Blloku neighbourhood, Chef Bledar Kola's Albanian food metamorphosis is hidden behind a row of grain mills and a wall of corn husks. Opened in February 2016, the restaurant is one of the pioneers of Albania's slow-food movement.

⭐ **Boutique de l'Artiste**        MEDITERRANEAN €€€
(Rr Ismail Qemali 12; mains 750-1500 lekë; ⊙ noon-midnight Mon-Fri, from 9am Sat & Sun; 🛜) Despite its rather pretentious name, this place is all understatement, with a restrained decor and passionate staff who effortlessly translate the daily specials from a giant blackboard into English for guests. There's also a full à la carte menu taking in various aspects of Mediterranean cooking with a strong Italian flavour. Brunch is popular here, as is the in-house patisserie.

**Uka Farm**                ALBANIAN €€€
(📞067 203 9909; Rr Adem Jashari, Laknas; mains 900-2500 lekë; ☺by reservation only) Uka Farm was founded in 1996 by former Minister of Agriculture Rexhep Uka, who started organic cultivation of agricultural products on a small plot of land. His son Flori, a trained winemaker and standout amateur chef, is now the driving force behind the restaurant, which opened in 2014. Guests can enjoy fresh, flavourful vegetables and locally sourced cheese and meat as well as quality homemade wine.

## 🍷 Drinking

★**Radio**                BAR
(Rr Ismail Qemali 29/1; ☺9am-1am; 🐾) Named for the owner's collection of antique Albanian radios, Radio is an eclectic dream with decor that includes vintage Albanian film posters and even a collection of communist-era propaganda books to read at the bar over a cocktail. It attracts a young, intellectual and alternative crowd. It's set back from the street, but it is well worth finding in otherwise rather mainstream Blloku.

**Bunker 1944**                BAR
(Rr Andon Zako Çajupi; ☺4pm-midnight Mon-Fri, to 3am Fri & Sat) This former bunker is now a bohemian bolthole amid a sea of fairly predictable Blloku bars. Inside it's stuffed full of communist-era furniture and antiques/junk including homemade paintings, old vinyl, clocks and radios. There's a great selection of beers available, including IPA, London Porter and London Pride, and a friendly international crowd.

**BUFE**                WINE BAR
(📞069 459 1203; Rr Reshit Çollaku; ☺10am-midnight; 🐾) Get a full *aperitivo* spread at this famed Tirana wine bar.

## ℹ Information

**Tirana Tourist Information Centre** (📞04 2223 313; www.tirana.gov.al; Rr Ded Gjo Luli; ☺9am-6pm Mon-Fri, to 2pm Sat) A friendly English-speaking staff makes getting information easy at this government-run initiative just off Sheshi Skënderbej.

## ℹ Getting There & Away

### AIR
The modern **Nënë Tereza International Airport** (Mother Teresa Airport; 📞04 2381 800; www.tirana-airport.com; Rinas) is at Rinas, 17km northwest of Tirana. The Rinas Express airport bus operates an on-the-hour (7am to 6pm) service, with departures from the corner of Rr Mine Peza and Rr e Durrësit (a few blocks from the National History Museum) for 250 lekë one way. The going taxi rate is 2000 lekë to 2500 lekë.

### BUS
There is no official bus station in Tirana. Instead, there are a large number of bus stops around the city centre from which buses to specific destinations leave. Do check at your hostel or hotel for the latest departure points, as they have been known to change.

Most international services depart from various parts of Blvd Zogu I, with multiple services to Skopje, Macedonia (€20, eight hours), and Pristina (via Prizren), Kosovo (€10, four hours), leaving from near the Tirana International Hotel, and services to Budva, Kotor and Podgorica in Montenegro (€15 to €25, four hours) leaving from in front of the **Tirana Tourist Information Centre** (p48).

*Furgons* (shared minibuses) to Durrës and Bajram Curri leave the Zogu i Zi roundabout at the intersection of Rr Durrësit and Rr Muhamet Gjollesha. Services to Shkodra leave from what's known as the Northern Bus Station on Rr Dritan Hoxha, a short distance from the Zogu i Zi roundabout.

Departures to the south leave from Rr Myhedin Llegami near the corner with Blvd Gjergj Fishta. These include services to Berat, Himara, Saranda and Gjirokastra. Services to Himara and Saranda will drop you off at any of the coastal villages along the way.

| DESTINATION | PRICE (LEKË) | DURA-TION | DISTANCE (KM) |
|---|---|---|---|
| **Berat** | 400 | 2½hr | 122 |
| **Durrës** | 130 | 1hr | 38 |
| **Elbasan** | 150 | 1½hr | 54 |
| **Fier** | 600 | 2hr | 113 |
| **Gjirokastra** | 1000 | 7hr | 232 |
| **Korça** | 500 | 4hr | 181 |
| **Kruja** | 150 | 30min | 32 |
| **Pogradec** | 500 | 3½hr | 150 |
| **Saranda** | 1500 | 7hr | 284 |
| **Shkodra** | 300 | 2hr | 116 |
| **Vlora** | 500-700 | 4hr | 147 |

## ℹ Getting Around

There's now a good network of city buses running around Tirana costing 30 lekë per journey (payable to the conductor), although most of the sights can be covered easily on foot.

# NORTHERN ALBANIA

## Shkodra

📧 022 / POP 111,000

Shkodra, the traditional centre of the Gheg cultural region, is one of the oldest cities in Europe. The ancient Rozafa Fortress has stunning views over Lake Shkodra, while a concerted effort to renovate the buildings in the Old Town has made wandering through Shkodra a treat for the eyes. Many travellers pass through here between Tirana and Montenegro, or en route to the Lake Koman Ferry and the villages of Theth and Valbona, but it's worth spending a night or two to soak up this welcoming place before hurrying on to the mountains, the coast or the capital.

## ⊙ Sights

### ★Rozafa Fortress                                  CASTLE

(200 lekë; ⊙ 8am-8pm summer, until 4pm winter) With spectacular views over the city and Lake Shkodra, the Rozafa Fortress is the most impressive sight in town. Founded by the Illyrians in antiquity and rebuilt much later by the Venetians and then the Turks, the fortress takes its name from a woman who was allegedly walled into the ramparts as an offering to the gods so that the construction would stand.

### ★Marubi National Photography Museum                       GALLERY

(Muzeu Kombëtari i Fotografise Marubi; Rr Kolë Idromeno 32; adult/student 700/200 lekë; ⊙ 9am-2pm & 4-7pm) Since moving to brand new premises on the *pedonalja* (pedestrianised Rr Kolë Idromeno) in 2016, the Marubi Museum has sealed its reputation as Albania's best photography collection. Here you can find the impressive work of the Marubi 'dynasty', Albania's first and foremost family of photographers, as well as high-quality temporary exhibits. The collection includes the first-ever photograph taken in Albania, by Pjetër Marubi in 1858, as well as fascinating portraits, street scenes and early photojournalism, all giving a fascinating glimpse into old Albania.

## 🛏 Sleeping

### Wanderers Hostel                                  HOSTEL €

(📞 069 2121 062; www.thewanderershostel.com; Rr Gjuhadol; dm/d incl breakfast €8/25; 🌐🛜) Stealing a march on much of the longer-established hostel competition in town, Wanderers is currently Shkodra's most pop-ular budget accommodation and attracts a young and fun crowd year-round. The place is a natural hangout, with a chilled-out garden, a bar area and a shared kitchen. Dorms are comfortable and clean, bike hire is €2 per day and the location is superb.

### Mi Casa Es Tu Casa                                HOSTEL €

(📞 069 3812 054; www.micasaestucasa.it; Blvd Skenderbeu 22; dm €9-13, d/apt €30/40, campsite per person with/without own tent €5/7; @🛜) English-speaking Alba is the matriarch of this impressive place, which has a central location, traditional atmosphere, a large kitchen, bright colour schemes and a garden where you can also pitch or hire a tent. Dorms can be a little crowded, but the cosy private rooms upstairs are excellent and are stuffed full of communist-era Albanian furniture. Bike hire is available for €5.

### Lake Shkodra Resort                            CAMPGROUND €

(📞 069 2750 337; www.lakeshkodraresort.com; campsite per tent €12, per person €5-6, cabins €65-85, glamping d €30; 🛜) Frequently appearing in lists of Europe's best campsites, this gorgeously located and superbly run place is not in Shkodra itself, but on the lakeside 7km from the city. There are spotless facilities, a huge range of activities including watersports on offer and, best of all, access to a great sandy beach perfect for swimming. There are also new cabins sleeping up to four people and even a glamping lodge to choose from.

### ★Tradita G&T                              BOUTIQUE HOTEL €€

(📞 068 2086 056, 022 809 683; www.hoteltradita. com; Rr Edith Durham 4; s/d/tr incl breakfast €43/64/81; 🅿🌐🛜) By far the best choice in town, this innovative, well-managed guesthouse is a delight. Housed in a painstakingly restored 17th-century mansion that once belonged to a famous Shkodran writer, the Tradita heaves with Albanian arts and crafts and has traditional yet very comfortable rooms with terracotta-roofed bathrooms and locally woven bed linen.

## ✖ Eating

### Sofra                                          ALBANIAN €

(Rr Kolë Idromeno; mains 200-500 lekë; ⊙ noon-midnight; 🛜) Right in the middle of the busy *petonalja* (pedestrianised Rr Kolë Idromeno), with tables on the street as well as a cosy upstairs dining room, this traditional place is an excellent opportunity to try a range of Albanian dishes, with the set meals being particularly good value.

**San Francisco** ALBANIAN €€
(Rr Kolë Idromeno; mains 300-800 lekë; ⊙6am-11pm; 🛜) This grand old place has a touch of the old world about it, particularly in its more formal upstairs dining room and spacious terrace where the best tables have superb views over the Great Mosque. This makes a great spot for breakfast, but full meals of traditional Albanian cooking are served all day long.

**Çoçja** ITALIAN €€
(Vila Bekteshi; Rr Hazan Riza; mains 250-1000 lekë; ⊙7am-11pm; 🛜) This classy converted mansion on a pleasant piazza in the centre of town is all gleaming white tablecloths, timber floors and smart design choices. The menu encompasses great pizza as well as more exciting fare such as veal ribs, grilled frogs, grilled trout, and chicken fillet with mushrooms and cream. There's also a courtyard garden that's perfect for summer drinks.

### ⓘ Getting There & Away

**BUS**
There is no bus station in Shkodra, but most services leave from around Sheshi Demokracia in the centre of town. There are hourly *furgons* (minibuses; 400 lekë) and buses (300 lekë) to Tirana (two hours, 6am to 5pm), which depart from outside Radio Shkodra near Hotel Rozafa. There are also several daily buses to Kotor, Ulcinj

and Podgorica in Montenegro (€5 to €8, two to three hours) from outside the Ebu Bekr Mosque.

To get up into the mountains, catch the 6.30am bus to Lake Koman (600 lekë, two hours) in time for the wonderful Lake Koman Ferry to Fierzë. Several *furgons* also depart daily for Theth between 6am and 7am (1200 lekë, four hours). In both cases hotels can call ahead to get the *furgon* to pick you up on its way out of town.

**TAXI**
It costs between €40 and €50 for the trip from Shkodra to Ulcinj in Montenegro, depending on your haggling skills.

## The Accursed Mountains

The 'Accursed Mountains' (Bjeshkët e Namuna) offer some of Albania's most impressive scenery, and the area has exploded in recent years as a popular backpacker destination. It's a totally different side of the country here: that of blood feuds, deep tradition, extraordinary landscapes and fierce local pride. It's absolutely a highlight of any trip to Albania and, indeed, it's quite extraordinary to get this far removed from modern life in 21st-century Europe.

### Valbona

Valbona has a gorgeous setting on a wide plain surrounded by towering mountain peaks, and its summer tourism industry is

---

### CROSSING LAKE KOMAN

One of Albania's undisputed highlights is this superb three-hour ferry ride (www.komanilakeferry.com/en/ferry-lines-in-the-komani-lake) across vast Lake Koman, connecting the towns of Koman and Fierza. Lake Koman was created in 1978 when the Drin River was dammed, with the result being that you can cruise through spectacular mountain scenery where many incredibly hardy people still live as they have for centuries, tucked away in tiny mountain villages.

The best way to experience the journey is to make a three-day, two-night loop beginning and ending in Shkodra, and taking in Koman, Fierza, Valbona and Theth. To do this, arrange to have the morning 6.30am *furgon* (shared minibus) from Shkodra to Koman (600 lekë, two hours) pick you up at your hotel, which will get you to the ferry departure point by 8.30am. There are normally two ferries daily (700 lekë, 2½ hours) and both leave from Koman at 9am. One of the two, the *Berisha*, carries up to 10 cars, which cost 700 lekë per square metre of space they occupy. There's also a big car ferry that leaves at 1pm, but it only runs when demand is high enough – call ahead to make a reservation.

On arrival in Fierza, the boats are met by *furgons* that will take you to either Bajram Curri (200 lekë, 15 minutes) or to Valbona (400 lekë, 15 minutes). There's no real reason to stop in Bajram Curri unless you plan to head to Kosovo. Hikers will want to head straight for Valbona, where you can stay for a night or two before doing the stunning day hike to Theth. After the hike you can stay for another night or two in glorious Theth before taking a *furgon* back to Shkodra.

increasingly well organised. The village itself consists virtually only of guesthouses and camping grounds, nearly all of which have their own restaurants attached. Most travellers just spend a night here before trekking to Theth, which is a shame as there are a wealth of other excellent hikes to do in the area – ask for guides or information at the superhelpful Hotel Rilindja (p51), or check out the excellent www.journeytovalbona. com website, a DIY-kit for the entire area.

## 🛏 Sleeping & Eating

★ **Hotel Rilindja**                    GUESTHOUSE €
(☑ 067 3014 637; www.journeytovalbona. com; Quku i Valbonës; tent/dm/d incl breakfast €4/12/35; 🛜) Pioneering tourism in Valbona since 2005, the Albanian-American–run Rilindja is hugely popular with travellers, who love the comfortable accommodation and excellent food. The five simple rooms in the atmospheric farmhouse share a bathroom, except for one with private facilities. The new Rezidenca up the road offers a far more upscale experience with en suite singles, double and triples.

**Hotel & Camping Tradita**              CHALET €
(☑ 067 3380 014, 067 3014 567; Valbona; dm/chalet €10/25) This collection of five chalets in the middle of the village has extraordinary views in all directions. The pine cabins each sleep three and come with hot water and private facilities. The owner, Isa, also offers six further rooms in his adjacent stone house. The good on-site restaurant is the social centre of the village.

## ℹ Getting There & Away

Valbona can be reached from Shkodra via the Lake Koman Ferry and a connecting *furgon* (minibus) from Fierzë (400 lekë, one hour). Alternatively it can be reached by *furgon* from Bajram Curri (200 lekë, 45 minutes).

## Theth

This unique mountain village easily has the most dramatic setting in Albania. Just the journey here is quite incredible, whether you approach over the mountains on foot from Valbona or by vehicle from Shkodra. Both a sprawling village along the valley floor amid an amphitheatre of distant mountains and a national park containing stunning landscapes and excellent hiking routes, Theth is now well on its way to being Albania's next big thing. An improved – though still incomplete – asphalt road from Shkodra has made access to this once virtually unknown village far easier in recent years, bringing with it the familiar problem of overdevelopment. Come quickly while Theth retains its incomparable romance and unique charm.

## 🛏 Sleeping & Eating

There are no normal restaurants in town, but nearly all guesthouses and homestays offer three meals a day.

★ **Guesthouse Rupa**                  GUESTHOUSE €
(☑ 068 2003 393, 022 244 077; rorupaog@yahoo. com; r per person incl full board €25; ⊙ Apr-Oct) This traditional stone guesthouse with a large garden is run by the formidable Roza, who speaks good English and is a great source of information about the area. There are only five rooms, but – rarely for Theth – all have private facilities, even if some of them are not in great shape. The excellent meals are taken communally around a big table.

**Vila Zorgji**                        GUESTHOUSE €
(☑ 068 3617 309; pellumbkola@gmail.com; r incl breakfast/full board per person €15/25; ⊙ Apr-Oct) One of the best new guesthouses in town, Zorgji is on the main track towards the church as you enter the village, next to the pink-painted school. The building on the road is the restaurant (which also has two rooms upstairs), while Zorgji's best accommodation is a couple of minutes up the hillside, where great wood-panelled rooms enjoy outstanding views.

## ℹ Getting There & Away

A new asphalt road from Shkodra ends 15km before reaching Theth. Do not attempt the last part unless you have a 4WD.

A daily *furgon* (1000 lekë, two hours) leaves from Shkodra at 7am and will pick you up from your hotel if your hotel owner calls ahead for you. The return trip leaves Theth between 1pm and 2pm, arriving late afternoon in Shkodra. During the summer months it's also easy to arrange a shared *furgon* transfer to Shkodra with other hikers from Valbona.

# CENTRAL ALBANIA

## Berat

🏛 032 / POP 35,000

Berat weaves its own very special magic and is easily a highlight of visiting Albania. Its most striking feature is the collection of white Ottoman houses climbing up the hill to its castle, earning it the title of 'town of a thousand windows' and helping it join Gjirokastra on the list of Unesco World Heritage sites in 2008. Its rugged mountain setting is particularly evocative when the clouds swirl around the tops of the minarets or break up to show the icy peak of Mt Tomorri. Despite now being a big centre for tourism in Albania, Berat has managed to retain its easygoing charm and friendly atmosphere.

## ◉ Sights

### ★Kalaja
CASTLE

(100 lekë; ⊙24hr) The Kala neighbourhood inside the castle's walls still lives and breathes; if you walk around this busy, ancient neighbourhood for long enough you'll invariably stumble into someone's courtyard thinking it's a church or ruin (no one seems to mind, though). In spring and summer the fragrance of camomile is in the air (and underfoot) and wildflowers burst from every gap between the stones, giving the entire site a magical feel.

### ★Onufri Museum
GALLERY

(200 lekë; ⊙ 9am-2pm & 4-7pm Mon-Sat, 9am-7pm Sun May-Sep, to 4pm Oct-Apr) The Onufri Museum is situated in the Kala quarter's biggest church, **Church of the Dormition of St Mary** (Kisha Fjetja e Shën Mërisë). The church itself dates from 1797 and was built on the foundations of an earlier 10th-century chapel. Today Onufri's spectacular 16th-century religious paintings are displayed along with the church's beautifully gilded 19th-century iconostasis. Don't miss the chapel behind the iconostasis, or its painted cupola, whose frescoes are now faded almost to invisibility.

### Ethnographic Museum
MUSEUM

(200 lekë; ⊙ 9am-2pm & 4-7pm Mon-Sat, 9am-7pm Sun May-Sep, to 4pm Oct-Apr) On the steep hillside that leads up to the castle is this excellent museum, which is housed in an 18th-century Ottoman house that's as interesting as the exhibits. The ground floor has displays of traditional clothes and the tools used by silversmiths and weavers, while the upper storey has kitchens, bedrooms and guest rooms decked out in traditional style.

## 🛏 Sleeping

### ★Berat Backpackers
HOSTEL €

(🏛069 7854 219; www.beratbackpackers.com; 295 Gorica; tent/dm/r €6/10/30; ⊙mid-Mar–Oct; @ 🛜) This transformed traditional house in the Gorica quarter houses one of Albania's friendliest hostels. The vine-clad establishment contains a basement bar and restaurant, an alfresco drinking area and a relaxed atmosphere that money can't buy. There are two airy dorms with original ceilings, and four gorgeous, excellent-value double rooms with antique furnishings. Shaded camping area and cheap laundry also available.

### Hotel Restaurant Klea
GUESTHOUSE €

(🏛032 234 970; Rr Shën Triadha, Kala; s/d/ incl breakfast €20/30) From the castle gates go straight ahead and you'll find this gorgeous hilltop hideaway, run by a friendly English-speaking family. There are just five compact wood-panelled rooms, each with its own clean and modern bathroom. The downstairs restaurant adjoins a wonderful garden and has a daily changing specials menu featuring tasty Albanian fare (200 lekë to450 lekë).

### ★Hotel Mangalemi
HOTEL €€

(🏛068 2323 238; www.mangalemihotel.com; Rr Mihail Komneno; s/d/tr from €30/40/55; P ✴ @ 🛜) A true highlight of Berat is this gorgeous place inside two sprawling Ottoman houses where all the rooms are beautifully furnished in traditional Berati style and balconies give superb views. Its terrace restaurant (mains 400 lekë to 600 lekë; reserve on summer evenings) is the best place to eat in town and has great Albanian food with bonus views of Mt Tomorri.

## 🍴 Eating

### ★Lili Homemade Food
ALBANIAN €

(🏛069 234 9362; mains 500-700 lekë; ⊙11am-10pm) This charming family home deep into the Mangalem Quarter underneath the castle is the setting for one of Berat's best restaurants. Lili speaks English and will invite you to take a table in his backyard where you can order a meal of traditional Berati cooking. We heartily recommend the *gjize ferges,* a delicious mash of tomato, garlic and cheese.

### Mangalemi Restaurant          ALBANIAN €€

(Rr Mihail Komneno; mains 300-800 lekë; ☺ noon-11pm; ⓢ) The restaurant of the excellent Hotel Mangalemi is the best place in town for traditional Albanian cooking, and summer nights on its breezy verandah are not to be missed. The large menu serves simple, home-cooked traditional Berati fare, including an excellent veal kebab, mouth-watering grilled halloumi cheese and *tavë kosi* (lamb and rice baked in yoghurt and eggs).

## ⓘ Information

**Information Centre** (Rr Antipatrea; ☺ 9am-noon & 2-6pm Mon-Fri) This brand new and rather sleek tourist information centre can be found on Berat's main square, and has lots of local information and English-speaking staff.

## ⓘ Getting There & Away

Berat now has a bus terminal, around 3km from the town centre on the main road to Tirana. Bus services run to Tirana (400 lekë, three hours, half-hourly until 3pm). There are also buses to Saranda (1600 lekë, six hours, two daily at 8am and 2pm), one of which goes via Gjirokastra (1000 lekë, four hours, 8am). To get to the bus station from the centre, ask locals to put you on a bus to 'Terminali Autobusave'.

# SOUTHERN COAST

# Saranda

☑ 0852 / POP 38,000

Saranda is the unofficial capital of the Albanian Riviera, and come the summer months it seems like half of Tirana relocates here to enjoy the busy beach and busier nightlife along its crowd-filled seaside promenade. What was once a sleepy fishing village is now a thriving city, and while Saranda has lost much of its charm in the past two decades, it has retained much of its charisma.

## ◎ Sights

### ★ Butrint          RUINS

(http://butrint.al/eng/; 700 lekë; ☺ 8am-7.30am) The ancient ruins of Butrint, 18km south of Saranda, are famed for their size, beauty and tranquillity. They're in a fantastic natural setting and are part of a 29-sq-km national park. The remains – Albania's finest – are from a variety of periods, spanning 2500 years. Set aside at least two hours to explore. Buses from Saranda (100 lekë, 20 minutes, hourly from 8.30am to 5.30pm) leave from outside the ZIT Information Centre (p54), returning from Butrint hourly on the hour.

## 🛏 Sleeping

### Hairy Lemon          HOSTEL €

(☑ 069 889 9196; www.hairylemonhostel.com; cnr Mitat Hoxha & E Arberit, 8th floor; dm incl breakfast from €10; ⓢ) With a prime 8th-floor location, a clean beach at its base and a friendly, helpful atmosphere, this Irish-run backpacker hostel is a good place to chill. There's an open-plan kitchen and lounge, and two dorm rooms with fans and sea breezes, not to mention unlimited pancakes for breakfast.

### Hotel Titania          HOTEL €€

(☑ 069 689 7826, 085 222 869; hoteltitania@yahoo.com; Rr Jonianët 13; r incl breakfast from €50; ⊗ⓢ) This place is a great bargain given that most of its rooms have sea views and the seafront promenade begins just meters from its front door. The rooms are spacious and modern, all with balconies and good bathrooms. An excellent breakfast is served on the delightful roof terrace that looks over the bay.

## ✕ Eating

### Gërthëla          SEAFOOD €€

(Rr Jonianët; mains 300-1000 lekë; ☺ 11am-midnight; ⓢ) One of Saranda's original restaurants, 'The Crab' is a long-standing taverna that only has fish and seafood on the menu, and locals will tell you with certainty that it offers the best-prepared versions of either available in town. The cosy glass-fronted dining room is full of traditional knick-knacks and there's a big wine selection to boot.

### ★ Mare Nostrum          INTERNATIONAL €€€

(Rr Jonianët; mains 700-1200 lekë; ☺ 7am-midnight Mar-Dec) This sleek restaurant immediately feels different to the others along the seafront. Here there's elegant decor that wouldn't look out of place in a major European capital; the buzz of a smart, in-the-know crowd; and an imaginative menu that combines the seafood and fish you'll find everywhere else with dishes such as Indonesian chicken curry and burgers.

## THE ALBANIAN RIVIERA

The Albanian Riviera was a revelation a decade or so ago, when backpackers discovered the last virgin stretch of the Mediterranean coast in Europe, flocking here in droves, setting up ad hoc campsites and exploring scores of little-known beaches. Since then, things have become significantly less pristine, with overdevelopment blighting many of the once-charming coastal villages. But worry not, while Dhërmi and Himara may be well and truly swarming, with a little persistence there are still spots to kick back and enjoy the empty beaches the region was once so famous for.

One such place is **Vuno**, a tiny hillside village above picturesque Jal Beach. Each summer Vuno's primary school is filled with blow-up beds and it becomes **Shkolla Hostel** (☑ 069 2119 596; www.tiranahostel.com/south-hostel; Vuno; tent/dm €4/8; ⊘ May-Sep). What it lacks in infrastructure and privacy it makes up for with its goat-bell soundtrack and evening campfire. Jal has two beaches; one has free camping while the other has a camping ground set back from the sea (including tent 2000 lekë). Fresh seafood is bountiful in Jal and there are plenty of beachside restaurants in summer.

## ℹ Information

**ZIT Information Centre** (☑ 069 324 3304; Rr Skënderbeu; ⊘ 8am-8pm Jul-Aug, to 4pm Mon-Fri Sep-Jun) Saranda's tiny but excellent ZIT information centre provides information about transport and local sights and is staffed by friendly and helpful English-speaking staff.

## ℹ Getting There & Away

### BUS

Most buses leave just uphill from the ruins on Rr Vangjel Pando, right in the centre of town. Buses to Tirana (1300 lekë, eight hours) go inland via Gjirokastra (300 lekë, two hours) and leave regularly between 5am and 10.30am There are later buses at 2pm and 10pm. The 7am Tirana bus takes the coastal route (1300 lekë, eight hours). There is also one bus a day to Himara at 11.30am (400 lekë, two hours), which can stop at any point along the way to let you off at riviera villages.

Municipal buses go to Butrint via Ksamil hourly on the half hour from 8.30am (100 lekë, 30 minutes), leaving opposite ZIT and returning from Butrint on the hour each hour.

### FERRY

**Finikas Lines** (☑ 085 226 057, 067 2022 004; www.finikas-lines.com; Rr Mithat Hoxha) at the port sells hydrofoil and ferry tickets for Corfu (adult/child €24/13, 45 minutes) with a daily departured 9am, 10.30am and 4pm in the summer months. From Corfu there are three ferries per day in summer: 9am, 1pm and 6.30pm. Note that Greek time is one hour ahead of Albanian time.

# EASTERN ALBANIA

## Gjirokastra

☑ 084 / POP 43,000

Defined by its castle, roads paved with chunky limestone and shale, imposing slate-roofed houses and views out to the Drina Valley, Gjirokastra is a magical hillside town described beautifully by Albania's most famous author, Ismail Kadare (b 1936), in *Chronicle in Stone*. There has been a settlement here for 2500 years, though these days it's the 600 'monumental' Ottoman-era houses in town that attract visitors. The town is also synonymous for Albanians with former dictator Enver Hoxha, who was born here and ensured the town was relatively well preserved under his rule; though he is not memorialised in any way here today. Far less touristy than Berat, the town is equally as charming and has several fascinating sights, as well as some excellent accommodation options.

## ◉ Sights

★ **Gjirokastra Castle**                     CASTLE
(200 lekë; ⊘ 9am-8pm summer, 9am-4pm winter) Gjirokastra's eerie hilltop castle is one of the biggest in the Balkans and is definitely worth the steep walk up from the Old Town. The castle remains somewhat infamous due to its use as a prison under the communists. Inside there's an eerie collection of armoury, two good museums, a recovered US Air Force jet shot down during the communist era, and a hilariously hard-to-use audio tour

that's included in your entry fee. The views across the valley are simply superb.

★ **Cold War Tunnel**   TUNNEL
(200 lekë; ⊙ 8am-4pm Mon-Fri, 10am-2pm Sat, 9am-3pm Sun) Gjirokastra's most interesting sight in no way relates to its traditional architecture, but instead to its far more modern kind: this is a giant bunker built deep under the castle for use by the local authorities during the full-scale invasion Hoxha was so paranoid about. Built in secret during the 1960s, it has 80 rooms and its existence remained unknown to locals until the 1990s. Personal guided tours run from the tourist information booth on the main square all day.

★ **Zekate House**   HISTORIC BUILDING
(200 leke; ⊙ 9am-6pm) This incredible three-storey house dates from 1811 and has twin towers and a double-arched facade. It's fascinating to nose around the almost totally unchanged interiors of an Ottoman-era home, especially the upstairs galleries, which are the most impressive. The owners live next door and collect the payments; to get here, follow the signs past the Hotel Kalemi and keep zigzagging up the hill.

### 🛏 Sleeping

★ **Stone City Hostel**   HOSTEL €
(📞 069 348 4271; www.stonecityhostel.com; Pazar; incl breakfast dm €10-11, d €25; ⊙ closed Nov-Mar; ✳ 🖥) This brand new hostel is a fantastic conversion of an Old Town house created and run by Dutchman Walter. The attention to detail and respect for traditional craftsmanship is extremely heartening, with beautiful carved wooden panels in all the rooms. Choose between the dorm rooms with custom-made bunks or the one double room, all of which share spotless communal facilities.

★ **Gjirokastra Hotel**   HOTEL €
(📞 068 4099 669, 084 265 982; hhotelgjirokastra@ yahoo.com; Rr. Sheazi Çomo; s/d €25/35, ste €40; ✳ 🖥) A great option that combines modern facilities with traditional touches, this lovely family-run hotel inside a 300-year-old house has rooms that boast huge balconies and gorgeously carved wooden ceilings. The suite is gorgeous, with a long Ottoman-style sofa, original wooden doors and ceiling, and magnificent stone walls: it's an absolute bargain at €40.

**Hotel Kalemi 2**   HOTEL €€
(www.kalemihotels.com; Rr Alqi Kondi; incl breakfast d €40-45, tr €55, ste €65-100; @ 🖥) The second of the two Kalemi hotels, this brand new place is a total renovation of a large stone mansion that has some beautiful fittings in its 16 individually decorated rooms. Modern bathrooms contrast with the elaborate traditional ceilings. The huge suite is easily worth its price and must rank among the most atmospheric sleeping options in Albania.

### 🍴 Eating

★ **Kujtimi**   ALBANIAN €€
(mains 350-650 lekë; ⊙ 11am-11pm) This wonderfully laid-back outdoor restaurant, run by the Dumi family, is an excellent choice. Try the delicious *trofte* (fried trout; 400 lekë), the *midhje* (fried mussels; 350 lekë) and *qifqi* (rice balls fried in herbs and egg, a local speciality). The terrace is the perfect place to absorb the charms of the Old Town with a glass of local wine.

**Taverna Kuka**   ALBANIAN €€
(Rr Astrit Karagjozi; mains 300-750 lekë; ⊙ 11am-midnight; 🖥) Just beyond Gjirokastra's old mosque, this largely outdoor terrace restaurant has a wonderful location and a menu full of delicious Albanian cooking, including *qofte* (meatballs), Saranda mussels, pork pancetta and grilled lamb. There's a surprisingly cool decor given the rural Albanian setting and its terrace is a firm local favourite on summer evenings.

---

### ESSENTIAL FOOD & DRINK

**Byrek** Pastry with cheese or meat.

**Fergesë** Baked peppers, egg and cheese, and occasionally meat.

**Konjak** Local brandy.

**Midhje** Wild or farmed mussels, often served fried.

**Paçë koke** Sheep's head soup, usually served for breakfast.

**Qofta** Flat or cylindrical minced-meat rissoles.

**Raki** Popular spirit made from grapes.

**Raki mani** Spirit made from mulberries.

**Sufllaqë** Doner kebab.

**Tavë** Meat baked with cheese and egg.

## ⓘ Information

**Information Centre** (◷ 8am-4pm Mon-Fri, to 2pm Sat, to 3pm Sun) In a kiosk on the main square at the entrance to the Old Town, the staff here don't speak a word of English, which isn't very helpful, but there are town maps for sale and well as information about tours in the local area. Tickets for the Cold War Tunnel are also on sale here.

## ⓘ Getting There & Away

Buses stop at the ad hoc bus station just after the Eida petrol station on the new town's main road. Services include Tirana (1200 lekë, seven hours, every one to two hours until 5pm), Saranda (300 lekë, one hour, hourly) and Berat (1000 lekë, four hours, 9.15am and 3.45pm). A taxi between the Old Town and the bus station is 300 lekë.

## ⓘ Getting Around

The new town (no slate roofs here) is on the main Saranda–Tirana road, and a taxi up to or back from the Old Town is 300 lekë.

# SURVIVAL GUIDE

## ⓘ Directory A–Z

### ACCOMMODATION

Hotels and guesthouses are easily found throughout Albania, as tourism continues to grow and grow. You will almost never have trouble finding a room for the night, though seaside towns are often booked out in late July and August.

---

### COUNTRY FACTS

**Area** 28,748 sq km

**Capital** Tirana

**Country Code** ☑ 355

**Currency** Lek (plural lekë); the euro (€) is widely accepted.

**Emergencies** ☑ 127 (Ambulance); ☑ 128 (Fire); ☑ 129 (Police)

**Language** Albanian

**Money** ATMs in most towns.

**Population** 2.77 million

**Visas** Nearly all visitors can travel visa-free to Albania.

---

### EATING PRICE RANGES

The following price categories are based on the cost of a main course.

**€** less than 300 lekë

**€€** 300 lekë to 600 lekë

**€€€** more than 600 lekë

---

### MONEY

The lek (plural lekë) is the official currency of Albania, though the euro is widely accepted; you'll get a better deal for things in general if you use lek. Accommodation is generally quoted in euros but can be paid in either currency. ATMs can be found in all but the most rural of Albania's towns, and many dispense cash in both currencies. Credit cards are accepted only in the larger hotels, shops and travel agencies, and few of these are outside Tirana.

### OPENING HOURS

**Banks** 9am to 3.30pm Monday to Friday

**Cafes & Bars** 8am to midnight

**Offices** 8am to 5pm Monday to Friday

**Restaurants** 8am to midnight

**Shops** 8am to 7pm; siesta time can be any time between noon and 4pm

### PUBLIC HOLIDAYS

**New Year's Day** 1 January

**Summer Day** 16 March

**Nevruz** 23 March

**Catholic Easter** March or April

**Orthodox Easter** March or April

**May Day** 1 May

**Mother Teresa Day** 19 October

**Independence Day** 28 November

**Liberation Day** 29 November

**Christmas Day** 25 December

### TELEPHONE

Albania's country phone code is ☑ 355.

### Mobile Phones

Albania has a good level of mobile coverage, though there are still some areas where getting a signal can be hard. It's very straightforward to buy a SIM card with mobile data from any internet provider. Prepaid SIM cards cost around 500 lekë and include credit. Mobile numbers begin with 06. To call an Albanian mobile number from abroad, dial +☑ 355 then either 67, 68 or 69 (ie drop the 0).

## ℹ Getting There & Away

### AIR

Nënë Tereza International Airport is a modern, well-run terminal 17km northwest of Tirana. There are no domestic flights within Albania. Airlines flying to and from Tirana include Adria Airways (www.adria.si), Alitalia (www.alitalia. com), Austrian Airlines (www.austrian.com), Lufthansa (www.lufthansa.com), Olympic Air (www.olympicair.com), Pegasus Airlines (www. flypgs.com) and Turkish Airlines (www.turkish airlines.com).

### LAND

There are no passenger trains into Albania, so your border-crossing options are buses, *furgons* (minibuses), taxis or walking to a border and picking up transport on the other side.

### Border Crossings

**Montenegro** The main crossings link Shkodra to Ulcinj (via Muriqan, Albania and Sukobin, Montenegro) and to Podgorica (Hani i Hotit).

**Kosovo** The closest border crossing to the Lake Koman Ferry terminal is Morina, and further south is Qafë Prush. Near Kukës use Morinë for the highway to Tirana.

**Macedonia** Use Blato to get to Debar, and Qafë e Thanës or Tushemisht, each to one side of Pogradec, for accessing Ohrid.

**Greece** The main border crossing to and from Greece is Kakavija on the road from Athens to Tirana.

### Bus

From Tirana, regular buses head to Pristina, Kosovo; to Skopje in Macedonia; to Ulcinj in Montenegro; and to Athens and Thessaloniki in Greece. *Furgons* and buses leave Shkodra for Montenegro, and buses head to Kosovo from Durrës. Buses travel to Greece from Albanian towns on the southern coast as well as from Tirana.

### SEA

Two or three boats per day ply the route between Saranda and Corfu, in Greece, and there are plenty of ferry companies making the journey to Italy from Vlora and Durrës. There are additional ferries from Vlora and Himara to Corfu in the summer.

# Belarus

## Includes →

## Best Places to Eat

→ Bistro de Luxe (p63)

→ Jules Verne (p67)

→ Kamyanyitsa (p63)

→ Time's Cafe (p67)

→ Lido (p62)

## Best Places to Stay

→ Hotel Manastyrski (p61)

→ Hermitage Hotel (p67)

→ Revolución Hostel (p61)

→ Kamyanyuki Hotel Complex (p68)

→ Neman Hotel (p66)

## Why Go?

Eastern Europe's outcast, Belarus (Беларусь) lies at the edge of the region and seems determined to avoid integration with the rest of the continent at all costs. Taking its lead from the Soviet Union rather than the European Union, this little-visited dictatorship may seem like a strange choice for travellers, but its isolation lies at the heart of its appeal.

While the rest of Eastern Europe has charged headlong into capitalism, Belarus allows the chance to visit a Europe with minimal advertising and no litter or graffiti. Outside the monumental Stalinist capital of Minsk, Belarus offers a simple yet pleasing landscape of cornflower fields, thick forests and picturesque villages. The country also has two excellent national parks and is home to Europe's largest mammal, the *zubr* (European bison). While travellers will always be the subject of curiosity, they'll also be on the receiving end of warm hospitality and a genuine welcome.

## When to Go
### Minsk

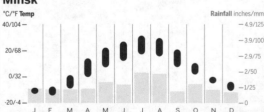

**Jun–Aug** Come to Belarus to escape the crowds elsewhere in Eastern Europe.

**Early Jul** On 6 July stay up all night for Kupalle, a fortune-telling festival with pagan roots.

**Oct** Pleasantly cool climate and fall foliage in Belavezhskaya Pushcha National Park near Brest.

## Belarus Highlights

**1 Minsk** (p60) Getting under the skin of Belarus' friendly and accessible capital, a showcase of Stalinist architecture.

**2 Brest** (p66) Strolling through the mellow pedestrian streets of this cosmopolitan city and gaping at its epic WWII memorials.

**3 Mir Castle** (p66) Training your lens on this fairy-tale 16th-century castle – and its equally famous reflection.

**4 Njasvizh** (p65) Exploring this tranquil provincial town's parks and impeccably restored castle.

**5 Belavezhskaya Pushcha National Park** (p68) Touring Europe's oldest wildlife refuge in search of rare European bison.

# MINSK MIHCK

17 / POP 1.915 MILLION

Minsk will almost certainly surprise you. The capital of Belarus is, contrary to its dreary reputation, a progressive, modern and clean place. Fashionable cafes, impressive restaurants and crowded nightclubs vie for your attention, while sushi bars and art galleries have taken up residence in a city centre once totally remodelled to the tastes of Stalin. Despite the strong police presence and obedient citizenry, Minsk is a thoroughly pleasant place that's easy to become fond of.

## ⊙ Sights

If you're short on time, have a wander around the attractive Old Town (Upper City). This was once the city's thriving Jewish quarter, and while most of it was destroyed in the war, a smattering of pre-war buildings along vul Internatsyanalnaya and a rebuilt **ratusha** (Town Hall; pl Svobody) on pl Svabody emit a whiff of history.

### ★ Museum of the Great Patriotic War MUSEUM

(17 2030 792; www.warmuseum.by; pr Peremozhtsau 8; adult/student BR7/3.50, photos BR1.50, guided tours BR30; ⊙10am-6pm Tue & Thu-Sun, 11am-7pm Wed) Located in a garish new building, Minsk's best museum houses an excellent display detailing Belarus' suffering and heroism during the Nazi occupation. With English explanations throughout, atmospheric dioramas and a range of real tanks, airplanes and artillery from WWII, it's one of the capital's few must-see attractions.

---

## ITINERARIES

### Three Days

Spend two days getting to know **Minsk**, whose Stalinist architecture belies a lively, friendly city. On the third day, take a day trip to **Njasvizh** and **Mir** with their historic castles and charming Belarusian countryside feel.

### One Week

Take a train to **Brest** and spend a couple of days there, including a day trip to **Belavezhskaya Pushcha National Park**. If you still have time, head north to pleasant **Hrodna** before exiting via Poland.

---

### Belarusian State Art Museum MUSEUM

(vul Lenina 20; adult/student BR5/2.50; ⊙11am-7pm Wed-Mon) This excellent state museum has been renovated and now includes a light-bathed extension out back that features local art from the 1940s to the 1970s. Don't miss Valentin Volkov's socialist realist *Minsk on July 3, 1944* (1944–5), depicting the Red Army's arrival in the ruined city. Several works by Yudel Pen, Chagall's teacher, are here, including his 1914 portrait of Chagall.

### Trinity Hill HISTORIC SITE

(Traetskae Pradmestse) Trinity Hill is a pleasant – if tiny – re-creation of Minsk's pre-war buildings on a pretty bend of the river just a little north of the centre. It has a few little cafes, restaurants and shops, and a walking bridge leads over to the **Island of Courage & Sorrow** (Island of Tears), an evocative Afghan war memorial known colloquially as the Island of Tears by locals.

### Stalin Line Museum MUSEUM

(http://stalin-line.by; Rt 28, Lashany; adult/student R10/5; ⊙10am-6pm) A must for military buffs is this impressive collection of tanks, missiles, helicopters and all other manner of Soviet war paraphernalia in an open field in Lashany, about 25km northwest of Minsk. While the theme is WWII, much of the military hardware is slightly more modern, generally dating from the 1960s and '70s. To get here take a Maladzechna-bound *marshrutka* (fixed-rate minivan) from the Druzhnaya (p64) stop behind Minsk's train station (R3.50, frequent).

### Zaslavsky Jewish Monument MONUMENT

(vul Melnikayte) This extremely moving sight, rather hidden away in a sunken gully amid trees off vul Melnikayte, commemorates the savage murder of 5000 Jews from Minsk at the hands of the Nazis on 2 March 1942.

## ⊊ Tours

### City Tour BUS

(17 392 5999; http://citytour.by; adult/child BR30/15; ⊙tours 11am, 1.30pm, 4pm & 6.30pm) Much of Minsk's most jaw-dropping architecture from the Soviet and Lukashenko eras is outside the centre, so these two-hour double-decker bus tours are a great way to see several of them at once. Tours kick off at the classic Stalinist 'City Gates' opposite the train station.

## MINSK'S MAIN DRAG

A walk along Minsk's inconspicuous **pr Nezalezhnastsi** (Independence Avenue) is a good way to take Minsk's pulse while also taking in a few sights. Formerly pr Fran-cyska Skaryny, it runs the length of the modern city, from stubbornly austere pl Nezalezhnastsi to the pinnacle of Lukashenko-approved hubris, the rhombicuboctahe-dron-shaped **National Library of Belarus**.

Heading out from pl Nezalezhnastsi, you'll pass the iconic Minsk Hotel, the ominous **KGB headquarters** (pr Nezalezhnastsi 17) and daunting **Oktyabrskaya pl** (pl Kastrych-nitskaya) before crossing the Svislach River, straddled by the city's two main parks. Just across the bridge, on the west bank, is the **former residence of Lee Harvey Oswald** (vul Kamyunistychnaya 4) – it's the bottom left apartment). The alleged assassin of former US president John F Kennedy lived here for a couple of years in his early 20s. He arrived in Minsk in January 1960 after leaving the US Marines and defecting to the USSR. Once here, he truly went native: he got a job in a radio factory, married a Minsk woman, had a child – and even changed his name to Alek. But soon he returned to the United States and...you know the rest.

Just 100m northeast of here, **pl Peramohi** (Victory Sq), ploshchad Pobedy in Russian), is marked by a giant **Victory Obelisk** and its eternal flame, which is directly beneath the obelisk underground. From here you can continue walking to **pl Jakuba Kolasa**, a leafy square occupied by an elephantine monument to the Belarusian writer, or hop on the Metro to go out to the National Library 5km away.

## 🛏 Sleeping

If you're here for more than a couple of nights, consider renting an apartment. You can go through online booking sites, but dealing with agents directly is better, especially if you require visa support. Two of the best are **Belarus Rent** (www.belarusrent.com; apts from US$45) and **Minsk4rent** (☑ 29 1114 817; www.minsk4rent.com; apts from US$35).

★**Revolución Hostel** HOSTEL €
(☑ 29 6146 465; www.revolucion.by; vul Revalyutsi-ynaya 16; dm US$8-10, d US$24-31; ➋ 🛜) Right in the heart of the Old Town, this friendly and pleasingly quirky hostel is festooned with photographs of various revolutionaries and even has a pet tortoise called Marseil-laise. The excellent four- to 12-bed dorms feature solid wooden bunk beds with individual plugs, and there are a couple of equally pleasing double rooms as well.

**Trinity Hostel** HOSTEL €
(☑ 29 3112 783; www.hostel-traveler.by; vul Stara-vilenskaya 12; dm from US$11, r without bathroom US$28-33; ➋ 🛜) This well-run hostel in a quiet courtyard is a great option. It's centrally located on Trinity Hill (p60), and has 40 beds in four- to eight-bed dorms and several excellent-value private rooms distributed between the main building and an adjoining

riverside annex. There's a no-alcohol rule and a strict ban on making noise after 11pm.

★**Hotel Manastyrski** HISTORIC HOTEL €€
(☑ 17 3290 300; http://monastyrski.by/en; vul Kiril-la i Mefodya 6; s/d incl breakfast from US$75/$96; ➋ ❋ 🛜) Housed in the converted remains of a Benedictine Monastery in the heart of Minsk's bustling Old Town, this 48-room gem cannot be beat for location or atmosphere. Rooms are smart and comfortably furnished with dark-wood fittings, while the impressive corridors are decorated with frescoes (found during the renovation) and wrought-iron chandeliers. Booking directly on its website nets a 10% discount.

**Hampton by Hilton** BUSINESS HOTEL €€
(☑ 17 2154 000; http://hamptoninn3.hilton.com; vul Talstoha 8; r incl breakfast from US$70; 🅿 ➋ ❋ @ 🛜) While not quite in the centre, the advantages of this shiny business-class hotel are many: slick service, comfortable beds, contemporary design, nice desks and functioning everything. Rooms are slightly on the cosy (as in small) side, but for this price and level of amenities, you're not complaining.

## 🍴 Eating

Minsk has a decent eating scene and plenty of choice – don't believe the hype about food

# Minsk

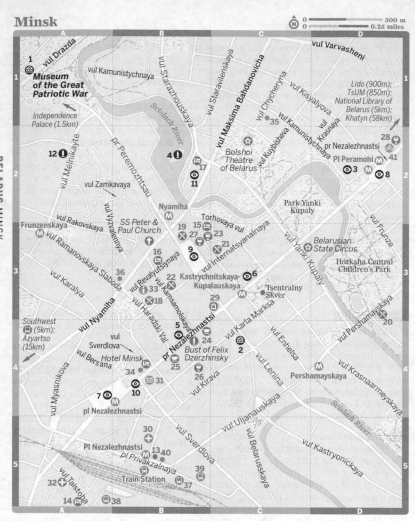

in Belarus; in the capital, at least, you'll eat well. Consider reserving tables at weekends.

### ★ Lido
CAFETERIA €

(pr Nezalezhnastsi 49/1; mains BR2.50-5; ☺8am-11pm Mon-Fri, from 11am Sat & Sun; ☺🍴) This large, upscale *stolovaya* (cafeteria) with Latvian roots has a huge array of food on display, so it's easy for non-Russian speakers: just point at what you want. Classic Russian soups and salads, grilled trout and chicken meatballs are highlights.

### Stolle
PIES €

(www.stolle.by; vul Rakovskaya 23; pies from BR2.50; ☺10am-11pm; 🛜) Stolle is a great option, with delicious, freshly baked sweet and savoury pies to eat in or take away. Unlike the many other branches in town, this well-located one features a full non-pie menu of traditional Russian and Belarusian cuisine.

Other central branches include those at **vul Internatsyonalnaya** (vul Internatsyonalnaya 23; ☺10am-11pm; 🛜), **vul Sverdlova** (vul Sverdlova 22; ☺10am-10pm; 🛜) and **pr Nezalezhnastsi** (pr Nezalezhnastsi 38; ☺8am-9pm).

# Minsk

**Kamyanitsa**      BELARUSIAN €€
(☑17 2945 124; vul Pershamayskaya 18; mains BR10-20; ◎noon-11pm; ☻) Wander a couple blocks southeast of the centre for some of the best traditional Belarusian cuisine in town. The *draniki* (potato pancakes) here are top-notch, or go for the *koldumy* (stuffed *draniki*) or quirky house specials like Granny Dunya's Meat Pot.

**Tapas Bar**      SPANISH €€
(☑29 3991 111; vul Internatsyanalnaya 9/17; mains BR10-20; ◎11am-midnight; ☻☏☑) This stylish joint with olive-coloured walls, friendly service and bright dining areas serves up good tapas from a large menu. All the classics are present, as well as a range of meaty mains and excellent *paella* (good for two).

**Gambrinus**      BELARUSIAN €€
(pl Svobody 2; mains BR15-25; ◎noon-midnight) This dungeon pub serves a mix of delicious Belarusian and European food and has a 'beer book' with over 100 beers (and about as many

cocktails, to boot). In the summer months you'll want to roost on the terrace and watch the action around the *ratusha* (town hall) directly opposite on central pl Svobody.

★**Bistro de Luxe**      BISTRO €€€
(44 7891 111; vul Haradski Val 10; mains BR20-45; ◎8am-midnight Mon-Fri, from 11am Sat & Sun; ☏) Housed in a gorgeous space with chandeliers, sleek brasserie-style furnishings, a chessboard floor and luxury toilets, Bistro de Luxe has charm and atmosphere that's hard to find elsewhere in Minsk. The food is excellent – it leans towards Italian – and service is impeccable. Breakfast served daily until midday.

## ▼ Drinking

Minsk's party scene is conveniently centred in the heart of the Old Town around pl Svobody. On summer weekend nights, vul Zybitskaya turns into a giant street party and the surrounding bars heave with life.

★ **Sweet & Sour**   COCKTAIL BAR
(vul Karla Marksa 14; ☺4pm-2am Mon-Sat; 🛜)
This dimly lit hideaway is for serious cocktail
aficionados. Kick back in scuffed leather
couches or belly up to the bar and order
US prohibition-era classics from smartly dressed bartenders. Some of the best
cocktails are off-menu, and there's a good
selection of single malts too.

**U Ratushi**   PUB
(pl Svobody; cover BR10 Fri & Sat; ☺10am-2am;
🛜) This multilevel pub-style restaurant is
packed with a raucous, fun-loving crowd
who come to drink cheap drinks and dance
to live rock music. It's one of the few places in the Old Town that caters to a not-so-
young clientele and is a great place to meet
fellow travelers and locals alike.

**Bessonitsa**   COCKTAIL BAR
(Insomnia; vul Hiersena 1; ☺noon-late) *The* place
in the Old Town for professional cocktails
(try the bourbon sour or a gimlet) and late-
night eats. It has Minsk's longest bar, a lively
interior and a bustling patio tailor-made for
people-watching.

**Stary Mensk**   CAFE
(pr Nezalezhnastsi 14; ☺10am-midnight Sun-
Thu, to 2am Fri & Sat) Itsy-bitsy Stary Mensk
and its teeny-weeny cousin, **London** (pr
Nezalezhnastsi 18; ☺10am-midnight Sun-Thu, to
2am Fri & Sat; 🛜), are two of the hippest cafes
in town, serving up coffees, fresh teas, imported beer, wine and hot grogs that are just
the tonic when the temperatures drop.

## 🛍 Shopping

★ Ў **Gallery & Shop**   GIFTS & SOUVENIRS
(pr Nezalezhnastsi 37a; gallery BR5; ☺10am-
10pm) This cool space, named after a letter
unique to the Belarusian language (called
'*u nieskladovaye*', and pronounced as a 'v')
is about as counter-cultural as Minsk gets.
The design, souvenir and clothes shop is
the ideal place for that quirky gift or T-shirt
to bring home. The gallery is attached to
Ў **Bar** (www.ybar.by; pr Nezalezhnastsi 37A;
☺10am-midnight) and showcases local
contemporary art.

**Minskikh Maestroy**
**Souvenir Market**   GIFTS & SOUVENIRS
(pl Svobody; ☺11am-9pm) This outdoor souvenir market on pl Svobody is where you can
haggle for local art, folk crafts, Soviet posters and coins, matryoshka dolls, etc.

## ❶ Information

### MEDICAL SERVICES

**Apteka #4** (vul Kirava 3; ☺24hr) All-day and
all-night pharmacy.

**Ecomedservice** (☎17 2077 474; www.ems.by;
vul Talstoha 4; ☺8am-9pm) Reliable, Western-style clinic. Bring a translator.

### MONEY

ATMs can be found throughout the city. Exchange bureaux dot the centre, while most
banks and hotels can change euros and US
dollars.

### POST

**Central Post Office** (pr Nezalezhnastsi 10;
☺8am-8pm Mon-Fri, 10am-5pm Sat & Sun) In
the centre of town.

### TOURIST INFORMATION

**BelarusTourService** (☎29 6770 011; www.
visa.by) Daria is an excellent source for visa
support, hotel bookings and transfers.

**Minsk Tourist Information Centre** (☎17 2033
995; www.minsktourism.by; vul Revalyutsi-
ynaya 13-119; ☺8.45am-1pm & 2-6pm Mon-Fri)
The friendly staff speak English, give out free
maps and can help find guides in English and
other languages.

## ❶ Getting There & Away

### AIR

**Minsk-2 International Airport** (☎17 2791 300;
www.airport.by) Minsk is well connected to the
rest of Europe and the Middle East from this
airport about 40km east of the centre. There
are no domestic flights in Belarus.

### BUS

**Ecolines** (☎29 3533 060; www.ecolines.net;
vul Babruyskaya 21) has useful international
buses to Kyiv (BR35, 11 hours, one daily), Riga
(BR30, nine hours, one daily), Vilnius (BR15,
four hours, one daily) and Warsaw (BR55, 11
hours, three daily).

The vast majority of intercity domestic and
international services leave from the **Central
bus station** (Tsentralny Awtavakzal; ☎114; vul
Babruyskaya 6), while the smaller **Southwest
bus station** (Yugo-Zapadnaya Awtavakzal;
Chyhunachnaya vul) and the **Druzhnaya bus
stop** serve some of Minsk's suburbs.

### TRAIN

The busy and modern **Minsk train station**
(☎17 2257 000, 105; pl Privakzalnaya; ☺24hr)
is pretty easy to deal with. You can buy tickets
here, or opposite the station at the less crowded
**International Train Ticket Office** (vul Kirava 2;
☺7am-8pm).

## ESSENTIAL FOOD & DRINK

Belarusian cuisine rarely differs from Russian cuisine, although there are a few dishes unique to the country.

**Belavezhskaya** A bitter herbal alcoholic drink.

**Draniki** Potato pancakes, usually served with sour cream *(smetana)*.

**Khaladnik** A local variation on cold *borshch*, a soup made from beetroot and garnished with sour cream, chopped-up hard-boiled eggs and potatoes.

**Kindziuk** A pig-stomach sausage filled with minced pork, herbs and spices.

**Kletsky** Dumplings stuffed with mushrooms, cheese or potato.

**Kolduni** Potato dumplings stuffed with meat.

**Kvas** A mildly alcoholic drink made from black or rye bread and commonly sold on the streets.

**Manchanka** Pancakes served with a meaty gravy.

Most services are standard Soviet *pasazhyrsky* (passenger) trains with *platskart* (3rd-class, hard sleeper) and pricier *kupe* (2nd-class, soft sleeper) options. Business-class express trains, with airplane-style seating, are an option on some intercity routes.

### ⓘ Getting Around

#### TO/FROM THE AIRPORT
From Minsk-2 International Airport, handy bus 300э goes to the train station in the centre of town via pr Nezalezhnasti (BR3.80, 55 minutes, every 30 to 60 minutes until 10pm). A taxi from the airport costs BR40 to BR60.

#### BICYCLE
Cycling is an ideal way to explore Minsk and its vast boulevards. **Speedy Go** (☑29 1445 030; http://speedygo.by; pr Nezalezhnasti 37A; bicycles per day BR15; ◷10am-10pm) hires out bicycles, or you can find more expensive bike rentals in most major parks.

#### CAR
Rental cars are widely available and work great for day trips out of town. As well as outlets at the airport, both **Avis** (☑17 2099 489; www.avis.by) and **Europcar** (☑29 1336 553; www.europcar. by ◷9am-6pm) can be found at Hotel Minsk at Nezalezhnasti 11; for a cheaper local option try **AvtoGurman** (☑29 6887 070; http://auto rent. by; vul Chycheryna 4; from €25 per day).

#### PUBLIC TRANSPORT
Minsk's metro system isn't hugely useful to travellers unless you're exploring the vast suburbs. It's open daily from dawn until just after midnight. One ride costs BR0.55.

Buses, trams and trolleybuses also cost 55 kopeks per ride, while swifter *marshrutky* (fixed-route minivans) cost BR0.80 to BR1.

#### TAXI
Ordering a taxi by phone will cost just BR8 to BR10 for trips within the centre. Dial ☑035 or ☑007. Drivers that hang out at taxi stands usually charge considerably more.

## AROUND MINSK

Mir and Njasvizh are near each other but are not connected by public transport so hiring a car makes sense to see them both in one day. Other worthwhile trips from the capital include **Khatyn** (www.khatyn.by; photo exhibit BR1; ◷complex 24hr, photo exhibit 11am-4pm Tue-Sun) FREE, a sobering memorial to a village wiped out by the Nazis 60km north of Minsk (accessible only by private transport); and **Dudutki** (☑29 602 5250; www.dudutki.by; adult/child BR10/6; audioguide BR3; ◷10am-5pm Tue-Wed, to 6pm Thu-Sun), an open-air folk museum 40km south of Minsk (take bus 323 from Minsk's Southwest bus station).

---

# Njasvizh     Нясвіж

This green and attractive town 120km southwest of Minsk is home to the splendid **Njasvizh Castle** (☑1770 20 602; www.niasvizh.by; adult/student BR13/6.50, excursion R36; ◷10am-7pm). It was erected by the Radziwill family in 1583 but was rebuilt and restored often over the centuries and encompasses many styles. With more than 30 fully refurbished state rooms, a very impressive inner courtyard and clearly labelled displays, you can easily spend a couple of hours looking around. Access to the castle is via a causeway leading away from the parking lot, with lovely lakes on either side.

**WORTH A TRIP**

## HRODNA ГРОДНА

If you're entering Belarus from northern Poland, or if you have extra time in the country, think about visiting Hrodna (or Grodno in Russian). It was one of the few Belarusian cities that *wasn't* bombed during WWII, so it's rife with old wooden homes and, although it's a major city, it definitely has a 'big village' sort of feel to it. The best hotel in terms of location and value is the **Neman Hotel** (☎152 791 700; www.hotel-neman.by; vul Stefana Batoryya 8; s/d from US$44/65; P✉🌐), which has functional rooms, including some cavernous suites, and two restaurants – one being a huge basement beer pub.

Five daily trains serve Minsk (from BR8, five to eight hours). For Brest, you're best off with a *marshrutka* (BR17, four hours, six daily) from the **Central bus station** (vul Chyrvonaarmeyskaya 7). To cross the Hrodna–Kuźnica border to Bialystok in Poland (about three hours), there are several minibuses (BR25) and a daily Ecolines bus (BR37). About four buses per day serve Vilnius (BR30, four hours).

From Minsk's Central bus station, there are four daily buses to and from Njasvizh (BR8, two hours).

## Mir                                    Mир

The charming small town of Mir, 85km southwest of Minsk, is dominated by the impossibly romantic 16th-century **Mir Castle** (☎1596 28 270; www.mirzamak.by; adult/student BR7/3.50; ◷castle 10am-6pm, closed last Wed of month; courtyard 24hr), which overlooks a small lake at one end of the town. It was once owned by the powerful Radziwill princes and has been under Unesco protection since 1994. A recent renovation has the place looking simply lovely, with gorgeous grounds, impressively restored interiors and a huge display on the life and times of the Radziwills.

The town of Mir itself is a delightful backwater and a great place to break your journey and experience a slice of rural Belarusian life. From Minsk's Central bus station, buses to Navahrudak (Novogrudok in Russian) stop in Mir (BR7, 1½ hours, at least hourly).

## BREST                              БРЕСТ

☎0162 / POP 309,800

This prosperous and cosmopolitan border town looks far more to the neighbouring EU than to Minsk. It has plenty of charm and has performed a massive DIY job on itself over the past few years in preparation for its millennial celebrations in 2019.

## ◉ Sights

Most sights are in and around Brest Fortress, which flanks the Bug and Mukhavets rivers just a whisper from the Polish border.

The fortress is about a 4km walk from central vul Savetskaya, a pleasant walking street lined with bars and restaurants.

★**Museum of Railway Technology**  MUSEUM
(pr Masherava 2; adult/student BR2.50/2; ◷9am-9pm Tue-Sun May-Sep, 8.30am-5.30pm Tue-Sun Oct-Apr) One of Brest's most popular sights is the outdoor Museum of Railway Technology, where there's a superb collection of locomotives and carriages dating from 1903 (eg the Moscow–Brest Express, with shower rooms and a very comfy main bedroom) to 1988 (far more proletarian Soviet passenger carriages).

**St Nikolaiv Church**                         CHURCH
(cnr vul Savetskaya & vul Mitskevicha) With its gold cupolas and yellow-and-blue facades shining gaily in the sunshine, the finely detailed 200-year-old Orthodox church is one of several lovely churches in Brest.

**Museum of Confiscated Art**           MUSEUM
(vul Lenina 39; adult/student BR22/15; ◷10am-6pm Tue-Sun) This museum has an extraordinary display of mostly 17th- to 18th-century icons, jewellery, antique furniture and Chinese porcelain seized from smugglers trying to get them across the border to Poland during the 1990s.

## ⌂ Sleeping

★**Dream Hostel**                          HOSTEL €
(☎162 531 499, 33 3610 315; www.dreamhostel.by; Apt 5, vul Mayakowskaha 17/1; dm US$10; ✉🌐) Brest's finest hostel is housed in an apartment building right in the middle of town. It's modern and bright, with clean bunks, a large TV room, kitchen and laundry. The entrance is 50m east of Bike N' Roll on vul Mayakowskaha; go through the first of two

adjacent archways and follow the footpath around to the right.

### Hotel Molodyozhnaya
HOTEL €

(☑162 216 376; www.molodezhnaya.by; vul Kamsamolskaya 6; s/d US$27/37; ☺☎) This small renovated Soviet-era hotel is ideally located opposite the train station, although it is susceptible to street noise. The rooms are comfortable and clean, all have private facilities, and the welcome is warm.

### Hermitage Hotel
HOTEL €€€

(☑162 276 000; www.hermitagehotel.by; vul Chkalava 7; s/d incl breakfast from US$115/143; P☺❄☎) This 55-room hotel is heads above the local competition and is priced accordingly. Housed in a sensitively designed modern building, it has more than a little old-world style, with spacious, grand and well-appointed rooms, as well as impressive public areas.

## ✕ Eating & Drinking

It's hard to beat dining outside on pedestrianized vul Savetskaya, but on summer evenings it can be hard to find a seat.

### ★ Jules Verne
INTERNATIONAL €€

(vul Hoholya 29; mains BR10-25; ☺noon-1am Sun-Thu, 5pm-1am Fri & Sat; ☎❂) It's almost a miracle that such a great restaurant exists in Brest. Decked out like a traditional gentlemen's club and with a travel theme, this dark, atmospheric joint manages to be refined without being stuffy. It serves up cracking dishes, from mouthwatering Indian curries and French specialities to sumptuous desserts and the best coffee in town. Don't miss it.

### Time's Cafe
EUROPEAN €€

(vul Savetskaya 30; mains BR10-20; ☺8.30am-11pm Mon-Fri, 11am-11pm Sat & Sun; ☎) This friendly and self-consciously cool place has a jazz and blues soundtrack and a summer terrace with views of pedestrianized vul Savetskaya. Dishes range from steak in a balsamic reduction to salmon carpaccio with scallops – quite different from the offerings of most places nearby.

### Korova
COCKTAIL BAR

(vul Savetskaya 73; ☺noon-2am Sun-Thu, to 4am Fri & Sat) Just an average grill and bar along vul Savetskaya by day, Korova morphs at night into a superb lounge-club, with slick bartenders serving expertly made cocktails and craft beer, while an all-types crowd gets their groove on to talented DJ acts and/or live bands.

### Coyote Bar
BAR

(vul Dzyarzhynskaha 14; BR10 after 11pm Fri & Sat; ☺noon-midnight Sun-Thu, to 3am Fri & Sat) Bartenders dancing on the bar and loud live music are the calling cards of this raucous bar. Terrific fun any night of the week, it really gets going on weekends, when the best bands play and shots fly.

## ❶ Information

**24-hour Pharmacy** (vul Hoholya 32; ☺24 hrs)
**Brest Intourist** (☑162 205 571, 162 200 510; Hotel Intourist, pr Masherava 15; ☺9am-6pm

---

## BREST FORTRESS

The city's main sight is the **Brest Fortress** (Brestskaya krepost; www.brest-fortress.by; pr Masherava) FREE, a moving WWII memorial where Soviet troops held out far longer than expected against the Nazi onslaught in the early days of Operation Barbarossa.

The fortress was built between 1833 and 1842, but by WWII it was being used mainly as a barracks. The two regiments bunking here when German troops launched a surprise attack in 1941 defended the fort for an astounding month and became venerated as national legends thanks to Stalin's propaganda machine.

Enter the Brest Fortress complex through a tunnel in the shape of a huge socialist star, then walk straight ahead several hundred metres to the fortresses' most iconic site – **Courage**, a chiselled soldier's head projecting from a massive rock, flanked by a skyscraping memorial obelisk.

There are several museums in and around the sprawling grounds, the most interesting of which are a pair museums that commemorate the siege and related events in WWII: the comprehensive **Defence of Brest Fortress Museum** (adult/student BR4/2, English-language audioguide BR3; ☺9am-6pm Tue-Sun) inside the fortresses' northern bastion; and the newer, more visual **Museum of War, Territory of Peace** (adult/student BR4/2, English-language audioguide BR3; ☺10am-7pm Wed-Mon) in the southern bastion.

Mon-Fri) The super-friendly English-speaking staff can arrange city tours, including 'Jewish Brest', and trips to the Belavezhskaya Pushcha National Park.

**Post Office** (pl Lenina; ⊗8am-8pm Mon-Sat, to 5pm Sat, to 3pm Sun)

### ⓘ Getting There & Away

#### BUS

The **bus station** (📞114; vul Mitskevicha) is in the centre of town. There are *marshrutky* (fixed-route minivans) to Hrodna (BR17, four hours, six daily), plus a slower bus or two. Buses serve Minsk (BR5 to BR8, five hours, three daily) but trains are preferable.

**Ecolines** (www.ecolines.net) buses to Warsaw (BR30, five hours, two daily) originate in Minsk. To Vilnius there are three midnight buses per week (BR35, 9½ hours).

#### TRAIN

The **train station** (📞105) is a short walk from the centre. There's a morning express train (BR9.50, 3¼ hours, one daily), and slower passenger (*pasazhirsky*) trains to Minsk (from BR8, 4½ hours to nine hours, frequent).

The number 9 train trundles to Warsaw (BR25, six hours, one daily).

### ⓘ Getting Around

For a taxi, call 📞5656 or have your hotel call for you.

**Bike N' Roll** (📞29 5051 286; http://bikenroll.net; vul Mayakowskaha 17/1; bicycles per day BR19.50; ⊗10am-7pm Mon-Fri, to 5pm Sat & Sun) Nice selection of mountain and city bikes available for hourly or daily rental.

**Easyday** (📞29 8882 007; www.easyday.by) Car rental for as low as €20 per day. No English.

---

### COUNTRY FACTS

**Currency** Belarusian rouble (BR)

**Language** Belarusian and Russian

**Money** ATMs taking international cards are widely available.

**Visas** Five-day visa-free travel for citizens of 80 countries arriving by air.

**Population** 9.57 million

**Area** 207,600 sq km

**Capital** Minsk

**Country Code** 📞375

**Emergency** Ambulance 📞03, Fire 📞01, Police 📞02

---

# AROUND BREST

## Belavezhskaya Pushcha National Park Белавежская Пушча

Unesco World Heritage Site **Belavezhskaya Pushcha National Park** (📞16 3156 200, 16 3156 398; www.npbp.by; varies per activity; ⊗ticket office 9am-5pm) is the oldest wildlife refuge in Europe and the pride of Belarus. At the National Park headquarters in Kamyanyuki, 55km north of Brest, you can arrange to tour the park by bus, bicycle or private car, and you can spend the night at one of several comfortable hotels in the **Kamyanyuki Hotel Complex** (📞1631 56 200; beltour07@mail.ru; d US$35-44; ⊗ 🛜 ❄) near the park entrance.

Some 1300 sq km of primeval forest survives in Belavezhskaya Pushcha National Park, half of which lies in Poland. At least 55 mammal species call this park home, but the area is most celebrated for its 300 or so European bison, the continent's largest land mammal. They were driven to near extinction then bred back from the 52 animals surviving in zoos. Now a total of about 3000 *zubr* exist, of which more than 300 are wild in the Belavezhskaya Pushcha.

You have a chance to spot these beasts in the wild on a tour of the park, although you have to be a bit lucky. The October-to-April period offers the best odds.

To get to the park from Brest take a bus or *marshrutka* from the bus station to the village of Kamyanyuki (BR3.80, 1¼ hours, about seven daily). An altogether easier option for visiting the park is to book a day trip from Brest with an English-speaking guide through Brest Intourist (p67).

# SURVIVAL GUIDE

### ⓘ Directory A–Z

#### BUSINESS HOURS

**Banks** 9am–5pm Monday to Friday
**Office hours** 9am–6pm Monday to Friday
**Shops** 9am/10am–9pm Monday to Saturday, to 6pm Sunday (if at all)

#### INSURANCE

You'll need a policy from an authorised state health-insurance provider as a requirement for obtaining a visa. This is best done through a travel agent. If you're eligible for the five-day visa-free scheme, then this health-insurance requirement is waived. However, we do recommend obtaining a legitimate international health-insurance policy that covers Belarus.

## MONEY

The Belarusian rouble is pinned to the US dollar at BR2-to-US$1 and is relatively stable. ATMs are widespread and most banks, supermarkets and higher-end hotels have currency-exchange facilities. Credit cards are widely used for payment in Minsk and other cities but are unlikely to be accepted in rural areas.

## TELEPHONE

There are four mobile-phone companies that can sell you a SIM-card package with oodles of data for next to nothing. Bring your passport, a Belarusian address and your unlocked phone.

To place a call or send a text from a local mobile phone, dial either +☎375 or ☎80, plus the nine-digit number.

## VISAS

From 2017, citizens of 80 countries can travel in Belarus visa-free for five days if arriving by air. For longer stays and if not arriving by air, most travellers need visas.

If you require a visa, you'll need to enlist the services of a Belarusian travel agency or prebooked hotel for letters of invitation and other visa-support documentation. For visa support, we recommend BelarusTourService (p64) or Belarus Rent (p61).

Belarusian visa regulations change frequently, so check the website of your nearest Belarusian embassy for the latest bureaucratic requirements.

### Registration

Keep the white slip you receive upon arrival in Belarus: you must have it registered and present it again upon departure if you are staying for more than five working days. Hotels do this automatically and the service is included in the room price.

## ℹ Getting There & Away

Flights into Minsk are the most popular means of entering Belarus. Common overland routes include bus or train to Brest or Hrodno from Poland; bus or train to Minsk from Vilnius, Lithu-

ania, and train to Homel or Minsk from Ukraine. Arriving overland from Russia is problematic as there are no border checkpoints between Russia and Belarus, so you won't be able to obtain a proper entry stamp.

### AIR

**Minsk-2 International Airport** (p64) is well connected by direct flights to Europe, the Middle East and the former Soviet Union.

Belarus' national airline, **Belavia** (☎17 2202 555; www.belavia.by; vul Nyamiha 14, Minsk), has lots of flights to Moscow and the Commonwealth of Independent States (CIS) and it also serves a few Western European cities including Amsterdam, Berlin, Frankfurt, London, Paris and Vienna. Belavia has a good safety record and modern planes. Other airlines that fly to Minsk include Aeroflot, Air Baltic, Austrian Airlines, El Al, LOT Polish Airlines and Lufthansa.

### LAND

Belarus has good overland bus and train links to all neighbouring countries and borders are generally hassle-free provided your papers are in order. Queues can plague any overland border crossing, of course, but they are usually not too bad. The one exception is the Hrodna–Kuźnica (Bialystok, Poland) crossing, where we've heard reports of long waits when crossing by train. We recommend taking the bus instead.

## ℹ Getting Around

Trains are extremely cheap and plenty comfortable, buses cheap but less comfortable. For train schedules and prices, www.rw.by and www.rzd.ru are great sites if you read Russian, or try www.bahn.de if you don't.

**Train** Super-cheap, efficient and usually on time. Try the business-class express trains for quick hops between cities.

**Car** Hiring a car is recommended for exploring around Minsk, with car hire widely available.

**Bus** A bit cheaper than trains, but can be slower. Zippy *marshrutky* (public minivans), on the other hand, are less comfortable but generally faster than buses or trains.

# Bosnia & Hercegovina

## Best Places to Eat

➡ Mala Kuhinja (p77)

➡ Hindin Han (p82)

➡ Manolo (p77)

➡ Babilon (p83)

➡ Park Prinčeva (p77)

## Best Places to Stay

➡ Muslibegović House (p82)

➡ Isabegov Hamam Hotel (p76)

➡ Ovo Malo Duše (p76)

➡ Hostel Balkanarama (p82)

## Why Go?

This craggily beautiful land retains some lingering scars from the heartbreaking civil war in the 1990s. But today visitors will more likely remember Bosnia and Hercegovina (BiH) for its deep, unassuming human warmth and for the intriguing East-meets-West atmosphere born of fascinatingly blended Ottoman and Austro-Hungarian histories.

Major drawcards are the reincarnated antique centres of Sarajevo and Mostar, where rebuilt historical buildings counterpoint fashionable bars and wi-fi–equipped cafes. Captivating Sarajevo is an architectural gem, with countless minarets amid the tile-roofed houses that rise steeply up its river flanks. Mostar is world famous for its extraordinary arc of 16th-century stone bridge, photogenically flanked by cute mill-house restaurants. The town is set at the heart of Hercegovina's sun-baked wine country, with waterfalls, a riverside sufi-house and an Ottoman fortress all nearby.

## When to Go
### Sarajevo

**Apr–Jun** Beat the heat in Hercegovina; blooming flowers in Bosnia.

**Jul–Aug** Gets sweaty and accommodation fills, but festivals keep things lively.

**Mid-Jan–mid-Mar** Skiing gets cheaper after the New Year holidays.

# Bosnia & Hercegovina Highlights

**1 Stari Most** (p79)
Gawping as young men throw themselves off Mostar's magnificently rebuilt stone arc.

**2 Baščaršija** (p72)
Padding around Old Sarajevo's fascinating Turkic era alleyways on soft flagstones that feel like chilled butter underfoot.

**3 Tunnel Museum** (p76)
Discovering more about the hopes and horrors of the 1990s civil war at this intensely moving museum.

**4 Mostar's Hinterland** (p83) Making a satisfyingly varied day trip from Mostar to Kravice Waterfalls and other gems of Hercegovina.

**5 Mountain Escapes** (p78) Heading for resorts like Jahorina and Bjelašnica in the hills around Sarajevo to ski in winter or hike in the summer sunshine.

# SARAJEVO

033 / POP 395,000

In the 1990s Sarajevo was besieged and on the edge of annihilation. Today, its restored historic centre is full of welcoming cafes and good-value lodgings, the bullet holes largely plastered over on the city's curious architectural mixture of Ottoman, Yugoslav and Austro-Hungarian buildings.

The antique stone-flagged alleys of Baščaršija give the delightful Old Town core a certain Turkish feel. Directly north and south, steep valley sides are fuzzed with red-roofed Bosnian houses and prickled with uncountable minarets, climbing towards green-topped mountain ridges. In winter, Sarajevo's mountain resorts Bjelašnica and Jahorina offer some of Europe's best-value skiing, barely 30km away.

## ☉ Sights & Activities

### ◉ Old Sarajevo

#### ★ Baščaršija                        AREA
Centred on what foreigners nickname Pigeon Sq, Baščaršija is the heart of old Sarajevo with pedestrians padding pale stone alleys and squares between lively (if tourist-centric) coppersmith alleys, grand Ottoman mosques, *caravanserai*-restaurants and lots of inviting little cafes and *ćevapi* serveries.

#### ★ Sarajevo City Hall               ARCHITECTURE
(Vijećnica; www.nub.ba; adult/child 5/3KM; ☉10am-8pm Jun-Sep, to 5pm Oct-May) Storybook neo-Moorish facades make the 1898 Vijećnica Sarajevo's most beautiful Austro-Hungarian–era building. Seriously damaged during the 1990s siege, it finally reopened in 2014 after laborious reconstruction. Its colourfully restored multi-arched interior and stained-glass ceiling are superb. And the ticket also allows you to peruse the excellent *Sarajevo 1914-1981* exhibition in the octagonal basement. This gives well-explained potted histories of the city's various 20th-century periods, insights into fashion and music subcultures, and revelations about Franz Ferdinand's love life.

#### Gazi-Husrevbey Mosque             MOSQUE
(www.vakuf-gazi.ba; Sarači 18; 3KM; ☉9am-noon, 2.30-3.30pm & 5-6.15pm May-Sep, 9am-11am only Oct-Apr, closed Ramadan) Bosnia's second Ottoman governor, Gazi-Husrevbey, funded a series of splendid 16th-century buildings of which this 1531 mosque, with its 45m minaret, forms the greatest centrepiece. The interior is beautifully proportioned and even if you can't look inside, it's worth walking through the courtyard with its lovely fountain and the tomb tower of Gazi-Husrevbey off to one side.

#### Franz Ferdinand's
#### Assassination Spot                 HISTORIC SITE
(cnr Obala Kulina Bana & Zelenih Beretki) On 28 June 1914, Archduke Franz Ferdinand, heir to the Habsburg throne of Austro-Hungary, was shot dead by 18-year-old Gavrilo Princip. This assassination, which would ultimately be the fuse that detonated WWI, happened by an odd series of coincidences on a street corner outside what is now the small **Sarajevo 1878–1918 museum** (Zelenih Beretki 2; 4KM; ☉10am-6pm Mon-Fri, to 3pm Sat mid-Apr–mid-Nov, to 4pm Mon-Fri, to 3pm Sat mid-Nov–mid-Apr).

---

## ITINERARIES

### Two Days
If you only have two days you're best concentrating your time on the two main cities. In **Sarajevo**, take time to wander the streets of the Old Town and visit the beautifully restored City Hall, but make sure you also venture out to the **Tunnel Museum**, perhaps as part of a guided tour. In **Mostar** you'll want plenty of time to take in views of the famous bridge, perhaps drinking or dining by the riverside. Both cities have plenty of quirky bars and cafes where you can get to know the locals.

### Four Days
With more time on your hands, extend your itinerary by joining a day tour ex-Mostar to visit historic **Počitelj**, quaint **Blagaj** and the impressive **Kravice** waterfalls. In Sarajevo, cafe-hop around Baščaršija's *caravanserais* and consider venturing up into the surrounding hills and mountains at Jahorina or Bjelašnica.

### Despića Kuća
MUSEUM

(☑033-215531; http://muzejsarajeva.ba; Despiće-va 2; adult/child 3/1KM, guide 5KM; ⊘10am-6pm Mon-Fri (to 4pm winter), to 3pm Sat) The Despića Kuća is one of the oldest surviving residential buildings in central Sarajevo, though you'd never guess so from the ho-hum facade. Inside, it's a house within a house, the original 1780 section retaining even the prison-style bars on stone window frames.

### Galerija 11-07-95
MUSEUM

(☑033-953170; http://galerija110795.ba; Trg fra Grge Martića 2, 3rd fl; admission/audioguide/tour 12/3/2KM; ⊘9am-10pm, guided tours 11.15am & 7.15pm) This new gallery uses stirring visual imagery and video footage to create a powerful memorial to more than 8000 victims of the Srebrenica massacre, one of the most infamous events of the Bosnian civil war. You'll need well over an hour to make the most of a visit, and it's worth paying the extra for the guide to get more insight.

## ◉ Bjelave & Vratnik

Bristling with little minarets amid tile-roofed houses and *doksat* box-windows, the appealingly untouristed areas of Bjelave and former citadel Vratnik (p73) rise steeply above the Old Town to the north and northeast. Random exploration highlights the fine viewpoints at Žuta Tabija and the eerie but even higher Bijela Tabija (p73).

### ★ Svrzo House
MUSEUM

(Svrzina Kuća; ☑033-535264; http://muzejsarajeva.ba; Glođina 8; 3KM; ⊘10am-6pm Mon-Fri, to 3pm Sat, closes early off-season) An oasis of white-washed walls, cobbled courtyards and partly vine-draped dark timbers, this 18th-century house-museum is brilliantly restored and appropriately furnished, helping visitors imagine Sarajevo life in eras past.

### War Childhood Museum
MUSEUM

(http://museum.warchildhood.com; Logavina 32; adult/child 10/5KM; ⊘11am-7pm Tue-Sun) A fascinating new museum focusing on the experiences of children who grew up during the 1990s conflict. Poignantly personal items donated by former war children, such as diaries, drawings and ballet slippers, are displayed alongside written and video testimonies.

### Vratnik
AREA

Built in the 1720s and reinforced in 1816, Vratnik Citadel once enclosed a whole area of the upper city. Patchy remnants of wall fragments, military ruins and gatehouses remain. The urban area is appealingly untouristed with many mosques and tile-roofed houses, and several superb viewpoints. Start with a 3KM taxi hop up to the graffiti-daubed **Bijela Tabija** (Poddžebhana bb) fortress-ruin viewpoint (or take buses 52 or 55 to **Višegradski Kaplja** (Carina 57a) gatehouse), then walk back.

### Žuta Tabija
VIEWPOINT

(Yellow Bastion; Jekovac bb) To gaze out across Sarajevo's red-roofed cityscape, one of the most appealing yet accessible viewpoints is from this chunk of old rampart-bastion, now sprouting mature trees and a popular place for picnickers and canoodling lovers.

## ◉ Novo Sarajevo

During the 1992–95 siege, the city's wide east–west artery road (Zmaja od Bosne) was dubbed 'sniper alley' because Serb gunmen in surrounding hills could pick off civilians as they tried to cross it. Most of the embattled journalists who covered that conflict sought refuge in what's now the Hotel Holiday, built in 1984 as the Holiday Inn and looking like a cubist still life of pudding and custard. Completely rebuilt, this business-oriented area now sports the nation's **tallest skyscraper** (www.avaztwisttower.ba; Tešanjska 24a; coffee/beer from 2/3KM; ⊘7am-11pm) and newest **shopping mall** (Sarajevo City Center; www.scc.ba; Vrbanja 1; ⊘10am-10pm, cafes 8am-11pm, parking 24hr; ⟦1, 3 Marijin Dvor) but is most interesting for two excellent museums.

### National Museum
MUSEUM

(Zemaljski Muzej Bosne-i-Hercegovine; www.zemaljskimuzej.ba; Zmaja od Bosne 3; adult/child 6/3KM; ⊘10am-7pm Tue-Fri, to 2pm Sat & Sun) Bosnia's biggest and best-endowed museum of ancient and natural history is housed in an impressive, purpose-built quadrangle of neoclassical 1913 buildings. It's best known for housing the priceless Sarajevo Haggadah but there's much more to see. Highlights include Illyrian and Roman carvings, Frankish-style medieval swords, beautifully preserved 19th-century room interiors and meteorites among the extensive cabinets full of geological samples. Many explanatory panels have English translations.

# Central Sarajevo

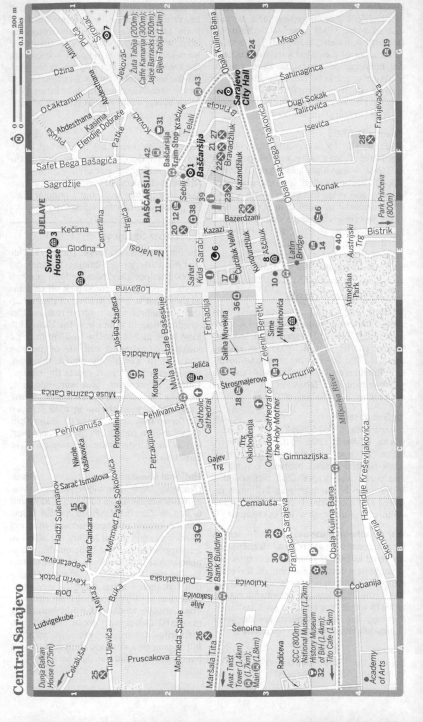

# Central Sarajevo

**History Museum of BiH**  MUSEUM
(☑ 033-226098; www.muzej.ba; Zmaja od Bosne 5; 5KM, person with disability 1KM; ☺9am-7pm) Somewhat misleadingly named, this small but engrossing museum has three exhibition rooms. Two feature changing themes, but while these are often fascinating (recently on German 1980s subcultures), the main attraction is the third hall's permanent *Surrounded Sarajevo* exhibition. This charts the Sarajevo people's life-and-death battle for survival between 1992 and 1995. Personal effects include self-made lamps, examples of food aid, stacks of Monopoly-style 1990s dinars and a makeshift siege-time 'home'.

## ⌖ Tours

Various companies run a range of tours in and beyond Sarajevo, many including the otherwise awkward-to-reach Tunnel Museum. Reliable operators include **Sarajevo Funky Tours** (☑062-910546; www.sarajevofunkytours.com; Besarina Čikma 5) and **Insider**

(☑061-190591; www.sarajevoinsider.com; Zelenih Beretki 30; ☺9am-6pm Mon-Fri, 9.30am-2pm Sat & Sun).

## ★彡 Festivals & Events

**Sarajevo Film Festival**  FILM
(www.sff.ba; ☺mid-Aug) During this globally acclaimed film fest, the whole city turns into a giant party with countless concerts and many impromptu bars opening on street counters.

## ⌁ Sleeping

**★ Seven Heavens**  GUESTHOUSE €
(☑062-191508; 3rd fl, Štrossmayerova 3; dm/d €12/30) Three floors up in the grand mansion above the Monument Jazz Club, this boutique hostel-guesthouse has bathrooms that would put a five-star hotel to shame, shared by just three smart rooms and one spacious dorm.

**DON'T MISS**

## TUNNEL MUSEUM

The most visceral of Sarajevo's many 1990s war-experience 'attractions' is the unmissable **Tunnel Museum** (Tunel Spasa; http://tunelspasa.ba; Tuneli bb 1; adult/student 10/5KM; ⊙9am-5pm, last entry 4.30pm Apr-Oct, 3.30pm Nov-Mar). The museum's centrepiece and raison d'être is a 25m section of the 1m wide, 1.6m high hand-dug tunnel under the airport runway. That acted as the city's lifeline to the outside world during the 1992–95 siege, when Sarajevo was virtually surrounded by hostile Serb forces.

Getting here by public transport is a bit of a fiddle. Take tram 3 to Ilidža, the far terminus (35 minutes), then take a taxi, the infrequent Kotorac-bound bus 12 (10 minutes) or walk (around 30 minutes). If you're alone, a group tour can prove cheaper than a taxi.

★**War Hostel** THEME HOSTEL €
(☎060-3171908; https://warhostel.com; Hrvatin 21; dm/d €10/40) 'You're not here just to sleep', says agent Zero-One who answers the door in a bulletproof vest. 'I want to change your experience'. A constant crackle of walkie-talkie messages form the soundscape to the seatless common room where you can discuss the immersion experience. Unforgettable.

**Hostel For Me** HOSTEL €
(☎062 328658, 033-840135; www.hostelforme.com; 4th fl, Prote Bakovica 2; dm €10; ❈ 🛜) Right within the Old Town, hidden away up four flights of stairs, this is one of Sarajevo's best-appointed modern hostels. It's worth the climb for good-headroom bunks, huge lockers, a decent lounge and a kitchen with fine views across the Old Town roofs to the Gazi-Husrevbegov Mosque.

★**Isabegov Hamam Hotel** HERITAGE HOTEL €€
(☎033-570050; www.isabegovhotel.com; Bistrik 1; s/d/q €80/100/120; ❈) After many years of restoration the classic 1462 Isabegov Hamam (bathhouse) reopened in 2015 with 15 hotel rooms designed to evoke the spirit of the age with lashings of handcrafted dark-wood furniture, ornately carved bedsteads and tube-glass chandeliers.

★**Ovo Malo Duše** BOUTIQUE GUESTHOUSE €€
(☎061-365100, 033-972800; http://ovo-malo-duse.com; Ćurčiluk Veliki 3; s/d 103/146KM; ⊙7am-10.30pm; ❈ 🛜) The six-room former Villa Wien has been rebranded and given a minor makeover but it retains an appealing mixture of comfort and old-world charm. Each room has its own idiosyncrasies. There's no reception so you will need to check in at the Wiener Café downstairs before 10.30pm when that closes.

**Hotel Latinski Most** HOTEL €€
(☎033-572660; www.hotel-latinskimost.com; Obala Isabega Isakovića 1; s/d/tr 117/158/178KM, off season 99/138/158KM) This cosy hotel is ideal for WWI aficionados who want to survey the Franz Ferdinand assassination spot from directly across the river. Three of the smaller rooms have petite balconies offering just that, and their double-glazing works remarkably well against street noise.

★**Hotel Central** HOTEL €€€
(☎033-561800; www.hotelcentral.ba; Ćumurija 8; d/ste 220/260KM; ❈ 🛜 ❈) Behind a grand Austro-Hungarian facade, most of this snazzy 'hotel' is in fact an amazing three-floor gym complex with professional-standard weight rooms, saunas and a big indoor pool manned by qualified sports training staff. The huge guest rooms are fashionably appointed but there are only 15. Book well in advance.

★**Hotel Michele** BOUTIQUE HOTEL €€€
(☎033-560310; www.hotelmichele.ba; Ivana Cankara 27; s/d €75/85, apt €120-175; ❈ 🛜) Behind the exterior of an oversized contemporary townhouse, this offbeat guesthouse-hotel welcomes you into a lobby-lounge full of framed portraits, pinned butterflies and elegant fittings. Antique-effect elements are in the 12 standard rooms but what has drawn celebrity guests such as Morgan Freeman and Kevin Spacey are the vast, indulgently furnished apartments with antique (if sometimes mismatching) furniture.

## ✖ Eating

**Bravadžiluk** STREET FOOD €
(mains from 3KM) For inexpensive snack meals look along Bravadžiluk or nearby Kundurdžiluk: **Buregdžinica Bosna** (Bravadžulik; potato/cheese/meat pies per 8/10/12kg, meal portions

2-3.50KM; ☺ 7am-11pm) is excellent for cheap, fresh *burek* sold by weight. Locals argue whether **Hodžić** (Sebilj Sq; small/large ćevapi 3.50/7KM; ☺ 8am-10pm), **Željo** (Kundurdžiluk 17 & 20; small/medium/large ćcvapi 3.5/7/10KM; ☺ 8am-10pm) or **Mrkva** (www.mrkva.ba; Bravadžulik 15; small/large ćevapi 3.5/7KM; ☺ 8am-10pm) serves the best *ćevapi,* and there is plenty of attractively styled competition.

### Barhana                    PIZZA, BOSNIAN €
(Ðugalina 8; pizza 5-12KM; ☺ 10am-midnight, kitchen to 11.30pm) Tourist-centric Barhana's remarkably reasonable prices pair unbeatably with its charming part-wooden cottage interior. The centrepiece is the large brick pizza oven and open kitchen, partly masked by collections of bottles and candles.

### ★Mala Kuhinja                    FUSION €€
(☎ 061-144741; www.malakuhinja.ba; Tina Ujevića 13; mains 12-25KM; ☺ 10am-11pm Mon-Sat; 🛜 🍴 ) Run by former TV celebrity chefs, the novel concept here is to forget menus and simply ask you what you do/don't like. Spicy? Vegan? No problem. And armed with this knowledge the team makes culinary magic in the show-kitchen. Superb.

### Manolo                    INTERNATIONAL €€
(Maršala Tita 21; mains 12-20KM, steaks 17-33KM; ☺ 8am-11pm) An exciting star in Sarajevo's culinary firmament, Manolo's panache for '60s and '70s retro design is backed by magicians in the kitchen. Beyond steaks and Italian mainstays, the menu's more imaginative dishes include wok-fried prawn and ginger, mustard chicken and spicy veal with sun-dried tomatoes. On colder days, closable glass panels convert the garden yard into a bright, wraparound veranda. No alcohol.

### Inat Kuća                    BOSNIAN €€
(Spite House; ☎ 033-447867; www.inatkuca.ba; Velika Alifakovac 1; mains 10-20KM; ☺ 11am-10pm; 🛜 🍴 ) This Sarajevo institution occupies a classic Ottoman-era house that's a veritable museum piece with central stone water trough, a case of antique guns and fine metal-filigree lanterns. A range of Bosnian specialities is served using pewter crockery at glass-topped display tables containing traditional local jewellery.

### Dunja Balkan House                    INTERNATIONAL €€
(☎ 033-214318; www.facebook.com/dunjasarajevo; Sumbala Avde 3; salads 6.20-13KM, mains 9-25KM; ☺ 8am-midnight Mon-Sat, 11am-6pm Sun) The house and garden seem to meld into one

another in this smart yet relaxed restaurant-cafe with a tree growing through the roof, birdcages, decanters on tables, and riding caps hanging on a hatstand. The menu includes excellent salads, some Bosnian fare, fish, grills and much to please the staff of the nearby Italian embassy.

### Pivnica HS                    INTERNATIONAL €€
(☎ 033-239740; Franjevačka 15; mains 14-23KM; ☺ 10am-1am, kitchen 10.30am-midnight; 🛜 📶 ) Wild West saloon, Munich bierkeller, Las Vegas fantasy or Willy Wonka masterpiece? However you describe its decor, Pivnica HS is a vibrant place for dining on well-presented (mainly meat-based) dishes or sampling the full range of Sarajevskaya tap beers brewed next door.

### Park Prinčeva                    BALKAN, EUROPEAN €€€
(☎ 033-222708; www.parkprinceva.ba; Iza Hidra 7; meals 16-32KM; ☺ 9am-11pm; 📶 ; 🚌 56) Gaze out over a superb city panorama from this hillside perch, like Bono and Bill Clinton before you. From the open-sided terrace the City Hall is beautifully framed between rooftops, mosques and twinkling lights. Waiters in bow ties and red waistcoats deliver dishes that go beyond Bosnian usuals, such as chicken in cherry sauce or *pizzaiolo* roll with capers and olives.

## 🍷 Drinking & Entertainment

### ★Zlatna Ribica                    BAR
(☎ 033-836348; Kaptol 5; ☺ 8am-late) Sedate and outwardly grand, this tiny and eccentric bar adds understated humour to a cosy treasure trove of antiques and kitsch, reflected in big art nouveau mirrors.

### ★Dekanter                    WINE BAR
(☎ 033-263815;    www.facebook.com/vinoteka. dekanter; Radićeva 4; ☺ 8am-midnight Mon-Sat, 6pm-midnight Sun; 🛜 ) It's easy to sit for hours sampling from more than 100 local and world vintages in this glorious, low-lit wine bar decorated with bottles, chateau-boxes and swirling ceiling sculptures of intertwined wires.

### Čajdžinica Džirlo                    TEAHOUSE
(www.facebook.com/cajdzinicadzirlo; Kovači 16; ☺ 8am-10pm) Minuscule but brimming with character, Džirlo brews some 50 types of tea, many of them made from distinctive Bosnian herbs. They are served in lovely little pots, each distinctive according to the blend.

## AROUND SARAJEVO

Mountains rise directly behind Sarajevo, offering convenient access to winter skiing and charming summer rambles. **Jahorina** is the larger resort, with multiple pistes and seven main ski lifts, whilst the more modest **Bjelašnica** offers night skiing and a web of magical mountain villages to explore.

To the east, **Visoko** attracts new-age mystics and curious tourists with its mysterious 'pyramid' and crystal vendors. To the south, **Konjic** is the nearest rafting centre to Sarajevo, with a gigantic atomic bunker that cost Yugoslavia billions to build.

**Cafe Barometar**　　　　　　　　BAR
(www.facebook.com/cafebarometar; Branilaca Sarajeva 23; ⊙7am-midnight Sun-Thu, to 2am Fri & Sat) Like an image of HG Wells' *Time Machine*, this little cafe-bar weaves together dials, pipes and wacky furniture crafted from axels, compressors and submarine parts.

★**Pink Houdini**　　　　　　　　JAZZ
(www.facebook.com/jazzbluesclubpinkhoudini; Branilaca Sarajeva 31; ⊙24hr) One of Sarajevo's rare 24-hour drinking spots, this quirky basement jazz bar has a tree of guitars, a wacky-fiesta themed abstract ceiling sculpture and UV lighting that makes your gin-and-tonic luminescent. Romping live blues gigs start at 10.30pm on Wednesdays, Fridays and Sundays.

★**National Theatre**　　　PERFORMING ARTS
(Narodno Pozorište; ☑033-226431; www.nps.ba; Obala Kulina Bana 9; ⊙box office 9am-noon & 4-7.30pm) Classically adorned with fiddly gilt mouldings, this proscenium-arched theatre hosts a ballet, opera, play or philharmonic concert virtually every night from mid-September to mid-June.

## 🛍 Shopping

★**Isfahan Gallery**　　　　　　　CARPETS
(☑033-237429; www.isfahans.com; Sarači 77, Morića Han; ⊙9am-11pm) Specialising in high-quality Persian carpets (with certificate), along with richly glazed ceramic work, this entrancing shop brings a barrage of beautiful colours to the already enticing Morića Han *caravanserai*.

★**Di Vina**　　　　　　　　　　WINE
(☑033-267400; www.divina.ba; Josipa Stadlera 10; 4-wine tasting 15KM; ⊙10am-8pm Mon-Fri, to 6pm Sat) There's nowhere better to start a wine-shopping spree than this well-stocked, super-friendly store run by a Bosnian family who returned to Sarajevo having lived in Canada. Drop-in wine tastings lasting around 20 minutes are available till an hour before closing.

**Bezistan**　　　　　　　　　　MARKET
(http://vakuf-gazi.ba/english/index.php; Gazi Husrevbegova; ⊙8am-9pm Mon-Sat, 10am-3pm Sun) The 16th-century stone-vaulted covered bazaar is little more than 100m long but squint and you could be in İstanbul. Many of the 70-plus shops sell inexpensive souvenirs, scarves, cheap handbags and knock-off sunglasses.

## ℹ Information

**Official Tourist Info Centre** (Turistički Informativni Centar; ☑033-580999; www.sarajevo-tourism.com; Sarači 58; ⊙9am-8pm Mon-Fri, 10am-6pm Sat & Sun, varies seasonally) Helpful tourist information centre. Beware of commercial imitations.

## ℹ Getting There & Away

### AIR

**Sarajevo International Airport** (Aerodrom; www.sia.ba; Kurta Schorka 36; ⊙closed 11pm-5am) Sarajevo's modern but compact international airport is about 12km southwest of Baščaršija. An hour is usually ample for check-in.

### BUS

From Sarajevo's **main bus station** (☑033-213100; www.centrotrans.com; Put Života 8; ⊙6am-10pm), beside the train station, there are frequent buses to Mostar (20KM, 2½ hours), several daily services to Zagreb, Split an Dubrovnik in Croatia, plus daily buses to Belgrade (Serbia). There are five more Belgrade services from the inconveniently distant **East Sarajevo (Lukovica) bus station** (Autobuska Stanica Istočno Sarajevo; ☑057-317377; www.balkanexpress-is.com; Srpskih Vladara bb; ⊙6am-11.15pm), 400m beyond the western terminus stop of trolleybus 103 or bus 31E. That bus station also has buses to Podgorica and Herceg Novi in Montenegro.

### TRAIN

There is a daily service to Zagreb (56KM, 9½ hours). Trains to Mostar were suspended at the time of research pending track reconstruction.

# ℹ Getting Around

## TO/FROM THE AIRPORT

Taxis should charge around 20KM for the 12km drive to Baščaršija. Beware taxi drivers refusing to use the meter and asking for vastly inflated fares.

An infrequent **Centrotrans** (www.centrotrans.com; Ferhadija 16) bus service marked Aerodrom-Baščaršija (5KM, pay on-board) departs from outside the terminal taking around 30 minutes to the Old Town area. A more frequent and cheaper alternative from the airport area is to take bus 31E or trolleybus 103 (1.80KM), which run every few minutes till around 11.30pm. The nearest stop to the airport is Konzum Dobrijna, around a 700m walk from the terminal.

## PUBLIC TRANSPORT

Single-ride tickets for bus, tram or trolleybus cost 1.60KM from kiosks, 1.80KM from drivers. They must be stamped once aboard.

**Tram 3** (every four to seven minutes) is the most useful for sightseeing. It loops anticlockwise around Baščaršija before heading out west past the National Museum to Ilidža, where you can catch bus 12 onward to the Tunnel Museum.

## TAXI

**Paja Taxis** (✆ 1522, 033-412555) This reliable taxi company charges on-the-metre fares of 2KM plus about 1KM per kilometre.

# MOSTAR

⤢ 036 / POP 105,800

Mostar's world-famous 16th-century stone bridge is the centrepiece of its alluring, extensively restored Old Town where, at dusk, the lights of numerous mill-house restaurants twinkle across gushing streamlets. Further from the centre a scattering of shattered building shells remain as a moving testament to the terrible 1990s conflict that divided the city. The surrounding sun-drenched Herzegovinian countryside produces excellent wines and offers a series of tempting day-trip attractions.

## ◉ Sights & Activities

★ **Stari Most**                                    BRIDGE

World-famous Stari Most (Old Bridge) is Mostar's indisputable visual focus. Its pale stone magnificently throws back the golden glow of sunset or the tasteful night-time floodlighting. The bridge's swooping arch was originally built between 1557 and 1566 on the orders of Suleyman the Magnificent. The current structure is a very convincing 21st-century rebuild following the bridge's 1990s bombardment during the civil war. Numerous well-positioned cafes and restaurants tempt you to sit and savour the splendidly restored scene.

**BOSNIA & HERCEGOVINA** MOSTAR

---

## BIH & THE 1990S CONFLICT

Today's BiH remains deeply scarred by a 1990s civil war that began when post-Tito-era Yugoslavia imploded. Seen very simply, the core conflict was a territorial battle between the Bosnians, Serbs and Croats. The war that ensued is often portrayed as 'ethnic', but in fact all sides were Slavs, differing only in their (generally secularised) religious backgrounds. Indeed, many Bosniaks (Muslims), Serbs (Orthodox Christians) and Croats (Catholics) had intermarried or were friends. Yet for nearly four years a brutal and extraordinarily complex civil war raged, with atrocities committed by all sides.

Best known is the campaign of 'ethnic' cleansing in northern and eastern BiH, which aimed at creating a Serb republic. Meanwhile in Mostar, Bosnian Croats and Bosniaks traded fire across a 'front line' with Croat bombardment eventually destroying the city's world-famous old bridge. Sarajevo endured a long siege and, in July 1995, Dutch peacekeepers monitoring the supposedly 'safe' area of Srebrenica proved unable to prevent a Bosnian Serb force from killing an estimated 8000 Muslim men in Europe's worst mass killings since WWII. By this stage, Croats had renewed their own offensive, expelling Serbs from western BiH and the Krajina region of Croatia.

Finally two weeks of NATO air strikes in September 1995 added force to an ultimatum to end the Serbs' siege of Sarajevo and a peace conference was held in Dayton, Ohio. The resultant accords maintained BiH's pre-war external boundaries but divided the country into a complex jigsaw of semi-autonomous 'entities' and cantons to balance 'ethnic' sensibilities. This succeeded in maintaining the fragile peace but the complex political structure resulting from the war has led to bureaucratic tangles and economic stagnation.

# Mostar

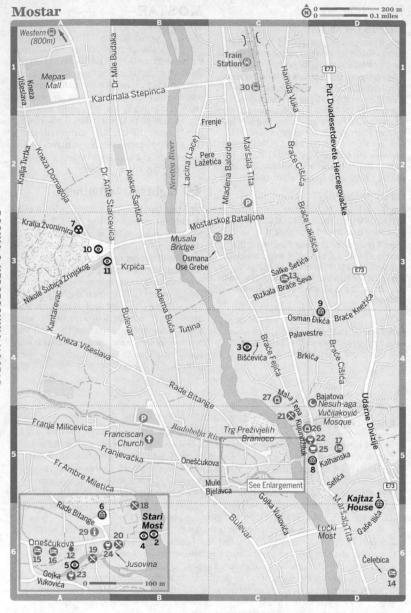

**Bridge Diver's Club** SPECTACLE
(☎ 061-388552; Stari Most; ☺ 10am-dusk) In
summer, young men leap from the parapet
of Stari Most, falling more than 20m into the
freezing cold Neretva. That's not a suicide attempt but a professional sport – donations
are expected from spectators and the divers
won't leap until 50KM has been collected.

# Mostar

**Crooked Bridge**　　　　　　　　　BRIDGE
(Kriva Ćuprija) Built as a miniature test run for Stari Most, the pint-sized Crooked Bridge crosses the tiny Rabobolja creek amid a series of picturesque mill-house restaurants.

**Hammam Museum**　　　　　　　　MUSEUM
(Dževanbeg Bathhouse; Rad Bitange bb; adult/student 5/3KM; ⊙10am-6pm Tue-Sun) This late-16th-century bathhouse has been attractively restored with whitewashed interior, bilingual panels explaining *hammam* (Turkish bath) culture and glass cabinets displaying associated traditional accoutrements.

**★ Kajtaz House**　　　　　　　　　MUSEUM
(Gaše Ilića 21; adult/child 4KM/free; ⊙9am-6pm Apr-Oct) Hidden behind tall walls, Mostar's most historic old house was once the harem section of a larger homestead built for a 16th-century Turkish judge. Full of original artefacts, it still belongs to descendants of the original family albeit now under Unesco protection. A visit includes a very extensive, personal tour.

**Bišćevića Ćošak**　　　　　　　　　HOUSE
(Turkish House; Bišćevića 13; adult/student 4/3KM; ⊙8.30am-7pm Apr-Oct, winter by tour only) Built in 1635, Bišćevića Ćošak is one of very few traditional Turkic-styled houses to retain its original appearance, albeit now with trin-

kets for sale and a fountain made of metal *ibrik* jugs. Three rooms are colourfully furnished with rugs, metalwork and carved wooden furniture. Spot the two tortoises.

**Spanski Trg**　　　　　　　　　HISTORIC SITE
In the early 1990s, Croat and Bosniak forces bombarded each other into the rubble across a 'front line' which ran along the Bulevar and Alese Šantića St. Even now, several shell-pocked skeletal buildings remain in ruins around Spanski Trg, notably the triangular tower that was once **Ljubljanska Banka** (Snipers' Nest; Kralja Zvonimira bb) but is now a concrete skeleton plastered with graffiti.

## ⌖ Tours
Virtually all hostels offer walking tours around town and/or great-value full-day Hercegovina trips visiting Blagaj, Počitelj and the Kravice Waterfalls (for around €30).

Requiring only a two-person minimum, **i-House** (✆036-580048, 063-481842; www.ihouse-mostar.com; Oneščukova 25; ⊙9am-9pm Jun-Sep, reduced hours Mar-May & Oct-Nov) has a similar around-Mostar option, does a fascinating 'Death of Yugoslavia' tour and offers numerous alternative possibilities, including wine tasting, paragliding, rafting and a Wednesday trip to **Tito's Nuclear Bunker**.

## 🛏 Sleeping

There are numerous small hostels, though some are dormant between November and April.

### ⭐ Hostel Balkanarama          HOSTEL €

(☑ 063-897832; www.facebook.com/balkanarama-hostel; Braće Seva 1A; dorm 20-30KM; ☺ bar 6pm-11pm, hostel closed Oct-Mar; 🛜) Run by a very creative Anglo-Bosnian, this excellent new hostel has quickly become one of Mostar's most popular. Quirky features include a central kitchen table fashioned from beer crates and seats made from container pallets augmenting floor cushions in the candle-lamp rooftop bar.

### Hostel Nina          HOSTEL €

(☑ 036-550520, 061-382743; www.hostelnina.ba; Čelebica 18; dm/s/d without bathroom €10/16/21; ⊛@🛜) This popular homestay-hostel is run by an obliging English-speaking lady whose husband is a war survivor and former bridge-jumper who pioneered and still runs regional Hercegovina day tours (€30) that just might end up with drinks at his Tabhana bar.

### Pansion Oskar          GUESTHOUSE €

(☑ 061-823649; www.pansionoskar.com; Oneščukova 33; per person €20; ⊛🛜) Pansion Oskar is essentially a pair of family homes above a delightful open-air garden bar-restaurant slap bang in the historic centre. The nine rooms are fairly simple – three have shared bathroom. Touches of oriental decor echo the feel of the impressive summer garden below. You might have to look for staff in reception if the bell remains unanswered.

### ⭐ Muslibegović House          HISTORIC HOTEL €€

(☑ 036-551379; www.muslibegovichouse.com; Osman Đikća 41; s/d/ste €60/90/105; ☺ museum 10am-6pm mid-Apr–mid-Oct; ⊛🛜) In summer, tourists pay 4KM to visit this beautiful, late-17th-century Ottoman courtyard house (extended in 1871). But it's also an extremely charming boutique hotel. Room sizes and styles vary significantly, mixing excellent modern bathrooms with elements of traditional Bosnian, Turkish or even Moroccan design.

### ⭐ Pansion City Star          HOTEL €€

(☑ 060-3328821, 036-580080; www.citystar.ba; Oneščukova 35; s/d/tr/q from 102/124/156/248KM; breakfast 10KM; ⊛🛜) Brand new in 2016, the building is designed to exacting traditional standards as befits the Unesco-protected Old Town zone, but room interiors are immaculately contemporary with a variety of mood lighting. The Swiss-made beds are super-comfortable and sepia wall photos of Mostar add visual focus.

### ⭐ Shangri-La          GUESTHOUSE €€

(☑ 061-169362; www.shangrila.com.ba; Kalhanska 10; r €49-65; Ⓟ⊛🛜) Behind an imposing 19th-century style facade, eight individually themed rooms are appointed to hotel standards, and there's a fine roof terrace with comfy parasol-shaded seating, dwarf citrus trees and panoramic city views. The English-speaking hosts are faultlessly welcoming without being intrusive. Breakfast costs €6 extra.

## 🍴 Eating

Cafes and restaurants with divine views of Stari Most cluster along the riverbank. Along Mala Tepa and the main central commercial street Braće Fejića you'll find supermarkets, a **vegetable market** (Mala Tepa; ☺ 6.30am-5pm) and several inexpensive places for *ćevapi* and other Bosnian snacks.

### Hindin Han          BALKAN €€

(☑ 061-153054, 036-581054; Jusovina bb; mains 10-18KM, seafood 14-24KM, ćevapi 7KM, wine per litre 15KM; ☺ 9am-11pm; 🛜🍽) Hindin Han is a rebuilt historic mill-cottage building with several layers of summer terrace perched

---

### ENTITIES & AREAS

Geographically BiH comprises Bosnia in the north and Hercegovina (pronounced her-tse-go-vina) in the south. However, the term 'Bosnian' refers to anyone from BiH, not just from Bosnia proper.

Politically, BiH is divided into two entirely different entities. Southwest and central BiH falls mostly within the Federation of Bosnia and Hercegovina, usually shortened to 'the Federation'. Meanwhile most areas bordering Serbia, Montenegro and the northern arm of Croatia are within the Serb-dominated Republika Srpska (abbreviated RS). A few minor practicalities (stamps, phonecards) appear in different versions and the Cyrillic alphabet is more prominent in the RS, but these days casual visitors are unlikely to notice immediately visible differences between the entities.

## AROUND MOSTAR

Many Mostar agencies and hostels combine the following for a satisfying day trip:

**Blagaj** This village's signature sight is a half-timbered sufi-house (*tekija*) standing beside the surreally blue-green Buna River, where it gushes out of a cliff-cave.

**Počitelj** A steeply layered Ottoman-era fortress village that's one of BiH's most picture-perfect architectural ensembles.

**Međugorje** Curious for its mixture of pilgrim piety and Catholic kitsch ever since the Virgin Mary was reputedly spotted in a series of 1981 visions.

**Kravice Waterfalls** BiH's splendid 25m mini Niagara. Some tours give you several hours here to swim in natural pools.

pleasantly above a side stream. Locals rate its food as better than most equivalent tourist restaurants. The stuffed squid we tried was perfectly cooked and generously garnished.

### Šadrvan
BALKAN €€
(☑ 036-579057; www.restoransadravan.ba; Jusovina 11; mains 10-25KM; ☺ 8am-11pm Feb-Dec; 🛜 🗋) On a vine- and tree-shaded corner where the pedestrian lane from Stari Most divides, this delightful tourist favourite has tables set around a trickling fountain made of old Turkish-style metalwork. Obliging costumed waiters can help explain a menu that covers many bases and takes a stab at some vegetarian options. Meat-free *đuveč* (KM8) tastes like ratatouille on rice.

### Babilon
BALKAN €€
(☑ 061-164912; Tabhana; mains 8-20KM; ☺ 9am-11pm summer, 11am-4pm Dec-Feb; 🗋) The Babilon has stupendous views across the river to the Old Town and Stari Most from an extensive series of terraces on five different layers.

### Urban Grill
BOSNIAN €€
(Mala Tepa 26; mains 8-18KM; ☺ 8am-11pm Mon-Sat, 9am-11pm Sun; 🗋) From street level Urban Grill seems to be a slightly upmarket Bosnian fast-food place. But the menu spans a great range and the big attraction is the lower terrace with unexpectedly perfectly framed views of the Old Bridge.

## 🍷 Drinking & Nightlife

### Black Dog Pub
PUB
(Crooked Bridge; beer/wine from 2/4KM; ☺ 10am-late) Old Mostar's best hostelry is a historic mill-house decked with flags and car number plates. It's about the only place you'll find draft ales from the local Oldbridz micro-brewery (www.facebook.com/oldbridz.

ale). Live bands play regularly midsummer, more rarely off season.

### Caffe Marshall
BAR
(www.apartmanimarshall.com; Oneščukova bb; coffee/beer from 2/3KM; ☺ 8am-1am) With a ceiling draped in musical instruments, this music-pumping box bar is named for an ancient Marshall speaker in the owner's collection, rather than for Tito, though a copper Tito head does now grace the cute stone building's facade.

### Terasa
CAFE
(Maršala Tita bb; coffee from 2KM; ☺ weather-dependent) Half a dozen tables on an open-air perch-terrace survey Stari Most and the Old Town towers from photogenic yet unexpected angles. Enter beside **MUM** (Museum of Mostar & Herzegovina; ☑ 036-551432; www.muzejhercegovine.ba; Maršala Tita 156; adult/student 5/3KM; ☺ 10am-4pm Tue-Sun).

### Ali Baba
BAR
(Kujundžiluk; beer/shots from 3/2KM; ☺ 7am-3am Jun-Sep) Take a gaping cavern in the raw rock, add fat beats and colourful flashing globe lamps and hey presto, you have this one-off party bar. A dripping tunnel leads out to a second entrance on Maršala Tita.

## 🛍 Shopping

### Edo Kurt's Workshop
ART
(☑ 061-772173; https://mostar-art.com; Kujundžiluk 5; ☺ 7.30am-4pm) For decades, coppersmith Ismet Kurt beat metal – notably shell casings – into beautiful works of art. His son Edo has now taken on the trade with similar skill in an intriguing little workshop on Kujundžiluk that's a veritable craft museum.

## ℹ️ Information

**Bosniak Post Office** (Braće Fejića bb; ⊘8am-8pm Mon-Fri, to 3pm Sat) The main BH Pošta office is right in the heart of town.

**Tourist Info Centre** (📞036-580275; www.hercegovina.ba; Trg Preživjelih Branioco; ⊘8am-8pm May–early Oct) This office is usefully central but not gushingly helpful.

## ℹ️ Getting There & Around

### BUS

The **main bus station** (📞036-552025; Trg Ivana Krndelja) beside the train station handles half a dozen daily services to Sarajevo, Split and Zagreb plus early morning departures to Belgrade, Herceg Novi, Kotor and Vienna. For Dubrovnik there are three or four direct buses (40KM, 4½ hours) each day.

### TRAIN

Trains to Sarajevo should leave morning and evening but services are currently suspended pending track renewal.

# SURVIVAL GUIDE

## ℹ️ Directory A–Z

### INTERNET ACCESS

Almost all hotels and most cafes offer free wi-fi.

### MONEY

Bosnia's convertible mark (KM or BAM), pronounced *kai-em* or *maraka*, is tied to the euro at

---

## COUNTRY FACTS

**Area** 51,129 sq km

**Capital** Sarajevo

**Country code** 📞387

**Currency** Convertible mark (KM, BAM)

**Emergency** Ambulance 📞124, Fire 📞123, Police 📞122

**Languages** Bosnian, Serbian and Croatian (all variants of the same language)

**Money** ATMs accepting Visa and MasterCard are ubiquitous

**Population** 3.53 million

**Useful phrases** *zdravo* (hello); *hvala* (thanks); *molim* (please), *koliko to košta?* (how much does it cost?)

**Visas** not required for most visitors (see www.mfa.ba)

---

## ESSENTIAL FOOD & DRINK

**Burek** Bosnian *burek* are cylindrical or spiral lengths of filo pastry filled with minced meat. *Sirnica* is filled instead with cheese, *krompiruša* with potato and *zeljanica* with spinach. Collectively these pies are called *pita*.

**Ćevapi (Ćevapčići)** Minced meat formed into cylindrical pellets and served in fresh bread with melting *kajmak*.

**Hurmastica** Syrup-soaked sponge fingers.

**Kajmak** Thick semi-soured cream.

**Pljeskavica** Patty-shaped *ćevapi*.

**Rakija** Grappa or fruit brandy.

**Sarma** Steamed dolma-parcels of rice and minced meat wrapped in cabbage or other green leaves.

**Tufahija** Whole stewed apple with walnut filling.

---

approximately €1=1.96KM. Though no longer officially sanctioned, many businesses still unblinkingly accept euros for minor purchases.

### OPENING HOURS

**Banks** 8am–6pm Monday to Friday, 8.30am–1.30pm Saturday

**Office hours** 8am–4pm Monday to Friday

**Shops** 8am–6pm daily; many stay open later

**Restaurants** 7am–10.30pm or last customer

### POST

BiH has three parallel postal organisations, each issuing their own stamps: BH Pošta (Federation; www.posta.ba), Pošte Srpske (RS; www.postes-rpske.com) and HP Post (Croat areas, western Mostar; www.post.ba).

### PUBLIC HOLIDAYS

Nationwide holidays:

**New Year's Day** 1 January

**Independence Day** 1 March

**May Day** 1 May

**National Statehood Day** 25 November

Additional holidays in the Federation:

**Kurban Bajram** (Islamic Feast of Sacrifice) 1 September 2017, 22 August 2018, 12 August 2019

**Ramazanski Bajram** (end of Ramadan) 26 June 2017, 15 June 2018, 5 June 2019

**Gregorian Easter** 14 and 17 April 2017, 31 March and 2 April 2018, 19 and 22 April 2019

**Gregorian Christmas** 25 December

Additional holidays in the Republika Srpska (RS):
**Orthodox Easter** 14 and 17 Apr 2017, 6 and 9 April 2018, 22 and 29 April 2019
**Orthodox Christmas** 6 January

### SAFE TRAVEL

Landmines and unexploded ordnance still affect 2.3% of Bosnia and Hercegovina's area (see www.bhmac.org). Stick to asphalt/concrete surfaces or well-worn paths and avoid exploring war-wrecked buildings.

### VISAS

Currently stays of less than 90 days require no visa for citizens of 77 counties including most European nations, plus Australia, Canada, Israel, New Zealand and the US. Other nationals should check www.mfa.ba for details.

Transit through Neum (coastal BiH between Split and Dubrovnik) is possible without a Bosnian visa assuming you have a double- or multiple-entry Croat visa.

## ⓘ Getting There & Away

The main gateway by air is busy little **Sarajevo International Airport** (p78). WizzAir budget flights from several north-European destinations arrive at **Tuzla International Airport** (TZL; ☑ 035-814605; http://tuzla-airport.ba; Dubrave Gornje; ⊙ closed midnight-3.30am or longer), there are regular summer links to several Italian cities from **Mostar Airport** (OMO; ☑ 036-350992; www.mostar-airport.ba), and

**Banja Luka Airport** (☑ 051-535210; www.ban-jaluka-airport.com) has an Air Serbia service to Belgrade with possible onward connections.

BiH cities have plenty of international bus services (notably to Belgrade, Dubrovnik, Munich, Split, Vienna and Zagreb), but the only international train is the daily Zagreb–Sarajevo service.

---

### EATING PRICE RANGES

The following price ranges refer to a main course.

**€** less than 10KM

**€€** 10KM–25KM

**€€€** more than 25KM

---

### SLEEPING PRICE RANGES

Except for in hostels, the following price ranges refer to a double room with bathroom during high season (June to September). Unless otherwise stated, breakfast is included in the price.

**€** less than 80KM

**€€** 80KM–190KM

**€€€** more than 190KM

BOSNIA & HERCEGOVINA GETTING THERE & AWAY

# Bulgaria

## Best Places to Eat

➜ MoMa Bulgarian Food & Wine (p92)

➜ Shtastliveca (p101)

➜ Rosé (p104)

➜ Made In Home (p92)

➜ Memory (p98)

## Best Places to Stay

➜ Hotel-Mehana Gurko (p100)

➜ At Renaissance Square (p97)

➜ Canapé Connection (p89)

➜ Hostel Old Plovdiv (p97)

➜ Yo Ho Hostel (p102)

## Why Go?

Soul-stirring mountains, golden beaches and cities that hum with music and art. There's a lot to love about Bulgaria (България): no wonder the Greeks, Romans, Byzantines and Turks all fought to claim it as their own. Billed as the oldest nation on the continent, Bulgaria is rich with ancient treasure. The mysterious Thracians left behind dazzling hauls of gold and silver, and tombs that can be explored to this day. The Romans built cities of breathtaking scale, the bathhouses, walls and amphitheatres of which sit nonchalantly in the midst of modern cities.

Centuries later, Bulgaria still beguiles with its come-hither coastline and fertile valleys laden with vines and roses. Plovdiv is the European Capital of Culture for 2019, Sofia has cool cred to rival any major metropolis, and lively Black Sea resorts teem with modern-day pleasure pilgrims.

## When to Go
### Sofia

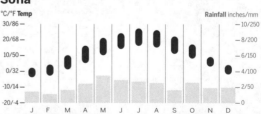

**Feb** Pop your cork at Melnik's Golden Grape Festival.

**Jun** Celebrate the sweetest harvest at Kazanlâk's Rose Festival.

**Jul–Sep** Spend lazy days on the Black Sea beaches and nights at Bulgaria's best clubs.

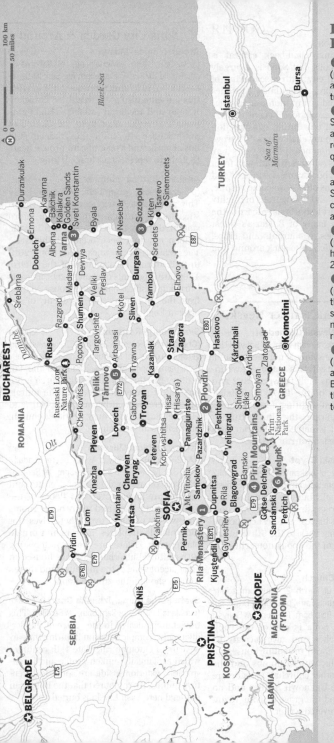

# Bulgaria Highlights

**1 Rila Monastery** (p95) Exploring artistic and religious treasures.

**2 Plovdiv** (p96) Soaking up the city's ancient ambience and revitalised artistic quarter.

**3 Sozopol** (p105) and **Varna** (p102) Sun-worshipping or clubbing all night long at Black Sea resorts.

**4 Pirin Mountains** (p95) Skiing or hiking among the 2000m peaks.

**5 Veliko Târnovo** (p100) Visiting the Tsars' medieval stronghold in this monumental, riverside town.

**6 Melnik** (p95) Sipping a glass or three of Bulgarian *vino* in this photogenic wine town.

# SOFIA СОФИЯ

☑ 02 / POP 1.2 MILLION

Bulgaria's pleasingly laid-back capital is no grand metropolis, but Sofia is a largely modern, youthful city, with a scattering of onion-domed churches, Ottoman mosques and stubborn Red Army monuments that lend an eclectic, exotic feel. Recent excavation work carried out during construction of the city's metro unveiled a treasure trove of Roman ruins from nearly 2000 years ago, when the city was called 'Serdica'. Away from the buildings and boulevards, vast parks and manicured gardens offer a welcome respite, and the ski slopes and hiking trails of mighty Mt Vitosha are just a short bus ride from the centre. Home to many of Bulgaria's finest museums, galleries, restaurants and clubs, Sofia may persuade you to stick around and explore further.

## ◉ Sights

### ◉ Ploshtad Aleksander Nevski

⭐**Aleksander Nevski Cathedral** CHURCH
(pl Aleksander Nevski; ⊘ 7am-7pm; Ⓜ Sofiyski Universitet) One of *the* symbols not just of Sofia but of Bulgaria itself, this massive, awe-inspiring church was built between 1882 and 1912 in memory of the 200,000 Russian soldiers who died fighting for Bulgaria's independence during the Russo-Turkish War (1877–78). It is named in honour of a 13th-century Russian warrior-prince.

**Aleksander Nevski Crypt** GALLERY
(Museum of Icons; pl Aleksander Nevski; adult/child 6/3 lv; ⊘ 10am-5.30pm Tue-Sun; Ⓜ Sofiyski Universitet) Originally built as a final resting place for Bulgarian kings, this crypt now houses Bulgaria's biggest and best collection of icons, stretching back to the 5th century. Enter to the left of the eponymous church's main entrance.

⭐**Sveta Sofia Church** CHURCH
(☑ 02-987 0971; ul Parizh 2; museum adult/child 6/2 lv; ⊘ church 7am-7pm Apr-Oct, to 6pm Nov-Mar, museum 9am-5pm Tue-Sun; Ⓜ Sofiyski Universitet) Sveta Sofia is one of the capital's oldest churches, and gave the city its name. A subterranean **museum** houses an ancient necropolis, with 56 tombs and the remains of four other churches. Outside are the Tomb of the Unknown Soldier and an eternal flame, and the grave of Ivan Vazov, Bulgaria's most revered writer.

### ◉ Sofia City Garden & Around

**Archaeological Museum** MUSEUM
(☑ 02-988 2406; www.naim.bg; ul Saborna 2; adult/child 10/2 lv; ⊘ 10am-5pm Tue-Sun; Ⓜ Serdika) Housed in a former mosque built in 1496, this museum displays a wealth of Thracian, Roman and medieval artefacts. Highlights include a mosaic floor from the Church of Sveta Sofia, a 4th-century BC Thracian gold burial mask, and a magnificent bronze head, thought to represent a Thracian king.

**Ancient Serdica Complex** RUINS
(pl Nezavisimost; ⊘ 6am-11pm; Ⓜ Serdika) FREE
This remarkable, partly covered excavation site, situated just above the Serdika metro station, displays the remains of Serdica, the Roman city that once occupied this area. The remains were unearthed from 2010 to 2012 during construction of the metro. There are fragments of eight streets, an early Christian basilica, baths and houses dating from the 4th to 6th centuries. Plenty of signage in English.

**Sveti Georgi Rotunda** CHURCH
(Church of St George; ☑ 02-980 9216; www.svgeorgi-rotonda.com; bul Dondukov 2; ⊘ services daily 8am, 9am & 5pm; Ⓜ Serdika) Built in the 4th century AD, this tiny red-brick church is Sofia's oldest preserved building. The murals inside were painted between the 10th and 14th centuries. It's a busy, working church, but visitors are welcome.

**Ethnographical Museum** MUSEUM
(☑ 02-988 1974; pl Knyaz Al Batenberg 1; adult/child 3/1 lv; ⊘ 10am-6pm Tue-Sun; Ⓜ Serdika) Displays on regional costumes, crafts and folklore are spread over two floors of the former royal palace, and many of the rooms are worth pausing over themselves for their marble fireplaces, mirrors and ornate plasterwork. There are some interesting 19th-century Bulgarian paintings housed in an adjacent wing of the museum, and there's a crafts shop on the ground floor.

**Sveta Petka Samardzhiiska Church** CHURCH
(bul Maria Luisa 2; ⊘ 9am-5pm; Ⓜ Serdika) This tiny church, located in the centre of the Serdika metro complex, was built during the early years of Ottoman rule (late 14th century), which explains its sunken profile and inconspicuous exterior. Inside are some 16th-century murals. It's rumoured that the Bulgarian national hero Vasil Levski is buried here.

### Sveta Nedelya Cathedral CHURCH
(☑02-987 5748; pl Sveta Nedelya; ☺8am-6pm; Ⓜ Serdika) Completed in 1863, this magnificent domed church is one of the city's major landmarks, and is noted for its rich, Byzantine-style murals. The church was targeted by communists on 16 April 1925 in a failed bomb attack aimed at assassinating Tsar Boris III.

### Museum of Socialist Art MUSEUM
(☑02-980 0093; ul Lachezar Stanchev 7, Iztok; 6 lv; ☺10am-5.30pm Tue-Sun; ⓂGM Dimitrov) If you wondered where all those unwanted statues of Lenin ended up, you'll find some here, along with the red star from atop Sofia's **Party House** (pl Nezavisimost; Ⓜ Serdika). There's a gallery of paintings, where you'll rejoice in catchy titles such as *Youth Meeting at Kilifarevo Village to Send Worker-Peasant Delegation to the USSR,* and stirring old propaganda films are shown.

## ☞ Tours

### Free Sofia Tour WALKING
(☑0988920461; www.freesofiatour.com; cnr ul Alabin & bul Vitosha; ☺11am & 6pm; Ⓜ Serdika) FREE Explore Sofia's sights in the company of friendly and enthusiastic English-speaking young locals on this two-hour guided walk. No reservation is needed; just show up outside the Palace of Justice.

### Balkan Bites FOOD & DRINK
(☑0877613992; www.balkanbites.bg; by donation; ☺tours 2pm; Ⓜ Sofiyski Universitet, 🚎9) This two-hour guided walking tour focuses on food and includes tastings and drinks at restaurants around town. The basic tour is free but a donation is expected. Walks depart at 2pm from the statue of Stefan Stambolov in Crystal Park.

### New Sofia Pub Crawl TOURS
(☑0877613992; www.thenewsofiapubcrawl.com; tours 20 lv; ☺9pm-1am; Ⓜ Sofiyski Universitet, 🚎9) Explore Sofia's secret haunts on this nightly knees-up. Expect lots of good chat and surprising insights into the social side of the city (plus the odd free drink). Meet by the statue of Stefan Stambolov in Crystal Park.

## 🛏 Sleeping

Accommodation in Sofia tends to be more expensive than elsewhere in Bulgaria, with hotel prices comparable to those in other large European cities. There are several modern hostels that offer dorm-bed accommodation (and often a couple of private rooms), plus free wi-fi, shared kitchens, and other perks.

### Art Hostel HOSTEL €
(☑02-987 0545; www.art-hostel.com; ul Angel Kânchev 21a; dm/s/d from 20/47/66 lv; @ 🛜; 🚎12) This bohemian hostel stands out from the crowd with its summertime art exhibitions, live music, dance performances and more. Dorms are appropriately arty and bright; private rooms are airy and very welcoming. There's a great basement bar and peaceful little garden at the back.

### ★ Canapé Connection GUESTHOUSE €
(☑02-441 6373; www.canapeconnection.com; ul William Gladstone 12a; s/d from 50/64 lv; 🛜🛁; 🚎1, 6, 7) Formerly a hostel, Canapé reinvented itself as a guesthouse in 2016, retaining its same attention to cleanliness and a refreshingly simple, rustic design. The six rooms are divided into singles and doubles, with a larger room upstairs to accommodate families. There's a quiet garden outside to relax in. Note there's no breakfast, but you'll find several coffee places nearby.

### ★ Hotel Niky HOTEL €€
(☑02-952 3058; www.hotel-niky.com; ul Neofit Rilski 16; r/ste from 90/130 lv; P 🐾❄🛜🛁; ⓂNDK, 🚎1) Offering excellent value and a good city-centre location, Niky has comfortable rooms and gleaming bathrooms; the smart little suites come with kitchenettes. It's a very popular place and frequently full; be sure to book ahead.

---

### ITINERARIES

#### One Week
Take a full day to hit **Sofia**'s main attractions, then take the bus to **Veliko Târnovo** for a few days of sightseeing and hiking. For the rest of the week, head to **Varna** for some sea and sand, or veer south to the ancient beach towns of **Nesebâr** and **Sozopol**.

#### Two Weeks
Spend a few extra days in Sofia, adding in a day trip to **Rila Monastery**, then catch a bus to **Plovdiv** to wander the cobbled lanes of the Old Town. From there, take the mountain air in majestic **Veliko Târnovo**. Make for the coast, with a few nights in **Varna** and lively **Sozopol**.

# Sofia

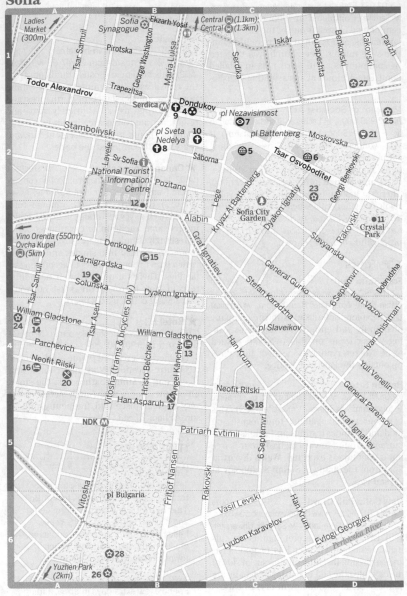

**BULGARIA** SOFIA

**Hotel Les Fleurs** BOUTIQUE HOTEL **€€€**
(☎02-810 0800; www.lesfleurshotel.com; bul Vitosha 21; r from 220 lv; P❖❈☎; MSerdika, 🚌10)
You can hardly miss this very central hotel with gigantic blooms on its facade. The flow-
ery motif is continued in the large, carefully styled rooms, and there's a very good restaurant on-site. The location, right at the start of the pedestrian-only stretch of bul Vitosha, is ideal.

BULGARIA SOFIA

cakes. Kiosks around town sell tasty local fast food such as *banitsa* (cheese pasties) and *palachinki* (pancakes).

**Vila Rosich**      BAKERY €
(📞02-954 3072; www.vilarosiche.com; ul Neofit Rilski 26; sandwiches & cakes 5-7 lv; ⊗8am-9pm; 🛜🍴; Ⓜ NDK) Step into the back garden of this hidden bakery and enter what feels like a secret world of fresh-made breads and cakes. It's a perfect spot for an afternoon sweet, or a light cheese-stuffed croissant sandwich.

# ✗ Eating

Sofia has some of the country's best restaurants, including traditional and international cuisines. In summer, cafes occupy every piece of garden and footpath, the best ones offering a refined setting for cocktails and

### ★MoMa Bulgarian
### Food & Wine
BULGARIAN €€

(☑0885622020; www.moma-restaurant.com; ul Solunska 28; mains 8-22 lv; ⊙11am-10pm; 🛜🖋; Ⓜ Serdika) An update on the traditional *mehana* (taverna), serving typical Bulgarian foods, such as grilled meats and meatballs, and wines, but in a more modern and understated interior. The result is one of the best nights out in town. Start off with a shot of *rakia* (Bulgarian brandy) and a salad, and move on to the ample main courses. Book ahead – this restaurant is popular.

### ★Made In Home
INTERNATIONAL €€

(☑0876884014; ul Angel Kânchev 30a; mains 12-22 lv; ⊙11am-9pm Mon, to 10pm Tue-Sun; 🛜🖋; Ⓜ NDK) Sofia's very popular entrant into the worldwide, locally sourced, slow-food trend (the name refers to the fact that all items are made in-house). The cooking is eclectic, with dollops of Middle Eastern (eg hummus) and Turkish items, as well as ample vegetarian and vegan offerings. The playfully rustic interior feels straight out of a Winnie-the-Pooh book. Reservations essential.

### Manastirska Magernitsa
BULGARIAN €€

(☑02-980 3883; www.magernitsa.com; ul Han Asparuh 67; mains 8-18 lv; ⊙11-2am; Ⓜ NDK) This traditional *mehana* (tavern) is among the best places in Sofia to sample authentic Bulgarian cuisine. The enormous menu features recipes collected from monasteries across the country, with dishes such as 'drunken rabbit' stewed in wine, as well as salads, fish, pork and game options. Portions are generous and the service attentive. Dine in the garden in nice weather.

## 🍷 Drinking & Nightlife

### Raketa Rakia Bar
BAR

(☑02-444 6111; ul Yanko Sakazov 15-17; ⊙11am-midnight; 🛜; 🚌11, Ⓜ Sofiyski Universitet) Unsurprisingly, this rakish communist-era retro bar has a huge selection of *rakia* (Bulgarian brandy) on hand; before you start working your way down the list, line your stomach with meat-and-cream-heavy snacks and meals. Reservations essential.

### One More Bar
BAR

(☑0882539592; ul Shishman 12; ⊙8.30am-2.30am; 🛜; Ⓜ Sofiyski Universitet) Inside a gorgeous old house, this shabby-chic hot spot wouldn't be out of place in Melbourne or Manhattan: an extensive cocktail list, a delightful summer garden and jazzy background music add to its cosmopolitan appeal.

### DaDa Cultural Bar
BAR

(☑0877062455; http://blog.dadaculturalbar.eu; ul Georgi Benkovski 10; ⊙24hr; 🛜; Ⓜ Serdika, 🚌20, 22) A local institution, DaDa bar is far more than a place to drink. The mission here is culture, and expect to find live music, art installations, readings or happenings. The website usually has an up-to-date program. Friendly staff and a welcoming vibe.

## ☆ Entertainment

If you read Bulgarian, or can decipher some Cyrillic, *Programata* is the most comprehensive source of entertainment listings; otherwise check out its excellent English-language website, www.programata.bg. You can book tickets online at www.ticketpro.bg.

### Live Music
### RockIT
LIVE MUSIC

(☑0888666991; ul Georgi Benkovski 14; ⊙9pm-4am Mon-Sat; Ⓜ Serdika, 🚌20, 22) If you're into rock and metal, get your horns up here. This huge two-level building shakes beneath the weight of heavy live bands, DJs, and lots and lots of hair.

### Sofia Live Club
LIVE MUSIC

(☑0886661045; www.sofialiveclub.com; pl Bulgaria 1; ⊙8pm-7am; Ⓜ NDK) This slick venue, located in the National Palace of Culture (NDK), is the city's largest live-music club. All swished up in cabaret style, it hosts local and international jazz, alternative, world-music and rock acts.

### Bulgaria Hall
CLASSICAL MUSIC

(☑tickets 02-987 7656; www.sofiaphilharmonie. bg; ul Aksakov 1; ⊙box office 9.30am-2.30pm, 3-7.30pm Mon-Fri, 9.30am-2.30pm Sat; Ⓜ Serdika) Home of the excellent Sofia Philharmonic Orchestra.

### Performing Arts

Ticket prices for theatre and live music vary enormously. For shows at the Opera House or the Ivan Vazov National Theatre, you might pay anything from 10 lv to 30 lv; shows at the National Palace of Culture (NDK) vary much more, with tickets costing from 30 lv to 80 lv for international acts and around 10 lv to 30 lv for local ones.

### National Palace of Culture
CONCERT VENUE

(NDK; ☑02-916 6300; www.ndk.bg; pl Bulgaria; ⊙ticket office 10am-8pm; 🛜; Ⓜ NDK) The NDK (as it's usually called) has 15 halls and is the country's largest cultural complex. It maintains a regular program of events throughout the year, including film screenings, trade shows and big-name international music acts.

### National Opera House
OPERA

(☑ tickets 02-987 1366; www.operasofia.bg; bul Dondukov 30; ☺ box office 9am-2pm & 2.30-7pm Mon-Fri, 11am-7pm Sat, 11am-4pm Sun; ☑ 20, 22) Opened in 1953, this monumental edifice is the venue for classical opera and ballet performances, as well as special concerts for children. Enter from ul Vrabcha.

### Cultural Centre G8
CINEMA

(☑ 02-995 0080; www.g8cinema.com; ul William Gladstone 8; tickets 6-8 lv; ☺ 9am-11pm; ☑ 1, 6, 7) This trendy, art-house cinema does triple duty as a contemporary art gallery and secluded, garden drinking spot.

## 🛍 Shopping

Bulevard Vitosha is Sofia's main shopping street, mostly featuring international brand-name boutiques interspersed with restaurants.

### Vino Orenda
WINE

(☑ 0889623606; www.vinoorenda.com; bul Makedonia 50a; ☺ 10.30am-7.30pm Mon-Fri; ☑ 4, 5) Small, knowledgeable wine shop offering products from a variety of independent producers around the country. The engaging owner is more than happy to guide you through your options.

### Centre of Folk Arts & Crafts
GIFTS & SOUVENIRS

(☑ 02-989 6416; www.craftshop-bg.com; ul Parizh 4; ☺ 9.30am-6.30pm Mon-Sat, by appointment Sun; ☑ Serdika, ☑ 20, 22) Typical Bulgarian souvenirs such as hand-woven rugs, pottery, silver jewellery, woodcarvings and CDs of Bulgarian music are available in this crowded shop, though prices are rather high. There's another branch inside the Royal Palace, at the exit from the Ethnographic Museum.

### Ladies' Market
MARKET

(Zhenski Pazar; ul Stefan Stambolov; ☺ dawn-dusk; ☑ Lavov most, ☑ 20, 22) Stretching several blocks between ul Ekzarh Yosif and bul Slivnitsa, this is Sofia's biggest market for fresh produce, meats, fish, cheeses and spices, with lots of Turkish items tossed into the mix. It's a great spot for self-caterers. Beware pickpockets.

## ℹ Information

**National Tourist Information Centre** (☑ 02-933 5826; www.bulgariatravel.org; pl Sveta Nedelya 1; ☺ 9am-5pm Mon-Fri; ☑ Serdika) The office is hidden near a small side street, a few steps southwest of pl Sveta Nedelya.

**Sofia Tourist Information Centre** (☑ 02-491 8344; www.info-sofia.bg; Sofiyski Universitet metro underpass; ☺ 8am-8pm Mon-Fri, 10am-6pm Sat & Sun; ☑ Sofiyski Universitet) Lots of free leaflets and maps, and helpful English-speaking staff.

**Pirogov Hospital** (☑ emergency 02-915 4411; www.pirogov.bg; bul General Totleben 21; ☑ 4, 5) Sofia's main public hospital for emergencies.

## ℹ Getting There & Away

### AIR

**Sofia Airport** (☑ info 24hr 02-937 2211; www.sofia-airport.bg; off bul Brussels; ☎; ☑ 84, ☑ Sofia Airport) is 10km east of the city centre. The only domestic flights within Bulgaria are between Sofia and the Black Sea coast. **Bulgaria Air** (☑ call centre 02-402 0400; www.air.bg; ul Ivan Vazov 2; ☺ 9.30am-noon & 12.30pm-5.30pm Mon-Fri; ☑ Serdika) flies daily to Varna, with two or three daily flights between July and September; the airline also flies to Burgas.

### BUS

Sofia's **central bus station** (Tsentralna Avtogara; ☑ info 0900 63 099; www.centralnaavtogara.bg; bul Maria Luisa 100; ☺ 24hr; ☎; ☑ Central Railway Station) is beside the train station and accessed by the same metro stop. There are dozens of counters for individual private companies, an information desk and an **OK-Supertrans taxi desk** (☑ 02-973 2121; www.oktaxi.net; Centrail Bus Station; ☺ 6am-10pm; ☑ Central Railway Station). Departures are less frequent between November and April. Frequent buses depart Sofia for Plovdiv (14 lv, 2½ hours), Veliko Târnovo (22 lv, four hours), Varna (33 lv, seven hours) and more; the easy-to-navigate www.bgrazpisanie.com/en has full local and international timetables and fare listings.

### TRAIN

The **central train station** (☑ info 02-931 1111, international services 02-931 0972, tickets 02-932 2270; www.bdz.bg; bul Maria Luisa 102a; ☺ ticket office 7am-8.15pm; ☑ Central Railway Station) has been extensively renovated but lacks many basic services. It's located in an isolated part of town about 1km north of the centre, though it's the terminus of a metro line and easy to reach. It's 100m (a five-minute walk) from the Central Bus Station.

Destinations for all domestic and international services are listed on timetables in Cyrillic, but

BULGARIA SOFIA

## MT VITOSHA & BOYANA

The Mt Vitosha range, 23km long and 13km wide, lies just south of Sofia; it's sometimes referred to as the 'lungs of Sofia' for the refreshing breezes it deflects onto the capital. The mountain is part of the 227 sq km Vitosha Nature Park (www.park-vitosha.org), the oldest of its kind in Bulgaria (created in 1934). The main activities are hiking in summer and skiing in winter (mid-December to April). All of the park's areas have good hiking; Aleko, the country's highest ski resort, is best for skiing.

On weekends chairlifts, starting around 4km from the village of **Dragalevtsi**, run all year up to Goli Vrâh (1837m); take bus 66 or 93. Another option is the six-person gondola at Simeonovo, reachable by buses 122 or 123 (also weekends only).

A trip out here could be combined with a visit to **Boyana**, home to the fabulous, Unesco-listed **Boyana Church** (☑02-959 0939; www.boyanachurch.org; ul Boyansko Ezero 3, Boyana; adult/child 10/1 lv, combined ticket with National Historical Museum 12 lv, guides 10 lv; ☉9.30am-5.30pm Apr-Oct, 9am-5pm Nov-Mar; ☐64, 107) (en route between central Sofia and the mountains). This tiny church is adorned with 90 colourful murals dating to the 13th century, considered among the most important examples of medieval Bulgarian art. A combined ticket includes entry to both the church and the **National Museum of History** (☑02-955 4280; www.historymuseum.org; ul Vitoshko Lale 16, Boyana; adult/child 10/1 lv, combined ticket with Boyana Church 12 lv, guided tours in English 30 lv; ☉9.30am-6pm Apr-Oct, 9am-5.30pm Nov-Mar; ☐63, 107, 111, ☐2), 2km away. Take bus 64 or 107 to reach Boyana.

departures (for the following two hours) and arrivals (for the previous two hours) are listed in English on a large screen on the ground floor.

Same-day tickets are sold at counters on the ground floor, while advance tickets are sold in the gloomy basement, accessed via an unsigned flight of stairs near some snack bars. Counters are open 24 hours, but normally only a few are staffed and queues are long, so don't turn up at the last moment to purchase your ticket, and allow some extra time to work out the confusing system of platforms (indicated with Roman numerals) and tracks.

Sample fast train routes include Sofia to Plovdiv (8 lv to 10 lv, 2½ to 3 hours) and Varna (31 lv to 39 lv, 7½ to 9 hours): see www.bgrazpisanie.com/en or www.bdz.bg/en for all domestic and international routes.

## 🏃 Getting Around

### TO/FROM THE AIRPORT

Sofia's metro connects Terminal 2 to the centre (Serdika station) in around 20 minutes. Buy tickets in the station, which is located just outside the terminal exit. Bus 84 also shuttles between the centre and both terminals. Buy tickets (1 lv, plus an extra fare for large luggage) from the driver. A taxi to the centre will cost anywhere from 10 lv to 15 lv. Prebook your taxi at the **OK-Supertrans Taxi** (p93) counter.

### CAR & MOTORCYCLE

Sofia's public transport is excellent and traffic can be heavy, so there's no need to drive a private or rented car in Sofia. If you wish to ex-

plore further afield, however, a car might come in handy. The **Union of Bulgarian Motorists** (☑02-935 7935, road assistance 02-91 146; www.uab.org) provides emergency roadside service. Numerous car-rental outlets have desks at Sofia Airport.

### PUBLIC TRANSPORT

Sofia has a comprehensive public transport system based on trams, buses, trolleybuses and underground metro. Public transport generally runs from 5.30am to around 11pm every day. The **Sofia Urban Mobility Centre** (☑info 0700 13 233; www.sofiatraffic.bg) maintains a helpful website with fares and an updated transport map.

Tickets for trams, buses and trolleybuses cost 1 lv each (8 lv for 10 trips) and can be purchased at kiosks near stops or from on-board ticket machines. Consider buying a day pass (4 lv) to save the hassle of buying individual tickets.

See www.sofiatraffic.bg for more information on public transport.

### TAXI

By law, taxis must use meters, but those that wait around the airport, luxury hotels and within 100m of pl Sveta Nedelya will often try to negotiate an unmetered fare – which, of course, will be considerably more. All official taxis are yellow, have fares per kilometre displayed in the window, and have obvious taxi signs (in English or Bulgarian) on top. **OK-Supertrans** (☑02-973 2121; www.oktaxi.net; 0.79/0.90 day/night rate) or **Yellow Taxi** (☑02-91 119; www.yellow333.com) are reliable operators.

# SOUTHERN BULGARIA

Some of Bulgaria's most precious treasures are scattered in the towns, villages and forests of the stunning south. The must-visit medieval Rila Monastery is nestled in the deep forest but easily reached by bus; tiny Melnik is awash in ancient wine; and the cobbled streets of Plovdiv, Bulgaria's second city, are lined with timeless reminders of civilisations come and gone.

The region is a scenic and craggy one; the **Rila Mountains** (www.rilanationalpark.bg) are just south of Sofia, the **Pirin Mountains** (www.pirin-np.com) rise towards the Greek border, and the **Rodopi Mountains** loom to the east and south of Plovdiv. There's great hiking to be had, and the south is also home to three of Bulgaria's most popular ski resorts: Borovets, Bansko and Pamporovo; see www.bulgariaski.com for information.

## Rila Monastery
### Рилски Манастир

Many Bulgarians say you haven't really been to Bulgaria until you've paid your respects to the truly heavenly, Unesco-listed **Rila Monastery**, 120km south of Sofia. Founded in AD 927 and inspired by the powerful spiritual influence of hermit monk Ivan Rilski, the monastery complex was heavily restored in 1469 after raids. It became a stronghold of Bulgarian culture and language during Ottoman rule. Set in a magnificent forested valley ideal for hiking, the monastery is rightfully famous for its mural-plastered **Church of Rozhdestvo Bogorodichno** (Church of the Nativity; Rila Monastery) dating from the 1830s. The attached **museum** (Rila Monastery; 8 lv; ⊙ 8.30am-4.30pm) is home to the astonishing **Rafail's Cross**, an early 19th-century double-sided crucifix, with biblical scenes painstakingly carved in miniature. The monastery compound is open from 6am to 10pm. Visitors should dress modestly.

If you have time, hike up to the **Tomb of St Ivan**, the founder of the monastery. The 15-minute walk begins along the road 3.7km east behind the monastery.

You can stay in simple **rooms** (☑ 0896872010; www.rilamonastery.pmg-blg.com; r 30-60 lv) at the monastery or, for something slightly more upmarket, try **Gorski Kut** (☑ 07054-2170, 0888710348; www.gorski-kut.eu; d/tr/ste 51/61/76 lv; P ❋ ), 5km west.

Tour buses such as **Rila Monastery Bus** (☑ 02-489 0883; www.rilamonasterybus.com; 50 lv) are a popular option for a day trip from Sofia. By public transport, one daily morning bus (22 lv, 2½ hours) goes from Sofia's Ovcha Kupel bus station, returning in the afternoon.

## Melnik     Мелник
☑ 07437 / POP 390

Steep sandstone pyramids form a magnificent backdrop in tiny Melnik, 20km north of the Bulgaria–Greece border. But it's a 600-year-old wine culture that has made Melnik famous, and the village's wonderfully restored National Revival architecture looks all the better through a haze of cabernet sauvignon.

### ⚜ Festivals & Events

**Golden Grapes Festival**     WINE
(⊙ 2nd weekend Feb) It's hardly Bacchanalian – this is small-town Bulgaria, after all – but this annual knees-up gathers local wine producers to showcase their wares and tempt tourists with wine tastings, all set to a backdrop of singing competitions and other folkish entertainment. It's usually on the second weekend of February; ask at the tourist office for details.

### ◎ Sights

The major sights here, unsurprisingly, are wineries. Melnik's wines, celebrated for more than 600 years, include the signature dark red, Shiroka Melnishka Loza; it was a favourite tipple of Winston Churchill. Shops and stands dot Melnik's cobblestone paths, with reds and whites starting from around 3 lv; better yet, learn the history and tools of Melnik's winemaking trade at the **Museum of Wine** (www.muzei-na-vinoto.com; ul Melnik 91; 5 lv; ⊙ 10am-7pm).

**Kordopulov House**     MUSEUM
(☑ 0877576120, 0887776917; www.kordopulova-house.com; 3 lv; ⊙ 9.30am-6.30pm Apr-Sep, to 4pm Oct-Mar) Reportedly Bulgaria's largest Revival-era building, this whitewashed and wooden mansion beams down from a cliff face at the eastern end of Melnik's main road. Dating from 1754, the four-storey mansion was formerly the home of a prestigious wine merchant family. Its naturally cool rooms steep visitors in luxurious period flavour, from floral stained-glass windows to

Oriental-style fireplaces and a sauna. There are touches of intrigue, too, such as the secret cupboard that allowed the whole family to eavesdrop on wine-trading deals.

## 🛏 Sleeping

Private rooms are a budget, no-frills option (15 lv to 20 lv per person), usually with shared bathrooms; look for English-language 'Rooms' signs.

### ★ Hotel Bolyarka                    HOTEL €€
(☑07437-2383; www.melnikhotels.com; ul Melnik 34; s/d/apt 40/60/100 lv; P🅿❄@🛜) The right blend of old-world nostalgia and modern comfort has made this one of Melnik's favourite hotels. The Bolyarka has elegant rooms, a snug lobby bar, a Finnish-style sauna and one of Melnik's best restaurants. For a touch of added charm, reserve a deluxe apartment (130 lv) with fireplace.

### Hotel Melnik                       HOTEL €€
(☑07437-2272, 0879131459; www.hotelmelnik. com; ul Vardar 2; s/d/apt 40/60/120 lv; P❄🛜) This pleasant hotel is shaded by fig and cherry trees, and peeps down over Melnik's main road. White-walled rooms with simple furnishings don't quite match the old-world reception and the *mehana* (tavern) with a bird's-eye view. But it's great value, smartly run and the location – up a cobbled lane, on the right as you enter the village – is convenient whether you arrive by car or bus.

## 🍴 Eating

### ★ Mehana Chavkova Kâshta   BULGARIAN €€
(☑0893505090; www.themelnikhouse.com; 7-12 lv) Sit beneath 500-year-old trees and watch Melnik meander past at this superb spot. Like many places in town, grilled meats and Bulgarian dishes are specialities (try the *satch,* a sizzling flat pan of meat and vegetables); the atmosphere and friendly service give it an extra nudge above the rest. It's 200m from the bus stop, along the main road.

## ℹ Information

**Melnik Tourist Information Centre** (Obshtina Building; ⊙9am-5pm) Located behind the bus stop, on the *obshtina* (municipality) building's upper floor, this centre advises on accommodation and local activities, though opening times can be spotty (especially outside summer). Bus and train timetables are posted outside.

Informative (but unofficial) tourism website http://melnik-bg.eu details history and local attractions.

## ℹ Getting There & Away

One daily direct bus connects Melnik with Sofia (17 lv, 4½ hours), though times vary. Two daily direct buses serve Blagoevgrad (7 lv, two hours) near the border with Macedonia.

# Plovdiv                        Пловдив
☑032 / POP 341,560

With an easy grace, Plovdiv mingles invigorating nightlife with millennia-old ruins. Like Rome, Plovdiv straddles seven hills; but as Europe's oldest continuously inhabited city, it's far more ancient. It is best loved for its romantic old town, packed with colourful and creaky 19th-century mansions that house museums, galleries and guesthouses.

Bulgaria's cosmopolitan second city has always been hot on the heels of Sofia, and a stint as European Capital of Culture 2019 seems sure to give Plovdiv the edge. Music and art festivals draw increasing crowds, while renovations in the Kapana artistic quarter and Tsar Simeon Gardens have given the city new confidence.

## ⊙ Sights

Most of Plovdiv's main sights are in and around the fantastic Old Town. Its meandering cobblestone streets, overflowing with atmospheric house museums, art galleries, antique stores, are also home to welcoming nooks for eating, drinking and people-watching.

### ★ Roman Amphitheatre          HISTORIC SITE
(ul Hemus; adult/student 5/2 lv; ⊙9am-6pm Apr-Oct, to 5pm Nov-Mar) Plovdiv's magnificent 2nd-century AD amphitheatre, built during the reign of Emperor Trajan, was uncovered during a freak landslide in 1972. It once held about 6000 spectators. Now largely restored, it's one of Bulgaria's most magical venues, once again hosting large-scale special events and concerts. Visitors can admire the amphitheatre for free from several lookouts along ul Hemus, or pay admission for a scarper around.

### Balabanov House                    MUSEUM
(☑032-627 082; ul K Stoilov 57; 3 lv; ⊙9am-6pm Apr-Oct, to 5.30pm Nov-Mar) One of Plovdiv's most beautiful Bulgarian National Revival-era mansions, Balabanov House is an enjoy-

## MYSTERIES OF THRACE

Plovdiv makes an excellent base for half-day trips to the windblown ruins and spiritual sights of Bulgarian Thrace.

Magnificent **Bachkovo Monastery** (www.bachkovskimanastir.com; Bachkovo; monastery free, refectory 6 lv, museum 2 lv, ossuary 6 lv; ⊙ 6am-10pm) FREE, founded in 1083, is about 30km south of Plovdiv. Its church is decorated with 1850s frescoes by renowned artist Zahari Zograf and houses a much-cherished icon of the Virgin Mary. Take any bus to Smolyan from Plovdiv's Rodopi bus station (4 lv), disembark at the turn-off about 1.2km south of Bachkovo village and walk about 500m uphill.

**Asen's Fortress** (Assenovgrad; adult/student 3/2 lv; ⊙ 10am-6pm Wed-Sun Apr-Oct, to 5pm Nov-Mar), 19km southeast of Plovdiv, squats precariously on the edge of a cliff. Over the centuries, Roman, Byzantine and Ottoman rulers admired its impenetrable position so much that they continued to build and rebuild, adding chapels and thickening its walls to a battering-ram-proof 3m. Taxis from Plovdiv will charge about 35 lv to 40 lv for a return trip to the fortress; better yet, negotiate for a driver to take you to both fortress and Bachkovo Monastery.

able way to experience old town nostalgia as well as contemporary art. The house was faithfully reconstructed in 19th-century style during the 1970s. The lower floor has an impressive collection of paintings by local artists, while upper rooms are decorated with antiques and elaborately carved ceilings.

**Ethnographical Museum**  MUSEUM
(☎ 032-624 261; www.ethnograph.info; ul Dr Chomakov 2; adult/student 5/2 lv; ⊙ 9am-6pm Tue-Sun May-Oct, to 5pm Nov-Apr) Even if you don't have time to step inside, it would be criminal to leave Plovdiv's old town without glancing into the courtyard of this stunning National Revival–era building. Well-manicured flower gardens surround a navy-blue mansion, ornamented with golden filigree and topped with a distinctive peaked roof. There is more to admire inside, especially the upper floor's sunshine-yellow walls and carved wooden ceiling, hovering above displays of regional costumes. The ground-floor displays of agrarian instruments are a shade less interesting.

## Tours

**Hristo Petrov**
(☎ 0879694681; hristo.petroff@yahoo.com) Knowledgeable Hristo can take small groups on day trips by car to surrounding attractions. A typical rate for visiting Buzludzha, a UFO-shaped Soviet relic in the central mountains, is around 150 lv.

**Patrick Penov**
(☎ 0887364711; www.guide-bg.com) For a tour with a personal touch, licensed guide Svet-

lomir 'Patrick' Penov crafts superb itineraries from Thracian treasures and wineries to horse riding, mountain biking and village life. Average daily rates are 200 lv to 250 lv.

## Sleeping

**Hikers Hostel**  HOSTEL €
(☎ 0896764854; www.hikers-hostel.org; ul Sâborna 53; 18-/12-bed dm 18/20 lv; @ 🖃) In a mellow Old-Town location, Hikers has wood-floored dorms and standard hostel perks such as a laundry and a shared kitchen. Bonuses such as a garden lounge, hammocks and mega-friendly staff make it a worthy option. Staff can help organise excursions to Bachkovo Monastery (southern mountains), Buzludzha Monument (central mountains) and more. Off-site private rooms (from 43 lv) are available in the Kapana area.

⭐ **Hostel Old Plovdiv**  HOSTEL €€
(☎ 032-260 925; www.hosteloldplovdiv. com; ul Chetvarti Yanuari 3; dm/s/d/tr/q 26/60/90/110/130 lv; 🅿 🖃) This marvellous old building (1868) is more akin to a boutique historical hotel than a run-of-the-mill hostel. Remarkably restored by charismatic owner Hristo Giulev and his wife, this genial place smack bang in the middle of the Old Town is all about warm welcomes and old-world charm.

⭐ **At Renaissance Square**  BOUTIQUE HOTEL €€€
(☎ 032-266 966; www.renaissance-bg.com; pl Vâzhrazhdane 1; s/d from 115/145 lv; 🅿 ❄ @ 🖃) Re-creating National Revival–era grandeur is a labour of love at this charming little

## TOMBS & BLOOMS: KAZANLÂK

For centuries Kazanlâk has been the sweet-smelling centre of European rose-oil production. This nondescript town is also the gateway to the Valley of the Thracian Kings, meaning you can combine fragrant flowers with awe-inspiring tombs in a single visit.

Roses (the aromatic *Rosa damascena*, to be precise) bloom around mid-May to mid-June. Their delicate oils are used in everything from moisturising balms, liqueurs, jams and candies. Kazanlâk's **Rose Festival** (☉first weekend Jun) is the highlight of the season. You can explore the history of rose-oil production year-round at the **Museum of Roses** (☑0431-64 057; bul Osvobozhdenie 10; adult/student 3/1 lv; ☉9am-6.30pm), or on a visit to **Enio Bonchev Rose Distillery** (☑02-986 3995; www.eniobonchev.com; Tarnichene; admission with/without rose picking 9.60/6 lv), 27km west of Kazanlâk (call or email in advance to fix a time).

Long before a single seed was sown, the Thracians – a fierce Indo-European tribe – ruled the roost. Archaeologists believe there are at least 1500 Thracian burial mounds and tombs in the vicinity. Most visitors head to the **Replica Thracian Tomb of Kazanlâk** (Tyulbe Park; adult/child 3/1 lv; ☉9am-5.30pm); at the time of research, the original was inaccessible to visitors. More tombs can be reached via tour bus or your own vehicle: between Kazanlâk and the village of Shipka you can step inside 4th-century BC **Shushmanets Tomb** (adult/student 3/1 lv; ☉9am-5pm May-Nov) and the mysterious **Ostrusha Tomb** (adult/student 3/1 lv; ☉9am-5pm May-Nov), whose sarcophagus was carved from a single slab of stone.

Day trips taking in both regions can be arranged at the Kazanlâk **tourist information centre** (☑0431-99 553; ul Iskra 4; ☉9am-1pm & 2-6pm Mon-Fri, 10am-4pm Sat & Sun). The **Roza Hotel** (☑0431-50 005; www.hotelrozabg.com; ul Rozova Dolina 2; r 50-110 lv; P❄@🖥) in town makes a comfortable and good-value base.

Buses run from Kazanlâk to Sofia (17 lv, three hours, five daily) and Plovdiv (9 lv, two hours, three daily). See www.bdz.bg/en for train schedules.

hotel, between the old town and Plovdiv's shopping streets. Its five rooms are individually decorated with handsome wood floors, billowy drapes, and floral wall and ceiling paintings. Friendly, English-speaking owner Dimitar Vassilev is a font of local knowledge who extends the warmest of welcomes.

## ✖ Eating

**Klebarnitsa Kapana**  BAKERY €
(☑0882330773; ul Ioakim Gruev 20; ☉9am-7pm; 🖉) This bakery has a sociable twist, with places to perch while you tuck into oven-warm bread, fresh pastries and other goodies.

**Happy Bar & Grill**  INTERNATIONAL €€
(☑0888181073; http://happy.bg; ul Patriarh Evtimii 13; mains 8-12 lv; ☉11am-11pm Mon-Sat, 11.30am-11.30pm Sun) Despite having the outward appearance of a Bulgarian TGI Friday's, this popular place serves impressive sushi, American-inspired caesar salads and steaks, alongside a gamut of fresh Bulgarian fare. Service is scantily clad but operates with razor-sharp efficiency.

**Memory**  EUROPEAN €€€
(☑032-626 103; http://memorybg.net; pl Saedinenie 3; mains 15-25 lv; ☉11am-1am) Candlelit tables in a secluded courtyard make Memory a venue to impress, with soul and jazz tunes completing the sultry mood. Its forte is creative interpretations of Western European flavours, such as lamb with mint risotto, and duck nestled in parsnip purée. Everything is lovingly presented and whisked to tables by polite (if slightly stiff) waiting staff.

## 🍷 Drinking & Nightlife

There are some great haunts in the Kapana district; the name means 'the trap', referring to its tight streets (north of pl Dzhumaya, between ul Rayko Daskalov to the west and bul Tsar Boris Obedinitel to the east).

★**Basquiat Wine & Art**  WINE BAR
(☑0895460493; https://basquiat.alle.bg; ul Bratya Pulievi 4; ☉9am-midnight) A smooth funk soundtrack and great selection of local wines lure an arty crowd to this small Kapana bar. House wines start at 2 lv per glass; for something more memorable, the *malina* (raspberry-scented) wine packs a syrupy punch.

## Kotka i Mishka
BAR

(☑0878407578; ul Hristo Dyukmedjiev 14; ⊙10am-midnight) The crowd at this hole-in-the-wall craft-beer hang-out spills onto the street – such is the bar's deserved popularity, even against stiff competition in buzzing Kapana, but it's too chilled to warrant its hipster label. Decorations – such as hamster cages hanging from the ceiling – in the industrial-feel brick bar are a nod to the name, meaning 'cat and mouse'.

## ℹ️ Information

**Tourist Information Centre** (☑032-656 794; www.visitplovdiv.com; pl Tsentralen 1; ⊙9am-6pm Mon-Fri, 10am-5pm Sat & Sun) Helpful centre near the post office; provides maps and info. There's another **office** (☑032-620 453; ul Sâborna 22; ⊙9am-1pm & 2pm-6pm Mon-Fri, 10am-1pm & 2-5pm Sat & Sun) in the Old Town.

## ℹ️ Getting There & Away

### BUS

Plovdiv's main station is **Yug bus station** (☑032-626 937; bul Hristo Botev 47). Yug is diagonally opposite the train station and a 15-minute walk from the centre. Taxis cost 5 lv to 7 lv; local buses 7, 20 and 26 stop across the street. Routes include Plovdiv to Sofia (8 lv to 14 lv, 2½ hours, half-hourly), Bansko (14 lv, 3½ hours, two daily) and Varna (22 lv to 26 lv, seven hours, two to five daily). Check out www.bgrazpisanie.com/en for full destination and fare info.

The **Sever bus station** (☑032-953 705; www.hebrosbus.com; ul Dimitar Stambolov 2) in the northern suburbs is accessed by bus route 99. It serves destinations to the north of Plovdiv, including Veliko Târnovo (18 lv, 4½hours).

### TRAIN

Daily direct services from the **train station** (bul Hristo Botev) include trains to Sofia (9 lv, three hours, 15 daily) and Burgas (14.60 lv, six hours, two daily); see www.bgrazpisanie.com/en or www.bdz.bg/en for all fares and timetables.

# CENTRAL BULGARIA

Bulgaria's mountainous centre is arguably the country's historic heart. Dramatic past events played out on both sides of the Stara Planina range: to the west is museum village Koprivshtitsa, while the lowlands town of Kazanlâk accesses Thracian tombs and the famously fragrant Valley of the Roses. The hub is magnificent Veliko Târnovo, former capital of the Bulgarian tsars, crowned with one of Europe's most spectacular citadels.

# Koprivshtitsa Копривщица

☑07184 / POP 2300

This museum-village immediately pleases the eye with its numerous restored National Revival–period mansions. It's a peaceful, touristy place, but Koprivshtitsa was once the heart of Bulgaria's revolution against the Ottomans. Historic houses are interspersed with rambling, overgrown lanes, making it a romantic getaway and a safe and fun place for children.

## 👁 Sights

Koprivshtitsa boasts six house museums. To buy a combined ticket for all (adult/student 5/3 lv), visit the souvenir shop Kupchinitsa, near the **tourist-information centre** (☑07184-2191; www.koprivshtitza.com; pl 20 April 6; ⊙9.30am-5.30pm Tue, Wed & Fri-Sun Apr-Oct, to 5pm Nov-Mar).

**Oslekov House**
MUSEUM

(ul Gereniloto 4; admission 3 lv; ⊙9.30am-5.30pm Apr-Oct, 9am-5pm Nov-Mar, closed Mon) With its triple-arched entrance and interior restored in shades from scarlet to sapphire blue, Oslekov House is arguably the most beautifully restored example of Bulgarian National Revival–period architecture in Koprivshtitsa. It was built between 1853 and 1856 by a rich merchant executed after his arrest during the 1876 April Uprising. Now a house museum, it features informative, multilingual displays (Bulgarian, English and French) about 19th-century Bulgaria.

**Kableshkov House**
MUSEUM

(ul Todor Kableshkov 8; adult/student 4/2 lv; ⊙9.30am-5.30pm Tue-Sun Apr-Oct, to 5pm Nov-Mar) Todor Kableshkov is revered as having (probably) been the person who fired the first shot in the 1876 uprising against the Turks. After his arrest, he committed suicide rather than allow his captors to decide his fate. This, his glorious former home (built 1845), contains exhibits about the April Uprising.

## 🛏 Sleeping & Eating

**Hotel Astra**
GUESTHOUSE €

(☑07184-2033; www.hotelastra.org; bul Hadzhi Nencho Palaveev 11; d/apt incl breakfast 45/66 lv; ℗) Set beautifully in a garden at the northern end of Koprivshtitsa, the hospitable Astra has large, well-kept rooms and serves an epic homemade breakfast spread of pancakes, thick yogurt and more.

**Dyado Liben**                    BULGARIAN €€

(🖃0887532096; bul Hadzhi Nencho Palaveev 47; mains 8-15 lv; ⊘11am-midnight; 🔊) Traditional fare is served at this atmospheric 1852 mansion with tables set in a warren of halls, graced with ornate painted walls and heavy, worn wood floors. Find it just across the bridge leading from the main square inside the facing courtyard.

## ℹ Information

There are ATMs and a post office/telephone centre in the village centre.

## ℹ Getting There & Away

Without private transport, getting to Koprivshtitsa can be inconvenient. Being 9km north of the village, to get to the train station requires a shuttle bus (2 lv, 15 minutes), which isn't always timed to meet trains. Trains come from Sofia (6 lv to 9 lv, 2½ hours, eight daily) and Karlovo (3 lv to 4 lv, one to 1½ hours, two to four daily). Koprivshtitsa's **bus stop** (🖃07184-3044; bul Palaveev 76) is more central; there are six daily buses to Sofia (13 lv, two hours) and one daily to Plovdiv (12 lv, two hours).

# Veliko Târnovo
## Велико Търново

🖉 062 / POP 68,780

Medieval history emanates from Veliko Târnovo's fortified walls and cobbled lanes. One of Bulgaria's oldest towns, Veliko Târnovo has as its centrepiece the breathtaking restored Tsarevets Fortress, citadel of the Second Bulgarian Empire.

## ⊙ Sights

★**Tsarevets Fortress**            FORTRESS

(adult/student 6/2 lv, scenic elevator 2 lv; ⊘8am-7pm Apr-Oct, 9am-5pm Nov-Mar) The inescapable symbol of Veliko Târnovo, this reconstructed fortress dominates the skyline and is one of Bulgaria's most beloved monuments. The former seat of the medieval tsars, it boasts the remains of more than 400 houses, 18 churches, the royal palace, an execution rock and more. Watch your step: there are lots of potholes, broken steps and unfenced drops. The fortress morphs into a psychedelic spectacle with a magnificent night-time **Sound & Light Show** (🖃0885080865; www.soundandlight.bg; ul N Pikolo 6; admission 20-25 lv).

**Ulitsa Gurko**                  HISTORIC SITE

The oldest street in Veliko Târnovo, ul Gurko is a must-stroll with arresting views towards the Yantra River and Asen Monument. Its charmingly crumbling period houses – which appear to be haphazardly piled on one another – provide a million photo ops and conversations that start with 'Imagine living here...' Sturdy shoes a must.

**Sarafkina Kâshta**                  MUSEUM

(ul General Gurko 88; adult/student 6/2 lv; ⊘9am-6pm Tue & Thu-Sat, noon-6pm Wed) Built for a wealthy banker in 1861, this National Revival-style house museum spans five storeys (when viewed from the river). Within, 19th-century earrings, bracelets and other delicate silverware are on display, alongside antique ceramics, woodcarvings and traditional costumes and jewellery.

## 🛏 Sleeping

**Hostel Mostel**                    HOSTEL €

(🖃0897859359; www.hostelmostel.com; ul Iordan Indjeto 10; campsites/dm/s/d incl breakfast 18/20/46/60 lv; @🔊) The famous Sofia-based Hostel Mostel has a welcoming branch in Târnovo, with clean, modern dorm rooms and doubles with sparkling bathrooms. It's just 150m from Tsarevets Fortress – good for exploring there, but a long walk from the city centre. Service is cheerful and multilingual, and there's barbecue equipment out back.

**Hotel Anhea**                    HOTEL €

(🖃062-577713; www.anheabg.com; ul Nezavisimost 32; s/d/tr from 30/45/55 lv; ❄🔊) This superb budget hotel in an early 1900s building has a restful air, despite its central location. Crisp beige and cream rooms are arranged across two buildings, between which lies a peaceful courtyard and breakfast area – this secret garden is decorated with pretty iron railings, fountains and overseen by resident rabbit Emma.

★**Hotel-Mehana Gurko**    HISTORIC HOTEL €€

(🖃0887858965; www.hotel-gurko.com; ul General Gurko 33; s/d/apt incl breakfast from 70/90/130 lv; ℙ❄@🔊) Sitting pretty on Veliko Târnovo's oldest street, with blooms spilling over its wooden balconies and agricultural curios littering the exterior, the Gurko is one of the best places to sleep (and eat) in town. Its 21 rooms are spacious and soothing, each individually decorated and offering great views.

## ✗ Eating

**★ Shtastliveca** BULGARIAN €€
(✆ 062-606 656; www.shtastliveca.com; ul Stefan Stambolov 79; mains 10-20 lv; ⏱11am-1am; 🛜) 🖋 Inventive dishes and amiable service have solidified the 'Lucky Man' as a favourite among locals and expats. Sauces pairing chocolate and cheese are drizzled over chicken, while strawberry and balsamic vinegar lend piquancy to meaty dishes, and there is a pleasing range for vegetarians.

**★ Han Hadji Nikoli** INTERNATIONAL €€€
(✆ 062-651 291; www.hanhadjinikoli.com; ul Rakovski 19; mains 17-30 lv; ⏱10am-11pm; 🛜) Countless Veliko Târnovo inns were ransacked under Ottoman rule, as they were popular meeting places for revolution-minded locals. Fortunately Han Hadji Nikoli survived, and today the town's finest restaurant occupies this beautifully restored 1858 building with an upstairs gallery. Well-executed dishes include Trakia chicken marinated in herbs and yoghurt, mussels sautéed in white wine and exquisitely prepared pork neck.

## 🍷 Drinking & Nightlife

**★ Tam** BAR
(✆ 0889879693; ul Marno Pole 2A; ⏱4pm-3am Mon-Sat) Open the nondescript door, and up the stairs you'll find the city's friendliest, most-open-minded hang-out. Tam is the place to feel the pulse of VT's arty crowd. You might stumble on art installations, movie screenings or language nights in English, French or Spanish. Punters and staff extend a genuine welcome and drinks flow late.

**Sammy's Bar** BAR
(✆ 0885233387; ul Nezavisimost; ⏱11am-3am) The lofty views from this bar and beer garden are as refreshing as the selection of herb-garnished lemonades (2.80 lv). So it's no wonder that Sammy's, just off busy ul Nezavisimost, has become a trusted local haunt.

## ☆ Entertainment

**Melon Live Music Club** LIVE MUSIC
(✆ 062-603 439; bul Nezavisimost 21; ⏱6pm-2am) Popular spot for live music, from rock and R&B to Latin jazz. Admission to live events is around 4 lv or 5 lv.

## 🛍 Shopping

**★ Samovodska Charshiya** ARTS & CRAFTS
(ul Rakovski) Veliko Târnovo's historic quarter is a true centre of craftsmanship, with genuine blacksmiths, potters and cutlers, among other artisans, still practising their trades here. Wander the cobblestone streets to discover bookshops and purveyors of antiques, jewellery and art, housed in appealing National Revival houses.

## ℹ Information

**Tourist Information Centre** (✆ 062-622 148; www.velikoturnovo.info; ul Hristo Botev 5; ⏱9am-6pm Mon-Sat Apr-Oct, Mon-Fri Nov-Mar) Helpful English-speaking staff offering local info and advice.

## ℹ Getting There & Away

### BUS
The most central bus terminal is **Hotel Etar Bus Station** (www.etapgroup.com; ul Ivailo 2), served by hourly buses to Sofia (20 lv, three to 3½ hours) and Varna (20 lv, 3½ hours). The station is just south of the tourist information centre.

Two non-central bus stations also serve Veliko Târnovo, with a broader range of destinations and services. **Zapad Bus Station** (✆ 062-640 908, 062-620 014; ul Nikola Gabrovski 74), about 3km southwest of the tourist information centre, is the main intercity one, serving Plovdiv (19 lv, four hours, four daily), Kazanlâk (9 lv, 2½ hours, five daily) and Burgas (18 lv to 25 lv, four hours, four daily). Local buses 10, 12, 14, 70 and 110 go to Zapad. Closer to the centre is **Yug Bus Station** (✆ 062-620 014; ul Hristo Botev 74), 700m south of the tourist information centre, serving Sofia and Varna.

### TRAIN
The slightly more walkable of the town's two stations is **Veliko Târnovo Train Station** (✆ 062-620 065), 1.5km west of town, served by one daily direct train to Plovdiv (12 lv, 4½ hours; alternatively, travel via Stara Zagora) and one direct service to Varna (14 lv, four hours).

**Gorna Oryakhovitsa train station** (✆ 062-826 118), 8.5km northeast of town, is along the main line between Sofia and Varna. There are daily services to/from Sofia (14.60 lv, four to five hours, eight daily), some via Tulovo or Mezdra. Direct trains also reach Varna (13 lv, 3½ to four hours, five daily). From Veliko Târnovo, minibuses wait opposite the market along ul Vasil Levski to get to this train station. Taxis cost about 12 lv to 15 lv.

# BLACK SEA COAST

Bulgaria's long Black Sea coastline is the country's summertime playground. The big, purpose-built resorts here have become serious rivals to those of Spain and Greece, while independent travellers will find plenty to explore away from the parasols and jet skis. Sparsely populated sandy beaches to the far south and north, the bird-filled lakes around Burgas, and picturesque ancient towns such as Nesebâr and Sozopol are rewarding destinations. The 'maritime capital' of Varna and its seaside rival, Burgas, are two of Bulgaria's most vibrant cities. Both are famous for summer festivals and nightlife.

## Varna                                 Варна

🗐 052 / POP 334,700

Cosmopolitan Varna is by far the most interesting town on the Black Sea coast. A combination of port city, naval base and seaside resort, it's an appealing place to while away a few days, packed with history yet thoroughly modern, with an enormous park to amble around and a lengthy, white-sand beach to lounge on. In the city centre you'll find Bulgaria's largest Roman baths complex and its finest archaeological museum, as well as a dynamic cultural and restaurant scene.

### ◉ Sights & Activities

★ **Archaeological Museum**                MUSEUM
(🗐 052-681 030; www.archaeo.museumvarna.com; ul Maria Luisa 41; adult/child 10/2 lv; ⊘ 10am-5pm Tue-Sun Apr-Sep, Tue-Sat Oct-Mar; 🚍 8, 9, 109, 409) Exhibits at this vast museum, the best of its kind in Bulgaria, include 6000-year-old bangles, necklaces and earrings said to be the oldest worked gold found in the world.

**Beach**                                  BEACH
(⊘ 9am-6pm) Varna has a long stretch of public beach, starting in the south, near the port, and stretching north some 4km. Generally, the quality of the sand and water improve and the crowds thin as you stroll north. The easiest way to access the beach is to walk south on bul Slivnitsa to Primorski Park and follow the stairs to the beach.

**Baracuda Dive Center**                    DIVING
(🗐 052-610 841; www.baracudadive.com; half-day beginning instruction from 110 lv) Offers diving instruction for beginners and advanced divers, as well as guided diving excursions along the Black Sea coast. Rates include equipment.

### ⌂ Sleeping

★ **Yo Ho Hostel**                          HOSTEL €
(🗐 0884729144; www.yohohostel.com; ul Ruse 23; dm/s/d from 14/30/40 lv; @ 🛜; 🚍 8, 9, 109) Shiver your timbers at this cheerful, pirate-themed place, with four- and 11-bed dorm rooms and private options. Staff offer free pick-ups and can organise camping and rafting trips. The location is an easy walk to the main sights.

**Hotel Odessos**                          HOTEL €€
(🗐 052-640 300; www.odessos-bg.com; bul Slivnitsa 1; s/d from 75/90 lv; P ❄ 🛜) Enjoying a great location opposite the main entrance to Primorski Park, this is an older establishment with smallish and pretty average rooms, but it's convenient for the beach. Only the pricier 'sea view' rooms have balconies.

### ✕ Eating

**Morsko Konche**                           PIZZA €
(🗐 052-600 418; www.morskokonche.bg; pl Nezavisimost, cnr ul Zamenhof; pizzas 5-10 lv; ⊘ 8.30am-10pm; 🛜 🗐; 🚍 8, 9, 109) The 'Seahorse' is a cheap and cheerful pizza place with a big menu featuring all the standard varieties, as well as some inventive creations of its own: the 'exotic' pizza comes with bananas and blueberries.

★ **Stariya Chinar**                        BULGARIAN €€
(🗐 0876520500; www.stariachinar.com; ul Preslav 11; mains 10-20 lv; ⊘ 8am-midnight) This is upmarket Balkan soul food at its best. Try the baked lamb, made to an old Bulgarian recipe, or the divine barbecue pork ribs; it also boasts some rather ornate salads. Outdoor seating is lovely in summer; park yourself in the traditional interior when the cooler weather strikes.

### ▾ Drinking & Nightlife

Some of Varna's best bars exist only during the summer: head down to Kraybrezhna aleya by the beach and take your pick.

**Sundogs**                                 PUB
(🗐 0988936630; www.sundogspub.com; ul Koloni 1; ⊘ 9am-midnight; 🛜) Big with expats and locals, this very welcoming watering hole is a great place to make new friends, chase down excellent pub grub with a good selection of beers, or show off your smarts at quiz nights.

**Palm Beach**                              CLUB
(🗐 0889422553; www.facebook.com/PalmBeach-Varna; Kraybrezhna aleya; ⊘ 24hr) By day, a great place to relax by the beach and enjoy coffee and drinks at the bar. By night, a beachside

nightclub, with music and dancing that can go all the way till morning.

## ☆ Entertainment

**Varna Opera Theatre**  OPERA
(☑ box office 052-665 022; www.tmpcvarna.com; pl Nezavisimost 1; ☺ ticket office 10am-1pm & 2-7pm; 📖 8, 9, 109, 409) Varna's grand opera house hosts performances by the Varna Opera and Philharmonic Orchestra all year, except July and August, when some performances are staged at the Open-Air Theatre in Primorski Park.

## ℹ Information

**Tourist Information Centre** (☑ 052-820 690; www.visit.varna.bg; pl Kiril & Metodii; ☺ 9am-7pm; 📖 8, 9, 109, 409) Plenty of free brochures and maps, and helpful multilingual staff. The Tourist Information Centre also operates free three-hour walking tours of the city on select days from June to September.

## ℹ Getting There & Away

### AIR

Varna's international **airport** (VAR; ☑ 052-573 323; www.varna-airport.bg; Aksakovo; 📖 409) has scheduled and charter flights from all over Europe, as well as regular flights to and from Sofia. From the centre, bus 409 goes to the airport.

### BUS

Varna's **central bus station** (Avtoexpress; ☑ information 052-757 044, tickets 052-748 349; www.bgrazpisanie.com; bul Vladislav Varenchik 158; ☺ 24hr; 📖 148, 409) is about 2km northwest of the city centre. There are regular buses to Sofia (33 lv, seven hours), Burgas (14 lv, 2½ hours) and other major destinations in Bulgaria: see www.bgrazpisanie.com/en for fares and schedules.

### TRAIN

Trains depart Varna's **train station** (☑ 052-662 3343; www.bdz.bg; pl Slaveikov; 📖 8, 9, 109) for Sofia (24 lv, seven to eight hours, seven daily) and Plovdiv (24 lv, seven hours, three daily).

# Nesebâr    Несебър

☑ 0554 / POP 11,600

Postcard-pretty Nesebâr (Ne-*se*-bar) – about 40km northeast of Burgas – was settled by Greek colonists in 512BC, though today it's more famous for its (mostly ruined) medieval churches. Though beautiful, Nesebâr is heavily commercialised, and transforms into one huge, open-air souvenir market during the high season. The Sunny Beach megaresort is 5km to the north.

## ◉ Sights & Activities

All of Nesebâr's main sights are in the Old Town; around 1.5km southwest of the peninsula is **South Beach**, where all the usual water sports are available, including jet-skiing and waterskiing.

**Archaeological Museum**  MUSEUM
(☑ 0554-46 019; www.ancient-nessebar.com; ul Mesembria 2; adult/child 6/3 lv; ☺ 9am-7pm Mon-Fri, 9.30am-2pm & 2.30-7pm Sat & Sun Jun-Sep, reduced hours Oct-May) Explore the rich history of Nesebâr – formerly Mesembria – at this fine museum. Greek and Roman pottery, statues and tombstones, as well as Thracian gold jewellery and ancient anchors, are displayed here. There's also a collection of icons recovered from Nesebâr's numerous churches.

**Sveti Stefan Church**  CHURCH
(☑ 0554-46 019; www.ancient-nessebar.com; ul Ribarska; adult/child 6/3 lv; ☺ 9am-7pm Mon-Fri, 10.30am-2pm & 2.30-7pm Sat & Sun May-Sep, 9am-5pm Mon-Fri, 10am-5pm Sat & Sun Oct-Apr) Built in the 11th century and reconstructed 500 years later, this is the best-preserved church in town. If you only visit one, this is the church to choose. Its beautiful 16th- to 18th-century murals cover virtually the entire interior. Come early, as it's popular with tour groups.

**Aqua Paradise**  WATER PARK
(☑ 0885208055; www.aquaparadise-bg.com; adult/child 40/20 lv, after 3pm 30/15 lv; ☺ 10am-6.30pm; ⊞) Organised watery fun is on hand at Aqua Paradise, a huge water park on the southern outskirts of Sunny Beach just as you enter Nesebâr, with a variety of pools, slides and chutes. A free minibus, running every 15 minutes, makes pick-ups at signed stops around Nesebâr and Sunny Beach.

## 🛏 Sleeping & Eating

★Boutique Hotel
**St Stefan**  BOUTIQUE HOTEL €€
(☑ 0554-43 603; www.hotelsaintstefan.com; ul Ribarska 11; r/ste 80/160 lv; ⊞✳🔊) One of the nicest hotels in Nesebâr, the St Stefan offers rooms with views out over the harbour and Black Sea. There's a small sauna on the premises as well as a terrace for drinks and light meals. Rooms feature original artwork by Bulgarian artists. Breakfast costs 8 lv. Book well in advance for summer dates.

BULGARIA NESEBÂR

★ **Gloria Mar** BULGARIAN €€€
(☑ 0893550055; www.gloriamar-bg.com; ul Krajbrezhna 9; mains 12-30 lv; ☉ 11am-11pm) For our money, the best dining option in touristy Nesebâr. Fresh seafood, wood-fired pizzas and grilled meats, as well as harder-to-find risottos and paellas. There's an extensive wine list and dining on three levels, including a rooftop terrace. It's on the southern side of old Nesebâr, facing the marina and passenger ferry terminal.

## 🛈 Getting There & Away

Nesebâr is well connected to coastal destinations by public transport; its bus station is on the small square just outside the city walls. The stop before this on the mainland is for the new town. There are buses every few minutes to Sunny Beach (1 lv, 10 minutes), and to Burgas (6 lv, one hour, hourly), Varna (14 lv, two hours, four daily) and Sofia (37 lv, seven hours, three daily).

**Fast Ferry.** (☑ 0885808001; www.fastferry. bg; Passenger Ferry Port; ☉ 8.30am-8.30pm Jun-Sep) operates a high-speed hydrofoil service to the uncrowded resort of Pomorie (one way/return from 11/20 lv, 25 minutes, three daily) and Sozopol (one way/return from 27/50 lv, 40 minutes, three daily).

# Burgas Бургас

☑ 056 / POP 200,000

For most visitors, the port city of Burgas (sometimes written as 'Bourgas') is no more than a transit point. But if you do decide to stop over, you'll find a well-kept city with a neat, pedestrianised centre, a long, uncrowded beach and some small but interesting museums. Nature lovers also arrive for the four lakes just outside the city, which are havens for bird life.

Burgas is also the jumping-off point for visits to St Anastasia Island (☑ 0882004124; www.anastasia-island.com; return boat trip adult/child 12/7 lv; ☉ departures 10am, 11.30am, 1pm, 3pm Jun-Aug), a small volcanic island that has served as a religious retreat, a prison and pirate bait (according to legend, a golden treasure is buried in its sands). Today it is dominated by a lighthouse and a monastery, where visitors can sample various healing herb potions.

## 🛏 Sleeping & Eating

**Old House Hostel** HOSTEL €
(☑ 056-841 558; www.burgashostel.com; ul Sofroniy 3; dm/d 17/33 lv; ❀ 🛜) This charming hostel makes itself right at home in a lovely 1895 house. Dorms are airy and bright (and bunk-free!), while doubles have access to a sweet little courtyard. The location is central and about 400m from the beach.

**Hotel Bulair** HOTEL €
(☑ 056-844 389; www.hotelbulair.com; ul Bulair 7; r 60 lv; 🅿 ❀ 🛜) In a converted 19th-century townhouse on a busy road, the 14-room Bulair is very handy for the bus and train stations. Guests have access to the spa and wellness centre at the nearby Primoretz Grand Hotel & Spa.

★ **Rosé** INTERNATIONAL €€
(☑ 0885855099; bul Aleko Bogoridi 19; mains 8-20 lv; ☉ 8am-11pm; 🛜) Choose from a wide menu of grilled meats and fish, including a superlative lamb-shank offering, or fresh pasta, at this superb restaurant in the city centre. Finish off with a cake or homemade ice cream. Rosé also does a very good breakfast, including a rarity for Bulgaria: gluten-free muesli.

## 🛈 Getting There & Away

### AIR

**Bulgaria Air** (www.air.bg) links **Burgas Airport** (BOJ; ☑ information 056-870 248; www. bourgas-airport.com; Sarafovo; 🛜; 🚌 15), 10km northeast of town, with Sofia daily (April to October). In summer, **Wizz Air** (www.wizzair. com) connects Burgas with London Luton, Budapest, Prague and Warsaw. Other carriers fly to destinations in Germany and Russia.

### BUS

**Yug bus station** (☑ 0884981220; www. bgrazpisanie.com; pl Tsaritsa Yoanna), outside the train station at the southern end of ul Aleksandrovska, is where most travellers arrive or leave. There are regular buses to coastal destinations, including Nesebâr (6 lv, 40 minutes, half-hourly), Varna (14 lv, two hours, half-hourly) and Sozopol (5 lv, 40 minutes, every 45 minutes). Several daily buses also go to and from Sofia (30 lv, seven to eight hours) and Plovdiv (20 lv, four hours). Departures are less frequent outside summer.

### TRAIN

The **train station** (☑ information 056-845 022; www.bdz.bg; ul Ivan Vazov; ☉ information office 6am-10pm) has clearly marked ticket windows for buying advance tickets for domestic and international services. Trains run to Plovdiv (16 lv, five to six hours, five daily) and Sofia (21 lv, seven to eight hours, five daily).

# Sozopol Созопол

**☑ 0550 / POP 5700**

Ancient Sozopol, with its charming old town of meandering cobbled streets and pretty wooden houses huddled together on a narrow peninsula, is one of the coast's real highlights. With two superb beaches, a genial atmosphere, plentiful accommodation and good transport links, it has long been a popular seaside resort and makes an excellent base for exploring the area. Although not quite as crowded as Nesebâr, it is becoming ever more popular with international visitors.

## ✵ Festivals

**Apollonia Arts Festival**                    ART, MUSIC
(www.apollonia.bg; ☺ end Aug–mid-Sep) This is the highlight of Sozopol's cultural calendar, with concerts, theatrical performances, art exhibitions, film screenings and more held across town.

## ◉ Sights & Activities

Sozopol has two great beaches: **Harmanite Beach** has all the good-time gear (waterslide, paddle boats, beach bar), while to the north, the smaller **Town Beach** packs in the serious sun-worshippers.

**Archaeological Museum**                    MUSEUM
(☑ 0550-22 226; ul Han Krum 2; adult/child 7/3 lv; ☺ 8.30am-6pm Jun-Sep, 8.30am-6pm Mon-Fri Oct-May) Housed in a drab concrete box near the port, this museum has a small but fascinating collection of local finds from its Apollonian glory days and beyond. In addition to a wealth of Hellenic treasures, the museum occasionally exhibits the skeleton of a local 'vampire', found with a stake driven through its chest. Enter from the building's northern side.

**Sveti Ivan**                    ISLAND
The largest Bulgarian island in the Black Sea (0.7 sq km), Sveti Ivan lies 3km north of Sozopol's Old Town. The island's history stretches back to Thracian and Roman times, and includes a monastery from the 4th century AD. Sveti Ivan made international headlines in 2010 with the purported discovery of the remains of St John the Baptist. There are no scheduled excursions to the island, but private trips can be arranged along the **Fishing Harbour**; expect to pay from around 50 lv.

BULGARIA SOZOPOL

---

## ESSENTIAL FOOD & DRINK

Fresh fruit, vegetables, dairy produce and grilled meat form the basis of Bulgarian cuisine, which has been heavily influenced by Greek and Turkish cookery. Pork and chicken are the most popular meats, while tripe also features heavily on traditional menus. You will also find recipes including duck, rabbit and venison, and fish is plentiful along the Black Sea coast, but less common elsewhere.

**Banitsa** Flaky cheese pastry, often served fresh and hot.

**Beer** You're never far from a cold beer in Bulgaria. Zagorka, Kamenitza and Shumensko are the most popular nationwide brands.

**Kavarma** This 'claypot meal', or meat stew, is normally made with either chicken or pork and is one of the country's most popular dishes.

**Kebabche** Thin, grilled pork sausage, a staple of every *mehana* (tavern) in the country.

**Mish Mash** Summer favourite made from tomatoes, capsicum, eggs, feta and spices.

**Musaka** Bulgarian moussaka bears more than a passing resemblance to its Greek cousin, but it's a delicious staple of cheap cafeteria meals.

**Shishcheta** Shish kebab consisting of chunks of chicken or pork on wooden skewers with mushrooms and peppers.

**Shkembe chorba** Traditional stomach soup is one of the more adventurous and offbeat highlights of Bulgarian cuisine.

**Tarator** On a hot day there's nothing better than this delicious chilled cucumber and yoghurt soup, served with garlic, dill and crushed walnuts.

**Wine** They've been producing wine here since Thracian times and there are some excellent varieties to try.

## 🛏 Sleeping & Eating

Hotel prices drop considerably in the off-season, when visitors will have Sozopol all to themselves. Cheap eats abound along the harbourfront ul Kraybrezhna in the Old Town; more upmarket restaurants are found on ul Morski Skali.

★ **Justa Hostel** HOSTEL **€**
(☑ 0550-22 175; ul Apolonia 20; dm 20 lv; 🛜) This clean, cosy, centrally located hostel sits in the centre of the Old Town, a few minutes' walk from the beach and offers dorm-bed accommodation with shared bath and shower. The price includes traditional breakfast (pancakes) and coffee.

★ **Art Hotel** HOTEL **€€**
(☑ 0550-24 081, 0878650160; www.arthotel-sbh. com; ul Kiril & Metodii 72; d/studios 80/100 lv; ❄🛜) This peaceful old house, belonging to the Union of Bulgarian Artists, is within a walled courtyard toward the tip of the peninsula, away from the crowds. It has a small selection of bright, comfortable rooms with balconies, most with sea views; breakfast is served on the terraces overlooking the sea.

**Panorama** SEAFOOD **€€**
(ul Morski Skali 21; mains 8-20 lv; ⊙11am-11pm) This lively place has an open terrace with a fantastic view toward Sveti Ivan island. Fresh, locally caught fish is the mainstay of the menu. It's one of the best of many seafood spots on this street.

## ℹ Getting There & Away

The small public **bus station** (☑ 0550-23 460; www.bgrazpisanie.com; ul Han Krum) is just south of the Old Town walls. Buses leave for Burgas (5 lv, 40 minutes) about every 30 minutes between 6am and 9pm in summer, and about once an hour in the low season. Buses run two to three times a day to Sofia (32 lv, seven hours).

**Fast Ferry** (☑ 0988908629, booking 0885808001; www.fastferry.bg; Sozopol Harbour) runs three ferries per day to/from Nesebâr (single/return from 27/54 lv, 40 minutes) between June and September.

# SURVIVAL GUIDE

## ℹ Directory A–Z

### ACCOMMODATION

Sofia, Plovdiv, Veliko Târnovo, Varna and Burgas all have hostels; for cheap accommodation

elsewhere, look out for signs reading 'стаи под наем' (rooms for rent). Many hotels offer discounts for longer stays or on weekends; prices may rise during summer.

### GAY & LESBIAN TRAVELLERS

Homosexuality is legal in Bulgaria but gay culture is very discreet as a result of prevailing macho attitudes and widespread homophobia. Attitudes among younger people are slowly changing, and there are a few gay clubs and bars in Sofia and in other major cities. Useful websites include www.gay.bg and www.gay-bulgaria.info.

### INTERNET RESOURCES

**Ministry of Tourism** (www.tourism.government.bg)

**National tourism portal** (www.bulgariatravel.org)

### TRAVELLERS WITH DISABILITIES

Bulgaria is not an easy destination for travellers with disabilities. Uneven and broken footpaths are common in towns and wheelchair-accessible toilets and ramps are rare outside the more expensive hotels.

### VISAS

Citizens of other EU countries, as well as Australia, Canada, New Zealand, the USA and many other countries do not need a visa for stays of up to 90 days. Other nationals should contact the Bulgarian embassy in their home country for current visa requirements.

## ℹ Getting There & Away

### AIR

Most international visitors come and/or go via **Sofia Airport** (p93); there are frequent flights between Sofia and other European cities. The national carrier is **Bulgaria Air** (www.air.bg).

### LAND

Although Sofia has international bus and train connections, it's not necessary to backtrack to the capital if you're heading to, for example,

Athens or İstanbul: Plovdiv offers regular buses to both. Heading to Belgrade by train means going through Sofia; for Skopje, you'll need to catch a bus from there, too.

### Bus

Most international buses arrive in Sofia. You'll have to get off the bus at the border and walk through customs to present your passport. When travelling out of Bulgaria by bus, the cost of entry visas for the countries concerned are not included in the prices of the bus tickets.

### Car & Motorcycle

In order to drive on Bulgarian roads, you will need to purchase a vignette (15/30 lv for one week/month), sold at all border crossings into Bulgaria, petrol stations and post offices. Rental cars hired within Bulgaria should already have a vignette.

### Train

There are a number of international trains from Bulgaria, including services to Serbia, Romania and Turkey. Sofia is the main hub, although trains stop at other towns.

##  Getting Around

### AIR

The only scheduled domestic flights within Bulgaria are between Sofia and Varna and Sofia and Burgas. Both routes are operated by **Bulgaria Air** (www.air.bg).

### BICYCLE

➡ Many roads are in poor condition; some major roads are always choked with traffic and bikes aren't allowed on highways.

➡ Many trains will carry your bike for an extra 2 lv.

---

**COUNTRY FACTS**
........................................

**Area** 110,879 sq km

**Capital** Sofia

**Country Code** ☑ 359

**Currency** Lev (lv)

**Emergency** ☑ 112

**Language** Bulgarian

**Money** ATMs are everywhere.

**Population** 7.19 million

**Visas** Not required for citizens of the EU, USA, Canada, Australia and New Zealand for stays of less than 90 days.

---

**EATING PRICE RANGES**
........................................

The following price ranges refer to a standard main course. Unless otherwise stated, service charge is included in the price.

€ less than 10 lv

€€ 10–20 lv

€€€ more than 20 lv

---

➡ Spare parts are available in cities and major towns, but it's better to bring your own.

### BUS

Buses link all cities and major towns and connect villages with the nearest transport hub. Though it isn't exhaustive, many bus and train schedules can be accessed at www.bgrazpisanie.com/en.

### CAR & MOTORCYCLE

Bulgaria's roads are among the most dangerous in Europe, and the number of road deaths each year is high. Speeding and aggressive driving habits are common; during summer (July to September), an increase in drink-driving and holiday traffic can contribute further to accidents.

The **Union of Bulgarian Motorists** (p94) offers 24-hour road assistance.

### Road Rules

➡ Drive on the right.

➡ Drivers and passengers in the front must wear seat belts; motorcyclists must wear helmets.

➡ Blood-alcohol limit is 0.05%.

➡ Children under 12 are not allowed to sit in front.

➡ Headlights must be on low beam at all times, year-round.

➡ Speed limits are 50km/h within towns, 90km/h on main roads and 130km/h on motorways.

### TRAIN

The Bulgarian State Railways (БДЖ; www.bdz. bg) boasts more than 4070km of tracks across the country, linking most sizeable towns and cities. Most trains tend to be antiquated and not especially comfortable, with journey times often slower than buses. On the plus side you'll have more room in a train compartment and the scenery is likely to be more rewarding.

Trains are classified as *ekspresen* (express), *bârz* (fast) or *pâtnicheski* (slow passenger). Unless you absolutely thrive on train travel or want to visit a more remote town, use a fast or express train.

# Croatia

## Best Places to Eat

➡ Pantarul (p129)

➡ Male Madlene (p116)

➡ Vinodol (p114)

➡ Restaurant 360° (p130)

➡ Zinfandel's (p114)

## Best Places to Stay

➡ Antique Split Luxury Rooms (p122)

➡ Art Hotel Kalelarga (p118)

➡ Karmen Apartments (p128)

➡ Studio Kairos (p113)

➡ Villa Skansi (p124)

## Why Go?

If your Mediterranean fantasies feature balmy days by sapphire waters in the shade of ancient walled towns, Croatia is the place to turn them into reality. The extraordinary Adriatic coastline, speckled with 1244 islands and strewn with historic towns, is Croatia's main attraction. The standout is Dubrovnik, its remarkable Old Town ringed by mighty defensive walls. Coastal Split showcases Diocletian's Palace, one of the world's most impressive Roman monuments, where dozens of bars, restaurants and shops thrive amid the old walls. In the heart-shaped peninsula of Istria, Rovinj is a charm-packed fishing port. The Adriatic isles hold much varied appeal, from glitzy Hvar Town on its namesake island to the secluded naturist coves of the Pakleni Islands just offshore. Away from the coast, Zagreb, Croatia's lovely capital has a booming cafe culture and art scene, while Plitvice Lakes National Park offers a verdant maze of turquoise lakes and cascading waterfalls.

## When to Go
### Zagreb

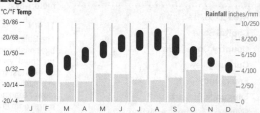

**May & Sep** Good weather, less tourists, full events calendar, great for hiking.

**Jun** Best time to visit: beautiful weather, fewer people, lower prices, the festival season kicks off.

**Jul & Aug** Lots of sunshine, warm sea and summer festivals; many tourists and highest prices.

# ZAGREB

POP 790,000

Zagreb has culture, arts, music, architecture, gastronomy and all the other things that make a quality capital city – it's no surprise that the number of visitors has risen sharply in recent years. Croatia's coastal attractions aside, Zagreb has finally been discovered as a popular city-break destination in its own right.

Visually, Zagreb is a mixture of straight-laced Austro-Hungarian architecture and rough-around-the-edges socialist structures, its character a sometimes uneasy combination of the two elements. This small metropolis is made for strolling the streets, drinking coffee in the permanently full cafes, popping into museums and galleries, and enjoying the theatres, concerts and cinema. It's a year-round outdoor city: in spring and summer everyone scurries to Jarun Lake in the southwest to swim or sail, or dance the night away at lakeside discos, while in winter Zagrebians go skiing at Mt Medvednica (only a tram or bus ride away).

## ◉ Sights

As the oldest part of Zagreb, the Upper Town (Gornji Grad) offers landmark buildings and churches from the earlier centuries of Zagreb's history. The Lower Town (Donji Grad) has the city's most interesting art museums and fine examples of 19th- and 20th-century architecture.

### ★ Museum of Broken Relationships
MUSEUM

(www.brokenships.com; Ćirilometodska 2; adult/concession 30/20KN; ⊙9am-10.30pm Jun-Sep, 9am-9pm Oct-May) Explore mementoes that remain after a relationship ends at Zagreb's quirkiest museum. The innovative exhibit toured the world until it settled here in its permanent home (it recently opened a second location in Hollywood). On display are donations from around the globe, in a string of all-white rooms with vaulted ceilings and epoxy-resin floors.

### Funicular Railway
FUNICULAR

(ticket 4KN; ⊙6.30am 10pm) The funicular railway, which was constructed in 1888, connects the Lower and Upper Towns of Zagreb.

### Dolac Market
MARKET

(⊙open-air market 6.30am-3pm Mon-Sat, to 1pm Sun, covered market 7am-2pm Mon-Fri, 7am-3pm Sat, 7am-1pm Sun) Zagreb's colourful fruit and vegetable market is just north of Trg Bana Jelačića. Traders from all over Croatia come to sell their products at this buzzing centre of activity. Dolac has been heaving since the 1930s, when the city authorities set up a market space on the 'border' between the Upper and Lower Towns.

### Zrinjevac
SQUARE

Officially called Trg Nikole Šubića Zrinskog but lovingly known as Zrinjevac, this verdant square at the heart of the city has become a vital part of Zagreb. It's filled with stalls almost year-round, and features festivals and events, be it summer or winter. Most are centred on the music pavilion (dating from 1891).

### Art Pavilion
GALLERY

(Umjetnički Paviljon; ☑01-48 41 070; www.umjetnicki-paviljon.hr; Trg Kralja Tomislava 22; adult/concession 40/25KN; ⊙11am-8pm Tue-Thu, Sat & Sun, to 9pm Fri) The yellow Art Pavilion presents changing exhibitions of contemporary art. Constructed in 1897 in stunning art nouveau style, the pavilion is the only space in Zagreb that was specifically designed to host large exhibitions.

### Museum of Contemporary Art
MUSEUM

(Muzej Suvremene Umjetnosti; ☑01-60 52 700; www.msu.hr; Avenija Dubrovnik 17; adult/concession 30/15KN; ⊙11am-6pm Tue-Fri & Sun, to 8pm Sat) Housed in a stunning city icon designed by local star architect Igor Franić, this swanky museum displays both solo and thematic group shows by Croatian and international artists in its 17,000 sq metres. The permanent display, *Collection in Motion,* showcases 620 edgy works by 240 artists, roughly half of whom are Croatian. There's a packed year-round schedule of film, theatre, concerts and performance art.

### Maksimir Park
PARK

(☑01-23 20 460; www.park-maksimir.hr; Maksimirski perivoj bb; ⊙info centre 10am-4pm Tue-Fri, to 6pm Sat & Sun) The park, a peaceful wooded enclave covering 18 hectares, is easily accessible by trams 11 and 12 from Jelačić square. Opened to the public in 1794, it was the first public promenade in southeastern Europe. It's landscaped like an English garden, with alleys, lawns and artificial lakes.

### Mirogoj
CEMETERY

(Aleja Hermanna Bollea 27; ⊙6am-8pm Apr-Oct, 7.30am-6pm Nov-Mar) A 10-minute ride north of the city centre (or a 30-minute walk

# Croatia Highlights

**1 Dubrovnik**
(p126) Circling the historic city's mighty walls and then catching the cable car up Mt Srđ for breathtaking views from above.

**2 Hvar Town**
(p124) Capping off endless beach days with sunset cocktails and back-lane boogie sessions.

**3 Split** (p119)
Discovering the city's ancient heart in Diocletian's Palace, a quarter that buzzes day and night.

**4 Zagreb** (p109)
Exploring the quirky museums and cafes of Croatia's cute little capital.

**5 Rovinj** (p116)
Roam the steep cobbled streets and piazzas of Istria's showpiece coastal town.

**6 Plitvice Lakes National Park**
(p119) Marvelling at the otherworldly turquoise lakes and dramatic waterfalls of arguably Croatia's top natural attraction.

**7 Zadar** (p117)
Exploring Roman ruins, intriguing museums, local eateries and hip bars within the marbled streets of the old town.

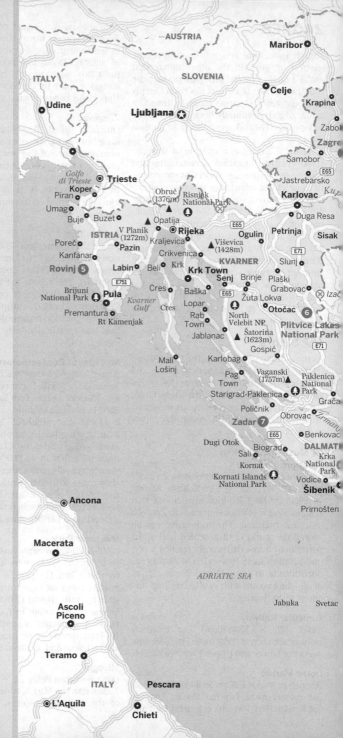

# Zagreb

N  0 ————————— 200 m
   0 ————————— 0.1 miles

Ribnjak

Zvonarnička

City Museum

Park Ribnjak

KAPTOL

Kaptol Square

St Mark's Church
Trg Svetog Marka
Sabor
Kamenita
Stone Gate

GRADEC

Croatian Museum of Naïve Art

**Museum of 1 Broken Relationships**

Vranicanijeva
Katarinin Trg
Cathedral of the Assumption of the

Karijola (450m);
Mali Bar (450m);
Studio Kairos (1km)

Aleksandrove stube

Strossmayerovo Šetalište

Grič Tunnel

Lotršćak Tower

**4**

Podzidom

Trg Bana Jelačića

Cesarčeva

**3**

Ilica

Zakmardijeve Stube

**8**

**9**

**6**

**11**

Trg Petra Preradovića

Oktogon

Petrićeva

Bogovićeva

Petrinjska

Croatian Design Superstore (350m)

Varšavska

Miškecov Prolaz

**13**

**12**

Teslina

Amruševa

Trg Nikole Šubića Zrinskog (Zrinjevac)

Masarykova

Berislavićeva

**5**

Prilaz Gjure Deželića

Preradovićeva

LOWER TOWN

Arts & Crafts Museum

Trg Maršala Tita

DONJI GRAD

Andrije Hebranga

Gallery of Modern Art

Strossmayer Gallery of Old Masters

Mažuranićev Trg

Museum Mimara

Rooseveltov Trg

Mažuranićev Trg

Kovačićeva

**10**

Katančićeva

Strossmayerov Trg

Kršnjavoga

Trg Braće Mažuranića

Vukotinovićeva

Jurja Žerjavića

Baruna Trenka

Svačićev Trg

**2**

Trg Kralja Tomislava

Marulićev Trg

Mihanovićeva

(1.2km)

Vodnikova

**7**

Starčevićev Trg

Branimirova

Grgurova

Zagreb Train Station

Botanical Garden

Crnatkova

Koturaška

Bednjanska

Trnjanska

## Zagreb

**Top Sights**
1 Museum of Broken Relationships ..... C2

**Sights**
2 Art Pavilion ..... D6
3 Dolac Market ..... D3
4 Funicular Railway ..... B3
5 Zrinjevac ..... D4

**Activities, Courses & Tours**
6 Blue Bike Tours ..... D3

**Sleeping**
7 Esplanade Zagreb Hotel ..... C6
8 Hotel Jägerhorn ..... C3
9 Swanky Mint Hostel ..... A3

**Eating**
10 Bistro 75 ..... C5
Le Bistro ..... (see 7)
11 Mundoaka Street Food ..... D3
12 Vinodol ..... C4
Zinfandel's ..... (see 7)

**Drinking & Nightlife**
13 Kino Europa ..... C4

**Shopping**
14 Bornstein ..... D1

through leafy streets) takes you to one of the most beautiful cemeteries in Europe, sited at the base of Mt Medvednica. It was designed in 1876 by Austrian-born architect Herman Bollé, who created numerous buildings around Zagreb. The majestic arcade, topped by a string of cupolas, looks like a fortress from the outside, but feels calm and graceful on the inside.

## Tours

**Secret Zagreb** TOURS
(www.secret-zagreb.com; per person 75KN) A thorough ethnographer and inspiring storyteller, Iva Silla is the guide who reveals the Zagreb of curious myths and legends and peculiar historical personalities. Take her hit walking tour Zagreb Ghosts and Dragons (which runs year-round) to peek into the city's hidden corners or forgotten graveyards, all set in the city centre.

**Blue Bike Tours** CYCLING
(☎098 18 83 344; www.zagrebbybike.com; Trg Bana Jelačića 15) To experience Zagreb on a bike, book one of the tours that run twice daily at 10am and 5pm from May through September (2pm only from October to April); choose between Ancient or Novi Zagreb. Tours last around 2½ hours and cost 190KN. The four-hour combo tour of both options costs 290KN. They also rent bikes for 100KN per day between 10am and 8pm.

## Sleeping

★**Studio Kairos** B&B $$
(☎01-46 40 680; www.studio-kairos.com; Vlaška 92; s 340-420KN, d 520-620KN; ❄ 📶) This adorable B&B in a street-level apartment has four well-appointed rooms decked out by theme – Writers', Crafts, Music and Granny's – and there's a cosy common space where a delicious breakfast is served. The interior design is gorgeous and the friendly owners are a fountain of knowledge. Bikes are also available for rent.

**Swanky Mint Hostel** HOSTEL $$
(☎01-40 04 248; www.swanky-hostel.com/mint; Ilica 50; dm from 150KN, s/d 360/520KN, apt 650-800KN; ❄ @ 📶 🏊) Inside a restored textile-dye factory from the 19th century, this cool hostel in the heart of town combines industrial chic with creature comforts in its rooms, dorms and apartments. Freebies include wi-fi, lockers, towels and a welcome shot of *rakija* (grappa). The garden bar serves breakfast and drinks, and there's even a small pool on site.

★**Esplanade Zagreb Hotel** HOTEL $$$
(☎01-45 66 666; www.esplanade.hr; Mihanovićeva 1; s/d 1165/1700KN; P ❄ @ 📶) Drenched in history, this six-storey hotel was built next to the train station in 1925 to welcome the *Orient Express* crowd in grand style. It has hosted kings, artists, journalists and politicians ever since. The art deco masterpiece is replete with walls of swirling marble, immense staircases and wood-panelled lifts.

**Hotel Jägerhorn** HOTEL $$$
(☎01-48 33 877; www.hotel-jagerhorn.hr; Ilica 14; s/d/apt 890/1000/1300KN; P ❄ @ 📶) A charming little hotel that sits right underneath Lotrščak Tower, the 'Hunter's Horn' has friendly service and 18 spacious, classic rooms with good views (you can gaze over leafy Gradec from the top-floor attic rooms). The downstairs terrace cafe is lovely. It's the oldest hotel in Zagreb, around since 1827.

## ✗ Eating

### Bistro 75
BISTRO $

(📞 01-48 40 545; Preradovićeva 34; mains 36-42KN; ⏰ 11am-11pm Mon-Thu, to 1am Fri & Sat) Tasty bites like oxtail sandwiches and falafel wraps, a set of daily specials, twisted cocktails and a great range of local craft beers (like Zmajska and Varionica) are all reasons to check out this sleek little bistro. It has a colourful wall mural and a banquette inside, plus tables on a streetside deck.

### ⭐Vinodol
CROATIAN $$

(📞 01-48 11 427; www.vinodol-zg.hr; Teslina 10; mains 48-160KN; ⏰ 10am-midnight) The well-prepared, central-European fare here is much-loved by local and overseas patrons. On warm days, eat on the covered patio (entered through an ivy-clad passageway off Teslina); the cold-weather alternative is the dining hall with vaulted stone ceilings. Highlights include the succulent lamb or veal and potatoes cooked under *peka* (a domed baking lid), as well as *bukovače* (local mushrooms).

### ⭐Mundoaka Street Food
INTERNATIONAL $$

(📞 01-78 88 777; Petrinjska 2; mains 65-85KN; ⏰ 9am-midnight Mon-Sat) This tiny eatery clad in light wood, with tables outside, serves up American classics – think chicken wings and pork ribs – and a global spectrum of dishes, from Spanish tortillas to *shakshuka* eggs. Great breakfasts, muffins and cakes, all prepared by one of Zagreb's best-known chefs. Reserve ahead.

### Mali Bar
TAPAS $$

(📞 01-55 31 014; Vlaška 63; dishes 45-120KN; ⏰ 12.30pm-midnight Mon-Sat) This spot by star chef Ana Ugarković shares the terraced space with **Karijola** (📞 01-55 31 016; www.pizzeria-karijola.com; Vlaška 63; pizzas 46-70KN; ⏰ 11am-midnight Mon-Sat, to 11pm Sun), hidden away in a *veža* (alleyway). The interior is cosy and earth-tone colourful, and the food is focused on globally inspired tapas-style dishes.

### Zinfandel's
INTERNATIONAL $$$

(📞 01-45 66 644; www.zinfandels.hr; Mihanovićeva 1; mains 150-295KN; ⏰ 6am-11pm Mon-Sat, 6.30am-11pm Sun) Some of the tastiest, most creative dishes in town are conjured up by chef Ana Grgić and served with flair here in the dining room of the Esplanade Zagreb Hotel (p113).

## 🍷 Drinking & Nightlife

In the Upper Town, the chic Tkalčićeva is throbbing with bars and cafes. With half a dozen bars and sidewalk cafes between Trg Petra Preradovića (known locally as Cvjetni trg) and Bogovićeva in the Lower Town, the scene on summer nights resembles a vast outdoor party. Things wind down by midnight though, and get quieter from mid-July through late August.

### Kino Europa
BAR

(www.kinoeuropa.hr; Varšavska 3; ⏰ 8.30am-midnight Mon-Thu, to 4am Fri & Sat, 11am-11pm Sun; 📶) Zagreb's oldest cinema, from the 1920s, now houses a splendid cafe, wine bar and *grapperia*. At this glass-enclosed space with an outdoor terrace you can enjoy great coffee, over 30 types of grappa and free wi-fi. The cinema hosts film screenings and occasional dance parties.

---

## ITINERARIES

### Three Days
Spend a day in dynamic **Zagreb**, delving into its vibrant cafe culture and nightlife and fascinating museums, then head down to **Rovinj** in Istria to spend a couple of days unwinding by the sea, wandering the cobbled streets and sampling the celebrated Istrian cuisine.

### One Week
Start with a weekend in Zagreb, then head south to take in one of the region's best sights: the Roman ruins of Diocletian's Palace in **Split** are a living part of this exuberant seafront city. Base yourself here for two days of sightseeing, beach fun and nightlife action. Next, take the winding coastal road to **Dubrovnik**, a magnificent walled city whose beauty is bound to blow you away with the jaw-dropping sights of its Old Town.

# 🔒 Shopping

### Croatian Design Superstore  DESIGN
(www.croatiandesignsuperstore.com; Martićeva 4; ☺9am-9pm Mon-Sat) This one-stop shop for the best of Croatian design stocks more than 130 curated items by 150 different creators. Clad in all red, the store showcases the cream of Croatia's homegrown design, from accessories and gifts to wine and lighting. It doubles as a platform for promoting Croatian design and also has a sweet little cafe serving healthy bites.

### Bornstein  WINE
(www.bornstein.hr; Kaptol 19; ☺9am-8pm Mon-Fri, to 4.30pm Sat) If Croatia's wine and spirits have gone to your head, get your fix here. Stocks an astonishing collection of brandy, wine and gourmet products. There's also a wine bar on site.

# ℹ️ Information

**Main Tourist Information Centre** (☑ information 0800 53 53, office 01-48 14 051; www.infozagreb.hr; Trg Bana Jelačića 11; ☺8.30am-9pm Mon-Fri, 9am-6pm Sat & Sun Jun-Sep, 8.30am-8pm Mon-Fri, 9am-6pm Sat, 10am-4pm Sun Oct-May) Distributes free city maps and leaflets. There are also tourist information centres at **Lotrščak Tower** (☑ 01-48 51 510; ☺9am-9pm Mon-Fri, 10am-9pm Sat & Sun Jun-Sep, 9am-5pm Mon-Fri, 10am-5pm Sat & Sun Oct-May); the **main railway station** (☺9am-9pm Mon-Fri, 10am-5pm Sat & Sun); the **main bus station** (☑ 01-61 15 507; ☺9am-9pm Mon-Fri, 10am-5pm Sat & Sun); and **Zagreb Airport** (☑ 01-62 65 091; ☺9am-9pm Mon-Fri, 10am-5pm Sat & Sun).

**Zagreb County Tourist Association** (☑ 01-48 73 665; www.tzzz.hr; Preradovićeva 42; ☺8am-4pm Mon-Fri) Has information and materials about attractions in Zagreb's surroundings, including wine roads and bike trails.

**KBC Rebro** (☑ 01-23 88 888; Kišpatićeva 12; ☺24hr) East of the city; provides emergency aid.

# ℹ️ Getting There & Away

### AIR
**Zagreb Airport** (☑ 01-45 62 170; www.zagreb-airport.hr) Located 17km southeast of Zagreb, this is Croatia's major airport, offering a range of international and domestic services.

### BUS
Zagreb's **bus station** (☑ 060 313 333; www.akz.hr; Avenija M Držića 4) is 1km east of the train station. If you need to store bags, there's a **garderoba** (☑ 01-60 08 649; Bus Station; per hour 5KN; ☺24hr). Trams 2 and 6 run from the bus station to the train station. Tram 6 goes to Trg bana Jelačića.

Domestic destinations include: Dubrovnik (191KN to 231KN, 9½ to 11 hours, nine to 12 daily), Rovinj (100KN to 195KN, 4 to 6 hours, 20 daily), Zadar (90KN to 135KN, 3½ to five hours, 31 daily) and Split (115KN to 205KN, five to 8½ hours, 32 to 34 daily).

### TRAIN
The **train station** (☑ 060 333 444; www.hzpp.hr; Trg Kralja Tomislava 12) is in the southern part of the city; there's a **garderoba** (locker per 24hr 15KN; ☺24hr). It's advisable to book train tickets in advance because of limited seating.

Domestic trains head to Split (190KN to 208KN, five to seven hours, four daily). There are international departures to Belgrade (184KN, 6½ hours, two daily), Ljubljana (68KN, 2½ hours, five daily), Sarajevo (165KN, eight to 9½ hours, daily) and Vienna (549KN, six to seven hours, two daily).

# ℹ️ Getting Around

### TO/FROM THE AIRPORT
The Croatia Airlines bus to the airport (30KN) leaves from the bus station every half-hour or hour from about 4.30am to 8pm, and returns from the airport on the same schedule.

Taxis cost between 110KN and 200KN to the city centre.

### PUBLIC TRANSPORT
Zagreb's public transport (www.zet.hr) is based on an efficient network of trams, although the city centre is compact enough to make them almost unnecessary. Tram maps are posted at most stations, making the system easy to navigate.

Buy tickets at newspaper kiosks or from the driver for 10KN (15KN at night). You can use your ticket for transfers within 90 minutes, but only in one direction. A *dnevna karta* (day ticket) is valid on all public transport until 4am the next morning; it's available for 30KN at most newspaper kiosks.

Make sure you validate your ticket when you get on the tram by pressing it on the yellow box.

# ISTRIA

Continental Croatia meets the Adriatic in Istria (Istra to Croats), the heart-shaped, 3600-sq-km peninsula just south of Trieste in Italy. While the bucolic interior of rolling hills and fertile plains attracts artsy visitors to its hilltop villages, rural hotels and farmhouse restaurants, the verdant indented coastline is enormously popular with the sun'n'sea set. Vast hotel complexes line much of the coast and its rocky beaches are not Croatia's best, but the facilities are wide-ranging, the sea is clean and secluded spots are still plentiful.

The coast gets flooded with tourists in summer, but you can still feel alone and undisturbed in 'Green Istria' (the interior), even in mid-August. Add acclaimed gastronomy (starring fresh seafood, prime white truffles, wild asparagus, top-rated olive oils and award-winning wines), sprinkle it with historical charm and you have a little slice of heaven.

# Rovinj

POP 14,300

Rovinj (Rovigno in Italian) is coastal Istria's star attraction. While it can get overrun with tourists in summer, it remains one of the last true Mediterranean fishing ports. Wooded hills and low-rise hotels surround the old town, which is webbed with steep cobbled streets and piazzas. The 14 green islands of the Rovinj archipelago make for a pleasant afternoon away; the most popular islands are Sveta Katarina and Crveni Otok (Red Island), also known as Sveti Andrija.

The old town is contained within an egg-shaped peninsula. About 1.5km south is the Punta Corrente Forest Park and the wooded cape of Zlatni Rt (Golden Cape), with its age-old oak and pine trees and several large hotels. There are two harbours: the northern open harbour and the small, protected harbour to the south.

## ◉ Sights

### ★ Church of St Euphemia          CHURCH
(Sveta Eufemija; Petra Stankovića; ☉10am-6pm Jun-Sep, to 4pm May, to 2pm Apr) FREE The town's showcase, this imposing church dominates the old town from its hilltop location in the middle of the peninsula. Built in 1736, it's the largest baroque building in Istria, reflecting the period during the 18th century when Rovinj was its most populous town. Inside, look for the marble **tomb of St Euphemia** behind the right-hand altar.

### ★ Punta Corrente Forest Park          PARK
(Zlatni Rt) Follow the waterfront on foot or by bike past Hotel Park to this verdant area, locally known as Zlatni Rt, about 1.5km south. Covered in oak and pine groves and boasting 10 species of cypress, the park was established in 1890 by Baron Hütterott, an Austrian admiral who kept a villa on Crveni Otok. You can swim off the rocks or just sit and admire the offshore islands.

## ⌑ Sleeping

### Porton Biondi          CAMPGROUND $
(☑052-813 557; www.portonbiondirovinj.com; Aleja Porton Biondi 1; campsites per person/tent 57/50KN; ☉Apr-Oct; ⊕) This beachside camping ground, which sleeps 1200, is about 700m north of the old town. It has a restaurant, snack bar and, oddly enough, a massage service.

### Villa Baron Gautsch          GUESTHOUSE $$
(☑052-840 538; www.baron-gautsch.com; IM Ronjgova 7; s/d 293/586KN; ✳🛜) This German-owned *pansion* (guesthouse), on the leafy street leading up from Hotel Park, has 17 spick-and-span rooms, some with terraces and views of the sea and the old town. Breakfast is served on the small terrace out the back. It's cash (kuna) only and prices almost halve in low season.

### Monte Mulini          HOTEL $$$
(☑052-636 000; www.montemulinihotel.com; A Smareglia bb; d from 3500KN; 🅿✳🛜⛱) This swanky and extremely pricey hotel slopes down towards Lone Bay, a 10-minute stroll from the old town along the Lungomare. Balconied rooms all have sea views and upscale trimmings. The spa and Wine Vault restaurant are both tops. There are three outdoor pools, and the design is bold and bright, but you'll need a fat wallet to enjoy it.

## ✕ Eating

### ★ Male Madlene          TAPAS $$
(☑052-815 905; Sv Križa 28; 5 courses fingerfood & wine 150KN; ☉11am-2pm & 7-11pm May-Sep) This adorable and popular spot is in the owner's tiny jumble sale of a living room hanging over the sea, where she serves creative finger food with market-fresh ingredients, based on old Italian recipes. Think tuna-filled zucchini, goat's-cheese-stuffed peppers and bite-size savoury pies and cakes. It has great Istrian wines by the glass. Reserve ahead, especially for evenings.

### ★ Barba Danilo          MEDITERRANEAN $$$
(☑052-830 002; www.barbadanilo.com; Polari 5; mains 90-280KN; ☉6-11.30pm) The last place you might expect to find one of Rovinj's best restaurants is on a campsite 3km from the centre, but that's where you'll find Barba Danilo. With just 45 seats in summer, book-

## MORE TO EXPLORE

**Poreč** This ancient Istrian town has at its heart a World Heritage–listed basilica and a medley of Gothic, Romanesque and baroque buildings.

**Pula** Don't miss Istria's main city, with its wealth of Roman architecture. The star of the show is the remarkably well-preserved amphitheatre dating back to the 1st century. About 10km south along the indented shoreline, the Premantura Peninsula hides a spectacular nature park, the protected cape of Kamenjak with its lovely rolling hills, wild flowers, low Mediterranean shrubs, fruit trees and medicinal herbs, and around 30km of virgin beaches and coves.

**Opatija** Genteel Opatija was the most chic seaside resort for the elite during the days of the Austro-Hungarian Empire – as evidenced by the many handsome belle-époque villas that the period bequeathed. The town sprawls along the coast between forested hills and the sparkling Adriatic, and the whole waterfront is connected by a promenade.

**Korčula** The Southern Dalmatian island of Korčula, rich in vineyards and olive trees, is the largest in an archipelago of 48, with plenty of opportunities for scenic drives, many quiet coves and secluded beaches, as well as Korčula Town, a striking walled town of round defensive towers, narrow stone streets and red-rooted houses that resembles a miniature Dubrovnik.

ing several days ahead is essential. Dishes by head chef Goran Glavan are modern takes on traditional Mediterranean fare with net-fresh seafood taking a star turn.

### ℹ Information

**Medical Centre** (☑ 052-840 702; Istarska bb; ☻24hr)

**Tourist Office** (☑ 052-811 566; www.tzgrovinj.hr; Pina Budicina 12; ☻8am-10pm Jun-Sep, to 8pm Apr-May & Oct-Nov) Just off Trg Maršala Tita.

### ℹ Getting There & Away

The **bus station** (Mattea Benussi) is just to the southeast of the old town. Destinations include Dubrovnik (402KN, 16 hours, one daily), Poreč (36KN to 47KN, 35 minutes to one hour, eight daily), Pula (33KN, 40 minutes, at least hourly), Split (285KN, 11 hours, one daily) and Zagreb (109KN to 150KN, 3¼ to 5½ hours, nine daily).

## DALMATIA

Roman ruins, spectacular beaches, old fishing ports, medieval architecture and unspoilt offshore islands make a trip to Dalmatia (Dalmacija) unforgettable. Occupying the central 375km of Croatia's Adriatic coast, Dalmatia offers a matchless combination of hedonism and historical discovery. The jagged coast is speckled with lush offshore islands and dotted with historic cities.

## Zadar

POP 75,100

Boasting a historic old town of Roman ruins, medieval churches, cosmopolitan cafes and quality museums set on a small peninsula, Zadar is an intriguing city. It's not too crowded, it's not overrun with tourists and its two unique attractions – the sound-and-light spectacle of the *Sea Organ* and the *Sun Salutation* – need to be seen and heard to be believed.

While it's not a picture-postcard kind of place, the mix of ancient relics, Habsburg elegance, coastal setting and unsightly tower blocks is what gives Zadar so much character. It's no Dubrovnik, but it's not a museum town either – this is a living, vibrant city, enjoyed by residents and visitors alike.

Zadar is also a key transport hub with superb ferry connections to the surrounding islands.

### ◉ Sights

★**Sea Organ**  MONUMENT
(Morske orgulje; Istarska Obala) **FREE** Zadar's incredible *Sea Organ*, designed by local architect Nikola Bašić, is unique. Set within the perforated stone stairs that descend into the sea is a system of pipes and whistles that exudes wistful sighs when the movement of the sea pushes air through it. The effect is hypnotic, the mellifluous tones increasing in volume when a boat or ferry passes by. You

**DON'T MISS**

## TROGIR

Gorgeous Trogir (called *Trau* by the Venetians) is set within medieval walls on a tiny island, linked by bridges to both the mainland and to the far larger Čiovo Island. On summer nights everyone gravitates to the wide seaside promenade, lined with bars, cafes and yachts – leaving the knotted, maze-like marble streets gleaming mysteriously under old-fashioned streetlights.

The old town has retained many intact and beautiful buildings from its age of glory between the 13th and 15th centuries. In 1997 its profuse collection of Romanesque and Renaissance buildings earned it World Heritage status.

While it's easily reached on a day trip from Split, Trogir also makes a good alternative base to the big city and a relaxing place to spend a few days.

Buses head here from Zagreb (from 149KN, 6½ hours, 11 daily), Zadar (80KN, 2½ hours, every half-hour), Split (21KN, 30 minutes, frequent) and Dubrovnik (140KN, 5½ hours, five daily).

can swim from the steps off the promenade while listening to the sounds.

★**Sun Salutation**　　　MONUMENT
(Pozdrav Suncu; Istarska Obala) Another wacky and wonderful creation by Nikola Bašić (along with the nearby Sea Organ; p117), this 22m-wide circle set into the pavement is filled with 300 multilayered glass plates that collect the sun's energy during the day. Together with the wave energy that makes the *Sea Organ's* sound, it produces a trippy light show from sunset to sunrise that's meant to simulate the solar system. It also collects enough energy to power the entire harbour-front lighting system.

**St Donatus' Church**　　　CHURCH
(Crkva Sv Donata; Šimuna Kožičića Benje bb; 20KN; ⊙9am-9pm May-Sep, to 4pm Oct-Apr) Dating from the beginning of the 9th century, this unusual circular Byzantine-style church was named after the bishop who commissioned it. As one of only a handful of buildings from the early Croatian kingdom to have survived the Mongol invasion of the 13th century, it's a particularly important cultural relic. The simple and unadorned interior includes two complete Roman columns, recycled from the Forum. Also from the Forum are the paving slabs that were revealed after the original floor was removed.

## 🛏 Sleeping

★**Drunken Monkey**　　　HOSTEL $
(☑023-314 406; www.drunkenmonkeyhostel. com; Jure Kastriotica Skenderbega 21; dm/r from 165/424KN; ❈@🛜🏊) Snuck away in a suburban neighbourhood, this friendly little hostel has brightly coloured rooms, a small pool, a guest barbecue and an all-round funky vibe. Staff can arrange trips to the Plitvice Lakes and the Krka National Park. If it's full, try the Drunken Monkey's nearby sister – the Lazy Monkey, with similar standards and rates.

★**Art Hotel Kalelarga**　　　HOTEL $$$
(☑023-233 000; www.arthotel-kalelarga.com; Majke Margarite 3; s/d 1340/1640KN; ❈🛜) Built and designed under strict conservation rules due to its old-town location, this 10-room boutique hotel is an understated and luxurious beauty. Exposed stonework and mushroom hues imbue the spacious rooms with plenty of style and character. The gourmet breakfast is served in the hotel's own stylish **restaurant** (Široka 23; breakfast 25-60KN; mains 60-140KN; ⊙7am-10pm).

## 🍴 Eating & Drinking

★**Kaštel**　　　MEDITERRANEAN $$
(☑023-494 950; www.hotel-bastion.hr; Bedemi Zadarskih Pobuna 13; mains 80-170KN; ⊙7am-11pm) Hotel Bastion's fine-dining restaurant offers contemporary takes on classic Croatian cuisine (octopus stew, stuffed squid, Pag cheese). France and Italy also make their presence felt, particularly in the delectable dessert list. Opt for the white-linen experience inside or dine on the battlements overlooking the harbour for a memorable evening's dining.

★**Pet Bunara**　　　DALMATIAN $$
(☑023-224 010; www.petbunara.com; Stratico 1; mains 60-165KN; ⊙11am-11pm) With exposed stone walls inside and a pretty terrace lined with olive trees, this is an atmospheric place

to tuck into Dalmatian soups and stews, homemade pasta and local faves such as octopus and turkey. Save room for a traditional Zadar fig cake or cherry torte.

**Foša**  SEAFOOD $$$
(☑ 023-314 421; www.fosa.hr; Kralja Dmitra Zvonimira 2; mains 95-225KN; ☺ noon-1am) With a gorgeous terrace that juts out into the harbour and a sleek interior that combines ancient stone walls with 21st-century style, Foša is a very classy place. The main focus of chef Damir Tomljanović is fresh fish, plucked from the Adriatic and served grilled or salt-baked.

**★ La Bodega**  WINE BAR
(www.labodega.hr; Široka 3; ☺ 7am-1am Sun-Thu, to 1.30am Fri & Sat) With its slick, eccentric, semi-industrial decor, a bar with a line of hams and garlic hanging above, Portuguese-style tiles and welcoming, open-to-the-street approach, this is one of Zadar's hippest bars. There's a good range of Croatian wines by the glass and an extraordinary selection by the bottle – to be enjoyed with a variety of cheese and prosciutto.

## ❶ Information

**Tourist Office** (☑ 023-316 166; www.zadar. travel; Mihe Klaića 5; ☺ 8am-11pm May-Jul & Sep, to midnight Aug, 8am-8pm Mon-Fri, 9am-2pm Sat & Sun Oct-Apr; ☏) Publishes a good colour map and rents audio guides (35KN) for a self-guided tour around the town. Also offers free wi-fi.

**Zadar General Hospital** (Opća Bolnica Zadar; ☑ 023-505 505; www.bolnica-zadar.hr; Bože Peričića 5)

## ❶ Getting There & Away

The **bus station** (☑ 060 305 305; www.liburnija-zadar.hr; Ante Starčevića 1) is about 1km southeast of the old town. Destinations include **Dubrovnik** (173KN, eight hours, six daily), **Pula** (176KN, seven hours, two daily), **Split** (80KN, three hours, hourly) and **Zagreb** (110KN, 3½ hours, hourly).

# Split

POP 178,000

Croatia's second-largest city, Split (*Spalato* in Italian) is a great place to see Dalmatian life as it's really lived. Always buzzing, this exuberant city has just the right balance of tradition and modernity. Step inside Diocletian's Palace (a Unesco World Heritage Site and one of the world's most impressive Roman monuments) and you'll see dozens of bars, restaurants and shops thriving amid the atmospheric old walls where Split life has been humming along for thousands of years.

To top it off, Split has a unique setting. Its dramatic coastal mountains act as the perfect backdrop to the turquoise waters of the Adriatic and help divert attention from the dozens of shabby high-rise apartment blocks that fill its suburbs. It's this thoroughly lived-in aspect of Split that means it will never be a fantasy land like Dubrovnik, but you could argue that it's all the better for that.

CROATIA SPLIT

WORTH A TRIP

## PLITVICE LAKES NATIONAL PARK

The absolute highlight of Croatia's Adriatic hinterland, this glorious expanse of forested hills and turquoise lakes is exquisitely scenic – so much so that in 1979 Unesco proclaimed the **park** (☑ 053-751 015; www.np-plitvicka-jezera.hr; adult/child 180/80KN Jul & Aug, 110/55KN Apr-Jun, Sep & Oct, 55/35KN Nov-Mar; ☺ 7am-8pm) a World Heritage Site.

Sixteen crystalline lakes tumble into each other via a series of waterfalls and cascades, whilst clouds of butterflies drift above. It takes upwards of six hours to explore the the 18km of wooden footbridges and pathways which snake around the edges of the rumbling water on foot, but you can slice two hours off by taking advantage of the park's free boats and buses (departing every 30 minutes from April to October).

While the park is beautiful year-round, spring and autumn are the best times to visit. In spring and early summer the falls are flush with water, while in autumn the changing leaves put on a colourful display. Winter is also spectacular, although snow can limit access and the free park transport doesn't operate. If possible, avoid the peak months of July and August, when the falls reduce to a trickle, parking is problematic and the sheer volume of visitors can turn the walking tracks into a conga line.

# Central Split

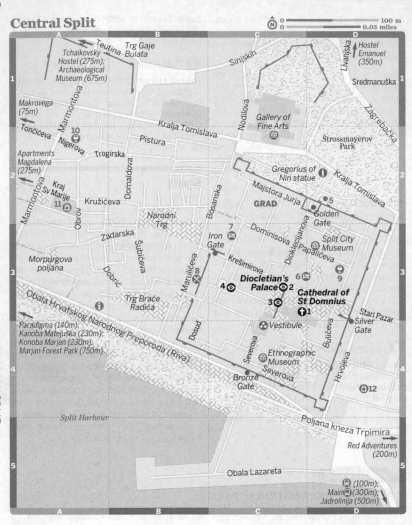

## 👁 Sights & Activities

### 👁 Diocletian's Palace

Facing the harbour, **Diocletian's Palace** is one of the most imposing Roman ruins in existence. Don't expect a palace though, nor a museum – this is the living heart of the city, its labyrinthine streets packed with people, bars, shops and restaurants.

It was built as a military fortress, imperial residence and fortified town, with walls reinforced by square corner towers. There are

220 buildings within the palace boundaries, which is home to about 3000 people.

**Peristil**                                           SQUARE
This picturesque, colonnaded, ancient Roman courtyard (or peristyle) lies at the very heart of Diocletian's Palace. In summer you can almost be guaranteed a pair of strapping local lads dressed as legionaries adding to the scene. Notice the black-granite sphinx sitting between the columns near the cathedral; dating from the 15th century BC, it was one of several imported from Egypt when the palace was constructed.

# Central Split

**Cathedral of St Domnius**    CHURCH
(Katedrala Sv Duje; Peristil; cathedral/belfry 35/20KN; ⊙8am-7pm Mon-Sat, 12.30-6.30pm Sun) FREE Split's octagonal cathedral is one of the best-preserved ancient Roman buildings standing today. It was built as a mausoleum for Diocletian, the last famous persecutor of the Christians, who was interred here in 311 AD. The Christians got the last laugh, destroying the emperor's sarcophagus and converting his tomb into a church in the 5th century, dedicated to one of his victims. Note that a ticket for the cathedral includes admission to its crypt, treasury and baptistery (Temple of Jupiter).

**Temple of Jupiter**    TEMPLE
(Jupiterov Hram; 10KN; ⊙8am-7pm Mon-Sat, 12.30-6.30pm Sun) Although it's now the cathedral's baptistery, this wonderfully intact building was originally an ancient Roman temple, dedicated to the king of the gods. It still has its original barrel-vaulted ceiling and a decorative frieze on the walls, although a striking bronze statue of St John the Baptist by Ivan Meštrović now fills the spot where the god once stood. Of the columns that once supported a porch, only one remains.

## ⊙ Other Areas

**Meštrović Gallery**    GALLERY
(Galerija Meštrović; ☑021-340 800; www.mestrovic.hr; Šetalište Ivana Meštrovića 46; adult/child 40/20KN; ⊙9am-7pm Tue-Sun May-Sep, to 4pm Tue-Sun Oct-Apr) At this stellar art museum, you'll see a comprehensive, well-arranged collection of works by Ivan Meštrović, Croatia's premier modern sculptor, who built the gallery as a personal residence in the 1930s. Although Meštrović intended to retire here, he emigrated to the USA soon after WWII. Admission includes entry to the nearby **Kaštelet** (☑021-358 185; www.mestrovic.hr; Šetalište Ivana Meštrovića 39; admission by Meštrović Gallery ticket; ⊙9am-7pm Tue-Sun May-Sep), a fortress housing other Meštrović works.

**Archaeological Museum**    MUSEUM
(Arheološki Muzej; ☑021-329 340; www.armus.hr; Zrinsko-Frankopanska 25; adult/concession 30/15KN; ⊙9am-2pm & 4-8pm Mon-Sat) A treasure trove of classical sculpture and mosaic is displayed at this excellent museum, a short walk north of the town centre. Most of the vast collection originated from the ancient Roman settlements of Split and neighbouring Salona (Solin), and there's also some Greek pottery from the island of Vis. There are displays of jewellery and coins, and a room filled with artefacts dating from the Paleolithic to the Iron Age.

**Salona**    ARCHAEOLOGICAL SITE
(☑021-213 358; Don Frane Bulića bb, Solin; adult/child 30/15KN; ⊙9am-7pm Mon-Sat, to 2pm Sun) The ruins of the ancient city of Salona, situated at the foot of the mountains just northeast of Split, are the most archaeologically important in Croatia. Start by paying your admission fee at the **Tusculum Museum**, near the entrance to the reserve, as you'll need the map from its brochure to help you navigate the vast, sprawling site. This small museum has lots of ancient sculpture and interesting displays on the archaeological team that uncovered the site.

**Marjan Forest Park**    WALKING
(Park šuma Marjan) Considered the lungs of the city, this hilly nature reserve offers trails through fragrant pine forests to scenic lookouts, medieval chapels and cave dwellings once inhabited by Christian hermits. For an afternoon away from the city buzz, consider taking a long walk through the park and descending to Kašjuni beach to cool off before catching the bus back.

## ACTIVITIES

Croatia is a great destination for outdoor activities. Cycling is tops, especially in Istria, which has over 60 marked trails through stunning scenery. Hiking is also incredible, particularly in the national parks like Plitvice. Croatia also has some great dive sites, including many wrecks. Other activities worth trying in Croatia are kayaking, rafting, rock climbing and caving.

## Tours

### Red Adventures                          ADVENTURE
(☑ 091 79 03 747; www.red-adventures.com; Kralja Zvonimira 8) Specialising in active excursions, this crew offers sea kayaking (from €38), rock climbing (from €50), hiking (from €30) and bike tours (from €45) around Split. It also rents bikes, kayaks and cars, charters yachts, provides transfers and arranges private accommodation.

### Split Walking Tours                        TOURS
(☑ 099 82 15 383; www.splitwalkingtour.com; Golden Gate; ⊙ Apr-Oct) Leads walking tours in English, Italian, German, Spanish and French, departing from the Golden Gate at set times during the day (check its website). Options include the 75-minute Diocletian's Palace Tour (100KN) and the two-hour Split Walking Tour (160KN), which includes the palace and the medieval part of town. It also offers kayaking, diving, cycling tours, boat trips and excursions.

## Sleeping

### Hostel Emanuel                         HOSTEL $
(☑ 021-786 533; hostelemanuel@gmail.com; Tolstojeva 20; dm €29; ❋@🖤) Run by a friendly couple, this hip little hostel in a suburban apartment block has colourful contemporary interiors and a relaxed vibe. In the two dorms (one sleeping five, the other 10), each bunk has a large locker, curtains, a reading light and a power outlet.

### Tchaikovsky Hostel                      HOSTEL $
(☑ 021-317 124; www.tchaikovskyhostel.com; Čajkovskoga 4; dm 180-200KN; ❋@🖤) This four-dorm hostel in an apartment block in the neighbourhood of Špinut is run by a German-born Croat. Rooms are neat and tidy, with bunks featuring built-in shelves. Freebies include cereal, espresso and tea.

★ Apartments Magdalena          APARTMENT $$
(☑ 098 423 087; www.magdalena-apartments.com; Milićeva 18; 450-580KN; ❋🖤) You may never want to leave Magdalena's top-floor apartment once you see the old-town view from the dormer window. The three apartments are nicely furnished and the hospitality offered by the off-site owners is exceptional: chocolates on arrival, beer in the fridge, a back-up toothbrush in the cupboard and even a mobile phone with credit on it.

★ Villa Split                               B&B $$$
(☑ 091 40 34 403; www.villasplitluxury.com; Bajamontijeva 5; r from €207; P❋🖤) Built into the Roman-constructed wall of Diocletian's Palace, this wonderful boutique B&B has only three rooms – the best of which is the slightly larger one in the attic. If you're happy to swap the ancient for the merely medieval, there are six larger rooms in a 10th-century building on the main square.

★ Antique Split Luxury Rooms      HOTEL $$$
(☑ 021-785 208; www.antique-split.com; Poljana Grgura Ninskog 1; r 2690-3845KN; ❋🖤) Palace living at its most palatial, this boutique complex has eight chic rooms with stone walls and impressive bathrooms. In some you'll wake up to incredible views over the cathedral.

## Eating

### Makrovega                          VEGETARIAN $
(☑ 021-394 440; www.makrovega.hr; Leština 2; mains 50-75KN; ⊙ 9am-9.30pm Mon-Fri, to 5pm Sat) Hidden away down a lane and behind a courtyard, this meat-free haven serves macrobiotic, vegetarian and some raw food. Think lots of seitan, tofu and tempeh, and excellent cakes.

★ Konoba Matejuška                   DALMATIAN $$
(☑ 021-355 152; www.konobamatejuska.hr; Tomića Stine 3; mains 85-160KN; ⊙ noon-11pm) This cosy, rustic tavern in an alleyway minutes from the seafront specialises in well-prepared seafood – as epitomised in its perfectly cooked fish platter for two. There are only four small tables outside and a couple of larger ones inside, so book ahead.

★ Zinfandel                            EUROPEAN $$
(☑ 021-355 135; www.zinfandelfoodandwinebar.com; Marulićeva 2; mains 90-145KN; ⊙ 8am-1am) The vibe might be more like an upmarket wine bar but the food is top-notch here, too. The menu includes delicious risotto, home-

made pasta, veal cheek *pašticada* (traditional Dalmatian stew), burgers, steaks and fish, and there's a huge choice of local wine by the glass to wash it down. The beer selection is good, too.

**Konoba Marjan**  DALMATIAN $$
(☎ 098 93 46 848; www.facebook.com/konobamarjan; Senjska 1; mains 78-139KN; ☺ noon-11pm; ☜) Offering great-quality Dalmatian fare, this friendly little Veli Varoš tavern features daily specials such as cuttlefish *brujet* (fish stew), goulash and prawn pasta. The wine list is excellent, showcasing some local boutique wineries, and there are a few seats outside on the street leading up to Marjan Hill.

**Paradigma**  MEDITERRANEAN $$$
(☎ 021-645 103; www.restoranparadigma.hr; Bana Josipa Jelačića 3; mains 100-175KN; ☺ 11am-midnight Jun-Sep, 11.30am-10.30pm Mon-Sat, to 4.30pm Sun Oct-May) Bringing culinary innovation to Split, this restaurant sports modern interiors with colourful paintings and a rooftop terrace with sea glimpses in an old building resembling a ship's bow. Dishes are presented like mini works of art – and while not everything tastes as exquisite as it looks, most of the dishes are sublime.

## 🍷 Drinking & Nightlife

**Marcvs Marvlvs Spalatensis**  WINE BAR
(www.facebook.com/marvlvs; Papalićeva 4; ☺ 5pm-midnight; ☜) Fittingly, the 15th-century Gothic home of the 'Dante of Croatia', Marko Marulić, now houses this wonderful little 'library jazz bar' – two small rooms crammed with books and frequented by ageless bohemians, tortured poets and wistful academics. Cheese, chess, cards and cigars are all on offer, and there's often live music.

**To Je To**  BAR
(www.tojetosplit.com; Nigerova 2; ☺ 8.30am-1am; ☜) If you're up for loud rock and hip hop, Croatian craft beer and Mexican food, this effortlessly hip little bar is the place to come. The chilled-out Honduran/US owners engender a feel-good Latin American party vibe, there's live music most nights and a crazy karaoke session on Fridays.

## 🛍 Shopping

**Green Market**  MARKET
(Hrvojeva bb; ☺ 6.30am-2pm) This open-air market is the place to come to stock up on fruit, vegetables and cut flowers. While it's busiest in the mornings, a few stallholders stay open to sell cherries and strawberries to tourists throughout the afternoon in the summer.

**Fish Market**  MARKET
(Ribarnica; Obrov 5; ☺ 6.30am-2pm) As stinky and chaotic a scene as you could possibly imagine, Split's indoor/outdoor fish market is a spectacle to behold. Locals head here on a daily basis to haggle for all their scaly and slimy requirements from their favourite chain-smoking vendors. It's all over by about 11am, bar the dregs.

## ℹ Information

**Tourist Office** (☎ 021-360 066; www.visitsplit.com; Obala hrvatskog narodnog preporoda 9; ☺ 8am-9pm Mon-Sat, to 7pm Sun Jun-Sep, 8am-8pm Mon-Sat, to 5pm Sun Apr, May & Oct, 9am-4pm Mon-Fri, to 1pm Sat Nov-Mar) Has info on Split and sells the Split Card (70KN), which offers free and reduced prices to Split attractions, plus discounts on car rental, restaurants, shops and theatres. You get the card for free if you're staying in Split more than three nights from October to May.

**University Hospital Split** (Klinički Bolnički Centar (KBC) Split; ☎ 021-556 111; www.kbsplit.hr; Spinčićeva 1)

## ℹ Getting There & Away

### AIR

**Split airport** (Zračna Luka Split; ☎ 021-203 507; www.split-airport.hr; Cesta dr Franje Tuđmana 1270, Kaštel Štafilić, Kaštela) is 20km west of town, just 6km before Trogir. **Croatia Airlines** (☎ 072 500 505; www.croatiaairlines.com) operates flights to Zagreb year-round and to Dubrovnik in summer, as well as various international destinations. In summer, dozens of airlines fly here from all over Europe, but the only year-round carriers are Germanwings (www.germanwings.com) and Lufthansa CityLine (www.lufthansacityline.com).

### BOAT

Split's ferry harbour is extremely busy and can be hard to negotiate, so you're best to arrive early. Most domestic ferries depart from Gat Sv Petra, the first of the three major piers, which has **ticket booths** for both Jadrolinija and Kapetan Luka. The giant international ferries depart from Gat Sv Duje, the second of the piers, where there's a large **ferry terminal** with ticketing offices for all the major lines.

For most domestic ferries you can't reserve tickets ahead of time; they're only available for purchase on the day of departure. In July and August it's often necessary to appear hours before departure for a car ferry, and put your car in the line for boarding. There is rarely a problem or a long wait obtaining a space off-season.

**Jadrolinija** (☑ 021-338 333; www.jadrolinija. hr; Gat Sv Duje bb) operates most of the ferries between Split and the islands, including catamarans to Hvar Town (55KN, one hour, two to four daily) and Korčula Town (80KN, three hours, daily).

**Kapetan Luka** (p126) has a fast catamaran operating daily from June to September, heading to **Hvar Town** (70KN, 65 minutes), **Korčula Town** (120KN, 1¾ hours) and **Dubrovnik** (190KN, 4¼ hours); services drop to four times per week in May and three per week in October.

### BUS

Most intercity and international buses arrive at and depart from the **main bus station** (Autobusni Kolodvor Split; ☑ 060 327 777; www.ak-split.hr; Obala kneza Domagoja bb) beside the harbour. In summer, it's best to purchase bus tickets with seat reservations in advance. If you need to store bags, there's a **garderoba** (Obala kneza Domagoja 12; 1st hr 5KN, then 1.50KN per hr; ⊙ 6am-10pm) nearby.

Domestic destinations include Zagreb (130KN, five hours, at least hourly), Pula (300KN, 10 hours, three daily), Zadar (100KN, 3½ hours, at least hourly) and Dubrovnik (130KN, 4½ hours, 21 daily).

### TRAIN

Five trains a day head to Split's **train station** (☑ 021-338 525; www.hzpp.hr; Obala kneza Domagoja 9; ⊙ 6am-10pm) from Zagreb (112KN, six hours, five daily). The train station has lockers (per day 15KN) that will fit suitcases but you can't leave bags overnight. There's another **garderoba** (☑ 098 446 780; Obala kneza Domagoja 6; per day 15KN; ⊙ 6am-10pm Jul & Aug, 7.30am-9pm Sep-Jun) nearby, out on the street.

# Hvar Island

POP 11,080

Long, lean Hvar is vaguely shaped like the profile of a holidaymaker reclining on a sun lounger, which is altogether appropriate for the sunniest spot in the country (2724 sunny hours each year) and its most luxurious beach destination.

Hvar Town, the island's capital, offers swanky hotels, elegant restaurants and a general sense that, if you care about seeing and being seen, this is the place to be. Rubbing shoulders with the posh yachties are hundreds of young partygoers, dancing on tables at the town's legendary beach bars.

The northern coastal towns of Stari Grad and Jelsa are far more subdued and low-key.

Hvar's interior hides abandoned ancient hamlets, craggy peaks, vineyards and the lavender fields that the island is famous for. It's worth exploring on a day trip, as is the southern end of the island, which has some of Hvar's most beautiful and isolated coves.

## ◉ Sights & Activities

**St Stephen's Cathedral**                    CATHEDRAL
(Katedrala svetog Stjepana; Trg Sv Stjepana bb; 10KN; ⊙ 9am-1pm & 5-9pm) Providing a grand backdrop to the main square, this baroque cathedral was built in the 16th and 17th centuries at the height of the Dalmatian Renaissance to replace one destroyed by the Turks. Parts of the older building are visible in the nave and in the carved 15th-century choir stalls. Its most distinctive feature is its tall, rectangular bell tower, which sprouts an additional window at each level, giving it an oddly top-heavy appearance.

**Fortica**                    FORTRESS
(Tvrđava Španjola; ☑ 021-742 608; Biskupa Jurja Dubokovica bb; adult/child 30/15KN; ⊙ 8am-9pm) Looming high above the town and lit with a golden glow at night, this medieval castle occupies the site of an ancient Illyrian settlement dating from before 500BC. The views looking down over Hvar and the Pakleni Islands are magnificent, and well worth the trudge up through the old-town streets. Once you clear the town walls it's a gently sloping meander up the tree-shaded hillside to the fortress – or you can drive to the very top.

## 🛏 Sleeping

Hvar Town has the lion's share of the island's best accommodation, but expect to pay more than you would at most places on the Dalmatian coast. However, a good crop of hostels and private apartments helps to keep things more affordable. Stari Grad and Jelsa are poorly served for both hotels and hostels; consider private accommodation as an alternative.

★**Villa Skansi**                    HOSTEL $
(☑ 021-741 426; hostelvillaskansi1@gmail.com; Domovinskog rata 18; dm/r from 250/750KN; ❄@🛜) Hvar's biggest and best hostel has brightly coloured dorms, fancy bathrooms, a great terrace with sea views, a barbecue, a bar, a book exchange and a laundry service,

## PAKLENI ISLANDS

Most visitors to Hvar Town visit the crystal-clear waters, hidden beaches and deserted lagoons of the Pakleni Islands (Pakleni Otoci), a gorgeous chain of wooded isles that stretch out immediately in front of the town. Although the name is often translated as 'Hell's Islands', its meaning is thought to derive from *paklina*, a pine resin that was once harvested here to waterproof boats.

The largest of the Pakleni Islands by far is **Sveti Klement**, which supports three villages in its 5 sq km. Palmižana village has a marina, accommodation, restaurants and a pebbly beach.

The closest of the islands to Hvar is **Jerolim**, which has a popular naturist beach. Stipanska bay on the nearby island of **Marinkovac** (40KN, 10 to 15 minutes), also has a clothing-optional section, although it's better known for its raucous beach club. Other popular options on Marinkovac include Ždrilca bay and pretty Mlini beach.

and rents scooters and boats. The private rooms are in a separate, newly built block next door, surrounded by citrus trees, pomegranates and bougainvillea. Plus there's a free pub crawl every night.

★**Apartments Ana Dujmović** APARTMENT **$**
(☑ 098 838 434; www.visit-hvar.com/apartments-ana-dujmovic; Biskupa Jurja Dubokovića 36; apt from €55; P❄☎) This brilliant brace of comfortable holiday apartments are set behind an olive grove, only a 10-minute walk from the centre of town and, crucially, five minutes from the beach and Hula-Hula bar. Call ahead and the delightful owner will pick you up from the town centre.

★**Earthers Hostel** HOSTEL **$$**
(☑ 099 26 79 889; www.earthershostel.com; Martina Vučetića 11; dm/r 250/640KN; ☺Apr-Sep; P❄☎) The advantages of Earthers' south-end-of-town location are the spacious surrounds and brilliant sunset views. The main hostel occupies a comfortable family home (which in the off-season reverts to being just that), and the well-appointed private rooms have their own swish house next door. A simple breakfast is included, and the friendly young owners host a barbecue every few days.

**Apartments Komazin** APARTMENT **$$$**
(☑ 091 60 19 712; www.croatia-hvar-apartments.com; Nikice Kolumbića 2; apt from 1025KN; P❄@☎⊞) With five bright apartments and one private room to rent, bougainvillea-draped Komazin is an attractive option at the upper end of the private-apartment heap.

### ✖ Eating

★**Fig Cafe Bar** CAFE **$$**
(☑ 099 42 29 721; www.figcafebar.com; Ivana Frane Biundovića 3; mains 60-100KN; ☺9am-10pm mid-Apr–Oct; ☎⊿) Run by an Aussie-Croat and an American, this great little place serves up delicious stuffed flatbreads (fig and farm cheese, pear and blue cheese, brie and prosciutto), vegetarian curries and, our favourite Hvar breakfast, spiced eggs. There are even some vegan options – a rarity in these parts.

★**Dalmatino** DALMATIAN **$$$**
(☑ 091 52 93 121; www.dalmatino-hvar.com; Sv Marak 1; mains 70-250KN; ☺noon-3pm & 5pm-midnight; ☎) Calling itself a 'steak and fish house', this place is always popular – due, in part, to the handsome waiters and the free-flowing *rakija* (brandy). Thankfully the food is also excellent; try their *gregada*, a fish fillet served on potatoes with a thick, broth-like sauce.

### 🍷 Drinking & Nightlife

★**Hula-Hula Hvar** BAR
(www.hulahulahvar.com; Šetalište Antuna Tomislava Petrića 10; ☺9am-11pm) *The* spot to catch the sunset to the sound of techno and house music, Hula-Hula is known for its après-beach party (4pm to 9pm), where all of young trendy Hvar seems to descend for sundowner cocktails. Dancing on tables is pretty much compulsory.

★**Kiva Bar** BAR
(www.kivabarhvar.com; Fabrika 10; ☺9pm-2am) A happening place in an alleyway just off the Riva, Kiva is packed to the rafters most nights, with crowds spilling out and filling

up the lane. DJs spin a crowd-pleasing mix of old-school dance, pop and hip-hop classics to an up-for-it crowd.

## ℹ️ Information

**Tourist Office** (☎ 021-741 059; www.tzhvar. hr; Trg Sv Stjepana 42; ☺ 8am-9pm Jul & Aug, 8am-8pm Mon-Sat, 8am-1pm & 4-8pm Sun Jun & Sep, 8am-2pm Mon-Fri, to noon Sat Oct-May) In the Arsenal building, right on St Stephen's Sq.

**Tourist Office Information Point** (☎ 021-718 109; Trg Marka Miličića; ☺ 8am-9pm Mon-Sat, 9am-1pm Sun Jun-Sep) A summertime annex of the main tourist office in the bus station.

## ℹ️ Getting There & Away

Hvar has two main car-ferry ports: one near Stari Grad and the other at Sućuraj on the eastern tip of the island. **Jadrolinija** (☎ 021-773 433; www. jadrolinija.hr) operates from both, with ferries from Split to Stari Grad (per adult/child/car/ motorcycle/bike 47/24/318/78/45KN, two hours, six daily June to September, three daily at other times) and from Drvenik to Sućuraj (16/8/108/30/16KN, 34 minutes, 10 daily). Note: bus services to/from Sućuraj are extremely limited.

Jadrolinija also has high-speed catamaran services to Hvar Town from Korčula Town (70KN, 1½ hours, two daily) and Split (55KN, 65 minutes, seven daily). From July to mid-September, there's also a daily catamaran to Hvar Town from Dubrovnik (190KN, four hours).

**Kapetan Luka** (Krilo; ☎ 021-645 476; www. krilo.hr) has a fast catamaran to Hvar Town from Dubrovnik (190KN, three hours), Korčula Town (90KN, 65 minutes) and Split (70KN, 65 minutes). Tickets can be purchased from **Pelegrini Tours** (☎ 021-742 743; www.pelegrini-hvar.hr; Obala Riva 20).

## ℹ️ Getting Around

Buses meet most ferries that dock at the ferry port near Stari Grad and go to Hvar Town (27KN, 20 minutes), central Stari Grad (13KN, 10 minutes) and Jelsa (33KN, 40 minutes). Buses also connect Hvar Town with Stari Grad (30KN, 30 minutes, 10 daily) and Jelsa (33KN, 50 minutes, eight daily); and Stari Grad with Jelsa (30KN, 25 minutes, 13 daily). Services are less frequent in the low season.

# Dubrovnik

POP 28,500

No matter whether you are visiting Dubrovnik for the first time or if you're returning to this marvellous city, the sense of awe and beauty when you set eyes on the Stradun (the Old Town's main street) never fades. It's hard to imagine anyone becoming jaded by the marble streets and baroque buildings or failing to be inspired by a walk along the ancient city walls that once protected a civilised, sophisticated republic for five centuries and that now look out onto the endless shimmer of the peaceful Adriatic.

## ◎ Sights

★ **City Walls & Forts** FORT
(Gradske zidine; adult/child 120/30KN; ☺ 8am-7.30pm Apr-Oct, 9am-3pm Nov-Mar) No visit to Dubrovnik would be complete without a walk around the spectacular city walls, the finest in the world and the city's main claim to fame. From the top, the view over the Old Town and the sparkling Adriatic is sublime. You can get a good handle on the extent of the shelling damage in the 1990s by gazing over the rooftops: those sporting bright new terracotta suffered damage and had to be replaced.

The first set of walls to enclose the city was built in the 9th century. In the middle of the 14th century the 1.5m-thick defences were fortified with 15 square forts. The threat of attacks from the Turks in the 15th century prompted the city to strengthen the existing forts and add new ones, so that the entire Old Town was contained within a stone barrier 2km long and up to 25m high. The walls are thicker on the land side – up to 6m – and range from 1.5m to 3m on the sea side.

The round **Minčeta Tower** (Tvrđava Minčeta; City Walls) protects the landward edge of the city from attack, the **Bokar Tower** (Tvrđava Bokar) and **Fort Lawrence** (Tvrđava Lovrjenac; admission 30KN; ☺ 8am-7.30pm) look west and out to sea, while **Fort Revelin** (Trg Oružja) and **Fort St John** (Tvrđava sv Ivana) guard the eastern approach and the Old Harbour.

There are entrances to the walls from near the Pile Gate, the Ploče Gate and the Maritime Museum. The Pile Gate entrance tends to be the busiest, and entering from the Ploče side has the added advantage of getting the steepest climbs out of the way first (you're required to walk in an anticlockwise direction). Don't underestimate how strenuous the wall walk can be, especially on a hot day. There's very little shelter and the few vendors selling water on the route tend to be overpriced.

## CAVTAT

Without Cavtat, there'd be no Dubrovnik, as it was refugees from the original Cavtat who established the city of Dubrovnik in 614. But Cavtat is interesting in itself. A lot more 'local' than Dubrovnik – read, not flooded by tourists on a daily basis – it has its own charm. Wrapped around a very pretty harbour that's bordered by beaches and backed by a curtain of imposing hills, the setting is lovely.

Cavtat's most famous personality is the painter Vlaho Bukovac (1855–1922), one of the foremost exponents of Croatian modernism. His paintings are liberally distributed around the town's main sights.

From June to September there are 11 sailings a day between Dubrovnik's Old Harbour and Cavtat (one way/return 50/80KN, 45 minutes). For the rest of the year this reduces to three to five a day, weather dependent. Bus 10 runs roughly half-hourly to Cavtat (25KN, 25 minutes) from Dubrovnik's bus station; the last buses return at 12.45am.

★ **Rector's Palace** PALACE
(Knežev dvor; ☎020-321 422; www.dumus.hr; Pred Dvorom 3; adult/child multimuseum pass 100/25KN; ⊘9am-6pm Apr-Oct, to 4pm Nov-Mar) Built in the late 15th century for the elected rector who governed Dubrovnik, this Gothic-Renaissance palace contains the rector's office, his private chambers, public halls, administrative offices and a dungeon. During his one-month term the rector was unable to leave the building without the permission of the senate. Today the palace has been turned into the **Cultural History Museum**, with artfully restored rooms, portraits, coats of arms and coins, evoking the glorious history of Dubrovnik.

★ **War Photo Limited** GALLERY
(☎020-322 166; www.warphotoltd.com; Antuninska 6; adult/child 40/30KN; ⊘10am-10pm daily Jun-Sep, 10am-4pm Wed-Mon May & Oct) An immensely powerful experience, this gallery features intensely compelling exhibitions curated by New Zealand photojournalist Wade Goddard, who worked in the Balkans in the 1990s. Its declared intention is to 'expose the myth of war...to let people see war as it is, raw, venal, frightening, by focusing on how war inflicts injustices on innocents and combatants alike'. There's a permanent exhibition on the upper floor devoted to the wars in Yugoslavia, but the changing exhibitions cover a multitude of conflicts.

★ **Lokrum** ISLAND
(www.lokrum.hr; adult/child incl boat 100/20KN; ⊘Apr-Nov) Lush Lokrum is a beautiful, forested island full of holm oaks, black ash, pines and olive trees, and is an ideal escape from urban Dubrovnik. It's a popular swimming spot, although the beaches are rocky.

To reach the nudist beach, head left from the ferry and follow the signs marked FKK; the rocks at the far end are Dubrovnik's de facto gay beach. Also popular is the small saltwater lake known as the **Dead Sea**.

## 🏃 Activities

★ **Cable Car** CABLE CAR
(Žičara; ☎020-414 355; www.dubrovnikcablecar.com; Petra Krešimira IV bb; return adult/child 120/50KN; ⊘9am-5pm Nov-Mar, to 9pm Apr, May, Sep & Oct, to midnight Jun-Aug) Dubrovnik's cable car whisks you from just north of the city walls to Mt Srđ in under four minutes. At the end of the line there's a stupendous perspective of the city from a lofty 405m, taking in the terracotta-tiled rooftops of the old town and the island of Lokrum, with the Adriatic and distant Elafiti Islands filling the horizon.

**Banje Beach** SWIMMING
(www.banjebeach.eu; Frana Supila 10) Banje Beach is the closest beach to the old town, just beyond the 17th-century Lazareti (a former quarantine station) outside Ploče Gate. Although many people rent lounge chairs and parasols from the beach club, there's no problem with just flinging a towel on the beach if you can find a space.

**Outdoor Croatia** KAYAKING
(☎020-418 282; www.outdoorcroatia.com; Sv Križa 3; day trip 400KN) Rents kayaks and offers day trips around the Elafiti Islands, along with multiday excursions and kayaking-cycling combos.

## 🛏 Sleeping

Dubrovnik is the most expensive city in the country, so expect to pay more for a room

# Dubrovnik

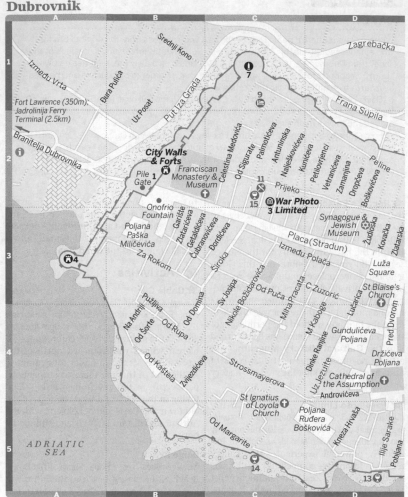

here (even hostels fall into our midrange category), and you should book well in advance, especially in summer. There's limited accommodation in the compact old town itself. If you want to combine a beach holiday with your city stay, consider the leafy Lapad peninsula, 4km west of the centre.

### Hostel Angelina
HOSTEL $

(☏ 091 89 39 089; www.hostelangelinaoldtown-dubrovnik.com; Plovani skalini 17a; dm 208KN; ✸ 🛜) Hidden away in a quiet nook of the old town, this cute little hostel offers bunk rooms, a small guest kitchen and a bougain-

villea-shaded terrace with memorable views over the rooftops. Plus you'll get a great glute workout every time you walk up the lane.

### ★ Karmen Apartments
APARTMENT $$

(☏ 098 619 282; www.karmendu.com; Bandureva 1; apt from €95; ✸ 🛜) These four inviting apartments enjoy a great location a stone's throw from Ploče harbour. All have plenty of character with art, splashes of colour, tasteful furnishings and books to browse. Apartment 2 has a little balcony while apartment 1 enjoys sublime port views. Book well ahead.

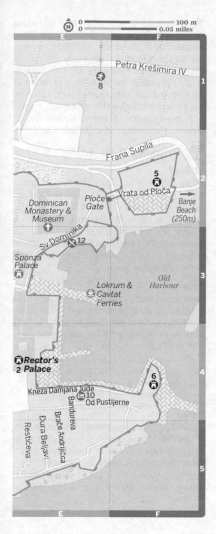

Map scale: 0 — 100 m / 0 — 0.05 miles

big hotel has more personality that you'd expect for its size, due in large part to its interesting art, slick design and charming staff. The breakfast buffet is excellent and the outdoor pool is pleasantly cool on a scorching day (the indoor one's warmer).

★**Villa Dubrovnik** HOTEL $$$
(☑020-500 300; www.villa-dubrovnik.hr; Vlaha Bukovca 6; r from €581; P❋🛜🖫) Gazing endlessly at the old town and Lokrum from its prime waterfront position, this elegant, low-slung boutique hotel gleams white against a backdrop of honey-coloured stone. The windows retract completely to bring the indoor pool into the outdoors, but sunseekers can laze on a lounger by the sea or commandeer a day bed in the rooftop prosciutto-and-wine bar.

## ✗ Eating

★**Pantarul** MODERN EUROPEAN $$
(☑020-333 486; www.pantarul.com; Kralja Tomislava 1; mains 70-128KN; ◷noon-4pm & 6pm-midnight) This breezy bistro serves exceptional homemade bread, pasta and risotto, alongside the likes of pork belly, steaks, ox cheeks, burgers and a variety of fish dishes. There's a fresh modern touch to most dishes, but chef Ana-Marija Bujić knows her

★**Villa Klaić** B&B $$
(☑091 73 84 673; www.villaklaic-dubrovnik.com; Šumetska 9; s/d from €70/90; P❋🛜🖫) Just off the main coast road, high above the old town, this outstanding guesthouse offers comfortable modern rooms and wonderful hospitality courtesy of the owner, Milo Klaić. Extras include a small swimming pool, continental breakfast, free pick-ups and free beer!

★**Hotel Kompas** HOTEL $$$
(☑020-299 000; www.adriaticluxuryhotels.com; Kardinala Stepinca 21; r/ste from €210/542; P❋🛜🖫) Right by the beach at Lapad, this

way around traditional Dalmatian cuisine too – she's got her own cookbook to prove it.

### ★ Nishta                    VEGETARIAN $$

(☑ 020-322 088; www.nishtarestaurant.com; Prijeko 29; mains 77-85KN; ☺ 11.30am-11.30pm; 🛜 🍴) The popularity of this tiny old-town eatery (expect to queue) is testament not just to the paucity of options for vegetarians and vegans in Croatia but to the excellent, imaginative food produced within. Alongside the expected curries, pastas and vegie burgers, the menu delivers more unusual options such as delicious eggplant tartare, 'tempehritos' and pasta-free zucchini 'spaghetti'.

### ★ Shizuku                     JAPANESE $$

(☑ 020-311 493; www.facebook.com/Shizuku-Dubrovnik; Kneza Domagoja 1f; mains 65-99KN; ☺ noon-midnight Tue-Sun; 🛜) Tucked away in a residential area between the harbour and Lapad Bay, this charming little restaurant has an appealing front terrace and an interior decorated with silky draperies, paper lampshades and colourful umbrellas. The Japanese owners will be in the kitchen, preparing authentic sushi, sashimi, udon and gyoza. Wash it all down with Japanese beer or sake.

### ★ Restaurant 360°      MODERN EUROPEAN $$$

(☑ 020-322 222; www.360dubrovnik.com; Sv Dominika bb; mains 240-290KN, 5-course degustation 780KN; ☺ 6.30-11pm) Dubrovnik's glitziest restaurant offers fine dining at its finest, with flavoursome, beautifully presented, creative cuisine and slick, professional service. The setting is unrivalled, on top of the city walls with tables positioned so you can peer through the battlements over the harbour.

### ★ Amfora                 INTERNATIONAL $$$

(☑ 020-419 419; www.amforadubrovnik.com; Obala Stjepana Radića 26; mains 145-185KN; ☺ noon-4pm & 7-11pm) From the street, Amfora looks like just another local cafe-bar, but the real magic happens at the six-table restaurant at the rear. Dalmatian favourites such as *pašticada* (stew with gnocchi) and black risotto sit alongside fusion dishes such as swordfish sashimi, veal kofte, and miso fish soup.

## 🍷 Drinking & Nightlife

### ★ Bard                              BAR

(off Ilije Sarake; ☺ 9am-3am) The more upmarket and slick of two cliff bars pressed up against the seaward side of the city walls, this one is lower on the rocks and has a shaded terrace where you can lose a day quite happily, mesmerised by the Adriatic vistas. At night the surrounding stone is lit in ever-changing colours.

### Cave Bar More                      BAR

(www.hotel-more.hr; Hotel More, Šetalište Nika i Meda Pucića; ☺ 10am-midnight) This little beach bar serves coffee, snacks and cocktails to bathers reclining by the dazzlingly clear waters of Lapad Bay, but that's not the half of it – the main bar is set in an actual cave. Cool off beneath the stalactites in the side chamber, where a glass floor exposes a water-filled cavern.

### D'vino                         WINE BAR

(☑ 020-321 130; www.dvino.net; Palmotićeva 4a; ☺ 10am-late; 🛜) If you're interested in sampling top-notch Croatian wine, this upmarket little bar is the place to go. As well as a large and varied wine list, it offers themed tasting flights (three wines for 50KN)

---

## ESSENTIAL FOOD & DRINK

Croatia's cuisine reflects the varied cultures that have influenced the country over the course of its history. You'll find a sharp divide between the Italian-style cuisine along the coast and the flavours of Hungary, Austria and Turkey in the continental parts. Istrian cuisine has been attracting international foodies in recent years for its long gastronomic tradition, fresh ingredients and unique specialities.

Here are a few essential food and drink items to be aware of while in Croatia:

**Beer** Two popular brands of Croatian pivo (beer) are Zagreb's Ožujsko and Karlovačko from Karlovac.

**Burek** Pastry stuffed with ground meat, spinach or cheese.

**Ćevapčići** Small spicy sausages of minced beef, lamb or pork.

**Rakija** Strong Croatian grappa comes in different flavours, from plum to honey.

**Ražnjići** Small chunks of pork grilled on a skewer.

accompanied by a thorough description by the knowledgable staff.

**Buža** BAR

(off Od Margarite; ☺8am-2am) Finding this ramshackle bar on a cliff feels like a real discovery as you duck and dive around the city walls and finally see the entrance tunnel. However, Buža's no secret – it gets insanely busy, especially around sunset. Wait for a space on one of the concrete platforms, grab a cool drink in a plastic cup and enjoy the vibe and views.

## ⓘ Information

Dubrovnik's tourist board has offices in **Pile** (☑020-312 011; www.tzdubrovnik.hr; Brsalje 5; ☺8am-9pm Jun-Sep, 8am-7pm Mon-Sat, 9am-3pm Sun Oct-May), **Gruž** (☑020-417 983; www.tzdubrovnik.hr; Obala Pape Ivana Pavla II 1; ☺8am-9pm Jun-Sep, to 3pm Mon-Sat Oct-May) and **Lapad** (☑020-437 460; www.tzdubrovnik. hr; Kralja Tomislava 7; ☺8am-8pm Mon-Fri, 9am-noon & 5-8pm Sat & Sun Jun-Sep) that dispense maps, information and advice.

**Dubrovnik General Hospital** (Opća bolnica Dubrovnik; ☑020-431 777; www.bolnica-du. hr; Dr Roka Mišetića 2; ☺emergency department 24hr) On the southern edge of the Lapad peninsula.

**Travel Corner** (☑020-492 313; Obala Stjepana Radića 40; internet per hr 25KN, left luggage 2hr 10KN then per hr 4KN, per day 40KN; ☺9am-8pm Mon-Sat, 9am-4.30pm Sun) This handy one-stop shop has a left-luggage service and internet terminals, dispenses tourist information, books excursions and sells Kapetan Luka ferry tickets.

## ⓘ Getting There & Away

### AIR

Daily flights to/from Zagreb and Split are operated by **Croatia Airlines** (☑01-66 76 555; www. croatiaairlines.hr). Dubrovnik airport is served by over a dozen other airlines from across Europe.

### BOAT

The **ferry terminal** (Obala Pape Ivana Pavla II 1) is in Gruž, 3km northwest of the old town. Ferries for **Lokrum and Cavtat** depart from the Old Harbour.

From July to mid-September, there's a daily **Jadrolinija** (☑020-418 000; www.jadrolinija. hr; Obala Stjepana Radića 40) catamaran to Korčula (120KN, 2¼ hours) and Hvar (190KN, four hours).

From June to September **Kapetan Luka** (Krilo; ☑021-872 877; www.krilo.hr) has a daily fast boat to/from Korčula (120KN, 1¾ hours), Hvar (190KN, three hours) and Split (190KN, 4¼ hours), dropping to four times per week in May and three per week in October.

### BUS

Buses out of Dubrovnik **bus station** (☑060 305 070; Obala Pape Ivana Pavla II 44a; ☎) can be crowded, so book tickets ahead in summer. All bus schedules are detailed at www.libertas-dubrovnik.hr.

## ⓘ Getting Around

**Dubrovnik Airport** (DBV, Zračna luka Dubrovnik; ☑020-773 100; www.airport-dubrovnik.hr) is in Čilipi, 19km southeast of Dubrovnik. Atlas runs the airport bus service (40KN, 30 minutes), timed around flights. Buses to Dubrovnik stop at the Pile Gate and the bus station; buses to the airport pick up from the bus station and from the bus stop near the cable car.

A taxi to the old town costs up to 280KN.

# SURVIVAL GUIDE

## ⓘ Directory A-Z

### ACCOMMODATION

Croatia is traditionally seen as a summer destination and good places book out well in advance in July and August. It's also very busy in June and September.

**Hotels** These range from massive beach resorts to boutique establishments.

**Apartments** Privately owned holiday units are a staple of the local accommodation scene, especially for families.

**Guesthouses** Usually family-run establishments where spare rooms are rented at a bargain price – sometimes with their own bathrooms, sometimes not.

**Hostels** Mainly in the bigger cities and more popular beach destinations, with dorms and sometimes private rooms, too.

**Campgrounds** Tent and caravan sites, often fairly basic.

### SLEEPING PRICE RANGES

The following price ranges refer to a double room with a bathroom in July and August.

€ less than 450KN

€€ 450–800KN

€€€ more than 800KN

## Registration & Sojourn Tax

Accommodation providers will handle travellers' registration with the local police, as required by Croatian authorities. To do this, they will ask for your passport when you check in. Normally they will note the details they require and photocopy or scan the relevant page, and then hand your passport straight back.

Part of the reason for this process is so that the correct 'sojourn tax' can be paid. This is a small amount (usually less than 10KN) that is charged for every day you stay in Croatia, no matter what type of accommodation you're staying in. It's quite normal for this to be additional to the room rate you've been quoted.

### OPENING HOURS

Opening hours vary throughout the year. We've provided high-season opening hours; hours generally decrease in the shoulder and low seasons.

**Banks** 8am or 9am to 8pm weekdays and 7am–1pm or 8am–2pm Saturdays.

**Cafes and Bars** 8am or 9am to midnight.

**Offices** 8am–4pm or 8.30am–4.30pm weekdays.

**Post Offices** 7am–8pm weekdays and 7am–1pm Saturdays. Longer hours in coastal towns in summer.

**Restaurants** Noon to 11pm or midnight. Often closed Sundays outside peak season.

**Shops** 8am–8pm weekdays, 8am to 2pm or 3pm Saturdays. Some take a 2pm–5pm break. Shopping malls have longer hours.

### PUBLIC HOLIDAYS

Croats take their holidays very seriously. Shops and museums are shut and boat services are reduced. On religious holidays, the churches are full; it can be a good time to check out the artwork in a church that is usually closed.

---

### COUNTRY FACTS

**Area** 56,538 sq km

**Capital** Zagreb

**Country Code** ☑ 385

**Currency** Kuna (KN)

**Emergency** Ambulance ☑ 94, police ☑ 92

**Language** Croatian

**Money** ATMs available; credit cards accepted in most hotels and many restaurants.

**Population** 4.3 million

**Visas** Not required for most nationalities for stays of up to 90 days.

---

### EATING PRICE RANGES

The following price ranges refer to a main course.

€ less than 70KN

€€ 70–120KN

€€€ more than 120KN

---

**New Year's Day** 1 January

**Epiphany** 6 January

**Easter Sunday & Monday** March/April

**Labour Day** 1 May

**Corpus Christi** 60 days after Easter

**Day of Antifascist Resistance** 22 June

**Statehood Day** 25 June

**Homeland Thanksgiving Day** 5 August

**Feast of the Assumption** 15 August

**Independence Day** 8 October

**All Saints' Day** 1 November

**Christmas** 25 & 26 December

### TELEPHONE
#### Mobile Phones

Users with unlocked phones can buy a local SIM card, which are easy to find. Otherwise, you may be charged roaming rates.

#### Phone Codes

➡ To call Croatia from abroad, dial your international access code, then ☑ 385 (the country code for Croatia), then the area code (without the initial 0) and the local number.

➡ To call from region to region within Croatia, start with the area code (with the initial 0); drop it when dialling within the same code.

➡ Phone numbers with the prefix 060 are either free or charged at a premium rate, so watch out for the small print. Phone numbers that begin with 09 are mobile phone numbers.

### TOURIST INFORMATION

The Croatian National Tourist Board (www.croatia.hr) is a good source of info.

### VISAS

Citizens of many countries, including EU member states, Australia, Brazil, Canada, Israel, Japan, New Zealand, Singapore and the USA do not need a visa for stays of up to 90 days within a 180-day period. (Note that this means that leaving the country just to get a stamp and return isn't a legal option.)

Other nationalities can check whether they need a visa and download application forms on the website of the Croatian Ministry for Foreign & European Affairs (www.mvep.hr).

## ❶ Getting There & Away

### AIR

There are direct flights to Croatia from a variety of European cities year-round, with dozens of seasonal routes and charters added in summer

### LAND

Croatia has border crossings with Slovenia, Hungary, Serbia, Bosnia and Hercegovina, and Montenegro.

Direct bus connections link Croatia to all of its neighbours and to as far afield as Norway. Useful websites include www.eurolines.com, www.buscroatia.com, www.getbybus.com and www.vollo.net.

Zagreb is Croatia's main train hub, with connections to Austria, Bosnia, Germany, Hungary, Serbia, Slovenia and Switzerland. Useful websites include www.raileurope.com and www.eurail.com.

### SEA

Regular ferries connect Croatia with Italy. Split is the main hub.

## ❶ Getting Around

Transport in Croatia is reasonably priced, quick and generally efficient.

**Air** A surprisingly extensive schedule of domestic flights, especially in summer.

**Boat** Extensive network of car ferries and faster catamarans all along the coast and the islands.

**Bus** Reasonably priced, with extensive coverage of the country and frequent departures.

**Car** Useful for travelling at your own pace or for visiting regions with minimal public transport. Cars can be hired in every city or larger town. Drive on the right.

**Train** Less frequent and much slower than buses, with a limited network.

# Czech Republic

## Includes ➡

## Best Places to Eat

➡ U Kroka (p144)

➡ Field (p144)

➡ Buffalo Burger Bar (p149)

➡ Pavillon (p155)

## Best Places to Stay

➡ Hotel 16 (p143)

➡ Savic Hotel (p143)

➡ Hotel garni Myší Díra (p152)

➡ Hostel Mitte (p154)

## Why Go?

Since the fall of communism in 1989 and the opening up of Central and Eastern Europe, Prague has evolved into one of Europe's most popular travel destinations. The city offers an intact medieval core that transports you back – especially when strolling the hidden streets of the Old Town – some 600 years. The 14th-century Charles Bridge, traversing two historic neighbourhoods across a slow-moving river, is one of the continent's most beautiful sights.

The city is not just about history. It's a vital urban centre with a rich array of cultural offerings. Outside the capital, in the provinces of Bohemia and Moravia, castles and palaces abound – including the audacious hilltop chateau at Český Krumlov – which illuminate the stories of powerful dynasties whose influence was felt throughout Europe. Olomouc, the historic capital of Moravia to the east, boasts much of the beauty of Prague without the crowds.

## When to Go
### Prague

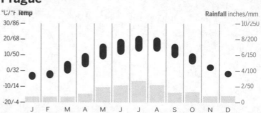

**May** Prague Spring Festival makes this the capital's most popular month.

**Sep** Autumn brings lovely strolling weather to West Bohemia's spa towns.

**Dec** *Svařák* (mulled wine) and music at Christmas markets in towns across the country.

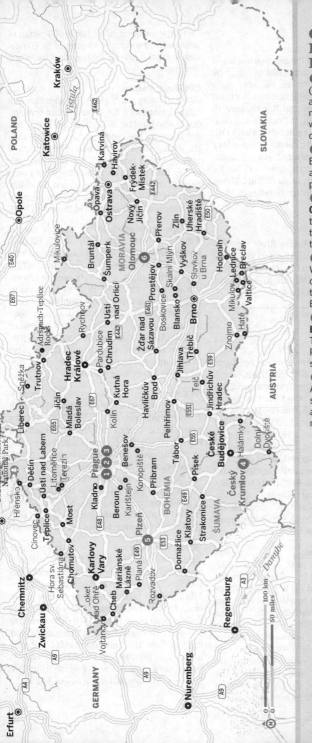

# Czech Republic Highlights

**1 Charles Bridge** (p138) Strolling across in the early morning or late evening when the crowds thin out.

**2 U Kroka** (p144) Enjoying an evening in an old-school Czech pub.

**3 Astronomical Clock** (p137) Joining the appreciative throngs at the top of the hour.

**4 Český Krumlov** Walking the streets of one of the prettiest towns in Central Europe.

**5 Pilsner Urquell Brewery** (p149) Touring this brewery in Plzeň to see where it all started.

**6 Olomouc** (p156) Ambling through this stately town, the most amazing place you've never heard of.

# PRAGUE

POP 1.3 MILLION

It's the perfect irony of Prague: you are lured here by the past, but compelled to linger by the present and the future. Fill your days with its illustrious artistic and architectural heritage – from Gothic and Renaissance to art nouveau and cubist. If Prague's seasonal legions of tourists wear you down, that's OK. Just drink a glass of the country's legendary lager, relax and rest reassured that quiet moments still exist: a private dawn on Charles Bridge, the glorious cityscape of Staré Město or getting lost in the intimate lanes of Malá Strana.

## ◉ Sights

Prague nestles on the Vltava River, separating **Hradčany** (the Castle district) and **Malá Strana** (Lesser Quarter) on the west bank, from **Staré Město** (Old Town) and **Nové Město** (New Town) on the east.

### ◉ Hradčany

#### ★ Prague Castle     CASTLE
(Pražský hrad; Map p137; ☑224 372 423; www.hrad.cz; Hradčanské náměstí 1; grounds free, sights adult/concession Tour A & C 350/175Kc, Tour B 250/125Kc; ⊙grounds 6am-11pm year-round, gardens 10am-6pm Apr-Oct, closed Nov-Mar, historic bldg 9am-5pm Apr-Oct, to 4pm Nov-Mar; Ⓜ Malostranská, 🚊22) Prague Castle – Pražský hrad, or just *hrad* to Czechs – is Prague's most popular attraction. Looming above the Vltava's left bank, its serried ranks of spires, towers and palaces dominate the city centre like a fairy-tale fortress. Within its walls lies a varied and fascinating collection of historic buildings, museums and galleries that are home to some of the Czech Republic's greatest artistic and cultural treasures.

#### ★ St Vitus Cathedral     CHURCH
(Katedrála sv Víta; Map p137; ☑257 531 622; www.katedralasvatehovita.cz; Third Courtyard, Prague Castle; admission incl with Prague Castle Tour A & B tickets; ⊙9am-5pm Mon-Sat, noon-5pm Sun Apr-Oct, to 4pm Nov-Mar; 🚊22) Built over a time span of almost 600 years, St Vitus is one of the most richly endowed cathedrals in central Europe. It is pivotal to the religious and cultural life of the Czech Republic, housing treasures that range from the 14th-century mosaic of the Last Judgement and the tombs of St Wenceslas and Charles IV, to the baroque silver tomb of St John of Nepomuck, the ornate Chapel of St Wenceslas, and art nouveau stained glass by Alfons Mucha.

#### Old Royal Palace     PALACE
(Starý královský palác; Map p137; admission with Prague Castle tour A & B tickets; ⊙9am-5pm Apr-Oct, to 4pm Nov-Mar; 🚊22) The Old Royal Palace is one of the oldest parts of Prague Castle, dating from 1135. It was originally used only by Czech princesses, but from the 13th to the 16th centuries it was the king's own palace. At its heart is the grand Vladislav Hall and the Bohemian Chancellery, scene of the famous Defenestration of Prague in 1618.

#### Lobkowicz Palace     MUSEUM
(Lobkovický palác; Map p137; ☑233 312 925; www.lobkowicz.com; Jiřská 3; adult/concession/family 275/200/690Kč; ⊙10am-6pm; 🚊22) This 16th-century palace houses a private museum known as the Princely Collections, which includes priceless paintings, furniture and musical memorabilia. Your tour includes an audio guide dictated by owner William Lobkowicz and his family – this personal connection really brings the displays to life, and makes the palace one of the castle's most interesting attractions.

#### ★ Loreta     CHURCH
(☑220 516 740; www.loreta.cz; Loretánské náměstí 7; adult/child/family 150/80/310Kč, photography permit 100Kč; ⊙9am-5pm Apr-Oct, 9.30am-4pm Nov-Mar; 🚊22) The Loreta is a baroque place of pilgrimage founded by Benigna Kateřina Lobkowicz in 1626, designed as a replica of the supposed Santa Casa (Sacred House; the home of the Virgin Mary) in the Holy Land. Legend says that the original Santa Casa was carried by angels to the Italian town of Loreto as the Turks were advancing on Nazareth.

#### ★ Strahov Library     HISTORIC BUILDING
(Strahovská knihovna; ☑233 107 718; www.strahovskyklaster.cz; Strahovské nádvoří 1; adult/child 100/50Kč; ⊙9am-noon & 1-5pm; 🚊22) Strahov Library is the largest monastic library in the country, with two magnificent baroque halls dating from the 17th and 18th centuries. You can peek through the doors but, sadly, you can't go into the halls themselves – it was found that fluctuations in humidity caused by visitors' breath was endangering the frescoes. There's also a display of historical curiosities.

# Prague Castle

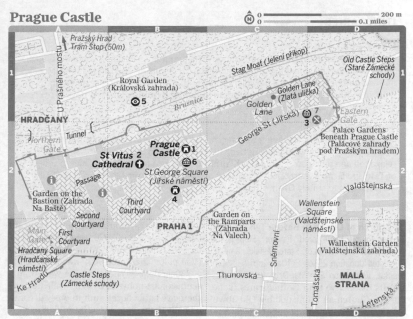

## ⊙ Staré Město

The Old Town (Staré Město) is the city's oldest quarter and home to its main market, **Old Town Square** (Staroměstské náměstí; Map p140; Ⓜ Staroměstská), often simply called Staromák. The square has functioned as the centre of the Old Town since the 10th century.

★**Old Town Hall** — HISTORIC BUILDING
(Staroměstská radnice; Map p140; ☑236 002 629; www.staromestskaradnicepraha.cz; Staroměstské náměstí 1; guided tour adult/child 100/70Kč, incl tower 180Kč; ☺11am-6pm Mon, 9am-6pm Tue-Sun; Ⓜ Staroměstská) Prague's Old Town Hall, founded in 1338, is a hotchpotch of medieval buildings acquired piecemeal over the centuries, presided over by a tall Gothic tower with a splendid Astronomical Clock. As well as housing the Old Town's main tourist information office, the town hall has several historic attractions, and hosts art exhibitions on the ground floor and the 2nd floor.

★**Astronomical Clock** — HISTORIC SITE
(Map p140; Staroměstské náměstí; ☺chimes on the hour 9am-9pm; Ⓜ Staroměstská) Every hour, on the hour, crowds gather beneath the Old

## Prague Castle

### ⊙ Top Sights
1 Prague Castle........................................B2
2 St Vitus Cathedral..............................B2

### ⊙ Sights
3 Lobkowicz Palace...............................C1
4 Old Royal Palace.................................B2
5 Royal Garden......................................B1
6 Story of Prague Castle.......................B2

### ⊗ Eating
7 Lobkowicz Palace Café......................D1

**Town Hall Tower** (Věž radnice; Map p140; ☑236 002 629; www.staromestskaradnicepraha.cz; Staroměstské náměstí 1; adult/child 130/80Kč, incl Old Town Hall tour 180Kč; ☺11am-10pm Mon, 9am-10pm Tue-Sun; Ⓜ Staroměstská) to watch the Astronomical Clock in action. Despite a slightly underwhelming performance that takes only 45 seconds, the clock is one of Europe's best-known tourist attractions, and a 'must-see' for visitors to Prague. After all, it's historic, photogenic and – if you take time to study it – rich in intriguing symbolism. The clock is scheduled to be out of action from spring 2017 to summer 2018 while the clock tower undergoes renovations.

## ITINERARIES

### One Week

Experience **Prague's** exciting combination of its tumultuous past and energetic present. Top experiences include the grandeur of Prague Castle, Josefov's Prague Jewish Museum, and getting lost amid the bewildering labyrinth of the Old Town. Take an essential day trip to **Karlštejn**, and then head south to **Český Krumlov** for a few days of riverside R&R.

### Two Weeks

Begin in **Prague** before heading west for the spa scene at **Karlovy Vary**. Balance the virtue and vice ledger with a few Bohemian brews in **Plzeň** before heading south for relaxation and rigour around **Český Krumlov**. Head east to the Renaissance grandeur of **Telč** and **Brno's** cosmopolitan galleries and museums. From Moravia's largest city, it's just a skip to stately **Olomouc**.

★**Church of Our Lady Before Týn**  CHURCH
(Kostel Panny Marie před Týnem; Map p140; ☑ 222 318 186; www.tyn.cz; Staroměstské náměstí; suggested donation 25Kč; ⊙ 10am-1pm & 3-5pm Tue-Sat, 10am-noon Sun Mar-Dec; Ⓜ Staroměstská) Its distinctive twin Gothic spires make the Týn Church an unmistakable Old Town landmark. Like something out of a 15th-century – and probably slightly cruel – fairy tale, they loom over the Old Town Square, decorated with a golden image of the Virgin Mary made in the 1620s from the melted-down Hussite chalice that previously adorned the church.

★**Church of St James**  CHURCH
(Kostel sv Jakuba; Map p140; http://praha.minorite.cz; Malá Štupartská 6; ⊙ 9.30am-noon & 2-4pm Tue-Sat, 2-4pm Sun; Ⓜ Náměstí Republiky) **FREE** The great Gothic mass of the Church of St James began in the 14th century as a Minorite monastery church, and was given a beautiful baroque facelift in the early 18th century. But in the midst of the gilt and stucco is a grisly memento: on the inside of the western wall (look up to the right as you enter) hangs a shrivelled human arm.

★**Municipal House**  HISTORIC BUILDING
(Obecní dům; Map p140; ☑ 222 002 101; www.obecnidum.cz; náměstí Republiky 5; guided tour adult/concession/child under 10yr 290/240Kč/free; ⊙ public areas 7.30am-11pm, information centre 10am-8pm; 🤚; Ⓜ Náměstí Republiky, 🚊 6, 8, 15, 26) Restored in the 1990s after decades of neglect, Prague's most exuberantly art-nouveau building is a labour of love, every detail of its design and decoration carefully considered, every painting and sculpture

loaded with symbolism. The **restaurant** (Map p140; ☑ 222 002 770; www.francouzskarestaurace.cz; mains 695Kč; ⊙ noon-11pm) and **cafe** (Map p140; ☑ 222 002 763; www.kavarnaod.cz; ⊙ 7.30am-11pm; 🤚) here are like walk-in museums of art-nouveau design, while upstairs there are half a dozen sumptuously decorated halls that you can visit by guided tour.

★**Apple Museum**  MUSEUM
(Map p140; ☑ 774 414 775; www.applemuseum.com; Husova 21; adult/child 300/140Kč; ⊙ 10am-10pm; Ⓜ Staroměstská) This shrine to all things Apple claims to be the world's biggest collection of Apple products, with at least one of everything made by the company between 1976 and 2012. Sleek white galleries showcase row upon row of beautifully displayed computers, laptops, iPods and iPhones like sacred reliquaries; highlights include the earliest Apple I and Apple II computers, an iPod 'family tree', and Steve Jobs' business cards.

## ⊙ Malá Strana

Across the river from the Old Town are the baroque backstreets of Malá Strana (the Lesser Quarter), built in the 17th and 18th centuries by victorious Catholic clerics and noblemen on the foundations of their predecessors' Renaissance palaces.

★**Charles Bridge**  BRIDGE
(Karlův most; Map p140; ⊙ 24hr; 🚊 2, 17, 18 to Karlovy lázně, 12, 15, 20, 22 to Malostranské náměstí) Strolling across Charles Bridge is everybody's favourite Prague activity. However, by 9am it's a 500m-long fairground, with an

army of tourists squeezing through a gauntlet of hawkers and buskers beneath the impassive gaze of the baroque statues that line the parapets. If you want to experience the bridge at its most atmospheric, try to visit it at dawn.

### ★ St Nicholas Church                      CHURCH
(Kostel sv Mikuláše; ☑ 257 534 215; www.stnicholas. cz; Malostranské náměstí 38; adult/child 70/50Kč; ☺ 9am-5pm Mar-Oct, to 4pm Nov-Feb; 🚊 12, 15, 20, 22) Malá Strana is dominated by the huge green cupola of St Nicholas Church, one of Central Europe's finest baroque buildings. (Don't confuse it with the other Church of St Nicholas on Old Town Square.) On the ceiling, Johann Kracker's 1770 *Apotheosis of St Nicholas* is Europe's largest fresco (clever trompe l'oeil technique has made the painting merge almost seamlessly with the architecture).

### ★ Museum of the
### Infant Jesus of Prague              MUSEUM
(Muzeum Pražského Jezulátka; ☑ 257 533 646; www.pragjesu.cz; Karmelitská 9; ☺ church 8.30am-7pm Mon-Sat, to 8pm Sun, museum 9.30am-5.30pm Mon-Sat, 1-6pm Sun, closed 1 Jan, 25 & 26 Dec & Easter Mon; 🚊 12, 15, 20, 22) **FREE** The Church of Our Lady Victorious (kostel Panny Marie Vítězné), built in 1613, has on its central altar a 47cm-tall waxwork figure of the baby Jesus, brought from Spain in 1628 and known as the Infant Jesus of Prague (Pražské Jezulátko). At the back of the church is a museum, displaying a selection of the frocks used to dress the Infant.

### ★ John Lennon Wall             HISTORIC SITE
(Velkopřevorské náměstí; 🚊 12, 15, 20, 22) After his murder on 8 December 1980, John Lennon became a pacifist hero for many young Czechs. An image of Lennon was painted on a wall in a secluded square opposite the French Embassy (there is a niche on the wall that looks like a tombstone), along with political graffiti and Beatles lyrics.

### ★ Petřín                                     HILL
(🚊 Nebozízek, Petřín) This 318m-high hill is one of Prague's largest green spaces. It's great for quiet, tree-shaded walks and fine views over the 'City of a Hundred Spires'. Most of the attractions atop the hill, including a lookout tower and mirror maze, were built in the late 19th to early 20th century, lending the place an old-fashioned, fun-fair atmosphere.

## ⊙ Nové Město

Nové Město (New Town) surrounds the Old Town on all sides and was originally laid out in the 14th century. Its main public area is **Wenceslas Square** (Václavské náměstí; Map p140; Ⓜ Můstek, Muzeum), lined with shops, banks and restaurants, and dotted by a **statue of St Wenceslas** (sv Václav; Map p140; Václavské náměstí; Ⓜ Muzeum) on horseback. The **National Museum** (Národní muzeum; Map p140; ☑ 224 497 111; www.nm.cz; Václavské náměstí 68; Ⓜ Muzeum), which dominates the top of the square, is closed for long-term renovation.

### ★ Mucha Museum                        GALLERY
(Muchovo muzeum; Map p140; ☑ 221 451 333; www.mucha.cz; Panská 7; adult/child 240/160Kč; ☺ 10am-6pm; 🚊 3, 5, 6, 9, 14, 24) This fascinating (and busy) museum features the sensuous art-nouveau posters, paintings and decorative panels of Alfons Mucha (1860–1939), as well as many sketches, photographs and other memorabilia. The exhibits include countless artworks showing Mucha's trademark Slavic maidens with flowing hair and piercing blue eyes, bearing symbolic garlands and linden boughs.

### ★ National Memorial to the
### Heroes of the Heydrich Terror      MUSEUM
(Národní památník hrdinů Heydrichiády; ☑ 224 916 100; www.pamatnik-heydrichiady.cz; Resslova 9; ☺ 9am-5pm Tue-Sun Mar-Oct, 9am-5pm Tue-Sat Nov-Feb; Ⓜ Karlovo Náměstí) **FREE** The Church of Sts Cyril & Methodius houses a moving memorial to the seven Czech paratroopers who were involved in the assassination of Reichsprotektor Reinhard Heydrich in 1942, with an exhibit and video about Nazi persecution of the Czechs. The church appeared in the 2016 movie based on the assassination, *Anthropoid*.

### ★ Prague City Museum               MUSEUM
(Muzeum hlavního města Prahy; ☑ 224 816 773; www.muzeumprahy.cz; Na Poříčí 52; adult/child 120/50Kč; ☺ 9am-6pm Tue-Sun; Ⓜ Florenc) This excellent museum, opened in 1898, is devoted to the history of Prague from prehistoric times to the 20th century (labels are in English as well as Czech). Among the many intriguing exhibits are an astonishing scale model of Prague, and the Astronomical Clock's original 1866 calendar wheel with Josef Mánes' beautiful painted panels representing the months – that's January at the

# Central Prague

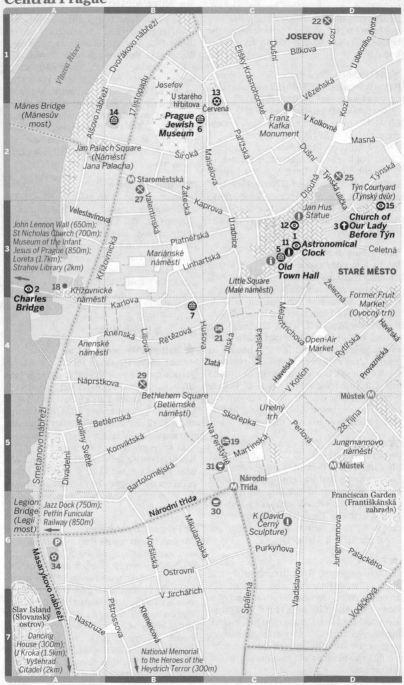

Vltava River

MáCHES Bridge
(Mánesův
most)

Dvořákovo nábřeží

Alšovo nábřeží

17. listopadu

Josefov

**22** ✕

**JOSEFOV**

Dušní

Bílkova

Kozí

U obecního dvora

Vězeňská

Kozí

U starého
hřbitova

**13** ✪
Červená

**Prague
Jewish
Museum** 🏛 **6**

Eliška Krasnohorské

Pařížská

Dušní

Franz
Kafka
Monument

V Kolkovně

Masná

**14** 🏛

Jan Palach Square
(Náměstí
Jana Palacha)

Široká

Maiselova

Týnská

Týnská ulička

Masná

T. Týnská

**25**

Týn Courtyard
(Týnský dvůr)

Ⓜ Staroměstská

**27**

Valentinská

Žatecká

Kaprova

Uradnice

Dlouhá

Jan Hus
Statue

**12** ◉

**11** 🏛 **Astronomical
Clock**

**5** 🏛
**Old
Town Hall**

**15** ◉

**Church of
3** ⛪**Our Lady
Before Týn**

Celetná

Veleslavínova

John Lennon Wall (650m);
St Nicholas Church (700m);
Museum of the Infant
Jesus of Prague (850m);
Loreta (1.7km);
Strahov Library (2km)

Platnéřská

Křižovnická

Mariánské
náměstí

Linhartská

Little Square
(Malé náměstí)

**STARÉ MĚSTO**

Železná

Former Fruit
Market
(Ovocný trh)

◉**2**
**Charles
Bridge**

**18** ●

Křížovnické
náměstí

Karlova

**7** 🏛

Husova

Anenská

Liliová

Řetězová

Jilská

Michalská

Melantrichova

Open-Air
Market

Havelská

Havířská

Rytířská

Provaznická

Anenské
náměstí

**21** 🍴

Zlatá

V Kotcích

Smetanovo nábřeží

Náprstkova

**29** ✕

Bethlehem Square
(Betlémské
náměstí)

Skořepka

Uhelný
trh

Perlová

Můstek Ⓜ

28. října

Karolíny Světlé

Betlémská

Konviktská

Na Perštýně

Martinská

Jungmannovo
náměstí

Divadelní

Bartolomějská

**19** 🍴

**31** 🍴

**Národní
Třída**

Ⓜ Můstek

Legion
Bridge
(Legii
most)

Jazz Dock (750m);
Petřín Funicular
Railway (850m)

**Národní třída**

**30** 🎭

Mikulandská

K (David
Černý
Sculpture) ❶

Franciscan Garden
(Františkánská
zahrada)

Palackého

Jungmannova

Masarykovo nábřeží

Ⓟ

**34** ✪

Voršilská

Ostrovní

Purkyňova

Vladislavova

Vodičkova

Slav Island
(Slovanský
ostrov)

Dancing
House (300m);
U Kroka (1.5km);
Vyšehrad
Citadel (2km)

Nástuze

Pštrossova

Křemencová

V Jirchářích

Spálená

National Memorial
to the Heroes of the
Heydrich Terror (300m)

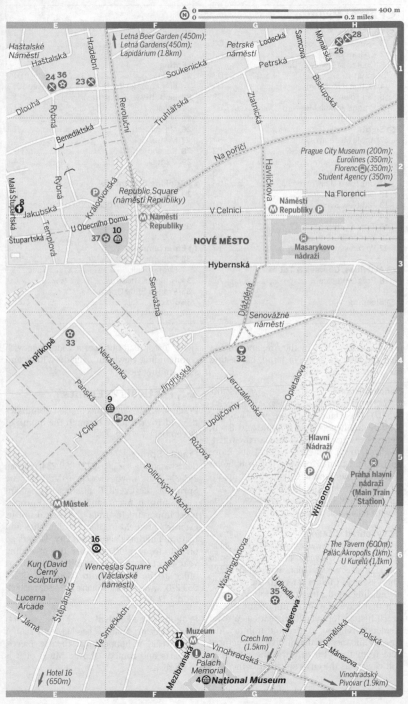

## Central Prague

top, toasting his toes by the fire, and August near the bottom, sickle in hand, harvesting the corn.

**Dancing House** ARCHITECTURE
(Tančící dům; http://tadu.cz; Rašínovo nábřeží 80; 🚊5, 17) The Dancing House was built in 1996 by architects Vlado Milunić and Frank Gehry. The curved lines of the narrow-waisted glass tower clutched against its more upright and formal partner led to it being christened the 'Fred & Ginger' building, after legendary dancing duo Fred Astaire and Ginger Rogers. It's surprising how well it fits in with its ageing neighbours.

**★ Vyšehrad Citadel** FORTRESS
(🚽261 225 304; www.praha-vysehrad.cz; information centre at V pevnosti 159/5b; admission to grounds free; ⊙grounds 24hr; Ⓜ Vyšehrad) **FREE** The Vyšehrad Citadel refers to the complex of buildings and structures atop Vyšehrad Hill that have played an important role in Czech history for over 1000 years as a royal residence, religious centre and military fortress. While most of the surviving structures date from the 18th century, the citadel is still viewed as the city's spiritual home. The

sights are spread out over a wide area, with commanding views out over the Vltava and surrounding city.

## ★ Festivals & Events

Prague's pretty Christmas market dominates the Old Town Square through the month of December.

**Prague Spring** MUSIC
(Pražské jaro; 🚽 box office 227 059 234, program 257 314 040; www.festival.cz; ⊙May) Prague Spring is the Czech Republic's biggest annual cultural event and one of Europe's most important festivals of classical music. Concerts are held in theatres, churches and historic buildings across the city. Tickets go on sale from mid-December the preceding year. Buy tickets online or at the festival box office at the **Rudolfinum** (Map p140; 🚽227 059 270; www.ceskafilharmonie.cz; Alšovo nábřeží 12; 🚊2, 17, 18).

**Prague Fringe Festival** ART
(www.praguefringe.com; ⊙late May/early Jun) A wild week of happenings, theatre pieces, concerts and comedy shows. Much of it is in English.

# 🛏 Sleeping

**⭐ Czech Inn** HOSTEL, HOTEL €
(☑ reception 267 267 612, reservations 267 267 600; www.czech-inn.com; Francouzská 76, Vršovice; dm 280-450Kč, s/d 1200/1600Kč, apt from 3000Kč; 🅿 🖾 @ 🛜; 🚊 4, 22) The Czech Inn calls itself a hostel, but the boutique label wouldn't be out of place. Everything seems sculpted by an industrial designer, from the iron beds to the brushed-steel flooring and minimalist square sinks. It offers a variety of accommodation, from standard hostel dorm rooms to good-value doubles (with or without private bathroom) and apartments.

**Ahoy! Hostel** HOSTEL €
(Map p140; ☑ 773 004 003; www.ahoyhostel. com; Na Perštýně 10; dm/tw 460/1350Kč; @ 🛜; Ⓜ Národní Třída, 🚊 2, 9, 18, 22) No big signs or branding here, just an inconspicuous card by the blue door at No 10. But inside is a very pleasant, welcoming and peaceful hostel (definitely not for the party crowd), with eager-to-please staff, some self-consciously 'arty' decoration, clean and comfortable six- or eight-bed dorms, and a couple of private twin rooms. Ideal location, too.

**⭐ Hotel 16** HOTEL €€
(☑ 224 920 636; www.hotel16.cz; Kateřinská 16; s/d from 2400/3500Kč; 🖾 🖾 @ 🛜 🖾; 🚊 4, 6, 10, 16, 22) Hotel 16 is a friendly, family-run little place with just 14 rooms, tucked away in a very quiet corner of town where you're more likely to hear birdsong than traffic. The rooms vary in size and are simply but smartly furnished; the best, at the back, have views onto the peaceful terraced garden. Staff are superb, and can't do enough to help.

**⭐ Fusion Hotel** BOUTIQUE HOTEL €€
(Map p140; ☑ 226 222 800; www.fusionhotels. com; Panská 9; r from 2650Kč; @ 🛜; 🚊 3, 5, 6, 9, 14, 24) Fusion has style in abundance, from the revolving bar and spaceship-like UV corridor lighting, to the individually decorated bedrooms that resemble miniature modern-art galleries. As well as doubles, triples and family rooms, there are 'theme rooms' decorated in vintage or romantic style, with works by young Czech artists; one even offers a communal bed for up to six people!

**⭐ Savic Hotel** HOTEL €€€
(Map p140; ☑ 224 248 555; www.savic.eu; Jilská 7; r from 4800Kč; 🖾 @ 🛜; Ⓜ Můstek) From the complimentary glass of wine when you arrive to the comfy king-size beds, the Savic certainly knows how to make you feel pampered. Housed in the former monastery of St Giles, the hotel is bursting with character and full of delightful period details including old stone fireplaces, beautiful painted timber ceilings and fragments of frescoes.

---

## PRAGUE'S JEWISH MUSEUM

The **Prague Jewish Museum** (Židovské muzeum Praha; Map p140; ☑ 222 749 211; www. jewishmuseum.cz; Reservation Centre, Maiselova 15; ordinary ticket adult/child 300/200Kč, combined ticket incl entry to Old-New Synagogue 480/320Kč; ☉ 9am-6pm Sun-Fri Apr-Oct, to 4.30pm Nov-Mar; Ⓜ Staroměstská), a collection of four synagogues – the **Maisel**, **Pinkas**, **Spanish** and **Klaus** – the former **Ceremonial Hall** and the **Old Jewish Cemetery**, is one of the city's treasures. The monuments are clustered together in Josefov, a small corner of the Old Town that was home to Prague's Jews for some 800 years before an urban renewal project at the start of the 20th century and the Nazi occupation during WWII brought this all to an end.

The monuments cannot be visited separately but require a combined-entry ticket good for all of the sights and available at ticket windows throughout Josefov. A fifth synagogue, the **Old-New Synagogue** (Staronová synagóga; Map p140; www.jewishmuseum.cz; Červená 2; adult/child 200/140Kč; ☉ 9am-6pm Sun-Fri Apr-Oct, to 4.30pm Nov-Mar; 🚊 17), is still used for religious services, and requires a separate ticket or additional fee.

The museum was first established in 1906 to preserve objects from synagogues that were demolished during the slum clearance at the turn of the 20th century. The collection grew richer as a result of one of the most grotesquely ironic acts of WWII. During the Nazi occupation, the Germans took over management of the museum in order to create a 'museum of an extinct race'. To that end, they brought in objects from destroyed Jewish communities throughout Bohemia and Moravia.

## ✖ Eating

### Lokál
CZECH €

(Map p140; ☑ 222 316 265; http://lokal-dlouha.ambi.cz; Dlouhá 33; mains 115-235Kč; ⊙ 11am-1am Mon-Sat, noon-midnight Sun; 🛜; 🚌 6, 8, 15, 26) Who'd have thought it possible? A classic Czech beer hall (albeit with slick modern styling); excellent *tankové pivo* (tanked Pilsner Urquell); a daily-changing menu of traditional Bohemian dishes; and smiling, efficient, friendly service! Top restaurant chain Ambiente has turned its hand to Czech cuisine, and the result has been so successful that the place is always busy, mostly with locals.

### ★ Mistral Café
BISTRO €

(Map p140; ☑ 222 317 737; www.mistralcafe.cz; Valentinská 11; mains 130-250Kč; ⊙ 10am-11pm; 🛜🚼; Ⓜ Staroměstská) Is this the coolest bistro in the Old Town? Pale stone, bleached birchwood and potted shrubs make for a clean, crisp, modern look, and the clientele of local students and office workers clearly appreciate the competitively priced, well-prepared food. Fish and chips in crumpled brown paper with lemon and black-pepper mayo – yum!

### Maitrea
VEGETARIAN €

(Map p140; ☑ 221 711 631; www.restaurace-maitrea.cz; Týnská ulička 6; mains 200-240Kč, weekday lunch 135Kč; ⊙ 11.30am-11.30pm Mon-Fri, noon-11.30pm Sat & Sun; 🍴📷🚼; Ⓜ Staroměstská) Maitrea (a Buddhist term meaning 'the future Buddha') is a beautifully designed space full of flowing curves and organic shapes, from the sensuous polished-oak furniture and fittings to the blossom-like lampshades. The menu is inventive and wholly vegetarian, with dishes such as Tex-Mex quesadillas, spicy goulash with wholemeal dumplings, and spaghetti with spinach, crispy shredded tofu and rosemary pesto.

### ★ Nejen Bistro
BISTRO €€

(☑ 222 960 515; www.nejenbistro.cz; Křižíkova 24, Karlín; mains 200-380Kč; ⊙ 10am-11pm; 🚌 3, 8, 24) 🍴 Nejen (Not Only) is emblematic of the new breed of restaurant that is transforming Karlín into one of Prague's hottest neighbourhoods. Its quirky interior was nominated for a slew of design awards. But just as much attention is lavished on the food, which makes the most of the kitchen's fancy Josper grill, turning out superb steaks, beef ribs and Nejen's signature Black Angus burger.

### ★ Sansho
ASIAN, FUSION €€

(Map p140; ☑ 222 317 425; www.sansho.cz; Petrská 25; lunch mains 190-245Kč, 6-course dinner 900-1200Kč; ⊙ 11.30am-2pm Tue-Fri, 6-11pm Tue-Sat, last orders 10pm; 🍴📷; 🚌 3, 8, 14, 24) 🍴 'Friendly and informal' best describes the atmosphere at this groundbreaking restaurant where British chef Paul Day champions Czech farmers by sourcing all his meat and vegetables locally. There's no menu as such – the waiter will explain what dishes are available, depending on market produce. Typical dishes include curried rabbit, pork belly with watermelon and hoisin, and 12-hour beef rendang. Reservations recommended.

### U Kroka
CZECH €€

(☑ 775 905 022; www.ukroka.cz; Vratislavova 12, Vyšehrad; mains 170-295Kč; ⊙ 11am-11pm; 🍴🛜; 🚌 2, 3, 7, 17, 21) Cap a visit to historic Vyšehrad Citadel with a hearty meal at this traditional pub that delivers not just excellent beer but very good food as well. Classic dishes like goulash, boiled beef, rabbit and duck confit are served in a festive setting. Daily lunch specials (around 140Kč) are available from 11am to 3pm. Reservations (advisable) are only possible after 3pm.

### ★ La Bottega Bistroteka
ITALIAN €€

(Map p140; ☑ 222 311 372; www.bistroteka.cz; Dlouhá 39; mains 265-465Kč; ⊙ 9am-10.30pm Mon-Sat, to 9pm Sun; 🚌 6, 8, 15, 26) You'll find smart and snappy service at this stylish deli-cum-bistro, where the menu makes the most of all that delicious Italian produce artfully arranged on the counter; the beef cheek canneloni with parmesan sauce and fava beans, for example, is just exquisite. It's best to book, but you can often get a walk-in table at lunchtime.

### ★ Field
CZECH €€€

(Map p140; ☑ 222 316 999; www.fieldrestaurant.cz; U Milosrdných 12; mains 590-620Kč, 6-course tasting menu 2800Kč; ⊙ 11am-2.30pm & 6-10.30pm Mon-Fri, noon-3pm & 6-10.30pm Sat, noon-3pm & 6-10pm Sun; 🍴; 🚌 17) 🍴 Prague's third Michelin-starred restaurant is its least formal and most fun. The decor is an amusing art-meets-agriculture blend of farmyard implements and minimalist chic, while the chef creates painterly presentations from the finest of local produce along with freshly foraged herbs and edible flowers. You'll have to book at least a couple of weeks in advance to have a chance of a table.

**V Zátiší**  CZECH, INDIAN €€€

(Map p140; ☑222 221 155; www.vzatisi.cz; Liliová 1; 2-/3-course meal 990/1190Kč; ☻noon-3pm & 5.30-11pm; ☻☎; ☐2, 17, 18) 'Still Life' is one of Prague's top restaurants, famed for the quality of its cuisine. The decor is bold and modern, with quirky glassware, boldly patterned wallpapers and cappuccino-coloured crushed-velvet chairs. The menu ranges from high-end Indian cuisine to gourmet versions of traditional Czech dishes – the South Bohemian duck with white cabbage and herb dumplings is superb.

## 🍷 Drinking & Nightlife

Czech beers are among the world's best. The most famous brands are Plzeňský Prazdroj (Pilsner Urquell), Budvar and Prague's own Staropramen. Independent microbreweries and regional Czech beers are also becoming more popular in Prague.

**★Vinograf**  WINE BAR

(Map p140; ☑214 214 681; www.vinograf.cz; Senovážné náměstí 23; ☻11.30am-midnight Mon-Sat, 5pm-midnight Sun; ☎; ☐3, 5, 6, 9, 14, 24) With knowledgeable staff, a relaxed atmosphere and an off-the-beaten-track feel, this appealingly modern wine bar is a great place to discover Moravian wines. There's good finger food to accompany your wine, mostly cheese and charcuterie, with food and wine menus (in Czech and English) on big blackboards behind the bar. Very busy at weekends, when it's worth booking a table.

**Vinohradský Pivovar**  PUB

(☑222 760 080; www.vinohradskypivovar.cz; Korunní 106, Vinohrady; ☻11am-midnight; ☎; ☐10, 16) This popular and highly recommended neighbourhood pub and restaurant offers its own home-brewed lagers as well as a well-regarded IPA. There's seating on two levels and a large events room at the back for concerts and happenings. The restaurant features classic Czech pub dishes (like *Wienerschnitzel* and pork medallions) at reasonable prices (180Kč to 230Kč). Book in advance for an evening meal.

**★Letná Beer Garden**  BEER GARDEN

(☑233 378 208; www.letenskyzamecek.cz; Letenské sady 341; ☻11am-11pm May-Sep; ☐1, 8, 12, 25, 26) No accounting of watering holes in the neighbourhood would be complete without a nod toward the city's best beer garden, with an amazing panorama, situated at the eastern end of the **Letná Gardens** (Letenské

sady; ☻24hr; ☖; ☐1, 8, 12, 25, 26 to Letenské náměstí). Buy a takeaway beer from a small kiosk and grab a picnic table, or sit on a small terrace where you can order beer by the glass and decent pizza.

**★Cross Club**  CLUB

(☑736 535 010; www.crossclub.cz; Plynární 23; admission free-200Kč; ☻cafe noon-2am, club 6pm-4am; ☎; Ⓜ Nádraží Holešovice) An industrial club in every sense of the word: the setting in an industrial zone; the thumping music (both DJs and live acts); and the interior, an absolute must-see jumble of gadgets, shafts, cranks and pipes, many of which move and pulsate with light to the music. The program includes occasional live music, theatre performances and art happenings.

**U Kurelů**  PUB

(www.ukurelu.cz; Chvalova 1, Žižkov; ☻5-11pm Tue-Sun; ☎; ☐5, 9, 15, 26) This reinvention of a classic Žižkov pub, originally opened in 1907, is the brainchild of the good folk at **The Tavern** (www.eng.thetavern.cz; Chopinova 26, Vinohrady; burgers 140-200Kč; ☻11.30am-10pm Mon-Fri, brunch from 11am Sat & Sun; ☻☎; Ⓜ Jiřího z Poděbrad, ☐11, 13), and the well-priced Pilsner Urquell (46Kč for 0.5L) and range of Czech microbrews is underpinned by the Tavern's famous smokehouse burgers, nachos and quesadillas.

**Pivnice U Černého Vola**  PUB

(☑220 513 481; Loretánské náměstí 1; ☻10am-10pm; ☐22) Many religious people make a pilgrimage to the Loreta, but just across the road, the 'Black Ox' is a shrine that pulls in pilgrims of a different kind. This surprisingly inexpensive beer hall is visited by real-ale aficionados for its authentic atmosphere and lip-smackingly delicious draught beer, Velkopopovický Kozel (31Kč for 0.5L), brewed in a small town southeast of Prague.

**Cafe Louvre**  CAFE

(Map p140; ☑224 930 949; www.cafelouvre.cz; 1st fl, Národní třída 22; ☻8am-11.30pm Mon-Fri, 9am-11.30pm Sat & Sun; ☐2, 9, 18, 22) The French-style Cafe Louvre is arguably the most amenable of Prague's grand cafes, as popular today as it was in the early 1900s when it was frequented by the likes of Franz Kafka and Albert Einstein. The atmosphere is wonderfully olde-worlde, and it serves good food as well as coffee. Check out the billiard hall and the ground-floor art gallery.

**U Medvídků**  BEER HALL
(At the Little Bear; Map p140; ☑224 211 916; www.umedvidku.cz; Na Perštýně 7; ⊘beer hall 11.30am-11pm, museum noon-10pm; ☎; Ⓜ Národní Třída, 🚊2, 9, 18, 22) The most micro of Prague's microbreweries, with a capacity of only 250L, U Medvídků started producing its own beer in 2005, though its trad-style beer hall has been around for many years. What it lacks in size, it makes up for in strength – the dark lager, marketed as X-Beer, is the strongest in the country, with an alcohol content of 11.8%.

## ☆ Entertainment

From dance to classical music to jazz, Prague offers plenty of entertainment options. Try the following ticket agencies to see what might be on during your visit, and to snag tickets online, check out **Bohemia Ticket** (Map p140; ☑224 215 031; www.bohemiaticket. cz; Na příkopě 16, Nové Město; ⊘10am-7pm Mon-Fri, to 5pm Sat, to 3pm Sun; Ⓜ Můstek).

### Performing Arts

**National Theatre**  OPERA, BALLET
(Národní divadlo; Map p140; ☑224 901 448; www.narodni-divadlo.cz; Národní třída 2; tickets 100-1290Kč; ⊘box offices 10am-6pm; 🚊2, 9, 18, 22) The much-loved National Theatre provides a stage for traditional opera, drama and ballet by the likes of Smetana, Shakespeare and Tchaikovsky, sharing the program alongside more modern works by composers and playwrights such as Philip Glass and John Osborne. The box offices are in the Nový síň building next door, in the Kolowrat Palace (opposite the Estates Theatre) and at the State Opera.

**Prague State Opera**  OPERA, BALLET
(Státní opera Praha; Map p140; ☑224 901 448; www.narodni-divadlo.cz; Wilsonova 4; ⊘box office 10am-6pm; Ⓜ Muzeum) The impressive neo-rococo home of the Prague State Opera provides a glorious setting for performances of opera and ballet. The building is closed for renovation work until 2018.

**Dvořák Hall**  CONCERT VENUE
(Dvořákova síň; Map p140; ☑227 059 227; www. ceskafilharmonie.cz; náměstí Jana Palacha 1, Rudolfinum; tickets 120-900Kč; ⊘box office 10am-12.30pm & 1.30-6pm Mon-Fri; Ⓜ Staroměstská) The Dvořák Hall in the neo-Renaissance Rudolfinum (p142) is home to the world-renowned Czech Philharmonic Orchestra (Česká filharmonie). Sit back and be impressed by some of the best classical musicians in Prague.

### Live Music

★**Palác Akropolis**  LIVE MUSIC
(☑296 330 913; www.palacakropolis.cz; Kubelíkova 27, Žižkov; tickets free-250Kč; ⊘club 6.30pm-5am; ☎; 🚊5, 9, 15, 26) The Akropolis is a Prague institution, a smoky, labyrinthine, sticky-floored shrine to alternative music and drama. Its various performance spaces host a smorgasbord of musical and cultural events, from DJs to string quartets to Macedonian Roma bands to local rock gods to visiting talent – Marianne Faithfull, the Flaming Lips and the Strokes have all played here.

**Roxy**  LIVE MUSIC
(Map p140; ☑224 826 296; www.roxy.cz; Dlouhá 33; tickets 150-700Kč; ⊘7pm-5am; 🚊6, 8, 15, 26) Set in the ramshackle shell of an art deco cinema, the legendary Roxy has nurtured the more independent and innovative end of Prague's club spectrum since 1987 – this is the place to see the Czech Republic's top DJs. On the 1st floor is NoD, an 'experimental space' that stages drama, dance, performance art, cinema and live music. Best nightspot in Staré Město.

**Jazz Dock**  JAZZ
(☑774 058 838; www.jazzdock.cz; Janáčkovo nábřeží 2, Smíchov; tickets 150-300Kč; ⊘4pm-3am; ☎; Ⓜ Anděl, 🚊9, 12, 15, 20) Most of Prague's jazz clubs are smoky cellar affairs, but this riverside club is a definite step up, with clean, modern decor and a decidedly romantic view out over the Vltava. It draws some of the best local talent and occasional international acts. Go early or book to get a good table. Shows normally begin at 7pm and 10pm.

## ℹ Information

The major banks are best for changing cash, but using a debit card in an ATM gives a better exchange rate. Avoid *směnárna* (private exchange booths), which advertise misleading rates and have exorbitant charges.

**Na Homolce Hospital** (☑257 271 111; www. homolka.cz; 5th fl, Foreign Pavilion, Roentgenova 2, Motol; 🚊167, 168 to Nemocnice Na Homolce) Widely considered to be the best hospital in Prague, equipped and staffed to Western standards, with staff who speak English, French, German and Spanish.

**Prague City Tourism** (Prague Welcome; Map p140; ☑221 714 714; www.prague. eu; Staroměstské náměstí 5, Old Town Hall;

⊙ 9am-7pm; Ⓜ Staroměstská) The busiest of the Prague City Tourism branches occupies the ground floor of the Old Town Hall (enter to the left of the Astronomical Clock).

**Relax Café-Bar** (☑ 224 211 521; www.relaxcafebar.cz; Dlážděná 4; per 10min 10Kč; ⊙ 8am-10pm Mon-Fri, 2-10pm Sat; ☎; Ⓜ Náměstí Republiky) A conveniently located internet cafe. Wi-fi is free.

## ⓘ Getting There & Away

There are very efficient overland and air routes to Prague and the Czech Republic.

## ⓘ Getting Around

### TO/FROM THE AIRPORT

To get into town from Prague airport, buy a full-price public transport ticket (32Kč) from the **Prague Public Transport Authority** desk in the arrivals hall and take bus 119 (20 minutes, every 10 minutes, 4am to midnight) to the Nádraží Veleslavín metro stop (line A), then continue by metro into the city centre (another 10 to 15 minutes; no new ticket needed).

If you're heading to the southwestern part of the city, take bus 100, which goes to the Zličín metro station (line B).

There's also an Airport Express bus (AE; 60Kč, 35 minutes, every half-hour from 5am to 10pm) that runs to Prague main train station, where you can connect to metro line C (buy ticket from driver, luggage goes free).

Several taxi companies operate from the airport. Count on about 30 minutes' drive time, depending on traffic, and a fare of 600Kč to and from the centre. You'll find taxi stands outside both arrivals terminals. Drivers usually speak some English and accept credit cards.

### PUBLIC TRANSPORT

Prague's excellent public-transport system combines tram, metro and bus services. It's operated by the **Prague Public Transport Authority** (DPP; ☑ 296 191 817; www.dpp.cz; ⊙ 7am-9pm), which has information desks in both terminals of Prague's Václav Havel Airport and in several metro stations, including the Můstek, Anděl, Hradčanská and Nádraží Veleslavín stations. The metro operates daily from 5am to midnight.

Tickets valid on all metros, trams and buses are sold from machines at metro stations (coins only), as well as at DPP information offices and many newsstands and kiosks. Tickets can be purchased individually or as discounted day passes valid for one or three days.

A full-price individual ticket costs 32/16Kč per adult/senior aged 65 to 70 and is valid for 90 minutes of unlimited travel. For shorter journeys, buy short-term tickets that are valid for 30 minutes of unlimited travel. These cost 24/12Kč

per adult/senior. One-day passes cost 110/55Kč per adult/senior; three-day passes cost 310Kč (no discount for seniors).

### TAXI

Taxis are frequent and relatively inexpensive. The official rate for licensed cabs is 40Kč flagfall plus 28Kč per kilometre and 6Kč per minute while waiting. On this basis, any trip within the city centre – say, from Wenceslas Sq to Malá Strana – should cost around 170Kč. A trip to the suburbs, depending on the distance, should run from 200Kč to 400Kč, and to the airport between 500Kč and 700Kč.

The following companies offer 24-hour service and English-speaking operators:

**AAA Radio Taxi** (☑ 14014, 222 333 222; www.aaataxi.cz) Operates a 24-hour taxi service from the airport, charging around 500Kč to 650Kč to get to the centre of Prague. You'll find taxi stands outside both arrivals terminals. Drivers usually speak some English and accept credit cards.

**City Taxi** (☑ 257 257 257; www.citytaxi.cz)
**ProfiTaxi** (☑ 14015; www.profitaxi.cz)

# AROUND PRAGUE

## Karlštejn

Rising above the village of Karlštejn, 30km southwest of Prague, medieval **Karlštejn Castle** (Hrad Karlštejn; ☑ tour bookings 311 681 617; www.hradkarlstejn.cz; adult/child Tour 1 270/180Kč, Tour 2 330/230Kč, Tour 3 150/100Kč; ⊙ 9am-6.30pm Jul & Aug, 9.30am-5.30pm Tue-Sun May, Jun & Sep, to 5pm Apr, to 4.30pm Oct, to 4pm Mar, shorter hrs Sat & Sun only Dec-Feb) is in such good shape it wouldn't look out of place at Disneyworld. The crowds come in theme-park proportions as well, but the peaceful surrounding countryside offers views of Karlštejn's stunning exterior that rival anything you'll see on the inside.

The castle was born of a grand pedigree, originally conceived by Emperor Charles IV in the 14th century as a bastion for hiding the crown jewels. Run by an appointed burgrave, the castle was surrounded by a network of landowning knight-vassals, who came to the castle's aid whenever enemies moved against it.

Karlštejn again sheltered the Bohemian and the Holy Roman Empire crown jewels during the Hussite Wars of the 15th century, but fell into disrepair as its defences became outmoded. Considerable restoration work in the late-19th century returned the castle to its former glory.

Castle visits are by guided tour only. Some tours must be reserved in advance by phone or via the castle website.

Three tours are available: **Tour 1** (50 minutes) passes through the Knight's Hall, still daubed with the coats-of-arms and names of the knight-vassals, Charles IV's Bedchamber, the Audience Hall and the Jewel House, which includes treasures from the Chapel of the Holy Cross and a replica of the St Wenceslas Crown.

**Tour 2** (70 minutes, May to October only) takes in the Marian Tower, with the Church of the Virgin Mary and the Chapel of St Catherine, then moves to the Great Tower for the castle's star attraction, the exquisite Chapel of the Holy Cross, its walls and vaulted ceiling adorned with thousands of polished semiprecious stones set in gilt stucco in the form of crosses, and with religious and heraldic paintings.

**Tour 3** (40 minutes, May to October only) visits the upper levels of the Great Tower, the highest point of the castle, which provides stunning views over the surrounding countryside.

From Prague, there are frequent train departures daily from Prague's main station. The journey takes 45 minutes and costs around 55Kč each way.

## Kutná Hora

In the 14th century, Kutná Hora, 60km southeast of Prague, rivalled the capital in importance because of the rich deposits of silver ore below the ground. The ore ran out in 1726, leaving the medieval townscape largely unaltered. Now with several fascinating and unusual historical attractions, the Unesco World Heritage–listed town is a popular day trip from Prague.

Interestingly, most visitors come not for the silver splendour but rather to see an eerie monastery, dating from the 19th century, with an interior crafted solely from human bones. Indeed, the remarkable **Sedlec Ossuary** (Kostnice; information centre 326 551 049; www.ossuary.eu; Zámecká 127; adult/concession 90/60Kč; 8am-6pm Mon-Sat, 9am-6pm Sun Apr-Sep, 9am-5pm Mar & Oct, 9am-4pm Nov-Feb), or 'bone church', features the remains of no fewer than 40,000 people who died over the years from wars and pestilence.

Closer to the centre of Kutná Hora is the town's greatest monument: the Gothic **Cathedral of St Barbara** (Chrám sv Barbora; 775 363 938; www.khfarnost.cz; Barborská; adult/concession 85/40Kč; 9am-6pm Apr-Oct, 10am-5pm Mon-Fri, 10am-6pm Sat & Sun Nov-Dec, 10am-4pm Jan-Mar). Rivalling Prague's St Vitus in size and magnificence, its soaring nave culminates in elegant, six-petalled ribbed vaulting, and the ambulatory chapels preserve original 15th-century frescoes. Other leading attractions include the **Hrádek** (České muzeum stříbra; 327 512 159; www.cms-kh.cz; Barborská 28; adult/concession Tour 1 70/40Kč, Tour 2 120/80Kč, combined 140/90Kč; 10am-6pm Jul & Aug, 9am-6pm May, Jun & Sep, 9am-5pm Apr & Oct, 10am-4pm Nov, closed Mon year-round) from the 15th century, which now houses the Czech Silver Museum.

Both buses and trains make the trip to Kutná Hora from Prague, though the train is usually a better bet. Direct trains depart from Prague's main train station to Kutná Hora hlavní nádraží every two hours (209Kč return, 55 minutes). It's a 10-minute walk from here to Sedlec Ossuary, and a further 2.5km (30 minutes) to the Old Town. Buses (136Kč return, 1¾ hours) depart from Prague's Háje bus station on the far southern end of the city. On weekdays, buses run hourly, with reduced services on weekdays.

# BOHEMIA

The Czech Republic's western province boasts surprising variety. Český Krumlov, with its riverside setting and dramatic Renaissance castle, is in a class by itself. Big cities like Plzeň offer urban attractions like great museums and restaurants. The spa towns of western Bohemia, such as Karlovy Vary, were world famous in the 19th century and retain old-world lustre.

## Plzeň

POP 188,190

Plzeň, the regional capital of western Bohemia and the second-biggest city in Bohemia after Prague, is best known as the home of the Pilsner Urquell Brewery, but it has a handful of other interesting sights and enough good restaurants and night-time pursuits to justify an overnight stay. Most of the sights are located near the central square, but the brewery itself is about a 15-minute walk outside the city centre.

# ◎ Sights

## ★ Pilsner Urquell Brewery                    BREWERY

(Prazdroj; ☑377 062 888; www.prazdrojvisit.cz; U Prazdroje 7; guided tour adult/child 200/120Kč; ⊙8.30am-6pm Apr-Sep, to 5pm Oct-Mar, English tours 1pm, 2.45pm & 4.30pm) Plzeň's most popular attraction is the tour of the Pilsner Urquell Brewery, in operation since 1842 and arguably home to the world's best beer. Entry is by guided tour only, with three tours in English available daily. Tour highlights include a trip to the old cellars (dress warmly) and a glass of unpasteurised nectar at the end.

## Underground Plzeň                    TUNNEL

(Plzeňské historické podzemí; ☑377 235 574; www.plzenskepodzemi.cz; Veleslavínova 6; tour in English adult/child 120/90Kč; ⊙10am-6pm Apr-Sep, to 5pm Oct-Dec & Feb-Mar, closed Jan, English tour 2.20pm daily Apr-Oct) This extraordinary tour explores the passageways below the old city. The earliest were probably dug in the 14th century, perhaps for beer production or defence; the latest date from the 19th century. Of an estimated 11km that have been excavated, some 500m of the tunnels are open to the public. Bring extra clothing – it's a chilly 10°C underground.

## ★ Techmania Science Centre                    MUSEUM

(☑737 247 585; www.techmania.cz; cnr Borská & Břeňkova, Areál Škoda; adult/child incl 3D planetarium 180/110Kč; ⊙8.30am-5pm Mon-Fri, 10am-7pm Sat, 10am-6pm Sun; P🔊♿; ☐15, 17) Kids will have a ball at this high-tech, interactive science centre where they can play with infrared cameras, magnets and many other instructive and fun exhibits. There's a 3D planetarium (included in the full-price admission) and a few full-sized historic trams and trains manufactured at the Škoda engineering works. Take the trolleybus; it's a 2km hike southwest from the city centre.

## Brewery Museum                    MUSEUM

(☑377 224 955; www.prazdrojvisit.cz; Veleslavínova 6; guided tour adult/child 120/90Kč, English text 90/60Kč; ⊙10am-6pm Apr-Sep, to 5pm Oct-Mar) The Brewery Museum offers an insight into how beer was made (and drunk) in the days before Pilsner Urquell was founded. Highlights include a mock-up of a 19th-century pub, a huge wooden beer tankard from Siberia and a collection of beer mats. All have English captions and there's a good printed English text available for those not taking the tour.

## Great Synagogue                    SYNAGOGUE

(Velká Synagoga; ☑377 223 346; www.zoplzen.cz; sady Pětatřicátníků 11; adult/child 70/40Kč; ⊙10am-6pm Sun-Fri Apr-Oct) The Great Synagogue, west of the Old Town, is the third-largest in the world – only those in Jerusalem and Budapest are bigger. It was built in the Moorish style in 1892 by the 2000 Jews who lived in Plzeň at the time. The building is now used for concerts and art exhibitions.

# 🛏 Sleeping

## Hotel Roudna                    HOTEL €

(☑377 259 926; www.hotelroudna.cz; Na Roudné 13; s/d 1150/1400Kč; P@🔊) Perhaps the city's best-value lodging, across the river to the north of the old town, the Roudna's exterior isn't much to look at, but inside rooms are well proportioned with high-end amenities such as flat-screen TV, minibar and desk. Breakfasts are fresh and ample, and reception is friendly. Note there's no lift.

## Hotel Rous                    BOUTIQUE HOTEL €€

(☑602 320 294; www.hotelrous.cz; Zbrojnicka 113/7; s/d from 1750/2150Kč; P@🔊) This 600-year-old building combines the historic character of the original stone walls alongside modern furnishings. Bathrooms are art deco cool in black and white. Breakfast is taken in a garden cafe concealed amid remnants of Plzeň's defensive walls. Downstairs, the Caffe Emily serves very good coffee.

# 🍴 Eating & Drinking

## Na Parkánu                    CZECH €

(☑377 324 485; www.naparkanu.com; Veleslavínova 4; mains 100-330Kč; ⊙11am-11pm Mon-Thu, to 1am Fri & Sat, to 10pm Sun; 🔊) Don't overlook this pleasant pub-restaurant, attached to the Brewery Museum. It may look a bit touristy, but the traditional Czech food is top rate, and the beer, naturally, could hardly be better. Try to snag a spot in the summer garden. Don't leave without trying the *nefiltrované pivo* (unfiltered beer). Reservations are an absolute must.

## ★ Buffalo Burger Bar                    AMERICAN €€

(☑733 124 514; buffaloburgerbar@gmail.com; Dominikánská 3; mains 165-385Kč; ⊙11am-11pm; 😊🔊) Tuck in to some of the best burgers in the Czech Republic at this American-style diner, with cool timber decor the colour of a well-done steak. Everything is freshly made, from the hand-cooked tortilla chips, zingy salsa and guacamole, to the perfect french fries, coleslaw and the juicy burgers themselves.

★ **Aberdeen Angus Steakhouse**  STEAK €€
(☑725 555 631; www.angussteakhouse.cz; Pražská 23; mains 215-715Kč; ⊗11am-11pm Sun-Thu, to midnight Fri & Sat; ⊜🐸) For our money, this may be the best steakhouse in all of the Czech Republic. The meats hail from a nearby farm, where the livestock is raised organically. There are several cuts and sizes on offer; lunch options include a tantalising cheeseburger. The downstairs dining room is cosy; there's also a creek-side terrace. Book in advance.

★ **Měšťanská Beseda**  PUB
(☑378 035 415; http://web.mestanska-beseda. cz; Kopeckého sady 13; ⊗9am-10pm Mon-Fri, 11am-10pm Sat & Sun; 🐸) Cool heritage cafe, sunny beer garden, expansive exhibition space and occasional art-house cinema – the elegant Art Nouveau Měšťanská Beseda is hands-down Plzeň's most versatile venue. The beautifully restored 19th-century pub is perfect for a leisurely beer or cafe. Check out who's performing at the attached theatre.

**Galerie Azyl**  BAR
(☑377 235 507; www.galerieazyl.cz; Veleslavíno-va 17; ⊗8am-11pm Mon-Thu, to 1am Fri, 6pm-1am Sat; 🐸) Locals kick off the morning with an excellent espresso here. Later in the day, Galerie Azyl morphs into Plzeň's classiest cocktail bar. Quirky artwork surrounds conversation-friendly booths.

## ❶ Information

**City Information Centre** (Informační centrum města Plzně; ☑378 035 330; www.pilsen.eu/ tourist; náměstí Republiky 41; ⊗9am-7pm Apr-Sep, to 6pm Oct-Mar; 🐸) Plzeň's well-stocked tourist information office is a first port of call for visitors. Staff here can advise on sleeping and eating options, and there are free city maps and a stock of brochures on what to see and do.

## ❶ Getting There & Away

Several trains leave daily from Prague's main train station (Hlavní nádraží; 160Kč, 1½ hours) to Plzeň's **train station** (Plzeň hlavní nádraží; www. cd.cz; Nádraží 102), which is 1km east of the historic centre.

From Prague, **Student Agency** (☑841 101 101; www.studentagency.cz; náměstí Republiky 9; ⊗9am-6pm Mon-Fri) runs half-hourly buses

during the day to Plzeň (100Kč, one hour). Plzeň **bus station** (Centrální autobusové nádraží, CAN; ☑377 237 237; www.csadplzen.cz; Husova 60), marked on maps and street signs as CAN, is 1km west of the centre.

# Český Krumlov

POP 61,100

Český Krumlov, in Bohemia's deep south, is one of the most picturesque towns in Europe. It's a little like Prague in miniature – a Unesco World Heritage Site with a stunning castle above the Vltava River, an old town square, Renaissance and baroque architecture, and hordes of tourists milling through the streets – but all on a smaller scale; you can walk from one side of town to the other in 20 minutes. Český Krumlov is best approached as an overnight destination; it's too far for a comfortable day trip from Prague. Consider staying at least two nights, and spend one of the days hiking or biking in the surrounding woods and fields.

## ⊙ Sights

★ **Český Krumlov State Castle**  CASTLE
(☑380 704 711; www.zamek-ceskykrumlov.eu; Zámek 59; adult/concession Tour 1 250/160Kč, Tour 2 240/140Kč, Theatre Tour 300/200Kč; ⊗9am-6pm Tue-Sun Jun-Aug, to 5pm Apr, May, Sep & Oct) Český Krumlov's striking Renaissance castle, occupying a promontory high above the town, began life in the 13th century. It acquired its present appearance in the 16th to 18th centuries under the stewardship of the noble Rožmberk and Schwarzenberg families. The interiors are accessible by guided tour only, though you can stroll the grounds on your own.

**Castle Museum & Tower**  MUSEUM, TOWER
(☑380 704 711; www.zamek-ceskykrumlov.eu; Zámek 59; combined entry adult/child 130/60Kč, museum only 100/50Kč, tower only 50/30Kč; ⊗9am-5pm Jun-Aug, to 4pm Apr, May, Sep & Oct, to 3pm Tue-Sun Nov-Mar) Located within the castle complex, this small museum and adjoining tower is an ideal option if you don't have the time or energy for a full castle tour. Through a series of rooms, the museum traces the castle's history from its origins through to the present day. Climb the tower for perfect photo-ops of the town below.

# Český Krumlov

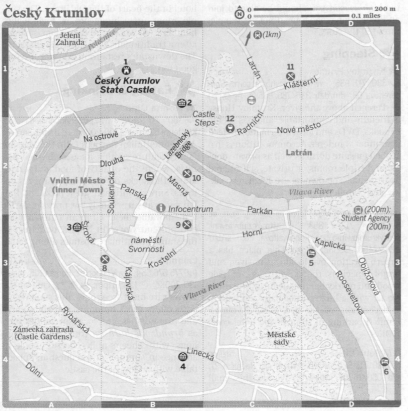

**Egon Schiele Art Centrum** MUSEUM
(☏380 704 011; www.schieleartcentrum.cz; Široká 71; adult/child under 6yr 160Kč/free; ☺10am-6pm Tue-Sun) This excellent private gallery houses a small retrospective of the controversial Viennese painter Egon Schiele (1890–1918), who lived in Krumlov in 1911, and raised the ire of the townsfolk by hiring young girls as nude models. For this and other sins he was eventually driven out. The centre also houses interesting temporary exhibitions.

**Museum Fotoateliér Seidel** MUSEUM
(☏736 503 871; www.seidel.cz; Linecká 272; adult/child 100/40Kč; ☺9am-noon & 1-6pm May-Sep, to 5pm Apr & Oct-Dec, to 5pm Tue-Sun Jan-Mar) This photography museum presents a moving retrospective of the work of local photographers Josef Seidel and his son František. Especially poignant are the images recording early-20th-century life in nearby villages. In

## Český Krumlov

the high season you should be able to join an English-language tour; if not, let the pictures tell the story.

## 🛏 Sleeping

### ★ Krumlov House                                  HOSTEL €

(☑ 380 711 935; www.krumlovhostel.com; Rooseveltova 68; dm/d/tr 335/785/935Kč; ☺ @ 🛜)
🍴 Perched above the river, Krumlov House is friendly and comfortable, and has plenty of books, DVDs and local information to feed your inner wanderer. Accommodation is in a six-bed en suite dorm as well as private double and triple rooms or private, self-catered apartments. The owners are English-speaking and traveller-friendly.

### ★ Hotel garni Myší Díra                         HOTEL €€

(☑ 380 712 853; http://cz.ubytovani. ceskykrumlov-info.cz; Rooseveltova 28; s/d/tr 2150/2450/2950Kč; P 🛜) This place has a superb location overlooking the river, and bright, spacious rooms with lots of pale wood and quirky handmade furniture; room No 12, with a huge corner bath and naughty decorations on the bed, is our favourite. Limited parking in front of the hotel costs 190Kč.

### U Malého Vítka                                  HOTEL €€

(☑ 380 711 925; www.vitekhotel.cz; Radniční 27; s/d 1050/1600Kč; P ☺ 🛜) We like this small hotel in the heart of the Old Town. The simple room furnishings are of high-quality, hand-crafted wood, and each room is named after a traditional Czech fairy-tale character. The downstairs restaurant and cafe are very good too.

## 🍴 Eating & Drinking

### ★ Nonna Gina                                    ITALIAN €

(☑ 380 717 187; www.pizzerianonnagina.wz.cz; Klášterní 52; mains 100-200Kč; ⏱ 11am-11pm; ☺) Authentic Italian flavours from the Massaro family feature at this long-established pizzeria, where the quality of food and service knock the socks off more expensive restaurants. Superb antipasti, great pizza and Italian wines at surprisingly low prices make for a memorable meal. Grab an outdoor table and pretend you're in Naples, or retreat to the snug and intimate upstairs dining room.

### Laibon                                          VEGETARIAN €

(☑ 775 676 654; www.laibon.cz; Parkán 105; mains 130-200Kč; ⏱ 11am-11pm; ☺ 🛜 ☑) One of the town's rare meat-free zones, this snug veggie oasis offers great hummus, couscous, curry and pasta dishes, and local specialities such as *bryndzové halušky* (tiny potato dumplings with sheep's-milk cheese). Book in advance in summer and request an outside table with a view of the castle.

---

**WORTH A TRIP**

### UNESCO HERITAGE ARCHITECTURE IN TELČ

The Unesco-protected town of Telč, perched on the border between Bohemia and Moravia, possesses one of the country's prettiest and best-preserved historic town squares.

The main attraction is the beauty of the square, **Náměstí Zachariáše z Hradce**, itself, which is lined with Renaissance burghers' houses. Most of the structures were built in the 16th century after a fire levelled the town in 1530. Famous houses include No 15, which shows the characteristic Renaissance sgraffito. The house at No 48 was given a baroque facade in the 18th century.

**Telč Chateau** (Zámek; ☑ 567 243 943; www.zamek-telc.cz; náměstí Zachariáše z Hradce 1; adult/concession Route A 120/80Kč, Route B 90/70Kč; ⏱ 10am-3pm Tue-Sun Apr & Oct, to 4pm May, Jun & Sep, to 4.30pm Jul & Aug), another Renaissance masterpiece, guards the northern end of the square. Entry is by guided tour only.

If you decide to spend the night, the **Hotel Celerin** (☑ 567 243 477; www.hotelcelerin. cz; náměstí Zachariáše z Hradce 43; s/d 980/1700Kč; ☺ ✳ 🛜) offers 12 comfortable rooms, with decor ranging from cosy wood to white-wedding chintz (take a look first).

There are a handful of daily buses that run from Prague's Florenc bus station (175Kč, 2½ hours), though many connections require a change in Jihlava. The situation is marginally better for bus travel to/from Brno (125Kč, two hours). Check the online timetable at http://jizdnirady.idnes.cz for times.

**Hospoda Na Louži** CZECH €
(☑380 711 280; www.nalouzi.cz; Kájovská 66; mains 120-240Kč; ☻) Nothing's changed in this wood-panelled *pivo* (beer) parlour for almost a century. Locals and tourists pack Na Louži for huge plates of Czech staples such as chicken schnitzels or roast pork and dumplings, as well as dark (and light) beer from the local Eggenberg brewery. Get the fruit dumplings for dessert if you see them on the menu.

★ **Krčma v Šatlavské** CZECH €€
(☑380 713 344; www.satlava.cz; Horní 157; mains 150-325Kč; ☺11am-midnight) This medieval barbecue cellar is hugely popular with visitors and your table mates are much more likely to be from Austria or China than from the town itself. The grilled meats served up with gusto in a funky labyrinth illuminated by candles are excellent and perfectly in character with Český Krumlov. Advance booking is essential.

**Zapa Cocktail Bar** COCKTAIL BAR
(☑380 712 559; www.zapabar.cz; Latrán 15; ☺6pm-1am; ☎) Most of Český Krumlov empties out after dinner, but Zapa keeps going until after midnight. Expect a relaxed vibe and the town's best cocktails.

### ⓘ Information

**Infocentrum** (☑380 704 622; www.ckrumlov. info; náměstí Svornosti 2; ☺9am-7pm Jun-Aug, to 6pm Apr, May, Sep & Oct, to 5pm Nov-Mar, closed lunch Sat & Sun) One of the country's best tourist offices. Good source for transport and accommodation info, maps, internet access (per five minutes 5Kč) and audio guides (per hour 100Kč). A guide for disabled visitors is also available.

### ⓘ Getting There & Away

The train from Prague (275Kč, 3½ hours, four to six daily) requires a change in České Budějovice. There's regular train service between České Budějovice and Český Krumlov (51Kč, 45 minutes). It is quicker and cheaper to take the bus. Český Krumlov **train station** (Vlakové nádraží; ☑840 112 113; www.cd.cz; Třída Míru 1) is located 2km north of the historic centre.

By bus, **Student Agency** (☑841 101 101; www. studentagency.cz; Nemocniční 586) coaches (200Kč, three hours, hourly) leave from Prague's Na Knížecí bus station at Anděl metro station (Line B). Book in advance for weekends or in July and August. Český Krumlov **bus station** (Autobusové nádraží; Nemocniční 586) is about a 10-minute walk east of the historic centre.

# MORAVIA

The Czech Republic's eastern province, Moravia is yin to Bohemia's yang. If Bohemians love beer, Moravians love wine. If Bohemia is towns and cities, Moravia is rolling hills and pretty landscapes. The Moravian capital, Brno, has the museums, but the northern city of Olomouc has the captivating architecture.

## Brno
POP 370,440
Among Czechs, Moravia's capital has a dull rep: a likeable enough place where not much actually happens. The reality, however, is very different. Tens of thousands of students who attend university here ensure a lively cafe and club scene that easily rival Prague's. The museums are great, too. Brno was one of the leading centres of experimental architecture in the early 20th century, and the Unesco-protected Vila Tugendhat is considered a masterwork of functionalist design.

### ◉ Sights

★ **Vila Tugendhat** ARCHITECTURE
(Villa Tugendhat; ☑515 511 015, tour bookings 731 616 899; www.tugendhat.eu; Černopolni 45; adult/concession basic tour 300/180Kč, extended tour 350/210Kč; ☺10am-6pm Tue-Sun Mar-Dec, 9am-7pm Wed-Sun Jan & Feb; ☐3, 5, 9) Brno had a reputation in the 1920s as a centre for modern architecture in the Bauhaus style. Arguably the finest example is this family villa, designed by modern master Mies van der Rohe for Greta and Fritz Tugendhat in 1930. The house was the inspiration for British author Simon Mawer in his 2009 bestseller *The Glass Room.* Entry is by guided tour booked in advance by phone or email. Two tours are available: basic (one hour) and extended (1½ hours).

**Capuchin Monastery** CEMETERY
(Kapucínský klášter; ☑511 145 796; www.kapucini.cz; Kapucínské náměstí; adult/concession 70/35Kč; ☺9am-noon & 1-6pm Mon-Sat, 11am-5pm Sun Apr-Oct, 10am-4pm Mon-Sat, 11am-4.30pm Sun Nov-Mar; ☐4, 8, 9) One of the city's leading attractions is this ghoulish cellar crypt that holds the mummified remains of several city noblemen from the 18th century. Apparently the dry, well-ventilated crypt has the natural ability to turn dead bodies into mummies. Up to 150 cadavers were

deposited here prior to 1784, the desiccated corpses including monks, abbots and local notables.

### Old Town Hall
HISTORIC BUILDING

(Stará radnice; ☑ 542 427 150; www.ticbrno.cz; Radnická 8; tower adult/concession 60/30Kč; ⊙ 10am-6pm; ☷ 4, 8, 9) No visit to Brno would be complete without a peek inside the city's medieval Old Town Hall, parts of which date back to the 13th century. The tourist office (p155) is here, plus oddities including a crocodile hanging from the ceiling (known affectionately as the Brno 'dragon') and a wooden wagon wheel with a unique story. You can also climb the tower.

### Labyrinth under the Cabbage Market
TUNNELS

(Brněnské podzemí; ☑ 542 427 150; www.ticbrno. cz; Zelný trh 21; adult/concession 160/80Kč; ⊙ 9am-6pm Tue-Sun; ☷ 4, 8, 9) In recent years, the city has opened several sections of extensive underground tunnels to the general public. This tour takes around 40 minutes to explore a number of cellars situated 6m to 8m below the Cabbage Market, which has served as a food market for centuries. The cellars were built for two purposes: to store goods and to hide in during wars.

### Špilberk Castle
CASTLE

(Hrad Špilberk; ☑ 542 123 611; www.spilberk.cz; Špilberk 210/1; combined entry adult/concession 280/170Kč, casemates only 90/50Kč, tower only 50/30Kč; ⊙ 9am-5pm May & Jun, 10am-6pm Jul-Sep, 9am-5pm Tue-Sun Oct-Apr) Brno's spooky hilltop castle is considered the city's most important landmark. Its history stretches back to the 13th century, when it was home to Moravian margraves and later a fortress. Under the Habsburgs in the 18th and 19th centuries, it served as a prison. Today it's home to the **Brno City Museum**, with several temporary and permanent exhibitions.

## 🛏 Sleeping

In February, April, August, September and October, Brno hosts major international trade fairs, and hotel rates increase by 40% to 100%. Book ahead if possible.

### ★Hostel Mitte
HOSTEL €

(☑ 734 622 340; www.hostelmitte.com; Panská 22; dm 400-500Kč, s/d 1000/1300Kč, all incl breakfast; ⊛@🛜; ☷ 4, 8, 9) Set in the heart of the Old Town, this clean and stylish hostel smells and looks brand new. The rooms are named after famous Moravians (eg Milan Kundera) or famous events (Austerlitz) and decorated accordingly. There are six-bed dorms and private singles and doubles. Cute cafe on the ground floor.

### Hostel Fléda
HOSTEL €

(☑ 731 651 005; www.hostelfleda.com; Štefánikova 24; dm/d from 250/800Kč; ⊛🛜; ☷ 1, 2, 4, 6, 8) One of Brno's best music clubs (p155) offers funky and colourful rooms and a good cafe and good bar reinforce the social vibe. It's a quick tram ride from the centre to the Hrnčirská stop.

### Hotel Europa
HOTEL €€

(☑ 515 143 100; www.hotel-europa-brno.cz; třída kpt Jaroše 27; s/d 1400/1800Kč; ℗⊛🛜; ☷ 3, 5, 9) Set in a quiet neighbourhood a 10-minute walk from the city centre, this self-proclaimed 'art' hotel (presumably for the futuristic furniture at the entrance) offers clean and tastefully furnished modern rooms in a historic 19th-century building. Rooms come in 'standard' and more expensive 'superior', with the chief difference being size. There is free parking out the front and in the courtyard.

### Barceló Brno Palace
LUXURY HOTEL €€€

(☑ national hotline 800 222 515, reception 532 156 777; www.barcelo.com; Šilingrovo nám 2; r from 3600Kč; ℗⊛✳@🛜; ☷ 1, 12) Five-star heritage luxury comes to Brno at the Barceló Brno Palace. The reception area blends glorious 19th-century architecture with thoroughly modern touches, and the spacious rooms are both contemporary and romantic. The location on the edge of Brno's Old Town is excellent.

## 🍴 Eating

### Špaliček
CZECH €

(☑ 542 211 526; www.facebook.com/restaurace. spalicek; Zelný trh 12; mains 80-160Kč; ⊙ 11am-11pm; ⊛🛜; ☷ 4, 8, 9) Brno's oldest (and maybe its 'meatiest') restaurant sits on the edge of the Cabbage Market. Ignore the irony and dig into huge Moravian meals, partnered with a local beer or something from the decent list of Moravian wines. The old-school tavern atmosphere is authentic and the daily lunch specials are a steal.

**Spolek** CZECH €
(☑774 814 230; www.spolek.net; Orli 22; mains 80-180Kč; ☉9am-10pm Mon-Fri, 10am-10pm Sat & Sun; 🛜☑🖕; 🖵4, 8, 9) You'll get friendly, unpretentious service at this coolly 'bohemian' (yes, we're in Moravia) haven with interesting salads and soups, and a concise but diverse wine list. Photojournalism on the walls is complemented by a funky mezzanine bookshop. It has excellent coffee, too.

**Bistro Franz** CZECH €€
(☑720 113 502; www.bistrofranz.cz; Veveří 14; mains 155-220Kč; ☉8am-11pm Mon-Fri, 10am-11pm Sat, 10am-9pm Sun; 🛜🛜☑; 🖵1, 3, 9, 11, 12) Colourfully retro Bistro Franz is one of a new generation of restaurants that focuses on locally sourced, organic ingredients. The philosophy extends to the relatively simple menu of soups, baked chicken drumsticks, curried lentils and other student-friendly food. The wine is carefully chosen and the coffee is sustainably grown. Excellent choice for morning coffee and breakfast.

**★Pavillon** INTERNATIONAL €€
(☑541 213 497; www.restaurant-pavillon.cz; Jezuitská 6; mains 250-385Kč; ☉11am-11pm Mon-Sat, noon-10pm Sun; 🛜🛜☑; 🖵1, 2, 4, 8) High-end dining in an elegant, airy space that recalls the city's heritage in functionalist architecture. The menu changes with the season, but usually features one vegetarian entree as well as mains with locally sourced ingredients, such as wild boar or lamb raised in the Vysočina highlands. Daily lunch specials (200Kč) including soup, main and dessert are a steal.

## 🍷 Drinking

**★Cafe Podnebi** CAFE
(☑542 211 372; www.podnebi.cz; Údolní 5; ☉8am-midnight Mon-Fri, from 9am Sat & Sun; 🛜🖕; 🖵4) This homey, student-oriented cafe is famous citywide for its excellent hot chocolate, but it also serves very good espresso drinks. There are plenty of baked goods and sweets to snack on. In summer the garden terrace is a hidden oasis, and there's a small play area for kids.

**Bar, Který Neexistuje** COCKTAIL BAR
(☑734 878 602; www.barkteryneexistuje.cz; Dvořákova 1; ☉5pm-2am; 🛜; 🖵4, 8, 9) 'The bar that doesn't exist' boasts a long, beautiful bar backed by every bottle of booze imagina-

ble. It anchors a row of popular, student-oriented bars along trendy Dvořákova. For a bar that 'doesn't exist', it gets quite crowded, so it's best to book ahead.

**Super Panda Circus** COCKTAIL BAR
(☑734 878 603; www.superpandacircus.cz; Šilingrovo náměstí 3, enter from Husova; ☉6pm-2am Mon-Sat; 🛜; 🖵1, 12) From the moment the doorman ushers you through an unmarked door into this bar, you feel you've entered a secret world like out of the movie *Eyes Wide Shut*. The dark interior, lit only in crazy colours emanating from the bar, and inventive drinks add to the allure. Hope for an empty table since it's not possible to book.

**U Richarda** PUB
(☑775 027 918; www.uricharda.cz; Údolní 7; ☉3.30pm-2.30am Mon-Sat; 🛜; 🖵4) This microbrewery is highly popular with students, who come for the great house-brewed, unpasteurised yeast beers, including a rare cherry-flavoured lager, and decent bar food like burgers and ribs (mains 110Kč to 149Kč). Book ahead.

## ☆ Entertainment

**Fléda** LIVE MUSIC
(☑533 433 432; www.fleda.cz; Štefánikova 24; tickets 200-400Kč; ☉7pm-2am; 🖵1, 2, 4, 6, 8) Brno's best up-and-coming bands, occasional touring performers and DJs all rock the stage at Brno's top music club. Buy tickets at the venue. Shows start around 9pm. Take the tram to the Hrnčířská stop.

**Brno Philharmonic Orchestra** CLASSICAL MUSIC
(Besední dům; ☑tickets 539 092 811; www.filharmonie-brno.cz; Komenského náměstí 8; tickets 290-390Kč; ☉box office 9am-2pm Mon & Wed, 1-6pm Tue, Thu & Fri, plus 1hr before performances; 🖵12, 13) The Brno Philharmonic is the city's leading orchestra for classical music. It conducts some 40 concerts each year, plus tours around the Czech Republic and Europe. It's particularly strong on Moravian-born, early 20th-century composer Leoš Janáček. Most performances are held at Besední dům concert house. Buy tickets at the box office, located around the corner from the main entrance on Besední.

## ℹ Information

**Tourist Information Centre** (TIC Brno; ☑542 427 150; www.gotobrno.cz; Radnická 8, Old

Town Hall; ⊘ 8.30am-6pm Mon-Fri, 9am-6pm Sat & Sun) Brno's main tourist office is located within the Old Town Hall complex. The office has loads of great information on the city in English, including events calendars and walking maps, and staff can help find accommodation. Lots of material on the city's rich architectural heritage is also available, as well as self-guided tours. There's a free computer to check email.

### ⓘ Getting There & Away

Express trains to Brno depart Prague's Hlavní nádraží (219Kč, three hours) every couple of hours during the day. Brno is a handy junction for onward train travel to Vienna (220Kč, two hours) and Bratislava (210Kč, 1½ hours).

There's regular coach service throughout the day to Prague (210Kč, 2½ hours), Bratislava (180Kč, two hours), Olomouc (100Kč, one hour) and Vienna (200Kč, two hours). **Student Agency** (🖉 Brno office 539 000 860, national hotline 800 100 300; www.studentagency.cz; náměstí Svobody 17; ⊘ 9am-6pm Mon-Fri) buses serve Prague, as well as other domestic and international destinations.

# Olomouc

POP 100,150

Olomouc (ol'-la-moats) is a sleeper. Practically unknown outside the Czech Republic and underappreciated even at home, the city is surprisingly majestic. The main square is among the country's nicest, surrounded by historic buildings and blessed with a Unesco-protected trinity column. The evocative central streets are dotted with beautiful churches, testament to the city's long history as a bastion of the Catholic church.

### ◎ Sights

**Holy Trinity Column**     MONUMENT
(Sloup Nejsvětější Trojice; Horní náměstí; ⊘ closed to the public) The town's pride and joy is this 35m-high (115ft) baroque sculpture that dominates Horní náměstí and is a popular meeting spot for local residents. The trinity column was built between 1716 and 1754 and is allegedly the biggest single baroque sculpture in Central Europe. In 2000 the column was added to Unesco's World Heritage Site list.

**Archdiocesan Museum**     MUSEUM
(Arcidiecézni muzeum; 🖉 585 514 111; www.olmuart. cz; Václavské náměstí 3; adult/concession 70/35Kč, Sun free, combined admission with Museum of Mod-

ern Art 100/50Kč; ⊘ 10am-6pm Tue-Sun; 🚌 2, 3, 4, 6) The impressive holdings of the Archdiocesan Museum trace the history of Olomouc back 1000 years. The thoughtful layout, with helpful English signage, takes you through the original Romanesque foundations of Olomouc Castle, and highlights the cultural and artistic development of the city during the Gothic and baroque periods. Don't miss the magnificent Troyer Coach, definitely the stretch limo of the 18th century.

**St Moritz Cathedral**     CHURCH
(Chrám sv Mořice; www.moric-olomouc.cz; Opletalova 10; ⊘ tower 9am-5pm Mon-Sat, noon-5pm Sun; 🚌 2, 3, 4, 6) **FREE** This vast Gothic cathedral is Olomouc's original parish church, built between 1412 and 1540. The western tower is a remnant of its 13th-century predecessor. The cathedral's amazing sense of peace is shattered every September with an International Organ Festival; the cathedral's organ is Moravia's mightiest. The tower (more than 200 steps) provides the best view in town.

**Museum of Modern Art**     MUSEUM
(Muzeum moderního umění; 🖉 585 514 111; www. olmuart.cz; Denisova 47; adult/child 70/35Kč, Sun & 1st Wed of month free, combined admission with Archdiocesan Museum 100/50Kč; ⊘ 10am-6pm Tue-Sun; 🚌 2, 3, 4, 6) On two floors, the museum showcases art from the 20th century under the heading 'A Century of Relativity'. The top floor focuses on movements from the first half of the century, including expressionism, cubism and surrealism. A second part, one floor below, features postwar movements such as abstraction and Czech trends from the 1970s and '80s.

**Civil Defence Shelter**     HISTORIC SITE
(Kryt Civilní Obrany; www.tourism.olomouc.eu; Bezručovy sady; 30Kč; ⊘ tours at 10am, 1pm & 4pm Thu & Sat mid-Jun–mid-Sep) Olomouc is all about centuries-old history, but this more-recent relic of the Cold War is also worth exploring on a guided tour. The shelter was built between 1953 and 1956 and was designed to keep a lucky few protected from the ravages of a chemical or nuclear strike. Tours are arranged by Olomouc Information Centre (p158), which is also where they start.

# 🛏 Sleeping

## Cosy Corner Hostel
HOSTEL €

(☑777 570 730; www.cosycornerhostel.com; 4th fl, Sokolská 1; dm/s/d 300/700/900Kč; ☺🛜; 🚌2, 3, 4, 6) The Australian-Czech couple who mind this friendly and exceptionally well-run hostel are a wealth of local information. There are dorms in eight-bed rooms, as well as private singles and doubles. Bicycles can be hired for 100Kč per day. In summer there's sometimes a two-night minimum stay, but Olomouc is worth it, and there's plenty of day-trip information on offer.

## ★ Penzión Na Hradě
PENSION €€

(☑585 203 231; www.penzionnahrade.cz; Michalská 4; s/d 1490/1990Kč; ☺✳🛜) In terms of price/quality ratio, this may be Olomouc's best deal, and worth the minor splurge if you can swing it. The location, tucked away in the shadow of St Michael's Church, is ideally central and the sleek, cool rooms have a professional design touch. There's also a small garden terrace for relaxing out the back. Book ahead in summer.

## Pension Royal
PENSION €€

(☑734 200 602; www.pension-royal.cz; Wurmova 1; r 1600/2000Kč; 🅿☺🛜; 🚌2, 3, 4, 6) With antique furniture, crisp white duvets and Oriental rugs on wood floors, the Royal is a spacious and splurge-worthy romantic getaway. Each room has a separate name and unique furnishings, though all go for an updated old-world feel. To get here catch a tram from the train station, jumping off at the U Domů stop.

# 🍴 Eating & Drinking

## ★ Svatováclavský Pivovar
CZECH €€

(☑585 207 517; www.svatovaclavsky-pivovar.cz; Mariánská 4; mains 180-290Kč; ☺9am-midnight Mon-Fri, 11am-midnight Sat, 11am-10pm Sun; ☺🛜; 🚌2, 3, 4, 6) This warm and inviting pub makes its own beer and serves plate-loads of Czech specialities such as duck confit and beer-infused goulash. Stop by for lunch midweek for an excellent value soup and main course for around 150Kč. Speciality beers include unpasteurised wheat and cherry-flavoured varieties. Useful for washing down some of Olomouc's signature stinky cheese, *tvarůžky*.

## Plan B
CZECH €€

(☑773 046 454; www.bar-planb.cz; Palachovo náměstí 1; mains 150-250Kč; ☺11am-midnight Mon-Fri, 4pm-midnight Sat; ☺🛜🚲; 🚌1, 3, 4, 6, 7) This homey, low-key bistro puts the emphasis on organic, locally sourced ingredients and traditional recipes. The daily lunch specials served during the week (11am to 2pm) feature a choice of four to five entrées (at least one vegetarian) plus soup for 120Kč. The evening menu changes week to week, so check the door or the website to see what's cooking during your visit.

## Vila Primavesi
INTERNATIONAL €€

(☑585 204 852; www.primavesi.cz; Univerzitní 7; mains 160-280Kč; ☺11am-11pm Mon-Sat, to 4pm Sun; ☺; 🚌2, 3, 4, 6) In an art nouveau villa that played host to Austrian artist Gustav Klimt in the early 20th century, the Vila Primavesi enjoys one of Olomouc's most exclusive settings. On summer evenings dine on dishes such as tuna steak and risotto on the terrace overlooking the city gardens. Lunch specials are better value than evening meals.

## ★ Cafe 87
CAFE

(☑585 202 593; www.cafe87.cz; Denisova 47; coffee 40Kč; ☺7.30am-9pm Mon-Fri, 8am-9pm Sat & Sun; 🛜; 🚌2, 3, 4, 6) Locals come in droves to this funky cafe beside the Olomouc Museum of Modern Art for coffee and its famous chocolate pie (50Kč). Some people still apparently prefer the dark chocolate to the white chocolate. When will they learn? It's a top spot for breakfast and toasted sandwiches, too. Seating is over two floors and there's a rooftop terrace.

## The Black Stuff
PUB

(☑774 697 909; www.blackstuff.cz; 1 máje 19; ☺4pm-2am Mon-Fri, 5pm-3am Sat, 5-11pm Sun; 🛜; 🚌2, 3, 4, 6) Cosy, old-fashioned Irish bar with several beers on tap and a large and growing collection of single malts and other choice tipples. Attracts a mixed crowd of students, locals and visitors.

# ☆ Entertainment

## Jazz Tibet Club
LIVE MUSIC

(☑585 230 399; www.jazzclub.olomouc.com; Sokolská 48; tickets 100-300Kč; 🛜) Blues, jazz and world music, including occasional international acts, feature at this popular spot, which also incorporates a good restaurant and wine bar. See the website for the program during your visit. Buy tickets at the venue on the day of the show or in advance at the Olomouc Information Centre (p158).

### Moravian Philharmonic Olomouc
CLASSICAL MUSIC

(Moravská Filharmonie Olomouc; ☑ 585 206 520, tickets 585 513 392; www.mfo.cz; Horní náměstí 23; tickets 80-220Kč) The local orchestra presents regular concerts and hosts Olomouc's International Organ Festival. Buy tickets one week in advance at the Olomouc Information Centre (p158) or at the venue one hour before the performance starts.

### ⓘ Information

**Olomouc Information Centre** (Olomoucká Informační Služba; ☑ 585 513 385; www.tourism.olomouc.eu; Horní náměstí; ⊙ 9am-7pm) Though Olomouc's information centre is short on language skills, it's very helpful when it comes to securing maps, brochures and tickets for events around town. It also offers regular daily sightseeing tours of the Town Hall (30Kč), and from mid-June to mid-September daily guided one-hour sightseeing tours of the city centre (70Kč).

### ⓘ Getting There & Away

Olomouc is on a main international rail line, with regular services from both Prague (220Kč, two to three hours) and Brno (100Kč, 1½ hours). From Prague, you can take normal trains or faster, high-end private trains run by **Student Agency's RegioJet** (RegioJet; ☑ 841 101 101; www.studentagency.cz; Riegrova 28; ⊙ 9am-6pm Mon-Fri; ☒ 2, 3, 4, 6) or **LEO Express** (☑ 220 311 700; www.le.cz; Jeremenkova 23, Main Train Station; ⊙ 5.45am-9.45pm; ☒ 1, 2, 3, 4, 5, 6, 7). Olomouc's train station is 2km east of the centre and accessible via several tram lines.

Olomouc is well-connected by bus to and from Brno (90Kč, 1¼ hours). The best way of getting to Prague, however, is by train. The **bus station** (Autobusové nádraží Olomouc; ☑ 585 313 848;

---

#### SLEEPING PRICE RANGES

The following price ranges refer to the cost of a standard double room per night in high season.

**€** less than 2000Kč

**€€** 2000Kč to 4000Kč

**€€€** more than 4000Kč

---

www.vlak-bus.cz; Sladkovského 142/37; ☒ 1, 2, 3, 4, 5, 6, 7) is located just behind the train station, about 2km east of the centre.

# SURVIVAL GUIDE

## ⓘ Directory A–Z

### ACCOMMODATION

The Czech Republic has a wide variety of accommodation options, from luxury hotels to pensions and camping grounds. Prague, Brno and Český Krumlov all have decent backpacker-oriented hostels.

➥ In Prague, hotel rates peak in spring and autumn, as well as around the Christmas and Easter holidays. Midsummer is considered 'shoulder season' and rates are about 20% off peak.

➥ The capital is a popular destination, so book in advance. Hotels are cheaper and less busy outside of Prague, but try to reserve ahead of arrival to get the best rate.

### BUSINESS HOURS

**Banks** 9am to 4pm Monday to Friday.

**Bars and clubs** 11am to 1am Tuesday to Saturday.

**Museums** 9am to 6pm Tuesday to Sunday; some attractions closed or have shorter hours October to April.

**Post offices** 8am to 7pm Monday to Friday, 9am to 1pm Saturday (varies)

**Restaurants** 11am to 11pm daily.

**Shops** 9am to 6pm Monday to Friday, 9am to 1pm Saturday (varies).

### GAY & LESBIAN TRAVELLERS

The Czech Republic is a relatively tolerant destination for gay and lesbian travellers. Homosexuality is legal, and since 2006, same-sex couples have been able to form registered partnerships.

Prague has a lively gay scene and is home to Europe's biggest gay pride march (www.praguepride.cz). Useful websites include **Travel Gay Europe** (www.travelgayeurope.com) and **Prague Saints** (www.praguesaints.cz).

### INTERNET RESOURCES

**CzechTourism** (www.czechtourism.com)

**National Bus & Train Timetable** (http://jizdnirady.idnes.cz)

**Prague Events Calendar** (www.pragueeventscalendar.com)

**Prague City Tourism** (www.prague.eu)

## MONEY

➡ The currency is the *koruna* (crown), abbreviated as Kč. The euro does not circulate.

➡ The best places to exchange money are banks or use your credit or debit card to withdraw money as needed from ATMs.

➡ Never exchange money on the street and avoid private exchange offices, especially in Prague, as they charge high commissions.

➡ Keep small change handy for use in public toilets and metro-ticket machines.

## PUBLIC HOLIDAYS

**New Year's Day** 1 January
**Easter Monday** March/April
**Labour Day** 1 May
**Liberation Day** 8 May
**Sts Cyril & Methodius Day** 5 July
**Jan Hus Day** 6 July
**Czech Statehood Day** 28 September
**Republic Day** 28 October
**Struggle for Freedom & Democracy Day** 17 November
**Christmas** 24 to 26 December

## TELEPHONE

➡ All Czech phone numbers have nine digits. Dial all nine numbers for any call.

➡ The Czech Republic's country code is ☑420.

➡ Mobile-phone coverage (GSM 900/1800) is compatible with most European, Australian or New Zealand handsets (though generally not with North American or Japanese models).

➡ Purchase a Czech prepaid SIM card from any mobile-phone shop. These allow you to make local calls at cheaper local rates.

## COUNTRY FACTS

**Area** 78,866 sq km

**Capital** Prague

**Country Code** ☑420

**Currency** Crown (Kč)

**Emergency** ☑112

**Language** Czech

**Money** ATMs all over; banks open Monday to Friday

**Population** 10.6 million

**Visas** Schengen rules apply; visas not required for most nationalities

➡ Local mobile numbers can be identified by prefix. Mobiles start with ☑601–608 or ☑720–779.

➡ Public phones operate via prepaid magnetic cards purchased at post offices or newsstands from 300Kč.

## VISAS

➡ The Czech Republic is part of the EU's Schengen area, and citizens of most developed countries can spend up to 90 days in the country in a six-month period without a visa.

## ❶ Getting There & Away

The Czech Republic lies at the centre of Europe and has good rail and road connections to surrounding countries. Prague's international airport is a major air hub for Central Europe.

## ESSENTIAL FOOD & DRINK

**Becherovka** A shot of this sweetish herbal liqueur from Karlovy Vary is a popular way to start (or end) a big meal.

**Beer** Modern *pils* (light, amber-coloured lager) was invented in the city of Plzeň in the 19th century, giving Czechs bragging rights to having the best beer (*pivo*) in the world.

**Braised Beef** Look out for svíčková na smetaně on menus. This is a satisfying slice of roast beef, served in a cream sauce, with a side of bread dumplings and a dollop of cranberry sauce.

**Carp** This lowly fish (kapr in Czech) is given pride of place every Christmas at the centre of the family meal. Kapr na kmíní is fried or baked carp with caraway seed.

**Dumplings** Every culture has its favourite starchy side dish; for Czechs it's *knedliky* – big bread dumplings that are perfect for mopping up gravy.

**Roast Pork** Move over beef, pork (*vepřové maso*) is king here. The classic Bohemian dish, seen on menus around the country, is vepřo-knedlo-zelo, local slang for roast pork, bread dumplings and sauerkraut.

## EATING PRICE RANGES

The following price ranges refer to the price of a main course at dinner:

€ less than 200Kč

€€ 200Kč to 500Kč

€€€ more than 500Kč

Flights, cars and tours can be booked online at lonelyplanet.com/bookings.

### AIR

Prague's **Václav Havel Airport** (Prague Ruzyně International Airport; ☑ 220 111 888; www.prg. aero; K letišti 6, Ruzyně; 🕿; 🖵 100, 119) is one of Central Europe's busiest airports, and daily flights connect the Czech capital with major cities throughout Europe, the UK, the Middle East and Asia. From April to October, direct flights link Prague to a handful of cities in North America.

### LAND

The Czech Republic has border crossings with Germany, Poland, Slovakia and Austria. These are all EU member states within the Schengen zone, meaning there are no passport or customs checks.

### Bus

➡ The main international terminal is Florenc bus station in Prague.

➡ Leading international bus carriers include Student Agency and Eurolines.

**Eurolines** (☑ 731 222 111; www.elines. cz; Křižíkova 2110/2b, ÚAN Praha Florenc; ⊘ 6.30am-7pm Sat-Thu, to 9pm Fri; 🕿; 🅼 Florenc) International bus carrier links Prague to cities around Europe. Consult the website for a timetable and prices. Buy tickets online or at Florenc bus station.

**Florenc Bus Station** (ÚAN Praha Florenc; ☑ 900 144 444; www.florenc.cz; Křižíkova 2110/2b, Karlín; ⊘ 5am-midnight; 🕿; 🅼 Florenc) Prague' s main bus station, servicing most domestic and long-haul international routes. There's an information counter, ticket windows, a left-luggage office and a small number of shops and restaurants. You can also usually purchase tickets directly from the driver.

**Student Agency** (☑ bus information 841 101 101, info 800 100 300; www.studentagency.cz; Křižíkova 2110/2b, ÚAN Praha Florenc; ⊘ 5am-11.30pm) This modern, well-run company operates comfortable, full-service coaches to major Czech cities as well as 60 destinations around Europe. Buses usually depart from Florenc bus

station, but may depart from other stations as well. Be sure to ask which station when you purchase your ticket.

### Train

➡ The country's main international rail gateway is **Praha hlavní nádraží** (Prague main train station). The station is accessible by public transport on metro line C.

➡ There is regular rail service from Prague to and from Germany, Poland, Slovakia and Austria. Trains to/from the south and east, including from Bratislava, Vienna and Budapest, also stop at Brno's main train station.

➡ In Prague, buy train tickets at ČD Centrum, located on the lower level of the station. Credit cards are accepted.

➡ Both InterRail and Eurail passes are valid on the Czech rail network.

**ČD Centrum** (☑ 840 112 113; www.cd.cz; Wilsonova 8, Praha hlavní nádraží; ⊘ 3am-midnight; 🅼 Hlavní nádraží) The main ticket office for purchasing train tickets for both domestic *(vnitrostátní jízdenky)* and international *(mezínárodní jizdenky)* destinations is located on the lower (park) level of the Prague's main train station. It also sells seat reservations, as well as booking couchettes and sleeping cars.

**LEO Express** (☑ 220 311 700; www.le.cz; Wilsonova 8, Praha hlavní nádraží; ⊘ ticket office 7.15am-9.30pm; 🅼 Hlavní Nádraží) Private company offering low-cost rail and bus transport to Brno, Olomouc and Ostrava, with onward bus connections to Lviv, Ukraine, and Kraków, Poland, among other destinations. Buy tickets online or at the ticket office in Prague's main train station (Praha hlavní nádraží).

**Praha hlavní nádraží** (Prague Main Train Station; ☑ 840 112 113; www.cd.cz; Wilsonova 8, Nové Město; ⊘ 3.30am-12.30am; 🅼 Hlavní nádraží) Prague's main train station, handling most international and domestic arrivals and departures.

## 🛈 Getting Around

### BUS

➡ Buses are often faster, cheaper and more convenient than trains.

➡ Many bus routes have reduced frequency (or none) on weekends.

➡ Check bus timetables and prices at http:// jizdnirady.idnes.cz.

➡ In Prague, many (though not all) buses arrive at and depart from Florenc bus station. Be sure to double-check the correct station.

➡ Try to arrive at the station well ahead of departure to secure a seat. Buy tickets at the station ticket window or directly from the driver.

**Student Agency** is the most popular, private bus company. It runs clean, comfortable coaches to cities around the country.

## CAR & MOTORCYCLE

⇒ For breakdown assistance anywhere in the country, dial 1230.

⇒ The minimum driving age is 18 and traffic moves on the right. Children aged under 12 are prohibited from sitting in the front seat.

⇒ Drivers are required to keep their headlights on at all times. The legal blood-alcohol limit is zero.

## TRAIN

⇒ Czech Railways provides efficient train services to almost every part of the country.

⇒ Private rail operators, such as LEO Express (p160) offer fast, high-speed trains between Prague and Olomouc, among other destinations.

⇒ For an online timetable, go to http://jizdni-rady.idnes.cz or www.cd.cz.

# Estonia

## Best Places to Eat

➜ Mr Jakob (p174)

➜ Ö (p170)

➜ Rataskaevu 16 (p170)

➜ Retro (p178)

➜ Altja Kõrts (p172)

## Best Places to Stay

➜ Pädaste Manor (p176)

➜ Antonius Hotel (p174)

➜ Georg Ots Spa Hotel (p177)

➜ Tabinoya (p168)

➜ Merekalda (p172)

## Why Go?

Estonia doesn't have to struggle to find a point of difference; it's completely unique. It shares a similar geography and history with Latvia and Lithuania, but it's culturally very different. Its closest ethnic and linguistic buddy is Finland, yet although they both may love to get naked together in the sauna, 50 years of Soviet rule have separated the two. For the past 300 years Estonia has been linked to Russia, but the two states have as much in common as a barn swallow and a bear (their respective national symbols).

In recent decades, and with a new-found confidence, Estonia has crept from under the Soviet blanket and leapt into the arms of Europe. The love affair is mutual: Europe has fallen for the chocolate-box allure of Tallinn and its Unesco-protected Old Town, while travellers seeking something different are tapping into Estonia's captivating blend of Eastern European and Nordic appeal.

## When to Go
### Tallinn

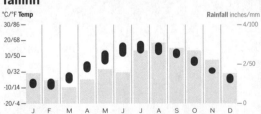

**Apr & May** See the country shake off winter's gloom.

**Jun–Aug** White nights, beach parties and loads of summer festivals.

**Dec** Christmas markets, mulled wine and long, cosy nights.

# Estonia Highlights

**① Tallinn** (p164)
Embarking on a medieval quest for atmospheric restaurants and hidden bars in the history-saturated lanes.

**② Lahemaa National Park** (p172) Wandering the forest paths, bog boardwalks, abandoned beaches and manor-house halls.

**③ Tartu** (p173) Furthering your education among the museums and student bars of Estonia's second city.

**④ Saaremaa** (p176) Unwinding among the windmills and exploring the island's castles, churches, cliffs, coast and crater.

**⑤ Muhu** (p176) Hopping over for frozen-in-island-time Koguva village and the gastronomic delights of Pädaste Manor.

**⑥ Pärnu** (p175) Strolling the golden sands and genteel streets of Estonia's 'summer capital'.

**⑦ Otepää** (p174) Getting back to nature, even if the snow's a no-show, at the 'winter capital'.

# TALLINN

POP 414,000

If you're labouring under the misconception that 'former Soviet' means dull and grey and that all tourist traps are soulless, Tallinn will delight in proving you wrong. This city has charm by the bucketload, fusing the modern and medieval to come up with a vibrant vibe all of its own. It's an intoxicating mix of church spires, glass skyscrapers, baroque palaces, appealing eateries, brooding battlements, shiny shopping malls, run-down wooden houses and cafes set on sunny squares – with a few Soviet throwbacks in the mix.

## ◉ Sights & Activities

### ◉ Old Town

Tallinn's medieval Old Town (Vanalinn) is without doubt the country's most fascinating locality. It's divided into Toompea (the upper town) and the lower town, which is still surrounded by much of its 2.5km defensive wall.

**Toompea**

Lording it over the Lower Town is the ancient hilltop citadel of Toompea. In German times this was the preserve of the feudal nobility, literally looking down on the traders and lesser beings below. It's now almost completely given over to government buildings, churches, embassies and shops selling amber knick-knacks and fridge magnets.

★**Alexander Nevsky Orthodox Cathedral**                    CATHEDRAL
(☑644 3484; http://tallinnanevskikatedraal.eu; Lossi plats 10; ☉8am-7pm, to 4pm winter) The positioning of this magnificent, onion-domed Russian Orthodox cathedral (completed in 1900) at the heart of the country's main administrative hub was no accident: the church was one of many built in the last part of the 19th century as part of a general wave of Russification in the empire's Baltic provinces. Orthodox believers come here in droves, alongside tourists ogling the interior's striking icons and frescoes. Quiet, respectful, demurely dressed visitors are welcome but cameras aren't.

**St Mary's Lutheran Cathedral**                    CHURCH
(Tallinna Püha Neitsi Maarja Piiskoplik toomkirik; ☑644 4140; www.toomkirik.ee; Toom-Kooli 6; church/tower €2/5; ☉9am-5pm daily May & Sep,

9am-6pm Jun-Aug, 9am-4pm Tue-Sun Oct, 10am-4pm Tue-Fri, 9am-4pm Sat & Sun Nov-Mar, 10am-5pm Tue-Fri, 9am-5pm Sat & Sun Apr) Tallinn's cathedral (now Lutheran, originally Catholic) was founded by at least 1233, although the exterior dates mainly from the 15th century, with the tower completed in 1779. This impressive building was a burial ground for the rich and titled, and the whitewashed walls are decorated with the elaborate coats-of-arms of Estonia's noble families. Fit viewseekers can climb the tower.

Toompea is named after the cathedral – the Estonian word 'toom' is borrowed from the German word 'dom' meaning cathedral. In English you'll often hear it referred to as the 'Dome Church', despite there being no actual dome.

**Lower Town**

Picking your way along the lower town's narrow, cobbled streets is like strolling into the 15th century – not least due to the tendency of local businesses to dress their staff up in medieval garb. The most interesting street is Pikk (Long St), which starts at the Great Coast Gate and includes Tallinn's historic guild buildings.

**Tallinn Town Hall**                    HISTORIC BUILDING
(Tallinna raekoda; ☑645 7900; www.raekoda.tallinn.ee; Raekoja plats; adult/student €5/2; ☉10am-4pm Mon-Sat Jul-Aug, by appointment Sep-Jun) Completed in 1404, this is the only surviving Gothic town hall in northern Europe. Inside, you can visit the Trade Hall (housing a visitor book dripping in royal signatures), the Council Chamber (featuring Estonia's oldest woodcarvings, dating from 1374), the vaulted Citizens' Hall, a yellow-and-black-tiled councillor's office and a small kitchen. The steeply sloped attic has displays on the building and its restoration.

★**Town Hall Square**                    SQUARE
(Raekoja plats) Raekoja plats has been the pulsing heart of Tallinn since markets began here in the 11th century. One side is taken up by the Gothic town hall, while the rest is ringed by pretty pastel-coloured buildings dating from the 15th to 17th centuries. Whether bathed in sunlight or sprinkled with snow, it's always a photogenic spot.

**Town Council Pharmacy**                    HISTORIC BUILDING
(Raeapteek; ☑5887 5701; www.raeapteek.ee; Raekoja plats 11; ☉10am-6pm Mon-Sat) Nobody's too sure on the exact date it opened but by 1422 this pharmacy was already on to its

third owner, making it the oldest continually operating pharmacy in Europe. In 1583 Johann Burchardt took the helm, and a descendant with the same name ran the shop right up until 1913 – 10 generations in all! Inside there are painted beams and a small historical display, or you can just drop in to stock up on painkillers and prophylactics.

**St Olaf's Church** CHURCH
(Oleviste kirik; ☑ 641 2241; www.oleviste.ee; Lai 50; tower adult/child €2/1; ☺ 10am-6pm Apr-Oct, to 8pm Jul & Aug) From 1549 to 1625, when its 159m steeple was struck by lightning and burnt down, this (now Baptist) church was one of the tallest buildings in the world. The current spire reaches a still respectable 124m and you can take a tight, confined, 258-step staircase up the tower for wonderful views of Toompea over the Lower Town's rooftops.

**Lower Town Wall** FORTRESS
(Linnamüür; ☑ 644 9867; Väike-Kloostri 3; adult/child €2/0.75; ☺ 11am-7pm Jun-Aug, 11am-5pm Fri-Wed Apr, May, Sep & Oct, 11am-4pm Fri-Tue Nov-Mar) The most photogenic stretch of Tallinn's remaining walls connects nine towers lining the western edge of the Old Town. Visitors can explore the barren nooks and crannies of three of them, with cameras at the ready for the red-rooftop views.

## ◉ Kalamaja

Immediately northwest of the Old Town, this enclave of tumbledown wooden houses and crumbling factories has swiftly transitioned into one of Tallinn's most interesting neighbourhoods. The intimidating hulk of Patarei Prison had seemed to cast a malevolent shadow over this part of town, so its transformation over the last few years has been nothing short of extraordinary. Major road projects and the opening of an impressive museum at Lennusadam are only the most visible elements of a revolution started by local hipsters opening cafes and bars in abandoned warehouses and rickety storefronts.

**Lennusadam** MUSEUM
(Seaplane Harbour; ☑ 620 0550; www.meremuuseum.ee; Vesilennuki 6; adult/child €14/7, incl Fat Margaret €16/8; ☺ 10am-7pm daily May-Sep, 10am-6pm Tue-Sun Oct-Apr; ℗) When this triple-domed hangar was completed in 1917, its reinforced-concrete shell frame construction was unique in the world. Resembling a classic Bond-villain lair, the vast space was completely restored and opened to the public in 2012 as a fascinating maritime museum, filled with interactive displays. Highlights include exploring the cramped corridors of a 1930s naval submarine, and the icebreaker and minehunter ships moored outside.

**Telliskivi Creative City** AREA
(Telliskivi Loomelinnak; www.telliskivi.eu; Telliskivi 60a; ☺ shops 8.30am-9pm Mon-Sat, 9am-7pm Sun) Once literally on the wrong side of the tracks, this set of 10 abandoned factory buildings is now Tallinn's most alternative shopping and entertainment precinct. All the cliches of hipster culture can be found here: cafes, a bike shop, bars selling craft beer, graffiti walls, artist studios, food trucks etc. But even the beardless flock to Telleskivi to peruse the fashion and design stores, sink espressos and rummage through the stalls at the weekly flea market.

## ◉ Kadriorg Park

About 2km east of the Old Town (take tram 1 or 3), this beautiful park's ample acreage is Tallinn's favourite patch of green. Together with the baroque Kadriorg Palace, it was commissioned by the Russian tsar Peter the

---

## ITINERARIES

### Three days

Base yourself in **Tallinn** and spend your first day exploring all the nooks and crannies of the **Old Town**. The following day, do what most tourists don't – step out of Old Town. Explore **Kadriorg Park** for a first-rate greenery and art fix, then hit the wonderful Estonian Open-Air Museum. On your last day, hire a car or take a day tour to **Lahemaa National Park**.

### One week

Spend your first three days in **Tallinn**, then allow a full day to explore **Lahemaa** before bedding down within the national park. The following day, continue on to **Tartu** for a night or two and then finish up in **Pärnu**.

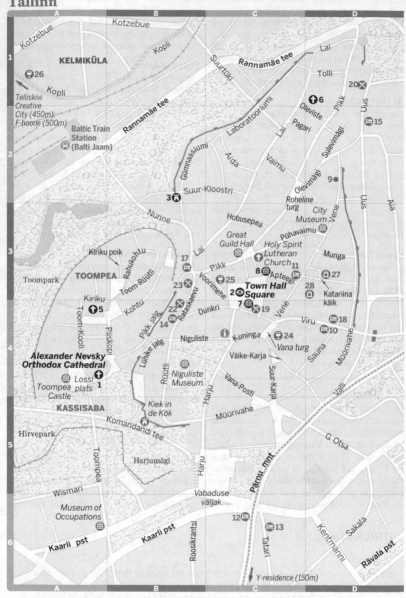

Great for his wife Catherine I soon after his conquest of Estonia (Kadriorg means Catherine's Valley in Estonian). Nowadays the oak, lilac and horse chestnut trees provide shade for strollers and picnickers, the formal pond and gardens provide a genteel backdrop for romantic promenades and wedding photos, and the children's playground is a favourite off-leash area for the city's youngsters.

# Tallinn

## ◎ Top Sights
| | | |
|---|---|---|
| 1 | Alexander Nevsky Orthodox Cathedral | A4 |
| 2 | Town Hall Square | C3 |

## ◎ Sights
| | | |
|---|---|---|
| 3 | Lower Town Wall | B2 |
| 4 | Rotermann Quarter | F3 |
| 5 | St Mary's Lutheran Cathedral | A4 |
| 6 | St Olaf's Church | D1 |
| 7 | Tallinn Town Hall | C4 |
| 8 | Town Council Pharmacy | C3 |

## ✦ Activities, Courses & Tours
| | | |
|---|---|---|
| 9 | City Bike | D2 |

## ▣ Sleeping
| | | |
|---|---|---|
| 10 | Hotel Cru | D4 |
| 11 | Hotel Telegraaf | C3 |
| 12 | Hotell Palace | C6 |
| 13 | Monk's Bunk | C6 |
| 14 | Old House Apartments | B4 |
| 15 | Old House Hostel & Guesthouse | D2 |
| 16 | Red Emperor | E3 |
| 17 | Tabinoya | B3 |
| 18 | Viru Backpackers | D4 |

## ✖ Eating
| | | |
|---|---|---|
| 19 | III Draakon | C4 |
| 20 | Leib | D1 |
| 21 | Ö | E2 |
| | Rataskaevu 16 | (see 14) |
| | Tchaikovsky | (see 11) |
| 22 | Vegan Restoran V | B4 |
| 23 | Von Krahli Aed | B3 |

## ◉ Drinking & Nightlife
| | | |
|---|---|---|
| 24 | Clazz | C4 |
| 25 | DM Baar | C3 |
| 26 | Speakeasy by Põhjala | A1 |

## ▣ Shopping
| | | |
|---|---|---|
| 27 | Katariina käik | D3 |
| 28 | Masters' Courtyard | D3 |
| 29 | Viru Keskus | F4 |

Oct-Apr) Kadriorg Palace, built by Peter the Great between 1718 and 1736, now houses a branch of the Estonian Art Museum devoted to Dutch, German and Italian paintings from the 16th to the 18th centuries, and Russian works from the 18th to early 20th centuries (check out the decorative porcelain with communist imagery upstairs). The building is exactly as frilly and fabulous as a palace ought to be and there's a handsome French-style formal garden at the rear.

★**Kadriorg Art Museum** PALACE
(Kardrioru kunstimuuseum; ☎606 6400; www.kadriorumuuseum.ekm.ee; A Weizenbergi 37; adult/child €6.50/4.50; ☉10am-6pm Tue & Thu-Sun, to 8pm Wed May-Sep, 10am-8pm Wed, to 5pm Thu-Sun

If tourists won't go to the countryside, let's bring the countryside to them. That's the modus operandi of the **Estonian Open-Air Museum** (Eesti vabaõhumuuseum; ☑ 654 9101; www.evm.ee; Vabaõhumuuseumi tee 12, Rocca Al Mare; adult/child May-Sep €8/5, Oct-Apr €6/4; ☉ 10am-8pm May-Sep, to 5pm Oct-Apr), an excellent, sprawling complex, where historic buildings have been plucked and transplanted among the tall trees. In summer the time-warping effect is highlighted by staff in period costume performing traditional activities among the wooden farmhouses and windmills.

★ **Kumu** GALLERY
(☑ 602 6000; www.kumu.ekm.ee; A Weizenbergi 34; all galleries adult/student €8/6, 5th floor only €4/3; ☉ 10am-8pm Thu, 10am-6pm Fri-Sun year-round, plus 10am-6pm Tue Apr-Sep, 10am-6pm Wed Oct-Mar) This futuristic, Finnish-designed, seven-storey building (2006) is a spectacular structure of limestone, glass and copper, nicely integrated into the landscape. Kumu (the name is short for *kunstimuuseum* or art museum) contains the country's largest repository of Estonian art as well as constantly changing contemporary exhibits.

◉ **Pirita**

Pirita's main claim to fame is that it was the base for the sailing events of the 1980 Moscow Olympics; international regattas are still held here. It's also home to Tallinn's largest and most popular beach.

Buses 1A, 8, 34A and 38 all run between the city centre and Pirita, with the last two continuing on to the TV Tower.

**Tallinn TV Tower** VIEWPOINT
(Tallinna teletorn; ☑ 686 3005; www.teletorn.ee; Kloostrimetsa tee 58a; adult/child €10/6; ☉ 10am-7pm) Opened in time for the 1980 Olympics, this futuristic 314m tower offers brilliant views from its 22nd floor (175m). Press a button and frosted glass disks set in the floor suddenly clear, giving a view straight down. Once you're done gawping, check out the interactive displays in the space-age pods. Daredevils can try the open-air 'edge walk' (€20).

⊂ **Tours**

**Tallinn Traveller Tours** TOURS
(☑ 5837 4800; www.traveller.ee) Entertaining, good-value tours – including a two-hour Old Town walking tour that departs at midday from outside the tourist information centre (it's nominally free but tips are encouraged). There are also ghost tours (€15), bike tours (from €19) and day trips to as far afield as Rīga (€55).

**City Bike** CYCLING
(☑ 511 1819; www.citybike.ee; Vene 33; ☉ 10am-7pm, to 6pm Oct-Apr) 'Welcome to Tallinn' tours (€19, two hours) depart at 11am year-round and include Kadriorg and Pirita. 'Other Side' tours take in Kalamaja and Stroomi Beach (from €19, 2½ hours), while 'Countryside Cycling & Old Town Walking' tours head out as far as the Open-Air Museum (€57, four hours). It also co-ordinates self-guided day trips and longer itineraries.

**Epic Bar Crawl** TOURS
(☑ 5624 3088; www.freetour.com; tour €12-15; ☉ 10pm Wed-Sat) The Epic Bar Crawl bills itself as 'the most fun and disorderly pub crawl in Tallinn' and the price includes a welcome beer or cider, a shot in each of three bars and entry to a nightclub. It also offers particularly ignominious packages designed for stags.

🛏 **Sleeping**

🛏 **Old Town**

★ **Tabinoya** HOSTEL €
(☑ 632 0062; www.tabinoya.com; Nunne 1; dm €17-19, d €50; @ 🖤) The Baltic's first Japanese-run hostel occupies the two top floors of a charming old building, with dorms and a communal lounge at the top, and spacious private rooms, a kitchen and a sauna below. Bathroom facilities are shared. The vibe's a bit more comfortable and quiet than most of Tallinn's hostels. Book ahead.

**Red Emperor** HOSTEL €
(☑ 615 0035; www.redemperorhostel.com; Aia 10; dm/s/d from €13/22/34; @ 🖤) Situated above a wonderfully grungy live-music bar, Red Emperor is Tallinn's premier party hostel for those of a beardy, indie persuasion. Facilities are good, with brightly painted rooms, wooden bunks and plenty of showers, and

there are organised activities every day (karaoke, shared dinners etc). Pack heavy-duty earplugs if you're a light sleeper.

### Old House Hostel & Guesthouse    HOSTEL €
(☑ 641 1281; www.oldhouse.ee; Uus 22 & Uus 26; dm/s/d €20/40/56; P @ 🖘) Although one is called a hostel and one a guesthouse, these twin establishments both combine a cosy guesthouse feel with hostel facilities (bunk-less dorm rooms, shared bathrooms, guest kitchens and lounges). The homey, old-world decor (antiques, wacky wallpaper, plants, lamps) and the relatively quiet Old Town location will appeal to budget travellers who like things to be nice and comfortable.

### Old House Apartments    APARTMENT €€
(☑ 641 1464; www.oldhouseapartments.ee; Rataskaevu 16; apt €99-109; P 🖘) Old House is an understatement for this wonderful 14th-century merchant's house. It's been split into eight beautifully furnished apartments (including a spacious two-bedroom one with traces of a medieval painted ceiling). There are a further 21 apartments scattered around the Old Town in similar buildings, although the quality and facilities vary widely.

### Viru Backpackers    HOSTEL €€
(☑ 644 6050; www.virubackpackers.com; 3rd fl, Viru 5; s/d €38/54; ✳ 🖘) This small, much flasher sibling of Monk's Bunk (p169) offers cosy, brightly painted private rooms, some of which have their own bathrooms. It's a quieter environment than the Monk, albeit in a noisier part of town.

### ★Hotel Cru    HOTEL €€€
(☑ 611 7600; www.cruhotel.eu; Viru 8; s/d/ste €105/130/270; 🖘) Behind its pretty powder-blue facade, this boutique 14th-century offering has richly furnished rooms with plenty of original features (timber beams and stone walls) scattered along a rabbit warren of corridors. The cheapest are a little snug.

### Hotel Telegraaf    HOTEL €€€
(☑ 600 0600; www.telegraafhotel.com; Vene 9; r €225-255; P ✳ 🖘 ▣) This upmarket hotel in a converted 19th-century former telegraph station delivers style in spades. It boasts a spa, a pretty courtyard, an acclaimed restaurant, swanky decor and smart, efficient service. 'Superior' rooms, in the older part of the building, have more historical detail but we prefer the marginally cheaper 'executive' rooms for their bigger proportions and sharp decor.

## 🛏 City Centre

### Monk's Bunk    HOSTEL €
(☑ 636 3924; www.themonksbunk.com; Tatari 1; dm €13-17, r €44-50; @ 🖘) Very much a party hostel; the only monk we can imagine fitting in here is, perhaps, Friar Tuck. There are organised activities every night, including legendary pub crawls. The facilities are good, with high ceilings, free lockers and underfloor heating in the bathrooms.

### ★Y-residence    APARTMENT €€
(☑ 502 1477; www.yogaresidence.eu; Pärnu mnt 32; apt €65-150; 🖘) The 'Y' stands for 'yoga', which is a strange name for what's basically a block of very modern, fresh and well-equipped apartments, a short stroll from the Old Town. You can expect friendly staff, a kitchenette and a washing machine. There is a second block north of the Old Town.

### Hotell Palace    HOTEL €€€
(☑ 680 6655; www.tallinnhotels.ee; Vabaduse Väljak 3; r €135-180; ✳ 🖘 ▣) A recent renovation has swept through this architecturally interesting 1930s hotel, leaving comfortable, tastefully furnished rooms in its wake. It's directly across the road from Freedom Sq and the Old Town. The complex includes an indoor pool, a spa, saunas and a small gym, although they're only free for those staying in superior rooms or suites.

### Swissôtel Tallinn    HOTEL €€€
(☑ 624 0000; www.swissotel.com; Tornimäe 3; r €235-390; ✳ 🖘 ▣) Raising the standards at the big end of town while stretching up 30 floors, this 238-room hotel offers elegant, sumptuous rooms with superlative views. The bathroom design is ultra-cool and, if further indulgence is required, there's an in-house spa. Friendly staff, too.

## ✗ Eating

## ✗ Old Town

### ★Vegan Restoran V    VEGAN €
(☑ 626 9087; www.vonkrahl.ee; Rataskaevu 12; mains €6-10; ⊙ noon-11pm Sun-Thu, noon-midnight Fri & Sat; 🖉) Visiting vegans are spoilt for choice in this wonderful restaurant. In summer everyone wants one of the four tables on the street but the atmospheric interior is just as great. The food is excellent; expect the likes of sweet potato peanut curry, spicy tofu with quinoa and stuffed zucchini.

**III Draakon**　　　　　　　　　CAFE €

(www.kolmasdraakon.ee; Raekoja plats 1; mains €1-3; ⊙9am-midnight) There's bucketloads of atmosphere at this Lilliputian tavern below the Town Hall, and super-cheap elk soup, sausages and oven-hot pies baked fresh on site. The historic setting is amped up – expect costumed wenches with a good line in tourist banter, and beer served in ceramic steins.

★**Rataskaevu 16**　　　　　　ESTONIAN €€

(✐642 4025; www.rataskaevu16.ee; Rataskaevu 16; mains €10-17; ⊙noon-11pm Sun-Thu, noon-midnight Fri & Sat; ☷) If you've ever had a hankering for braised roast elk, this is the place to come. Although it's hardly a traditional eatery, plenty of Estonian faves fill the menu – fried Baltic herrings, grilled pork fillet and Estonian cheeses among them. Finish with a serve of its legendary chocolate cake.

**Von Krahli Aed**　　　　MODERN EUROPEAN €€

(✐626 9088; www.vonkrahl.ee; Rataskaevu 8; mains €13-17; ⊙noon-midnight Mon-Sat, noon-11pm Sun; ☏✐) You'll find plenty of greenery on your plate at this rustic, plant-filled restaurant (*aed* means 'garden'). The menu embraces fresh flavours and wins fans by noting vegan, gluten-, lactose- and egg-free options.

★**Tchaikovsky**　　　　RUSSIAN, FRENCH €€€

(✐600 0610; www.telegraafhotel.com; Vene 9; mains €24-26; ⊙noon-3pm & 6-11pm Mon-Fri, 1-11pm Sat & Sun) Located in a glassed-in pavilion at the heart of the Hotel Telegraaf, Tchaikovsky offers a dazzling tableau of blinged-up chandeliers, gilt frames and greenery. Service is formal and faultless, as is the classic Franco-Russian menu, all accompanied by live chamber music.

★**Leib**　　　　　　　　　　ESTONIAN €€€

(✐611 9026; www.leibresto.ee; Uus 31; mains €13-22; ⊙noon-3pm & 6-11pm Mon-Fri, noon-11pm Sat) An inconspicuous gate opens onto a large lawn guarded by busts of Sean Connery and Robert Burns. Welcome to the former home of Tallinn's Scottish club (really!), where 'simple, soulful food' is served along with homemade *leib* (bread). The slow-cooked meat and grilled fish dishes are exceptional.

### ✕ City Centre

★**Ö**　　　　　　　　　　　NEW NORDIC €€€

(✐661 6150; www.restoran-o.ee; Mere pst 6e; degustations €59-76; ⊙6-11pm Mon-Sat, closed Jul) Award-winning Ö (pronounced 'er') has carved a unique space in Tallinn's culinary world, delivering inventive degustation menus showcasing seasonal Estonian produce. There's a distinct 'New Nordic' influence at play, and the understated dining room nicely counterbalances the theatrical cuisine.

### ✕ Kalamaja

**F-hoone**　　　　　　　　　PUB FOOD €

(✐5322 6855; www.fhoone.ee; Telliskivi 60a; mains €5-10; ⊙kitchen 9am-11pm Mon-Sat, 9am-9pm Sun; ☏✐) The trailblazer of the überhip Telliskivi complex, this cavernous place embraces industrial chic and offers a quality menu of pasta, burgers, stews, grilled vegies and felafels. Wash it down with a craft beer from the extensive selection.

★**Moon**　　　　　　　　　RUSSIAN €€

(✐631 4575; www.restoranmoon.ee; Võrgu 3; mains €10-20; ⊙noon-11pm Mon-Sat, 1-9pm Sun, closed Jul) The best restaurant in ever-increasingly hip Kalamaja, Moon is informal but excellent, combining Russian and broader European influences to delicious effect. Save room for dessert.

**Klaus**　　　　　　　　　　CAFE €€

(✐5691 9010; www.klauskohvik.ee; Kalasadama; mains €9.50-14; ⊙9am-11pm; ☏) There's a fresh, designery feel to this informal cafe down by the water. The menu is full of tasty snacks and more substantial meals, including lamb koftas, pasta and steaks. We wholeheartedly endorse the 'Cubanos' pulled pork sandwich, although we don't suggest tackling this messy beast on a date.

### ✕ Pirita

★**NOA**　　　　　　　　　　INTERNATIONAL €€€

(✐508 0589; www.noaresto.ee; Ranna tee 3; mains €12-24; ⊙noon-11pm Mon-Thu, noon-midnight Fri & Sat, noon-10pm Sun; ✐) It's worth the trek out to the far side of Pirita to this elegant eatery which opened in 2014 and was rated the best in Estonia that very year. It's housed in a stylish low-slung pavilion that gazes back over Tallinn Bay to the Old Town. Choose between the more informal à la carte restaurant and the degustation-only Chef's Hall.

## 🍷 Drinking & Nightlife

**Speakeasy by Põhjala**　　　　　　　BAR

(www.speakeasy.ee; Kopli 4; ⊙6pm-2am Wed-Sat) It's pretty basic – particleboard walls, junkstore furniture and a courtyard surrounded by derelict buildings – but this hip little bar is a showcase for one of Estonia's best microbreweries. Expect lots of beardy dudes discussing the relative merits of the India Pale Ale over the Imperial Baltic Porter.

**DM Baar** BAR
(✆ 644 2350; www.depechemode.ee; Voorimehe 4; ⊗ noon-4am) If you just can't get enough of Depeche Mode, this is the bar for you. The walls are covered with all manner of memorabilia, including pictures of the actual band partying here. And the soundtrack? Do you really need to ask? If you're not a fan, leave in silence.

**Clazz** BAR
(✆ 666 0003; www.clazz.ee; Vana turg 2; ⊗ 6pm-2am Tue-Thu, noon-3am Fri & Sat) Behind the cheesy name (a contraction of 'classy jazz') is a popular lounge bar featuring live music every night of the week, ranging from jazz to soul, funk, blues and Latin.

## 🛍 Shopping

**Viru Keskus** SHOPPING CENTRE
(www.virukeskus.com; Viru väljak 4; ⊗ 9am-9pm) Tallinn's showpiece shopping mall is home to fashion boutiques, a great bookstore (Rahva Raamat) and a branch of the Piletilevi event ticketing agency. At the rear it connects to the Kaubamaja department store. The main terminal for local buses is in the basement.

**Masters' Courtyard** ARTS & CRAFTS
(Meistrite Hoov; www.hoov.ee; Vene 6; ⊗ 10am-6pm) Rich pickings here, with the cobbled courtyard not only home to a cosy cafe but also small stores and artisans' workshops selling quality ceramics, glass, jewellery, knitwear, woodwork and candles.

**Katariina käik** ARTS & CRAFTS
(St Catherine's Passage; www.katariinagild.eu; off Vene 12) This lovely lane is home to the Katariina Gild comprising several artisans' studios where you can happily browse ceramics, textiles, patchwork quilts, hats, jewellery, stained glass and beautiful leather-bound books.

## ℹ Information

**East-Tallinn Central Hospital** (Ida-Tallinna Keskhaigla; ✆ 666 1900; www.itk.ee; Ravi 18) Offers a full range of services, including a 24-hour emergency room.

**Tallinn Tourist Information Centre** (✆ 645 7777; www.visittallinn.ee; Niguliste 2; ⊗ 9am-5pm Mon-Sat, 10am-3pm Sun Oct-Mar, 9am-6pm Mon-Sat, 9am-4pm Sun Apr, May & Sep, 9am-7pm Mon-Sat, 9am-6pm Sun Jun-Aug) Brochures, maps, event schedules and other info.

## ℹ Getting There & Away

### BUS
The **Central Bus Station** (Tallinna bussijaam; ✆ 12550; www.bussijaam.ee; Lastekodu 46; ⊗ 5am-1am) is about 2km southeast of the Old Town (tram 2 or 4). Destinations include Rakvere (€3.50 to €7, 1½ hours, 19 daily), Tartu (€7 to €12, 2½ hours, at least every half-hour), Otepää (€13, 3½ hours, daily), Pärnu (€6.50 to €11, two hours, at least hourly) and Kuressaare (€15 to €17, four hours, 11 daily). **TPilet** (www.tpilet.ee) has times and prices for all national bus services.

### TRAIN
The **Central Train Station** (Balti Jaam; Toompuiestee 35) is on the northwestern edge of the Old Town. Destinations include Rakvere (€5.50, 1½ hours, three daily), Tartu (€11, two to 2½ hours, eight daily) and Pärnu (€7.60, 2¼ hours, three daily).

## ℹ Getting Around

### TO/FROM THE AIRPORT
➔ **Tallinn Airport** (Tallinna Lennujaam; ✆ 605 8888; www.tallinn-airport.ee; Tartu mnt 101) is 4km from the centre.

➔ Bus 2 runs every 20 to 30 minutes (6am to around 11pm) from the A Laikmaa stop, opposite the Tallink Hotel, next to Viru Keskus. From the airport, bus 2 will take you to the centre. Buy tickets from the driver (€1.60); journey time depends on traffic but rarely exceeds 20 minutes.

➔ A taxi between the airport and the city centre should cost less than €10.

### PUBLIC TRANSPORT
Tallinn has an excellent network of buses, trams and trolleybuses that run from around 6am to midnight. The major **local bus station** is on the basement level of the Viru Keskus shopping centre, although some buses terminate their routes on the surrounding streets. All local public transport timetables are online at www.tallinn.ee.

Public transport is free for Tallinn residents. Visitors still need to pay, either from the driver with cash (€1.60 for a single journey) or by using the e-ticketing system. Buy a plastic smartcard (€2 deposit) and top up with credit, then validate the card at the start of each journey using the orange card-readers. Fares using the e-ticketing system cost €1.10/3/6 for an hour/day/five days.

The Tallinn Card includes free public transport. Travelling without a valid ticket runs the risk of a €40 fine.

ESTONIA TALLINN

## TAXI

Taxis are plentiful, but each company sets its own fare. The base fare ranges from €2 to €5, followed by 50c to €1 per kilometre. To avoid suprises, try **Krooni Takso** (☑ 1212; www.kroonitakso.ee; base fare €2.50, per km 6am-11pm €0.50, 11pm-6am €0.55) or **Reval Takso** (☑ 1207; www.reval-takso.ee; base fare €2.29, per km €0.49).

# LAHEMAA NATIONAL PARK

The perfect country retreat from the capital, Lahemaa takes in a stretch of coast indented with peninsulas and bays, plus 475 sq km of pine-fresh forested hinterland. Visitors are looked after with cosy guesthouses, remote seaside campgrounds and a network of pine-scented forest trails.

## ☉ Sights

**Palmse Manor**                           HISTORIC BUILDING
(☑ 5559 9977; www.palmse.ee; adult/child €7/5; ☉ 10am-5pm, to 6pm summer) Fully restored Palmse Manor is the showpiece of Lahemaa National Park, housing the visitor centre in its former stables. The pretty manor house (1720, rebuilt in the 1780s) is now a museum containing period furniture and clothing. Other estate buildings have also been restored and put to new use: the distillery is a hotel, the steward's residence is a guesthouse, the lakeside bathhouse is a summertime restaurant and the farm labourers' quarters became a tavern.

**Altja**                                           VILLAGE
First mentioned in 1465, this fishing village has many restored or reconstructed traditional buildings, including a wonderfully ancient-looking tavern that was actually built in 1976. Altja's Swing Hill (Kiitemägi), complete with a traditional Estonian wooden swing, has long been the focus of Midsummer's Eve festivities in Lahemaa. The 3km circular **Altja Nature & Culture Trail** starts at Swing Hill and takes in net sheds, fishing cottages and the stone field known as the 'open-air museum of stones'.

## 🍴 Sleeping & Eating

**Lepispea Caravan & Camping** CAMPGROUND €
(☑ 5450 1522; www.lepispea.eu; Lepispea 3; tent per person €6, caravan €17, plus per person €2; ☉ May-Sep; P 🕯) In Lepispea, 1km west of Võsu, this campground is spread over a large

field fringed by trees and terminating in a little reed-lined beach. Facilities are good, including a sauna house for rent. It also hires bikes (per day €10).

**★ Merekalda**                           APARTMENT €€
(☑ 323 8451; www.merekalda.ee; Neeme tee 2, Käsmu; r €49, apt €69-99; ☉ May-Sep; P 🕯) At the entrance to Käsmu, this peaceful retreat is set around a lovely large garden right on the bay. Ideally you'll plump for an apartment with a sea view and terrace, but you'll need to book ahead. Boat and bike hire are available.

**★ Toomarahva Turismitalu**      GUESTHOUSE, CAMPGROUND €€
(☑ 505 0850; www.toomarahva.ee; Altja; tent/hayloft per person €3/5, caravan €10, cottage €30, d €50, apt €70-120; 🕯) This atmospheric farmstead comprises thatch-roofed wooden buildings and a garden full of flowers and sculptures. Sleeping options include two cute and comfortable rooms that share a bathroom, and an apartment that can be rented with either one or two bedrooms, or you can even doss down in the hayloft in summer. Plus there's a traditional sauna for hire.

**★ Altja Kõrts**                           ESTONIAN €
(☑ 324 0070; www.palmse.ee; Altja; mains €6-8; ☉ noon-8pm) Set in a thatched, wooden building with a large terrace, this uber-rustic place serves delicious plates of traditional fare (baked pork with sauerkraut etc) to candlelit wooden tables. It's extremely atmospheric and a lot of fun.

## ℹ Information

**Lahemaa National Park Visitor Centre**
(☑ 329 5555; www.loodusegakoos.ee; ☉ 9am-5pm or 6pm daily mid-Apr–mid-Oct, 9am-5pm Mon-Fri mid-Oct–mid-Apr) This excellent centre stocks the essential map of Lahemaa (€1.90), as well as information on hiking trails, accommodation and guiding services. It's worth starting your park visit with the free 17-minute film titled *Lahemaa – Nature and Man*.

## ℹ Getting There & Away

Hiring a car will give you the most flexibility, or you could take a tour from Tallinn. Exploring the park using public transport requires patience and time. Buses to destinations within the park leave from the town of Rakvere (connected by bus to Tallinn, Tartu and Pärnu), which is 35km southeast of Palmse. Once you've arrived in the park, bike hire is easy to arrange.

# TARTU

POP 98,000

Tartu was the cradle of Estonia's 19th-century national revival and lays claim to being the nation's cultural capital. Locals talk about a special Tartu *vaim* (spirit), created by the time-stands-still feel of its wooden houses and stately buildings, and by the beauty of its parks and riverfront. It's also Estonia's premier university town, with students making up nearly one fifth of the population – guaranteeing a vibrant nightlife for a city of its size.

## ⊙ Sights

Rising to the west of the town hall, Toomemägi (Cathedral Hill) is the original reason for Tartu's existence, functioning on and off as a stronghold from around the 5th or 6th century. It's now a tranquil park, with walking paths meandering through the trees and a pretty-as-a-picture rotunda which serves as a summertime cafe.

### ★ University of Tartu Museum    MUSEUM
(Tartu Ülikool muuseum; ☑ 737 5674; www.muuseum.ut.ee; Lossi 25; adult/child €5/4; ⊙10am-6pm Tue-Sun May-Sep, 11am-5pm Wed-Sun Oct-Apr) Atop Toomemägi are the ruins of a Gothic cathedral, originally built by German knights in the 13th century. It was substantially rebuilt in the 15th century, despoiled during the Reformation in 1525, used as a barn, and partly rebuilt between 1804 and 1809 to house the university library, which is now a museum. Inside there are a range of interesting exhibits chronicling student life.

### ★ Town Hall Square    SQUARE
(Raekoja plats) Tartu's main square is lined with grand buildings and echoes with the chink of glasses and plates in summer. The centrepiece is the Town Hall itself, fronted by a statue of students kissing under a spouting umbrella. On the south side of the square, look out for the communist hammer-and-sickle relief that still remains on the facade of number 5.

### Science Centre AHHAA    MUSEUM
(Teaduskeskus AHHAA; www.ahhaa.ee; Sadama 1; adult/child €13/10, planetarium €4, flight simulator €1, 4D theatre €2.50; ⊙10am-7pm Sun-Thu, 10am-8pm Fri & Sat) Head under the dome for a whizz-bang series of interactive exhibits that are liable to bring out the mad scientist in kids and adults alike. Allow at least a couple of hours. And you just haven't lived until you've set a tray of magnetised iron filings

'dancing' to Bronski Beat's *Smalltown Boy*. Upstairs there's a nightmarish collection of pickled organs and deformed foetuses courtesy of the university's medical faculty.

### ★ Estonian National Museum    MUSEUM
(Eesti rahva muuseum; ☑ 736 3051; www.erm.ee; Muuseumi tee 2; adult/child €12/8; ⊙10am-7pm Tue & Thu-Sun, 10am-9pm Wed) This immense, low-slung, architectural showcase is a striking sight and had both Estonian patriots and architecture-lovers purring when it opened in late 2016. The permanent exhibition covers national prehistory and history in some detail. Fittingly, for a museum built over a former Soviet airstrip, the Russian occupation is given in-depth treatment, while the 'Echo of the Urals' exhibition gives an overview of the various peoples speaking tongues in the Estonian language family. There's also a restaurant and cafe.

## ⊨ Sleeping & Eating

### Terviseks    HOSTEL €
(☑ 565 5382; www.terviseksbbb.com; top fl, Raekoja plats 10; dm €15-17, s/d €22/44; @ ﹫ ⏃) Occupying a historic building in a perfect main-square location, this excellent 'backpacker's bed and breakfast' offers dorms (maximum four beds, no bunks), private rooms, a full kitchen and lots of switched-on info about the happening places in town. It's like staying in your rich mate's cool European pad. *Terviseks* (cheers) to that.

### ★ Domus Dorpatensis    APARTMENT €€
(☑ 733 1345; www.dorpatensis.ee; Raekoja plats 1; apt €50-85; ⏃) Run by an academic foundation, this block of 10 apartments offers an unbeatable location and wonderful value for money. The units range in size but all have writing desks (it's run by scholars, after all) and almost all have kitchenettes. The staff are particularly helpful – dispensing parking advice and directing guests to the communal laundry. The entrance is on Ülikooli.

### Tampere Maja    GUESTHOUSE €€
(☑ 738 6300; www.tamperemaja.ee; Jaani 4; s/d/tr/q from €45/72/89/132; P ﹡ @ ﹫ ⏃) With strong links to the Finnish city of Tampere (Tartu's sister city), this cosy guesthouse features six warm, light-filled guest rooms. Breakfast is included and each room has access to cooking facilities. And it wouldn't be Finnish if it didn't offer an authentic sauna (one to four people €15; open to nonguests).

**Villa Margaretha** BOUTIQUE HOTEL €€

(📞731 1820; www.margaretha.ee; Tähe 11/13; s €55-85, d €65-95, ste €175; P🐾) Like something out of a fairy tale, this wooden art nouveau house has a sweet little turret and romantic rooms decked out with sleigh beds and artfully draped fabrics. The cheaper rooms in the modern extension at the rear are bland in comparison. It's a little away from the action but still within walking distance of the Old Town.

★ **Antonius Hotel** HOTEL €€€

(📞737 0377; www.hotelantonius.ee; Ülikooli 15; s/d/ste from €95/120/220; ✳️🐾) Sitting plumb opposite the main university building, this first-rate, 18-room boutique hotel is loaded with antiques and period features. Breakfast is served in the 18th-century vaulted cellar, which in the evening morphs into a top-notch restaurant.

**Cafe Truffe** MODERN EUROPEAN €€

(📞742 8840; www.truffe.ee; Raekoja plats 16; mains €11-19; ⊙11am-11pm Mon-Thu, 11am-1am Fri & Sat, 11am-10pm Sun) Truffe calls itself a cafe, although it feels more like an upmarket bar, and the food is absolutely restaurant quality. One thing's for certain, it's the best eatery on Town Hall Sq and one of Tartu's finest. In summer, grab a seat on the large terrace and tuck into a steak with truffle sauce or a delicately smoked duck breast.

### ℹ️ Information

**Tartu Tourist Information Centre** (📞744 2111; www.visittartu.com; Town Hall, Raekoja plats; ⊙9am-6pm Mon-Fri, 10am-5pm Sat & Sun May–mid-Sep, 9am-6pm Mon, 9am-5pm Tue-Fri, 10am-2pm Sat mid-Sep–Apr) Stocks local maps and brochures, books accommodation and tour guides, and has free internet access.

### ℹ️ Getting There & Away

#### BUS

From the **bus station** (Tartu Autobussijaam; Turu 2 (enter from Soola); ⊙6am-9pm), buses run to and from Tallinn (€7 to €12, 2½ hours, at least every half hour), Rakvere (€7 to €9, three hours, eight daily), Otepää (€2 to €3.50, one hour, 10 daily), Pärnu (€9.60 to €12, 2¾ hours, 12 daily) and Kuressaare (€18, 5½ hours, two daily).

#### TRAIN

Tartu's beautifully restored **train station** (📞673 7400; www.elron.ee; Vaksali 6) is 1.5km southwest of the old town (at the end of Kuperjanovi street). Four express (2½-hour) and four regular (two-hour) services head to Tallinn daily (both €11),

# OTEPÄÄ

POP 1900

The small hilltop town of Otepää, 44km south of Tartu, is the centre of a picturesque area of forests, lakes and rivers. The district is beloved by Estonians for its natural beauty and its many possibilities for hiking, biking and swimming in summer, and cross-country skiing in winter. It's often referred to as Estonia's winter capital, and winter weekends here are busy and loads of fun. Some have even dubbed the area (tongue firmly in cheek) the 'Estonian Alps' – a reference not to its peaks but to its excellent ski trails. The 63km Tartu Ski Marathon kicks off here every February but even in summer you'll see professional athletes and enthusiasts hurtling around on roller skis.

The main part of Otepää is centred on the intersection of the Tartu, Võru and Valga highways, where you'll find the main square, shops and some patchy residential streets. A small swathe of forest separates it from a smaller settlement by the lakeshore, 2km southwest.

### 🛏️ Sleeping & Eating

**Murakas** HOTEL €€

(📞731 1410; www.murakas.ee; Valga mnt 23a; s/d €50/60; P🐾) With only 10 bedrooms, Murakas is more like a large friendly guesthouse than a hotel. Stripey carpets, blonde wood and balconies give the rooms a fresh feel and there's a similarly breezy breakfast room downstairs.

★ **Mr Jakob** MODERN ESTONIAN €€€

(📞5375 3307; www.otepaagolf.ee; Mäha küla; mains €14-18; ⊙noon-9pm, closed Mon-Thu Nov-Mar; 🐾) Otepää's best restaurant is hidden away at the golf club, 4km west of Pühajärv. The menu is as contemporary and playful as the decor, taking Estonian classics such as pork ribs and marinated herring fillets and producing something quite extraordinary. Add to that charming service and blissful views over the course and surrounding fields.

### ℹ️ Information

**Otepää Tourist Information Centre** (📞766 1200; www.otepaa.eu; Tartu mnt 1; ⊙10am-5pm Mon-Fri, to 3pm Sat & Sun mid-May–mid-Sep, 10am-5pm Mon-Fri, to 2pm Sat rest of year) A well-informed staff distribute maps and brochures, and make recommendations for activities, guide services and lodging in the area.

## ℹ️ Getting There & Away

The **bus station** (Tartu mnt 1) is next to the tourist office. Destinations include Tallinn (€13, 3½ hours, daily) and Tartu (€2 to €3.50, one hour, 10 daily).

# PÄRNU

POP 39,800

Local families, young party-goers and German, Swedish and Finnish holidaymakers join together in a collective prayer for sunny weather while strolling the golden-sand beaches, sprawling parks and picturesque historic centre of Pärnu (*pair*-nu), Estonia's premier seaside resort.

The main thoroughfare of the old town is Rüütli, lined with splendid buildings dating back to the 17th century.

## ◉ Sights

### ★ Pärnu Beach                                                     BEACH

Pärnu's long, wide, sandy beach – sprinkled with volleyball courts, cafes and changing cubicles – is easily the city's main drawcard. A curving path stretches along the sand, lined with fountains, park benches and an excellent playground. Early-20th-century buildings are strung along Ranna pst, the avenue that runs parallel to the beach. Across the road, the formal gardens of **Rannapark** are ideal for a summertime picnic.

### ★ Museum of New Art                                 GALLERY

(Uue kunstimuuseum; ☑ 443 0772; www.mona. ee; Esplanaadi 10; adult/child €4/2; ☉ 9am-9pm Jun-Aug, 9am-7pm Sep-May) Pärnu's former Communist Party headquarters now houses one of Estonia's edgiest galleries. As part of its commitment to pushing the cultural envelope, it stages an international nude art exhibition every summer. Founded by film-maker Mark Soosaar, the gallery also hosts the annual Pärnu Film Festival.

## 🛏️ Sleeping

In summer it's worth booking ahead; outside high season you should be able to snare a good deal (rates can be up to 50% lower).

### Embrace                                                          B&B €€

(☑ 5887 3404; www.embrace.ee; Pardi 30; r €110; ☉ Mar-early Jan; P ✳ 🛜) Snuggle up in an old wooden house in a suburban street, close to the beach and water park. Rooms strike a nice balance between antique and contemporary,

and there's a set of four modern, self-contained apartments in a neighbouring annex.

### Inge Villa                                            GUESTHOUSE €€

(☑ 443 8510; www.ingevilla.ee; Kaarli 20; s/d/ ste €56/70/82; ♿ 🛜) Describing itself as a 'Swedish-Estonian villa hotel', low-key and lovely Inge Villa occupies a prime patch of real estate near the beach. Its 11 rooms are simply decorated in muted tones with Nordic minimalism to the fore. The garden, lounge and sauna seal the deal.

### Villa Ammende                                           HOTEL €€€

(☑ 447 3888; www.ammende.ee; Mere pst 7; s/d/ ste €225/275/475; P ✳ 🛜) Luxury abounds in this refurbished 1904 art nouveau mansion, which lords it over handsomely manicured grounds. The gorgeous exterior – looking like one of the cooler Paris metro stops writ large – is matched by an elegant lobby and individually antique-furnished rooms. Rooms in the gardener's house are more affordable but lack a little of the wow factor. It's a lot cheaper outside of July.

## 🍴 Eating

### ★ Piccadilly                                                    CAFE €

(☑ 442 0085; www.kohvila.com; Pühavaimu 15; dishes €4-6; ☉ 9am-7pm Mon-Thu, 11am-midnight Fri-Sat, 11am-7pm Sun; 🖉) Piccadilly offers a down-tempo haven for wine-lovers and vegetarians and an extensive range of hot beverages. Savoury options include delicious salads, sandwiches and omelettes, but really it's all about the sweeties, including moreish cheesecake and handmade chocolates.

### ★ Lime Lounge                              INTERNATIONAL €€€

(☑ 449 2190; www.limelounge.ee; Hommiku 17; mains €8-19; ☉ noon-11pm Mon-Thu, noon-midnight Fri & Sat; 🛜🍴) Bright and zesty Lime Lounge feels more like a cocktail bar than a restaurant, although the food really is excellent. The well-travelled menu bounds from Russia (borscht) to France (duck breast), Italy (delicious pasta) and all the way to Thailand (*tom kha gai* soup).

## ℹ️ Information

**Pärnu Tourist Information Centre** (☑ 447 3000; www.visitparnu.com; Uus 4; ☉ 9am-6pm mid-May–mid-Sep, 9am-5pm Mon-Fri, 10am-2pm Sat & Sun mid-Sep–mid-May) A very helpful centre stocking maps and brochures, booking accommodation and rental cars (for a small fee), and providing a left-luggage service (per day €2). There's a small gallery attached as well as a toilet and showers.

## ⓘ Getting There & Away

Pärnu's **bus station** is right in the centre of town, with services to/from Tallinn (€6.50 to €11, two hours, at least hourly), Rakvere (€9 to €11, 2¾ to four hours, three daily), Tartu (€9.60 to €12, 2¾ hours, 12 daily) and Kuressaare (€13, 3½ hours, four daily).

# MUHU

POP 1560

Connected to Saaremaa by a 2.5km causeway, the island of Muhu has the undeserved reputation as the 'doormat' for the bigger island – lots of people passing through on their way from the ferry, but few stopping. In fact, Estonia's third-biggest island offers plenty of excuses to hang around, not least one of the country's best restaurants and some excellent accommodation options. There's no tourist office on the island, but there's lots of good information online at www.muhu.info.

## ⊙ Sights

**Muhu Museum**                                    MUSEUM

(☑ 454 8872; www.muhumuuseum.ee; Koguva; adult/concession €3/2; ⊙ 9am-6pm mid-May–mid-Sep, 10am-5pm Tue-Sat rest of year) Koguva, 6km off the main road on the western tip of Muhu, is an exceptionally well-preserved, old-fashioned island village, now protected as an open-air museum. One ticket allows you to wander through an old schoolhouse, a house displaying beautiful traditional textiles from the area (including painstakingly detailed folk costumes) and a farm that was the ancestral home of author Juhan Smuul (1922–71). You can poke around various farm buildings, one of which contains a collection of Singer sewing machines.

## ⌣ Sleeping & Eating

★**Pädaste Manor**                                HOTEL €€€

(☑ 454 8800; www.padaste.ee; Pädaste; r €254-481, ste €416-875; ⊙ Mar-Oct; P 🎧) If money's no object, here's where to part with it. This manicured bayside estate encompasses the restored manor house (14 rooms and a fine-dining restaurant), a stone carriage house (nine rooms and a spa centre) and a separate stone 'sea house' brasserie. The attention to detail is second-to-none, from the pop-up TVs to the antique furnishings and Muhu embroidery.

## ⓘ Getting There & Away

**BOAT**

➠ Car ferries run by **Praamid** (☑ 1310; www.praamid.ee; adult/child/car €3/1.50/8.40) make the 25-minute crossing between Virtsu on the mainland and Kuivastu on Muhu.

➠ Boats depart Virtsu from roughly 5.35am until midnight, with at least one or two sailings per hour up until 10.15pm.

➠ A 50% surcharge applies to vehicles heading to the island after 1pm on Fridays and departing the island after 1pm on Sundays.

➠ Up to 70% of each boat's capacity is presold online; the website has a real-time indicator showing what percentage has already been sold. The remaining 30% is kept for drive-up customers and offered on a first-in, first-on basis. You should definitely consider prebooking at busy times, particularly around weekends in summer.

➠ Tickets purchased online must either be printed out or loaded as an electronic ticket onto a smartphone.

➠ If you miss your prebooked boat, your ticket will be valid for the regular queue on subsequent boats for up to 48 hours.

**BUS**

Buses take the ferry from the mainland and continue through to Saaremaa via the causeway, stopping along the main road. Major destinations include Tallinn (€12 to €14, three hours, 11 daily), Tartu (€17, five hours, two daily), Pärnu (€8.80, 2½ hours, four daily) and Kuressaare (€5 to €5.60, one hour, 18 daily).

# SAAREMAA

POP 31,600

Saaremaa (literally 'island land') is synonymous to Estonians with space, spruce and fresh air – and bottled water, vodka and killer beer. Estonia's largest island (roughly the size of Luxembourg) is still substantially covered in forests of pine, spruce and juniper, while its windmills, lighthouses and tiny villages seem largely unbothered by the passage of time.

During the Soviet era the entire island was off limits to visitors (due to an early-radar system and rocket base stationed there), even to 'mainland' Estonians, who needed a permit to visit. This resulted in a minimum of industrial build-up and the unwitting protection of the island's rural charm.

This unique old-time setting goes hand-in-hand with inextinguishable Saaremaan pride. Saaremaa has always had an

## ESSENTIAL FOOD & DRINK

Estonian gastronomy mixes Nordic, Russian and German influences, and prizes local and seasonal produce.

**Desserts** On the sweet side, you'll find delicious chocolates, marzipan and cakes.

**Favourite drinks** Õlu (beer) is the favourite alcoholic drink. Popular brands include Saku and A Le Coq, and aficionados should seek out the product of the local microbreweries such as Tallinn's Põhjala. Other tipples include vodka (Viru Valge and Saremaa are the best-known local brands) and Vana Tallinn, a syrupy sweet liqueur, also available in a cream version.

**Other favourites** Include black bread, sauerkraut, black pudding, smoked meat and fish, creamy salted butter and sour cream, which is served with almost everything.

**Pork and potatoes** The traditional stodgy standbys, prepared a hundred different ways.

**Seasonal** In summer, berries enter the menu in both sweet and savoury dishes, while everyone goes crazy for forest mushrooms in the autumn.

independent streak and was usually the last part of Estonia to fall to invaders. Its people have their own customs, songs and costumes. They don't revere mainland Estonia's *Kalevipoeg* legend, for Saaremaa has its own hero, Suur Tõll, who fought many battles around the island against devils and fiends.

Kuressaare, the capital of Saaremaa, is on the south coast (75km from the Muhu ferry terminal) and is a natural base for visitors. It's here among the upmarket hotels that you'll understand where the island got its nickname, 'Spa-remaa'. When the long days arrive, so too do the Finns and Swedes, jostling for beach and sauna space with Estonian urban-escapees. More information is online at www.saaremaa.ee.

### ⊙ Sights

The long stretch of pine-lined sand from **Mändjala** to **Järve**, west of Kuressaare, is Saaremaa's main beach resort. The shallow beach curves languidly towards the south, where the 32km **Sõrve Peninsula** takes over. This beautiful but sparsely populated finger of land comes to a dramatic end at **Sääre**, with a lighthouse and a narrow sand spit extending out to sea.

The peninsula saw heavy fighting during WWII and the battle scars remain. Various abandoned bunkers and battlements, and the remnants of the Lõme-Kaimri anti-tank defence lines, can still be seen.

★**Kuressaare Castle**　　　CASTLE
(www.saaremaamuuseum.ee) Majestic Kuressaare Castle stands facing the sea at the southern end of the town, on an artificial island ringed by a moat. It's the best-preserved castle in the Baltic and the region's only medieval stone castle that has remained intact. The castle grounds are open to the public at all times but to visit the keep you'll need to buy a ticket to Saaremaa Museum.

**Panga Pank**　　　VIEWPOINT
Saaremaa's highest cliffs run along the northern coast near Panga for 3km. The highest point (21.3m) was a sacred place where sacrifices were made to the sea god; gifts of flowers, coins, vodka and beer are still sometimes left here. It's a pretty spot, looking down at the treacherous waters below.

### 🛏 Sleeping & Eating

The tourist office can organise beds in private apartments and farms across the island. Hotel prices are up to 50% cheaper from September through April. Most hotel spa centres are open to nonguests. All of the following are in Kuressaare, unless otherwise noted.

★**Georg Ots Spa Hotel**　　　HOTEL €€
(Gospa; ☑ 455 0000; www.gospa.ee; Tori 2; r €185-225, ste €295; 🅿 ❄ 🛜 🛅 ♿) Named after a renowned Estonian opera singer, Gospa has modern rooms with wildly striped carpet, enormous king-sized beds and a warm but minimalist design. Most rooms have balconies and there's a fitness centre and excellent spa centre, including a pool and multiple saunas. Separate freestanding 'residences' are also available, and families are very well catered for. Prices vary widely.

★ **Piibutopsu** APARTMENT €€
(☑ 5693 0288; www.piibutopsu.ee; Ülejõe 19a, Nasva; d/tr/q €60/90/120; P 🖥) Set on the ample lawn of a private residence down a side street in Nasva (the first little settlement west of Kuressaare), Piibutopsu offers four well-equipped holiday apartments in a new custom-built block. The units are grouped around a central lounge with a wood fire, and there's even a mini spa centre on site. All in all, an excellent option.

★ **Ekesparre** BOUTIQUE HOTEL €€€
(☑ 453 8778; www.ekesparre.ee; Lossi 27; r €172-215; ⊙ Apr-Oct; P 🖥) Holding pole position on the castle grounds, this elegant 10-room hotel has been returned to its art nouveau glory. Period wallpaper and carpet, Tiffany lamps and a smattering of orchids add to the refined, clubby atmosphere, while the 3rd-floor guests' library is a gem. As you'd expect from the price, it's a polished operator.

★ **Retro** CAFE €
(☑ 5683 8400; www.kohvikretro.ee; Lossi 5; mains €7.50-14; ⊙ noon-10pm Mon-Thu, to midnight Fri & Sat, to 8pm Sun; 🖥 🍴) The menu at this hip little cafe-bar is deceptively simple (pasta, burgers, steak, grilled fish), but Retro takes things to the next level, making its own pasta and burger buns and using the best fresh local produce. Desserts are delicious, too. There's also a great selection of Estonian craft beer, perfect for supping on the large rear terrace.

## ℹ Information

**Kuressaare Tourist Office** (☑ 453 3120; www. kuressaare.ee; Tallinna 2; ⊙ 9am-6pm Mon-Fri, 10am-4pm Sat & Sun mid-May–mid-Sep, 9am-5pm Mon-Fri rest of year) Inside the old town hall, it sells maps and guides, arranges accommodation and has information on boat trips and island tours.

**Leisi Tourist Office** (☑ 457 3073; www. leisivald.ee; Kuressaare mnt. 11; ⊙ 1-7pm Jun-Aug; 🖥) If you're arriving from Hiiumaa via the Sõru-Triigi ferry, pick up maps and get general Saaremaa information at the tiny Leisi tourist office, inside the pretty, vine-covered restaurant, Sassimaja.

## ℹ Getting There & Away

Most travellers reach Saaremaa by taking the ferry from Virtsu to Muhu and then crossing the 2.5km causeway connecting the islands.

## ℹ Getting Around

Local buses putter around the island, but not very frequently. The main terminus is **Kuressaare bus station** (Kuressaare Bussijaam; ☑ 453 1661; www.bussipilet.ee; Pihtla tee 2) and there's a route planner online at www.bussipilet.ee.

# SURVIVAL GUIDE

## ℹ Directory A–Z

### ACCOMMODATION

If you like flying by the seat of your pants when you're travelling, you'll find July and August in Estonia very problematic. The best accommodation books up quickly and in Tallinn, especially on weekends, you might find yourself scraping for anywhere at all to lay your head. In fact, Tallinn gets busy most weekends, so try to book about a month ahead anytime from May through to September (midweek isn't anywhere near as bad).

High season in Estonia means summer. Prices drop off substantially at other times. The exception is Otepää, when there's also a corresponding peak in winter.

### GAY & LESBIAN TRAVELLERS

Today's Estonia is a fairly tolerant and safe home to its gay and lesbian citizens, but only Tallinn has any gay venues. Homosexuality was decriminalised in 1992 and since 2001 there has been an equal age of consent for everyone (14 years). In 2014 Estonia became the first former Soviet republic to pass a law recognising same-sex registered partnerships.

### TELEPHONE

There are no area codes in Estonia. All landline numbers have seven digits; mobile numbers have seven or eight digits, beginning with ☑ 5.

### TOURIST INFORMATION

Most major destinations have tourist offices. The national tourist board has an excellent website (www.visitestonia.com).

---

## SLEEPING PRICE RANGES

The following price ranges refer to a double room in high (but not necessary peak) seaon.

€ less than €35

€€ €35–100

€€€ more than €100

## VISAS

EU citizens can spend unlimited time in Estonia, while citizens of Australia, Canada, Japan, New Zealand, the USA and many other countries can enter visa-free for a maximum 90-day stay over a six-month period. Travellers holding a Schengen visa do not need an additional Estonian visa. For information, see the website of the Estonian Ministry of Foreign Affairs (www.vm.ee/en).

## ⓘ Getting There & Away

### AIR

Eleven European airlines have scheduled services to Tallinn year-round, with additional routes and airlines added in summer. There are also direct flights from Helsinki to Tartu Airport.

### LAND
### Bus

The following bus companies all have services between Estonia and the other Baltic states:

**Ecolines** (www.ecolines.net) Major routes: Tallinn–Pärnu–Rīga (seven daily), two of which continue on to Vilnius; Tallinn–St Petersburg (four daily); Tartu–Valga–Rīga (daily); Vilnius–Rīga–Tartu–Narva–St Petersburg (daily).

**Lux Express & Simple Express** (www.luxexpress.eu) Major routes: Tallinn–Pärnu–Rīga (10 to 12 daily), six of which continue on to Panevėžys and Vilnius; Tallinn–Rakvere–Sillamäe–Narva–St Petersburg (six to nine daily); Tallinn–Tartu–Võru–Moscow (daily); Rīga–Valmiera–Tartu–Sillamäe–Narva–St Petersburg (nine to 10 daily).

**UAB Toks** (www2.toks.lt) Tallinn–Pärnu–Rīga–Panevėžys–Vilnius buses (two daily), with one continuing on to Kaunas and Warsaw.

### Train

**GoRail** (www.gorail.ee) has direct trains to Tallinn from St Petersburg and Moscow. There are no direct trains to Latvia; you'll need to change at Valga.

### SEA

**Eckerö Line** (www.eckeroline.fi; Passenger Terminal A, Varasadam; adult/child/car from €19/12/19) Twice-daily car ferry from Helsinki to Tallinn (2½ hours).

---

### EATING PRICE RANGES

The following Estonian price ranges refer to a standard main course.

€ less than €10

€€ €10 to €15

€€€ more than €15

---

### COUNTRY FACTS

**Area** 45,226 sq km

**Capital** Tallinn

**Country Code** ☑ 372

**Currency** euro €

**Emergency** Ambulance & fire ☑ 112, police ☑ 110

**Language** Estonian

**Money** ATMs all over.

**Visas** Not required for citizens of the EU, USA, Canada, New Zealand and Australia.

---

**Linda Line** (☑ 699 9331; www.lindaliini.ee; Linnahall Terminal) Small, passenger-only hydrofoils travel between Helsinki and Tallinn at least two times daily from late March to late December (from €25, 1½ hours). Weather dependent.

**Tallink** (☑ 640 9808; www.tallink.com; Terminal D, Lootsi 13) Four to seven car ferries daily between Helsinki and Tallinn (passenger/vehicle from €31/26). The huge *Baltic Princess* takes 3½ hours; newer high-speed ferries take two hours. They also have an overnight ferry between Stockholm and Tallinn, via the Åland islands (passenger/vehicle from €39/62, 18 hours).

**Viking Line** (☑ 666 3966; www.vikingline.com; Terminal A, Varasadam; passenger/vehicle from €29/26) Two daily car ferries between Helsinki and Tallinn (2½ hours).

## ⓘ Getting Around

### BUS

Buses are a good option domestically, as they're more frequent than trains and cover many destinations not serviced by the limited rail network. **TPilet** (www.tpilet.ee) has schedules and prices for all services.

### TRAIN

Trains are handy for getting between Tallinn and Tartu, but services to Pärnu are extremely limited.

# Hungary

## Best Places to Eat

➡ Borkonyha (p188)

➡ Macok Bistro & Wine Bar (p199)

➡ Zeller Bistro (p188)

➡ Barack & Szilva (p188)

➡ Nem Kacsa (p194)

## Best Places to Stay

➡ Four Seasons Gresham Palace Hotel (p187)

➡ Hotel Senator Ház (p199)

➡ Shantee House (p185)

➡ Bohem Art Hotel (p187)

➡ Tiszavirág Hotel (p197)

## Why Go?

Stunning architecture, vital folk art, thermal spas and Europe's most exciting capital after dark: Hungary is just the place to kick off a European adventure. Lying virtually in the centre of the continent, this land of Franz Liszt and Béla Bartók, paprika-lashed dishes, superb wines and the romantic Danube River continues to enchant visitors. The allure of Budapest, once an imperial city, is immediate at first sight, and it also boasts the region's hottest nightlife.

Pécs, the warm heart of the south, and Eger, wine capital of the north, also have much to offer travellers, as does the Great Plain, where cowboys ride and cattle roam. And how about lazing in an open-air thermal spa while snow patches glisten around you? That's at Hévíz at the western edge of Lake Balaton, continental Europe's largest lake and Hungary's 'inland sea', which offers innumerable opportunities for rest and recreation.

## When to Go
### Budapest

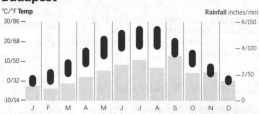

**May** Spring is in full swing, meaning reliable weather, cool temperatures and flowers.

**Jul–Aug** Sunny but often hot; decamp to the hills or Lake Balaton (book ahead).

**Sep–Oct** Blue skies, mild temperatures and grape-harvest festivals – a rewarding time to visit.

## Hungary Highlights

**1 Budapest** (p181)
Losing yourself in Europe's best nightlife – the 'ruin pubs', wine bars and nightclubs of Hungary's capital.

**2 Eger** (p198)
Understanding the sobering history of Turkish attacks, and sampling the region's famed Bull's Blood wine.

**3 Pécs** (p196) Absorbing the Mediterranean-like climate and historic architecture, including the iconic Mosque Church.

**4 Lake Balaton** (p193)
Taking a pleasure cruise across Central Europe's largest body of fresh water.

**5 Hévíz** (p195) Easing your aching muscles year-round in the warm waters of this thermal lake.

**6 Hortobágy National Park** (p198) Watching Hungarian cowboys' spectacular shows in this romantic region of the Great Plain.

**7 Szentendre** (p191)
Mill about with artists, freethinkers and day trippers at this too-cute-for-words town.

# BUDAPEST

🗹 1 / POP 1.7 MILLION

The beauty of Hungary's capital is both natural and man-made. Straddling a gentle curve in the Danube, the city is flanked by the Buda Hills on the west bank and the beginnings of the Great Plain to the east. Architecturally, the city is a treasure trove of baroque, neoclassical, Eclectic and art nouveau buildings. The city is also blessed with an abundance of hot springs, and in recent years Budapest has taken on the role of the region's party town.

Budapest is paradise for explorers; keep your senses primed and you'll discover something wonderful at every turn.

## 👁 Sights & Activities

### 👁 Buda

Castle Hill (Várhegy) is Budapest's biggest tourist draw and a first port of call for any visit to the city. Here, you'll find most of Budapest's remaining medieval buildings, the Royal Palace and sweeping views of Pest across the river.

You can walk to Castle Hill up the **Király lépcső**, the 'Royal Steps' that lead northwest off Clark Ádám tér, or else take the **Sikló** (Map p184; www.bkv.hu; I Szent György tér; one-way/return adult 1200/1800Ft, 3-14yr 700/1100Ft; ☺7.30am-10pm, closed 1st & 3rd Mon of month; ☐16, 16A, ☐19, 41), a funicular railway built in 1870 that ascends from Clark Ádám tér to Szent György tér near the Royal Palace.

### ★ Fishermen's Bastion            MONUMENT

(Halászbástya; Map p184; I Szentháromság tér; adult/concession 800/400Ft; ☺9am-8pm Mar–mid-Oct; ☐16, 16A, 116) The bastion, a neo-Gothic masquerade that looks medieval and offers some of the best views in Budapest, was built as a viewing platform in 1905 by Frigyes Schulek, the architect behind Matthias Church. Its name was taken from the medieval guild of fishermen responsible for defending this stretch of the castle wall. The seven gleaming white turrets represent the Magyar tribes that entered the Carpathian Basin in the late 9th century.

### ★ Matthias Church            CHURCH

(Mátyás templom; Map p184; ☑1-355 5657; www.matyas-templom.hu; I Szentháromság tér 2; adult/concession 1500/1000Ft; ☺9am-5pm Mon-Sat, 1-5pm Sun; ☐16, 16A, 116) Parts of Matthias Church date back 500 years, notably the carvings above the southern entrance. But basically Matthias Church (so named because King Matthias Corvinus married Beatrix here in 1474) is a neo-Gothic confection designed by the architect Frigyes Schulek in 1896.

### ★ Citadella            FORT

(Citadel; Map p184; ☐27) The Citadella is a fortress that never saw a battle. Built by the Habsburgs after the 1848–49 War of Independence to defend the city from further insurrection, the structure was obsolete by the time it was ready in 1851 due to the change in political climate. Today the fortress contains some big guns peeping through the loopholes, but the interior has now been closed to the public while its future is decided.

### ★ Memento Park            HISTORIC SITE

(☑1-424 7500; www.mementopark.hu; XXII Balatoni út & Szabadkai utca; adult/student 1500/1000Ft; ☺10am-dusk; ☐101, 150) Home to more than 40 statues, busts and plaques of Lenin, Marx, Béla Kun and others whose likenesses have ended up on trash heaps elsewhere, Memento Park, 10km southwest of the city centre, is truly a mind-blowing place to visit. Ogle the socialist realism and try to imagine that some of these relics were erected as recently as the late 1980s.

---

## ITINERARIES

### One Week

Spend at least three days in **Budapest**, checking out the sights, museums, cafes and 'ruin pubs'. On your fourth day take a day trip to a Danube Bend town such as **Szentendre** or **Esztergom**. Day five can be spent getting a morning train to **Pécs** to see Turkish remains, museums and galleries. If you've still got the travel bug, on day six head for **Eger**, a baroque town set in red-wine country. On your last day recuperate back in one of Budapest's wonderful thermal baths.

### Two Weeks

After a week in Budapest and the Danube Bend towns, spend two days exploring the towns and grassy beaches around **Lake Balaton**. **Tihany** is a rambling hillside village set on a protected peninsula, **Keszthely** is an old town with a great palace in addition to beaches, and **Hévíz** has a thermal lake. On day 10, head to the **Great Plain – Szeged** is a splendid university town on the Tisza River, and **Kecskemét** a centre of art nouveau. Finish your trip in **Tokaj**, home of Hungary's famous sweet wine.

★**Gellért Baths**      BATHHOUSE
(Gellért gyógyfürdő; ☑1-466 6166; www.gellert bath.hu; XI Kelenhegyi út 4, Danubius Hotel Gellért; with locker/cabin Mon-Fri 5100/5500Ft, Sat & Sun 5300/5700Ft; ☺6am-8pm; ▣7, 86, Ⓜ︎M4 Szent Gellért tér, ▣18, 19, 47, 49) Soaking in the art nouveau Gellért Baths, open to both men and women in mixed sections (so bring a swimsuit), has been likened to taking a bath in a cathedral. The eight thermal pools (one outdoors) range in temperature from 19°C to 38°C, and the water is said to be good for pain in the joints, arthritis and blood circulation.

👁 **Margaret Island**

The island's gardens and shaded walkways are lovely places to stroll or cycle, plus there is a dense concentration of swimming pools and spas. The largest and best series of outdoor pools in the capital is **Palatinus Strand** (☑1-340 4505; www.palatinusstrand.hu; XIII Margitsziget; adult/child Mon-Fri 2800/2100Ft, Sat & Sun 3200/2300Ft; ☺9am-7pm May-Sep; ▣26), with upward of a dozen pools (two with thermal water), wave machines, water slides and kids' pools.

👁 **Pest**

★**Parliament**      HISTORIC BUILDING
(Országház; Map p186; ☑1-441 4904; www.hungarianparliament.com; V Kossuth Lajos tér 1-3; adult/student EU citizen 2200/1200Ft, non-EU citizen 5400/2800Ft; ☺8am-6pm Mon-Fri, to 4pm Sat, to 2pm Sun; Ⓜ︎M2 Kossuth Lajos tér, ▣2) The Eclectic-style Parliament, designed by Imre Steindl and completed in 1902, has 691 sumptuously decorated rooms, but you'll only get to see several of these and other features on a guided tour of the North Wing: the **Golden Staircase**; the **Domed Hall**, where the **Crown of St Stephen**, the nation's most important national icon, is on display; the **Grand Staircase** and its wonderful landing; Loge Hall; and **Congress Hall**, where the House of Lords of the one-time bicameral assembly sat until 1944.

★**Heroes' Square**      SQUARE
(Hősök tere; ▣105, Ⓜ︎M1 Hősök tere) Heroes' Sq is the largest and most symbolic square in Budapest, and contains the Millenary Monument *(Ezeréves emlékmű)*, a 36m-high pillar topped by a golden Archangel Gabriel. Legend has it that he offered Stephen the crown of Hungary in a dream. At the column's base

are Prince Árpád and other chieftains. The colonnades behind the pillar feature various illustrious leaders of Hungary. It was designed in 1896 to mark the 1000th anniversary of the Magyar conquest of the Carpathian Basin.

★**Basilica of St Stephen**      CATHEDRAL
(Szent István Bazilika; Map p186; ☑06 30 703 6599, 1-311 0839; www.basilica.hu; V Szent István tér; requested donation 200Ft; ☺9am-7pm Mon-Sat, 7.45am-7pm Sun; Ⓜ︎M3 Arany János utca) Budapest's neoclassical cathedral was built over half a century and completed in 1905. Much of the interruption during construction had to do with a fiasco in 1868 when the dome collapsed during a storm, and the structure had to be demolished and then rebuilt from the ground up. The basilica is rather dark and gloomy inside, but take a trip to the top of the **dome** for incredible views.

★**House of Terror**      MUSEUM
(Terror Háza; Map p186; ☑1-374 2600; www.terrorhaza.hu; VI Andrássy út 60; adult/concession 2000/1000Ft, audioguide 1500Ft; ☺10am-6pm Tue-Sun; Ⓜ︎M1 Oktogon) The headquarters of the dreaded secret police is now the startling House of Terror, focusing on the crimes and atrocities of Hungary's fascist and Stalinist regimes in a permanent exhibition called Double Occupation. But the years after WWII leading up to the 1956 Uprising get the lion's share of the exhibition space (almost three-dozen spaces on three levels). The reconstructed prison cells in the basement and the **Perpetrators' Gallery**, featuring photographs of the turncoats, spies and torturers, are chilling.

★**Hungarian National
Museum**      MUSEUM
(Magyar Nemzeti Múzeum; Map p186; ☑1-338 2122; www.hnm.hu; VIII Múzeum körút 14-16; adult/concession 1600/800Ft; ☺10am-6pm Tue-Sun; ▣47, 49, Ⓜ︎M3/4 Kálvin tér) The Hungarian National Museum houses the nation's most important collection of historical relics in an impressive neoclassical building, purpose built in 1847. Exhibits trace the history of the Carpathian Basin from earliest times to the end of the Avar period, and the ongoing story of the Magyar people from the conquest of the basin to the end of communism. Don't miss King Stephen's crimson silk coronation mantle and the Broadwood piano, used by both Beethoven and Liszt.

# Buda

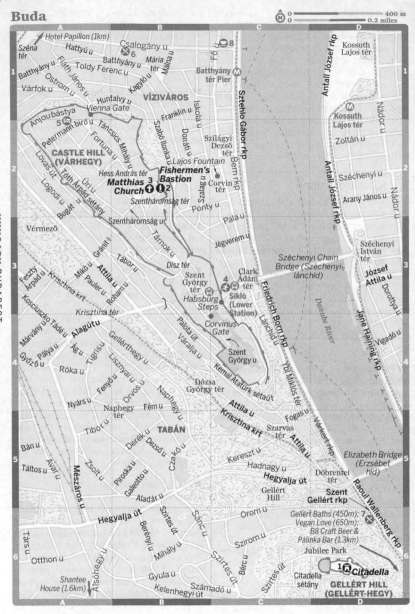

★**Great Synagogue**                          SYNAGOGUE
(Nagy Zsinagóga; Map p186; ☎1-462 0477; www.
dohany-zsinagoga.hu; VII Dohány utca 2; adult/
concession incl museum 3000/2000Ft; ⊙10am-
6pm Sun-Thu, to 4pm Fri Mar-Oct, 10am-4pm Sun-
Thu, to 2pm Fri Nov-Feb; Ⓜ M2 Astoria, 🚊47, 49)

Budapest's stunning Great Synagogue is the
largest Jewish house of worship in the world
outside New York City. Built in 1859, the
synagogue has both Romantic and Moorish
architectural elements. Inside, the **Hungarian Jewish Museum & Archives** (Magyar

Zsidó Múzeum és Levéltár; Map p186; ☑1-343 6756; www.milev.hu; incl in synagogue entry adult/concession 3000/2000Ft) contains objects relating to both religious and everyday life. On the synagogue's north side, the **Holocaust Tree of Life Memorial** (Map p186; Raoul Wallenberg Memorial Park, opp VII Wesselényi utca 6) presides over the mass graves of those murdered by the Nazis.

★**Kerepesi Cemetery**　　　CEMETERY
(Kerepesi temető; ☑06 30 331 8822; www.nemzetisirkert.hu; VIII Fiumei út 16; ☉7am-8pm May-Jul, to 7pm Apr & Aug, to 6pm Sep, to 5pm Mar & Oct, 7.30am-5pm Nov-Feb; Ⓜ M2/4 Keleti train station, ◻24) **FREE** Budapest's equivalent of London's Highgate or Père Lachaise in Paris, this 56-hectare necropolis was established in 1847 and holds some 3000 gravestones and mausoleums, including those of statesmen and national heroes Lajos Kossuth, Ferenc Deák and Lajos Batthyány. Maps indicating the location of noteworthy graves are available free at the entrance. Plot 21 contains the graves of many who died in the 1956 Uprising.

★**Széchenyi Baths**　　　BATHHOUSE
(Széchenyi Gyógyfürdő; ☑1-363 3210; www.szechenyibath.hu; XIV Állatkerti körút 9-11; tickets incl locker/cabin Mon-Fri 4700/5200Ft, Sat & Sun 4900/5400Ft; ☉6am-10pm; Ⓜ M1 Széchenyi fürdő) These thermal baths are particularly popular with visitors and have helpful, English-speaking attendants. Its mix of indoor and outdoor pools includes 12 thermal pools (water temperatures up to 40°C), a swimming pool and an activity pool with whirlpool. The baths are open year-round, and it's quite a sight to watch men and women playing chess on floating boards when it's snowing.

## 🎉 Festivals & Events

★**Sziget Festival**　　　MUSIC
(http://szigetfestival.com; ☉mid-Aug) One of the biggest and most popular music festivals in Europe, held in mid-August on Budapest's Hajógyár (Óbuda) Island, with some 500,000 revellers (in 2016) and a plethora of Hungarian and international bands.

★**Budapest International Wine Festival**　　　WINE
(www.aborfesztival.hu; ☉mid-Sep) Hungary's foremost winemakers introduce their wines at this ultrapopular event in the Castle District. The tipples are accompanied by a cornucopia of edibles along the Gastro Walkway.

★**CAFe Budapest**　　　PERFORMING ARTS
(Contemporary Art Festival; www.budapestbylocals.com/event/budapest-autumn-festival; ☉Oct) Contemporary art takes on many forms during this two-week-long festival: poetry slams, contemporary fashion design, modern theatre, a jazz marathon and the 'Night of the Contemporary Galleries', to name a few. Design Week, the Art Market Budapest and the Mini Festival of Contemporary Music in Várkert Bazaar are all part of the celebrations.

## 🛏 Sleeping

### Buda

★**Shantee House**　　　HOSTEL €
(☑1-385 8946; www.backpackbudapest.hu; XI Takács Menyhért utca 33; beds in yurt €10-13, dm small/large from €12/16, d €38-52; ℗@🛜; ◻7, 7A, ◻19, 49) Budapest's first hostel (originally known as the Back-Pack Guesthouse), the Shantee has added two floors to its colourfully painted suburban 'villa' in south Buda. It's all good and the fun (and sleeping bodies in high season) spills out into a lovely landscaped garden, with hammocks, a yurt and a gazebo. Two of the five doubles are en suite.

★**Hotel Papillon**　　　HOTEL €€
(☑1-212 4750; www.hotelpapillon.hu; II Rózsahegy utca 3/b; s/d/tr €44/54/69, apt €39-99; ℗✳🛜♒; ◻4, 6) This cosy hotel in Rózsadomb (Rose Hill) has a delightful back garden with a small swimming pool, and some of the 20 rooms have balconies.

# Central Pest

N
0 — 400 m
0 — 0.2 miles

HUNGARY BUDAPEST

Szinyei Merse u
Bajnok u
Szív u

Palatinus
Strand (2.1km)

Hegedűs Gyula u
Visegrádi u
Katona József u
Kádár u
Váci út

Szent István krt

Nyugati
Train Station

Podmaniczky u
Izabella u
Vörösmarty u
Csengery u

TERÉZVÁROS

Balaton u
Stollár Béla u

Nyugati pu

Jókai u
Szobi u
Szondi u
Eötvös u
Teréz krt

Heroes' Square (950m);
City Park (1km);
Budapest Info (1.1km);
Sparty (1.8km);
Széchenyi Baths (1.8km)

Falk Miksa u
Honvéd tér
Markó u
Bihari János u
Bajcsy-Zsilinszky út

Balassi Bálint u
Honvéd u
Nagy Ignác u

Antall József rkp
Szechenyi rkp

Vajkay u
Szalay u

Alkotmány u

Weiner Leó u

House of Terror
Andrássy út
Vörösmarty u

**Parliament**
5

Kossuth
Lajos tér

Báthory u
Kálmán Imre u

Lovag u
Dessewffy u
Zichy Jenő u
Jókai u
Aradi u

Hunyadi tér

Garibaldi u
Vécsey u
Aulich u
Hold u
Vadász u

Zeller Bistro
(250m)

LIPÓTVÁROS
Zoltán u
Perczel M u
Nagysándor u J u

Oktogon
Jókai tér

Steindl Imre u
Szabadság tér

ERZSÉBETVÁROS

Antall József rkp
Széchenyi u

Bank u
Podmaniczky
Frigyes tér
Arany
János u

Hegedű u
Nagymező u
Király u
Hársfa u
Erzsébet krt

Arany János u
Lázár u
Révay u

20
Opera
Andrássy út

Vasvári Pál u
Kis Diófa u
Csányi u
Dob u
Kertész u

19
Szent
István tér
Paulay Ede u
14

Vigyázó
Ferenc u

**Basilica of
St Stephen**
1

Klauzál
tér

13
Sas u
Hercegprímás u
Oktober 6 u

15

Zrínyi u

12

József Attila u

Király u
Kazinczy u
Akácfa u

16
Klauzál u
11

Bajcsy-
Zsilinszky út

18

Széchenyi
Chain Bridge
(Széchenyi
lánchíd)
9

Mérleg u

Madách Imre út
Gozsdu
Udvar
10

Nyár u

Eötvös
tér
Széchenyi
István tér
Dorottya u

József
nádor tér
Bécsi u

Erzsébet
tér

Memento Park Bus
Deák
Ferenc tér

Rumbach
Sebestyén u

6
7
2

Wesselényi u

17
Vigadó u
Deák
Ferenc u

Barczy I u

Károly krt

Síp u

**Great
Synagogue**

Dohány u

Danube River

Jane Haining rkp

Vörösmarty
tér

Fehér Hajó u

Genczy u

Astoria

Rákóczi út

Keleti
(1.2km); Kerepesi
Cemetery (1.2km);
Piety Museum
(1.6km)

Vigadó
tér
Váci u
Városház u

Vármegye u

Kossuth Lajos u
Múzeum krt
Puskin u

Vas u

Vigadó tér
Pier

Petőfi
tér

Haris köz

Piarista u
Kígyó u
Ferenciek
tere

Szabadsajtó út

JÓZSEFVÁROS

Bródy Sándor u
Horánszky u

Elizabeth Bridge
(Erzsébet
híd)

Március
15 tér

Irányi u
Durán
Károlyi M u

Veres Pálné u
Egyetem
tér

**Hungarian
National
Museum**
4

Pollack
Mihály tér
Szentkirályi u

Szent Gellért rkp

Nyáry Pál u
Vaci u
Szerb u
Kecskeméti u
Király Pál u

Múzeum u
Mikszáth
Kálmán tér
Reviczky u
Lőrinc
pap tér

Mahart
PassNave
8

Képíró u
Kálvin
tér

Kálvin tér
Szabó
E tér

Baross u

International
Ferry Pier

Jane Haining rkp

Molnár u
Bástya u
Havas u
Só u

Vámház krt

Erkel u
Ráday u
Üllői út

Raoul Wallenberg rkp

Liberty Bridge
(Szabadság
híd)

Fővám
tér

22

Fővám
tér

Pipa u
Gönczy u
Lónyay u

Csarnok
tér

Mátyás u
Köztelek u
Markusovszky
tér

## Central Pest

There are also four apartments available in the same building, one boasting a lovely roof terrace, as well as more apartments (studio to three-bedroom) next door. The staff are on the ball and helpful.

★ **Baltazár** BOUTIQUE HOTEL €€€
(Map p184; ☑1-300 7051; http://baltazarbudapest.com/; I Országház utca 31; r/ste from €135/214; ❋☏; ☐16, 16A, 116) This family-run boutique hotel at the northern end of the Castle District has 11 individually decorated rooms decked out with vintage furniture and striking wallpaper. Nods to more recent times include street art on the walls and a rain shower in the bathrooms. One of the rooms has a lovely little balcony with views to the castle. Excellent value.

### Pest

★ **Hive Hostel** HOSTEL €€
(Map p186; ☑06 30 826 6197; www.thehive.hu; VII Dob utca 19; dm €15-25, d €60-100; @☏; M M1/2/3 Deák Ferenc tér) This enormous and very central place with more than 50 rooms of all sizes and shapes over several levels is for the slightly better-heeled budget traveller. There's a big common area and kitchen and a wonderful rooftop bar that looks down on a courtyard with two large chestnut trees and a popular ruin garden. A wonderful place, with equally great staff.

★ **Bohem Art Hotel** BOUTIQUE HOTEL €€
(Map p186; ☑1-327 9020; www.bohemarthotel.hu; V Molnár utca 35; r/ste incl breakfast from

€95/118; P❋☏; M M4 Fővám tér, M3/4 Kálvin tér, ☐47, 48, 49) Though the rooms at this delightful small hotel are a little on the compact side, each one is decorated in its own individual style (the suites are done by local artists – we particularly like Room 302), with giant prints, bold touches of colour amid monochrome decor and ultramodern furnishings present throughout. Indulgent buffet breakfast.

★ **Four Seasons Gresham Palace Hotel** HOTEL €€€
(Map p186; ☑1-268 6000; www.fourseasons.com/budapest; V Széchenyi István tér 5-6; r/ste from €295/815; P❋@☏☒; ☐16, 105, ☐2) This one-of-a-kind 179-room hotel was created out of the long-derelict art nouveau Gresham Palace (1907) and a lot of blood, sweat and tears. No expense was spared to piece back together the palace's Zsolnay tiles, mosaics and celebrated wrought-iron Peacock Gates leading north, west and south from the enormous lobby – the hotel is truly worthy of its name.

## ✗ Eating

### ✗ Buda

**Vegan Love** VEGAN €
(www.veganlove.hu; Bartók Béla út 9; mains 1490-1590Ft; ⊙11am-8pm Mon-Sat, noon-8pm Sun; ☑; M M4 Móricz Zsigmond körtér, ☐18, 19, 47, 49) Vegan fast (sorry, street) food doesn't get much better than at this hole-in-the-wall eatery on up-and-coming Bartók Béla út. Try the likes

of sweet potato or curry lentil burgers, or the vegan chilli tofu hotdog. Small/large servings from the salad bar cost 590/1120Ft.

### ⭐Rudas
**Restaurant & Bar** INTERNATIONAL €€

(Map p184; 🖉 06 20 921 4877; www.rudasrestaurant. hu; Döbrentei tér 9, Rudas Baths; mains 2450-4350Ft; ⊗11am-10pm; 🚊7, 86, 🚊18, 19) We love, love, love this place with its turquoise interior and stunning views of the Danube and bridges. It sits above the Rudas Baths Wellness Centre (ask about inclusive packages) so it's just the ticket after a relaxing massage or treatment. The smallish outside terrace is a delight in summer (though it can be noisy).

### ⭐Csalogány 26 INTERNATIONAL €€

(Map p184; 🖉1-201 7892; www.csalogany26.hu; I Csalogány utca 26; mains 3800-5300Ft; ⊗noon-3pm & 7-10pm Tue-Sat; 🚊11, 111) Definitely one of the better restaurants in town, this intimate place with spartan decor turns its creativity to its superb food. Try the suckling *mangalica* (a kind of pork) with savoy cabbage (4900Ft) or other meat-heavy dishes that make the most of local ingredients. A three-course set lunch is a budget-pleasing 2900Ft.

---

## ✖ Pest

The **Nagycsarnok** (Great Market Hall; Map p186; 🖉1-366 3300; www.piaconline.hu; IX Vámház körút 1-3; ⊗6am-5pm Mon, to 6pm Tue-Fri, to 3pm Sat; Ⓜ M4 Fővám tér) is a vast historic market built of steel and glass. Head here for fruit, vegetables, deli items, fish and meat.

### Kisharang HUNGARIAN €

(Map p186; 🖉1-269 3861; www.kisharang.hu; V Október 6 utca 17; mains 1000-2350Ft; ⊗11.30am-10pm; 🚊15, 115) Centrally located 'Little Bell' is an *étkezde* (canteen serving simple Hungarian dishes) that's top of the list with students and staff of the nearby Central European University. The daily specials are something to look forward to and the retro decor is fun. *Főzelék* (370Ft to 490Ft), the traditional Hungarian way of preparing vegetables and sometimes served with meat, is always a good bet.

### ⭐Borkonyha HUNGARIAN €€

(Wine Kitchen; Map p186; 🖉1-266 0835; www. borkonyha.hu; V Sas utca 3; mains 3150-7950Ft; ⊗noon-4pm & 6pm-midnight Mon-Sat; 🚊15, 115, Ⓜ M1 Bajcsy-Zsilinszky út) Chef Ákos Sárközi's approach to Hungarian cuisine at this

Michelin-starred restaurant is contemporary, and the menu changes every week or two. Go for the signature foie gras appetiser wrapped in strudel pastry and a glass of sweet Tokaj wine. If *mangalica* (a special type of Hungarian pork) is on the menu, try it with a glass of dry *furmint*.

### ⭐Barack & Szilva HUNGARIAN €€

(Map p186; 🖉1-798 8285; www.barackesszilva. hu; VII Klauzál utca 13; mains 3200-5500Ft; ⊗6pm-midnight Mon-Sat; Ⓜ M2 Blaha Lujza tér) This is the kind of perfectly formed restaurant that every neighbourhood wishes it could boast. Run by a husband-and-wife team, the 'Peach & Pear' serves high-quality and exceptionally well-prepared Hungarian provincial food in a bistro setting. Try the duck pâté with dried plums and the red-wine beef *pörkölt* (goulash). Lovely terrace in summer too.

### ⭐Zeller Bistro HUNGARIAN €€

(🖉06 30 651 0880, 1-321 7879; VII Izabella utca 38; mains 2900-5400Ft; ⊗noon-3pm & 6-11pm Tue-Sat; Ⓜ M1 Vörösmarty utca, 🚊4, 6) You'll receive a very warm welcome at this lovely candlelit cellar where the attentive staff serve food sourced largely from the owner's family and friends in the Lake Balaton area. The Hungarian home cooking includes some first-rate dishes such as grey beef, duck leg, oxtail and lamb's knuckle. Superb desserts too. Popular with both locals and expats; reservations are essential.

##  Drinking

### 🍷 Buda

### ⭐Kávé Műhely COFFEE

(Map p184; 🖉06 30 852 8517; www.facebook. com/kavemuhely; II Fő utca 49; ⊗7.30am-6.30pm Mon-Fri, 9am-5pm Sat & Sun; Ⓜ M2 Batthyány tér, 🚊19, 41) This tiny coffee shop is one of the best in the city. These guys roast their own beans, and their cakes and sandwiches are fantastic. Too hot for coffee? They've got craft beers and homemade lemonades, too. The attached gallery stages vibrant contemporary art exhibitions.

### B8 Craft Beer & Pálinka Bar CRAFT BEER

(B8 Kézműves Sör és Pálinkabár; 🖉1-791 3462; www. facebook.com/b8pub; Bercsényi utca 8; ⊗4-11pm Mon, noon-11pm Tue-Fri, 5-11pm Sat; Ⓜ M4 Móricz Zsigmond körtér, 🚊18, 19, 47, 49) Our favourite new watering hole in Buda, this pint-sized place (though there are three floors) has

## BUDAPEST'S RUIN PUBS

Ruin pubs (romkocsmák) began to appear in the city from the early 2000s, when entrepreneurial free thinkers took over abandoned buildings and turned them into pop-up bars. At first a very word-of-mouth scene, the ruin bars' popularity grew exponentially and many have transformed from ramshackle, temporary sites full of flea-market furniture to more slick, year-round fixtures. Start with **Anker't** (Map p186; www.facebook.com/ankertbar; VI Paulay Ede utca 33; ⊙2pm-2am Mon-Wed & Sun, to 4am Thu-Sat; 🛜; M M1 Opera), an achingly cool, grown-up courtyard pub surrounded by seriously ruined buildings, and **Füge Udvar** (Fig Court; Map p186; ☑1-782 6990; VII Klauzál utca 19; ⊙4pm-4am; M M2 Blaha Lujza tér, 🚋4, 6), an enormous ruin pub with a large covered courtyard (both are on the Pest side).

more than two-dozen craft beers available from Hungary's 52 (at last count) breweries. Look for the names Legenda, Monyo and Etyeki and try the last's Belga Búza (Belgian Wheat). Harder stuff? Some 10 types of *pálinka* (fruit brandy), from Japanese plum to Gypsy cherry.

## 🍷 Pest

### ★ Instant                                                    CLUB
(Map p186; ☑06 30 830 8747, 1-311 0704; www.instant.co.hu; VII Akácfa utca 51; ⊙4pm-6am, M M1 Opera) We still love this 'ruin bar' on one of Pest's most vibrant nightlife strips and so do all our friends. It has 26 rooms, seven bars, seven stages and two gardens with underground DJs and dance parties. It's always heaving.

### ★ DiVino Borbár                                         WINE BAR
(Map p186; ☑06 70 935 3980; www.divinoborbar.hu; V Szent István tér 3; ⊙4pm-midnight Sun-Wed, to 2am Thu-Sat; M M1 Bajcsy-Zsilinszky út) Central and always heaving, DiVino is Budapest's most popular wine bar, as the crowds spilling out onto the square in front of the Basilica of St Stephen in the warm weather will attest. Choose from more than 140 wines produced by 36 winemakers under the age of 35, but be careful: those 0.15dL (15mL) glasses (650Ft to 3500Ft) go down quickly.

### ★ Gerbeaud                                                    CAFE
(Map p186; ☑1-429 9001; www.gerbeaud.hu; V Vörösmarty tér 7-8; ⊙noon-10pm; M M1 Vörösmarty tér) Founded on the northern side of Pest's busiest square in 1858, Gerbeaud has been the most fashionable meeting place for the city's elite since 1870. Along with exquisitely prepared cakes and pastries, it serves continental/full breakfasts and a smattering of nicely presented Hungarian dishes with international touches. A visit is mandatory.

### Tütü Bar                                                         GAY
(Map p186; ☑06 70 353 4074; http://tutubudapest.hu; V Hercegprímás utca 18; ⊙10pm-5am Thu-Sat; M M3 Arany János utca) Budapest's newest gay club is a basement bar that serves up a lot more than just drinks and attitude. From pole-dancers and acrobats to drag and fashion shows, they are out to entertain you. A barrel of laughs.

## ☆ Entertainment

Handy websites for booking theatre and concert tickets are www.kulturinfo.hu and www.jegymester.hu.

### Performing Arts

### ★ Liszt Music Academy                        CLASSICAL MUSIC
(Liszt Zeneakadémia; Map p186; ☑1-462 4600, box office 1-321 0690; www.zeneakademia.hu; VI Liszt Ferenc tér 8; ⊙box office 10am-6pm; M M1 Oktogon, 🚋4, 6) Performances at Budapest's most important concert hall are usually booked up at least a week in advance, but more expensive (though still affordable) last-minute tickets can sometimes be available. It's always worth checking.

### ★ Hungarian State Opera House            OPERA
(Magyar Állami Operaház; Map p186; ☑1-814 7100, box office 1-353 0170; www.opera.hu; VI Andrássy út 22; ⊙box office 10am-8pm; M M1 Opera) The gorgeous neo-Renaissance opera house is worth a visit as much to admire the incredibly rich decoration inside as to view a performance and hear the perfect acoustics.

## 🛍 Shopping

### ★ Ecseri Piac                                              MARKET
(Ecseri Market; www.piaconline.hu; XIX Nagykőrösi út 156; ⊙8am-4pm Mon-Fri, 5am-3pm Sat, 8am-1pm Sun; 🚌54, 84E, 89E 94E) One of the biggest flea markets in Central Europe, Ecseri sells everything from antique jewellery and Soviet army watches to Fred Astaire–style top hats.

Take bus 54 from Pest's Boráros tér, or for a quicker journey, express bus 84E, 89E or 94E from the Határ út stop on the M3 metro line in Pest and get off at the Fiume utca stop.

## ℹ Information

There are ATMs everywhere, including in the train and bus stations and at the airport. Avoid moneychangers (especially those on V Váci utca) in favour of banks if possible. Arrive about an hour before closing time to ensure the bureau de change desk is still open.

**Budapest Info** (☎ 1-438 8080; www.budapest info.hu; Olof Palme sétány 5, City Ice Rink; ☺ 9am-7pm; Ⓜ M1 Hősök tere) Helpful tourist office branch with bicycles for rent.

**Déli Gyógyszertár** (☎ 1-355 4691; www. deligyogyszertar.hu; XII Alkotás utca 1/b; ☺ 24hr; Ⓜ M2 Déli pályaudvar) All-night pharmacy.

**FirstMed Centers** (☎ 1-224 9090; www. firstmedcenters.com; I Hattyú utca 14, 5th fl; ☺ 8am-8pm Mon-Fri, to 2pm Sat, urgent care 24hr; Ⓜ M2 Széll Kálmán tér)

**SOS Dent** (☎ 1-269 6010, 06 30 383 3333; www.sosdent.hu; VI Király utca 14; ☺ 8am-8pm Mon-Sat; Ⓜ M1/2/3 Deák Ferenc tér) Dental consultations from 5000Ft.

**Vista@netcafe** (☎ 06 70 585 3924; http:// vistanetcafe.com; XIII Váci út 6; per hour 250Ft; ☺ 24hr; Ⓜ M3 Nyugati pályaudvar) One of the very few internet cafes open round the clock.

## ℹ Getting There & Away

### AIR

Budapest's **Ferenc Liszt International Airport** (BUD; ☎ 1-296 7000; www.bud.hu) has two modern terminals side by side 24km southeast of the city centre.

### BOAT

**Mahart PassNave** (Map p186; ☎ 1-484 4013; www.mahartpassnave.hu; V Belgrád rakpart; ☺ 9am-4pm Mon-Fri; ⛴ 2) runs a hydrofoil service on the Danube River between Budapest and Vienna (5½ to 6½ hours) from late April to late September. Hydrofoils arrive at and depart from the **International Ferry Pier** (Nemzetközi hajóállomás; Map p186; ☎ 1-484 4013; www. mahartpassnave.hu; V Belgrád rakpart; ☺ 9am-4pm Mon-Fri; ⛴ 2), which is between Elizabeth and Liberty Bridges on the Pest side.

### BUS

All international buses and domestic ones to/ from western Hungary arrive at and depart from **Népliget bus station** (☎ 1-219 8030; IX Üllői út 131; Ⓜ M3 Népliget) in Pest. The international ticket office is upstairs. **Eurolines** (www. eurolines.hu) is represented here, as is its Hun-

garian associate, **Volánbusz** (☎ 1-382 0888; www.volanbusz.hu). There are left-luggage lockers on the ground floor. Népliget is on the blue metro M3 (station: Népliget).

**Stadion bus station** (☎ 1-219 8086; XIV Hungária körút 48-52; Ⓜ M2 Stadionok, ⛴ 1) generally serves cities and towns in eastern Hungary. The ticket office and left-luggage lockers are on the ground floor. Stadion is on the red metro M2 (station: 2 Stadionok).

**Árpád Híd bus station** (☎ 1-412 2597; XIII Árbóc utca 1; Ⓜ M3 Árpád Híd), on the Pest side of Árpád Bridge, is the place to catch buses for the Danube Bend and parts of the Northern Uplands.

### CAR & MOTORCYCLE

Border formalities with Austria, Slovenia and Slovakia are virtually nonexistent. However, one may only enter or leave Hungary via designated border crossing points during opening hours when travelling to/from Croatia, Romania, Ukraine and Serbia, especially since, in the wake of the Syrian refugee crisis, a controversial border wall now stretches along Hungary's border with Serbia and Croatia. For the latest on border formalities, check www.police.hu.

All major international rental firms, including **Avis** (☎ 1-318 4240; www.avis.hu; V Arany János utca 26-28; ☺ 7am-6pm Mon-Fri, 8am-2pm Sat & Sun; Ⓜ M3 Arany János utca) and **Europcar** (☎ 1-505 4400; www.europcar.hu; V Erzsébet tér 7-8; ☺ 8am-6pm Mon & Fri, to 4.30pm Tue-Thu, to noon Sat; Ⓜ M1/2/3 Deák Ferenc tér), have offices in the city and at the airport.

### TRAIN

**MÁV** (Magyar Államvasutak, Hungarian State Railways; ☎ 1-349 4949; www.mavcsoport. hu) runs the country's extensive rail network. Contact the **MÁV-Start passenger service centre** (☎ 1-512 7921; www.mav-start.hu; V József Attila utca 16; ☺ 9am-6pm Mon-Fri; Ⓜ M1/M2/M3 Deák Ferenc tér) for information on domestic train departures and arrivals. Its website has a useful timetable in English for planning routes.

Buy tickets at one of Budapest's three main train stations or the passenger service centre. **Keleti train station** (Keleti pályaudvar; VIII Kerepesi út 2-6; Ⓜ M2/M4 Keleti pályaudvar) handles most international trains as well as domestic ones from the north and northeast.

For some international destinations (eg Romania), as well as domestic ones to/from the Danube Bend and Great Plain, head for **Nyugati train station** (Western Train Station; VI Nyugati tér). For trains bound for Lake Balaton and the south, eg Osijek in Croatia and Sarajevo in Bosnia, go to **Déli train station** (Déli pályaudvar; I Krisztina körút 37; Ⓜ M2 Déli pályaudvar). All three stations are on metro lines.

# ℹ Getting Around

## TO/FROM THE AIRPORT

To get into the city centre from Ferenc Liszt International Airport, minibuses, buses and trains run from 4am to midnight (350Ft to 3200Ft); taxis cost from 6500Ft.

**MiniBUD** (☑1-550 0000; www.minibud.hu; one way from 1900Ft) shuttles passengers from the airport directly to their accommodation. Tickets are available at a clearly marked desk in the arrivals hall, though you may have to wait while the van fills up.

## PUBLIC TRANSPORT

Public transport operates from 4.15am to between 9am and 11.30pm. After hours some 41 night buses run along main roads. Tram 6 on the Big Ring Rd runs round the clock.

A single ticket for all forms of transport is 350Ft (60 minutes of uninterrupted travel on the same metro, bus, trolleybus or tram line without transferring/changing; a book of 10 tickets is 3000Ft. A 'transfer ticket' allowing unlimited stations with one change within one hour costs 530Ft.

The three-day travel card (4150Ft) or the seven-day pass (4950Ft) make things easier, allowing unlimited travel inside the city limits. The fine for riding without a ticket is 8000Ft on the spot, or 16,000Ft if you pay within 30 days at the **BKK office** (☑1-325 5255; www.bkk.hu; VII Akácfa utca 22; ☉7am-8pm Mon-Fri, 8am-2pm Sat; Ⓜ M2 Blaha Lujza tér).

## TAXI

Taxis in Budapest are fully regulated, with uniform flag fall (450Ft) and per-kilometre charges (280Ft). Never get into a taxi that does not have a yellow licence plate and dashboard identification badge (required by law), plus the logo of a reputable firm on the outside and a table of fares clearly visible on the right-side back door. Reliable companies include **Budapest Taxi** (☑1-777 7777; www.budapesttaxi.hu), **City Taxi** (☑1-211 1111; www.citytaxi.hu), **Fő Taxi** (☑1-222 2222; www.fotaxi.hu) and **Taxi 4** (☑1-444 4444; www.taxi4.hu). Note that rates are higher at night and early morning.

# THE DANUBE BEND

The Danube Bend is where hills on both banks force the river to turn sharply and flow southward. It is the most beautiful stretch of the Danube, where several historical towns vie for visitors' attention. Szentendre has its roots in Serbian culture and became an important centre for art early in the 20th century. Round the bend is tiny Visegrád, Hungary's 'Camelot' in the 15th century.

Esztergom is a sleepy town with the nation's biggest cathedral.

# ℹ Getting There & Away

## BUS & TRAIN

Regular buses serve towns on the west bank of the Danube. Trains reach Szentendre and, on a separate line, Esztergom. For Visegrád, you can take one of the regular trains from Budapest to the opposite bank of the river and then take a ferry across (timings linked to train arrivals).

## BOAT

Regular **Mahart PassNave** (☑1-484 4013; www.mahartpassnave.hu; ☉8am-4pm Mon-Fri) boats run to and from Budapest over the summer months. From May to September, a boat departs Budapest's Vigadó tér at 10am Tuesday to Sunday bound for Szentendre (one way/return 2000/3000Ft, 1½ hours), returning at 5pm; the service runs on Saturday only in April. In July and August, the boat continues to Visegrád (one way/return 2500/3750Ft).

Between May and late August there's a daily ferry from Vigadó tér in Budapest at 9am, calling in at Visegrád (noon, 2500/3750Ft) before carrying on to Esztergom (2pm, 3000/4500Ft).

Hydrofoils travel from Budapest to Visegrád (one way/return 4000/6000Ft, one hour) and Esztergom (one way/return 5000/7500Ft, 1½ hours) on Friday, Saturday and Sunday from early May to September; boats leave at 9.30am and return at 5pm from Esztergom and 5.30pm from Visegrád.

---

# Szentendre

☑26 / POP 25,542

Pretty little Szentendre (*sen-ten-dreh*), 19km north of Budapest, is an art colony turned tourist centre. The charming old centre around Fő tér (Main Square) has plentiful cafes and galleries, as well as beautiful baroque Serbian Orthodox churches. Meanwhile the Art Mill (Művészet Malom; ☑26-301 701; www.muzeumicentrum.hu; Bogdányi utca 32; adult/6-26yr 2000/1200Ft; ☉10am-6pm) exhibits cutting-edge art installations across three floors. The Tourinform (☑26-317 965, www.szentendreprogram.hu; Dumtsa Jenő utca 22; ☉9am-6pm) office hands out maps.

The most convenient way to get to Szentendre is to take the HÉV suburban train from Buda's Batthyány tér (630Ft, 40 minutes, every 10 to 20 minutes). There are efficient ferry services to Szentendre from Budapest between late March and late October.

HUNGARY SZENTENDRE

# Visegrád

☑ 26 / POP 1842

History and spectacular views pull visitors to soporific, leafy Visegrád (*vish*-eh-grahd).

The mighty 13th-century **Citadel** (Fellegvár; ☑ 26-598 080; www.parkerdo.hu; Várhegy; adult/concession 1800/900Ft; ⊙ 9am-5pm mid-Mar–Apr & Oct, to 6pm May-Sep, to 3pm Nov–mid-Mar) looms over Visegrád atop a 350m hill; the views are well worth the climb. The partly reconstructed **Royal Palace** (Királyi Palota; ☑ 26-597 010; www.visegrad.hu; Fő utca 29; adult/concession 1100/550Ft; ⊙ 9am-5pm Tue-Sun Mar-Oct, 10am-4pm Tue-Sun Nov-Feb) stands at the foot of the hills, closer to the centre of town. Seek information from **Visegrád Info** (☑ 26-597 000; www.palotahaz.hu; Dunaparti út 1; ⊙ 10am-6pm Apr-Oct, to 4pm Tue-Sun Nov-Mar).

Buses are very frequent (745Ft, 1¼ hours) to/from Budapest's Újpest-Városkapu train station, Szentendre (465Ft, 45 minutes, every 45 minutes) and Esztergom (560Ft, 45 minutes, hourly). Regular ferry services travel to Visegrád from Budapest between late April and late September.

# Esztergom

☑ 33 / POP 27,990

Esztergom's massive basilica sits high above the town and Danube River. But Esztergom's attraction goes deeper than the domed structure: the country's first king, St Stephen, was born here in 975. It was a royal seat from the late 10th to the mid-13th centuries, as well as the seat of Roman Catholicism in Hungary for more than a thousand years.

Hungary's largest church is **Esztergom Basilica** (Esztergomi Bazilika; ☑ 33-402 354; www.bazilika-esztergom.hu; Szent István tér 1; basilica free, crypt 200Ft, dome adult/concession 700/500Ft, treasury adult/concession 900/450Ft; ⊙ 8am-6pm, crypt & treasury 9am-5pm, dome 9am-6pm). At the southern end of the hill is the extensive **Castle Museum** (Vármúzeum; ☑ 33-415 986; www.mnmvarmuzeuma.hu; Szent István tér 1; tours adult 1500-2000Ft, tours concession 750-1000Ft, joint ticket with Balassa Bálint Museum 3400/1700Ft; ⊙ 10am-6pm Tue-Sun), housed in the former Royal Palace built during Esztergom's golden age. Below Castle Hill in the former Bishop's Palace, the **Christian Museum** (Keresztény Múzeum; ☑ 33-413 880; www.christianmuseum.hu; Mindszenty hercegprímás tere 2; adult/concession 900/450Ft; ⊙ 10am-5pm Wed-Sun Mar-Nov; 🛜) contains the finest collection of medieval religious art in Hungary.

Frequent buses run to/from Budapest (930Ft, 1¼ hours), Visegrád (560Ft, 45 minutes) and Szentendre (930Ft, 1¼ hours). Trains depart from Budapest's Nyugati train station (1120Ft, 1¼ hours) at least hourly. Ferries travel regularly from Budapest to Esztergom between May and September.

# WESTERN HUNGARY

A visit to this region is a boon for anyone wishing to see remnants of Hungary's Roman legacy, medieval heritage and baroque splendour. Because it largely managed to avoid the Ottoman destruction of the 16th and 17th centuries, towns like Sopron retain their medieval cores; exploring their cobbled streets and hidden courtyards is a magical experience.

# Sopron

☑ 99 / POP 61,887

Sopron (*showp*-ron) is the most beautiful town in western Hungary. Its medieval Inner Town (*Belváros*) is intact and its cobbled streets are a pleasure to wander. It's also surrounded by flourishing vineyards and famous for its wine.

## ⊙ Sights

⭐ **Storno House** MUSEUM
(Storno Ház és Gyűjtemény; ☑ 99-311 327; www.muzeum.sopron.hu; Fő tér 8; adult/concession Storno Collection 1000/500Ft, Boundless Story 700/350Ft; ⊙ 10am-6pm Tue-Sun) Storno House, built in 1417, has an illustrious history: King Matthias stayed here in 1482–83, and Franz Liszt played a number of concerts here in the mid-19th century. Later it was taken over by the Swiss-Italian family of Ferenc Storno, chimney sweep turned art restorer, whose recarving of Romanesque and Gothic monuments throughout Transdanubia divides opinions to this day. Don't miss the **Storno Collection**, the family's treasure trove. The **Boundless Story** exhibition of local history is also worth a peek.

## 🛌 Sleeping

⭐ **Braun Rooms Deluxe** GUESTHOUSE €€
(☑ 06 70 300 6460; http://braun-rooms-deluxe-sopron.bedspro.com; Deák tér 15; s/d €30/38; ➳❄🛜) Halfway between the Old Town and the train station, this great place consists of just three spotless, super-comfortable

doubles, with sunken bathtubs, climate control, coffee makers and murals on the walls. And if you want your teeth done, you're in an ideal location – right above a dental surgery.

### ★ Pauline-Carmelite Monastery of Sopronbanfalva
MONASTERY €€€

(Sopronbánfalvi Pálos-Karmelita; ☑99-505 895; www.banfalvakolostor.hu; Kolostorhegy utca 1; s/d/ste €84/128/164; ☜) Having worn many hats over the centuries – home for coal miners, Carmelite nunnery, mental hospital, museum – this 15th-century monastery has now been sensitively restored as a beautiful hotel/retreat. The vaulted singles and light-filled doubles look out on to the forest. Upstairs there's an art gallery and a tranquil common space, the library. The **refectory** (Kolostorhegy utca 2; mains 2750-6850Ft, tasting menus 7200Ft; ⊙noon-3pm & 6-9pm; ☑) serves the best meals in Sopron.

## ✖ Eating & Drinking

### ★ Erhardt
INTERNATIONAL €€

(☑99-506 711; www.erhardts.hu; Balfi út 10; mains 2990-4590Ft; ⊙11.30am-10pm Sun-Thu, to 11pm Fri & Sat; ☑) An excellent restaurant where a pleasant garden terrace, a wooden-beamed ceiling and paintings of rural scenes complement imaginative dishes such as paprika catfish with oyster mushrooms and crispy duck leg with cabbage noodles. There's an extensive selection of Sopron wines to choose from (also available for purchase at its wine cellar).

### ★ Cezár Pince
WINE BAR

(☑99-311 337; www.cezarpince.hu; Hátsókapu utca 2; ⊙noon-midnight Mon-Sat, 4-11pm Sun; ☜) Atmospheric bar in a 17th-century cellar, where you can imbibe a wide selection of local wines while sharing large platters of cured meats, local cheeses, pâtés and salami.

## ℹ Information

**OTP Bank** (Várkerület 96/a) Handy ATM.

**Tourinform** (☑99-517 560; http://turizmus. sopron.hu; Liszt Ferenc utca 1, Ferenc Liszt Conference & Cultural Centre; ⊙9am-5pm Mon-Fri, to 1pm Sat year-round, 9am-1pm Sun Mar-Sep only) Some information on Sopron and surrounds, including local vintners.

## ℹ Getting There & Away

### BUS
There are direct buses to Keszthely (2520Ft, three hours, four daily) and to Balatonfüred (3130Ft, four hours, daily).

### TRAIN
Direct services from the **train station** (Állomás utca), a 10-minute walk from the heart of Sopron, run to Budapest's Keleti train station (4735Ft, 2½ hours, six daily) and Vienna's Haufbahnhof and Miedling (5000Ft, 1½ hours, up to 12 daily).

# LAKE BALATON

Extending roughly 80km, at first glance Lake Balaton seems to simply be a happy, sunny expanse of fresh water in which to play. But step beyond the beaches of Europe's biggest and shallowest body of water and you'll encounter vine-filled forested hills, a national park and a wild peninsula jutting out 4km, nearly cutting the lake in half.

# Balatonfüred

☑87 / POP 13,082

Balatonfüred (*bal*-ah-ton fuhr-ed) is the oldest and most fashionable resort on the lake. In its glory days in the 19th century the wealthy and famous built large villas along its tree-lined streets, hoping to take advantage of the health benefits of the town's thermal waters. The town now sports the most stylish marina on the lake.

## 🏃 Activities

The lake is ideal for water sports, such as windsurfing, kayaking and stand-up paddleboarding. Hire your gear from **Surf Pro Center** (☑06 30 936 6969; www.surfpro.hu; Széchenyi utca 10; ⊙9am-6pm Apr-Oct); windsurfing lessons also available. The 210km Balaton cycle path runs through Balatonfüred, and you can rent bicycles from **Eco Bike** (☑06 20 924 4995, 06 70 264 2299; www. greenspark.hu; Széchenyi utca 8; per half-/1/2 days from 1900/2755/5655Ft; ⊙9am-8pm) at the western end of the promenade.

**Kisfaludy Strand** (www.balatonfuredistrandok.hu; Aranyhíd sétány; adult/child 600/400Ft; ⊙8.30am-7pm mid-Jun–mid-Aug, 8am-6pm mid-May–mid-Jun & mid-Aug–mid-Sep) is the best of the three public beaches.

## 🛏 Sleeping

### Aqua Haz
PENSION €€

(☑8/-342 813; www.aquahaz.hu; Garay utca 2; s/d/tr 9350/11,000/15,500Ft; ℙ☜) Family-run, mustard-yellow, three-storey house, conveniently located between the lake and the train/bus station. The operators go out of their way

HUNGARY BALATONFÜRED

**WORTH A TRIP**

## HISTORIC TIHANY

While in Balatonfüred, don't miss the chance to visit Tihany (population 1383), a peninsula jutting 5km into the lake and the place with the greatest historical significance on Lake Balaton. Tihany is home to the celebrated **Benedictine Abbey Church** (Bencés Apátság Templom; 🖉 87-538 200; http://tihany.osb.hu; András tér 1; adult/concession incl museum 1000/700Ft; ⊙ 9am-6pm Apr-Sep, 10am-5pm Oct, 10am-4pm Nov-Mar), filled with fantastic altars, pulpits and screens carved in the mid-18th century by an Austrian lay brother; all are baroque-rococo masterpieces. The church attracts a lot of tourists, but the peninsula itself has an isolated, almost wild feel. Hiking is one of Tihany's main attractions; a good map outlining the trails is available from the **Tourinform** (🖉 87-448 804; www.tihany.hu; Kossuth Lajos utca 20; ⊙ 9am-7pm Mon-Fri, 10am-6pm Sat & Sun mid-Jun–mid-Sep, 10am-4pm Mon-Fri mid-Sep–mid-Jun) office just down from the church. Buses bound for Tihany depart from Balatonfüred's bus/train station (310Ft, 30 minutes, 15 daily).

to make you feel right at home, most rooms feature bright balconies, and free bikes are available for tooling around town. Excellent breakfast.

### ★ Club Hotel Füred    RESORT €€€
(🖉 87-341 511, 06 70 458 1242; www.clubhotelfured. hu; Anna sétány 1-3; r/ste from 22,100/60,000Ft; ❈ 🛜 ⛱) This stunner of a resort hotel, right on the lake, about 1.5km from the town centre, has 43 rooms and suites in several buildings spread over 2.5 hectares of parkland and lush gardens. There's an excellent spa centre with sauna, steam room and pool, but the real delight is the private beach at the end of the garden. Stellar service.

## ✕ Eating & Drinking

### ★ Nem Kacsa    HUNGARIAN €€
(🖉 06 70 364 7800; www.facebook.com/nemkacsa etterem; Zákonyi Ferenc utca; mains from 3300Ft; ⊙ noon-11pm Wed-Sun) The gourmet stylings of chef Lajos Takács stand out against the town's largely mediocre offerings. The kitchen delivers beautifully crafted dishes featuring freshly grown produce from the farm it shares with the chef of **Bistro Sparhelt** (🖉 06 70 639 9944; http://bistrosparhelt.hu; Szent István tér 7; mains 2790-6390Ft; ⊙ noon-10pm Wed-Sun; 🖉). Duck stands out, but it's hard to go wrong with other meats or the homemade Italian pasta. Marina views and local wines seal the deal.

### Kredenc Borbisztró    WINE BAR
(🖉 06 20 518 9960; www.kredencborbisztro.hu; Blaha Lujza utca 7; ⊙ noon-10pm Mon-Fri, 10am-midnight Sat & Sun) This family-run combination wine bar and bistro is a peaceful retreat near the lakefront. The menu is stacked with

oodles of local wines and the owner is often on hand to thoughtfully recommend the best tipple according to your tastes. The wine bar sells bottles of everything served, plus an extensive selection of regional wines. Weekend DJ sets.

## 🛈 Information

**Tourinform** (🖉 87-580 480; www.balatonfured. info.hu; Blaha Lujza utca 5; ⊙ 9am-7pm Mon-Sat, 10am-4pm Sun) is the main tourist office. Useful websites include www.balatonfured.hu and www.welovebalaton.hu.

## 🛈 Getting There & Away

### BOAT
From April to June and September to late October, at least four daily **Balaton Shipping Co** (Balatoni Hajózási Rt; 🖉 84-310 050; www. balatonihajozas.hu; Krúdy sétány 2, Siófok) ferries link Balatonfüred with Siófok and Tihany (adult/concession 1300/650Ft). Up to seven daily ferries serve these ports from July to August.

### BUS
Buses reach Tihany (310Ft, 30 minutes, 15 daily) and Keszthely (1300Ft, one to 1½ hours, three daily). Buses and trains to Budapest (both 2520Ft, three hours) are much of a muchness but bus departures are more frequent (up to eight daily).

## Keszthely

🖉 83 / POP 19,910

At the very western end of Lake Balaton sits Keszthely (*kest*-hey), the lake's main town and a place of grand townhouses and a gentle ambience.

## ◉ Sights & Activities

### ★ Festetics Palace                                    PALACE
(Festetics Kastély; ☎ 83-312 194; www.helikon kastely.hu; Kastély utca 1; Palace & Coach Museum adult/6-26yr 2500/1250Ft; ⊘ 9am-6pm) The glimmering white, 100-room Festetics Palace was begun in 1745; the two wings were extended out from the original building 150 years later. Some 18 splendid rooms in the baroque south wing are now part of the **Helikon Palace Museum**, as is the palace's greatest treasure, the **Helikon Library**, with its 100,000 volumes and splendid carved furniture.

### Helikon Beach                                          BEACH
(Helikon Strand; adult/concession 500/350Ft; ⊘ 8am-7pm May–mid-Sep) Reedy Helikon Beach, north of City Beach, is good for swimming and sunbathing. It has a unique view of both the north and south shores of the lake.

## ⊨ Sleeping

### ★ Ilona Kis Kastély Panzió         PENSION €€
(☎ 83-312 514; Móra Ferenc utca 22; s/d/apt 9400/12,130/16,980Ft; ❄ 🅿) Its pointy turrets covered in creepers, this delightful pension resembles a miniature castle. The rooms might be on the compact side, but some have balconies, while the apartments are positively spacious. A generous, varied breakfast is included. What sets this place apart is the attitude of its owners, who can't do enough to make their guests feel welcome.

## ✖ Eating

### Lakoma Étterem                             HUNGARIAN €€
(☎ 83-313 129; Balaton utca 9; mains 1990-3200Ft; ⊘ 11am-10pm; 🖉) With a good vegetarian and fish selection (trout with almonds, grilled perch-pike), meaty stews and roasts, plus a back garden that transforms itself into a convivial dining area in the summer months, it's hard to go wrong with Lakoma.

### ★ Paletta Keszthely                          BISTRO €€
(☎ 06 70 431 7413; www.facebook.com/Paletta Keszthely; Libás Strand; mains 1700-3300Ft; ⊘ 9am-11pm May–mid-Oct) On a summer terrace by the marina, this appealing spot mixes international fare such as bouillabaisse and its signature Basalt Burger. The dishes on the succinct menu are well-executed and the staff are friendly and prompt.

---

**WORTH A TRIP**

## HOT SPRINGS OF HÉVÍZ

Hévíz (population 4721), just 8km northwest of Keszthely, is the most famous of Hungary's spa towns because of the **Gyógy-tó** (Hévíz Thermal Lake; ☎ 83-342 830; www.spaheviz.hu; Dr Schulhof Vilmos sétány 1; 3hr/4hr/whole day 2600/3000/4500Ft; ⊘ 8am-7pm Jun-Aug, 9am-6pm May & Sep, 9am-5.30pm Apr & Oct, 9am-5pm Mar & Nov-Feb) – Europe's largest 'thermal lake'. A dip into this water lily–filled lake is essential for anyone visiting the Lake Balaton region.

Fed by 80 million litres of thermal water daily, Thermal Lake is an astonishing sight. The temperature averages 33°C and never drops below 22°C in winter, allowing bathing even when there's ice on the fir trees of the surrounding Park Wood.

Buses link Hévíz with Keszthely (250Ft, 15 minutes) every half-hour.

## ⓘ Information

**Tourinform** (☎ 83-314 144; www.keszthely.hu; Kossuth Lajos utca 30; ⊘ 9am-7pm mid-Jun–Aug, to 5pm Mon-Fri, to noon Sat Sep–mid-Jun) An excellent source of information on Keszthely and the west Balaton area. Brochures in English are available, and English spoken. Bicycles for rent, too.

**www.welovebalaton.hu** A handy listings website.

## ⓘ Getting There & Away

### BUS

Buses link Keszthely with Hévíz (250Ft, 15 minutes, half-hourly), Budapest (3410Ft, 2½ to four hours, up to nine daily) and Pécs (2830Ft, 3½ hours, up to four daily).

### TRAIN

Keszthely has train links to Budapest (3705Ft, three hours, seven daily). To reach towns along Lake Balaton's northern shore, such as Balatonfüred (1490Ft, 1½ hours, 10 daily) by train, you have to change at Tapolca.

# SOUTHERN HUNGARY

Southern Hungary is a place to savour life at a slower pace. It's only marginally touched by tourism and touring through the countryside is like travelling back in time.

# Pécs

📞 72 / POP 145,347

Blessed with a mild climate, an illustrious past and a number of fine museums and monuments, Pécs (pronounced *paich*) is one of the most pleasant and interesting cities to visit in Hungary. Many travellers put it second only to Budapest on their Hungary 'must-see' list.

## 👁 Sights

### ★ Zsolnay Cultural Quarter
NOTABLE BUILDING

(📞 72-500 350; www.zskn.hu; adult/concession 4500/2500Ft; ⊗ 9am-6pm Apr-Oct, to 5pm Nov-Mar) The biggest project to evolve out of the 2010 Capital of Culture has been the Zsolnay Cultural Quarter, built on the grounds of the original Zsolnay Family Factory. Divided into four quarters (craftsman, family and children's, creative and university), it's a lovely place to stroll around. Highlights include the street of artisans' shops and the functioning **Zsolnay Factory** (Zsolnay utca 37, Zsolnay Cultural Quarter; adult/concession 1200/700Ft; ⊗ 10am-6pm Tue-Sun Apr-Oct, to 5pm Nov-Mar), which now takes up just a section of the grounds.

### ★ Mosque Church
MOSQUE

(Mecset templom; 📞 72-321 976; Hunyadi János út 4; adult/concession 1000/500Ft; ⊗ 9am-5pm Mon-Sat, 1-5pm Sun) The largest building from the time of the Turkish occupation, the former Pasha Gazi Kassim Mosque (now the Inner Town Parish Church) dominates the main square in Pécs. Turks built the square mosque in the mid-16th century with the stones of the ruined Gothic Church of St Bertalan. The Catholics moved back in the early 18th century. The Islamic elements include windows with distinctive Turkish ogee arches, a *mihrab* (prayer niche), faded verses from the Koran and lovely geometric frescos.

## 🛏 Sleeping

### Nap Hostel
HOSTEL €

(📞 72-950 684; www.naphostel.com; Király utca 23-25; dm €10-15, d €44; @ 🛜) This friendly hostel has three dorm rooms, with between six and eight beds each, and a double with washbasin on the 1st floor of a former bank (1885). One of the six-bed dorm rooms has a corner balcony, and there's a little garden at the rear. There's a large communal kitchen and great

on-site **bar** (📞 72-585 705; www.facebook.com/nappali.bar; ⊗ 10am-2am). Enter through the bar's main entrance.

### ★ Szinbád Panzió
PENSION €€

(📞 72-221 110; www.szinbadpanzio.hu; Klimó György utca 9; s/d from €37/48; 🞵 🛜) A cosy, standard pension with excellent service and well-maintained, snug, wood-panelled rooms with cable TV, just outside the walls of Old Town. The warm welcome from the staff is much appreciated.

## 🍴 Eating & Drinking

### Cellárium
HUNGARIAN €€

(📞 72-314 453; http://cellariumetterem.hu; Hunyadi János út 2; mains 2850-4370Ft; ⊗ 11am-10pm Mon-Sat) This subterranean eatery with vaulted stone ceilings offers good value for money and imaginative dishes (juniper-braised venison, tarragon lamb with feta...). Weekends bring a variety of live music – often a small folk band or just a guy playing guitar.

### ★ Csinos Presszó
RUIN PUB

(📞 06 30 357 0004; www.facebook.com/csinos presszo; Váradi Antal utca 8; ⊗ 10am-midnight Mon-Thu, noon-2am Fri & Sat, noon-midnight Sun) Between the alfresco garden with mismatched furniture painted in bright pastels and the Christmas lights strung from the trees it's easy to see why Csinos packs in relaxed patrons. A small snack menu accompanies an inventive drinks menu (a number of the cordials are house-made) and in the afternoon it's also a prime spot to grab a coffee and press pause.

## ℹ Information

**Tourinform** (📞 06 30 681 7195; www.irany pecs.hu; Széchenyi tér; ⊗ 8am-8pm Mon-Fri, 9am-8pm Sat, 10am-6pm Sun Apr-Oct, 8am-8pm Mon-Fri, 10am-6pm Sat & Sun Nov-Mar) Knowledgable staff; copious information on Pécs and surrounds.

## ℹ Getting There & Away

### BUS

Daily buses connect Pécs with Budapest (3690Ft, 4½ hours, five daily), Szeged (3690Ft, 3½ hours, two daily) and Kecskemét (3410Ft, 4¼ hours, daily).

### TRAIN

Up to nine direct trains daily connect Pécs with Budapest's Keleti station (4485Ft, 237km, three hours). Most destinations in Southern Transdanubia are best reached by bus.

# GREAT PLAIN

Like the Outback for Australians or the Wild West for Americans, the Nagyalföld (Great Plain) – also known as the *puszta* – holds a romantic appeal for Hungarians. Many of these notions come as much from the collective imagination, paintings and poetry as they do from history, but there's no arguing the spellbinding potential of big-sky country. The Great Plain is home to cities of graceful architecture and history such as Szeged and Kecskemét.

## Szeged

☑ 62 / POP 162,600

Szeged (*seh*-ged) is a bustling border town with a handful of historic sights that line the embankment along the Tisza River and a clutch of sumptuous art nouveau town palaces. Importantly, it's also a big university town, which means lots of culture, lots of partying and an active festival scene that lasts throughout the year.

### ⚜ Festivals & Events

Annual events include the 10-day **Szeged Wine Festival** (Szegedi Borfesztivál; www. szegediborfesztival.hu; ☉ May), the pretty (and fragrant) three-day **Rose Festival** (Rózsafesztivál; www.rozsaunnep.hu; ☉ Jun), and the tasty, but less fragrant **International Tisza Fish Festival** (Nemzetközi Tiszai Halfesztivál; www. halfesztival.hu; ☉ Sep).

★**Szeged Open-Air Festival**            MUSIC
(Szegedi Szabadtéri Játékok; ☑ 62-541 205; www. szegediszabadteri.hu; ☉ Jul & Aug) The Szeged Open-Air Festival held in Dom tér in July and August is the largest festival in Hungary outside Budapest. The outdoor theatre in front of the Votive Church seats some 6000 people. Main events include an opera, an operetta, a play, folk dancing, classical music, ballet and a rock opera.

### ☉ Sights & Activities

**Reök Palace**            ARCHITECTURE
(Reök Palota; ☑ 62-541 205; www.reok.hu; Tisza Lajos körút 56; ☉ 10am-6pm Tue-Sun) The Reök Palace is a mind-blowing green-and-lilac art nouveau structure, built in 1907, that looks like a decoration at the bottom of an aquarium. It's been polished up to regain its original lustre in recent years and now hosts regular photography and visual-arts exhibitions.

**Anna Baths**            SPA
(☑ 62-553 330; www.szegedsport.hu/intezmenyek/ anna-furdo; Tisza Lajos körút 24; adult/child 1650/1350Ft; ☉ 6am-8pm) The lovely cream-coloured Anna Baths were built in 1896 to imitate the tilework and soaring dome of a Turkish bath. Rich architectural detail surrounds all the modern saunas and bubbly pools you'd expect.

### 🛏 Sleeping

**Familia Vendégház**            GUESTHOUSE €€
(Family Guesthouse; ☑ 62-441 122; www.familia panzio.hu; Szentháromság utca 71; s/d/tr 7500/ 11,000/14,000Ft; ❋ ☎) Families and international travellers often book up this family-run guesthouse with contemporary, if nondescript, furnishings in a great old building close to the train station. The two-dozen rooms have high ceilings, lots of wood and brick walls, and loads of light from tall windows.

★**Tiszavirág Hotel**            BOUTIQUE HOTEL €€€
(☑ 62-554 888; http://tiszaviragszeged.hu; Hajnóczy utca 1/b; s/d/ste €80/90/140; ❋ ☎) Wow. Our favourite new boutique hotel in Szeged is a jaw-dropper. Set in a historic townhouse built by a wealthy goldsmith in 1859, it counts 12 rooms, many with original features and all with fabulous modern artwork. There's a new wing too, separated from the old one by a splendid glass-enclosed inner courtyard perfect for lounging.

### ⚔ Eating & Drinking

★**Malata**            BURGERS €€
(www.facebook.com/malatakezmuves; Somogyi utca 13; mains 1190-3000Ft; ☉ 2-11pm Mon-Thu, 2pm-1am Fri, noon-1am Sat, noon-11pm Sun) This great new hipster hang-out is part ruin garden, part pub/cafe and counts upwards of two dozen craft beers on tap and by the bottle. The food is mostly gourmet burgers (1450Ft to 1850Ft) though not exclusively so; order and pay at the bar. In winter and rain, sit in the colourful cafe with upended umbrellas dangling from the ceiling.

### ❶ Information

**Tourinform** (☑ 62-488 690; www.szeged tourism.hu; Dugonics tér 2; ☉ 9am-5pm Mon-Fri year-round, plus 9am-1pm Sat Apr-Oct) This exceptionally helpful office is tucked away in a courtyard near the university. There is a seasonal **Tourinform kiosk** (Széchenyi tér; ☉ 8am-8pm Jun-Sep) in Széchenyi tér.

## DEBRECEN: CULTURE & COWBOY COUNTRY

Debrecen is Hungary's second-largest city, and its array of museums and thermal baths will keep you busy for a day or two. Start with the colourful **Calvinist College** (Református Kollégium; ☑ 52-614 370; www.reformatuskollegium.ttre.hu; Kálvin tér 16; adult/concession 900/500Ft; ⊙10am-4pm Mon-Fri, 10am-1pm Sat), before splashing around the slides and waterfalls within **Aquaticum Debrecen Spa** (☑ 52-514 111; www.aquaticum.hu; Nagyerdei Park 1; adult/concession 3000/2450Ft; ⊙9am-7pm); you can sleep here, too.

Next take a trip to **Hortobágy National Park**, 40km west, once celebrated for its sturdy *csikósok* (cowboys), inns and Gypsy bands. You can see a staged recreation at **Máta Stud Farm** (Mátai Ménes; ☑ 52-589 369, 06 70 492 7655; www.hortobagy.eu/hu/matai-menes; Hortobágy-Máta; adult/child 2600/1400Ft; ⊙10am, noon & 2pm mid-Mar–Oct, plus 4pm Apr–mid-Oct).

Buses reach Debrecen from Eger (2520Ft, 2½ hours, eight daily) and Szeged (3950Ft, 4½ hours, three daily), while trains go direct from Budapest (3950Ft, 3½ hours, hourly). Six buses stop daily at Hortobágy village on runs between Debrecen (745Ft, 40 minutes) and Eger (1680Ft, 1¾ hours).

## ❶ Getting There & Away

### BUS

Buses run to Pécs (3410Ft, 3½ hours, seven daily) and Debrecen (3950Ft, five hours, three daily). You can also get to the Serbian city of Novi Sad (2510Ft, 3½ hours) up to four times a day by bus.

### TRAIN

Szeged is on the main rail line to Budapest's Nyugati train station (3705Ft, 2½ hours, hourly); many trains also stop halfway along in Kecskemét (1680Ft, one hour).

# NORTHEASTERN HUNGARY

This is the home of Hungary's two most famous wines – honey-sweet Tokaj and Eger's famed Bull's Blood – and a region of microclimates conducive to wine production. The chain of wooded hills in the northeast constitutes the foothills of the Carpathian Mountains, which stretch along the Hungarian border with Slovakia.

## Eger

☑ 36 / POP 54,500

Filled with baroque buildings, Eger (*egg-air*) is a jewellery box of a town. Explore the bloody history of Turkish occupation and defeat at the hilltop castle, listen to an organ performance at the colossal basilica, or relax in a renovated Turkish bath. Then traipse from cellar to cellar in the Valley of Beautiful

Women, tasting celebrated Eger Bull's Blood (Egri Bikavér) from the cask.

## ◉ Sights & Activities

### ★ Eger Castle                                     FORTRESS

(Egri Vár; ☑ 36-312 744; www.egrivar.hu; Vár köz 1; castle grounds adult/child 800/400Ft, incl museum 1600/800Ft; ⊙exhibits 10am-5pm Tue-Sun May-Oct, 10am-4pm Tue-Sun Nov-Apr, castle grounds 8am-8pm May-Aug, to 7pm Apr & Sep, to 6pm Mar & Oct, to 5pm Nov-Feb) Climb up cobbled Vár köz from Tinódi Sebestyén tér to reach the castle, erected in the 13th century after the Mongol invasion. Models, drawings and artefacts like armour and Turkish uniforms in the **Castle History Exhibition**, on the 1st floor of the former Bishop's Palace (1470), painlessly explain the castle's story. On the eastern side of the complex are foundations of the 12th-century **St John's Cathedral**. Enter the **castle casemates** (Kazamata) hewn from solid rock via the nearby **Dark Gate**.

### ★ Lyceum Library                                    LIBRARY

(Liceumi Könyvtár; ☑ 36-520 400 ext 2214; Eszterházy tér 1, Lyceum; adult/child 1000/500Ft; ⊙9.30am-1.30pm Tue-Sun Mar & Apr, 9.30am-3.30pm Tue-Sun May-Sep, by appointment Oct-Feb) This awesome 60,000-volume all-wood library on the 1st floor of the Lyceum's south wing contains hundreds of priceless manuscripts, medical codices and incunabula. The trompe l'oeil ceiling fresco painted by Bohemian artist Johann Lukas Kracker in 1778 depicts the Counter-Reformation's Council of Trent (1545–63), with a lightning bolt setting heretical manuscripts ablaze. It was Eger's

– and its archbishop's – response to the Enlightenment and the Reformation.

### ★ Valley of the Beautiful Women    WINE

(Szépasszony-völgy Hétvége) More than two dozen cellars are carved into rock at the evocatively named Valley of the Beautiful Women, where wine tasting is popular. Try ruby-red Bull's Blood or any of the whites: *leányka*, *olaszrizling* and *hárslevelű* from nearby Debrő. The choice of wine cellars can be a bit daunting so walk around and have a look yourself. The valley is a little over 1km southwest across Rte 25 and off Király utca.

### 🛌 Sleeping

**Agria Retur Vendégház**    GUESTHOUSE €

(☑ 36-416 650; www.returvendeghaz.hu; Knézich Károly utca 18; s/d/tr 4200/7600/10,600Ft; @ 🛜) You couldn't receive a warmer welcome than the one you'll get at this guesthouse near the minaret. Walking up three flights of stairs, you enter a cheery communal kitchen/eating area central to four mansard rooms. Out the back is a huge garden with tables and a barbecue at your disposal.

### ★ Hotel Senator Ház    BOUTIQUE HOTEL €€€

(Senator House Hotel; ☑ 36-320 466; www.senator haz.hu; Dobó István tér 11; s/d €47/64; ❄ @ 🛜) Eleven warm and cosy rooms with traditional white furnishings fill the upper floors of this delightful 18th-century inn on Eger's main square. The ground floor is shared between a quality restaurant and a reception area stuffed with antiques and curios.

### ✕ Eating & Drinking

### ★ Macok Bistro & Wine Bar    HUNGARIAN €€€

(Macok Bisztró és Borbár; ☑ 36-516 180; www. imolaudvarhaz.hu/en/the-macok-bistro-wine-bar. html; Tinódi Sebestyén tér 4; mains 2190-4900Ft; ⊙ noon-10pm Sun-Thu, to 11pm Fri & Sat) This stylish eatery at the foot of the castle, with its inventive menu and excellent wine cellar, has been named among the top dozen restaurants in Hungary.

**Bíboros**    CLUB

(☑ 06 70 199 2733; www.facebook.com/biboroseger; Bajcsy-Zsilinszky utca 6; ⊙ 11am-3am Mon-Fri, 1pm-3am Sat, 3pm-midnight Sun) A subdued ruin bar by day, the 'Cardinal' transforms into a raucous dance club late in the evening; the cops at the door most weekend nights are a dead giveaway. Enjoy.

### ⓘ Information

**Tourinform** (☑ 36-517 715; www.eger.hu; Bajcsy-Zsilinszky utca 9; ⊙ 8am-6pm Mon-Fri, 9am-1pm Sat & Sun Jul & Aug, 8am-5pm Mon-Fri, 9am-1pm Sat May, Jun, Sep & Oct, 8am-5pm Mon-Fri Nov-Apr) Helpful office that promotes both the town and areas surrounding Eger.

### ⓘ Getting There & Away

#### BUS

From Eger, buses serve Debrecen (2520Ft, 2¾ hours, six daily), Kecskemét (3130Ft, four hours, two daily) and Szeged (3950Ft, 5½ hours, two daily).

#### TRAIN

Up to seven direct trains a day head to Budapest's Keleti train station (2905Ft, two hours).

# SURVIVAL GUIDE

## ⓘ Directory A–Z

### DISCOUNT CARDS

The **Hungary Card** (www.hungarycard.hu) offers free entry to many museums; 50% off on a number of return train fares and some bus and boat travel; up to 20% off selected accommodation; and 25% off the price of the **Budapest Card** (www.budapestinfo.hu). It's available at Tourinform offices.

### INTERNET RESOURCES

**Budapest Tourism** (www.budapestinfo.hu)
**Hungary Museums** (www.museum.hu)
**Hungarian National Tourist Office** (www.gotohungary.com)

---

### COUNTRY FACTS

**Area** 93,030 sq km

**Capital** Budapest

**Country Code** 36

**Currency** Forint (Ft)

**Emergency** Ambulance ☑ 104, emergency assistance ☑ 112, fire ☑ 105, police ☑ 107

**Language** Hungarian

**Money** ATMs widely available

**Population** 9.82 million

**Visas** None for EU, USA, Canada, Australia and New Zealand

## EATING PRICE RANGES

The following price ranges refer to a main course in the provinces and the cost of a two-course meal with drink in Budapest.

**Budapest**

€ less than 3500Ft

€€ 3500Ft–7500Ft

€€€ more than 7500Ft

**Provinces**

€ less than 2000Ft

€€ 2000Ft–3500Ft

€€€ more than 3500Ft

### MONEY

The unit of currency is the Hungarian forint (Ft). Coins come in denominations of five, 10, 20, 50, 100 and 200Ft, and notes are denominated in 500, 1000, 2000, 5000, 10,000 and 20,000Ft. ATMs are everywhere, even in small villages. Tip waiters, hairdressers and bar staff approximately 10% of the total, and round up taxi fares.

### TELEPHONE

Hungary's country code is 36. To make an outgoing international call, dial ☑ 00 first. For an intercity landline call within Hungary and whenever ringing a mobile telephone, dial ☑ 06, followed by the area code and phone number. All localities in Hungary have a two-digit city code, except for Budapest, where the code is ☑ 1.

Hungary has extensive mobile phone network coverage. Local SIM cards can be used in European, Australian and some North American phones. Other phones must be set to roaming, which can be pricey (check with your service provider). The three main mobile phone providers are Telenor, T-Mobile and Vodafone. You can purchase a rechargeable or prepaid SIM card from any of the three providers.

### TOURIST INFORMATION

The **Hungarian National Tourist Office** (HNTO; http://gotohungary.com) has a chain of some 130 **Tourinform** (☑ from abroad 36 1 438 80 80; www.tourinform.hu; ☺ 8am-8pm Mon-Fri) information offices across the country.

### VISAS

Citizens of all European countries and of Australia, Canada, Israel, Japan, New Zealand and the USA do not require visas for visits of up to 90 days. Check current visa requirements on the website of the **Ministry of Foreign Affairs** (http://konzuliszolgalat.kormany.hu/).

## ⓘ Getting There & Away

There are direct train connections from Budapest to major cities in all of Hungary's neighbours. International buses head in all directions and in the warmer months you can take a ferry along the Danube to reach Vienna in Austria.

### AIR

Ferenc Liszt International Airport (p190) has flights to/from Schengen countries at Terminal 2A, while Terminal 2B serves non-Schengen countries. Between April and November, **Hévíz-Balaton Airport** (SOB; ☑ 83-200 304; www.hevizairport.com; Repülőtér 1, Sármellék) receives flights from German destinations and Moscow.

### LAND
#### Bus

Most international buses arrive at the Népliget bus station (p190) in Budapest and most services are run by **Eurolines** (www.eurolines. com) in conjunction with its Hungarian affiliate, Volánbusz (p190). Useful international routes include buses from Budapest to Vienna in Austria, Bratislava in Slovakia, Subotica in Serbia, Rijeka, Dubrovnik and Split in Croatia, Prague in the Czech Republic, Kraków in Poland and Sofia in Bulgaria.

#### Car & Motorcycle

Drivers and motorbike riders will need the vehicle's registration papers, liability insurance and an international driver's permit in addition to their domestic licence.

Travel on Hungarian motorways requires pre-purchase of a highway pass *(matrica)* available from petrol stations and post offices (see www.autopalya.hu for more details).

#### Train

MÁV (p190) links up with international rail networks in all directions, and its schedule is available online. Most larger train stations in

## SLEEPING PRICE RANGES

The following price ranges refer to a double room with bathroom in high season:

**Budapest**

€ less than 15,000Ft

€€ 15,000Ft–33,500Ft

€€€ more than 33,500Ft

**Provinces**

€ less than 9000Ft

€€ 9000Ft–16,500Ft

€€€ more than 16,500Ft

## ESSENTIAL FOOD & DRINK

Traditional Hungarian food is heavy and rich. Meat, sour cream and fat abound and the omnipresent seasoning is paprika. Things are lightening up though, with increasingly available vegetarian, 'New Hungarian' and world cuisines.

**Gulyás** (goulash) Hungary's signature dish, though here it's more like a soup than a stew and made with beef, onions and tomatoes.

**Halászlé** Highly recommended fish soup made from poached freshwater fish, tomatoes, green peppers and paprika.

**Lángos** Street food; fried dough topped with cheese and/or *tejföl* (sour cream).

**Palacsinta** Thin crêpes eaten as a main course or filled with jam, sweet cheese or chocolate sauce for dessert.

**Pálinka** A strong brandy distilled from all kinds of fruit but especially plums and apricots.

**Paprika** The omnipresent seasoning in Hungarian cooking, which comes in two varieties: strong (*erős*) and sweet (*édes*).

**Pörkölt** Paprika-infused stew; closer to what we would call goulash.

**Wine** Two Hungarian wines are known internationally: the sweet dessert wine Tokaji Aszú and Egri Bikavér (Eger Bull's Blood), a full-bodied red.

Hungary have left-luggage rooms open from at least 9am to 5pm.

Seat reservations are required for international destinations, and are included in the price of the ticket. Some direct train connections from Budapest include Austria, Slovakia, Romania, Ukraine, Croatia, Serbia, Germany, Slovenia, Czech Republic, Poland, Switzerland, Italy and Bulgaria.

### RIVER

Mahart PassNave (p190) runs daily hydrofoil services on the Danube River between Budapest and Vienna (5½ to 6½ hours) from mid-May to late September. Adult one-way/return fares for Vienna are €99/125. For the return journey, consult **Mahart PassNave Wien** (☑ 01 72 92 162, 01 72 92 161; Handelskai 265, Reichsbrücke pier, Vienna) in Vienna.

## ⓘ Getting Around

Hungary does not have any scheduled domestic flights.

### BOAT

In summer there are regular passenger ferries on the Danube from Budapest to Szentendre, Visegrád and Esztergom as well as on Lake Balaton.

### BUS

Domestic buses, run by the Volánbusz (p190), an association of coach operators, cover an extensive nationwide network.

### CAR & MOTORCYCLE

There is a 100% ban on alcohol when you are driving, and this rule is strictly enforced. Headlights must be on at all times outside built-up areas. Motorcyclists must illuminate headlights too, but at all times and everywhere. Helmets are compulsory. Most cities and towns require that you pay for street parking (usually 9am to 6pm workdays) by buying temporary parking passes from machines or a warden.

### LOCAL TRANSPORT

Public transport is efficient and extensive in Hungary, with bus and, in many towns, trolleybus services. Budapest, Szeged and Debrecen also have trams, and there's an extensive metro and a suburban commuter railway in Budapest. Purchase tickets at newsstands before travelling and validate them once aboard. Inspectors frequently check tickets.

### TRAIN

**MÁV** (p190) operates reliable train services. Schedules are available online and computer information kiosks are popping up at train stations around the country.

IC trains are express trains and are the most comfortable and modern. *Gyorsvonat* and *sebesvonat* ('fast trains', indicated on the timetable by boldface type, a thicker route line and/or an 'S') take longer and use older cars; *személyvonat* (passenger trains) stop at every village along the way. Seat reservations (*helyjegy*) cost extra and are required on IC and some fast trains; these are indicated on the timetable by an 'R' in a box or a circle (a plain 'R' means seat reservations are available but not required).

In all stations a yellow board indicates departures (*indul*) and a white board is for arrivals (*érkezik*). Express and fast trains are indicated in red, local trains in black.

Both **InterRail** (www.interrail.eu) and **Eurail** (www.eurail.com) passes cover Hungary.

# Kosovo

## Best Places to Eat

➡ Tiffany (p206)

➡ Renaissance (p206)

➡ Soma Book Station (p206)

➡ Art Design (p209)

## Best Places to Stay

➡ Swiss Diamond Hotel (p205)

➡ Dukagjini Hotel (p208)

➡ Driza's House (p209)

➡ Han Hostel (p205)

## Why Go?

Europe's newest country, Kosovo is a fascinating land at the heart of the Balkans rewarding visitors with welcoming smiles, charming mountain towns, incredible hiking opportunities and 13th-century domed Serbian monasteries – and that's just for starters. It's perfectly safe to travel here now, but despite this, Kosovo remains one of the last truly off-the-beaten-path destinations in Europe.

Kosovo declared independence from Serbia in 2008, and while it has been diplomatically recognised by 112 countries, there are still many nations that do not accept Kosovan independence, including Serbia. The country has been the recipient of massive aid from the international community, particularly the EU and NATO, which effectively run the entity politically and keep peace between the ethnic Albanian majority and the minority Serbs. Barbs of its past are impossible to miss, however: roads are dotted with memorials to those killed in 1999, while NATO forces still guard Serbian monasteries.

## When to Go
### Pristina

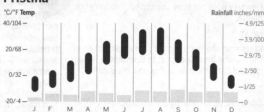

**Dec–Mar**
Hit the powder on the still largely virgin ski slopes of Brezovica.

**May–Sep**
Pleasant weather for hiking in the Rugova Mountains.

**Aug**
The excellent DokuFest in Prizren is Kosovo's best arts event.

## Kosovo Highlights

**1 Prizren's old town** (p209) Discovering the picturesque, mosque-studded streets of Prizren's charming old quarter and getting a breathtaking view from the fortress.

**2 Rugova Mountains** (p208) Trekking around the stunning landscapes of Kosovo's most impressive mountains, which rise to the west of Peja.

**3 Peja's Cheese Market** (p208) Breathing deep at Peja's Saturday Cheese Market inside the town's colourful bazaar.

**4 Visoki Dečani Monastery** (p208) Taking in gorgeous frescoes and then buying monk-made wine and cheese at this serene 14th-century Serbian monastery.

**5 Bear Sanctuary Pristina** (p207) Visiting the rescued bears living in excellent conditions at this wonderful lakeside sanctuary that's just a short trip from the capital.

**6 Pristina** (p203) Exploring Europe's youngest country through its plucky and idiosyncratic capital city, and enjoying its excellent dining and nightlife.

# PRISTINA

038 / POP 211,000

Pristina (pronounced 'prish-*tee*-na') is a city changing fast and one that feels full of optimism and potential, even if its traffic-clogged streets and mismatched architectural styles don't make it an obviously attractive place. Far more a provincial town than great city, Pristina makes for an unlikely national capital, and yet feels more cosmopolitan than the capitals of many larger Balkan nations due to the number of foreigners working here: the UN and EU both have large presences and the city feels rich and more sophisticated as a result.

# Pristina

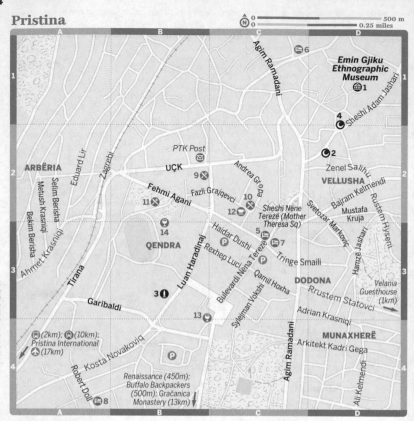

## Pristina

## ⊙ Sights

### ★ Emin Gjiku Ethnographic
Museum                          HISTORIC BUILDING
(Rr Iliaz Agushi; ⊙10am-5pm Tue-Sat, to 3pm Sun)
FREE This wonderful annex of the Museum of Kosovo is located in two beautifully preserved Ottoman houses enclosed in a large walled garden. The English-speaking staff will give you a fascinating tour of both properties and point out the various unique pieces of clothing, weaponry, jewellery and household items on display in each. There's no better introduction to Kosovar culture.

**Jashar Pasha Mosque** MOSQUE
(Rr Ylfete Humolli; ⊙ dawn-dusk) This mosque, which was fully renovated as a gift from the Turkish government, reopened in 2015 and has vibrant interiors that exemplify Turkish baroque style.

**Sultan Mehmet Fatih Mosque** MOSQUE
(Xhamia e Mbretit; Rr Ilir Konushevci; ⊙ dawn-dusk) The 'imperial mosque' (Xhamia e Mbretit), as locals call it, was built on the orders of Mehmed the Conqueror around 1461, and although it was converted to a Catholic church during the Austro-Hungarian era, it was renovated again after WWII and is now the city's most important mosque. It has some beautiful interiors, as well as striking painted ceilings over the main entrance.

**Newborn Monument** MONUMENT
These iconic block letters in downtown Pristina look a bit scrappy and worn these days, but they captured the imagination of the fledgling nation when they were unveiled on 17 February 2008, the day Kosovo declared its independence from Serbia and began its painful (and still incomplete) journey to full international recognition.

## 🏃 Activities

**Be In Kosovo** TOURS
(☑ 049 621 768; www.beinkosovo.com) This ambitious and fast-growing company offers tours and services throughout Kosovo, and its Kosovar guides know the country well – including the Serbian monasteries and the Serb minorities of North Mitrovica. The company also has offices in neighbouring countries and can easily organise multinational itineraries.

**Traveks** ADVENTURE
(☑ 044 484 444; www.traveks.com) This operator offers a variety of tours including horse riding around the village of Brod in southern Kosovo, and 'Taste of Kosovo' cultural tours which include raki and wine tasting.

## 🛏 Sleeping

**★ Han Hostel** HOSTEL €
(☑ 044 396 852, 044 760 792; www.hostelhan.com; Rr Fehmi Agani 2/4; dm €12-14, s/d €20/30; @ 🛜) Pristina's best hostel is on the 4th floor of a residential building right in the heart of town. Cobbled together from two apartments that have been joined and converted, this great space has a large communal kitchen, balconies and smart rooms with clean

bathrooms. It's well set up for backpackers and run by an extremely friendly local crew.

**White Tree Hostel** HOSTEL €
(☑ 049 166 777; www.whitetreehostel.com; Rr Mujo Ulqinaku 15; dm €9-12, d €30; ❄ 🛜) This hostel is run by a group of well-travelled locals who took a derelict house into their care, painted the tree in the courtyard white and gradually began to attract travellers with a cool backpacker vibe. It feels more like an Albanian beach resort than a downtown Pristina bolthole.

**Buffalo Backpackers** HOSTEL €
(☑ 377 643 261; www.buffalobackpackers.com; Rr Musine Kokalari 25; dm/camping incl breakfast €12/6; 🛜) This charming dorm-only hostel has some of the cheapest and most chilled-out accommodation in the country, as well as friendly staff and a pleasant location in a house south of Pristina's busy city centre.

**Hotel Begolli** HOTEL €€
(☑ 038 244 277; www.hotelbegolli.com; Rr Maliq Pashë Gjinolli 8; s/d incl breakfast €40/50, apt from €50; ❄ @ 🛜) While it may have gone overboard with its '90s-style furniture, Begolli is a pleasant, rather sprawling place to stay. The apartment has a Jacuzzi and a kitchen and is good value, while the normal rooms are on the small side but comfy. A good breakfast is served in the ground-floor bar.

**★ Swiss Diamond Hotel** LUXURY HOTEL €€€
(☑ 038 220 000; www.swissdiamondhotelprishtina.com; Sheshi Nënë Tereza; s/d incl breakfast from €145/165; 🅿 ❄ ❄ @ 🛜 ⊠) This international-

standard five-star hotel is the choice of those who can afford it. Opened in 2012 in the heart of the city, this place is all marble floors, obsequious staff and liveried attendants. The rooms are lavish and the suites are immense, all decorated with expensive furnishings and many enjoying great city views.

 ## Eating

### ★Soma Book Station    MEDITERRANEAN €€

(4/A Fazli Grajqevci; mains €5-11; ⊙8am-midnight Mon-Sat; ) Despite existing for just a couple of years, Soma is already a local institution, and nearly all visitors to Pristina end up here at some point. The shady garden hums with activity at lunchtime, while the interior has a club-like atmosphere. Food combines various tastes of the Mediterranean, including tuna salad, beef carpaccio, grilled fish, steaks and burgers.

### ★Tiffany    BALKAN €€

(☑038 244 040; off Rr Fehmi Agani; meals €12; ⊙9am-10.30pm Mon-Sat, from 6pm Sun; ) The organic menu here (delivered by efficient, if somewhat terse, English-speaking staff) is simply dazzling: sit on the sun-dappled terrace and enjoy the day's grilled special, beautifully cooked seasonal vegetables drenched in olive oil, and freshly baked bread. Understandably much prized by the foreign community, this brilliant place is unsigned and somewhat hidden behind a well-tended bush on Fehmi Agani.

---

### ESSENTIAL FOOD & DRINK

'Traditional' food is generally Albanian – most prominently, stewed and grilled meat and fish. Kos (goat's-cheese yoghurt) is eaten alone or with almost anything. Turkish kebabs and gjuveç (baked meat and vegetables) are common.

**Byrek** Pastry with cheese or meat.

**Gjuveç** Baked meat and vegetables.

**Fli** Flaky pastry pie served with honey.

**Kos** Goat's-milk yoghurt.

**Pershut** Dried meat.

**Qofta** Flat or cylindrical minced-meat rissoles.

**Tavë** Meat baked with cheese and egg.

**Vranac** Red wine from the Rahovec region of Kosovo.

---

### ★Renaissance    BALKAN €€

(Renesansa; ☑044 118 796; Rr Musine Kokollari; set meals €15; ⊙6pm-midnight) This atmospheric place might just be Pristina's best-kept secret, if only for the fact that it seems to move premises with alarming speed. At its newest location, wooden doors open to a traditional dining room where tables are brimming with local wine and delicious meze and meaty main courses prepared by the family's matriarch. Vegetarians can be catered for but should call ahead. The restaurant can be rather tricky to find, as it's unsigned: taxi drivers usually know it.

### Home Bar & Restaurant    INTERNATIONAL €€

(Rr Luan Haradinaj; mains €5-12; ⊙7am-11pm Mon-Sat, 11am-11pm Sun; ) Having been here since the dark days of 2001, this is the closest Pristina has to an expat institution. It lives up to its name, too: it's exceptionally cosy and friendly and is peppered with curios and antiques. The menu, which has some Lebanese influence, includes comfort foods such as spring rolls, hummus, curries, wraps, burgers and fajitas.

 ## Drinking

### ★Dit' e Nat'    CAFE

(www.ditenat.com/en; Rr Fazli Grajqevci 5; ⊙8am-midnight Mon-Sat, noon-midnight Sun; ) 'Day and night', a bookshop-cafe-bar-performance space, is a home away from home for bookish expats and locals alike. There's a great selection of books in English, strong espresso, excellent cocktails, friendly English-speaking staff and occasional live music in the evenings, including jazz. Recently the establishment has started serving vegetarian food to boot.

### Sabaja Craft Brewery    BREWERY

(Stadioni i Prishtinës; ⊙9am-11pm; ) This American-Kosovar venture is Pristina's first microbrewery; its several wonderful brews include an IPA and a Session pale ale. There are also various seasonal products available. To complement that, there's a relaxed vibe and a good international menu (mains €2 to €5) available.

### Rooftop 13    CLUB

(☑045 628 628; www.rooftop13.com; 13th fl, Grand Hotel, Blvd Nënë Tereza; ⊙11pm-5am Wed, Fri & Sat) Despite its rather unlikely location on top of the gargantuan and grotesque state-run Grand Hotel, Rooftop 13 pulls off the impressive feat of being a smart and stylish club. Revelers come to drink cocktails until the early hours while enjoying incredible views of

## GRAČANICA MONASTERY & BEAR SANCTUARY PRISTINA

Explore beyond Pristina by heading southeast to two of the country's best sights. Dusty fingers of sunlight pierce the darkness of **Gračanica Monastery** (⊙ 6am-5pm) FREE, completed in 1321 by Serbian King Milutin. It's an oasis in a town that is the cultural centre of Serbs in central Kosovo. Take a Gjilan-bound bus (€0.50, 15 minutes, every 30 minutes); the monastery's on your left. Do dress respectably (that means no shorts or sleeveless tops for anyone, and head scarves for women) and you'll be very welcome to look around this historical complex and to view the gorgeous icons in the main church.

Further along the road to Gjilan is the excellent **Bear Sanctuary Pristina** (☑ 045 826 072; www.vier-pfoten.eu; Mramor; adult/student €1.50/0.50c; ⊙ 9am-6pm Apr-Oct, 10am-4pm Nov-Mar), in the village of Mramor. Here you can visit a number of brown bears that were rescued from cruel captivity by the charity Four Paws. All the bears here were once kept in tiny cages as mascots for restaurants, but when the keeping of bears was outlawed in Kosovo in 2010, Four Paws stepped in to care for these wonderful animals. Sadly some of them still suffer from trauma and don't socialise well, but their excellent conditions are heartening indeed. Ask to be let off any Gjilan-bound bus by the Delfina gas station at the entrance to Mramor, then follow the road back past the lakeside, and then follow the track around to the right.

the city. Dress to impress – locals do and you'll feel out of place if you don't make an effort.

### ℹ Information

**American Hospital** (☑ 038 221 661; www. ks.spitaliamerikan.com; Rr Shkupi) The best hospital in Kosovo offers American-standard healthcare, although not always the language skills to match. It's just outside the city in the Serbian-majority town of Gračanica.

**Barnatore Pharmacy** (Blvd Nënë Tereza; ⊙ 8am-10pm)

**PTK Post** (Rr UÇK; ⊙ 8am-8pm Mon-Sat) Post and special delivery services.

### ℹ Getting There & Around

#### AIR

There is currently no public transport from **Pristina International Airport** (☑ 038 501 502 1214; www.airportpristina.com), so you'll have to get a taxi into the city. Taxis charge €25 for the 20-minute, 18km trip to the city centre.

#### BUS

The **bus station** (Stacioni i Autobusëve; ☑ 038 550 011; Rr Lidja e Pejes) is 2km southwest of the centre off Blvd Bil Klinton. Taxis to the centre should cost €2.

International buses from Pristina include Belgrade (€21, seven hours, 11pm) and Novi Pazar (€5.50, three hours, 10am) in Serbia; Tirana, Albania (€10.50, five hours, every one to two hours), Skopje, Macedonia (€5.50, two hours, hourly from 5.30am to 5pm); Podgorica (€15.50, seven hours, 7pm) and Ulcinj (€15.50, seven hours, 8am & 9pm) in Montenegro .

Domestically there are buses to all corners of the country, including Prizren (€4, 75 minutes, every 20 minutes) and Peja (€4, 1½ hours, every 20 minutes).

#### TRAIN

Trains run from Pristina to Peja (€3, at 8.01am and 4.41pm, two hours) and, internationally, to Skopje in Macedonia (€4, 7.22am, three hours).

## AROUND PRISTINA

Kosovo is a small country, which can be crossed by car in any direction in around an hour. Not far in distance, but worlds away from the chaotic capital, the smaller towns of Peja and Prizren both offer a different pace and a new perspective on Kosovar life.

## Peja (Peć)

☑ 039 / POP 97,000

Peja (known as Peć in Serbian) is Kosovo's third-largest city and one flanked by sites vital to Orthodox Serbians. With a Turkish-style bazaar at its heart and the dramatic but increasingly accessible Rugova Mountains all around it, it's a diverse and progressive place that's fast becoming Kosovo's tourism hub.

### ◉ Sights

**Patriarchate of Peć**　　　　　MONASTERY
(Pećka Patrijaršija; ☑ 044 150 755; ⊙ 9am-6pm) This church and nunnery complex on the outskirts of Peja are a slice of Serbian Orthodoxy that has existed here since the late 13th

## VISOKI DEČANI MONASTERY

This imposing whitewashed **monastery** ( 049 776 254; www.decani.org; 11am-1pm & 4-5.30pm), 15km south of Peja, is one of Kosovo's absolute highlights. Located in an incredibly beautiful spot beneath the mountains and surrounded by a forest of pine and chestnut trees, the monastery has been here since 1327 and is today heavily guarded by Nato's Kosovo Force (KFOR). Despite occasional attacks from locals who'd like to see the Serbs leave – most recently a grenade attack in 2007 – the 25 Serbian monks living here in total isolation from the local community have stayed.

Buses go to the town of Dečani from Peja (€1, 30 minutes, every 15 minutes) on their way to Gjakovë. It's a pleasant 1km walk to the monastery from the bus stop. From the roundabout in the middle of town, take the second exit if you're coming from Peja. You'll need to surrender your passport while visiting.

century. You're welcome to enter to visit the church, which is divided into four separate chapels containing superb frescoes. The entire complex dates from between the 1230s and the 1330s. Since 2013, the buildings have been guarded by Kosovo's police force, and you will need your passport to enter.

### Cheese Market
MARKET

( 8am-4pm Sat) The town's bustling daily bazaar makes you feel like you've just arrived in İstanbul, and it's a great place to see local farmers and artisans hawking their wares. The highlight is when farmers gather in a busy courtyard at the centre of the market area each Saturday with wooden barrels of goat's cheese. You can actually just follow your nose and you'll find it.

## ⚡ Activities

Peja has established itself as the country's tourism hub and there's an impressive number of activities on offer in the nearby Rugova Mountains, including rock climbing, mountain biking, skiing, hiking and white-water rafting.

### ★ Rugova Experience
ADVENTURE

( 044 137 734, 044 350 511; www.rugovaexperience.org; Rr Mbretëreshë Teuta) ∅ This excellent, locally run company is championing the Rugova region for hikers and cultural tourists. It organises homestays in mountain villages, runs very good trekking tours, enjoys great local access and works with English-speaking guides. Its helpful office has maps and plenty of information about Peja's local trekking opportunities.

### Balkan Natural Adventure
ADVENTURE

( 049 661 105; www.bnadventure.com) Balkan Natural Adventure is the best local resource to book your via ferrata, zipline, caving, rock climbing or snowshoeing adventure in the Rugova region. It also leads the Peaks of the Balkans hiking tours.

### Rugova Hiking
HIKING

( 049 126 443; www.rugovahiking.com; Rr Filip Shiroka 16) This highly regarded local firm offers hiking, biking and skiiing tours of the Rugova Mountains to groups of up to 20 people. There's a number of tried and tested itineraries on offer, but tailor-made tours are also possible. One popular tour is a 43km downhill biking tour (€39 per person, 4-5 hours) run with Belgian cycling tour operator Cyclistes Sans Frontières.

## 🛏 Sleeping

### Hostel Saraç
HOSTEL €

( 049 247 391; hostelsarac@gmail.com; Vëllezërit Bakir e Adem Gjuka 22; dm €10; 🛜) Opened in 2015, this new hostel inside a family home has a spacious garden and a common area scattered with traditional Albanian musical instruments. The accommodation is in one big dorm upstairs, which is partially divided into two areas that all share a small kitchen and bathroom. Private rooms are planned. It's central, English-speaking and ideal for groups.

### ★ Dukagjini Hotel
HOTEL €€

( 038 771 177; www.hoteldukagjini.com; Sheshi i Dëshmorëve 2; s/d incl breakfast €50/70; ⊕✳🛜🏊) The regal Dukagjini boasts international standards, which you probably didn't expect in a small city in Kosovo. Rooms can be rather small but are grandly appointed and have supremely comfortable beds; many on the 1st floor have huge terraces overlooking the central square. There's a pool and gym and a huge restaurant with views of the river.

## ✖ Eating

★ **Art Design** BALKAN €
(📞 049 585 885; Rr Enver Hadri 53; mains €2.50-6; ⊘ 8am-midnight) Despite sounding flash and modern, Art Design is actually an old house brimming with character and full of local arts and crafts. Choose between dining outside over a little stream or in one of the two rather chintzy dining rooms. Traditional dishes here include *sarma* (meat and rice rolled in grape leaves) and *speca dollma* (peppers filled with meat and rice).

**Kulla e Zenel Beut** BALKAN €€
(Rr William Walker; mains €3-7; ⊘ 8am-midnight; 🛜) This charming option in the centre of town has a pleasant terrace and a cosy dining room. The dishes to go for here are the *tava* (various traditional specialties served in clay pots), though fresh fish, baked mussels, grills and even a breakfast menu are on offer, too. There's only one English menu, so you may have to wait your turn.

## ℹ Information

**Tourist Information Centre** (📞 039 423 949; www.pejatourism.org; Rr Mbretëreshë Teuta; ⊘ 8am-noon & 1-4pm Mon-Fri) This little office in the centre of town is run by friendly English-speaking staff. They can offer you lots of advice, maps and other information about exploring Peja and the surrounding region, and help organise trips into the Rugova Mountains.

## ℹ Getting There & Away

### BUS

The town's bus station is on Rr Adem Jashari, a short walk from the town centre. Frequent buses run to Pristina (€4, 1½ hours, every 20 minutes), Prizren (€4, 80 minutes, hourly), Gjakova (€2.50, 50 minutes, hourly) and Dečani (€1, 20 minutes, hourly). International buses link Peja with Ulcinj (€16, 10 hours, 10am and 8.30pm) and Podgorica in Montenegro (€15, seven hours, 10am).

### TRAIN

Trains depart Peja for Pristina (€3, two hours, twice daily) from the town's small train station. To find the station, walk away from the Dukagjini Hotel down Rr Emrush Miftari for 1.4km.

# Prizren

📞 029 / POP 185,000
Picturesque Prizren is Kosovo's second city and it shines with post-independence enthusiasm that's infectious. If you're passing through between Albania and Pristina, the charming mosque- and church-filled old town is well worth setting aside a few hours to wander about in. It's also worth making a special journey here if you're a documentary fan: Prizren's annual DokuFest is Kosovo's leading arts event and attracts documentary makers and fans from all over the world every August.

## ⊙ Sights

**Prizren Fortress** CASTLE
(Kalaja; ⊘ dawn-dusk) FREE It's well worth making the steep 15-minute hike up from Prizren's old town (follow the road past the Orthodox church on the hillside; it's well signed and pretty obvious) for the superb views over the city and on into the distance. The first fortress here was built by the Byzantines and was expanded by successive Serbian kings in the 12th to 14th centuries before becoming a seat of power for the Ottoman rulers of Kosovo until their expulsion in 1912.

**Sinan Pasha Mosque** MOSQUE
(Xhamia e Sinan Pashës; Vatra Shqiptare; ⊘ dawn-dusk) Dating from 1615, the Sinan Pasha Mosque is the most important in Prizren, and it sits right at the heart of the old town, overlooking the river and the town's Ottoman Bridge. Its impressive dome, minaret and colonnaded facade form a fabulous sight from the street, though it's also well worth going inside (outside of prayer times) to see the striking interior.

**Church of Our Lady of Ljeviš** CHURCH
(Bogorodica Ljeviška; Rr Xhemil Fluku; admission €3) Prizren's most important site is the Orthodox Church of Our Lady of Ljeviš, a 14th-century Serbian church that was used as a mosque by the local population until 1911. The church was badly damaged in 2004 by the town's Albanian population and placed on Unesco's World Heritage in Danger list in 2006. Restoration work on its magnificent frescoes has recently begun.

## 🛏 Sleeping

★ **Driza's House** HOSTEL €
(📞 049 618 181; www.drizas-house.com; Remzi Ademaj 7; dm €9-15, tw/tr €25/40; ❄🛜) New in 2016, this former family home in a courtyard just off the river embankment is an atmospheric option full of local charm. Made up of two dorms with custom-made bunk beds (which include curtains, reading lights, personal electricity plugs and lockable storage cupboards), the place feels very communal – but worlds away from your average hostel.

### Prizren City Hostel
HOSTEL €

(☑049 466 313; www.prizrencityhostel.com; Rr Iljaz Kuka 66; dm incl breakfast €11, d incl breakfast with/without bathroom €33/28; ❂❅➔) Over four floors and a short wander from the heart of the old town, Prizren's original hostel is a great place to stay, with a friendly, international vibe and a chilled-out roof terrace bar complete with hammocks, awesome city views and regular BBQs. There are good bathrooms, tours can be arranged and the friendly owner decidedly encourages drinking.

### Classic Hotel
HOTEL €€

(☑029 223 333; www.classic-hotel-prizren.com; Shuaip Spahiu; s/d €49/69; P❅➔) This plush and atmospheric spot in the heart of the old town is an ideal place to stay if you'd like some comfort and a bit of pampering. The spacious rooms have safes, flat-screen TVs, minibars and marble bathrooms. Gold flourishes abound, and service is gracious and attentive.

## ✗ Eating

### Ego
INTERNATIONAL €

(Sheshi i Shadërvanit; mains €2.50-7; ❂8am-11pm Mon-Fri, 11am-11pm Sat & Sun; ➔) Right on Prizren's pretty main cobblestone square, this place stands out from the many cafes and restaurants here with its sophisticated international menu, abundant vegetarian options, smart decor and charming staff. Have lunch on the terrace, drinks inside or a more formal dinner in the upstairs dining room.

### Ambient
BALKAN €€

(Rr Vatrat Shqiptare; mains €3-9; ❂8am-midnight; ➔) With views over the old town and by far the most charming location in Prizren – beside a waterfall cascading down the cliffside by the river – this is a place to come for a romantic dinner or sundowner. The menu includes a Pasha burger, steaks, seafood and a catch of the day cooked to your specification.

## ▼ Drinking

### Te Kinezi
PUB

(Sheshi i Shadërvanit; ❂noon-midnight Sun-Thu, until 2am Fri & Sat) This little place is riotously popular and rightly so: it has excellent brews on tap from Pristina's Sabaja Craft Brewery (p206). There's a full range of other drinks, too, and an in-the-know crowd that's more bohemian and interesting than most you'll meet in town.

### Corner Bar
BAR

(Sheshi i Shadërvanit; ❂noon-11pm) In the thick of the bars that surround the old town's main square, this raucous and popular place stands out for its young, cool crowd and eclectic local DJs. There's a big cocktail list, and the owner will often join in the fun himself while the crowds spill out onto the street during the summer.

## ⓘ Getting There & Away

Prizren is well connected by bus to Pristina (€4, two hours, every 20 minutes), Peja (€4, two hours, six daily), Skopje in Macedonia (€6, three hours, two daily) and Tirana in Albania (€12, three hours, seven daily). The bus station is on the right bank of the river, a short walk from the old town: follow the right-hand side of the river embankment away from the castle until you come to the traffic circle, then turn left onto Rr De Rada. The bus station will be on your left after around 200m.

# SURVIVAL GUIDE

## ⓘ Directory A–Z

### ACCOMMODATION
Accommodation is booming in Kosovo, with most large towns now offering a good range of options.

### INTERNET RESOURCES
**UN Mission in Kosovo Online** (http://unmik. unmissions.org) A good overview of the UN's work in Kosovo and the latest security situation.

**Balkan Insight** (www.balkaninsight.com) Quality news and analysis about the Balkans, with a good section on Kosovo.

**Kosovo Guide** (www.kosovoguide.com) An excellent Kosovo travel wiki.

**Balkanology** (www.balkanology.com) A popular website about the Balkans with strong Kosovo coverage.

**Lonely Planet** (www.lonelyplanet.com/kosovo) Destination information, hotel bookings, traveller forum and more.

### MONEY
Kosovo's currency is the euro, despite not being part of the eurozone or the EU. It's best to arrive with small denominations, and euro coins are particularly useful. ATMs are common and established businesses accept credit cards.

### OPENING HOURS
Opening hours vary, but these are the usual hours of business.

**Banks** 8am–5pm Monday to Friday, until 2pm Saturday

**Bars** 8am–11pm
**Shops** 8am–6pm Monday to Friday, until 3pm Saturday
**Restaurants** 8am–midnight

### POST
PTK post and telecommunications offices operate in Kosovo's main towns.

### PUBLIC HOLIDAYS
**New Year's Day** 1 January
**Independence Day** 17 February
**Kosovo Constitution Day** 9 April
**Labour Day** 1 May
**Europe Day** 9 May

### TELEPHONE
Kosovo's country code is  381.

### VISAS
Kosovo is visa-free for EU, Australian, Canadian, Japanese, New Zealand, South African and US passport holders. All passports are stamped on arrival for a 90-day stay.

## ⓘ Getting There & Away

### AIR
**Pristina International Airport** (p207) is 18km from the centre of Pristina. Airlines flying to Kosovo include Air Pristina, Adria, Austrian Airlines, easyJet, Norwegian, Pegasus and Turkish Airlines.

### LAND
Kosovo has good bus connections between Albania, Montenegro and Macedonia, with regular services from Pristina, Peja and Prizren to Tirana (Albania), Skopje (Macedonia) and Podgorica (Montenegro). There's also a train line from Pristina to Macedonia's capital, Skopje. You can take international bus trips to and from all neighbouring capital cities; note that buses to and from Belgrade in Serbia travel via Montenegro.

### Border Crossings
**Albania** There are three border crossings between Kosovo and Albania. To get to Albania's Koman Ferry, use the Qafa Morina border crossing west of Gjakova. A short distance further south is the Qafë Prush crossing, though the road continuing into Albania is bad here. The busiest border is at Vërmicë, where a modern motorway connects to Tirana.

**Macedonia** There are crossings to Blace from Pristina and Gllobocicë from Prizren.

**Montenegro** The main crossing is the Kulla/Rožaje crossing on the road between Rožaje and Peja.

**Serbia** There are six border crossings between Kosovo and Serbia. Be aware that Kosovo's independence is not recognised by Serbia, so

---

if you plan to continue to Serbia but entered Kosovo via Albania, Macedonia or Montenegro, officials at the Serbian border will deem that you entered Serbia illegally and you will not be let in. You'll need to exit Kosovo to a third country and then enter Serbia from there. If you entered Kosovo from Serbia, there's no problem returning to Serbia.

## ⓘ Getting Around

### BUS
Buses stop at distinct blue signs, but can be flagged down anywhere. Bus journeys are generally cheap, but the going can be slow on Kosovo's single-lane roads.

### CAR
Drivers should carry their licences with them whenever on the road, as police checks are not uncommon. Road conditions in Kosovo are generally good, though watch out for potholes on some poorly maintained stretches.

European Green Card vehicle insurance is not valid in the country, so you'll need to purchase vehicle insurance at the border when you enter with a car; this is a hassle-free and inexpensive procedure.

It's perfectly easy to hire cars here and travel with them to neighbouring countries (with the exception of Serbia). Note that Serbian-plated cars have been attacked in Kosovo, and rental companies do not let cars hired in Kosovo travel to Serbia and vice versa.

### TRAIN
The train system is something of a novelty, but services connect Pristina to Peja and to Skopje in Macedonia. Locals generally take buses.

# Latvia

## Why Go?

A tapestry of sea, lakes and woods, Latvia is best described as a vast unspoilt parkland with just one real city – its cosmopolitan capital, Rīga. The country might be small, but the amount of personal space it provides is enormous. You can always secure a chunk of pristine nature all for yourself, be it for trekking, cycling or dreaming away on a white-sand beach amid pine-covered dunes. Having been invaded by every regional power, Latvia has more cultural layers and a less homogenous population than its neighbours. People here fancy themselves to be the least pragmatic and the most artistic of the Baltic lot. They prove the point with myriad festivals and a merry, devil-may-care attitude – well, a subdued Nordic version of it.

## Best Places to Eat

➡ Vincents (p220)

➡ Fazenda Bazārs (p219)

➡ 36.Line (p222)

➡ 3 Pavaru (p219)

➡ Skroderkrogs (p225)

## Best Places to Stay

➡ Ekes Konvents (p218)

➡ Hotel Bergs (p219)

➡ Neiburgs (p218)

➡ Hotel Cēsis (p223)

➡ 2 Baloži (p224)

## When to Go
### Rīga

°C/°F Temp          Rainfall inches/mm

**Jun–Aug** Summer starts with an all-night solstice romp, then it's off to the beach.

**Sep** Refusing to let summer go, Rīgans sip lattes under heat lamps at al fresco cafes.

**Dec** Celebrate the festive season in the birthplace of the Christmas tree.

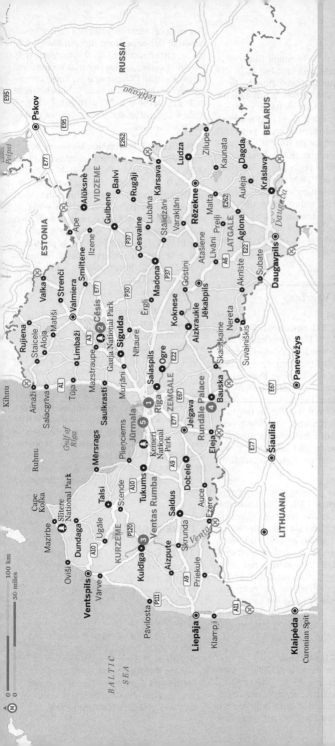

# Latvia Highlights

**❶ Rīga** (p214)
Clicking your camera at the nightmarish menagerie of devilish gargoyles, mythical beasts, praying goddesses and twisting vines that inhabits the city's surplus of art nouveau architecture.

**❷ Cēsis** (p223)
Launching lighting raids into Gauja National Park from the castle fortress.

**❸ Ventas Rumba** (p224) Joining swarms of fish trying to jump over the waterfall, the widest (and possibly the shortest) in Europe.

**❹ Rundāle Palace** (p215) Sneaking away from the capital and indulging in aristocratic decadence.

**❺ Jūrmala** (p221) Hobnobbing with Russian jetsetters in the heart of the swanky spa scene.

# RĪGA

POP 643,000

The Gothic spires that dominate Rīga's cityscape might suggest austerity, but it is the flamboyant art nouveau that forms the flesh and the spirit of this vibrant cosmopolitan city, the largest of all three Baltic capitals. Like all northerners, it is quiet and reserved on the outside, but there is some powerful chemistry going on inside its hip bars and modern art centres, and in the kitchens of its cool experimental restaurants. Standing next to a gulf named after itself, Rīga is a short drive from jet-setting sea resort, Jūrmala, which comes with a stunning white-sand beach. But if you are craving solitude and a pristine environment, gorgeous sea dunes and blueberry-filled forests, begin right outside the city boundaries.

## ◉ Sights

### ◉ Old Rīga (Vecrīga)

#### ★ Rīga Cathedral                    CHURCH
(Rīgas Doms; ☑ 6722 7573; www.doms.lv; Doma laukums 1; admission €3; ☺ 10am-5pm Oct-Jun, 9am-6pm Sat-Tue, 9am-5pm Wed-Fri Jul-Sep) Founded in 1211 as the seat of the Rīga diocese, this enormous (once Catholic, now Evangelical Lutheran) cathedral is the largest medieval church in the Baltic. The architecture is an amalgam of styles from the 13th to the 18th centuries: the eastern end, the oldest portion, has Romanesque features; the tower is 18th-century baroque; and much of the rest dates from a 15th-century Gothic rebuilding.

#### St Peter's Church                    CHURCH
(Sv Pētera baznīca; www.peterbaznica.riga.lv; Skārņu iela 19; adult/child €9/3; ☺ 10am-6pm Tue-Sat, noon-6pm Sun, to 7pm May-Aug) Forming the centrepiece of Rīga's skyline, this Gothic church is thought to be around 800 years old, making it one of the oldest medieval buildings in the Baltic. Its soaring red-brick interior is relatively unadorned, except for heraldic shields mounted on the columns. A colourful contrast is provided by the art exhibitions staged in the side aisles. At the rear of the church, a lift whisks visitors to a viewing platform 72m up the steeple.

#### ★ Art Museum Rīga Bourse           MUSEUM
(Mākslas muzejs Rīgas Birža; ☑ 6732 4461; www.lnmm.lv; Doma laukums 6; adult/child €6/3; ☺ 10am-6pm Tue-Thu, Sat & Sun, to 8pm Fri) Rīga's lavishly restored stock exchange building is a worthy showcase for the city's art treasures.

The elaborate facade features a coterie of deities that dance between the windows, while inside, gilt chandeliers sparkle from ornately moulded ceilings. The Oriental section features beautiful Chinese and Japanese ceramics and an Egyptian mummy, but the main halls are devoted to Western art, including a Monet painting and a scaled-down cast of Rodin's *The Kiss*.

#### Rīga History & Navigation Museum   MUSEUM
(Rīgas vēstures un kuģniecības muzejs; ☑ 6735 6676; www.rigamuz.lv; Palasta iela 4; adult/child €4.27/0.71; ☺ 10am-5pm May-Sep, 11am-5pm Wed-Sun Oct-Apr) Founded in 1773, this is the oldest museum in the Baltic, situated in the old cathedral monastery. The permanent collection features artefacts from the Bronze Age all the way to WWII, ranging from lovely pre-Christian jewellery to preserved hands removed from Medieval forgers. A highlight is the beautiful neoclassical Column Hall, built when Latvia was part of the Russian empire.

#### Museum of Decorative
#### Arts & Design                       MUSEUM
(Dekoratīvi lietišķās mākslas muzejs; ☑ 6722 7833; www.lnmm.lv; Skārņu iela 10/20; adult/child €5/2.50; ☺ 11am-5pm Tue & Thu-Sun, till 7pm Wed) The former St George's Church houses a museum devoted to applied art from the art nouveau period to the present, including an impressive collection of furniture, woodcuts, tapestries and ceramics. The building's foundations date back to 1207 when the Livonian Brothers of the Sword erected their castle here. Since the rest of the original knights' castle was levelled by rioting citizens at the end of the same century, it is the only building that remains intact since the birth of Rīga.

---

### ITINERARIES

#### Three Days
Fill your first two days with a feast of **Rīga's** architectural eye candy and then take a day trip to opulent **Rundāle Palace**.

#### One Week
Spend day four lazing on the beach and coveting the gracious wooden houses of **Jūrmala**. The following morning head west to **Kuldīga** before continuing on to **Ventspils**. Spend your last days exploring **Sigulda** and **Cēsis** within the leafy confines of **Gauja National Park**.

## THE BALTIC VERSAILLES

Built as a grand residence for the Duke of Courland, the magnificent **Rundāle Palace** (Rundāles pils; ☑ 6396 2274; www.rundale.net; whole complex/house longroute/short route/garden/short route & garden €9/6/4/4/7.50; ☉ 10am-5pm Nov-Apr, 10am-6pm May-Oct) is a monument-to 18th-century aristocratic ostentation, and rural Latvia's architectural highlight. It was designed by Italian baroque genius Bartolomeo Rastrelli, who is best known for the Winter Palace in St Petersburg. About 40 of the palace's 138 rooms are open to visitors, as are the wonderful formal gardens, inspired by those at Versailles.

★**Blackheads House**  HISTORIC BUILDING
(Melngalvju nams; ☑ 6704 3678; www.melngalvjunams.lv; Rātslaukums 7) Built in 1344 as a veritable fraternity house for the Blackheads guild of unmarried German merchants, the original house was decimated in 1941 and flattened by the Soviets seven years later. Somehow the original blueprints survived and an exact replica of this fantastically ornate structure was completed in 2001 for Rīga's 800th birthday.

★**Arsenāls Exhibition Hall**  GALLERY
(Izstāžu zāle Arsenāls; ☑ 6732 4461; www.lnmm.lv; Torņa iela 1; adult/child €3.50/2; ☉ 11am-6pm Tue, Wed & Fri, to 8pm Thu, noon-5pm Sat & Sun) Behind a row of spooky granite heads depicting Latvia's most prominent artists, the imperial arsenal, constructed in 1832 to store weapons for the Russian tzar's army, is now a prime spot for international and local art exhibitions, which makes it worth a visit whenever you are in Rīga. Also check out the massive wooden stairs at the back of the building – their simple yet funky geometry predates modern architecture.

## ◉ Central Rīga (Centrs)

**Freedom Monument**  MONUMENT
(Brīvības bulvāris) Affectionately known as 'Milda', Rīga's Freedom Monument towers above the city between Old and Central Rīga. Paid for by public donations, the monument was designed by Kārlis Zāle and erected in 1935 where a statue of Russian ruler Peter the Great once stood.

**Latvian National Museum of Art**  GALLERY
(Latvijas Nacionālā mākslas muzeja; ☑ 6732 4461; www.lnmm.lv; K Valdemāra iela 10a; adult/child €6/3; ☉ 10am-6pm Tue-Thu, to 8pm Fri, to 5pm Sat & Sun) Latvia's main gallery, sitting within the Esplanāde's leafy grounds, is an impressive building built in a baroque-classical style in 1905. Well-displayed paintings form a who's who of Latvian art from the 18th to late 20th centuries. Temporary exhibitions supplement the permanent collection.

★**Alberta iela**  ARCHITECTURE
It's like a huge painting, which you can spend hours staring at, as your eye detects more and more intriguing details. But in fact this must-see Rīga sight is a rather functional street with residential houses, restaurants and shops. Art nouveau, otherwise known as Jugendstil, is the style, and the master responsible for most of these is Mikhail Eisenstein (father of filmmaker Sergei Eisenstein). Named after the founder of Rīga, Bishop Albert von Buxthoeven, the street was the architect's gift to Rīga on its 700th anniversary.

**Nativity of Christ Cathedral**  CHURCH
(Kristus Piedzimšanas katedrāle; ☑ 6721 1207; www.pravoslavie.lv; Brīvības bulvāris 23; ☉ 7am-7pm) With gilded cupolas peeking through the trees, this Byzantine-styled Orthodox cathedral (1883) adds a dazzling dash of Russian bling to the skyline. During the Soviet period the church was converted into a planetarium but it's since been restored to its former use. Mind the dress code – definitely no shorts; women are asked to cover their heads.

## ◉ Moscow Suburb (Maskavas forštate)

This old part of Rīga takes its name from the main road to Moscow which runs through it. During the Nazi occupation it was the site of the Rīga Ghetto. In October 1941 the city's entire Jewish population (around 30,000 people) was crammed into the blocks east of Lāčplēša iela and enclosed by barbed wire. Later that year most of them were marched 10km to the Rumbula Forest where they were shot and buried in mass graves.

★**Rīga Central Market**  MARKET
(Rīgas Centrāltirgus; ☑ 6722 9985; www.rct.lv; Nēģu iela 7; ☉ 7am-6pm) Haggle for your huckleberries at this vast market, housed in a series of WWI Zeppelin hangars and spilling outdoors as well. It's an essential Rīga experience, providing bountiful opportunities both for

# Rīga

LATVIA RĪGA

Rīga Passenger
Terminal (400m)

Elizabetes iela

Pulkveža Brieža iela

Strēlnieku iela

Dzirnavu iela

Alberta iela

**QUIET CENTRE
(KLUSAIS CENTRS)**

28

E Melngaiļa iela

31

Antonijas iela

Elizabetes iela

K Valdemāra iela

30

Lāčplēša iela

14

Skolas iela

19

23

Kalpaka bulvāris

Alunana iela

8 **CENTRAL RĪGA
(CENTRS)**

Baznīcas iela

Mīķeļa iela

K Valdemāra iela

Kronvalda parks

Kronvalda bulvāris

Citadeles iela

Esplanāde

Kalpaka bulvāris

10

Rīga
(12km)

K Valdemāra iela

Bastēja bulvāris

Raiņa bulvāris

Brīvības bulvāris

Tērbatas iela

Jēkaba iela

Bastejkalns

Torņa iela

1

**Arsenāls
Exhibition Hall**

22

13

ZA Meierovica bulvāris

6

Elizabetes iela

Pils
laukums

Trokšņu iela

**OLD RĪGA
(VECRĪGA)**

Smilšu iela

Vērmanesdārzs

33

Maza Pils iela

25

Valņu iela

Architektu iela

**Art Museum
Rīga Bourse**

Zirgu iela

Anglikāņu

16

2

Livu
laukums

32

Alfrēda Kalnina iela

**Rīga Cathedral**

Doma
laukums

4

Kalēju iela

Valņu iela

Vāgnera iela

26

Škūņu iela

Kaļķu iela

Teatra iela

Merķeļa iela

11

21

9

Aspazijas bulvāris

Audēju iela

15

Kungu iela

17

**Rātslaukums**

12

34

20

Audēju iela

Satekles iela

Stacijas
laukums

**Blackheads
House**

3

Grēciņieku
iela

**Central
Train
Station**

**Latviešu
Strēlnieku
laukums**

Kaļķu iela

29

Peldu iela

Mārstaļu iela

Kungu iela

Alberta
laukums

Kalēju iela

Akmens Bridge

11 novembra krastmala iela

13 janvāra iela

Rīga
**International
Bus Station**

Gogoļa iela

Gogoļa iela

Daugava River

City Canal
(Pilsētas
kanāls)

27

**Riga
Central
Market**

5

Nēģu iela

Pragas iela

Rīga Ghetto &
Latvian Holocaust
Museum (150m)

people-watching and to stock up for a picnic lunch. Although the number of traders is dwindling, the dairy and fish departments, each occupying a separate hangar, present a colourful picture of abundance that activates ancient foraging instincts in the visitors.

LATVIA RĪGA

## Rīga Ghetto & Latvian Holocaust Museum MUSEUM

(☑ 6799 1784; www.rgm.lv; Maskavas iela 14A; adult/child €5/3; ◷ 10am-6pm Sun-Fri) FREE
The centrepiece of this rather modest museum is a wooden house with a reconstructed flat, like those where Jews had to move into when in 1941 the Nazis established a ghetto in this area of Rīga. Models of synagogues that used to stand in all major Latvian towns are exhibited in the ground floor of the house. Outside, there is a photographic exhibition detailing the Holocaust in Latvia.

## Latvian Academy of Science HISTORIC BUILDING

(Latvijas Zinātņu Akadēmija; www.panoramariga. lv; Akadēmijas laukums 1; adult/child €5/1; ◷ 9am-10pm Apr-Nov) Rising above the Moscow suburb, this Stalinesque tower is in fact a not-so-welcome present from the Russian capital, which has seven towers like it, only bigger. Construction of what is often dubbed 'Stalin's birthday cake' commenced in 1951 but wasn't completed until 1961, by which time Stalin had run out of birthdays. Those with an eagle eye will spot hammers and sickles hidden in the convoluted facade. The wonderful viewing terrace at floor 17 is Rīga's best vantage point.

## ⛬ Tours

### E.A.T. Rīga WALKING, CYCLING

(☑ 22469888; www.eatriga.lv; tours from €15) Foodies may be initially disappointed to discover that the name stands for 'Experience Alternative Tours' and the focus is on off-the-beaten-track themed walking tours (Old Rīga, Art Nouveau, Alternative Rīga, Retro Rīga). But don't fret – Rīga Food Tasting is an option. It also offers a cycling tour of Jūrmala.

### Rīga By Canal BOATING

(☑ 2591 1523; www.rigabycanal.lv; adult/child €18/9; ◷ 10am-8pm May–mid-Oct) Enjoy a different perspective of the city aboard the century-old *Darling,* a charming wooden canal cruiser that belonged to the family of ABBA producer Stig Anderson and saw the entire band on board. There are three other boats in the fleet that paddle along the same loop around the city canal and Daugava River.

## 🛏 Sleeping

### 🛏 Old Rīga (Vecrīga)

#### ★ Naughty Squirrel HOSTEL €

(☑ 6722 0073; www.thenaughtysquirrel.com; Kalēju iela 50; dm €10-18, f €48-58; ✳ @ 🛜) Slashes of bright paint and cartoon graffiti brighten up the city's capital of backpackerdom, which buzzes with travellers rattling the foosball table and chilling out in the TV room. Sign up for regular pub crawls, day trips to the countryside and summer BBQs.

#### ★ Cinnamon Sally HOSTEL €

(☑ 22042280; www.cinnamonsally.com; Merķeļa iela 1; dm €10-14; @ 🛜) Convenient for the train/bus stations, Cinnamon Sally comes with perfectly clean rooms, very helpful staff and a common area cluttered with sociable characters. It might feel odd to be asked to take off your shoes at the reception, but it's all part of its reffort to create a homey atmosphere.

#### ★ Ekes Konvents HOTEL €€

(☑ 6735 8393; www.ekeskonvents.lv; Skārņu iela 22; r €60; 🛜) Not to be confused with Konventa Sēta next door, the 600-year-old Ekes Konvents oozes wobbly medieval charm from every crooked nook and cranny. Curl up with a book in the adorable stone alcoves on the landing of each storey. Breakfast is served down the block.

#### ★ Dome Hotel HOTEL €€€

(☑ 6750 9010; www.domehotel.lv; Miesnieku iela 4; r €149-380; 🛜) It's hard to imagine that this centuries-old structure was once part of a row of butcheries. Today a gorgeous wooden staircase leads guests up to a charming assortment of uniquely decorated rooms that sport eaved ceilings, wooden panelling, upholstered furniture and picture windows with city views.

#### ★ Neiburgs HOTEL €€€

(☑ 6711 5522; www.neiburgs.com; Jaun iela 25/27; r €194-244; ✳ 🛜) Occupying one of Old Rīga's finest art nouveau buildings, Neiburgs blends preserved details with contemporary touches to achieve its signature boutique-chic style. Try for a room on one of the higher floors – you'll be treated to a view of a colourful clutter of gabled roofs and twisting medieval spires.

## Central Rīga (Centrs)

### ★ Art Hotel Laine
HOTEL €€

(☑ 6728 8816; www.laine.lv; Skolas iela 11; s €55, d €65-77, superior d €126; 🅿🛜) Embedded into an apartment block, with an antiquated lift taking guests to the reception on the 3rd floor, this place brings you closer to having your own home in Rīga than most hotels can or indeed wish to do. Dark green walls and armchair velvet, art on the walls, yesteryear bathtubs and furniture only complement the overall homey feeling.

### Hotel Valdemārs
HOTEL €€

(☑ 6733 4462; www.nordicchoicehotels.com; K Valdemāra iela 23; s/d €130/146; ❄🛜) Hidden within an art nouveau block, this Clarion Collection hotel is an excellent choice for those happy to trade fancy decor for reasonable rates. Most surprisingly, the hotel lays on breakfast, afternoon snacks and a simple dinner buffet for all guests. Prices drop significantly outside July.

### Hotel Bergs
HOTEL €€€

(☑ 6777 0900; www.hotelbergs.lv; Elizabetes iela 83/85; ste from €187; 🅿❄🛜) A refurbished 19th-century building embellished with a Scandi-sleek extension, Hotel Bergs embodies the term 'luxury'. The spacious suites are lavished with high-quality monochromatic furnishings and some have kitchens. There's even a 'pillow menu', allowing guests to choose from an array of different bed pillows based on material and texture.

##  Eating

### Old Rīga (Vecrīga)

### LIDO Alus Sēta
LATVIAN €

(☑ 6722 2431; www.lido.lv; Tirgoņu iela 6; mains around €5; ☺11am-10pm; 🛜) The pick of the LIDO litter (Rīga's ubiquitous smorgasbord chain), Alus Sēta feels like an old Latvian brew house. It's popular with locals as well as tourists – everyone flocks here for cheap but tasty traditional fare and homemade beer. Seating spills onto the cobbled street during the warmer months.

### Ķiploku Krogs
EUROPEAN €€

(Garlic Pub; ☑ 6721 1451; www.kiplokukrogs.lv; Jēkaba iela 3/5; mains €7-14; ☺noon-11pm) Vampires beware – *everything* at this joint contains garlic, even the ice cream. The menu is pretty hit-and-miss, but no matter what, it's

best to avoid the garlic pesto spread – it'll taint your breath for days (trust us). Enter from Mazā Pils.

### ★ 3 Pavaru
MODERN EUROPEAN €€€

(☑ 20370537; www.3pavari.lv; Torņa iela 4; mains €17-28; ☺noon-11pm) The stellar trio of chefs who run the show have a jazzy approach to cooking, with improvisation at the heart of the compact and ever-changing menu. The emphasis is on experiment (baked cod with ox-tail stew, anyone?) and artful visual presentation that could have made Joan Miró gasp in admiration.

### Le Dome Fish Restaurant
SEAFOOD €€€

(☑ 6755 9884; www.zivjurestorans.lv; Miesnieku iela 4; mains €18-30; ☺7am-11pm Mon-Fri, 8am-11pm Sat & Sun; 🛜) The Dome Hotel's restaurant quickly reminds diners that Rīga sits near a body of water that's full of delicious fish. Service is impeccable and dishes (including some meat and vegetarian options) are expertly prepared, reflecting the eclectic assortment of recipes in the modern Latvian lexicon.

### Central Rīga (Centrs)

### ★ Fazenda Bazārs
MODERN EUROPEAN €€

(☑ 6724 0809; www.fazenda.lv; Baznīcas iela 14; mains €7-12; ☺9am-10pm Mon-Fri, 10am-10pm Sat, 11am-10pm Sun) Although right in the centre, this place feels like you've gone a long way and suddenly found a warm tavern in the middle of nowhere. Complete with a

LATVIA RĪGA

## AN ENCHANTING FOREST

If you don't have time to visit the Latvian countryside, a stop at the **Latvian Ethnographic Open-Air Museum** (Latvijas etnogrāfiskais brīvdabas muzejs; ☑ 6799 4106; www.brivdabasmuzejs.lv; Brīvības gatve 440; adult/child €4/1.40; ⊘ 10am-5pm, to 8pm May-Oct) is a must. Sitting along the shores of Lake Jugla just northeast of the city limits, this stretch of forest contains more than 100 wooden buildings (churches, windmills, farmhouses etc) from each of Latvia's four cultural regions. Take bus 1 from the corner of Merķeļa iela and Tērbatas iela to the 'Brīvdabas muzejs' stop.

tiled stove, this wooden house oozes megatonnes of charm and the food on offer feels as homey as it gets, despite its globalist fusion nature.

★ **Kasha Gourmet** MODERN EUROPEAN €€
(☑ 20201444; www.kasha-gourmet.com; Stabu iela 14; mains €8-17; ⊘ 10am-10pm Mon-Thu, 10am-11pm Fri & Sat, 10am-8pm Sun) It might be that it does succeed in making the food feel tastier by turning the plate into a piece of modern art, or perhaps it's the post-modernist mixture of ingredients, but this is one of the most unusual and undervalued restaurants in Rīga. We are particularly fond of its set breakfasts beautifully laid out on wooden slabs.

★ **Vincents** EUROPEAN €€€
(☑ 6733 2830; www.restorans.lv; Elizabetes iela 19; mains €28-37; ⊘ 6-10pm Tue-Sat) 🍴 Rīga's ritziest restaurant has served royalty and rock stars (Emperor Akihito, Prince Charles, Elton John) amid its eye-catching van Gogh–inspired decor. The head chef, Martins Ritins, is a stalwart of the Slow Food movement and crafts his ever-changing menu mainly from produce sourced directly from small-scale Latvian farmers.

## 🍴 Moscow Suburb (Maskavas forštate)

**Siļķītes un Dillītes** SEAFOOD €€
(www.facebook.com/SilkitesUnDillites; Centrāltirgus iela 3; mains €7-10; ⊘ 9am-5pm) Having explored fish stalls at the Rīga Central Market, one might ask: Where do I get it cooked? Well, Herring & Dill, as the name of this grungy kitchen-cum-bar translates, is right here and it'll do the cooking for you. Pick your fish and some minutes later it will be fried and served with veggies and chips. It's located in the passage between the fish and vegetable departments of the market.

## 🍷 Drinking & Nightlife

★ **Folksklub Ala Pagrabs** BEER HALL
(☑ 27796914; www.folkklubs.lv; Peldu iela 19; ⊘ noon-midnight Sun, to 1am Mon & Tue, to 3am Wed, to 4am Thu & Fri, 2pm-4am Sat) A huge cavern filled with the bubbling magma of relentless beer-infused joy, folk-punk music, dancing and Latvian nationalism, this is an essential Rīga drinking venue, no matter what highbrowed locals say about it. The bar strives to reflect the full geography and diversity of Latvian beer production, but there is also plenty of local cider, fruit wine and *šmakouka* moonshine.

**Left Door Bar** COCKTAIL BAR
(☑ 26300368; www.theleftdoorbar.lv; Antonijas iela 12; ⊘ noon-midnight Mon-Thu, noon-1am Fri, 6pm-1am Sat, 6pm-midnight Sun) Rīga's grand lodge of cocktails masters masquerades as an assuming bar in the art nouveau district. Never satisfied with past achievements, the award-winning prodigies in charge are constantly experimenting with the aim to impress globetrotting connoisseurs, not your average Joe. Each cocktail comes in individually shaped glasses.

★ **Kaņepes Kultūras Centrs** BAR
(☑ 29404405; www.kanepes.lv; Skolas iela 15; ⊘ 1pm-2am or later) The crumbling building of a former musical school, which half of Rīgans over 40 seem to have attended, is now a bar with a large outdoor area filled with an artsy studenty crowd. Wild dancing regularly erupts in the large room, where the parents of the patrons once suffered through their violin drills.

**Piens** BAR, CLUB
(Milk; www.klubspiens.lv; Aristida Briāna iela 9; noon-midnight Sun-Tue, to 4pm Wed-Sat) Located up in the Miera iela area, this bar-club hybrid occupies a large chunk of industrial land. There's an appealing mix of eclectic decor, old sofas and sunny terraces.

## ☆ Entertainment

**Latvian National Opera** OPERA, BALLET
(Latvijas Nacionālajā operā; ☑ 6707 3777; www.opera.lv; Aspazijas bulvāris 3) With a hefty international reputation as one of the finest opera companies in all of Europe, the national

opera is the pride of Latvia. It's also home to the Rīga Ballet; locally born lad Mikhail Baryshnikov got his start here.

**Arena Rīga** LIVE MUSIC
(☑ 6738 8200; www.arenariga.com; Skantes iela 21) This is the main venue for the most popular spectator sports, ice hockey and basketball. The 10,000-seat venue hosts dance revues and pop concerts when it is not being used for sporting events.

## 🛍 Shopping

**Hobbywool** ARTS & CRAFTS
(☑ 27072707; www.hobbywool.com; Mazā Pils iela 6; ☉ 10am-6pm Mon-Sat, 11am-3pm Sun) It feels like walking into a Mark Rothko painting – the little shop is filled from top to bottom with brightly coloured knitted shawls, mittens, socks and jackets.

**Latvijas Balzāms** DRINKS
(☑ 6708 1213; www.lb.lv; Audēju iela 8; ☉ 9am-10pm) One of myriad branches of a popular chain of liquor stores selling the trademark Latvian Black Balzām.

## ⓘ Getting There & Away

Rīga is connected by air, bus, train and ferry to various international destinations.

### BUS
Buses depart from **Rīga International Bus Station** (Rīgas starptautiskā autoosta; ☑ 9000 0009; www.autoosta.lv; Prāgas iela 1), located behind the railway embankment just beyond the southeastern edge of Old Rīga. Destinations include Sigulda (€2.15, one hour, every 45 minutes), Cēsis (€4.15, two hours, hourly), Kuldīga (€6.40, 2½ hours to 3½ hours, 11 daily) and Ventspils (€7.55, three hours, hourly).

### TRAIN
Rīga's **central train station** (Centrālā stacija; ☑ 6723 2135; www.pv.lv; Stacijas laukums 2) is housed in a conspicuous glass-encased shopping centre near the Central Market. Destinations include Jūrmala (€1.40, 30 minutes, half-hourly), Sigulda (€2.35, 1¼ hours, 10 daily) and Cēsis (€3.50, 1¾ hours, five daily).

## ⓘ Getting Around

### TO/FROM THE AIRPORT
**Rīga International Airport** (Starptautiskā Lidosta Rīga; ☑ 1817; www.riga-airport.com; Mārupe District; ☒ 22) is in Skulte, 20km west of the city centre.

The cheapest way to get to central Rīga is bus 22 (€2, 25 minutes), which runs every 10 to 30 minutes and stops at several points around town. Taxis cost €12 to €15 and take about 15 minutes.

### BICYCLE
Zip around town with **Sixt Bicycle Rental** (Sixt velo noma; ☑ 6767 6780; www.sixtbicycle.lv; per 30min/day €0.90/9). A handful of stands are conveniently positioned around Rīga and Jūrmala; simply choose your bike, call the rental service and receive the code to unlock your wheels.

### PUBLIC TRANSPORT
The centre of Rīga is too compact for most visitors even to consider public transport, but trams, buses or trolleybuses may come in handy if you are venturing further out. For routes and schedules, consult www.rigassatiksme.lv. Tickets cost €1.15 (€0.30 for ISIC-holding students). Unlimited tickets are available for 24 hours (€5), three days (€10) and five days (€15). Tickets are available from Narvessen newspaper kiosks as well as vending machines on board new trams and in the underground pass by the train station.

### TAXI
Taxis charge €0.60 to €0.80 per kilometre. Insist on having the meter on before you set off. Meters usually start running at around €1.50. It shouldn't cost more than €5 for a short journey (like crossing the Daugava for dinner in Ķīpsala). There are taxi ranks outside the bus and train stations, at the airport and in front of a few major hotels in Central Rīga, such as Radisson Blu Hotel Latvija.

# AROUND RĪGA

If you're on a tight schedule, it's easy to get a taste of the Latvian countryside on day trips from Rīga. Within 75km of the capital are national parks, the country's grandest palace and long stretches of flaxen beach.

## Jūrmala
POP 56,600

The Baltic's version of the French Riviera, Jūrmala is a long string of townships with grand wooden beach houses belonging to Russian oil tycoons and their supermodel trophy wives. Even during the height of communism, Jūrmala was a place to see and be seen. On summer weekends, jet-setters and day-tripping Rīgans flock to the resort town for some serious fun in the sun.

If you don't have a car or bicycle, you're best to head straight to the townships of Majori and Dzintari, the heart of the action. A 1km-long pedestrian street, Jomas iela, connects the two and is considered to be Jūrmala's main drag.

## ESSENTIAL FOOD & DRINK

**Black Balzām** The jet-black, 45%-proof concoction is a secret recipe of more than a dozen fairy-tale ingredients including oak bark, wormwood and linden blossoms. A shot a day keeps the doctor away, so say most of Latvia's pensioners. Try mixing it with a glass of cola to take the edge off.

**Mushrooms** A national obsession; mushroom-picking takes the country by storm during the first showers of autumn.

**Alus** For such a tiny nation there's definitely no shortage of *alus* (beer) – each major town has its own brew. You can't go wrong with Užavas (Ventspils' contribution).

**Smoked fish** Dozens of fish shacks dot the Kurzeme coast – look for the veritable smoke signals rising above the tree line. Grab 'em to go; they make the perfect afternoon snack.

**Kvass** Single-handedly responsible for the decline of Coca Cola at the turn of the 21st century, Kvass is a beloved beverage made from fermented rye bread. It's surprisingly popular with kids!

**Rye Bread** Apart from being tasty and arguably healthier than their wheat peers, these large brown loafs have aesthetic value too, matching nicely the dark wood of Latvia's Nordic interiors.

The highway connecting Rīga to Jūrmala was known as '10 Minutes in America' during Soviet times, because locally produced films set in the USA were always filmed on this busy asphalt strip. Motorists driving the 15km into Jūrmala must pay a €2 toll per day, even if they are just passing through. Keep an eye out for the multilane self-service toll stations sitting at both ends of the resort town.

### ◉ Sights

**Jūrmala City Museum** MUSEUM
(☑ 6776 1915; www.facebook.com/JurmalasPilse-tasMuzejsJurmalaCityMuseum; Tirgoņu iela 29; ◷ 10am-6pm Wed-Sun) FREE After a pricey renovation, this museum now features a beautiful permanent exhibit detailing Jūrmala's colourful history as *the* go-to resort town in the former USSR.

### ⌂ Sleeping & Eating

★**Hotel MaMa** BOUTIQUE HOTEL €€€
(☑ 6776 1271; www.hotelmama.lv; Tirgoņu iela 22; r €175-360; 🛜) The bedroom doors have thick, mattress-like padding on the interior (psycho-chic?) and the suites themselves are a veritable blizzard of white drapery. A mix of silver paint and pixie dust accents the ultramodern furnishings and amenities. If heaven had a bordello, it would look something like this.

★**36.Line** LATVIAN €€€
(☑ 22010696; www.36line.com; Līnija 36; mains €14-33; ◷ 11am-11pm; 🍴) Popular local chef Lauris Alekseyevs delivers modern twists on traditional Latvian dishes at this wonderful restaurant, occupying a slice of sand at the eastern end of Jūrmala. Enjoy the beach, then switch to casual attire for lunch or glam up for dinner. In the evening it's not uncommon to find DJs spinning beats.

### ℹ Getting There & Away

Two to three trains per hour link central Rīga to the sandy shores of Jūrmala. Most visitors disembark at Majori station (€1.50, 30 minutes).

The river boat *New Way* departs from Rīga Riflemen Sq and docks in Majori near the train station. The journey takes one hour, and only runs on weekends.

## Sigulda
POP 16,700

With a name that sounds like a mythical ogress, it's fitting that the gateway to Gauja National Park is an enchanted little spot. Locals proudly call their pine-peppered town the 'Switzerland of Latvia', but if you're expecting a mountainous snowcapped realm, you'll be rather disappointed. Instead, Sigulda is a magical mix of scenic walking and cycling trails, extreme sports and 800-year-old castles steeped in colourful legends.

### ◉ Sights

★**Turaida Museum Reserve** CASTLE
(Turaidas muzejrezervāts; ☑ 6797 1402; www.turai-da-muzejs.lv; Turaidas iela 10; adult/child €5/1.15, in winter €3/0.70; ◷ 9am-8pm May-Sep, 9am-7pm Oct, 10am-5pm Nov-Mar, 10am-7pm Apr) Turaida means 'God's Garden' in ancient Livonian,

and this green knoll capped with a fairy-tale castle is certainly a heavenly place. The red-brick castle with its tall cylindrical tower was built in 1214 on the site of a Liv stronghold. A museum inside the castle's 15th-century granary offers an interesting account of the Livonian state from 1319 to 1561, and additional exhibitions can be viewed in the 42m-high Donjon Tower, and the castle's western and southern towers.

## Activities

**Bobsled Track** ADVENTURE SPORTS
(Bob trase; ☑ 6797 3813; www.bobtrase.lv; Šveices iela 13; ⊙ noon-5pm Sat & Sun) Sigulda's 1200m bobsled track was built for the Soviet team. In winter you can fly down the 16-bend track at 80km/h in a five-person Vučko **soft bob** (per adult/child €10/7, from November to March). Summer speed fiends can ride a wheeled **summer bob** (per adult/child €10/7, from May to September).

**Aerodium** ADVENTURE SPORTS
(☑ 28384400; www.aerodium.lv; 2min/4min €45/65) The one-of-a-kind aerodium is a giant wind tunnel that propels participants up into the sky as though they were flying. Instructors can get about 15m high, while first-timers usually rock out at about 3m. To find the site, look for the sign along the A2 highway, 4km west of Sigulda.

**Cable Car Bungee Jump** ADVENTURE SPORTS
(☑ 28383333; www.bungee.lv; Poruka iela 14; bungee jump from €40; ⊙ 6.30pm, 8pm & 9.30pm Wed-Sun Apr-Oct) Take your daredevil shenanigans to the next level with a 43m bungee jump from the bright-orange cable car that glides over the Gauja River. For an added thrill, jump naked.

## Sleeping & Eating

**Līvkalni** B&B €€
(☑ 22825739; livkalnisigulda@gmail.com; Pēteralas iela 2; s/d from €45/55; P ❉ 🐾) No place is more romantically rustic than this idyllic retreat next to a pond on the forest's edge. The rooms are pine-fresh and sit among a campus of adorable thatch-roof manors.

**Mr Biskvīts** CAFE, BAKERY €
(☑ 6797 6611; www.mr.biskvits.lv; Ausekļa iela 9; mains €4-8; ⊙ 8am-9pm Mon-Fri, 9am-9pm Sat, 9am-7pm Sun) Naughty Mr Biskvīts' candy-striped lair is filled with delicious cakes and pastries, but it's also a good spot for a cooked breakfast, a lunchtime soup or sand-wich, and an evening pasta or stir-fry. The coffee's great too.

## ℹ️ Getting There & Around

Trains run to/from Rīga (€2.35, one or 1¼ hours) and Cēsis (€2, 40 minutes, five daily).

There are also buses to Rīga (€2.15, one hour, every 30 minutes between 8am and 10.30pm) and Cēsis (€1.85, 1½ hours, daily).

# Cēsis

With its stunning medieval castle, cobbled streets, green hills and landscaped garden, Cēsis is simply the cutest little town in the whole of Latvia. There is a lot of history there, too. The place started eight centuries ago as a Livonian Order's stronghold in the land of unruly pagans and saw horrific battles right under (or inside) the castle walls. Although it's an easy day trip from Rīga, Cēsis is definitely worth a longer stay, especially since there is the whole of Gauja National Park around it to explore.

## Sights

⭐ **Cēsis Castle** CASTLE
(Cēsu pils; ☑ 6412 1815; www.cesupils.lv; both castles adult/student €5/2.50, tours from €35; ⊙ 10am-6pm daily May-Sep, 10am-5pm Tue-Sat, 10am-4pm Sun Oct-Apr) It is actually two castles in one. The first is the sorrowful dark-stone towers of the old Wenden castle. Founded by Livonian knights in 1214, it was sacked by Russian tsar Ivan the Terrible in 1577, but only after its 300 defenders blew themselves up with gunpowder. The other is the more cheerful castle-like 18th-century manor house once inhabited by the dynasty of German counts von Sievers. It houses a museum that features original fin de siècle interiors.

## Sleeping & Eating

**Hotel Cēsis** HOTEL €€
(☑ 6412 0122; www.facebook.com/hotelcesis; Vienības laukums 1; s/d €45/60; @ 🐾) The exterior is vaguely neoclassical while the inside features rows of standard upmarket rooms. The in-house restaurant serves top-notch Latvian and European cuisine in a formal setting or outdoors in the pristine garden.

⭐ **Izsalkušais Jānis** MODERN EUROPEAN €€
(☑ 29262001; www.izsalkusaisjanis.lv; Valmieras iela 1; mains €9-16; ⊙ noon-11pm) The town's old fire depot has changed profession and now helps to extinguish hunger and thirst with a

compact but powerful menu that takes Cēsis to a metropolitan level of culinary sophistication. Hot trout salad is our personal fave. It also bakes its own delicious bread.

### ① Getting There & Away

Four to five trains a day travel to/from Rīga (€3.50, 1¾ hours) and Sigulda (€2, 45 minutes).

There are also buses to Rīga (€4.15, two hours, hourly) and Sigulda (€1.85, 1½ hours, daily).

# WESTERN LATVIA

Latvia's westernmost province, Kurzeme (Courland), offers the simple delights of beautiful beaches and a scattering of historic towns. It's hard to imagine that this low-key region once had imperial aspirations but during the 17th century, while still a semi-independent vassal of the Polish-Lithuanian Commonwealth, the Duchy of Courland had a go at colonising Tobago and the Gambia. The Great Northern War put paid to that, after which the Duchy was subsumed into the Russian Empire.

## Kuldīga

Lovely old Kuldīga would be a hit even if it didn't have its own Niagara of sorts, with salmon flying over its chute for good measure. Home to what Latvians brand 'the widest waterfall in Europe', Kuldīga is also the place where your immersion into the epoch of chivalry won't be spoiled by day-tripping camera-clickers – the place is simply too far from Rīga.

In its heyday, Kuldīga (or Goldingen, as its German founders called it) served as the capital of the Duchy of Courland (1596–1616), but it was badly damaged during the Great Northern War and never quite able to regain its former lustre. Today, this blast from the past is a favourite spot to shoot Latvian period-piece films.

### ◉ Sights

**Ventas Rumba**
**(Kuldīga Waterfall)**                    WATERFALL
In a country that is acutely short of verticals but rich on horizontals, landscape features appear to be blatantly two-dimensional – even waterfalls. Spanning 240m, Ventas Rumba is branded Europe's widest, but as it is hardly taller than a basketball player, it risks being dismissed by vile competitors as a mere rapid, if it decides to attend an international waterfall congress. That said, it does look like a cute toy Niagara, when observed from the Kuldīga castle hill.

### 🛏 Sleeping & Eating

★**2 Baloži**                    GUESTHOUSE €€
(☑ 29152888; www.facebook.com/2balozi; Pasta iela 5; r from €50) Perched above the Alekšupīte stream, this old wooden house has newly refurbished rooms designed in the laconic Scandinavian style with lots of aged wood that creates a pleasant nostalgic ambience. Goldingen Room restaurant across the square serves as the reception.

★**Pagrabiņš**                    INTERNATIONAL €€
(☑ 6632 0034; www.pagrabins.lv; Baznīcas iela 5; mains €5-15; ⊙ 11am-11pm Mon-Thu, to 3am Fri & Sat, noon-11pm Sun; ☑) Pagrabiņš inhabits a cellar that was once used as the town's prison. Today a combination of Latvian and Asian dishes are served under low-slung alcoves lined with honey-coloured bricks. In warmer weather, enjoy your snacks on the small verandah, which sits atop the trickling Alekšupīte stream out the back.

### ① Getting There & Away

Buses run to/from Rīga (€6.40, three hours, 11 daily) and Ventspils (€6, 1¼ hours, six daily).

# Ventspils

Fabulous amounts of oil and shipping money have given Ventspils an economic edge over Latvia's other small cities, and although locals coddle their Užavas beer and claim that there's not much to do, tourists will find a weekend's worth of fun in the form of brilliant beaches, well-maintained parks and interactive museums.

### ◉ Sights

**Open-Air Museum of the Coast**        MUSEUM
(Ventspils jūras zvejniecības brīvdabas muzejs; ☑ 6322 4467; www.muzejs.ventspils.lv; Riņķu iela 2; adult/child €1.40/0.60; ⊙ 10am-6pm Tue-Sun May-Oct, by appointment winter) For centuries, life in Kurzeme revolved around seafaring and fishing. Occupying vast parkland territory, the museum features a collection of fishing crafts, anchors and traditional log houses, brought from coastal villages north and south of Ventspils. A bonus attraction is a narrow-gauge railway, built by the occupying Germans in 1916.

## 🛏 Sleeping & Eating

**Kupfernams**      B&B €€
(☑ 27677107; www.hotelkupfernams.lv; Kārļa iela 5; s/d €44/65; ☎) Our favourite spot to spend the night, this charming wooden house at the centre of the Old Town has a set of cheery upstairs rooms with slanted ceilings, opening onto a communal lounge. Below, there's a cafe and a hair salon.

**Skroderkrogs**      LATVIAN €€
(☑ 6362 7634; Skroderu iela 6; mains €6-13; ⊙ 11am-10pm) If you're after big serves of Latvian comfort food in a pleasant local setting (candles and flowers on tables fashioned from old sewing machines), this is the place to come.

## ⓘ Getting There & Away

Ventspils is served by buses to/from Rīga (€7.50, 2¾ to four hours, hourly) and Kuldīga (€3, 1¼ hours, five daily).

# SURVIVAL GUIDE

## ⓘ Directory A–Z

### FESTIVALS & EVENTS

Check out Kultura (www.culture.lv) for a yearly listing of festivals and events across the country. At midsummer, the cities empty out as locals head to the countryside for traditional celebrations.

### GAY & LESBIAN TRAVELLERS

Homosexuality was decriminalised in 1992 and an equal age of consent applies (16 years). However, negative attitudes towards gays and lesbians are the norm and violent attacks occasionally occur. Rīga has a few gay venues and in 2015 it became the first former-Soviet city to host Europride.

### INTERNET RESOURCES

**Latvia Travel** www.latvia.travel
**Latvian Institute** www.li.lv
**Latvian Yellow Pages** www.1188.lv

### TELEPHONE

There are no area codes in Latvia. All telephone numbers have eight digits; landlines start with 6 and mobile numbers with 2.

## ⓘ Getting There & Away

### AIR

Fifteen European airlines fly into Rīga, including the national carrier airBaltic.

---

### COUNTRY FACTS

**Area** 64,589 sq km

**Capital** Rīga

**Country Telephone Code** ☑ 371

**Currency** euro (€)

**Emergency** ☑ 112

**Language** Latvian

**Money** ATMs easy to find.

**Population** 2 million

**Visas** Not required for citizens of the EU, Australia, Canada, New Zealand and the USA, among others, for stays of up to 90 days. For further information, visit www.mfa.gov.lv.

---

### LAND

In 2007 Latvia acceded to the Schengen Agreement, which removed all border control between Estonia and Lithuania. Carry your travel documents with you at all times, as random border checks do occur.

### Bus

**Ecolines** Routes include Rīga–Parnu–Tallinn (€17, four to 4¾ hours, seven daily), Rīga–Tartu (€7, four hours, two daily), Rīga–Vilnius (€17, four hours, seven daily), Rīga–Vilnius–Minsk (€24, eight hours, daily) and Rīga–Moscow (€60, 14 hours, daily).

**Kautra/Eurolines** (www.eurolines.lt) Operates buses on the Rīga–Vilnius–Warsaw–Berlin–Cologne route (€116, 29 hours).

**Lux Express & Simple Express** Routes include Rīga–Pärnu–Tallinn (from €13, 4½ hours, 11 daily), Rīga–Tartu–St Petersburg (from €23, 12 hours, four daily), Rīga–Vilnius (from €11, four hours, 10 daily) and Rīga–Kaliningrad (€20, eight hours, daily).

### Train

International trains head from Rīga to Moscow (16 hours), St Petersburg (15 hours) and Minsk (12 hours) daily. There are no direct trains to Estonia; you'll need to change at Valka.

## ⓘ Getting Around

### BUS

➧ Buses are generally more frequent than trains and serve more of the country.
➧ Updated timetables are available at www.1188.lv and www.autoosta.lv.

### CAR & MOTORCYCLE

➧ Driving is on the right-hand side.

# Lithuania

## Best Places to Eat

➜ Balzac (p231)
➜ Senoji Kibininė (p233)
➜ Lokys (p231)
➜ Sweet Root (p231)

## Best Places to Stay

➜ Bernardinu B&B (p229)
➜ Miško Namas (p237)
➜ Litinterp Guesthouse (p236)
➜ Domus Maria (p230)

## Why Go?

Little Lithuania has so much to offer. Those with a passion for baroque architecture, ancient castles and archaeological treasures will find plenty in the capital and beyond. There are sculpture parks and interactive museums for the historically curious; modern art spaces for the more contemporary-minded; and all-night clubbing for those requiring something less cerebral.

Away from the cities, the pristine beaches and giant sand dunes on the west coast are a must-see. The Hill of Crosses is an unexpected delight. Elsewhere, the country's woods and lakes come alive in summer with cyclists, berry pickers and campers.

## When to Go
### Vilnius

**Apr** Some of the world's best jazz performers are at the Kaunas International Jazz Festival.

**Jun & Jul** The loveliest time to explore the forests and sand dunes of the Curonian Spit.

**Sep** Vilnius Capital Days, a celebration of the capital with street theatre, music and fashion.

## Lithuania Highlights

**1 Vilnius** (p227) Exploring Lithuania's beautiful baroque capital with its cobbled streets, church spires, bars and bistros.

**2 Curonian Spit** (p237) Breathing pure air amid fragrant pine forests and high sand dunes.

**3 Hill of Crosses** (p235) Hearing the wind whistle between thousands of crosses at this eerie pilgrimage site, near Šiauliai.

**4 Trakai** (p233) Wandering this historic city, home of the Karaite people and a stunning island castle.

**5 Grūtas Park** (p233) Experiencing a taste of Lithuania's communist past.

**6 Ninth Fort** (p234) Taking in the poignant WWII history of Kaunas' memorial.

# VILNIUS

📝 5 / POP 546,700

Lithuania's capital, Vilnius, doesn't get the attention it deserves. The city's surprising Old Town is a dazzling assemblage of bright baroque houses, inviting alleyways and colourful churches built around quiet courtyards. But this is no museum piece. The city's cosmopolitan heritage, enriched by Polish, Jewish and Russian influences, lends a sophisticated vibe, and thousands of students keep the energy level high.

## ⊙ Sights

### ⊙ Cathedral Square & Gediminis Hill

Cathedral Square (Katedros aikštė), dominated by Vilnius Cathedral (p228) and its 57m-tall belfry, marks the centre of Vilnius

## ITINERARIES

### Three Days
Devote two days to exploring the baroque heart of **Vilnius**, then day trip to **Trakai** for its island castle and the homesteads of the Karaite people, stopping off at **Paneriai** on the way.

### One Week
Spend four nights in **Vilnius**, with day trips to both **Trakai** and the **Kernavė Cultural Reserve.** Travel cross-country to the **Hill of Crosses**, near Šiauliai, then explore some serious nature on the **Curonian Spit** for two or three days. Head back east via **Klaipėda** and **Kaunas**.

and is home to the city's most important sights.

**Gediminas Castle & Museum**   MUSEUM
(Gedimino Pilis ir Muziejus; ☑ 5-261 7453; www.lnm.lt; Gediminas Hill, Arsenalo gatvė 5; adult/child €2/1; ⊙ 10am-7pm daily Apr-Sep, 10am-5pm Tue-Sun Oct-Mar) With its prime hilltop location above the junction of the Neris and Vilnia rivers, Gediminas Castle is the last of a series of settlements and fortified buildings occupying this site since Neolithic times. This brick version, built by Grand Duke Vytautas in the early 15th century, offers commanding 360-degree views of Vilnius, and an exhibition tracing the history of the castle across the centuries, complete with scale models.

★**Palace of the
Grand Dukes of Lithuania**   MUSEUM
(Valdovų Rumai; ☑ 5-212 7476; www.valdovurumai.lt; Katedros aikštė 4; adult/student €3/1.50, guided tour €22; ⊙ museum 10am-6pm Tue, Wed, Fri & Sat, to 8pm Thu, to 4pm Sun) On a site that has been settled since at least the 4th century AD stands the latest in a procession of fortified palaces, repeatedly remodelled, extended, destroyed, and rebuilt over the centuries. What visitors now see is a painstaking restoration of its final grand manifestation, the baroque palace built for the Grand Dukes in the 17th century. While the gleamingly white complex is evidently new, it contains fascinating historical remains, and is a potent symbol of revitalised, independent Lithuania.

**National Museum of Lithuania**   MUSEUM
(Lietuvos Nacionalinis Muziejus; ☑ 5-262 7774; www.lnm.lt; Arsenalo gatvė 1; adult/child €2/1; ⊙ 10am-6pm Tue-Sun) FREE Building on the collections complied by the Museum of Antiquities since 1855, this splendid museum shows artefacts from Lithuanian life from Neolithic times to the 20th century. It has special collections devoted to the country's different folk traditions, to numismatics (including some of the very first Lithuanian coins) and to burial goods. A statue of Mindaugas, Lithuania's sole king, stands guard over the entrance.

**Vilnius Cathedral**   CATHEDRAL
(Vilniaus Arkikatedra; ☑ 5-261 0731; www.katedra.lt; Katedros aikštė 1; crypts adult/child €4.50/2.50; ⊙ 7am-7pm, crypts 10am-4pm Mon-Sat) Known in full as the Cathedral of St Stanislav and St Vladislav, this national symbol occupies a spot originally used for the worship of Perkūnas, the Lithuanian thunder god. Seventeenth-century St Casimir's Chapel, with its a baroque cupola, coloured marble and frescoes of the saint's life, is the showpiece, while the crypts (10am to 4pm Monday to Saturday, adult/child €4.50/2.50) are the final resting place of many prominent Lithuanians, including Vytautas the Great (1350–1430). The website has details of Mass.

## ◉ Old Town

★**Vilnius University**   HISTORIC BUILDING
(Vilniaus Universitetas; ☑ 5-268 7298; www.muziejus.vu.lt; Universiteto gatvė 3; architectural ensemble adult/child €1.50/0.50; ⊙ 9am-6pm Mon-Sat Mar-Oct, 9.30am-5.30pm Mon-Sat Nov-Feb) Founded in 1579 during the Counter-Reformation, Vilnius University was run by Jesuits for two centuries and became one of the greatest centres of Polish learning. It produced many notable scholars but was closed by the Russians in 1832 and didn't reopen until 1919. Today it has 23,000 students and Lithuania's oldest library, shelving five million books (including one of two originals of *The Catechism* by Martynas Mažvydas, the first book ever published in Lithuanian).

**Gates of Dawn**   HISTORIC BUILDING
(Aušros Vartai; ☑ 5-212 3513; www.ausrosvartai.lt; Aušros Vartų gatvė 12; ⊙ 6am-7pm) FREE The southern border of Old Town is marked by the last-standing of five portals that were once built into the city walls. A suitably grand way to enter one of the best-preserved

## JEWISH VILNIUS

Over the centuries Vilnius developed into one of Europe's leading centres of Jewish life and scholarship until the community was brutally wiped out by the occupying Nazis and their Lithuanian sympathisers during WWII. The former Jewish quarter lay in the streets west of Didžioji gatvė, including present-day Žydų gatvė (Jews St) and Gaono galvė, named after Vilnius' most famous Jewish resident, Gaon Elijahu ben Shlomo Zalman (1720–97).

The **Tolerance Centre** (📞 5-262 9666; www.jmuseum.lt; Naugarduko gatvė 10/2; adult/concession €3/1.50; ⊗ 10am-6pm Mon-Thu, to 4pm Fri & Sun), a beautifully restored former Jewish theatre, houses thought-provoking displays on the history and culture of Jews in Lithuania before the Shoah (Holocaust) and occasional art exhibitions. The **Holocaust Museum** (Holokausto Muziejus; 📞 5-262 0730; www.jmuseum.lt; Pamėnkalnio gatvė 12; adult/child €3/1.50; ⊗ 9am-5pm Mon-Thu, 9am-4pm Fri, 10am-4pm Sun), in the so-called Green House, is an unvarnished account detailing the suffering of the Lithuanian Jews in an unedited display of horrific images and letters by local Holocaust survivors.

Vilnius' only remaining synagogue, the **Choral Synagogue** (Choralinė Sinagoga; 📞 5-261 2523; Pylimo gatvė 39; donations welcome; ⊗ 10am-2pm Mon-Fri) FREE, was built in a Moorish style in 1903 and survived only because the Nazis used it as a medical store.

---

sections of the Old Town, it's also the site of the Gate of Dawn Chapel of Mary the Mother of Mercy and the 'Vilnius Madonna', a 17th-century painting of Our Lady said to work miracles.

### St Anne's Church
CHURCH

(Šv Onos Bažnyčia; 📞 8-698 17731; www.onosbaznycia.lt; Maironio gatvė 8-1; ⊗ 10.30am-6.30pm Tue-Sat, 8am-5pm May-Sep, 4.30-6.30pm Tue-Fri, 10.30am-6.30pm Sat, 8am-5pm Sun Oct-Apr) This gorgeous, late-15th-century Gothic church is a tiny confection of red brick, glass and arches, dwarfed by the Bernadine Church outside which it stands. Marrying 33 different kinds of brick into a whole that many regard as the most beautiful in Vilnius, it's reputed that Napoleon was so charmed by St Anne's that he wanted to relocate it to Paris.

---

## 👁 New Town & Outside the City Centre

### ★ Museum of Genocide Victims
MUSEUM

(Genocido Aukų Muziejus; 📞 5-249 8156; www.genocid.lt/muziejus; Aukų gatvė 2a; adult/discount €4/1; ⊗ 10am-6pm Wed-Sat, to 5pm Sun) This former headquarters of the KGB (and before them the Gestapo, Polish occupiers and Tsarist judiciary) houses a museum dedicated to thousands of Lithuanians who were murdered, imprisoned or deported by the Soviet Union from WWII until the 1960s. Memorial plaques honouring those who perished tile the outside of the building. Inside, floors cover the harsh realities of Soviet occupa-

tion, including gripping personal accounts of Lithuanian deportees to Siberia.

### ★ Antakalnis Cemetery
CEMETERY

(off Karių kapų gatvė; ⊗ 9am-dusk) One of Eastern Europe's most beautiful graveyards lies in this leafy suburb, a short stroll east of the centre. Those killed by Soviet special forces on 13 January 1991 are buried here; a sculpture of the Madonna cradling her son memorialises them. Another memorial honours Napoleonic soldiers who died of starvation and injuries in Vilnius while retreating from the Russian army. The remains of 2000 of them were only found in 2002.

## 🛏 Sleeping

### Jimmy Jumps House
HOSTEL €

(📞 5-231 3847; www.jimmyjumpshouse.com; Savičiaus gatvė 12-1; dm €11-13, r from €30; ⊗ @ 🖵) This clean, well-run, centrally located hostel is justifiably popular among backpackers. The pine-wood bunks are modest in four- to 12-bed rooms, but extras like free walking tours, themed pub crawls and a free breakfast add up to money well spent. Offers discounts if booked directly via email. No credit cards.

### ★ Bernardinu B&B
GUESTHOUSE €€

(📞 5-261 5134; www.bernardinuhouse.com; Bernardinų gatvė 5; r without bathroom €45-50, r with bathroom €50-70; 🅿 ❄ 🖵) This charming family-owned guesthouse is on one of the most picturesque lanes in the Old Town. The 18th-century townhouse has been sensitively renovated, preserving elements like

# Central Vilnius

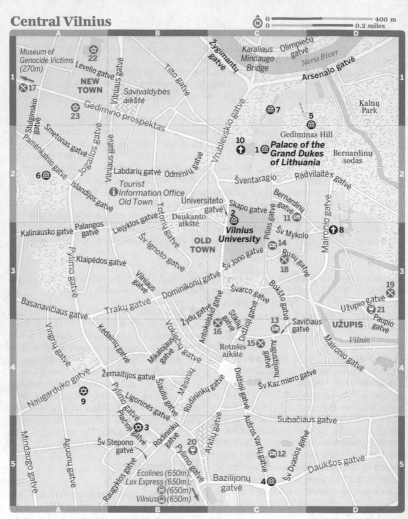

old timber flooring and ceilings, and with stripped patches of brick allowing you to see through the patina of the years. Breakfast (€4) is brought to your door on a tray.

**Domus Maria** GUESTHOUSE €€
(☑ 5-264 4880; www.domusmaria.lt; Aušros Vartų gatvė 12; s/d €62/85; 🅿 ➔ @ 🛜) The guesthouse of the Vilnius archdiocese is housed in a former monastery dating to the 17th century and oozes charm. Accommodation is in the monks' chambers, but they've been given a thorough, stylish makeover. Two rooms, 207 and 307, have views of the Gates of Dawn and are usually booked far in advance. Breakfast is served in the vaulted refectory.

★ **Narutis** HISTORIC HOTEL €€€
(☑ 5-212 2894; www.narutis.com; Pilies gatvė 24; r €109-139; 🅿 ✳ @ 🛜) Housed in a red-brick townhouse built in 1581, this classy pad has been a hotel since the 16th century. Breakfast and dinner are served in a vaulted Gothic cellar, there's wi-fi access throughout, and free apples at reception add a tasty touch. Booking over the internet can yield substantial savings.

# Central Vilnius

## ✖ Eating

### ⭐ Senamiesčio Krautuvė     LITHUANIAN €
(☑ 5-231 2836; www.senamiesciokrautuve.lt; Literatų gatvė 5; ☺ 10am-8pm Mon-Sat, 11am-5pm Sun) Look no further than this wonderful, quiet hobbit-hole for the very best Lithuanian comestibles, many unique to the country. Cured meats, fresh sausages, cheeses, fresh fruit and vegetables, honey and preserves, breads and pastries: all are arranged in irresistible profusion around the walls of this snug trove on Literatų gatvė.

### Radharanė     VEGETARIAN €
(☑ 5-212 3186; www.radharane.lt; Gediminio prospektas 32; mains €4; ☺ 11am-9pm Mon-Fri, 11.30am-9pm Sat & Sun; ☑) In a town where light, tasty vegetarian fare isn't thick on the ground, Radharanė's Indian-with-a-Lithuanian-twist fare is a godsend. Try the kofta, paneer with eggplant, channa dahl: all served with rice and salad, it's all good.

### ⭐ Balzac     FRENCH €€
(☑ 8-614 89223; www.balzac.lt; Savičiaus gatvė 7; mains €12-15; ☺ 11.30am-11pm Mon-Thu, to midnight Fri & Sat, to 9pm Sun) This classic French bistro serves what may be the best French food in Vilnius. Alongside bistro staples, such as *tournedos de boeuf* and duck confit, you'll find a great selection of seafood, some flown fresh from France. While there's a summer terrace, the dining area is small, so book to avoid disappointment.

### ⭐ Lokys     LITHUANIAN €€€
(☑ 5-262 9046; www.lokys.lt; Stiklių gatvė 8; mains €10-19; ☺ noon-midnight) Track down the big wooden bear to find this Vilnius institution, making merry in the vaulted 16th-century cellars of a former merchant's house since 1972. As a 'hunters' restaurant', it does a strong line in game, including roast venison and boar, game sausages, quail with pear and cowberry, and even beaver stewed with mushrooms. Folk musicians play in summer.

### Sweet Root     LITHUANIAN €€€
(☑ 8-685 60767; www.sweetroot.lt; Užupio gatvė 22; 7-course degustation €65; ☺ 6-11pm Tue-Sat) Sweet Root is proof that the (ironically international) trend towards 'locavorism' has reached high-end dining in Vilnius. In a smart if formulaic modern dining room (complete with open kitchen and tattooed chefs) you can enjoy modern dishes using Lithuanian ingredients, such as dock leaves, catmint, snails, beetroot leaves and freshwater fish.

## 🍷 Drinking & Nightlife

### Bukowski     BAR
(☑ 8-640 58855; www.facebook.com/bukowski-pub; Visų Šventų gatvė 7; ☺ 11am-midnight Sun-Wed, to 5am Thu-Sat) The eponymous Barfly is the spiritual patron of this charismatic boho bar in a less-trodden pocket of the Old Town. It has a back terrace for finer weather, great beers on tap, a full program of poetry, music and other events, and a welcoming, unpretentious atmosphere. One of Vilnius' best.

### Špunka     BAR
(☑ 8-652 32361; www.spunka.lt; Užupio gatvė 9; ☺ 3-10pm Tue-Sun, from 5pm Mon) This tiny, charismatic bar does a great line in craft

ales from Lithuania and further afield. If you need sustenance to keep the drink and chat flowing, local cheese and charcuterie are on hand.

## ☆ Entertainment

**Lithuanian National
Opera & Ballet Theatre** OPERA
(Lietuvos Nacionalinis Operos ir Baleto Teatras; ☑ 5-262 0727; www.opera.lt; Vienuolio gatvė 1; ☺ box office 10am-7pm Mon-Fri, to 6.30pm Sat, to 3pm Sun) This stunning (or gaudy, depending on your taste) Soviet-era building, with its huge, cascading chandeliers and grandiose dimensions, is home to Lithuania's national ballet and opera companies. You can see world-class performers for as little as €4 (or as much as €200...).

**Small Theatre of Vilnius** THEATRE
(Vilniaus Mažasis Teatras; ☑ 5-249 9869; www.vmt.lt; Gedimino prospektas 22) Founded just before Lithuania achieved legal Independence from the Soviet Union, in March 1990, the Small Theatre has occupied its present premises since 2005. The brainchild of artistic director Rimas Tuminas, it stages productions of classic works (Chekov, Beckett) alongside plays by Lithuanian writers and Tuminas' own repertoire.

## ⓘ Information

**Tourist Information Office Old Town** (☑ 5-262 9660; www.vilnius-tourism.lt; Vilniaus gatvė 22; ☺ 9am-6pm) The head office of Vilnius' tourist information service is great for brochures, advice and accommodation bookings.

**University Emergency Hospital** (☑ 5-236 5000; www.santa.lt; Santariškių gatvė 2; ☺ 24hr) This teaching hospital takes serious and emergency cases.

## ⓘ Getting There & Away

### BUS

The **bus station** (Autobusų Stotis; ☑ information 1661; www.autobusustotis.lt; Sodų gatvė 22) handles both domestic and international

coach services and is situated about 1km south of Old Town, across the street from the train station. The main international bus operators include **Ecolines** (☑ 5-213 3300; www.ecolines.net; Geležinkelio gatvė 15; ☺ 8am-9.30pm Mon-Fri, 9am-9.30pm Sat & Sun), **Lux Express** (☑ 5-233 6666; www.luxexpress.eu; Sodų 20b-1; ☺ 8am-7pm Mon-Fri, 9am-7pm Sat & Sun) or one of the affiliated carriers under **Eurolines** (☑ 5-2335 2774; www.eurolines.lt; Sodų gatvė 22; ☺ 6.30am-9.30pm).

### TRAIN

From the **train station** (Geležinkelio Stotis; ☑ information 233 0088; www.litrail.lt; Geležinkelio gatvė 16), Vilnius is linked by rail to various international destinations, including Warsaw, Minsk and Moscow, though most trains run through Belarus and require a transit visa.

## ⓘ Getting Around

### TO/FROM THE AIRPORT

Bus 1 runs between **Vilnius International Airport** (p238), 5km south of the city centre, and the train station. A shuttle train service runs from the train station 17 times daily between 5.44am and 9.07pm (around €0.75). A taxi from the airport to the city centre should cost around €15.

### BICYCLE

Vilnius is becoming increasingly bike-friendly, although bike lanes are rarer outside the Old Town and along the banks of the Neris. Orange Cyclocity stations dot the city, the Tourist Office has free cycling maps, and BaltiCCycle (www.balticcycle.lt) is good for ideas and information.

### PUBLIC TRANSPORT

The city is efficiently served by buses and trolleybuses from 5.30am or 6am to midnight; Sunday services are less frequent. Single-trip tickets cost: €1 from the driver; €0.64 if you have a Vilniečio Kortelė (an electronic ticket sold at kiosks); or nothing if you have a Vilnius City Card with public transport included (sold in tourist information centres).

### TAXI

Taxi rates in Vilnius can vary, and are generally cheaper if ordered in advance by telephone than if hailed directly off the street or picked up at a taxi stand. Ask the hotel reception desk or restaurant to call one for you.

# PANERIAI

During WWII the Nazis – aided by Lithuanian accomplices – murdered 100,000 people, around 70,000 of them Jews, at this site in the forest, 8km southwest of Vilnius.

---

### ⓘ VILNIUS CITY CARD

If you're planning to do epic amounts of sightseeing within a short period of time, the Vilnius City Card provides free or discounted entry to many attractions, as well as free transport.

## GRŪTAS PARK – THE GRAVEYARD OF COMMUNISM

Both entertaining and educational, **Grūtas Park** (Grūto Parkas; ☑ 6824 2320; www.grutoparkas.lt; Grūtas; adult/child €6/3 Oct-Apr, €7.50/4 May-Sep; ⊙ 9am-10pm summer, to 5pm rest of year; 🖐 ), 125km south of Vilnius, near the spa town of Druskininkai, has been an enormous hit since it opened in 2001. The sprawling grounds, built to resemble a Siberian concentration camp, feature the entire Marxist pantheon and dozens of other statuesque examples of Soviet realism, as well as assorted communist paraphernalia, exhibits on Soviet history (with a focus on the oppression of Lithuania) and loudspeakers bellowing Soviet anthems.

From the entrance a path leads to the small **Paneriai Museum** (☑ tours 6999 0384; www.jmuseum.lt; Agrastų gatvė 15; ⊙ 9am-5pm Tue-Sun May-Sep, by appointment Oct-Apr) **FREE**, with a graphic display of photographs and personal belongings of those who died here, and the grassed-over pits where the Nazis burnt the exhumed bodies of their victims.

# TRAKAI

☑ 528 / POP 5400

With its picturesque red-brick castle, Karaite culture, quaint wooden houses and pretty lakeside location, Trakai is a highly recommended day trip, within easy reach of the capital.

The Karaite people are named after the term *kara,* which means 'to study the scriptures' in both Hebrew and Arabic. The sect originated in Baghdad and practices strict adherence to the Torah (rejecting the rabbinic Talmud). In around 1400 the grand duke of Lithuania, Vytautas, brought about 380 Karaite families to Trakai from Crimea to serve as bodyguards. Only a dozen families remain in Trakai today and their numbers are dwindling rapidly.

Trakai's trophy piece is the fairy-tale **Trakai Castle** (Trakų Pilis; www.trakaimuziejus.lt; adult/senior/student & child €6/4/3; ⊙ 10am-7pm May-Sep, 10am-6pm Tue-Sun Mar, Apr & Oct, 9am-5pm Tue-Sun Nov-Feb; 🖐 ), occupying a small island in Lake Galvė. A footbridge links the island castle to the shore. The red-brick Gothic castle, painstakingly restored from original blueprints, dates from the late 14th century. Inside the castle, the Trakai History Museum tells the story of the structure. There's a bewildering variety of objects on show – hoards of coins, weaponry and porcelain, as well as interactive displays.

You can sample *kibinai* (meat-stuffed Karaite pastries similar to empanadas or Cornish pasties) either at **Senoji Kibininė**

(☑ 528-55 865; www.kibinas.lt; Karaimų gatvė 65; mains €4-8; ⊙ 10am-10pm) or at **Kybynlar** (☑ 8-698 06320; www.kybynlar.lt; Karaimų gatvė 29; mains €7-12; ⊙ noon-9pm Mon, 11am-9pm Tue-Thu, 11am-10pm Fri & Sat, 11am-9pm Sun).

# KAUNAS

☑ 37 / POP 353,000

Lithuania's second city has a compact Old Town, an entertaining array of museums and plenty of vibrant, youthful energy provided by its large student population. A good time to visit is in late April, during the Kaunas Jazz Festival (www.kaunasjazz.lt), when homegrown and international artists perform in venues across the city.

## ◉ Sights

### ◉ Old Town

The heart of Kaunas' lovely Old Town is **Rotušės Aikštė**, home of the city's former **Town Hall** (Kauno rotušė; ☑ 37-203 572; www.kaunas.lt; Rotušės aikštė 15), now known as the 'Palace of Weddings', and surrounded by 15th- and 16th-century German merchants' houses.

**St Francis Xavier Church & Monastery** CHURCH
(☑ 37-432 098; www.jesuit.lt; Rotušės aikštė 7-9; tower €1.50; ⊙ 4-6pm Mon-Fri, 7am-1pm & 4-6pm Sun) The southern side of Rotušės aikštė is dominated by the twin-towered St Francis Xavier Church, college and Jesuit monastery complex, built between 1666 and 1720. Take a peek inside and then climb the tower for the best aerial views of Kaunas.

**Maironis Lithuanian Literary Museum** MUSEUM
(Maironio Lietuvos Literatūros Muziejus; ☑ 37-206 842; www.maironiomuziejus.lt; Rotušės aikštė 13;

adult/child €1.45/0.58; ⊙ 9am-6pm Tue-Sat) This 18th-century mansion was, between 1910 and 1932, the home of Jonas Mačiulis (Maironis), the Kaunas poet-priest who stirred Lithuania's national ambitions in the late 19th and early 20th centuries. It's now a museum dedicated to his life and works, and Lithuanian literature more broadly.

## ◉ New Town

Laisvės alėja, a 1.7km-long pedestrian street lined with bars, shops and restaurants, runs east from Old Town to New Town, ending at the white, neo-Byzantine **St Michael the Archangel Church** (Šv Archangelo Mykolo Rektoratas; ☑ 37-226 676; www.kaunoarkivyskupija.lt; Nepriklausomybės aikštė 14; ⊙ 9am-6pm).

### ★ MK Čiurlionis
### National Museum of Art   GALLERY
(MK Čiurlionio Valstybinis Dailės Muziejus; ☑ 37-229 475; www.ciurlionis.lt; Putvinskio gatvė 55; adult/child €4/2; ⊙ 11am-5pm Tue, Wed & Fri-Sun, to 7pm Thu) In this, Kaunas' leading gallery, you'll find extensive collections of the romantic paintings of Mikalojus Konstantinas Čiurlionis (1875–1911), one of Lithuania's greatest artists and composers, as well as Lithuanian folk art and 16th- to 20th-century European applied art.

### Museum of the Ninth Fort   MUSEUM
(IX Forto Muziejus; ☑ 37-377 750; www.9fortomuziejus.lt; Žemaičių plentas 73; adult/child €3/1.50; ⊙ 10am-6pm Wed-Mon Apr-Oct, 10am-4pm Wed-Sun Nov-Mar) A poignant memorial to the tens of thousands of people, mainly Jews, who were murdered by the Nazis, the excellent Museum of the Ninth Fort, 7km north of Kaunas, comprises an old WWI-era fort and the bunker-like church of the damned. Displays cover deportations of Lithuanians by the Soviets and graphic photo exhibitions track the demise of Kaunas' Jewish community. Various guided tours of different aspects of the fort are offered.

### Kaunas Picture Gallery   GALLERY
(Kauno Paveikslų Galerija; ☑ 37-221 779; www.ciurlionis.lt; Donelaičio gatvė 16; adult/student €2/1; ⊙ 11am-5pm Tue, Wed & Fri-Sun, to 7pm Thu) This underrated gem, another branch of the many-tentacled MK Čiurlionis National Museum of Art, exhibits works by late-20th-century Lithuanian artists, with a room devoted to Jurgis Mačiūnas, the father of the Fluxus avant-garde movement.

## 🛌 Sleeping

### Kauno Arkivyskupijos
### Svečių Namai   GUESTHOUSE €
(☑ 37-322 597; www.kaunas.lcn.lt/sveciunamai; Rotušės aikštė 21; s/d/tr without bathroom €15/25/32, d with bathroom €35-48; ℗ ✳ @) 🍃 This Catholic archdiocesan guesthouse couldn't have a better location, snuggled between venerable churches and overlooking the Old Town square. Rooms are spartan but spacious, and breakfast is not included. Book well in advance, since it fills up fast.

### Daugirdas   BOUTIQUE HOTEL €€
(☑ 37-301 561; www.daugirdas.lt; T Daugirdo gatvė 4; s/d/tr €60/72/90; ✳ 🛜) This stylish boutique hotel, wedged between central Old Town and the Nemunas, is one of the most charismatic in Kaunas. The standard doubles are perfectly acceptable, with good-quality beds and bathrooms (with heated floors), but for something a little out of the ordinary, try the timber ceiling, enormous bed and Jacuzzi of the Gothic Suite.

### Radharanė   GUESTHOUSE €€
(☑ 37-320 800; www.radharane.lt; M Daukšos gatvė 28; d €48-60; ℗ @ 🛜) Atmospheric guesthouse with an excellent Old Town location. The rooms have been recently renovated and the vegetarian restaurant below is well worth investigating.

## 🍴 Eating

### Motiejaus Kepyklėlė   BAKERY €
(☑ 8-616 15599; Vilniaus gatvė 7; ⊙ 8am-7pm Mon-Sat, 9am-6pm Sun) Perhaps the best bakery in Kaunas, Motiejaus has settled into grand new red-brick digs in the heart of Vilniaus gatvė. Alongside Lithuanian cookies and pastries you'll find excellent international dainties, such as canelles, cupcakes, macaroons and croissants. The coffee can also be counted on.

### ★ Moksha   INDIAN, THAI €€
(☑ 8-676 71649; www.facebook.com/cafemoksha; Vasario 16-osios gatvė 6; mains €5-8; ⊙ 11am-10pm Mon-Sat; 🥢) This tiny place with whitewashed brick walls and fresh flowers everywhere lures you in with exotic smells. You can expect such daily specials as lamb kofta curry or crispy duck with persimmon salad, and there are even vegan options such as lentil soup. On top of that, the service is super-friendly; a rarity in these parts.

## THE HILL OF CROSSES

One of Lithuania's most awe-inspiring sights is the legendary **Hill of Crosses** (Kryžių kalnas; ☑41-370 860; Jurgaičiai). The sound of the thousands of crosses – which appear to grow on the hillock – tinkling in the breeze is wonderfully eerie.

Planted here since at least the 19th century and probably much older, the crosses were bulldozed by the Soviets, but each night people crept past soldiers and barbed wire to plant more, risking their lives or freedom to express their national and spiritual fervour.

Some of the crosses are devotional, others are memorials (many for people deported to Siberia) and some are finely carved folk-art masterpieces.

LITHUANIA KLAIPĖDA

**Senieji Rūsiai** EUROPEAN €€
(Old Cellars; ☑37-202 806; www.seniejirusiai.lt; Vilniaus gatvė 34; mains €9-16; ⊙11am-midnight Mon-Thu, 11am-1am Fri, noon-1am Sat, noon-11pm Sun; ☜) Named for its 17th-century subterranean vaults, lined with candlelit frescoes, 'Old Cellars' is one of the most atmospheric places in Kaunas to eat substantial pan-European dishes. Alongside frogs' legs, trout and other local delicacies, you can shell out extra for fillet with *foie gras,* or steak flame grilled at your table.

## 🍷 Drinking & Nightlife

**Kultūra Kavinė** CAFE
(☑8-676 25546; www.facebook.com/kauno.kultura; Donelaičio gatvė 14-16; ⊙noon-10pm Sun-Thu, noon-2am Fri & Sat; ☜) It calls itself a cafe, but this alternative meeting spot covers the bases from pub to cocktail bar to cosy spot to grab a cup of coffee. The clientele is skewed towards students and thinkers, and the space is a bit of fresh air for anyone looking to escape trendier, commercial bars. Excellent bar food, salads and wings, too.

**Skliautas** BAR
(☑37-6864 2700; www.skliautas.com; Rotušės aikštė 26; ⊙11am-midnight Mon-Thu, to 2am Fri & Sat, to 11pm Sun) Great for cheap Lithuanian food and a boisterous atmosphere, Skliautas bursts with energy most times of the day and night, and in summer its crowd basically takes over the adjoining alley. Also good for coffee and cake.

## ℹ Information

**Tourist Office** (☑37-323 436; www.visit.kaunas.lt; Laisvės alėja 36; ⊙9am-7pm Mon-Fri, 10am-3pm Sat & Sun Apr-Oct, 9am-6pm Mon-Thu, 9am-5pm Fri Nov-Mar) Books accommodation, sells maps and guides, and arranges bicycle rental and guided tours of the Old Town.

## ℹ Getting There & Away

Kaunas' bus and train stations are located not far from each other, about 2km south of the city centre. From the bus station, frequent services leave for Klaipėda (€14, three hours) and Vilnius (€6, 1¾ hours). From the train station there are plenty of trains each day to Vilnius (€5-6, 1¼ to 1¾ hours).

# KLAIPĖDA

☑46 / POP 161,300
Klaipėda, Lithuania's main seaport, is known mainly as the gateway to the Curonian Spit, though it has a fascinating history as the East Prussian city of Memel long before it was incorporated into modern Lithuania in the 1920s. It was founded in 1252 by the Teutonic Order, who built the city's first castle, and has served as a key trading port through the centuries to modern times. It was retaken by Nazi Germany in WWII and housed a German submarine base. Though it was heavily bombed in the war, it retains a unique Prussian feel, particularly in the quiet backstreets of the historic **Old Town**.

## ⊙ Sights

**Klaipėda Castle Museum** MUSEUM
(Klaipėda Pilies Muziejus; ☑46-410 527; www.mlimuziejus.lt; Pilies gatvė 4; adult/child €1.74/0.87; ⊙10am-6pm Tue-Sat) This small museum is based inside the remains of Klaipėda's old moat-protected castle, which dates back to the 13th century. It tells the castle's story through the ages until the 19th century, when most of the structure was pulled down. You'll find fascinating photos from WWII and the immediate postwar years, when the city was rebuilt by Soviet planners.

### History Museum of Lithuania Minor
MUSEUM

(Mažosios Lietuvos Istorijos Muziejus; ☑46-410 524; www.mlimuziejus.lt; Didžioji Vandens gatvė 6; adult/child €1.45/0.72; ☉10am-6pm Tue-Sat) This small museum traces the origins of 'Lithuania Minor' (Kleinlitauen) – as this coastal region was known during several centuries as part of East Prussia. It exhibits Prussian maps, coins, artefacts of the Teutonic order, traditional weaving machines and traditional folk art.

## 🛏 Sleeping

### Litinterp Guesthouse
GUESTHOUSE €

(☑46-410 644; www.litinterp.com; Puodžių gatvė 17; s without/with bathroom €23/28, d without/with bathroom €40/46; ℗🕙) A commercial building since the 18th century, this guesthouse retains timber stairs, brick arches and other lovely old touches. Its 19 rooms are spotless, with light pine furnishings. The breakfast (€3) is spartan, but with overall value this good we're not complaining.

### ★ Hotel Euterpė
HOTEL €€

(☑46-474 703; www.euterpe.lt; Daržų gatvė 9; s/d €73/93; ℗🕙@🕙) Our bet for the best small hotel in Klaipėda is this upscale number, tucked among former German merchant houses in the Old Town. Expect a warm welcome at reception and snug rooms in earthy colours and a neat, minimalist look. The downstairs restaurant is excellent and there's a small terrace to enjoy your morning coffee.

## 🍴 Eating & Drinking

### Friedricho Pasazas
INTERNATIONAL €€

(☑46-301 070; www.pasazas.lt; Tiltų gatvė 26a; mains €5-10; ☉11am-1am Mon-Sat, noon-midnight Sun; 🕙) Lining this snug carriageway on the southern side of the Old Town you'll find Friedricho Pasazas – not just one restaurant, but a whole complex of them. Friedricho Restoranas, the main show, is top of the pile, with creative Mediterranean dishes and wine to match. Following closely behind, there's a pizzeria, a steakhouse and a Lithuanian tavern.

### ★ Momo Grill
STEAK €€€

(☑8-693 12355; www.momogrill.lt; Liepų gatvė 20; mains €10-18; ☉11am-10pm Tue-Fri, noon-10pm Sat; 🕙🕙) This tiny, modern, minimalist steakhouse is foodie heaven and the hardest table to book in town. The small menu consists of just three cuts of beef plus grilled fish

and leg of duck, and allows the chef to focus on what he does best. The austere interior of white tiles is soothing and the wine list is excellent.

### Žvejų Baras
BAR

(☑8-686 60405; www.zvejubaras.lt; Kurpių gatvė 8; ☉5pm-midnight Sun-Wed, to 2am Thu, to 4am Fri & Sat) The beautiful, lead-lit, timbered interior of this portside pub (the name means 'Fisherman's Bar') is one of Klaipėda's nicest places to catch live music, or chat over a few interesting beers.

## ℹ Information

**Tourist Office** (☑46-412 186; www.klaipedainfo.lt; Turgaus gatvė 7; ☉9am-7pm Mon-Fri, 10am-4pm Sat & Sun Apr-Oct, 9am-6pm Mon-Fri Nov-Mar) Exceptionally efficient tourist office selling maps and locally published guidebooks, and arranging accommodation, tours and more. Operates reduced hours outside high season, closing on Sundays.

## ℹ Getting There & Away

The train and bus stations are situated near each in the modern part of town, about 2km north of Old Town. Three daily trains run to Vilnius (€18, four hours). There's also regular bus services to Vilnius (€18, four to 5½ hours) and Kaunas (€14, 2¾ to four hours).

# CURONIAN SPIT

☑469 / POP 3100

This magical sliver of land, covered by pine forest, hosts some of Europe's most precious sand dunes and a menagerie of elk, deer and avian wildlife. Recognised by Unesco as a World Heritage Site, the fragile spit is divided evenly between Lithuania and Russia's Kaliningrad region, with Lithuania's half protected as **Curonian Spit National Park** (☑46-402 256; www.nerija.lt; Smiltynės gatvė 11, Smiltynė; ☉9am-5pm Sun-Thu, to 6pm Fri & Sat).

Smiltynė, where the ferries from Klaipėda dock, draws weekend crowds with the delightful aquarium and the **Ethnographic Sea Fishermen's Farmstead** (Smiltynės gatvė; ⊙ dusk-dawn) . Further south, the village of Juodkrantė is awaft with the tempting smells of smoked fish (*žuvis*), while picture-perfect Nida is home to the unmissable 52m-high **Parnidis Dune** (Parnidžio kopos), with its panoramic views of the 'Lithuanian Sahara' – coastline, forest and sand extending towards Kaliningrad. Stay in one the town's handsomely painted fisherman's houses and eat the famous Curonian smoked fish at **Tik Pas Jona** (☑8-620 82084; www.facebook.com/RukytosZuvysTikPas-Jona; Naglių gatvė 6-1; mains €3; ⊙10am-10pm Apr-Nov, Sat & Sun only Dec-Mar).

A flat cycling trail runs all the way from Nida to Smiltynė, passing the massive colony of grey herons and cormorants near Juodkrantė, and you stand a good chance of seeing wild boar and other wildlife along the path. Bicycles are easy to hire (around €9/12 per 12/24 hours) in Nida.

The tourist office in Klaipėda can help arrange transport and accommodation; **Miško Namas** (☑469-52 290; www.miskonamas.com; Pamario gatvė 11; d €75-85, 2-/4-person apt €95/100; P @ 🛜 🐾 ) and **Vila Banga** (☑8-686 08073; www.nidosbanga.lt; Pamario gatvė 2; d/ apt €98/135; 🛜 ) are both fine choices.

## ❶ Getting There & Away

To get to the Spit, board a ferry at the **Old Ferry Port** (Senoji perkėla; ☑46-311 117; www.keltas.lt; Danės gatvė 1; per passenger/bicycle €0.80/free) just west of Klaipėda's Old Town (€0.90, 10 minutes, half-hourly). Vehicles must use the **New Ferry Port** (Naujoji perkėla; ☑46-311 117; www.keltas.lt; Nemuno gatvė 8; per passenger/car €0.80/11.05, bicycle free), 2.5km south of the passenger terminal (per car €12, at least hourly).

# SURVIVAL GUIDE

## ❶ Directory A–Z

### ACCOMMODATION
➡ Book ahead in the high season for Vilnius and the Curonian Spit. High-season prices are around 30% higher than low-season prices. Prices are higher in Vilnius.

➡ Vilnius has numerous youth hostels. Budget accommodation is easy to find outside the capital.

### RESOURCES
**Lithuania Travel** (www.lithuania.travel) The State Department of Tourism's visitor portal

**Vilnius Tourism** (www.vilnius-tourism.lt/en/) Handy, always up-to-date site covering most of what the capital has to offer

**Lithuania Railways** (www.litrail.lt/en) Train schedules, fares and information.

**Autobusubilietai** (www.autobusubilietai.lt) Bus fares, schedules and information.

### MONEY
Lithuania adopted the euro (€) on 1 January 2015.

➡ Exchange money with your credit or debit card at ATMs located around the country or at major banks.

➡ Credit cards are widely accepted for purchases.

➡ Some banks still cash travellers cheques, though this is increasingly uncommon.

➡ Tip 10% in restaurants to reward good service.

### OPENING HOURS
**Banks** 8am–3pm Monday to Friday
**Bars** 11am–midnight Sunday to Thursday, 11am–2am Friday and Saturday

---

## ESSENTIAL FOOD & DRINK

**Beer and mead** Šytutys, Utenos and Kalnapilis are top beers; midus (mead) is a honey-tinged nobleman's drink.

**Beer snacks** No drinking session is complete without a plate of smoked pigs' ears and *kepta duona* (deep-fried garlicky bread sticks).

**Beetroot delight** Cold, creamy *šaltibarščiai* (beetroot soup) is a summer speciality, served with a side of fried potatoes.

**Potato creations** Try the cepelinai (potato-dough 'zeppelin' stuffed with meat, mushrooms or cheese), bulviniai blynai (potato pancakes) or žemaičių blynai (heart-shaped mashed potato stuffed with meat and fried), or the vedarai (baked pig intestines stuffed with mashed potato).

**Smoked fish** The Curonian Spit is famous for its smoked fish, particularly the superb rukytas unguris (smoked eel).

**Unusual meat** Sample the game, such as beaver stew or bear sausages.

**Clubs** 10pm–5am Thursday to Saturday

**Post offices** 8am–8pm Monday to Friday, 10am–9pm Saturday, 10am–5pm Sunday

**Restaurants** noon–11pm; later on weekends

**Shops** 9am or 10am–7pm Monday to Saturday; some open on Sunday

### TELEPHONE

➡ Dial 8 and wait for the tone before calling both landlines (followed by the city code and phone number) and mobile phones (followed by the eight-digit number).

➡ To make an international call dial 00 before the country code.

➡ Mobile companies **Bitė** (www.bite.lt), **Omnitel** (www.omnitel.lt) and **Tele 2** (www.tele2.lt) sell prepaid SIM cards; Tele2 offers free roaming with its prepaid cards – making it the best choice for those also travelling in Estonia, Latvia and Poland – and has the cheapest rates.

➡ Payphones – increasingly rare given the widespread use of mobiles – only accept phonecards, sold at newspaper kiosks.

## ⓘ Getting There & Away

Lithuania has frequent air, bus, train and ferry links to neighbouring countries, though be sure to route your travel to avoid Belarus or the Russian province of Kaliningrad if you don't have the right transit visas. Latvia and Poland are both members of the EU's Schengen zone and there are no passport controls at these borders. Vilnius is the country's hub for air travel, with an increasing number of direct services to many European cities. Sweden and Germany can be reached by ferry from Klaipėda, Lithuania's international seaport.

Flights, tours and rail tickets can be booked online at www.lonelyplanet.com/bookings.

### AIR

Most international traffic to Lithuania goes through **Vilnius International Airport** (Tarptautinis Vilniaus Oro Uostas; ☑ 6124 4442; www.vno.lt; Rodūnios kelias 10a; 🛜; 🚌1, 2), which has connections to a good cross-section of Europe's cities..

➡ Major carriers that service Vilnius include airBaltic, Austrian Airlines, Lufthansa, LOT and Scandinavian Airlines.

➡ Budget carriers include Ryanair and Wizz Air.

### BOAT

From Klaipėda's **International Ferry Port** (☑ 46-395 051; www.dfdsseaways.lt; Perkėlos gatvė 10), **DFDS Seaways** (☑ 46-395 000; www.dfdsseaways.com; Šaulių gatvė 19) runs passenger ferries to/from Kiel (from €80, six weekly, 22 hours) in Germany and Karlshamn, Sweden (from €75, 14 hours, daily).

### BUS

The main international bus companies operating in Lithuania are **Lux Express** (https://luxexpress.eu) and **Ecolines** (https://ecolines.net).

### CAR & MOTORCYCLE

➡ There are no passport or customs controls if entering from Poland or Latvia.

➡ A valid entry or transit visa is required to enter or drive through Belarus and the Russian province of Kaliningrad.

### TRAIN

➡ Many international train routes, including to Warsaw and Moscow, pass through Belarus and require a transit visa.

➡ Consult the timetable at **Lithuanian Railways** (www.litrail.lt/en) for further information.

## ⓘ Getting Around

### BICYCLE

➡ Lithuania is mostly flat and easily explored by bike.

➡ Large cities and areas popular with visitors have bike-rental and repair shops.

➡ Information about bike touring in Lithuania can be found on **BaltiCCycle** (www.balticcycle.lt)

## COUNTRY FACTS

**Area** 65,303 sq km

**Capital** Vilnius

**Country Code** ☑ 370

**Currency** euro (€)

**Emergency** ☑ 112

**Language** Lithuanian

**Money** ATMs everywhere

**Population** 2.9 million

**Visas** Not required for citizens of the EU, Australia, Canada, Israel, Japan, New Zealand, Switzerland or the US for stays of 90 days

## EATING PRICE RANGES

The following Lithuanian budgets are based on a typical main meal offered.

**€** less than €7

**€€** €7–14

**€€€** more than €14

### BUS

➡ The bus network is extensive, efficient and relatively inexpensive.

➡ See www.autobusubilietai.lt for national bus timetables.

### CAR & MOTORCYCLE

➡ Drivers must be at least 18 years old and have a valid driving licence (with photo) in their country of residence.

➡ The speed limit is 50km/h in cities, 70km/h to 90km/h on two-lane highways, and 110km/h to 130km/h on motorways.

➡ The blood-alcohol limit is 0.04% (or 0.2% for drivers of less than two years' experience).

➡ International and local car-rental agencies are well represented at Vilnius International Airport. Expect to pay around €150 per week for a basic compact manual.

### LOCAL TRANSPORT

➡ Lithuanian cities generally have good public transport, based on buses, trolleybuses and minibuses.

➡ A ride usually costs around €1.

### TRAIN

➡ The country's efficient train network, **Lithuanian Rail** (see www.litrail.lt, with timetables in English) links Vilnius to Kaunas, Klaipėda and Trakai, though for some journeys, including Kaunas to Klaipėda, buses are faster.

# Macedonia

## Best Places to Eat

➡ Letna Bavča Kaneo (p252)

➡ Hotel Tutto (p249)

➡ Vila Raskrsnica (p256)

➡ Kebapčilnica Destan (p245)

## Best Places to Stay

➡ Vila Raskrsnica (p256)

➡ Villa Dihovo (p256)

➡ Sunny Lake Hostel (p251)

➡ Villa Jovan (p251)

➡ Urban Hostel & Apartments (p244)

## Why Go?

Part Balkan, part Mediterranean and rich in Greek, Roman and Ottoman history, Macedonia (Македонија) has a fascinating past and complex national psyche. Glittering Lake Ohrid and the historic waterside town of Ohrid itself have etched out a place for Macedonia on the tourist map, but this small nation is far more than just one great lake.

Skopje may be the Balkans' most bonkers and unfailingly entertaining capital city, thanks to a government-led building spree of monuments, museums and fountains. What has emerged is an intriguing jigsaw where ancient history and buzzing modernity collide.

The rest of Macedonia is a stomping ground for adventurers. Mountains are omnipresent and walking trails blissfully quiet. The national parks of Mavrovo, Galičica and Pelister are also cultivating some excellent cultural and food tourism initiatives; these gorgeous regions are criminally underexplored. If you want to get off the beaten track in Europe, this is it.

## When to Go
### Skopje

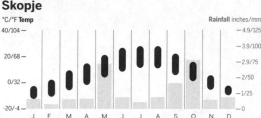

**Jun–Aug** Enjoy Ohrid's Summer Festival and dive into its 300m-deep lake.

**Sep–Oct** Partake in Skopje's jazz festival or the Tikveš region's Kavadarci Wine Carnival.

**Dec–Feb** Ski Mavrovo, snuggle up in chalet-style lodges and experience Ohrid out of season.

## Macedonia Highlights

**1 Ohrid Old Town**
(p249) Exploring the
distinctive historic quarter,
right to the end of the
boardwalk and pebble beach,
and up to the clifftop Church
of Sveti Jovan.

**2 Skopje** (p241) Diving
into the historic Čaršija
(Old Turkish Bazaar) of
Macedonia's capital, then
marvelling at its super-sized
new riverside monuments.

**3 Pelister National Park**
(p255) Eating your fill at
food-focused village tourism
initiatives in this underrated
national park, and walking it
off the next day.

**4 Golem Grad** (p254)
Chasing ghosts, pelicans and
tortoises around this eerie
Lake Prespa island, fecund
with overgrown ruins.

**5 Popova Kula** (p253)
Sipping and slurping your
way through Macedonia's
premier wine region, Tikveš,
using this could-be-in-Italy
winery hotel as your base.

**6 Sveti Jovan Bigorski
Monastery** (p248) Taking
tea with monks at this
majestic complex, teetering
in the hills of Mavrovo
National Park.

# SKOPJE СКОПЈЕ

02 / POPULATION 2.02 MILLION

In the past few years, the central riverside
area of Skopje has hammered out the look of
a set design for an ancient civilisation. Towering warrior statues gaze down on you and
gleaming Italianate power buildings make
visitors feel very small indeed. Marble-clad
museums have mushroomed alongside hypnotic new mega-fountains, and the Macedonian capital has become a thoroughly entertaining Balkan metropolis – a bit surreal
and at times garish, maybe, but never dull.

Yet peel back the veneer and Skopje has a genuine historic core that warrants just as much attention as its new wonders. Ottoman- and Byzantine-era sights are focused around the city's delightful Čaršija (old Turkish bazaar), bordered by the 15th-century Kameni Most (Stone Bridge) and Tvrdina Kale Fortress – Skopje's guardian since the 5th century.

##  Sights

### ◉ Ploštad Makedonija & the South Bank

**Ploštad Makedonija**                    SQUARE
(Macedonia Sq) This gigantic square is the centrepiece to Skopje's audacious nation-building-through-architecture project and has massive statues dedicated to national heroes in it, as well as an incongruous Triumphal Arch in the southeast corner. The towering, central Warrior on a Horse is bedecked by fountains that are illuminated at night. Home to a number of cafes and hotels, it's a popular stomping ground for locals as well as tourists, particularly when the sun goes down.

**Memorial House of Mother Teresa**  MUSEUM
(✆02 3290 674; ul Makedonija 9; ⊙9am-8pm Mon-Fri, to 2pm Sat-Sun) **FREE** This extraordinary retro-futuristic memorial is the most unique church you'll see in Macedonia. Inside the building there's a small 1st-floor museum displaying memorabilia relating to the famed Catholic nun of Calcutta, born in Skopje in 1910. On the 2nd floor there is a mind-boggling chapel, with glass walls wrought in filigree (a revered traditional craft of Skopje). Silhouettes of doves are worked into the filigree to symbolise peace, as a homage to Mother Teresa.

### ◉ North Bank & Čaršija

**★Čaršija**                    AREA
(Old Turkish Bazaar) Čaršija is the hillside Turkish old town of Skopje and evokes the city's Ottoman past with its winding lanes filled with teahouses, mosques, craftsmen's stores, and even good nightlife. It also boasts Skopje's best historic structures and a handful of museums, and is the first place any visitor should head. Čaršija runs from the Stone Bridge to the Bit Pazar, a big vegetable and household goods market. Expect to get pleasantly lost in its maze of narrow streets.

**★Archaeological Museum of Macedonia**                    MUSEUM
(www.amm.org.mk; Bul Goce Delčev; adult/student & child 300/150MKD; ⊙10am-6pm Tue-Sun) All gleaming and shiny new, this supersized pile of Italianate-styled marble has been a giant receptacle for Skopje's recent splurge on government-led monuments to boost national pride. Inside, there are three floors displaying the cream of Macedonian archaeological excavations beneath the dazzle of hundreds of tiny lights. Highlights include Byzantine treasures; sophisticated 3D reconstructions of early Macedonian faces from skulls; a pint-sized replica of an early Christian basilica showing the life phases of mosaic conservation; and a Phoenician royal necropolis.

**Sveti Spas Church**                    CHURCH
(Church of the Holy Saviour; Makarije Frčkoski 8; adult/student 120/50MKD; ⊙9am-5pm Tue-Fri, to 3pm Sat & Sun) Partially submerged 2m underground (the Ottomans banned churches from being taller than mosques), this church dates from the 14th century and is the most historically important in Skopje. Its sunken design means it doesn't look like a church, so you might not notice it at first: it's opposite the Old Town Brewery – look for the pretty bell tower that watches over it, built into its outer courtyard wall. Inside the church an elaborate carved iconostasis shines out of the dark.

**★Tvrdina Kale Fortress**                    FORTRESS
(Samoilova; ⊙7am-7pm) **FREE** Dominating the skyline of Skopje, this *Game of Thrones*-worthy 6th-century AD Byzantine (and later, Ottoman) fortress is an easy walk up from the Čaršija and its ramparts offer great views over the city and river. Inside the ruins, two mini museums were being built at the time of writing to house various archaeological finds from neolithic to Ottoman times. This will be a welcome addition to the site, as there are no information boards at the fortress at present.

**National Gallery of Macedonia**  GALLERY
(Daut Paša Amam; www.nationalgallery.mk; Kruševska 1a; admission adult/student & child 50/20MKD; ⊙10am-8pm Tue-Sun Apr-Sep, to 6pm Oct-Mar) The Daut Paša Amam (1473) were once the largest Turkish baths outside of İstanbul and they make a magical setting for the permanent collection of Skopje's national art gallery, just by the entrance to the

# Skopje

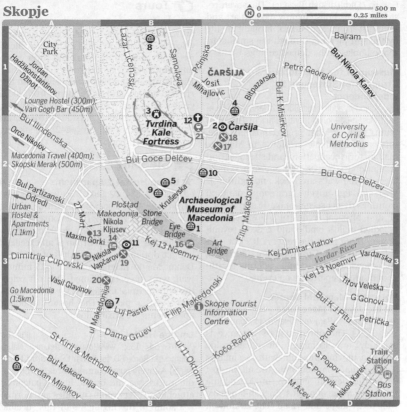

0    500 m
0    0.25 miles

MACEDONIA SKOPJE

# Skopje

### ◉ Top Sights

### ◉ Sights

### ◉ Activities, Courses & Tours

### ◉ Sleeping

### ◉ Eating

### ◉ Drinking & Nightlife

Čaršija (Old Turkish Bazaar). The seven restored rooms house mainly modern art and sculpture from Macedonia, brought to life by the sun piercing through the small star-shaped holes in the domed ceilings.

### Museum of the Macedonian Struggle for Statehood & Independence
MUSEUM

(Iljo Vojvodo; adult/child 300/120MKD; ⊙10am-6pm, closed 1st Mon of month) Part history museum, part national propaganda machine, this is a formidable memorial to Macedonia's historic occupation, land struggles and revolutionary heroes. The museum is dark, literally (the walls are black and lighting is low) and figuratively (gruesome giant oil paintings depict scenes of battle and betrayal, and physical reconstructions include a bloodied child's cradle and a dead revolutionary hung from the rafters). It's not suitable for children. The guides are interesting and knowledgeable (despite offering a rather one-sided perspective on events).

### Holocaust Memorial Center for the Jews of Macedonia
MUSEUM

(Iljo Vojvoda; ⊙9am-7pm Tue-Fri, to 3pm Sat & Sun) FREE The mirrored-glass entrance is bizarrely unwelcoming, but once inside this is a moving museum with fascinating displays that commemorate the all-but-lost Sephardic Jewish culture of Macedonia through a range of photos, English-language wall texts, maps and video. The exhibition documents the Jewish community's history in the Balkans, ending in WWII when some 98% of Macedonian Jews perished in the Holocaust. In the central atrium, 7144 beads hang to represent the individuals who died.

### Museum of Contemporary Art
MUSEUM

(NIMoCA; ☏02 3117 734; www.msuskopje.org.mk; Samoilova 17; admission 300MKD, free 1st Fri of month; ⊙10am-5pm Tue-Sat, 9am-1pm Sun) This museum was formed in the aftermath of Skopje's devastating 1963 earthquake, with artists and collections around the world donating works to form a collection that now includes works by Picasso, Léger, Hockney, Meret Oppenheim and Bridget Riley. It's housed in an impressive contemporary building, with floor-to-ceiling windows, perched atop a hill with wonderful city views. Unfortunately, its collection isn't always on display – you may come here and find its exhibitions extraordinary or mundane, depending on what's been put on display.

##  Tours

### Skopje Walks
WALKING

(www.skopjewalks.com; ul Makedonija; donations welcome; ⊙10am daily) FREE These excellent free tours run for 2½ hours and cover every important corner of Skopje's inner city. Highly recommended for an insight into the city, its history and its residents from local guides who are passionate about showing Skopje off. Tours meet outside the Memorial House of Mother Teresa (p242) – look out for the blue ID badge.

## 🛏 Sleeping

### ★ Urban Hostel & Apartments
HOSTEL €

(☏078 432 384, 02 6142 785; www.urbanhostel.com.mk; Adolf Ciborovski 22; dm €10-13, s/d €24/35, apt €35-70; ❈ 🛜) In a converted residential house with a sociable front garden for summer lounging, Urban is an excellent budget option on the outskirts of the leafy Debar Maalo neighbourhood, a 15-minute walk west of central Skopje. Decor is eclectic, with a fireplace for cosy winter nights and even a piano. The hostel's modern apartments are great value.

### Lounge Hostel
HOSTEL €

(☏076 547 165; www.loungehostel.mk; Naum Naumovski Borče 80, 1st fl; dm €9-12, s/d €17/25; ❈ 🛜) A lovely large common area, orthopaedic mattresses and bright, breezy balconies attached to every room (privates and dorms) are some of the highlights of this sociable retro-styled hostel with a view over the City Park. Staff are a little less clued-up here than at some other hostels, but will bend over backwards to help make guests' lives easier.

### Bed & Breakfast London
BOUTIQUE HOTEL €€

(☏02 3116 146; www.londonbnb.mk; Maksim Gorki 1; s/d/ste €50/60/90; ❈ 🛜) The theme at this hotel is a little random, but all is forgiven when you see the front-row Ploštad view it has – rooms at the front are in gawping distance of the Alexander the Great fountain, though the hotel is set back slightly from the main square and windows are thick enough that sound from the cafe-bar below doesn't disturb too much.

### Senigallia
HOTEL €€

(☏02 3224 044; www.senigallia.mk; Kej 13 Noemvri 5S; s/d €65/75 ste €90-110; ❈ 🛜) You see that splendid ship docked opposite the grand Archaeological Museum? It's not a pirate ship; it's a rather swish hotel that just so happens to blend in perfectly with the government's weird and wonderful building drive along the Vardar river. The hotel's interior is all wood panelling, rooms have mini fridges and there's a terrace bar on the top deck.

★ **Hotel Solun** HOTEL €€€
(☑ 02 3232 512, 071 238 599; www.hotelsolun.com; Nikola Vapčarov 10; s/d from €83/103; ✳@🖥✉) The 55-room Solun sits in a different stratosphere to most of Macedonia's faded 'high-end' hotels (though you wouldn't know it from the dated hotel signage around the Ploštad). It's a stylish and design-conscious property that wouldn't feel out of place in any European capital, accessed through an alley just off the main square.

## ✗ Eating

★ **Kebapčilnica Destan** KEBAB €
(ul 104 6; set meal 180MKD; ⏲7am-11pm) Skopje's best beef kebabs, accompanied by seasoned grilled bread, peppers and a little raw onion, are served at this classic Čaršija place. There's no menu, everyone gets the same thing, but the terrace is usually full – that's how good it is. Ten stubby kebabs constitute a serious meat feast (180MKD); or you can ask for a half portion (120MKD).

**Rock Kafana Rustikana** GRILL €
(☑ 02 72 561 450; off Dimitrije Čupovski; 140-300MKD; ⏲8am-midnight Mon-Sat; 🖥📶) Just a block from the Ploštad but rocking a decidedly more local vibe, this humble bar-restaurant prides itself on good music, friendly service and simple dishes of grilled meats, sandwiches and inventive bar snacks such as zucchini with sour cream and garlic. Its setting amid an unkempt, mildly post-apocalyptic green space behind the Rekord Hostel only adds to its kooky charm.

**Restaurant Pelister** INTERNATIONAL €€
(Ploštad Makedonija; mains 260-400MKD; ⏲7am-1am daily Jun-Sep, 7am-1am Fri-Sat, to midnight Sun-Thu Oct-May; 🖥📶) This cafe-restaurant is a real local fixture with a prime spot on Skopje's Ploštad and the feel of a Mitteleuropa grand cafe, attracting a diverse crowd. It's a good spot for coffee and people-watching, and it also serves a vast array of decent pastas.

★ **Pivnica An** MACEDONIAN €€€
(Beerhouse An; ☑ 02 3212 111; www.pivnicaan.mk; Kapan An; mains 250-750MKD; ⏲10am-midnight; 🖥📶) Skopje's Čaršija is still home to a couple of *ans* – ancient Ottoman inns, similar to desert *caravanserai* – and the Kapan An houses this upmarket restaurant, serving some of the city's best Macedonian fare. Try butter-soft *sarma* (stuffed vine leaves) or roasted pork ribs and observe history echoing through the sumptuous central courtyard, where Pivnica's partially covered patio offers a tranquil bolt-hole. It's tricky to find: it's through an archway off the busy little square in the heart of the Čaršija where the kebab restaurants are concentrated.

**Skopski Merak** MACEDONIAN €€€
(☑ 02 3212 215; Debarca 51; mains 200-1000MKD; ⏲8am-1am; 🖥📶) This hugely popular place packs locals in with its pretty timber-framed terrace, live music most evenings and huge menu of *skara* (grilled meats) and other Macedonian specialities. Its chef's choice platters of smoked meats, local cheeses and grilled veg are particularly impressive, but not on the menu: ask for *daska* (around 500MKD for two people). It's worth booking for dinner.

MACEDONIA SKOPJE

---

## ITINERARIES

### One Week

Plan to spend at least a couple of days in the capital **Skopje** (p241) marvelling at the statues and visiting its **Čaršija** (p242). Leave time for a day trip to Canyon Matka (p247), then head southwest to historic **Ohrid** (p249) for some R&R by the lake.

Complete the week with a couple of nights at a village guesthouse on the edge of **Pelister National Park** (p255), and a visit to **Golem Grad** (p254) island.

### Two Weeks

Between Skopje and Ohrid, add in a trip through **Mavrovo National Park** (p248), stay in a village and visit the impressive **Sveti Jovan Bigorski Monastery** (p248). From Pelister National Park take a trip to the cultured city of Bitola, with its ancient **Heraclea Lyncestis** (p256) ruins. Before heading back to Skopje, spend a night at Macedonia's fabulous winery hotel, **Popova Kula** (p253).

## Drinking & Nightlife

The steep Čaršija street called Teodosij Gologanov is the centre of Skopje's nightlife.

★ **Old Town Brewery** CRAFT BEER
(Gradište 1; ⊙10am-1am; 🛜) The siren call of tasty craft beer sings to locals and tourists alike at Skopje's only microbrewery, which is justifiably popular for its Weiss beer, IPA, Golden Ale and dark beer – all brewed on-site and accompanied by a dependable menu of international pub grub. Its sunny terrace, sandwiched between the fortress walls and the Sveti Spas Church, crowns its appeal.

**Van Gogh Bar** BAR
(📞02 3121 876; Mikhail Cokov 4; ⊙8am-1am) Whisky nights, cocktail nights, live-music nights...there's something going on every day of the week at Van Gogh, a poky bar with a lively local crew that spills onto the street. The bar is a haunt of local bikers, but all sorts of characters drink here and it's always good fun. It's close to the City Park, in Debar Maalo.

## ⓘ Information

### INTERNET ACCESS

Free wi-fi is widespread in cafes, restaurants and hotels, though it's often unadvertised – don't feel cheeky asking staff for password details. Some hotels have desktop computers for guest use.

### MEDICAL SERVICES

**City Hospital** (📞02 3235 000; 11 Oktomvri 53; ⊙24hr)
**Neuromedica Private Clinic** (📞02 3133 313; www.neuromedica.com.mk; Partizanski Odredi 42; ⊙24hr)

### TOURIST INFORMATION

Skopje's tourist offices are neglected, not always open and not very useful. The staff in your hotel are likely to be far better sources of information.
**Skopje Tourist Office** (Filip Makedonski; ⊙8.30am-4.30pm)

### TRAVEL AGENCIES

**Go Macedonia** (📞02 3064 647; www.gomacedonia.com; ul Ankarska 29a)
**Macedonia Experience** (📞075 243 944; www.macedoniaexperience.com; ul Nikola Kljusev 3, Skopje)
**Macedonia Travel** (📞02 3112 408; www.macedoniatravel.com; Orce Nikolov 109/1, 3rd fl)

## ⓘ Getting There & Away

### AIR

**Skopje Alexander the Great Airport** (📞02 3148 333; www.airports.com.mk; 1043, Pet-

rovec) is located 21km east of the city centre. Skopje has direct air services to many cities throughout Europe, Turkey and the Gulf.

### BUS

Skopje's **bus station** (📞02 2466 313; www.sas.com.mk in Macedonian; bul Nikola Karev), with ATM, exchange office and English-language information office, adjoins the train station. Bus schedules are only available online in Macedonian (your hotel/hostel staff should be more than happy to translate for you, though). Buy tickets on the day or in advance from the window counters inside the station.

#### Domestic Buses

**Bitola** (480MKD, three hours, 11 daily)
**Kavadarci** (270MKD, two hours, 10 daily)
**Mavrovo** (350MKD, two hours, two Monday to Saturday)
**Ohrid** (500MKD, three hours, 14 daily)

#### International Buses

**Belgrade** (1400MKD, six to eight hours, 10 daily)
**İstanbul** (1900MKD, 12 hours, five daily)
**Ljubljana** (3800MKD, 14 hours, one daily )
**Pristina** (330MKD, two hours, 14 daily)
**Sarajevo** (3170MKD, 14 hours, 8pm Wednesday and Sunday)
**Sofia** (1040MKD, 5½ hours, five daily)
**Thessaloniki** (1300MKD, four hours, 6am and 5pm Monday, Wednesday and Friday)
**Zagreb** (3200MKD, 12 hours, 5pm daily)

### CAR

For car hire try **Balkan Rent-A-Car** (📞02 6091 112, 070 206 157; balkanrentacar@yahoo.com; Vladimir Polezinovski 30; 1-5 days from €27 per day).

### TRAIN

The **train station** (Zheleznička Stanica; bul Jane Sandanski) serves local and international destinations.

#### Domestic Trains

The 5.10pm daily service to Bitola is an express train, taking two hours 40 minutes. All trains to Bitola stop at Prilep first.
**Bitola** (320MKD, 3½ hours, four daily)
**Negotino** (200MKD, 1¾ hours, two daily)
**Prilep** (250MKD, three hours, four daily)

#### International Trains

Disagreements with the Greek government have led to periodically suspended train routes with Greece. At the time of writing, the Skopje–Thessaloniki ticket being sold by the train station involved a train to Gevgelija and then a bus across the border to Thessaloniki (760MKD, five hours, 4.45am daily).

A train serves Belgrade (1430MKD, 10 hours, 10.19pm daily), and another heads for Pristina (three hours, 4.10pm daily) in Kosovo; for Pristina, the train station will only sell you a ticket to the border (100MKD) and at the border you need to buy another ticket for your onward travel to the capital, costing €2.50.

## ℹ️ Getting Around

### TO/FROM THE AIRPORT

Airport shuttle bus **Vardar Express** (📞 02 3118 263; www.vardarexpress.com) runs between the airport and the city; check the website for its timetable. Taxis to the airport cost 800MKD to 1000MKD. From the airport to the city centre, taxis cost 1200MKD.

### BUS

Skopje's public city buses cost 35MKD and follow numbered routes. You can buy and validate tickets on board. Buses congregate under the bus/train station.

### TAXI

Skopje's taxis aren't bad value, with the first kilometre costing just 40MKD, and 25MKD for subsequent kilometres. Drivers rarely speak English, but they do use their meters (if they don't, just ask or point). Central destinations cost 60MKD to 150MKD.

# Around Skopje

Monasteries, mountains plunging into a spectacular canyon and an impressive new ethno village surround Skopje's urban core, and make worthwhile day trips.

## ◎ Sights

**Macedonian Village**               MUSEUM, HOTEL
(📞 02 3077 600; www.macedonianvillage.mk; Gorno Nerezi village) FREE Across the road from ancient **Sveti Pantelejmon Monastery** (Gorno Nerezi village; admission 120MKD; ⊙10am-5pm Tue-Sun), it is something of a surprise to come face to face with this elaborate, no-money-spared reconstruction of a Macedonian village. The village – also a quirky heritage hotel with restaurants and a bar – consists of 12 houses typical of each region of Macedonia, showcasing traditional styles of architecture. Tours of the village are free and finish at a small ethnographic museum. A taxi from Skopje city centre takes about 20 minutes and should cost around 350MKD.

**Mt Vodno**                          MOUNTAIN
(gondola round-trip 100MKD) Framing Skopje to the south, Vodno's towering mass – pin-pointed by the 66m Millennium Cross – is an enduring symbol of the city. A popular (shaded) hiking trail cuts a swathe up its wooded slopes and there's also a gondola that climbs the mountainside from halfway up, where a couple of restaurants cater to day-trippers. To get here, take the 'Millennium Cross' special bus (35MKD, 12 daily) from the bus station to the gondola. A taxi to the gondola costs about 200MKD.

## ℹ️ Getting There & Away

At the time of writing, there were plans to run a bus line up to the Sveti Pantelejmon Monastery and ethno village, but it wasn't yet in operation.

## Canyon Matka (Матка)

Ah, Matka. Early Christians, ascetics and anti-Ottoman revolutionaries picked a sublime spot when they retreated into the hills here from Ottoman advances: the setting is no less than reverential.

Churches, chapels and monasteries have long been guarded by these forested mountains, though most have now been left to rack and ruin.

These days, locals and tourists alike come to walk the breadth of the canyon and dip a toe in the tempting clear waters of the dammed lake. Brace yourself: the temperature hovers at around 14°C year-round.

Canyon Matka is a popular day trip from Skopje and crowded at weekends; if you want peace and quiet, come very.

## ◎ Sights

There are also several atmospheric churches (mostly ruins) scaling the canyon cliffs but getting to them is tricky. **Sveti Spas**, close to the village of Gorna Matka, has a modern bell tower and crumbling, ancient chapel (often locked), with the ruins of **Sveta Trojca** adjoining the site; **Sveta Nedela** is the highest and most spectacularly located atop a rocky outcrop, but the scramble up there is scary indeed.

**Church of Sveti Andrej**              CHURCH
(Lake Matka; ⊙9/10am-4pm) FREE The most easily accessible of Canyon Matka's 14th-century churches and also one of the finest, the petite Church of St Andrew (1389) is practically attached to the Canyon Matka Hotel and backed by the towering massif of the canyon walls. Inside, well-preserved painted frescoes depict apostles, holy warriors and archangels. Opening hours can be a bit erratic.

**Sveta Bogorodica Monastery**   MONASTERY
(Lake Matka; ⊘8am-8pm) FREE Bogorodica is
an extremely sweet spot. Framed by mountains and blessed with some interesting architectural features, the monastery is still
home to nuns and an air of peace prevails
(cover shoulders and knees when visiting).
The wooden-balustraded living quarters date
to the 18th century and the frescoed chapel to the 14th century, though a church has
stood on this spot since the 6th century. Bogorodica is clearly signposted from the road
that leads to the Canyon Matka car parks.

**Cave Vrelo**   CAVE
(Matka boat kiosk; 400MKD; ⊘9am-7pm) A team
of scuba divers from Italy and Belgium have
explored Matka's underwater caverns to a
depth of 212m and still not found the bottom,
making these caves among the deepest in Europe. Cave Vrelo is open to the public and the
chug down the canyon by boat to reach it is a
popular excursion – offering visitors a chance
to get out on the water as well as enter the
inky depths of the bat-inhabited cave. Boats
depart from Canyon Matka Hotel.

## 🏃 Activities

While it's theoretically possible to do some
hiking at Lake Matka, most of the trails are
not maintained and it's not recommended
you attempt any serious walking without a
guide (book in Skopje) or reliable GPS.

The area's easiest amble is a 5km walkway that clings precariously to one side of
the steep canyon walls, though tragically its
appeal is dampened by the volume of cigarette butts carelessly littering the path.

You can rent **kayaks** (single/double kayak
per 30 mins 150/250MKD; ⊘9am-7pm) at the
boat kiosk for a gentle paddle.

## 🛏 Sleeping & Eating

**Canyon Matka Hotel**   LODGE €€
(☑02 2052 655; www.canyonmatka.mk; Lake Matka;
d €40-50) Its premium lakefront setting by the
canyon walls makes this hotel a fine place for
a night's rest, but it's a bit more rough around
the edges than might be expected and ultimately feels like an adjunct to the excellent
restaurant below. Rooms on the 2nd floor
have characterful wooden beams but are
slightly smaller than those on the 1st floor.

## ❶ Getting There & Away

From Skopje, catch bus 60 from bul Partizanski
Odredi or from the bus/train station (return
70MKD, 40 minutes, nine daily). From the bus
and taxi (450MKD) drop-off point at Matka, it's
a scenic 10- to 15-minute walk to the main lake
area. There are also two free car parks here.

# WESTERN MACEDONIA

## Mavrovo National Park
### Маврово Национален Парк

The gorges, pine forests, karst fields and
waterfalls of Mavrovo National Park offer a
breath of fresh, rarefied air for visitors travelling between Skopje and Ohrid. Locally
the park is best known for its ski resort (the
country's biggest) near Mavrovo town, but by
international standards the skiing is fairly average. In summertime, this area is glorious.

Driving in the park is extremely scenic,
but a word of caution: car GPS doesn't work
well here and signposting is poor.

## ⊙ Sights & Activities

★**Sveti Jovan Bigorski**
**Monastery**   MONASTERY
(⊘services 5.30am, 4pm, 6pm) FREE This revered 1020 Byzantine monastery is located, fittingly, up in the gods along a track
of switchbacks off the Debar road, close to
Janče village. Legend attests an icon of Sveti
Jovan Bigorski (St John the Baptist) miraculously appeared here; since then the monastery has been rebuilt often – the icon occasionally reappearing too. The complex went
into demise during Communist rule but has
been painstakingly reconstructed and today
is as impressive as ever, with some excellent views over Mavrovo's mountains. Hang
about and the monks might approach for a
chat and offer a tea or coffee. The monastery
also offers comfy **hostel accommodation**
(☑Father Serges 070 304 316, Father Silvan 078
383 771; www.bigorski.org; Mavrovo National Park;
dm €15-20; ✲🛜); call a day ahead to book.

**Janče**   VILLAGE
The small village of Janče is one of the few
places in Mavrovo (beside the ski resort)
where it's possible to get decent accommodation (p249). It's a picturesque spot that
scales the hillside, with awesome views and
some fascinating examples of decaying rural
architecture.

Note that although Janče and Galičnik
are very close to each other as the crow flies
(6km), there is no road between the two and

to visit both involves a drive of about 1½ hours looping through the national park. A picturesque walking trail connects the two villages but some parts can be tricky to follow; if at all possible, take a GPS with you if you plan to do this walk.

### Galičnik
VILLAGE

Up a winding, tree-lined road ending in a rocky moonscape 17km southwest of Mavrovo, almost depopulated Galičnik features traditional houses along the mountainside. It's also famed for its traditional cheese making. The village is placid except for during the **Galičnik Wedding Festival** in mid-July.

### Horse Club Bistra Galičnik
HORSE RIDING

(☑ 077 648 679; www.horseriding.com.mk) Offers daily rides (as well as multiday excursions) through Mavrovo's mountain valleys, departing from the village of Galičnik and dropping by traditional villages. The shortest treks offered are two, three or four hours and involve a stop for cheese tasting.

## Sleeping & Eating

### Hotel Tutto
HOTEL €€

(☑ 042 470 999; www.tutto.com.mk; Janče; s/d/t €30/50/60; P❄❤️🅟) A foodie hotel with a broad brushstroke of a dining terrace wrapped around it, fronting a ramshackle village of crumbling 19th-century stone houses high in the hills of Mavrovo: welcome to one of Macedonia's most enterprising community projects. Service is a bit hit and miss, but the 1st-floor rooms are exceedingly comfy: ask for one at the front to appreciate the view from your balcony. Tutto's owner also rents a handful of nice apartments (one- to two-bed, €40 to €50; email for details) in two restored houses in the village and has grand ambitions to help support the community by turning the entire village into an eco-project.

## Getting There & Away

Without your own wheels, it's difficult to reach the various places of interest in the national park independently, or do any hiking.

Two buses a day run from Skopje to Mavrovo town Monday to Saturday (350MKD, 9.30am and 2.45pm).

For Sveti Jovan Bigorski Monastery, buses transiting Debar for Ohrid or Struga will be able to drop you off. The monastery is very close to the village of Janče, so you would no doubt be able to make it to the village if you can get as far as the monastery (even if it means walking between the two – it's about 5km).

# Ohrid
Охрид

POP 55,749

Sublime Ohrid is Macedonia's most seductive destination, with an atmospheric old quarter cascading down a graceful hill, crammed full of beautiful churches and topped by the bones of a medieval castle. Its cobbled streets are flanked by traditional restaurants and lakeside cafes, but it's not a complete tourist circus just yet and still has a lived-in feel.

Best of all is that you can be skipping through historic monuments one minute and lying on a deck chair with your toes in the water the next – its location right on the edge of serene Lake Ohrid is hard to beat. A holiday atmosphere prevails all summer; Ohrid's busiest time is from mid-July to mid-August, during the popular **summer festival** (☑ 046 262 304; www.ohridsummer.com.mk; Kej Maršal Tito; ☺ box office 9am-10pm Jul & Aug).

## ⊙ Sights

★ **Church of Sveti Jovan at Kaneo** CHURCH

(Kaneo; 100MKD; ☺ 9am-6pm) This stunning 13th-century church is set on a cliff over the lake, about a 15-minute walk west of Ohrid's port area, and is possibly Macedonia's most photographed structure. Peer down into the azure waters and you'll see why medieval monks found spiritual inspiration here. The small church has original frescoes behind the altar. Little bobbing boats cluster beneath the church around the cliff base, waiting to whisk passengers back to the harbour (300MKD) if you don't fancy the walk.

★ **Ohrid Boardwalk & City Beach** BEACH

Skimming the surface of the water along Ohrid's shore, snaking towards Kaneo fishing village and the town's most famous church, this over-water boardwalk propels people towards a gorgeous outcrop of rocky beaches and a handful of small restaurants and bars. On a hot day, the area is thronged by bathers, drinkers and diners. The cool waters are translucent and inviting, the cliff-backed setting is sublime and strolling this stretch of coast up to the Church of Sveti Jovan is an Ohrid must.

### Plaošnik
CHURCH

(adult/student & child 100/30MKD; ☺ 8am-7pm) Saluting the lake from Ohrid's hilltop, Plaošnik is home to the multidomed medieval Church of Sveti Kliment i Pantelejmon, the foundations of a 5th-century basilica and a garden of intricate Early Christian

# Ohrid

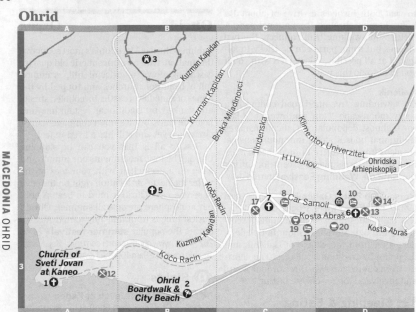

flora-and-fauna mosaics. The central church was restored in 2002; though it lacks the ancient wall frescoes of many other Macedonian churches, it is unusual in having glass floor segments revealing the original foundations and framed relics from the medieval church, which dated to the 9th century. At the time of writing, Plaošnik's once-woody environs were a building site, paving the way for the construction of a ginormous School of Theology that will also house a museum and gallery of icons.

### Sveta Bogorodica Bolnička & Sveti Nikola Bolnički CHURCH
(off Car Samoil; admission to each church 50MKD; ⊙9am-1pm) *Bolnica* means 'hospital' in Macedonian; during plagues visitors faced 40-day quarantines inside the confines of these petite churches that are thought to date to the 14th century. Sandwiched between Car Samoil and Kosta Abras in the Old Town, the churches have somewhat irregular opening hours, but are worth a look if you're passing and they are accessible. Both churches are small and low-lying, but have intricate interiors heaving under elaborate icons.

### Sveta Sofija Cathedral CHURCH
(Car Samoil; adult/student & child 100/30MKD; ⊙9am-7pm) Ohrid's grandest church, 11th-cen-

tury Sveta Sofija is supported by columns and decorated with elaborate, if very faded, Byzantine frescoes, though they are well preserved and very vivid in the apse, still. Its superb acoustics mean it's often used for concerts. To one side of the church there's a peaceful, manicured garden providing a small oasis of green in the heart of the Old Town.

### National Museum MUSEUM
(Robev Family House Museum; Car Samoil 62; adult/student & child 100/50MKD; ⊙9am-3pm Tue-Sun) Ohrid's National Museum is housed over three floors of this remarkably well-preserved Old Town house, which dates to 1863 and was once owned by the Robev family of merchants. The creaking timbered building has just been renovated; on the top two floors displays include Roman archaeological finds, a 5th-century golden mask from Ohrid and local wood carving, while the ground floor is reserved for art exhibitions. Across the road the Urania Residence, a further part of the museum, has an ethnographic display.

### Car Samoil's Fortress CASTLE
(Kuzman Kapidan; 30MKD; ⊙9am-7pm) The massive, turreted walls of Ohrid's 10th-century castle indicate the power of the medieval Bulgarian state. The ramparts offer fantastic views over the town and lake, but there's lit-

# Ohrid

◎ **Top Sights**
| | | |
|---|---|---|
| 1 | Church of Sveti Jovan at Kaneo | A3 |
| 2 | Ohrid Boardwalk & City Beach | B3 |

◎ **Sights**
| | | |
|---|---|---|
| 3 | Car Samoil's Fortress | B1 |
| 4 | National Museum | D2 |
| 5 | Plaošnik | B2 |
| 6 | Sveta Bogorodica Bolnička & Sveti Nikola Bolnički | D2 |
| 7 | Sveta Sofija Cathedral | C2 |

✈ **Activities, Courses & Tours**
| | | |
|---|---|---|
| | Free Pass Ohrid | (see 19) |

🛏 **Sleeping**
| | | |
|---|---|---|
| 8 | Jovanovic Guest House | C2 |
| 9 | Sunny Lake Hostel | E1 |
| 10 | Villa Jovan | D2 |
| 11 | Villa Lucija | C3 |

✴ **Eating**
| | | |
|---|---|---|
| 12 | Letna Bavča Kaneo | A3 |
| 13 | Pizzeria Leonardo | D2 |
| 14 | Restaurant Antiko | D2 |
| 15 | Restoran Cun | E2 |
| 16 | Tinex Supermarket | E2 |
| 17 | Via Sacra | C2 |

🍷 **Drinking & Nightlife**
| | | |
|---|---|---|
| 18 | Havana Club | F2 |
| 19 | Jazz Inn | C3 |
| 20 | Liquid | D3 |

tle else to come here for – the site itself is in a bit of a woeful state.

## 🏃 Activities

**Free Pass Ohrid** TOURS
(📞070 488 231; www.freepassohrid.mk; Kosta Abraš 74) This alternative tourism company organises stacks of cultural and adventure tours from its base in Ohrid, including winery tours to Tikveš, hiking in Galičica National Park and paragliding over Lake Ohrid.

## 🛏 Sleeping

★**Sunny Lake Hostel** HOSTEL €
(📞075 629 571; www.sunnylakehostel.mk; 11 Oktombri 15; dm €10-12, d €25 Jul–mid-Sep, dm €8-9, d €22 mid-Sep–Jun; ❄️ 🛜) This excellent hostel is a bustling hub for backpackers stopping off in Ohrid. Space is a little cramped, but nobody cares because they have such a good time here. The common areas are a highlight: a snug upstairs terrace with lake views and a garden down below for beer drinking. Facilities include laundry, free breakfast, a kitchen, lockers and bike hire (€5 per day).

★**Villa Jovan** HISTORIC HOTEL €
(📞076 236 606; vila.jovan@gmail.com; Car Samoli 44; s/d/ste €25/35/49; ❄️ 🛜) There are nine rooms within this 1856 mansion in the heart of Ohrid's Old Town, and they're charmingly rustic with old-world furnishings and wooden beams. The rooms are a little on the small side but they're bright and have more character than anything else in town. Two of the rooms have quirky sunken baths and tiny sun-trap terraces.

**City Hostel** HOSTEL €
(📞078 208 407; jedidooel@yahoo.com; bul Makedonski Prosvetiteli 22; dm/d €10/€30 incl breakfast; ❄️ 🛜) In a modern block a 10-minute walk north of Ohrid's harbour, everything at this family-run hostel feels fresh and new. The quirky interior takes inspiration from Ohrid's timbered Old Town houses – even down to the lanterns. The common area is a little dark and there's no communal outside chilling space, but the rooms are bright and all have balconies and ensuite bathrooms.

**Villa Lucija** GUESTHOUSE €
(📞046 265 608, 077 714 815; www.vilalucija.com.mk; Kosta Abraš 29; s/d/tr/apt €25/35/40/55; ❄️ 🛜) Lucija is in the thick of the Old Town with

possibly the most enviable location: right on the lake front with a patio and decking by the water's edge, complete with lounge chairs. A homely feel pervades, with a communal kitchen and lovingly decorated, breezy rooms with lake-view balconies. Rooms cost €5 less per night from mid-September to mid-June.

★ **Jovanovic Guest House**  GUESTHOUSE €€
(📞070 589 218; jovanovic.guesthouse@hotmail.com; Boro Sain 5; apt €40-65; ❉🛜📶) This property has two studio apartments, both of which sleep four, set in the heart of the Old Town. Each is well equipped and comes with a shady balcony. The apartment on the 1st floor is slightly bigger, but the top-floor apartment's balcony is more private and has one of the best views in town, right over the lake and Sveta Sofija Cathedral.

## 🍴 Eating

The best place for self-caterers to stock up is the **fruit and vegetable market** (off Goce Delčev; ☉7am-9pm Mon-Sat, to 2pm Sun, closes 2 hrs earlier Mon-Sat in winter), just north of the Činar tree, and the **supermarkets** (bul Makedonski Prosvetiteli) at the foot of Makedonski Prosvetiteli, by the harbour.

**Via Sacra**  PIZZA €
(📞075 440 211; www.viasacra.mk; Ilindenska 36; mains 160-350MKD; ☉9am-1am; 🛜📶) Pleasantly fusing the best of Italian and Macedonian fare, Via Sacra offers up crisp and tasty pizzas as well as a good selection of Macedonian national cooking and wines. Service is excellent and its location is a big draw too: facing the lovely Sveta Sofija Cathedral on a cobbled Old Town street. Breakfast is also served, a rarity in Ohrid.

★ **Letna Bavča Kaneo**  SEAFOOD €€
(📞046 250 975; Kočo Racin 43; mains 220-370MKD; ☉9am-midnight; 🛜) There are three terrace restaurants dipping their toes in the water at Kaneo and this one is marginally considered the best. A fry-up of *plasnica* (a diminutive fish commonly eaten fried in the Balkans; 190MKD), plus salad, feeds two cheaply, or try other Lake Ohrid specialities such as eel, carp or local lake fish *belvica* – the location doesn't come much better than this.

**Restoran Cun**  MACEDONIAN €€
(📞046 255 603; Kosta Abraš 4; mains 180-480MKD; 📶) There's a vaguely nautical air about this whitewashed restaurant with large lakefront windows and a breezy elevated terrace, housed in a traditional-style Ohrid Old Town building. Of all the restaurants on this prime strip, Cun is the classiest. Across the road there's a strip of streetside tables close enough to dive into the harbour; a great spot for breakfast.

**Restaurant Antiko**  MACEDONIAN €€
(Car Samoil 30; mains 200-800MKD; ☉11am-11pm; 📶) In an old Ohrid mansion in the middle of the Old Town, the famous Antiko has great traditional ambience and is a good place to try classic Macedonian dishes such as *tavče gravče* (beans cooked in spices and peppers), and top-quality Macedonian wines.

## 🍷 Drinking & Nightlife

Ohrid's main nightclub is **Havana Club** (www.cubalibreohrid.com; Partizanska 2; ☉1am-5am) FREE, just outside the Old Town.

★ **Jazz Inn**  BAR
(Kosta Abraš 74; ☉9pm-1am) This unassuming little jazz-themed bar sways to a different rhythm to the strip of bars down on Ohrid's lakefront, with an alternative vibe, a different soundtrack and grungier clientele. Tucked down a cobbled backstreet away from the touristy hubbub, the low-lit interior has a speakeasy feel, though revellers can be found spilling out onto the road by midnight on weekends and throughout summer.

**Liquid**  CAFE
(Kosta Abraš 17; ☉10am-1am; 🛜📶) Ohrid's most stylish lakefront bar is a relaxed chill-out place by day, serving coffee and drinks (no food). At night it morphs into the town's most lively bar with a beautiful crowd and

## TASTING TIKVEŠ WINES

On the cusp of eastern Macedonia, Tikveš is the country's most lauded and well-developed wine region. Although many vineyards are theoretically open for tastings, beware that in practice it's difficult to tour them independently. Signposting is extremely poor and virtually none of the wineries accept walk-ins. If you want to visit, you'll need to plan appointments to taste and tour by calling ahead (and arrange a taxi, at a cost of about €25 per car for five or so hours, to escort you around).

If you want to visit this area, your best bet is to book a night at the region's excellent winery hotel and restaurant, **Popova Kula** (☑ 043 367 400; www.popovakula.com.mk; bul Na Vinoto 1, Demir Kapija; s €35-€45, d €45-60) in Demir Kapija. Tours of the property are held four times a day for guests and non-guests, rooms have wonderful vineyard views and its restaurant offers food and wine pairing menus.

If you don't have time to stay over, it's also possible to take a tour of the region from Ohrid (a long day) with **Free Pass Ohrid** (p251).

pumping music. Its patio jutting into the lake has the best views and ambience on this strip. During the day this place is kid-friendly, too.

### ℹ Information

Ohrid no longer has an official tourist office (despite the fact that many city maps suggest it does); www.visitohrid.org is the municipal website.

Once you leave Ohrid town, ATMs are surprisingly hard to find elsewhere around the lake. There's a reliable one in the foyer of Hotel Bellevue, just south of Ohrid town.

### ℹ Getting There & Around

#### AIR

Ohrid's **St Paul the Apostle Airport** (☑ 046 252 820; www.airports.com.mk) is 10km north of the town.

There is no public transport to and from the airport. Taxis cost 500MKD one way (it's a set fare) and are easy to pick up without pre-booking.

#### BUS

Ohrid's **bus station** (cnr 7 Noemvri & Klanoec) is 1.5km northeast of the town centre. Tickets can either be bought at the station itself or from the **Galeb** (www.galeb.mk; Partizanska; ⊙ 9am-5pm) bus company ticket office just outside Ohrid Old Town. A taxi to Ohrid's bus station from the port area on the edge of the Old Town is a set fare of 150MKD. Destinations include the following:

**Skopje via Kičevo** (490MKD, three hours, seven daily)

**Skopje via Bitola** (550MKD, five hours, two daily)

**Bitola** (190MKD, 1½ hours, six daily)

**Kavadarci/Tikveš** (420MKD, 3¼ hours, one daily)

**Belgrade, Serbia** Three buses a day but only one direct, departing at midday (1790MKD, nine hours)

**Tirana, Albania** (1000MKD, four hours, one daily)

**Kotor, Montenegro** (1530MKD, 8½ hours, one daily)

It's also possible to cross into Albania by taking the bus or a taxi to Sveti Naum, from where you can cross the border and take a taxi (€5, 6km) to Pogradeci.

## Around Ohrid

The rippling, rock-crested massif of Galičica lies to the east of Ohrid, separating Lakes Ohrid and Prespa. To the south, a long, wooded coast conceals pebble beaches, churches and a **camp site** (per tent €10; ⊙ 24hr reception) at Gradište. Much of the area surrounding Lake Ohrid is protected within the 228-sq-km **Galičica National Park**, stretching down to Sveti Naum.

At 300m deep, 34km long and three million years old, Lake Ohrid is among Europe's deepest and oldest. The Macedonian portion is inscribed on the Unesco World Heritage list and is considered the most biodiverse lake of its size in the world.

### ⊙ Sights

★ **Sveti Naum Monastery**  MONASTERY
(Lake Ohrid; 100MKD, parking 50MKD; ⊙ 7am-8pm Jun-Aug, closes at sunset rest of year) Sveti Naum, 29km south of Ohrid, is an imposing sight on a bluff near the Albanian border and a popular day trip from Ohrid. Naum was a contemporary of St Kliment, and their monastery an educational centre. The iconostasis inside the church date to 1711 and the frescoes to the 19th century, and it's well worth paying the fee to enter. Sandy beaches hem the mon-

astery in on two sides and are some of the best places to swim around Lake Ohrid.

Surrounding the core of the complex is a tranquil garden looped by fountains, with roses and peacocks (mind the peacocks – they're cranky!). Boat trips to the **Springs of St Naum** (per boat 600MKD) are also worthwhile, and there's a good-value **hotel** (☑046 283 080; www.hotel-stnaum.com.mk; s/d/ste from €30/40/50; 🐾).

If you come by car, you have to pay for parking at the entrance to the monastery.

### ★ Golem Grad                                    ISLAND

(Lake Prespa) Adrift on Lake Prespa, Golem Grad was once the summer playground of Car Samoil but is now home to wild tortoises, cormorants and pelicans, and perhaps a few ghosts. A settlement endured here from the 4th century BC to the 6th century AD and during medieval times there was a monastery complex. The ruins, birdlife and otherworldly beauty make it well worth exploration. Trips can be organised through Vila Raskrsnica (p256) in the village of Brajčino or Dzani Dimovski (☑070 678 123), who owns the cafe at Dupeni Beach.

An hour or so on the island and return boat transfers from Dupeni Beach costs €65 for up to three to four people.

### Museum on Water – Bay of the Bones                MUSEUM

(☑078 909 806; adult/student & child 100/30MKD; ⊙9am-7pm Jul-Aug, to 4pm rest of year, closed Mon Oct-Apr) In prehistoric times Lake Ohrid was home to a settlement of pile dwellers who lived literally on top of the water, on a platform supported by up to 10,000 wooden piles anchored to the lake bed. The remains of the settlement were discovered at this spot and between 1997 and 2005 they were gradually excavated by an underwater team – the Museum on Water is an elaborate reconstruction of the settlement as archaeologists think it would have looked between 1200 and 600 BC.

### Vevčani                                         VILLAGE

(Lake Ohrid) Keeping one sleepy eye on Lake Ohrid from its mountain perch, Vevčani dates to the 9th century and is a quiet rural settlement beloved by locals for its traditional restaurants and **natural springs** (Vevchani, Lake Ohrid; adult/child 20/10MKD; ⊙9am-5pm). The old brick streets flaunt a distinctive 19th-century rural architecture and the village is watched over by the Church of St Nicholas. Vevčani lies 14km north of Struga, at the northerly edge of the lake. Buses from Struga run hourly (50MKD); a taxi should cost around 400MKD.

## 🛏 Sleeping

### Robinson Sunset House                         HOSTEL €

(☑075 727 252; www.ohridhotel.org; Lagadin, Lake Ohrid; dm/d/apt €12/30/45; ❄🐾👪) Sweeping lake views, free surfboards (for paddling) and a sprawling garden with lots of relaxing nooks and crannies make this ramshackle hostel a winner if you don't fancy the bustle of Ohrid itself. It sits on a hill above the village of Lagadin, a short bus ride south of Ohrid town. Rooms are spacious and charming, if a little rough around the edges.

## 🍴 Eating & Drinking

### Kutmičevica                             MACEDONIAN €€

(☑046 798 399; kutmicevica@yahoo.com; Vevčani; mains 250-900MKD; ⊙10am-11pm; 🅿) This restaurant, which reverberates with the chatter of locals, is a great find: the views from its dining room are immense, right out over the lake, and it spills onto a terrace on sunny days. The traditional wood-beamed setting

---

## ESSENTIAL FOOD & DRINK

**Ajvar** Sweet red-pepper dip; accompanies meats and cheeses.

**Lukanci** Homemade chorizo-like pork sausages, laced with paprika.

**Pita** A pie made of a coil of flaky pastry stuffed with local cheese and spinach or leek.

**Rakija** Grape-based fruit brandy.

**Šopska salata** Tomatoes, onions and cucumbers topped with grated sirenje (white cheese).

**Tavče gravče** Baked beans cooked with spices, onions and herbs and served in earthenware.

**Vranec** and **Temjanika** Macedonia's favourite red/white wine varietals.

matches the menu, where you'll see some Macedonian specialities you won't see on the menus in Ohrid, and some inventive takes on classic foods.

If you want to stay in Vevčani, this place also offers a few rooms.

**Restaurant Ostrovo**     MACEDONIAN €€
(Острово; Sveti Naum Monastery; mains 120-850MKD; ☺8am-9pm) Of all the restaurants at Sveti Naum, this one has the prettiest setting by the water. Cross the little bridge and there's a seemingly endless garden for dining as well as a unique feature: moored pontoons that you can eat on. Staff speak very little English but are friendly and helpful. Fish features heavily on the menu and breakfast here is good.

**Orevche Beach Bar**     BAR
(Orevche, Lake Ohrid; ☺10am-8pm; 🅢) A twisted cliffside path sloping steeply downwards into the unknown makes Orevche feel like a secret hideaway, and really it is because hardly anybody knows it's here. The Lake Ohrid water is clear and it would be easy to lose a few hours lounging on the rustic beach bar's day beds and swimming, particularly at sunset. It's not quite Ibiza, but it's lovely.

As well as alcohol, coffee and a short lunch menu is served, or there are toasted sandwiches outside of lunch hours.

### ❶ Getting Around

Frequent buses ply the Ohrid–Sveti Naum route (€1) in summer, stopping off at various points along the lake road, including the village of Lagadin and the Bay of Bones.

From Ohrid town harbour, boats run to Sveti Naum (€10 return) every day at 10am, returning at 4pm, and it's 1.5 hours each way; taxis take half an hour and cost €16 one way or €32 return, and for that price the driver will stop at the Bay of Bones as well.

# CENTRAL MACEDONIA

# Pelister National Park
Пелистер

Macedonia's oldest national park, created in 1948, Pelister covers 125 sq km of the country's third-highest mountain range. Eight peaks top 2000m, crowned by Mt Pelister (2601m). Two glacial lakes, known as 'Pelister's Eyes', sit at the top.

Pelister has excellent village guesthouses in its foothills and the historic town of Bitola is just 30 minutes away by car. With its fresh alpine air and good day hikes, the park is an underrated Macedonian stopover.

### ◎ Sights & Activities

**Dihovo**     VILLAGE
Propping up the base of Pelister, just 5km from Bitola, the 830m-high mountainside hamlet of Dihovo is a charming spot, surrounded by thick pine forests and rushing mountain streams. The village's proximity to the main access road into Pelister National Park makes it a popular base for walkers, and locals have shown impressive initiative in developing their traditional community into a pioneering village tourism destination.

**Brajčino**     VILLAGE
Cradled by the foothills on the western edge of Pelister, little Brajčino's lungs are fit to bursting with fresh mountain air, making it a thoroughly idyllic place to pitch up. Rushing water resounds around the village, cherry trees blossom in summer and migrating swallows stop by; traditional rural architecture adds further charm. There are five churches and a monastery hidden in the leafy environs circling this well-kept village and a two- to -three-hour, well-marked trail takes in all of them.

**Mt Pelister & Lakes**     WALKING
Pelister's signature hike is the full-day ascent to the national park's highest peak (2601m) and nearby mountain lakes – Big Lake and Small Lake – that puncture the mountain top like a pair of deep blue eyes, hence their nickname, 'Pelister's Eyes'. There are numerous starting points for the hike but none are reliably marked so it's advisable to take a guide.

Guides can be arranged for about €50 through Villa Dihovo (p256) or Vila Raskrsnica (p256) and most speak English. If your budget won't stretch to a guide at the very least take a detailed map, which can be purchased from the national park information centre for 120MKD.

**First World War Trail**     WALKING
During WWI the Macedonian Front was stationed in and around Bitola and tasked with fighting off Bulgarian and German forces. Villages in the shadow of Pelister were dragged into the turmoil and suffered greatly. This gentle trail starting at the national park's headquarters meanders uphill through Pelister's cool alpine forests, and

**WORTH A TRIP**

## BITOLA & HERACLEA LYNCESTIS

Buttressing Pelister National Park, elevated Bitola (Битола; 660m) has a sophistication inherited from its Ottoman days as the 'City of Consuls'. Macedonians wax lyrical about its elegant 18th- and 19th-century buildings, nationally important ruins and cafe culture.

The main promenade and heart of the city is pedestrianised Širok Sokak. Bitola's quaint, workaday Čaršija (Old Turkish Bazaar) is worth a look, particularly for its interesting food market in the eastern corner. Bitola's headline attraction is the **Heraclea Lyncestis** (adult/child 100MKD/20MKD; ⊙ daylight-8pm) ruins, 1km south of the city centre. It is among Macedonia's best archaeological sites – though the neglected state of the on-site museum might make you think otherwise.

The bus and train stations are adjacent on Nikola Tesla, 1km south of the centre and within walking distance of Heraclea Lyncestis. Buses serve Skopje (450MKD, 3¼ hours, hourly) and Ohrid (210MKD, 1¾ hours, four daily). There are five trains a day to Skopje (314MKD to 365MKD, 3¼ hours).

is accompanied by engaging information boards (in English) exploring this chapter in Macedonian history. The trail is easy enough to follow without a map or GPS.

### 🛏 Sleeping & Eating

⭐ **Vila Raskrsnica**  BOUTIQUE HOTEL €
(📞047 482 322; vila.raskrsnica@gmail.com; Brajčino; d €40; P☀🛜) It's worth detouring from the tourist trail between Skopje and Ohrid just to stay at this utterly lovely village hotel, which offers five rooms in a chalet-style house and lip-smacking country food. Rooms are relatively luxurious, with exposed stone walls and wooden floors, but it's the expansive mountain-backed garden, its rustic picnic tables and peeping view of Lake Prespa that make Raskrsnica so special.

⭐ **Villa Dihovo**  GUESTHOUSE €€
(📞070 544 744, 047 293 040; www.villadihovo.com; Dihovo; 🛜) A remarkable guesthouse, Villa Dihovo comprises three traditionally decorated rooms in a historic house that's home to former professional footballer Petar Cvetkovski and family. There's a big, private flowering lawn and cosy living room with open fire place for winter. The only fixed prices are for the homemade wine, beer and *rakija* (fruit brandy); all else, room price included, is your choice.

Petar himself is a mine of information, deeply involved in the Slow Food movement, and can arrange everything from food tastings to hikes to Pelister's lakes, to mountain-bike rides to an evening of wine tasting in his cellar. Ask about cooking classes (€20 per person).

### ℹ Information

**Pelister National Park Information Centre**
(📞 047 237 010; www.park-pelister.com; ⊙9am-3pm Tue-Sun) The information centre at Pelister National Park sells a detailed map of the park and its trails (120MKD) and has information on various routes and their starting points. There's also an exhibition of the park's flora and fauna inside, though unfortunately it's not free (20MKD). The centre is accessible from the Dihovo road shortly after you enter the park.

### ℹ Getting There & Away

There is one main road into Pelister, which enters from the eastern side coming from Bitola and skirts very close to the village of Dihovo. If you enter the park in your own car, you'll be stopped at a checkpoint and charged 50MKD.

Public transport does not service the park. If you're staying in one of the surrounding villages, your host will be able to organise transfers. A taxi from Bitola or Dihovo costs 360MKD one way.

## SURVIVAL GUIDE

### ℹ Directory A–Z

**MONEY**
Most tourist businesses, including lower to midrange hotels, accept cash only. ATMs are wide-

---

**SLEEPING PRICE RANGES**

The following price indicators are for a high-season double room:

**€** less than 3000MKD/€50

**€€** 3000MKD/€50 – 5000MKD/€80

**€€€** more than 5000MKD/€80

spread in major towns, but surprisingly hard to find around Lake Ohrid except in Ohrid town itself.

##  Getting There & Away

Skopje and Ohrid are well connected to other Balkan tourist hubs, as well as some international destinations further afield.

### AIR

The long-awaited arrival of budget airlines has improved Skopje's modest number of air connections, and it's now connected pretty well to major European cities. International flights to Ohrid have also increased in the past few years, particularly coming from the UK (with Wizz Air).

### LAND
#### Bus

International routes from Macedonia generally arrive and depart from Skopje or Ohrid. Pristina, Tirana, Sofia, Belgrade and Thessaloniki are the most common connections.

From Skopje it's also possible to get to Ljubljana, İstanbul and Zagreb; some Ohrid buses travel to various destinations in Montenegro.

#### Train

Macedonian Railway runs antiquated trains. They are often the cheapest mode of transport, however the network is limited and trains are less frequent than buses.

Trains connect Skopje to Pristina, Belgrade and Thessaloniki (though the last is currently via a train-and-bus combo because of the fraught relationship with Greece).

##  Getting Around

### BUS

Skopje serves most domestic destinations. Larger buses are new and air conditioned; *kombi* (minibuses) are usually not. During summer, pre-book for Ohrid. Sunday is often the busiest day for inter-city bus travel among locals, so if you plan to travel that day book ahead if you can.

### CAR & MOTORCYCLE

There are occasional police checkpoints; make sure you have the correct documentation. Call 196 for roadside assistance.

Motorway toll points are common in the north of Macedonia on roads leading from and to Skopje.

---

### COUNTRY FACTS

**Area** 25,713 sq km

**Capital** Skopje

**Currency** Macedonian denar (MKD)

**Country Code** ☑389

**Emergency** Ambulance ☑194; Fire ☑193; Police ☑192

**Language** Macedonian, Albanian

**Population** 2.02 million

**Visas** None for EU, US, Australian, Canadian or New Zealand citizens for stays of up to three months.

---

The toll is usually 40MKD to 60MKD and cheaper if you pay in denars (you can also pay in euros). The toll can be paid in cash or by credit card.

### Driver's Licence

Your national driver's licence is fine, though an International Driving Permit is best.

### Hire

Economy cars (small) average €25 a day, including basic insurance, but you can negotiate down to €20 to €21 a day if you're renting for one to two weeks. Bring your passport, driver's licence and credit card; some agencies will even drop the car off at your hotel door (ask!).

Note that it's virtually impossible to hire a car with automatic transmission in Macedonia: manual-only here.

### Road Rules
➜ Drive on the right.

➜ Speed limits are 120km/h on motorways, 80km/h for open road and 50km/h to 60km/h in towns. Speeding fines start from 1500MKD.

➜ Seatbelt and headlight use is compulsory (yes – headlights even during the day).

➜ Cars must carry replacement bulbs, two warning triangles and a first-aid kit (usually supplied by the hire company – if you're driving your own car, this kit is available to buy at big petrol stations).

➜ From 15 November to 15 March snow tyres must be used, otherwise you can be fined, and chains should be on-board too.

➜ Police also fine for drink driving (blood alcohol limit 0.05%). Fines are payable immediately.

### TRAIN

Domestic trains are reliable but slow. From Skopje, one train line runs to Negotino and another to Bitola via Veles and Prilep. A smaller line runs Skopje–Kičevo. Ohrid does not have a train station.

---

### EATING PRICE RANGES

The following prices are for a main meal:

**€** less than 200MKD

**€€** 200MKD – 350MKD

**€€€** more than 350MKD

# Moldova

## Best Places to Eat

➡ Grill House (p262)
➡ Gok-Oguz (p261)
➡ Kumanyok (p268)
➡ Vatra Neamului (p263)
➡ Pani Pit (p263)

## Best Places to Stay

➡ Art Rustic Hotel (p261)
➡ City Park Hotel (p261)
➡ Eco-Resort Butuceni (p265)
➡ Hotel Russia (p268)
➡ Hotel Codru (p261)

## Why Go?

The world is finally waking up to the charms of this little nation wedged between Romania and Ukraine. Famously dubbed the world's least happy place in a bestselling book almost a decade ago, Moldova is increasingly known more for its unspoiled countryside and superb wine tours.

As one of Europe's least visited countries, Moldova retains a certain off-the-beaten-track charm. But even that's changing as budget flights from London and other European cities make the lively capital, Chişinău, a popular weekend break. Meanwhile, those looking to plant the flag in a land few others have visited still have their Shangri-La in the form of the breakaway republic of Transdniestr, where the Soviet Union still reigns supreme.

As for Moldova's 'unhappy' reputation? Well it's shed that, too, thank you very much. According to the most recent UN survey on the subject, Moldova is now the world's 55th *happiest* country.

## When to Go
### Chişinău

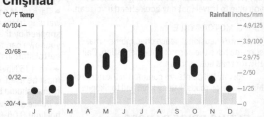

**Jun** Parks and restaurant terraces fill with students, and the weather is warm.

**Jul** High season hits its peak with hiking, wine tours and camping in full operation.

**Oct** The wine festival takes place during the first weekend of October in Chişinău.

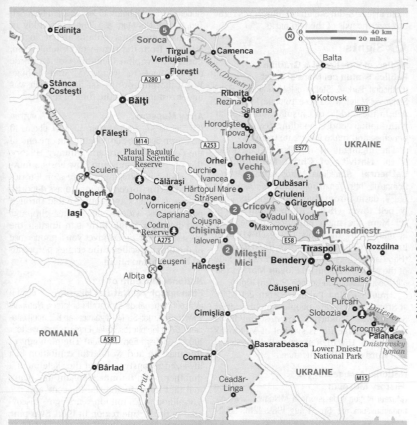

## Moldova Highlights

**1** **Chişinău** (p259)
Strolling the tree-lined streets and parks of Moldova's friendly capital.

**2** **Wineries** (p265)
Designating a driver for tours of Cricova, one of

several world-famous wine cellars outside Chişinău.

**3** **Orheiul Vechi** (p260)
Exploring this historic cave monastery, burrowed by 13th-century monks.

**4** **Transdniestr** (p266)
Leaving Europe behind in this surreal, living homage to the Soviet Union.

**5** **Soroca** (p266) Ogling gypsy-king mansions in Moldova's Roma capital, and visiting its medieval fortress.

# CHIŞINĂU

🎵 22 / POP 750,000

The capital Chişinău is by far Moldova's largest and liveliest city and its main transport hub. While the city's origins date back six centuries to 1420, much of Chişinău was levelled in WWII and a tragic earthquake that struck in 1940. The city was rebuilt in Soviet style from the 1950s onwards, and is dominated by utilitarian (and frankly not very attractive) buildings.

That said, Chişinău does have a few architectural gems remaining, and is surprisingly green and peaceful. It's a pleasant city to wander about and discover as you go – with frequent cafe breaks and all-you-can-carry wine-shopping sprees.

Most visitors confine their stay to the centre, defined by two large, diagonally opposed parks. The best museums, hotels, restaurants and cafes are no more than a leisurely 10- or 15-minute walk away. The impressive main artery, B-dul Ştefan cel Mare, cuts right through the axis of the two parks.

## ⊙ Sights

### ★ Parcul Catedralei & Grădina Publică Ştefan cel Mare şi Sfînt PARK

(Cathedral Park & Ştefan cel Mare Park; B-dul Ştefan cel Mare; 🚶) These two parks, smack dab in the middle of Chişinău, are popular with families and canoodling teenagers on benches, and make for great strolling.

The highlight of the Parcul Catedralei is the **Nativity of Christ Metropolitan Cathedral** (Catedrala Mitropolitană Naşterea Domnului; http://en.mitropolia.md; ⊙ 9am-8pm) **FREE**, dating from the 1830s, and its lovely bell tower (1836). Along B-dul Ştefan cel Mare the main entrance to the park is marked by the Holy Gates (1841), also known as Chişinău's own **Arc de Triomphe** (Holy Gates) **FREE**. On the northwestern side of the park is a colourful **Flower Market** (Str Mitropolit G Bănulescu-Bodoni; ⊙ 10am-10pm).

Parcul Grădina Publică Ştefan cel Mare şi Sfînt is a first-rate people-watching area. Ştefan was Moldavia's greatest medieval prince and ubiquitous symbol of Moldova's brave past. His 1928 **statue** (B-dul Ştefan cel Mare) lords over the entrance.

### National Archaeology & History Museum MUSEUM

(Muzeul Naţional de Istorie a Moldovei; www.nationalmuseum.md; Str 31 Aug 1989, 121a; adult/

---

### ITINERARIES

#### Three Days

Use the capital **Chişinău** (p259) as your base for a long-weekend getaway. Make day trips out to the stunning cave monastery at **Orheiul Vechi** (Butuceni) and, if you don't mind a bit of driving, the intriguing Roma capital **Soroca** (p266). On day three take a day trip to one of the big-name **vineyards** (p265) around Chişinău for a tour and tasting.

#### One Week

Spend a night or two in surreal **Transdniestr** (p266), a bastion of Russianness on the fringes of Europe-leaning Moldova. Take an overnight trip to **Soroca** (p266) to see the impressive fortress on the lazy Dniestr River. Lastly, reserve two or three days to explore Moldova's great outdoors (p267).

---

student 10/5 lei, photos 15 lei; ⊙ 10am-6pm Sat-Thu, to 5pm Nov-Mar; 🐾) The grandaddy of Chişinău's museums contains archaeological artefacts from the region of Orheiul Vechi, north of the capital, including Golden Horde coins; Soviet-era weaponry; and a huge WWII diorama on the 1st floor (which was under restoration at the time of research).

### Army Museum MUSEUM

(Str Tighina 47; adult/student 10/3 lei, photos 10 lei; ⊙ 9am-5pm Tue-Sun) Occupying one end of the Centre of Culture and Military History, this once-musty museum now hosts a moving exhibit on Soviet-era repression. Stories of Red Terror, forced famines, mass deportations and gulag slave labor are told through photographs, videos, newspaper clippings and dioramas. While little is in English, the museum nevertheless gives you a good sense of the horrific scale of the crimes perpetrated by Lenin and Stalin.

### National Museum of Ethnography & Natural History MUSEUM

(Muzeul Naţional de Etnografie şi Istorie Naturală; www.muzeu.md; Str M Kogălniceanu 82; adult/student 15/10 lei, photos 10 lei, English-language tour 100 lei; ⊙ 10am-6pm Tue-Sun) The highlight of this massive and wonderful exhibition is a life-sized reconstruction of the skeleton of a dinothere – an 8-tonne elephant-like mammal that lived during the Pliocene epoch – 5.3 million to 1.8 million years ago – discovered in the Rezine region in 1966. Sweeping dioramas depict national customs and dress, while other exhibits cover geology, botany and zoology (including bizarre deformed animals in jars). Allow at least an hour to see all the displays. English-language tours need to be arranged in advance.

### Pushkin Museum MUSEUM

(✏ 022 924 138; Str Anton Pann 19; adult/student 10/5 lei, per photo 10 lei, excursion 100 lei; ⊙ 10am-4pm Tue-Sun) This is where Russia's national poet Alexander Pushkin (1799–1837) spent three years exiled between 1820 and 1823. You can view his tiny cottage, filled with original furnishings and personal items, including a portrait of his beloved Byron on his writing desk. There's also a three-room literary museum in the building facing the cottage, which documents Pushkin's dramatic life.

## ⌖ Tours

Chişinău has several highly competent travel agencies that specialise in day or multi-day trips out of the capital. All do the standard wine and monastery tours in addition to more specialised offerings. **Tatra-Bis** (☑ 022 844 304; www.tatrabis.md; Str Alexandru Bernardazzi 59; ⏱ 9am-7pm Mon-Fri) and **Amadeus Travel** (Lufthansa City Center; ☑ 022 221 644; www.amadeus.md; Str Puşkin 24; ⏱ 9am-7pm Mon-Fri) are two of the better ones. **Valery Bradu** (☑ 079 462 986, 022 227 850; valbradu@yahoo.com) is a recommended English-speaking driver for excursions outside Chişinău.

## 🛏 Sleeping

Rates on business hotels tend to go down at the weekends, so be sure to inquire. Renting an apartment is always an option - check out **Adresa** (☑ 022 544 392; www.adresa.md; B-dul Negruzzi 1; 1-bedroom apt €35-70), **Marisha.net** (☑ 022 488 258, 069 155 753; www.marisha.net; apt 500-600 lei) or **Natalia Raiscaia** (☑ 079 578 217; www.domasha.net; per person €8-15). The latter offers homestays.

**Tapok Hostel**      HOSTEL €
(☑ 068 408 626; www.tapokhostel.com; Str Armenească 27a; dm €8-10, d €20; P ⊖ 🛜) This friendly, modern youth hostel offers accommodation in four-, six- and eight-bed dorms in a quiet location near the centre and handy to the city's best bars and restaurants. The kitchen is tiny but the tall dark-wood bunks with individual plugs and lights are a bonus.

**★ Art Rustic Hotel**      HOTEL €€
(☑ 022 232 593; www.art-rustic.md; Str Alexandru Hajdeu 79/1; s/d incl breakfast from €35/45; P ⊖ ❄ 🛜) This small boutique hotel, a 10- to 15-minute walk from the centre, offers excellent value. The 13 rooms are individually and imaginatively furnished (some feature antiques). Rooms come in two classes: 'standart' and cheaper 'econom', with the former being much bigger, and the latter boasting balconies. And a dalmatian greets you at the entrance. Note there's no lift.

**★ City Park Hotel**      HOTEL €€
(☑ 022 249 249; www.citipark.md; Str E Doga 2; s/d incl breakfast €70/80; P ⊖ 🛜) This fashionable hotel on the main walking street in town is very popular, so book ahead if you want to enjoy its bold, bright rooms, crisp English-speaking service and excellent breakfast in its street-side beer restaurant. Phone or walk-in bookings net a substantial discount, just make sure you ask for it.

---

**WORTH A TRIP**

## GAGAUZIA

The autonomous region of Gagauzia (Gagauz Yeri) lies 100km due south of Chişinău but is a world apart from the cosmopolitan capital. This Turkic-influenced Christian ethnic minority forfeited full independence for autonomy in the early '90s, thus making it subordinate to Moldova constitutionally and for defence. But politically the Gagauz generally look toward Russia for patronage.

**Comrat**, the capital, is little more than an intriguing cultural and provincial oddity, but makes an easy day trip from Chişinău, with hourly *marshrutky* departures from the South Bus Station (45 lei, two hours). The Chişinău-based owner of Tiraspol Hostel (p268) runs excellent tours to Gagauzia that cover both Comrat and smaller villages, with plenty of Gagauzian food and wine consumed along the way.

**MOLDOVA** CHIŞINĂU

**Hotel Codru**      HOTEL €€
(☑ 022 208 104; www.codru.md; Str 31 August 1989, 127; s/d incl breakfast from €70/79; P ⊖ ❄ @ 🛜) Go through the cavernous lobby and ascend the tiny lift to find no-nonsense, business-standard rooms that become downright plush when you reach 'luxury' classification. The location, across the street from the park and near the main entertainment and dining strip, is just about perfect.

## 🍴 Eating

Chişinău has a surprising number of good restaurants. Most are clustered in the centre in the shady neighbourhood along Str Bucureşti and Str 31 August 1989. Pedestrianised Str E Doga is another cafe and restaurant row.

**★ Gok-Oguz**      GAGAUZIAN €
(☑ 022 468 852; Str Calea Orheiului 19a; mains 75-125 lei; ⏱ 10am-11pm) It's well worth the short taxi ride north of the centre to Chişinău's only Gagauzian restaurant. Gagauzian food has Turkic, Romanian and Russian influences, and the offerings here include *carne de miel po Gheorhievski* (baked mutton with rice and vegetables), lamb *cavurma* (a spicy stew) and *ghiozlemea* (gözleme – or Turkic pastries) with ewes' milk cheese.

# Central Chişinău

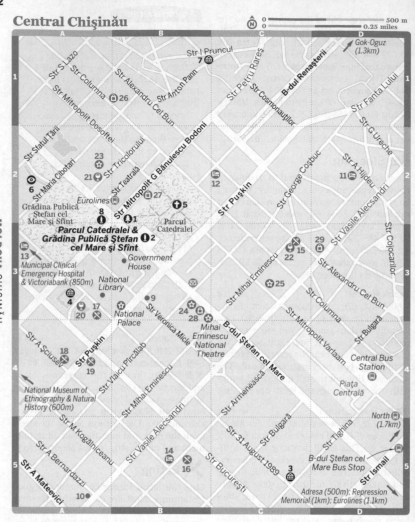

MOLDOVA CHIŞINĂU

★**Coffee Molka** CAFE €

(Str Alexandru cel Bun; ⏰8am-10pm; 🛜) The charismatic owner's love of coffee is on display everywhere at Coffee Molka, from Turkish coffee faithfully prepared according to an ancient style, to shelves of antique coffee grinders that make up part of the on-site coffee 'museum' and library. Vintage furniture and groovy lighting only add to the ambience. Light bites available.

**Propaganda Cafe** INTERNATIONAL €

(📞060 096 666; Str Alexei Şciusev 70; mains 85-150 lei; ⏰11am-1am; 🌐🛜🍴) This highly recommended, popular student-oriented cafe serves very good mains built around chicken, pork and beef, as well as inventive salads and desserts – all at very reasonable prices. The playfully antique interior, done up like a 19th-century dollhouse, is worth the trip alone.

★**Grill House** INTERNATIONAL €€

(📞022-224 509; Str Armeneasca 24/2; mains 100-250 lei; ⏰11am-midnight; 🌐🛜) It may not look like much from the street, but inside this sleek place you'll find the best steaks in town served up by attentive staff from the glassed-in, fire-oven kitchen. Creative pasta dishes

# Central Chişinău

MOLDOVA CHIŞINĂU

complement the array of hearty meat, seafood and fish, and there's a great wine list to boot. Go down the atmospheric alley off the street.

**Vatra Neamului** MOLDOVAN €€
(☑022 226 839; www.vatraneamului.md; Str Puşkin 20b; mains 115-230 lei; ⊙11am-11pm; ⊜🖥) This superb place boasts charming old-world decor, unfailingly genial staff and – by night – a duet strumming traditional Moldovan instruments. A long menu of imaginatively dressed-up meats – think stewed pork with *mămăligă* (boiled corn meal), baked rabbit and salmon in pastry, not to mention *varenyky* (Ukrainian dumplings) and *plăcintă* (stuffed pastries) – may prompt repeat visits.

**Pani Pit** MOLDOVAN €€
(☑022 240 127; Str 31 August 1989, 115; mains 100-300 lei; ⊙11am-11pm; 🖥) In the heart of Chişinău's main drinking and dining area is this charming courtyard restaurant with cushioned cast-iron chairs, vines and a small waterfall. It features peasant-uniformed staff serving Moldovan dishes with a modern twist, such as pork and apples in teriyaki sauce, beef tartare and trout fried in almonds.

## 🍷 Drinking & Nightlife

**Teatru Spălătorie** CLUB
(Str Mihai Eminescu 72; ⊙9pm-late Thu-Sat) This chic, grey-slate basement joint is the night-

club of choice for the young creative set, who gather to listen to great DJs and occasional live music. Usually closes for most of the summer.

**Mojito** BAR
(Str Tricolorului; ⊙24hr) Love it or hate it, you have to acknowledge there's a reason for its unbridled popularity. That patio was put there by the gods, broad and beckoning with warm blankets when it gets chilly, and the cocktails are almost grotesquely large. Tack on an absurdly good location flanking the opera house? No wonder it draws the cool crowd.

**Military Pub** CLUB
(Str 31 August 1989, 68; 100 lei; ⊙10pm-6am Fri & Sat) This is the most happening spot in town, conveniently located in the middle of the bar-packed alley off Str 31 Aug 1989. It gets packed early and stays that way until the wee hours, drawing all kinds.

## ☆ Entertainment

**Opera & Ballet Theatre** OPERA
(www.nationalopera.md; B-dul Ştefan cel Mare 152; ⊙box office 10am-6pm) Home to the esteemed national opera and ballet company, which puts on productions from September to June.

**Organ Hall** CLASSICAL MUSIC
(Sala cu Orgă; www.organhall.md; B-dul Ştefan cel Mare 81; ⊙box office 11am-6pm, performances

6pm) Classical concerts and organ recitals are held in the neoclassical Organ Hall, one of Chişinău's fin de siècle architectural gems.

##  Shopping

The main tourist sites have souvenir shops attached, or head to **Kishinŏsky Arbat** (B-dul Ştefan cel Mare 81; ⊙9am-6.30pm), a row of souvenir vendors next to the Organ Hall. **Carpe Diem** (www.wineshop.md; Str Columna 136, 3a; ⊙11am-11pm) is the best wine shop in town, with highly knowledgeable, English-speaking owners.

## ❶ Information

**Moldinconbank** (B-dul Ştefan cel Mare 123; ⊙6am-6pm Mon-Sat, 9am-2pm Sun) All banking services, including Western Union and Moneygram.

**Municipal Clinical Emergency Hospital** (☑903; cnr Str 31 August 1989 & Str Toma Ciorba; ⊙24hr) Has emergency services, although finding English-speaking staff could be a challenge.

## ❶ Getting There & Away

### AIR

Moldova's only international airport is the modern **Chişinău International Airport** (KIV; ☑022 525 111; www.airport.md; Str Aeroportului 80/3), 13km southeast of the city centre, with regular flights to many major European capitals. There are no domestic flights.

*Marshrutka* No 165 departs every 20 minutes until 9pm between the airport and the **B-dul Ştefan cel Mare bus stop** (cnr B-dul Ştefan cel Mare & Str Ismail) in the centre (3 lei, 35 minutes). Taxis from the airport cost a fixed 100 lei.

### BUS

Buses heading south to Bucharest and east to Transdniestr and Odesa (via Tiraspol) use the **Central Bus Station** (Gara Centrala; ☑022 271 476; www.autogara.md; Str Mitropolit Varlaam). The **North Bus Station** (Autogara Nord; ☑022 411 338) serves Soroca and points north, and has international departures to Kyiv, Moscow and Odesa via Palanca (these avoid Transdniestr). The **South Bus Station** (Autogara Sud; ☑022 713 983; Şoseaua Hînceşti 143) serves Comrat and most southern destinations, and also serves Iaşi, Romania.

With offices at the **train station** (☑022 549 813; www.eurolines.md; Aleea Garii 1; ⊙9am-6pm Mon-Fri) and in the **centre** (☑022 222 827; www.eurolines.md; Str Teatrului 4/1), Eurolines has nicer buses to major cities around Europe.

### TRAIN

International trains depart from the beautiful, recently renovated **train station** (Gara Feroviară Chişinău; Aleea Gării).

From Chişinău trains serve Bucharest (from 720 lei, 14 hours, 4.45pm daily); Odesa (200 lei, five hours, 7.45am Saturday & Sunday) via Tiraspol; Moscow (from 1710 lei, 29 to 32 hours, two to three daily) via Kyiv; and St Petersburg (2100 lei, 37 hours, odd days) via Vinnytsia, Ukraine, and Zhlobin, Belarus.

## ❶ Getting Around

Buses (2 lei), trolleybuses (2 lei) and *marshrutky* (3 lei) run from 6am until about midnight. Trolleybuses 4, 5, 8 and 28 connect the train station with the centre via main drag B-dul Ştefan cel Mare. From the centre, bus 11 serves the South Bus Station while buses 24 and 38 go to the North Bus Station.

Taxis ordered by phone are dirt cheap – only 25 lei or so for trips around the centre. Call 14 222, 14 009, 14 022 or 14 700.

## BUSES FROM CHIŞINĂU

| DESTINATION | PRICE (LEI) | DURATION (HR) | DEPARTURES |
| --- | --- | --- | --- |
| **Bucharest** | 260-340 | 8-9 | hourly |
| **Comrat (marshrutky)** | 45 | 2 | hourly |
| **Iaşi** | 140 | 4 | hourly |
| **Kyiv** | 300 | 12 | several daily |
| **Moscow** | 600 | 28hr | several daily |
| **Odesa** | 150 | 5 | hourly |
| **Soroca (marshrutky)** | 75 | 2½ | every 30min |
| **Tiraspol (via Bendery; marshrutky)** | 37 | 1¾ | every 20min |

## TOURING MOLDOVA'S WINE COUNTRY

Moldova was the Rhone Valley of the Soviet Union, and two of the largest wineries in the world are within 20km of Chişinău. More intimate wine-tasting experiences are also possible, though you'll have to travel a bit further to reach these. Moldova's **wine festival** (⊘Oct) kicks off the first weekend in October in downtown Chişinău and elsewhere. A run-down of the top wineries:

**Cricova** (☑069 077 734; www.cricova.md; Str Ungureanu 1, Cricova; ⊘10am-5pm Mon-Fri) This underground wine kingdom 15km north of Chişinău is one of Europe's biggest. Some 60km of the 120km-long underground limestone tunnels – dating from the 15th century – are lined wall-to-wall with bottles. Reserve well in advance as these tours are often booked out. The basic tour with tasting costs 310 lei; it's 410 lei with snacks, and 695 lei (minimum four persons) with lunch.

**Mileştii Mici** (www.milestii-mici.md; Str Vasile Alecsandri 137; ⊘9am-7pm Mon-Fri, to 5pm Sat, to 3pm Sun) The impressive wine cellars at Mileştii Mici, 20km south of Chişinău, stretch for some 200km, holding about 1.5 million bottles – which makes this the world's largest wine collection, according to the *Guinness Book of World Records*. You must email or call ahead to book a tour, and you'll need to arrive in a private car to navigate the vast underground cave network.

**Château Vartely** (☑022 829 891; Str Eliberării 170b, Orhei (New Orhei)) This up-and-coming winery, established in 2008, offers not just very good whites and reds, but excellent food and cosy accommodation (rooms from €82) in one of 12 pretty wooden bungalows, just 50km north of Chişinău.

**Château Purcari** (☑024 230 411; www.purcari.md; Purcari) Nestled in the extreme southeast corner of Moldova, about 115km from Chişinău and 95km west of Odesa, Purcari's wines are arguably Moldova's finest. Tours here can last from one to several days, with luxurious lakeside accommodation (single/double rooms from €46/56), excellent food and an array of activities to squeeze in between tastings.

# AROUND CHIŞINĂU

Even the furthest reaches of Moldova are a reasonable day trip from Chişinău, though an overnight somewhere is a good idea to experience the tranquil rural atmosphere. Moldova Holiday (www.moldovaholiday travel) lists rural guesthouses in Trebujeni, Mileştii Mici and elsewhere.

# Orheiul Vechi

The archaeological and ecclesiastical complex at Orheiul Vechi (Old Orhei), about 50km north of Chişinău, is the country's most important historical site and a place of stark natural beauty. Occupying a remote cliff high above the Răut River, the complex is known for its **Cave Monastery** (Mănăstire în Peşteră; Orheiul Vechi; voluntary donation; ⊘8am-6pm) **FREE**, but also includes baths, fortifications and ruins dating back as much as 2000 years.

The complex is in the village of Butuceni, where a small bridge over the Răut takes you to the trailhead for a 15-minute hike up to the Cave Monastery, dug by Orthodox monks in the 13th century. Dress appropriately at the monastery: long skirts or pants for women, long shorts or trousers for men, and no tank tops.

Excursions in English (150 lei) are possible via the **Orheiul Vechi Exhibition Centre** (☑079 292 125, 068 440 761; Butuceni; museum adult/student 10/5 lei; ⊘9am-5pm Tue-Sun), located just before the bridge. The exhibition centre also has a museum and some basic rooms, but you are better off staying in Butuceni proper at **Eco-Resort Butuceni** (☑079 617 870, 023 556 906; www. pensiuneabutuceni.md; Butuceni; d with/without meals 1200/1000 lei; ☂☀), a rambling complex with fantastic cottage-style rooms and a swimming pool.

From Chişinău, *marshrutky* to Butuceni depart from Str Mitropolit Varlaam directly opposite the Central Bus Station entrance (27 lei, 1¼ hours, five or six daily). Placards will say 'Butuceni', 'Trebujeni' or 'Orheiul Vechi'. The last trip back is at 4.15pm (6.20pm in the summer). A taxi round-trip shouldn't cost more than €35.

MOLDOVA ORHEIUL VECHI

# SOROCA

📞 230 / POP 37,000

The northern city of Soroca occupies a prominent position on the Dniestr River and is Moldova's unofficial 'Roma capital'. The incredibly gaudy, fantastical mansions of the Roma 'kings' that line the streets up on the hill above the centre are a sight to behold.

## 👁 Sights

### Soroca Fortress
FORTRESS

(Cetatea Soroca; 📞 069 323 734; Str Petru Rareş 1; adult/student 5/3 lei, photos 3 lei, tours in English 100 lei; ⊙9am-1pm & 2-6pm Wed-Sun) This gloriously solid behemoth on the Dniestr dates from 1499 when Moldavian Prince Ştefan cel Mare built a wooden fortress here. It was rebuilt in stone less than 50 years later and given its circular shape, with five bastions. Today those bastions contain medieval-themed exhibits, with a few English placards posted about that shed light on the history of the fortress.

### Candle of Gratitude
MONUMENT

You can get fantastic views of the Dniestr and the perfectly partitioned fields of Ukraine beyond from this curious obelisk, which was erected in 2004 to honour the 'anonymous heroes' responsible for preserving Moldova's culture over the years. It's accessible by a 660-step (not an exact count) stairway on the town's southern outskirts.

## 🛏 Sleeping & Eating

### Hotel Central
HOTEL €

(📞 0230 23 456; www.soroca-hotel.com; Str M Kogălniceanu 20; s/d from €20/30; ❋ ❋ 🛜) The best lodging in town is this small, partly renovated hotel opposite the mothballed Dacia Theatre in the centre of town. The ground level rooms are mediocre, but the situation improves dramatically upstairs, where amenities such as spruced-up bathrooms, balconies and luggage racks await.

### Andy's Pizza
PIZZA €

(Parcu Central; mains 60-100 lei; ⊙9am-11pm) The local branch of this national chain is a burst of fresh air on the bleak Soroca dining scene. Besides the eponymous pizza, you'll find burgers, salmon and a range of Russian and Moldovan favourites on the menu. You can't miss it in the very centre of town opposite the central park.

## ℹ Getting There & Away

There are *marshrutky* to Chişinău's North Bus Station every 45 minutes or so until 6pm (75 lei, 2½ hours).

# TRANSDNIESTR

POP 505,000

The self-declared republic of Transdniestr (sometimes called Transnistria), a narrow strip of land on the eastern bank of the Dniestr River, is one of the strangest places in Eastern Europe. Unrecognised by anybody else, it's a ministate with its own currency, police force, army and borders.

From the Moldovan perspective, Transdniestr is still officially part of its sovereign territory that was illegally grabbed in the early 1990s with Russian support. Officials in Transdniestr see it differently and proud-

---

## ℹ CROSSING INTO TRANSDNIESTR

Entering Transdniestr is fairly straightforward and formalities take about five minutes. You'll be given a 'migration card' that allows for a stay of up to 24 hours. You're required to keep this paper with your passport and surrender it when leaving (so don't lose it!).

It's easy to extend your stay beyond the 24-hour time frame. The better hotels and hostels do this automatically, or you and your host can handle it at the OVIR (📞 053 379 038; ul Kotovskogo 2a; ⊙9am-5pm Mon-Tue & Thu-Fri) immigration office in Tiraspol.

If you are entering Transdniestr from Ukraine and continuing on to Moldova proper, you will not obtain a Moldovan entry stamp upon exiting Transdniestr. Register instead at one of the following within three days of arriving in Moldova proper:

➡ **Center for State Information Resources 'Registru'** (Str Puşkin 42, Chişinău)

➡ **Bureau for Migration and Asylum** (B-dul Ştefan cel Mare 124, Chişinău)

➡ Any local passport office outside of Chişinău.

Be prepared to present valid proof of arrival in the form of a bus or train ticket. You may be fined or worse when leaving Moldova if you fail to comply.

ly point to the territory having won its 'independence' in a bloody civil war in 1992. A bitter truce has ensued ever since.

# Tiraspol

📞 533 / POP 136,000

The 'capital' of Transdniestr is also, officially at least, the second-largest city in Moldova. But don't expect it to be anything like the chaotic Moldovan capital: here time seems to have stood still since the end of the Soviet Union. Tiraspol (from the Greek, meaning 'town on the Nistru') will be one of the strangest places you'll ever visit.

If you get here, be sure to add neighbouring Bendery to your itinerary. Site of a wonderful old fortress on the Dniestr River, this pleasantly provincial town is an easy 20-minute drive from Tiraspol.

## ◉ Sights & Activities

Do have a stroll along the river, where a pedestrian bridge behind the **War Memorial** leads to a **public beach**, and party boats depart on one-hour **river cruises** (per person 25 roubles) in the summer. The main drag, ul 25 Oktober, has some foreboding Soviet buildings, including the **Presidential Palace** (⊘ closed to the public) and the **House of Soviets**, both fronted by Lenin statues.

**Bendery Fortress**                    FORTRESS

(Tighina Fortress; 📞 055 248 032, 077 908 728; www.bendery-fortress.com; ul Kosmodemyanskoi 10; admission 50 roubles, tours in English 75 roubles; ⊘ 9am-6pm Tue-Sun) This impressive Ottoman fortress on the outskirts of Bendery was built in the 16th century, and saw keen fighting between Turkish and Russian forces before falling to Tsarist Russia permanently in the early 19th century. Today it's Transdniestr's top tourist attraction. You can walk along the ramparts taking in the fine views of the Dniestr River, have a picnic on the grounds, and visit several museums onsite that document the fort's long and rich history.

**Noul Neamţ Monastery**          MONASTERY

(Kitskany Monastery; Kitskany Village) A stunning 70m bell tower marks this serene monastery (1861) 7km south of Tiraspol. You can climb the bell tower for a birds'-eye view of the monastery's four churches and a sweeping panorama of the countryside. You'll need to ask around for the key to be let up. To get here, cross the Dniestr via the classic Sovi-

## INTO THE WILD

Moldova has several playgrounds for lovers of the great outdoors, but to experience it you'll want to find a capable guide with the right equipment. The travel agents in Chişinău providing guided tours (p260) all offer some variety of outdoor fun. Another option is to base yourself at **Costel Hostel** (📞 069 072 674; www.costelhostel.com; Rosu Village, Cahul; s/d from €10/20; 🛜), just north of Cahul; owner Constantin knows the lower Prut River basin inside and out.

But to really get into the wild, you're best off contacting English-speaking Leonid of **Explore Moldova** (📞 069 258 006; leonidros@gmail.com) in Chişinău. Leonid has fleets of kayaks and mountain bikes, and you can combine both with hiking or rock-climbing on a multi-day excursion. Highlights include a three-day kayaking and camping expedition on the Dniestr River in the northern Soroca District; birdwatching with professional ornithologists in the Prutul de Jos (lower Prut) Natural Scientific Reserve; and biking or cross-country skiing along the Troyanov Val – a defence wall in the extreme south that dates back to Roman times.

et-era **car ferry** (car/passenger 10/1.50 roubles) near the Hotel Aist in Tiraspol, then pick up a *marshrutka* on the other side (4 roubles, 15 minutes, frequent).

**Tiraspol National History Museum**          MUSEUM

(ul 25 Oktober 46; 39 roubles; ⊘ 8.30am-5pm Mon-Fri, 9.30am-6.30pm Sat & Sun) No period of Transdniestran history is ignored at this relatively interesting museum, starting with photos of late-19th-century Tiraspol, moving to the Soviet period and the Great Patriotic War, to the war of 1992.

**Kvint Factory**                    FACTORY

(📞 053 392 025; www.kvint.biz; ul Lenina 38; ⊘ store 8am-9pm) Since 1897, Kvint has been making some of Moldova's finest brandies. Book private tasting tours in English a day in advance (US$32 to US$100 per person, depending on what you're tasting), or join one-hour standard tours of the factory (in Russian), which take place Monday to Friday at 3pm (180 roubles per person).

## ESSENTIAL FOOD & DRINK

**Brânză** Moldova's most common cheese is a slightly salty-sour sheep's milk product that often comes grated. Put it on *mămăligă*.

**Fresh produce** Moldova is essentially one big, very rewarding farmers market.

**Mămăligă** Cornmeal mush with a consistency between porridge and bread that accompanies many dishes.

**Muşchi de vacă/porc/miel** A cutlet of beef/pork/lamb.

**Piept de pui** The ubiquitous chicken breast.

**Sarma** Cabbage-wrapped minced meat or pilau rice packages, similar to Turkish dolma or Russian *goluptsy*.

## 🛏 Sleeping

Both hostels in town arrange interesting tours of the city and beyond.

**Go Tiraspol Hostel** HOSTEL €
(📞 068 188 352, 077 758 005; www.gotiraspol. wordpress.com; ul Lenina 28; dm €13) Tiraspol's newest hostel has nine beds a few floors up in a large apartment building between the train station and the centre. You'll need to call ahead to access the entrance, which is around the back.

**Tiraspol Hostel** HOSTEL €
(📞 068 571 472; www.moldovahostels.com; ul Krasnodonskaya 46/22; dm €15; 🖥🛜) This welcoming hostel occupies a homey apartment in a quiet residential area a bit outside the centre. Prices include a tour. There are just a few dorm beds and a small but well-appointed kitchen. It's hard to find, so call for a pick-up.

**Hotel Russia** HOTEL €€
(📞 053 338 000; www.hotelrussia.biz; ul Sverdlova 69; r from €50; 🅿🖥❄🛜) This large and smartly furnished hotel is definitely the mainstay for business people and anyone wanting comfort. It has a super-central location near the House of Soviets. Rooms come with flat-screen TVs, smart bathrooms and comfortable beds. Breakfast costs €10.

## 🍴 Eating & Drinking

⭐ **Kumanyok** UKRAINIAN €
(📞 053 372 034; ul Sverdlova 37; mains 50-100 roubles; ⊗9am-11pm; 🛜) This smart, super-

friendly, traditional Ukrainian place is set in a kitsch faux-countryside home, where diners are attended to by a fleet of peasant-dressed waitresses. The menu is hearty Ukrainian fare; think *varenyky, bliny, golubtsi* (stuffed cabbage rolls), fish, mutton and, above all, excellent, authentic borscht.

**Cafe Larionov** INTERNATIONAL €
(ul K Liebknechta 397; mains 25-70 roubles; ⊗8am-11pm Mon-Fri, noon-midnight Sat & Sun; 🛜) Named for Tiraspol's own avant-garde modernist painter Mikhail Larionov (1881–1964), this cafe has a menu featuring local cuisines drawing from the cultural influences (Russian, Jewish, Moldovan) common in Larionov's time, with an emphasis on soups, stews and grilled meats.

**Vintage** CLUB
(www.clubvintage.ru; ul Klary Tsetkin 14/2; free weekdays, from 100 roubles weekends; ⊗7pm-6am) The hottest club in Tiraspol, often pulling top DJs from Moscow and elsewhere. Serious fun.

## ℹ Information

You can exchange dollars, euros, Russian roubles or Moldovan lei for Transdniestran roubles at exchange kiosks and banks. Credit cards are not accepted in the republic. The Bank of the Republic of Transdniestr (www.cbpmr.net) posts daily exchange rates.

## ℹ Getting There & Around

The bus station and train station share a parking lot about 1.5km north of the centre. Trolleybus 1

## COUNTRY FACTS

**Area** 33,851 sq km

**Capital** Chişinău

**Country Code** 📞373

**Currency** Moldovan leu (plural lei)

**Emergency** Ambulance 📞903, fire 📞901, police 📞902

**Language** Moldovan

**Money** ATMs abundant in Chişinău; less common in smaller cities and towns.

**Population** 3.5 million (including Transdniestr)

**Visas** None for EU, USA, Canada, Japan, Australia and New Zealand citizens, but required for South Africa and many other countries.

takes you into the centre via ul Lenina and ul 25 Oktober (2.50 roubles).

From the bus station, *marshrutky* go to Odesa in Ukraine (60 roubles, 2½ hours to three hours, at least five daily) and Chişinău (40 roubles, 1¾ hours, every 20 minutes).

To get from Tiraspol to Bendery, hop on trolleybus 19 (3 roubles, 25 minutes) or various *marshrutky* (3.50 roubles, 20 minutes) heading west along ul 25 Oktober.

# SURVIVAL GUIDE

## Directory A–Z

### BUSINESS HOURS
**Banks** 9am to 3pm Monday to Friday
**Businesses** 8am to 7pm Monday to Friday, to 4pm Saturday
**Shops** 9am or 10am to 6pm or 7pm Monday to Saturday

### MONEY
Moldova's currency, the leu (plural lei), has been stable for several years. Use ATMs to withdraw lei, or exchange dollars, euros or pounds for lei at banks or higher-end hotels.

The only legal tender in Transdniestr is the wonderfully quirky Transdniestran rouble, not recognised anywhere outside Transdniestr.

### PUBLIC HOLIDAYS
**New Year's Day** 1 January
**Orthodox Christmas** 7 January
**International Women's Day** 8 March
**Orthodox Easter** April/May
**Victory (1945) Day** 9 May
**Independence Day** 27 August
**National Language Day** 31 August

### VISAS
The maximum stay for visa-free countries is 90 days within a six-month period. For South Africans (and some others), visa on arrival is avail-

able at Chişinău International Airport and at the following land border crossings with Romania: Sculeni/Sculeni; Leuşeni/Albiţa; Oancea/Cahul. South Africans and others who require visas also require letter of invitation, obtainable from a travel agent, hotel or individual. Visas on arrival are not available if arriving by train.

## Getting There & Away

### AIR
Moldova's only **international airport** (p264) is in Chişinău.

### LAND
#### Bus
Chişinău is well linked by bus (p264) to Romania, Russia and Ukraine. For bus journeys between Chişinău and Odesa, we advise taking the route going through the southeast Palanca border crossing, circumnavigating Transdniestr.

#### Car & Motorcyle
On arriving at the border, drivers need to show valid vehicle registration, insurance (Green Card), driving licence (US and EU licences OK) and passport. Motorists must purchase a highway sticker (vignette) to drive on Moldovan roads. Buy these at the border crossing. Rates per 7/15/30 days are €2/4/7.

#### Train
Only a handful of international trains serve Moldova, all of them terminating in Chişinău.

## Getting Around

Moldova has a comprehensive network of buses running to most towns and villages. *Marshrutky*, or fixed-route minivans (also known by their Romanian name, maxitaxis), follow the same routes as the buses and are quicker.

Car hire makes sense as Moldova's roads are in great shape these days and you can reach just about any part of the country on a day trip out of Chişinău. Car hire is readily available at Chişinău International Airport (p264).

# Montenegro

## Includes →

## Best Places to Eat

## Best Places to Stay

## Why Go?

If all the world's a stage, then Montenegro struts upon it, continuously playing out the most dramatic act. There's not an iota of the insipid to be found here; from its backdrop of majestic mountains and captivating coastline to its passionate populace and lively, living history, this is a country with charisma.

Most visitors make a beeline to Montenegro's spectacular seaside, where mountains jut sharply from crystal-clear waters, ancient walled towns cling to the rocks and cosmopolitan jetsetters mingle with traditional fisherfolk. But there's more to Montenegro than sun and sand; its native name – Crna Gora (Црна Гора) – means 'Black Mountain', and it's in the rugged highlands that the country's profound and adventurous soul reveals itself.

Smaller than the state of Connecticut and roughly two-thirds the size of Wales, miniscule Montenegro proves once and for all that good things do indeed come in small packages.

## When to Go

### Podgorica

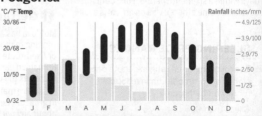

**Jun** Enjoy balmy weather without the peak season prices and crowds.

**Sep** Warm water but fewer bods to share it with; shoulder season prices.

**Oct** The leaves turn golden, making a rich backdrop for walks in the national parks.

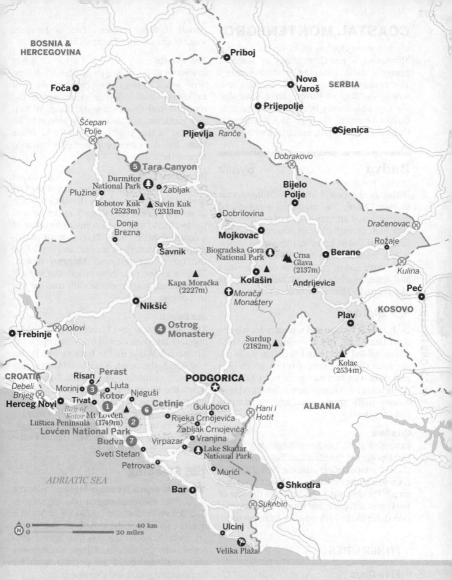

# Montenegro Highlights

**1 Kotor** (p274) Randomly roaming the atmospheric streets until you're at least a little lost.

**2 Lovćen National Park** (p277) Driving the vertiginous route from Kotor to the Njegoš Mausoleum.

**3 Perast** (p276) Admiring the baroque palaces and churches.

**4 Ostrog Monastery** (p278) Seeking out the spiritual at this impressive cliff-clinging monastery.

**5 Tara Canyon** (p279) Floating through paradise,

rafting between the plunging walls of this canyon.

**6 Cetinje** (p278) Diving into Montenegro's history, art and culture in the old royal capital.

**7 Budva** (p272) Watching the beautiful people over the rim of a coffee cup in the cobbled Old Town lanes.

# COASTAL MONTENEGRO

It's not even 300km from tip to toe, but Montenegro's coastline crams in some of Europe's most stunning seaside scenery. The commanding cliffs and dazzling waters of the **Bay of Kotor** (Boka Kotorska) are brain-blowingly beautiful; the Adriatic Coast's beautiful beaches and charismatic Old Towns are equally enrapturing.

## Budva    Будва

🎵 033 / POP 13,400

Budva is the poster child of Montenegrin tourism. Easily the country's most-visited destination, it attracts hordes of holidaymakers intent on exploring its atmospheric Stari Grad (Old Town), sunning themselves on the bonny beaches of the Budva Riviera and partying until dawn; with scores of buzzy bars and clanging clubs, it's not nicknamed 'the Montenegrin Miami' for nothing.

### ◉ Sights

Budva's best feature and star attraction is the Stari Grad (Old Town) – a mini-Dubrovnik with marbled streets and Venetian walls rising from the clear waters below. Much of it was ruined by two earthquakes in 1979 but it has since been completely rebuilt and now houses more shops, bars and restaurants than residences.

**Citadela** FORTRESS
(admission €2.50; ⏱ 9am-midnight May-Oct, to 5pm Nov-Apr) At the Stari Grad's seaward end, the old citadel offers striking views, a small museum and a library full of rare tomes and maps. It's thought to be built on the site of the Greek acropolis, but the present incarnation dates to the 19th century Austrian occu-

---

**ITINERARIES**

••••••••••••••••••••••••••••••••••••••

### Five Days

Basing yourself in **Kotor**, spend an afternoon in Perast and a whole day in Budva. Allow another day to explore **Lovćen National Park** and **Cetinje**.

### One Week

For your final two days, head north to **Durmitor National Park**, making sure to stop at **Ostrog Monastery** on the way. Spend your time hiking, rafting (in season) and canyoning.

---

pation. Its large terrace serves as the main stage of the annual Theatre City festival.

**Town Walls** FORTRESS
(admission €1.50) A walkway about a metre wide leads around the landward walls of the Stari Grad, offering views across the rooftops and down on some beautiful hidden gardens. Admission only seems to be charged in the height of summer; at other times it's either free or locked. The entrance is near the Citadela.

**Ričardova Glava** BEACH
(Richard's Head) Immediately south of the Old Town, this little beach has the ancient walls as an impressive backdrop. Wander around the headland and you'll come to a **statue** of a naked dancer, one of Budva's most-photographed landmarks. Carry on and you'll find the quiet, double-bayed **Mogren Beach**. There's a spot near here where the fearless or foolhardy leap from the cliffs into the waters below.

**Jaz Beach** BEACH
The blue waters and broad sands here look spectacular when viewed from high up on the Tivat road. While it's not built up like Budva and Bečići, the beach is still lined with loungers, sun umbrellas and beach bars; head down the Budva end of the beach for a little more seclusion. If peace and privacy is what you're after, steer clear in mid-July, when Jaz is overrun by more than 100,000 merrymakers boogeying it up at the **Sea Dance Festival** (www.seadancefestival.me).

### 🛏 Sleeping

⭐ **Montenegro Freedom Hostel** HOSTEL €
(☎ 067-523 496; montenegrofreedom@gmail.com; Cara Dušana 21; dm/tw/d €18/50/66; ❋ 🛜) In a quieter section of the Old Town, this beloved, sociable hostel has tidy little rooms scattered between three buildings. The terraces and small courtyard are popular spots for impromptu guitar-led singalongs.

**Montenegro Hostel** HOSTEL €
(☎ 069-039 751; www.montenegrohostel.com; Vuka Karadžića 12; dm €17.50, r per person from €20; ❋ 🛜) With a right-in-the-thick-of-it Old Town location (pack earplugs), this colourful little hostel provides the perfect base for hitting the bars and beaches. Each floor has its own kitchen and bathroom, and there's a communal space at the top for fraternisation.

**Sailor House** GUESTHOUSE €€
(www.sailor-house-guest-house-budva.bedspro.
com; Vuka Karadžića 25; r from €50; ❋ 🛜) Come
for the budget prices and great Old Town
location, stay for the warm hospitality. The
five cosy rooms are kept immaculate, and
there's a shared kitchen for socialising. Bike
rentals available. Online bookings only.

★**Hotel Poseidon** HOTEL €€€
(🖉033-463 134; www.poseidon-jaz.com; Jaz
Beach; d/apt per person €59/47; 🅿 ❋ 🛜) This
glorious seaside hotel has been sitting by the
sands of Jaz Beach since 1967, and while the
clean, spacious rooms don't show their age,
its excellent service certainly echoes decades
of experience. The views from every room
– many of which have kitchens – are picture-perfect, and the hotel has its own small
slice of private beach with sunbeds and umbrellas free for guests' use.

★**Avala Resort & Villas** RESORT €€€
(www.avalaresort.com; Mediteranska 2; d/villa/
ste from €225/316/360; 🅿 ❋ 🛜 ⛶) Stunning,
breathtaking, luxurious: and that's just
the views from the sea-facing rooms. This
modern resort is a decadent delight, with
a prime location right on Ričardova Glava,
and an array of simple yet elegant rooms
and sumptuous suites to choose from. The
eye-smartingly blue outdoor pool makes direct eye contact with the Old Town and Sveti
Nikola; you'd better waterproof your camera, as this is prime selfie scenery.

## ✗ Eating

★**Grill Bistro Parma** MONTENEGRIN €€
(🖉069-028 076; Mainski Put 70; mains €3-10;
⊘24hr) A good grill (roštilj) is easy to find in
meat-loving Montenegro, but if you're looking for one that's great, get your carnivorous
self to Parma post-haste. Everything from
ćevapi to chicken is barbecued to perfection
here; their punjena pljeskavica (stuffed
spicy hamburger) will inspire daydreams and
drooling for months after your meal. Portions
are massive. The restaurant is friendly and
often packed; they also do deliveries.

★**Mercur** MONTENEGRIN €€
(Katunska Trpeza; 🖉067-570 483; Budva bus station; mains €3-12) Bus stations and top nosh
are usually mutually exclusive territories, but
this marvellous restaurant is the exception
to the rule. For starters, it sits in a gorgeous
green oasis populated by peacocks, deer and
goats; there's also a playground. The menu is

Montenegrin to the core, with superb grilled
and baked (ispod sač) meats, spicy soups and
local seafood. The prices are ridiculously low.

**Jadran kod Krsta** MONTENEGRIN, SEAFOOD €€
(🖉069-030 180; www.restaurantjadran.com;
Šetalište bb; mains €6-20; ⊘7am-1am; 🛜) With
candlelit tables directly over the water, this
extremely popular, long-standing restaurant
offers all the usual seafood suspects along
with classic Montenegrin dishes from the interior. It may seem incongruous, but there's
a rip-roaring bar – the Beer & Bike Club –
out the back.

**Konoba Portun** MONTENEGRIN, SEAFOOD €€
(🖉068-412 536; Mitrov Ljubiše 5; mains €7-20;
⊘noon-midnight) Hidden within the Old Town's
tiny lanes, this atmospheric eatery has only
three outdoor tables and a handful inside; it
feels like you're eating in a long-lost relative's
home. The traditional dishes are beautifully
presented. Don't miss out on their house speciality, hobotnica ispod sača (octopus cooked
under a metal lid with hot coals on top).

**Taste of Asia** ASIAN €€
(🖉033-455 249; Popa Jola Zeca bb; mains €7-15;
⊘11am-11pm) Spicy food is virtually nonexistent in Montenegro, which makes this
attractive little eatery such a welcome surprise. The menu ambles through Southeast
Asia, with dishes from Indonesia, Malaysia,
Singapore and Vietnam, but lingers longest
in Thailand and China.

## 🍷 Drinking & Nightlife

**Greco** BAR
(Njegoševa bb; ⊘9am 2am) On summer nights,
the little square that Greco shares with its
neighbour/rival Cafe Jef is packed from wall
to wall with revellers. It's easily the busiest
spot in the Old Town.

**Top Hill** CLUB
(www.tophill.me; Topliški Put; events €10-25;
⊘11pm-5am Jul & Aug) The top cat of Montenegro's summer party scene attracts up
to 5000 revellers to its open-air club atop
Topliš Hill, offering them top-notch sound
and lighting, sea views, big-name touring
DJs and performances by local pop stars.

## ℹ Information

**Tourist Office** (🖉033-452 750; www.budva.
travel; Njegoševa 28; ⊘9am-9pm Mon-Sat,
5-9pm Sun Jun-Aug, 8am-8pm Mon-Sat Sep-
May) Small but helpful office in the Old Town.

MONTENEGRO BUDVA

## ℹ️ Getting There & Away

The **bus station** (📞 033-456 000; Popa Jola Zeca bb) has frequent services to Kotor (€3.75, 40 minutes) and Cetinje (€3.75, 40 minutes), and a daily bus to Žabljak (€16, five hours).

---

## Kotor
## Котор

📞 032 / POP 5340

Wedged between brooding mountains and a moody corner of the bay, the achingly atmospheric Kotor is perfectly at one with its setting. Hemmed in by staunch walls snaking improbably up the surrounding slopes,

the town is a Middle Ages maze of museums, churches, cafe-strewn squares and Venetian palaces and pillories. Come nightfall, Kotor's spectacularly lit-up walls glow as serenely as a halo; behind the bulwarks, the streets buzz with bars, live music – from soul to serenades – and castle-top clubbing.

## ◉ Sights & Activities

The best thing to do in Kotor is to let yourself get lost and found again in the maze of winding streets. You'll soon know every nook and cranny, but there are plenty of old churches to pop into, palaces to ogle and

## Kotor

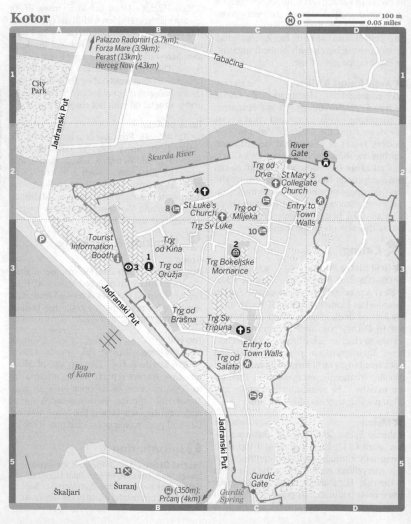

many coffees and/or vinos to be drunk in the shady squares.

### Sea Gate GATE

(Vrata od Mora) The main entrance to the town was constructed in 1555 when it was under Venetian rule (1420–1797). Look out for the winged lion of St Mark, Venice's symbol, which is displayed prominently on the walls here and in several other spots around the town. Above the gate, the date of the city's liberation from the Nazis is remembered with a communist star and a quote from Tito. An enormous (and inexplicable) bench outside the entrance makes for amusing happy snaps.

As you pass through the gate, look for the 15th-century stone relief of the Madonna and Child flanked by St Tryphon and St Bernard. Stepping through onto Trg od Oružja (Weapons Sq), you'll see a strange stone pyramid in front of the **clock tower** (1602); it was once used as a pillory to shame wayward citizens.

### Town Walls FORTRESS

(admission €3; ⊘24hr, fees apply 8am-8pm May-Sep) Kotor's fortifications started to head up St John's Hill in the 9th century and by the 14th century a protective loop was completed, which was added right up until the 19th century. The energetic can make a 1200m ascent up the fortifications via 1350 steps to a height of 260m above sea level; the views from up here are glorious. There are entry points near the North Gate and behind Trg od Salate; avoid the heat of the day and bring lots of water.

### St Tryphon's Cathedral CHURCH

(Katedrala Sv Tripuna; Trg Sv Tripuna; admission €2.50; ⊘8am-7pm) Kotor's most impressive building, this Catholic cathedral was consecrated in the 12th century but reconstructed after several earthquakes. When the entire frontage was destroyed in 1667, the baroque bell towers were added; the left one remains unfinished. The cathedral's gently hued interior is a masterpiece of Romanesque architecture with slender Corinthian columns alternating with pillars of pink stone, thrusting upwards to support a series of vaulted roofs. Its gilded silver bas-relief altar screen is considered Kotor's most valuable treasure.

### St Nicholas' Church CHURCH

(Crkva Sv Nikole; Trg Sv Luke) Breathe in the smell of incense and beeswax in this relatively unadorned Orthodox church (1909). The silence, the iconostasis with its silver bas-relief panels, the dark wood against bare grey walls, the filtered light through the dome and the simple stained glass conspire to create a mystical atmosphere.

### Maritime Museum of Montenegro MUSEUM

(Pomorski muzej Crne Gore; www.museummaritimum.com; Trg Bokeljske Mornarice; adult/child €4/1; ⊘8am-6.30pm Mon-Sat, 9am-1pm Sun Apr-Oct, 9am-5pm Mon-Sat, to noon Sun Nov-Mar) Kotor's proud history as a naval power is celebrated in three storeys of displays housed in a wonderful early 18th-century palace. An audio guide helps explain the collection of photographs, paintings, uniforms, exquisitely decorated weapons and models of ships.

### Kotor Open Tour BUS

(tickets €20; ⊘9am-5pm, departing every 30min) On sunny days during summer, these open-top, hop-on-hop-off sightseeing buses ply the busy road between Kotor, Perast and Risan, showing off the hot spots (apart from the pedestrian-free Stari Grad, of course) and providing histories and explanations via multi-language audio guides. The ticket price includes admission to the museums in Perast and Risan.

You can't pre-book a ticket; just look out for the women wearing red T-shirts near the Sea Gate, or ask at the tourism information booth.

## 🍴 Sleeping & Eating

Although the Stari Grad is a charming place to stay, you'd better pack earplugs. In summer, the bars blast music onto the streets until 1am every night, rubbish collectors clank around at 6am and the chattering starts at the cafes by 8am. Some of the best options are just out of Kotor in quieter Dobrota.

MONTENEGRO KOTOR

★**Old Town Hostel**  HOSTEL €

(📋 032-325 317; www.hostel-kotor.me; near Trg od Salata; dm €18-22, d with/without bathroom €50/30, apt €55; ❀ 🛜) If the ghosts of the Bisanti family had any concerns when their 13th-century palazzo was converted into a hostel, they must be overjoyed now. Sympathetic renovations have brought the place to life, and the ancient stone walls now echo with the cheerful chatter of happy travellers, mixing and mingling beneath the Bisanti coat of arms.

★**Palazzo Drusko**  GUESTHOUSE €€

(📋 032-325 257; www.palazzodrusko.me; near Trg od Mlijeka; s/d from €50/88; ❀ 🛜) Loaded with character and filled with antiques, this venerable 600-year-old palazzo is a memorable place to stay, right in the heart of the Old Town. Thoughtful extras include a guest kitchen, 3D TVs and old-fashioned radios rigged to play Montenegrin music.

**Hotel Marija**  HOTEL €€

(📋 032-325 062; www.hotelmarija.me; Stari Grad; r €65-130; ❀) This charming little hotel occupies a beautiful palazzo in the centre of the Old Town. Although the decor of the rooms is a little old-fashioned, it's very comfortable, clean and has a romantic feel, despite its dated furnishings. One room has a balcony. The location is unbeatable, but be warned: the walls aren't soundproofed.

★**Hotel Hippocampus**  BOUTIQUE HOTEL €€€

(📋 068-889 862; www.hotelhippocampus.com; near Trg od Mlijeka; d €140-260; ❀ 🛜) The hippocampus is the part of the brain responsible for memories, and you'll have plenty of those after a stay at this gorgeous boutique hotel. The owner is an architect, and it shows: every inch of the place is elegant, interesting and evocative. They haven't placed style over substance, though: the beds are comfortable, the rooms are spacious and the staff attentive.

**Restoran Galerija**  MONTENEGRIN, SEAFOOD €€

(📋 068-825 956; www.restorangalerija.com; Šuranj bb; mains €7-20; ⏱11am-11.30pm) This bustling place on the waterfront excels in both meat and seafood, as well as fast and attentive service (along the coast, you'll often find these things are mutually exclusive). Try the prawns or mixed seafood in *buzara* sauce, a deceptively simple – yet spectacularly sublime – blend of olive oil, wine, garlic and mild spices.

## ℹ Information

**Tourist Information Booth** (📋 032-325 950; www.tokotor.me; outside Vrata od Mora; ⏱8am-8pm Apr-Nov, 8am-5pm Dec-Mar) Stocks free maps and brochures, and can help with contacts for private accommodation.

## ℹ Getting There & Away

The **bus station** (📋 032-325 809; ⏱ticket sales 6am-8pm) is to the south of town, just off the road leading to the Tivat tunnel. Buses head to Budva (€4, 55 minutes) at least hourly and to Žabljak (€17, 4 hours) twice daily.

A taxi to Tivat airport should cost between €7 to €10.

# Perast                               Пераст

📋 032 / POP 350

Looking like a chunk of Venice that has floated down the Adriatic and anchored itself onto the bay, Perast hums with melancholy memories of the days when it was rich and powerful. Despite having only one main street, this tiny town boasts 16 churches and 17 formerly grand palazzos. Perast's most famous landmarks aren't on land at all: two peculiarly picturesque islands with equally peculiar histories.

## ◉ Sights

**Gospa od Škrpjela**  ISLAND

(Our-Lady-of-the-Rock Island) This iconic island was artificially created (on 22 July 1452, to be precise) around a rock where an image of the Madonna was found; every year on that same day, the locals row over with stones to continue the task. The magnificent church was erected in 1630 and has sumptuous Venetian paintings, hundreds of silver votive tablets and a small museum (admission €1). The most unusual – and famous – exhibit is an embroidered icon of the Madonna and Child partly made with the hair of its maker.

Boats (€5 return) run between Perast and the island during summer.

**Sveti Djordje**  ISLAND

(St George's Island) Sveti Djordje, rising from a natural reef, is the smaller of Perast's two islands. It houses a Benedictine monastery shaded by cypresses, and a large cemetery, earning it the local nickname 'Island of the Dead'. Legend has it that the island is cursed…but it looks pretty heavenly to us.

**Perast Museum**     MUSEUM
(Muzej grada Perasta; adult/child €2/1; ⊙9am-7pm) The Bujović Palace, dating from 1694, has been lovingly preserved and converted into a museum showcasing the town's proud seafaring history. It's worth visiting for the building alone and for the wondrous photo opportunities afforded by its balcony.

## 🛏 Sleeping & Eating

**Bogišić Rooms & Apartments**     APARTMENT €
(📷067-440 062; www.bogisicroomsapartment.com; Obala Marka Martinovića bb; s €25, d without bathroom €42, apt €70; P❄🌀) This welcoming place offers great value for money. The rooms aren't massive, but they're comfortable, cute and right on the waterfront. The hosts have Montenegrin hospitality down pat; you'll want for naught here. The single room and two-bedroom apartment have kitchenettes.

**★ Palace Jelena**     BOUTIQUE HOTEL €€€
(📷032-373 549; www.palacejelena-perast.com; Obala Marka Martinovića bb; d €80-140; ❄🌀) This quaint hotel isn't suffering from delusions of grandeur; its four atmospheric rooms and lovely restaurant are actually located within a palace (the Lučić-Kolović-Matikola Palace to be precise). It's so close to the shore that you can hear waves lapping from your room. All rooms have gorgeous sea and island views; the most expensive has a balcony.

**★ Konoba Školji**     SEAFOOD, MONTENEGRIN €€
(📷069-419 745; Obala Marka Martinovića bb; mains €7-17; ⊙11am-11pm) This cute, traditional waterfront restaurant is all about the thrill of the grill; fresh seafood and falling-off-the-bone meats are barbecued to perfection in full view of salivating diners. Thankfully, they're not shy with the portion sizes; the delightful/maddening smell of the cooking and the sea air will have you ravenous by the time your meal arrives.

## ℹ Getting There & Away

Paid parking is available on either approach to town; car access into the town itself is restricted.

There's no bus station but buses to and from Kotor (€1.50, 25 minutes) stop at least every 30 minutes on the main road at the top of town

# CENTRAL MONTENEGRO

The heart of Montenegro – physically, spiritually and politically – is easily accessed as a day trip from the coast, but it's well deserving

**WORTH A TRIP**

### TIVAT

With bobbing super yachts, a posh promenade and rows of elegant edifices, visitors to Tivat could be forgiven for wondering if they're in Monaco or Montenegro. The erstwhile village's impossibly glamorous **Porto Montenegro** (www.portomontenegro.com) complex houses boutiques, bars, an excellent naval **museum** (Zbirka Pomorskog Nasljeđa; Porto Montenegro; adult/child €2/1; ⊙9am-4pm Mon-Fri, 1-5pm Sat) and a marina. It's also home to some of the country's most eclectic eateries, including the luxurious **Byblos** (📷063-222 023; www.byblos.me; Porto Montenegro; mains €8-27; ⊙7am-1am) Lebanese restaurant. Tivat, renowned as one of the sunniest spots in Boka Kotorska, is an easy day trip from Kotor (11km away).

of a longer exploration. This really is the full monty, with soaring peaks, hidden monasteries, steep river canyons and historic towns

## Lovćen National Park
Ловћен

Directly behind Kotor is Mt Lovćen (1749m), the black mountain that gave Crna Gora (Montenegro) its name; *crna/negro* means 'black', and *gora/monte* means 'mountain' in Montenegrin and Italian respectively. This locale occupies a special place in the hearts of all Montenegrins. For most of its history it represented the entire nation – a rocky island of Slavic resistance in an Ottoman sea. The old capital of Cetinje nestles in its foothills.

The national park's 6220 hectares are criss-crossed with well-marked hiking paths.

## ◉ Sights

**★ Njegoš Mausoleum**     MONUMENT
(Njegošev Mauzolej; admission €3; ⊙8am-6pm) Lovćen's star attraction, this magnificent mausoleum (built 1970–1974) sits at the top of its second-highest peak, Jezerski Vrh (1657m). Take the 461 steps up to the entry where two granite giantesses guard the tomb of Montenegro's greatest hero. Inside under a golden mosaic canopy, a 28-ton Petar II Petrović Njegoš rests in the wings of an eagle, carved from a single block of black granite.

**DON'T MISS**

## OSTROG MONASTERY

Clinging improbably – miraculously? – to a cliff face 900m above the Zeta valley, the gleaming white Ostrog Monastery (1665) is a strangely affecting place that attracts up to one million visitors each year.

A guesthouse near the Lower Monastery offers tidy single-sex dorm rooms (€5); in summer, sleeping mats are provided for free to pilgrims in front of the Upper Monastery. There's no public transport but numerous tour buses head here from the coast.

### Njeguši                                    VILLAGE

On the northern edge of the park, this endearing collection of stone houses is famous for being the home village of the Petrović dynasty, Montenegro's most important rulers, and for making the country's best *pršut* (smoke-dried ham) and *sir* (cheese). Roadside stalls sell both, along with honey, *rakija* (fruit brandy), hand-woven mats and souvenirs. In the nearby village of **Erakovic**, Petar II Petrović Njegoš' birth house has been turned into a small **museum** (admission €2).

### ℹ️ Information

**National Park Visitor Centre** (www.nparkovi. me; Ivanova Korita; ⊙9am-5pm) The centre has loads of information on the national park, and it also rents bikes (per hour €2) and offers accommodation in four-bed bungalows (€40).

### ℹ️ Getting There & Away

If you're driving, the park (entry €2) can be approached from either Kotor (20km) or Cetinje (7km) . Tour buses are the only buses that head into the park.

## Cetinje                           Цетиње

☑ 041 / POP 16,700

Rising from a green vale surrounded by rough grey mountains, Cetinje is an odd mix of erstwhile capital (it was the seat of Montenegro until 1946) and overgrown village, where single-storey cottages and stately mansions share the same street.

### ⊙ Sights

Cetinje's collection of four museums and two galleries is known collectively as the National Museum of Montenegro. A joint ticket (adult/child €10/5) will get you into all of them or you can buy individual tickets.

### Biljarda                                   PALACE

(Njegoš Museum, Njegošev muzej; www.mnmuseum. org; Dvorski Trg; adult/child €3/1.50; ⊙9am-5pm) This castle-like palace was the residence of Montenegro's favourite son, prince-bishop and poet Petar II Petrović Njegoš. It was built and financed by the Russians in 1838 and housed the nation's first billiard table (hence the name). The bottom floor is devoted to military costumes, photos of soldiers with outlandish moustaches and exquisitely decorated weapons. Upstairs are Njegoš' personal effects, including his bishop's cross and garments, documents, fabulous furniture and, of course, the famous billiard table.

### History Museum                            MUSEUM

(Istorijski muzej; ☑041-230 310; www.mnmuseum. org; Novice Cerovića 7; adult/child €3/1.50; ⊙9am-5pm) Housed in the imposing former parliament building (1910), this fascinating museum follows a timeline from the Stone Age to 1955. There are few English signs but the enthusiastic staff will give you an overview. Bullet holes are a theme of some of the most interesting relics: there are three in the back of the tunic that Prince Danilo was wearing when assassinated; Prince Nikola's standard from the battle of Vučji Do has 396; while, in the communist section, there's a big gaping one in the skull of a fallen comrade.

### Montenegrin Art Gallery                   GALLERY

(Crnogorska galerija umjetnosti; www.mnmuseum. org; Novice Cerovića 7; adult/child €4/2; ⊙9am-5pm) All of Montenegro's great artists are represented here, with the most famous (Milunović, Lubarda, Đurić etc) having their own separate spaces. There's a small collection of icons, the most important being the precious 9th-century Our Lady of Philermos, traditionally believed to be painted by St Luke himself. It's spectacularly presented in its own blue-lit 'chapel', but the Madonna's darkened face is only just visible behind its spectacular golden casing mounted with diamonds, rubies and sapphires.

### Cetinje Monastery                         MONASTERY

(Cetinjski Manastir; ⊙8am-6pm) It's a case of four times lucky for the Cetinje Monastery, having been repeatedly destroyed during Ottoman attacks and rebuilt. This sturdy incarnation dates from 1786, with its only exterior ornamentation being the capitals of columns recycled from the original building, founded in 1484. The chapel to the right of the courtyard holds the monastery's proudest possessions: a shard of the True Cross (the pièce de résistance of many of Europe's churches) and the mummified right hand of St John the Baptist.

## 🛏 Sleeping & Eating

### ★ La Vecchia Casa
B&B €

(☑ 067-629 660; www.lavecchiacasa.com; Vojvode Batrica 6; s/d/apt €17/28/40; P❄🛜) With its gorgeous garden, traditional hospitality and pervading sense of tranquility, this remarkably renovated period house wouldn't be out of place in a quaint mountain village. Instead, it's right in the centre of Cetinje, offering a rural-feeling retreat with all of the historical capital's attractions, shops and restaurants a short stroll away. Clean, simple rooms retain a sense of the home's history; good-sized apartments have kitchens.

### ★ Kole
MONTENEGRIN, EUROPEAN €€

(☑ 041-231 620; www.restaurantkole.me; Bul Crnogorskih Junaka 12; mains €4-15; ⊘7am-midnight) They serve omelettes and pasta at this snazzy modern eatery, but it's the local specialities that truly shine. Try the memorable Njeguški *ražanj*, smoky spit-roasted meat stuffed with *pršut* and cheese.

## ℹ Information

**Tourist Information** (☑ 041-230 250; www.cetinje.travel; Novice Cerovića bb, Njegošev Park; ⊘8am-6pm Mar-Oct, to 4pm Nov-Feb) Helpful tourist information, though be aware that they often charge for brochures that elsewhere might be free. The website could use an update, but it's a good place to start your pre-Cetinje research.

## ℹ Getting There & Away

Buses stop at the run-down Trg Golootočkih Žrtava, two blocks from the main street. There are regular services to Budva (€4, 40 minutes) and Kotor (€5, 1½ hours).

# Durmitor National Park
## Дурмитор

The impossibly rugged and dramatic Durmitor National Park (entry €3) is one of Montenegro's – and Mother Nature's – showpieces. Carved out by glaciers and underground streams, the Durmitor range has 48 limestone peaks soaring to over 2000m; the highest, **Bobotov Kuk**, hits 2523m. Scattered in between are 18 glacial lakes known as *gorske oči* (mountain eyes); the largest, **Black Lake** (Crno jezero), is a 3km walk from **Žabljak**, the park's principal gateway. Slicing through the mountains at the northern edge of the national park, the **Tara River** forms one of the world's deepest canyons (1300m; the Grand Canyon plummets a mere 200m deeper).

From December to March, Durmitor is a major ski resort, while in summer it's popular for hiking, rafting and other active pursuits.

## 🏃 Activities

Durmitor is rough, rugged and ripe for adventure, with tons of outdoor activities on offer, from canyoning to high-altitude hiking; the visitors centre can help with thrill-seeking quests. Rafting along the Tara is the country's

---

**WORTH A TRIP**

## MORE TO EXPLORE

**Herceg Novi** A bustling waterfront promenade runs below a small fortified centre, with cafes and churches set on sunny squares.

**Sveti Stefan** Gazing down on this impossibly picturesque walled island village (now an exclusive luxury resort) provides one of the biggest 'wow' moments on the entire Adriatic coast.

**Ulcinj** Minarets and a hulking walled town dominate the skyline, providing a dramatic background for the holidaymakers on the beaches.

**Podgorica** The nation's modern capital has a buzzy cafe scene, lots of green space and some excellent galleries.

**Lake Skadar National Park** The Balkans' largest lake is dotted with island monasteries and provides an important sanctuary for migrating birds.

**Prokletije National Park** The 'Accursed Mountains' offer heavenly hiking in a forgotten corner of Europe.

## ESSENTIAL FOOD & DRINK

Loosen your belt; you're in for a treat. By default, most Montenegrin food is local, fresh and organic, and hence very seasonal. The food on the coast is virtually indistinguishable from Dalmatian cuisine: lots of grilled seafood, garlic, olive oil and Italian dishes. Inland it's much more meaty and Serbian-influenced. The village of Njeguši in the Montenegrin heartland is famous for its *pršut* (prosciutto, air-dried ham) and *sir* (cheese). Anything with Njeguški in its name is going to be a true Montenegrin dish and stuffed with these goodies. Eating in Montenegro can be a trial for vegetarians and almost impossible for vegans. Pasta, pizza and salad are the best fallback options.

Here are some local favourites:

**Riblja čorba** Fish soup, a staple of the coast.

**Crni rižoto** Black risotto, coloured and flavoured with squid ink.

**Lignje na žaru** Grilled squid, sometimes stuffed (*punjene*) with cheese and smoke-dried ham.

**Jagnjetina ispod sača** Lamb cooked (often with potatoes) under a metal lid covered with hot coals.

**Rakija** Domestic brandy, made from nearly anything. The local favourite is grape-based *loza*.

**Vranac & Krstač** The most famous indigenous red and white wine varietals (respectively).

premier outdoor attraction (May to October). Most of the day tours from the coast traverse only the last 18km of the river – this is outside the national park and hence avoids hefty fees. This section also has the most rapids – but don't expect much in the way of white water.

**Summit Travel Agency** ADVENTURE
(☑ 069-016 502; www.summit.co.me; Njegoševa 12, Žabljak; half-/1-/2-day rafting trip €45/110/200) As well as rafting trips, this long-standing agency can arrange 4WD tours, mountain-bike hire and canyoning expeditions. It also has accommodation in the form of cabins (€70) and a guesthouse (from €15) in Žabljak.

## 🛏 Sleeping

### ★ Eko-Oaza
**Suza Evrope** CABINS, CAMPGROUND €
(☑ 069-444 590; ekooazatara@gmail.com; Dobrilovina; campsites per tent/person/campervan €5/1/10, cabins €50; ⊙ Apr-Oct) Consisting of four comfortable wooden cottages (each

---

**EATING PRICE RANGES**

The following price categories refer to a standard main meal. Tipping isn't expected, though it's common to round up to the nearest euro.

**€** up to €5

**€€** €5 to €8

**€€€** over €9

---

sleeping five people) and a fine stretch of lawn above the river, this magical, family-run 'eco oasis' offers a genuine experience of Montenegrin hospitality. Home-cooked meals are provided on request, and rafting trips and 4WD safaris can be arranged.

### ★ Hikers Den HOSTEL €
(☑ 067-854 433; www.hostelzabljak.com; Božidara Žugića bb, Žabljak; dm €13-15, s/d €22/35; 🛜) Split between three neighbouring houses, this laid-back and sociable place is by far the best hostel in the north. If you're keen on a rafting or canyoning trip, the charming English-speaking hosts will happily make the arrangements.

### ★ Etno Selo Šljeme CABIN €€
(☑ 063-229 294; www.etnoselosljeme.com; Smrčevo brdo bb, Žabljak; cabin €90; 🅿 🛜) With majestic mountain views and lashings of local cuisine on offer, a stay here is a wonderful way to soak up the scenic splendour of Durmitor. The five two-bedroom cabins are more swish than some of the other 'etno' offerings in the area; there's also a playground and bikes for hire. It's close to the ski centres and Žabljak town, but isolated enough to get a feel for the northern wilderness.

## 🛈 Information

**National Park Visitors Centre** (☑ 052-360 228; www.nparkovi.me; ⊙ 7am-5pm Mon-Fri, 10am-5pm Sat & Sun Jan & Jun–mid-Sep, 7am-3pm Mon-Fri mid-Sep–Dec & Feb-May) On the road to the Black Lake, this centre has a wonderful micromuseum focusing on the park's flora and fauna. Maps, books and permits are sold here; they can also organise local guides (from €60).

## ⓘ Getting There & Away

The bus station is at the southern edge of Žabljak, on the Šavnik road. Destinations include Kotor (€17, four hours, two daily) and Budva (€16, five hours, daily).

# SURVIVAL GUIDE

## ⓘ Directory A–Z

### ACCOMMODATION

Private accommodation and hotels form the bulk of the sleeping options, although there are some hostels in the more touristed areas. Campgrounds operate in summer and some of the mountainous areas have cabin accommodation in 'eco villages' or mountain huts. In the peak summer season, some places require minimum stays (three days to a week). Many establishments on the coast close during winter. An additional tourist tax (usually less than €1 per night) is added to the rate for all accommodation types.

### INTERNET RESOURCES

**Montenegrin National Tourist Organisation** (www.montenegro.travel)
**National Parks of Montenegro** (www.nparkovi.me)
**Visit Montenegro** (www.visit-montenegro.com)

## ⓘ Getting There & Away

### AIR

Montenegro has two international airports – **Tivat** (TIV; ☑ 032-670 930; www.montenegroairports.com) and **Podgorica** (TGD; ☑ 020-444 244; www.montenegroairports.com) – although many visitors use Croatia's Dubrovnik Airport, which is very near the border.

Montenegro Airlines (www.montenegroairlines.com) is the national carrier.

---

### SLEEPING PRICE RANGES

The following price indicators refer to a double room in the shoulder season (June and September). Expect to pay more in the absolute peak months (July and August).

**€** less than €45
**€€** €45 to €100
**€€€** more than €100

---

### COUNTRY FACTS

**Area** 13,812 sq km
**Capital** Podgorica
**Country Code** ☑ 382
**Currency** euro (€)
**Emergency** Ambulance ☑ 124, fire ☑ 123, police ☑ 122
**Language** Montenegrin
**Money** ATMs in larger towns.
**Population** 676,870
**Visas** None for citizens of EU, Canada, USA, Australia, New Zealand and many other countries.

### LAND
#### Bus

There's a well-developed bus network linking Montenegro with major cities in the neighbouring countries, including Dubrovnik, Sarajevo, Belgrade, Pristina and Shkodra.

#### Car & Motorcycle

Vehicles need a locally valid insurance policy (such as European Green Card vehicle insurance); otherwise, insurance must be bought at the border.

#### Train

At least two trains head between Bar and Belgrade daily (€21, 11 hours); see www.zcg-prevoz.me for details.

### SEA

**Montenegro Lines** (www.montenegrolines.com) operates car ferries between Bar to Bari, Italy, at least twice weekly from May to September.

## ⓘ Getting Around

### BUS

The bus network is extensive and reliable. Buses are usually comfortable and air-conditioned, and are rarely full.

### CAR & MOTORCYCLE

Cars drive on the right-hand side and headlights must be kept on at all times. Drivers are recommended to carry an International Driving Permit (IDP) as well as their home country's driving licence. Traffic police are everywhere, so stick to speed limits. Sadly requests for bribes do happen (especially around the Durmitor area), so don't give the police any excuse to pull you over.

Allow more time than you'd expect for the distances involved, as the terrain will slow you down.

The major international car-hire companies have a presence in various centres.

# Poland

## Best Places to Eat

➡ Warszawa Wschodnia (p288)

➡ Glonojad (p293)

➡ Kardamon (p296)

➡ Drukarnia (p303)

➡ Tawerna Mestwin (p306)

## Best Places to Stay

➡ Hotel Rialto (p287)

➡ Mundo Hostel (p292)

➡ Hotel Piast (p300)

➡ Hotel Stare Miasto (p302)

➡ Hotel Petite Fleur (p308)

## Why Go?

If they were handing out prizes for 'most eventful history', Poland would score a gold medal. The nation has spent centuries at the pointy end of history, grappling with war and invasion. Nothing, however, has succeeded in suppressing Poles' strong sense of nationhood and cultural identity. As a result, bustling centres like Warsaw and Kraków exude a sophisticated energy that's a heady mix of old and new.

Away from the cities, Poland is surprisingly diverse, from its northern beaches to a long chain of mountains on its southern border. In between, towns and cities are dotted with ruined castles, picturesque market squares and historic churches.

Although prices have steadily risen in the postcommunist era, Poland is still good value. As the Poles continue to reconcile their distinctive national identity with their location at the heart of Europe, it's a fascinating time to pay a visit.

## When to Go
### Warsaw

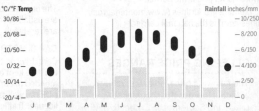

**May–Jun** Stately Kraków returns to life after a long winter.

**Jul–Aug** A brief but hot summer is good for swimming in the Baltic Sea or hiking in the mountains.

**Sep–Oct** Warm and sunny enough for an active city break to Warsaw.

## Poland Highlights

**1 Kraków** (p289)
Experiencing the beauty and history of the Old Town.

**2 Wrocław** (p299)
Enjoying the city's student-fuelled party vibe.

**3 Auschwitz-Birkenau** (p295) Remembering the victims of the Nazi German genocide.

**4 European Solidarity Centre** (p306) Reliving Poland's inspirational anticommunist struggle in Gdańsk.

**5 Zakopane** (p297)
Skiing or hiking the Tatra mountains from this alpine resort.

**6 Museum of the History of Polish Jews** (p285)
Being dazzled by the museum in Warsaw.

# WARSAW

POP 1.74 MILLION

Once you've travelled around Poland, you realise this: Warsaw is different. Rather than being centred on an old market square, the capital is spread across a broad area with diverse architecture: restored Gothic, communist concrete, modern glass and steel.

This jumble is a sign of the city's tumultuous past. Warsaw has suffered the worst history could throw at it, including virtual destruction at the end of World War II – and survived. As a result, it's a fascinating collection of neighbourhoods, landmarks and fine museums charting its culture and history.

It's not all about the past, however, as Warsaw's restaurant and entertainment scene is the best in Poland. This gritty city knows how to have fun.

# ◉ Sights

## ◉ Old Town

Warsaw's Old Town looks old but dates from the post-WWII era. It was rebuilt from the ground up after being reduced to rubble during the conflict. The reconstruction, which took place between 1949 and 1963, aimed at restoring the appearance of the city from the 17th and 18th centuries. Its centre is the rebuilt **Old Town Square** (Rynek Starego Miasta).

★**Royal Castle**                    CASTLE
(Zamek Królewski; ☑ 22 3555 338; www.zam-ek-krolewski.pl; Plac Zamkowy 4; adult/concession 30/20zł; ⊙ 10am-6pm Mon-Sat, 11am-6pm Sun) This massive brick edifice, a copy of the original blown up by the Germans in WWII, began life as a wooden stronghold of the dukes of Mazovia in the 14th century. Its heyday came in the mid-17th century, when it became one of Europe's most splendid royal residences. It then served the Russian tsars and, in 1918, after Poland regained independence, became the residence of the president. Today it is filled with period furniture and works of art.

Highlights of the castle tour include the Great Apartment and its magnificent Great Assembly Hall, which has been restored to its 18th-century decor of dazzling gilded stucco and golden columns. The enormous ceiling painting, *The Disentanglement of Chaos,* is a postwar re-creation of a work by Marcello Bacciarelli showing King Stanisław bringing order to the world. The king's face also appears in a marble medallion above the main door, flanked by the allegorical figures of Peace and Justice.

The neighbouring National Hall was conceived by the king as a national pantheon; the six huge canvases (surviving originals) depict pivotal scenes from Polish history. A door leads off the hall into the smaller Marble Room, decorated in 16th-century style with coloured marble and trompe l'oeil paintwork. The room houses 22 portraits of Polish kings, from Bolesław Chrobry to a large gilt-framed image of Stanisław August Poniatowski himself.

Further on from the National Hall is the lavishly decorated Throne Room. Connected by a short corridor is the King's Apartment, the highlight of which is the Canaletto Room at the far end. An impressive array of 23 paintings by Bernardo Bellotto (1721–80), better known in Poland as Canaletto, captures Warsaw's mid-18th-century heyday in great detail. The works were of immense help in reconstructing the city's historic facades.

**Barbican**                    FORTRESS
(Barbakan; ul Nowomiejska) Heading north out of the Old Town along ul Nowomiejska you'll soon see the redbrick Barbican, a semicircular defensive tower topped with a decorative Renaissance parapet. It was partially dismantled in the 19th century, but reconstructed after WWII, and is now a popular spot for buskers and art sellers.

## ◉ Royal Way

This 4km historic route connects the Old Town with the modern city centre, running south from about Plac Zamkowy along elegant ul Krakowskie Przedmieście and ul Nowy Świat all the way to busy Al Jerozolimskie.

**Church of the Holy Cross**                    CHURCH
(Kościół św Krzyża; ☑ 22 826 8910; ul Krakowskie Przedmieście 3; ⊙ 10am-4pm) FREE Of Warsaw's many impressive churches, this is the one most visitors want to visit. Not so much to admire the fine Baroque altarpieces that miraculously survived the Warsaw

---

## ITINERARIES

### One Week

Spend a day exploring **Warsaw**, with a stroll around the Old Town and a stop at the Museum of the History of Polish Jews. Next day, head to historic **Kraków** for three days, visiting the beautiful Old Town, Wawel Castle and former Jewish district of Kazimierz. Take a day trip to **Auschwitz-Birkenau**, the former Nazi German extermination camp. Afterward, head to **Zakopane** for a day in the mountains.

### Two Weeks

Follow the above itinerary, then travel to **Wrocław** for two days, taking in its graceful town square. Head north to Gothic **Toruń** for a day, then onward to **Gdańsk** for two days, exploring the museums and bars of the main town and visiting the magnificent castle at **Malbork**.

Rising reprisals, but to glimpse a small urn by the second pillar on the left side of the nave. This urn, adorned with an epitaph to Frédéric Chopin, contains what remains of the composer's heart. It was brought here from Paris after the great man's death.

★ **Chopin Museum** MUSEUM
(☑22 441 6251; www.chopin.museum; ul Okólnik 1; adult/concession 22/13zł, Sun free; ☺11am-8pm Tue-Sun) High-tech, multimedia museum within the Baroque Ostrogski Palace, showcasing the work of the country's most famous composer. You're encouraged to take your time through four floors of displays, including stopping by the listening booths in the basement where you can browse Chopin's oeuvre to your heart's content. Limited visitation is allowed each hour; your best bet is to book your visit in advance by phone or email.

◉ **City Centre & Beyond**

★ **Palace of Culture
& Science** HISTORIC BUILDING
(Pałac Kultury i Nauki; www.pkin.pl; Plac Defilad 1; observation terrace adult/concession 20/15zł; ☺9am-8.30pm) Love it or hate it, every visitor to Warsaw should visit the iconic, socialist realist PKiN (as its full Polish name is abbreviated). This 'gift of friendship' from the Soviet Union was built in the early 1950s, and at 231m high remains the tallest building in Poland. It's home to a huge congress hall, theatres, a multiscreen cinema and museums. Take the high-speed lift to the 30th-floor (115m) observation terrace to take it all in.

The building has never sat well with the locals, who have branded it with one uncomplimentary moniker after another; the 'Elephant in Lacy Underwear', a reference both to the building's size and the fussy sculptures that frill the parapets, is a particular favourite. However, though there are occasional calls for it to be demolished, the Palace is gradually becoming accepted (even embraced) as a city icon.

★ **Warsaw Rising Museum** MUSEUM
(Muzeum Powstania Warszawskiego; www.1944. pl; ul Grzybowska 79; adult/concession 20/16zł, Sun free; ☺8am-6pm Mon, Wed & Fri, to 8pm Thu, 10am-6pm Sat & Sun; Ⓜ Rondo Daszyńskiego, Ⓖ 9, 22 or 24 along al Jerozolimskie) One of Warsaw's best, this museum traces the history of the city's heroic but doomed uprising against the German occupation in 1944 via three levels of interactive displays, photographs,

film archives and personal accounts. The volume of material is overwhelming, but the museum does an excellent job of instilling in visitors a sense of the desperation residents felt in deciding to oppose the occupation by force, and of illustrating the dark consequences, including the Germans' destruction of the city in the aftermath.

The ground floor begins with the division of Poland between Nazi Germany and the Soviet Union in 1939 and moves through the major events of WWII. A lift then takes you to the 2nd floor and the start of the uprising in 1944. The largest exhibit, a Liberator bomber similar to the planes that were used to drop supplies for insurgents, fills much of the 1st floor.

★ **Łazienki Park** GARDENS
(Park Łazienkowski; www.lazienki-krolewskie.pl; ul Agrykola 1; ☺dawn-dusk) Pronounced wah-zhen-kee, this park is a beautiful place of manicured greens and wild patches. Its popularity extends to families, peacocks and fans of classical music, who come for the alfresco Chopin concerts on Sunday afternoons at noon and 4pm from mid-May through September. Once a hunting ground attached to Ujazdów Castle, Łazienki was acquired by King Stanisław August Poniatowski in 1764 and transformed into a splendid park complete with palace, amphitheatre, and various follies and other buildings.

◉ **Former Jewish District**

The suburbs northwest of the Palace of Culture & Science were once predominantly inhabited by Warsaw's Jewish community.

★ **Museum of the
History of Polish Jews** MUSEUM
(Polin; ☑22 471 0301; www.polin.pl; ul Anielewicza 6; adult/concession 25/15zł, incl temporary exhibits 30/20zł; ☺10am-6pm Mon, Wed-Fri & Sun, to 8pm Sat; Ⓖ4, 15, 18 or 35 along ul Marszałkowska) This exceptional museum's permanent exhibition opened in late 2014. Impressive multimedia exhibits document 1000 years of Jewish history in Poland, from accounts of the earliest Jewish traders in the region through waves of mass migration, progress and pogroms, all the way to WWII and the destruction of Europe's largest Jewish community. It's worth booking online first, and you can hire an audioguide (10zł) to get the most out of the many rooms of displays, interactive maps, photos and videos.

# Central Warsaw

Museum of the History
of Polish Jews (500m);
Hotel Maria (1.4km)

Polyester
(250m)

Świętojerska

Długa

Miodowa

**2 Old Town**
⊚ **Square**

5

Warsaw
Tourist
Office

Świętojańska

Jezuicka

8

Bugaj

Podwale

4 ⊕ **Royal**
**Castle**

Vistula

Długa

Al Solidarności

Senatorska

Kozia

Molera

Bednarska

Furmańska

Dobra

Ⓜ **Ratusz-**
**Arsenał**

Generała Andersa

Senatorska

Wierzbowa

Trębacka

Krakówskie Przedmieście

Browarna

Elektoralna

12

Saxon
Gardens

*Plac*
*Piłsudskiego*

*Plac*
*Małachowskiego*

Traugutta

6 ✝

Obożna

Sewerynów

Dynasy

Warsaw Rising
Museum
(1.4km)

Grzybowska

Marszałkowska

Królewska

Kredytowa

Jasna

Plac
Dąbrowskiego

13

15 ✪

Czackiego

Mazowiecka

Świętokrzyska

**Nowy Świat -**
Ⓜ **Uniwersytet**

Tamka

**Chopin**
**Museum**

1 🏛

Plac
Próżna
Grzybowski

Zielna

9

Świętokrzyska
Ⓜ

Warecka

Plac
Powstańców
Warszawy

Nowy Świat

Ordynacka

Kopernika

Okólnik

Twarda

Moniuszki

14 ✿
Sienkiewicza

Jasna

Szpitalna

Górskiego

11 ✕

Foksal

**Palace of**
**Culture &**
**Science**

Plac
Defilad

Marszałkowska

Złota

Zgoda

Chmielna

7

Smolna

Sienna

Emilii Plater

3 🏢

Warsaw
Tourist Office

Centrum
Ⓜ

Widok

✕ 10

Bracka

Al Jerozolimskie

Złota

Warszawa
Śródmieście
Train Station

Nowogrodzka

Książąca

Warszawa
Centralna
Train Station

Al Jerozolimskie

Żurawia

Wspólna

Plac Trzech
Krzyży

Wiejska

Warszawa Zachodnia
Terminal
(2.2km)

Emilii Plater

Wspólna

Poznańska

Marszałkowska

Hoza

Krucza

Wilcza

Mokotowska

Al Ujazdowskie

Niepodległości

Hoża

Hotel Rialto
(100m)

Charlotte Chleb i
Wino (500m)

Łazienki
Park (1km)

POLAND WARSAW

# Central Warsaw

## 👁 Praga

⭐ **Neon Museum**                                    MUSEUM
(Muzeum Neonów; 🖊 665 711635; www.neon-muzeum.org; ul Mińska 25; adult/concession 10/8zł; ⊙ 12-5pm Wed-Sun; 🚍 22 from al Jerozolimskie) Situated within the cool Soho Factory complex of old industrial buildings housing designers and artists, this museum is devoted to the preservation of the iconic neon signs of the communist era. The collection is arrayed within a historic factory, with many large pieces fully lit. Other exhibits are dotted around the complex and are illuminated after dark. It's well worth the trek across the river. Alight the tram at the Bliska stop.

## 🛏 Sleeping

**Apartments Apart** (🖊 22 351 2250; www.apartmentsapart.com; ul Nowy Świat 29/3; apt from 200zł; 🛜) offers short-term apartment rentals in the Old Town and city centre.

⭐ **Oki Doki Hostel**                                    HOSTEL €
(🖊 22 828 0122; www.okidoki.pl; Plac Dąbrowskiego 3; dm 29-90zł; s/d from 100/128zł; 🛜) Arguably Warsaw's most popular hostel, and certainly one of the best. Each of its bright, large rooms is individually named and dec-

orated. Accommodation is in three- to eight-bed dorms, with a special three-bed dorm for women only. The owners are well travelled and know the needs of backpackers, providing a kitchen and a laundry service. Breakfast available (15zł).

⭐ **Castle Inn**                                    HOTEL €€
(🖊 22 425 0100; www.castleinn.pl; ul Świętojańska 2; s/d from 280/300zł; ⊛🛜) Nicely decorated 'art hotel', housed in a 17th-century town house. All rooms overlook either Castle Sq or St John's Cathedral, and come in a range of playful styles. Our favourite would be No 121, 'Viktor', named for a reclusive street artist, complete with tasteful graffiti and a gorgeous castle view. Breakfast costs an extra 35zł.

**Hotel Maria**                                    HOTEL €€
(🖊 22 838 4062; www.hotelmaria.pl; al Jana Pawła II 71; s/d 323/384zł; 🅿⊛🛜) Rambling old house masquerading as a hotel set on three floors (no lifts, just steep wooden stairs), with friendly staff, a delightful restaurant and breakfast nook, and spacious rooms. The location is outside the centre, but convenient to the Jewish sights and just a few tram stops away from the Old Town.

Rooms at the back are slightly quieter than those at the front, along busy al Jana Pawła II. Weekend bookings slice about 100zł off the price.

⭐ **Hotel Rialto**                                    HOTEL €€
(🖊 22 584 8700; www.rialto.pl; ul Wilcza 73; s/d from 279/319zł; 🅿⊛🛜) This converted town house is a monument to early 20th-century design. Each room is individually decorated in Art Nouveau or Art Deco style, with antique and reproduction furniture, period fittings, and tiled or marbled baths. There are plenty of modern touches where it counts, such as power showers, and a sauna and steam room. Cheaper rates click into place at weekends.

## 🍴 Eating

⭐ **Charlotte Chleb i Wino**                                    FRENCH €
(www.bistrocharlotte.pl; al Wyzwolenia 18; mains 8-18zł; ⊙ 7am-midnight Mon-Thu, to 1am Fri, 9am-1am Sat, 9am-10pm Sun; 🛜) Dazzling French bakery and bistro facing Plac Zbawiciela. It dishes up tantalising croissants and pastries at the break of dawn, then transitions to big salads and crusty sandwiches through the lunch and dinner hours, and finally to wine on the terrace in the evening. Great value for money.

### ★ Mango
VEGAN €

(☑535 533 629; www.mangovegan.pl; ul Bracka 20; mains 13-25zł; ⏰11am-10pm Sun-Thu, to 10.30pm Fri & Sat; 📶🌿) Mango is a stylish all-vegan eatery with a simple contemporary interior and pleasant outdoor seating. Excellent menu items range from veggie burgers to mango sticky rice. The 'Mango Plate' (Talerz Mango) of hummus, mango, falafel, eggplant, olives, sweet peppers and harissa paste served with pita bread is top value at 22zł.

### Socjal
MEDITERRANEAN €€

(☑787 181 051; ul Foksal 18; mains 18-39zł; ⏰noon-midnight) Hypercool restaurant and bar with pared-back interiors and an open kitchen. The menu is Mediterranean-influenced, with *piadine* (stuffed Italian flatbreads), pasta, and pizzas of a more adventurous stripe (asparagus pizza, anyone?). The outdoor deck is a great people-watching space.

### ★ Warszawa Wschodnia
EUROPEAN €€€

(☑22 870 2918; www.sohofactory.pl; ul Mińska 25; mains 25-80zł; ⏰24hr; 🔊) Fabulous restaurant within a huge industrial building in the Soho Factory complex, taking its name from a neon sign salvaged from the nearby train station of the same name. Serves a modern interpretation of Polish cuisine, with French influences. Mains are priced between 60zł and 80zł, so you can't beat the 25zł three-course set lunch menu served noon to 4pm Monday to Friday.

## 🍸 Drinking & Nightlife

Good places for pub crawls include along ul Mazowiecka in the centre, in Praga across the Vistula River, and the Powiśle district near the university.

### Capitol
CLUB

(☑608 089 504; ul Marszałkowska 115; ⏰10pm-late Fri & Sat) If scarcity excites you, squeeze through the doors of this oh-so-cool club on the two nights of the week it's open – Friday and Saturday. Low lighting gleams off pillars, retro decor and the shining faces of Warsaw's beautiful people as they gyrate within the dance-floor throng.

### Polyester
BAR

(ul Freta 49/51; ⏰noon-midnight; 🔊) Smooth establishment with fashionably retro furnishings and a laid-back vibe – arguably the hippest cocktail bar in the vicinity of the Old Town. Serves excellent cocktails, as well as a range of coffee drinks and light food. Also hosts regular jazz and other live music.

### Enklawa
CLUB

(☑22 827 3151; www.enklawa.com; ul Mazowiecka 12; ⏰10pm-4am Tue-Sat) Blue and purple light illuminates this space with comfy plush seating, mirrored ceilings, two bars and plenty of room to dance. Check out the extensive drinks menu, hit the dance floor or observe the action from a stool on the upper balcony. Wednesday night is 'old school' night, with music from the '70s to the '90s.

## ☆ Entertainment

### Filharmonia Narodowa
CLASSICAL MUSIC

(National Philharmonic; ☑22 551 7127; www.filharmonia.pl; ul Jasna 5; ⏰box office 10am-2pm & 3-7pm Mon-Sat) Home of the world-famous National Philharmonic Orchestra and Choir of Poland, founded in 1901, this venue has a concert hall (enter from ul Sienkiewicza 10) and a chamber-music hall (enter from ul Moniuszki 5), both of which stage regular concerts. The box office entrance is on ul Sienkiewicza.

### Tygmont
LIVE MUSIC

(☑22 828 3409; www.tygmont.com.pl; ul Mazowiecka 6/8; ⏰9pm-late) Hosting both local and international acts, the live music here (occasionally including jazz) is both varied and plentiful. Concerts start around 10pm; it fills up early, so either reserve a table or turn up at opening time. Dinner is also available.

## ⓘ Information

**Warsaw Tourist Information** (www.warsawtour.pl) operates three helpful branches at various points around town: **Old Town** (www.warsawtour.pl; Rynek Starego Miasta 19/21; ⏰9am-8pm May-Sep, to 6pm Oct-Apr; 🔊), the **Palace of Culture & Science** (www.warsawtour.pl; Plac Defilad 1, enter from ul Emilii Plater; ⏰8am-8pm May-Sep, to 6pm Oct-Apr; 🔊) and **Warsaw-Frédéric Chopin Airport** (www.warsawtour.pl; Terminal A, Warsaw Frédéric Chopin Airport, ul Żwirki i Wigury 1; ⏰9am-7pm). They offer free city maps as well as advice on what to see and where to stay.

## ⓘ Getting There & Away

### AIR

Warsaw's main international airport, **Warsaw-Frédéric Chopin Airport** (Lotnisko Chopina Warszawa; ☑22 650 4220; www.lotnisko-chopina.pl; ul Żwirki i Wigury 1), 10km from the city centre, handles most flights in and out of the city. The terminal has ATMs, restaurants and a branch of the Warsaw Tourist Information office.

Some budget flights, including Ryanair services, use outlying **Warsaw Modlin** (☑801 80

1880; www.modlinairport.pl; ul Generała Wiktora Thommée 1a), 35km north of the city.

### BUS

Warsaw's main bus station is **Warszawa Zachodnia** (☑ 708 208 888; www.dworzeconline.pl; al Jerozolimskie 144; ⊘ information & tickets 6am-9pm), southwest of the centre and adjoining Warszawa Zachodnia train station. This sprawling terminal handles most (but not all) international and domestic routes.

Trains are usually more convenient than buses to Poland's major cities, with the exception of the comfortable coach services run by private company Polski Bus. These usually depart from the small **Wilanowska bus station** (Dworzec Autobusowy Wilanowska; ul Puławska 145) near the Wilanowska metro station. Check the bus company's website (www.polskibus.com) for further information and give yourself plenty of time to find the bus station. Fares vary by date and demand, so buy your tickets online.

### TRAIN

Warsaw has several train stations and is connected directly to a number of international destinations. The station most travellers use is **Warszawa Centralna** (Warsaw Central; www.pkp.pl; al Jerozolimskie 54; ⊘ 24hr), but it's not always where trains start or finish so be sure to board promptly.

Regular international train services run to Berlin (from €60, six hours, five daily), Prague (€50, eight hours, three daily), Bratislava (€90, eight hours, daily), Kyiv (from €90, 11 hours, daily), Minsk (from €80, 10 hours, daily) and Moscow (€130, 19 hours).

### ❶ Getting Around

#### TO/FROM THE AIRPORT

Regular train services run between the airporT's **Warszawa Lotnisko Chopina** (ul Żwirki i Wigury) station and Warszawa Centralna (4.40zł, 20 minutes). Some trains also link the airport to **Warszawa Śródmieście station** (al Jerozolimskie), next to the Palace of Culture.

Bus 175 (4.40zł) terminates at Plac Piłsudskiego, about a 500m walk from the Old Town. A taxi fare between the airport and city centre is around 50zł.

From Warsaw Modlin, the easiest way to the centre is aboard the regular **Modlin bus** (☑ 22 290 5090; www.modlinbus.com) (33zł). A taxi will cost from 160zł to 200zł.

#### PUBLIC TRANSPORT

Warsaw has a reliable system of trams, buses and metro cars. Trams running east–west across busy Al Jerozolimskie are particularly handy.

Buy tickets from machines (have coins or small bills handy) or from news kiosks near stops. A standard ticket (4.40zł) is valid for one ride by bus, tram or metro. Day passes are available for 15zł. Be sure to validate the ticket on boarding.

# MAŁOPOLSKA

Małopolska (literally 'Lesser Poland') covers southeastern Poland from the former royal capital of Kraków to the eastern Lublin Uplands. The name does not refer to size or relative importance, but rather that Lesser Poland was mentioned in atlases more recently than Wielkopolska ('Greater Poland'). It's a colourful region filled with remnants of traditional life and historic cities.

## Kraków

POP 761,000

Many Polish cities are centred on an attractive Old Town, but none compare to Kraków (pronounced krak-oof) for effortless beauty. As it was the royal capital of Poland until 1596 and miraculously escaped destruction in WWII, Kraków is packed with appealing historic buildings and streetscapes. One of the most important sights is Wawel Castle, from where the ancient Polish kingdom was once ruled.

South of the castle lies the former Jewish quarter of Kazimierz. Its silent synagogues are a reminder of the tragedy of WWII. These days, the quarter has been injected with new life and is home to some of the city's best bars and clubs.

### ◉ Sights

#### ◉ Wawel Hill

South of Old Town, this prominent hilltop is crowned with the former Royal Castle and Cathedral – both enduring symbols of Poland.

★ **Wawel Royal Castle** CASTLE
(Zamek Królewski na Wawelu; ☑ Wawel Visitor Centre 12 422 5155; www.wawel.krakow.pl; Wawel Hill; grounds admission free, attractions priced separately; ⊘ grounds 6am-dusk; 🚃 6, 8, 10, 13, 18) As the political and cultural heart of Poland through the 16th century, Wawel Castle is a potent symbol of national identity. It's now a museum containing five separate sections: Crown Treasury & Armoury; State Rooms; Royal Private Apartments; Lost Wawel; and the Exhibition of Oriental Art. Each

# Kraków – Old Town & Wawel

0
200 m
0
0.1 miles

Kurniki

Bus Station

Polski Bus – Kraków

Fenn'a

Długa

Paderewskiego

Warszawska

Plac Matejki

11

Worcella

Zacisze

Pawia

Plac Kolejowy

Bosacka

Basztowa

Pijarska

Basztowa

Kraków Główny Train Station

Lubicz

Strzelecka

Reformacka

Pjarska

Św Tomasza

13

Sławkowska

Św Jana

Floriańska

Szpitalna

Plac Św Ducha

Zamenhofa

Szczepańska

14

Św Marka

Skłodowskiej-Curie

Rynek Główny

Szewska

Jagiellońska

InfoKraków – Old Town

Św Tomasza

Rynek Underground

2

St Mary's Basilica

Św Krzyża

Westerplatte

Radziwiłłowska

17

6

Wiślna

Bracka

InfoKraków – Cloth Hall

3

Plac Mariacki

Mikołajska

Mikołajska

Kopernika

Gołębia

OLD TOWN

Mały Rynek

Blich

Filharmonia Krakowska (80m)

Franciszkańska

Grodzka

Stolarska

Sienna

Planty

Zyblikiewicza

Kołłątaja

Gen Sołtyka

Plac Dominikańska

Dominikańska

Wielopole

Bonerowska

WESOŁA

Plac Wszystkich Świętych

Poselska

12

Senacka

Starowiślna

10

8

Metalowców

Plac Św Marii Magdaleny

Kanonicza

Grodzka

Św Gertrudy

Sarego

9

Bogusławskiego

Wrzesińska

Siedleckiego

Straszewskiego

Podzamcze

Św Idziego

Św Sebastiana

Dietla

Dietla

4

Wawel Cathedral

Wawel Royal Castle

5

Wawel Hill

Droga do Zamku

Bernardyńska

Stradomska

Św Idziego

Joselewicza

Starowiślna

Smocza

Koletek

Św Agnieszki

Krakowska

Brzozowa

Podbrzezie

Miodowa

Św Sebastiana

Jakuba

Szeroka

Schindler's Factory (1.1km)

Dajwor

Most Grunwaldzki

Dietla

Dietla

Sukiennicza

Orzeszkowej

Meiselsa

Meiselsa

Bożego Ciała

Paulińska

Józefa

Plac Nowy

16

Estery

Nowa

KAZIMIERZ

InfoKraków – Kazimierz

Marchewka z Groszkiem (200m)

Warszauera

Izaaka

Józefa

15

7

Wąska

Bartosza

Św Wawrzyńca

Galicia Jewish Museum

1

Kurniki

## Kraków – Old Town & Wawel

requires a separate ticket. Of the five, the State Rooms and Royal Private Apartments are most impressive. There's also a special display here of the city's most valuable painting, Leonardo da Vinci's *The Lady with an Ermine*.

The Renaissance palace you see today dates from the 16th century. An original, smaller residence was built in the early 11th century by King Bolesław I Chrobry. Kazimierz III Wielki (Casimir III the Great) turned it into a formidable Gothic castle, but when it burned down in 1499, Zygmunt I Stary (Sigismund I the Old; 1506–48) commissioned a new residence. Within 30 years, the current Italian-inspired palace was in place. Despite further extensions and alterations, the three-storey structure, complete with a courtyard arcaded on three sides, has been preserved to this day.

Repeatedly sacked and vandalised by the Swedish and Prussian armies, the castle was occupied in the 19th century by the Austrians, who intended to make Wawel a barracks, while moving the royal tombs elsewhere. They never got that far, but they did turn the royal kitchen and coach house into a military hospital and raze two churches. They also built a new ring of massive brick walls, largely ruining the original Gothic fortifications.

After Kraków was incorporated into re-established Poland after WWI, restoration work began and continued until the outbreak of WWII. The work was resumed after the war and has been able to recover a good deal of the castle's earlier external form and interior decoration.

★ **Wawel Cathedral** CHURCH
(☏ 12 429 9515; www.katedra-wawelska.pl; Wawel 3, Wawel Hill; cathedral free, combined entry for crypts, bell tower & museum adult/concession 12/7zł; ⊙ 9am-5pm Mon-Sat, from 12.30pm Sun; 🚍 6, 8, 10, 13, 18) The Royal Cathedral has witnessed many coronations, funerals and burials of Poland's monarchs and strongmen over the centuries. This is the third church on this site, consecrated in 1364. The original was founded in the 11th century by King Bolesław I Chrobry and replaced with a Romanesque construction around 1140. When that burned down in 1305, only the Crypt of St Leonard survived. Highlights include the Holy Cross Chapel, Sigismund Chapel, Sigismund Bell, and the Crypt of St Leonard and Royal Crypts.

### ◉ Old Town

This vast Rynek Główny (main square) is the focus of the Old Town, and is Europe's largest medieval town square (200m by 200m).

**Cloth Hall** HISTORIC BUILDING
(Sukiennice; www.mnk.pl; Rynek Główny 1/3; 🚍 1, 6, 8, 13, 18) FREE Dominating the middle of Rynek Główny, this building was once the centre of Kraków's medieval clothing trade. Created in the early 14th century when a roof was put over two rows of stalls, it was extended into a 108m-long Gothic structure, then rebuilt in Renaissance style after a 1555 fire; the arcades were a late 19th-century addition. The ground floor is now a busy trading centre for crafts and souvenirs; the upper floor houses the recently renovated **Gallery of 19th-Century Polish Painting** (☏ 12 433 5400; www.mnk.pl; Rynek Główny 1; adult/concession 14/8zł, Sun free; ⊙ 10am-6pm Tue-Sun; 🚍 1, 6, 8, 13, 18).

The gallery's collection features works by Józef Chełmoński, Jacek Malczewski, Aleksander Gierymski and the leader of monumental historic painting, Jan Matejko.

POLAND KRAKÓW

★**Rynek Underground** MUSEUM
(☑ 12 426 5060; www.podziemiarynku.com; Rynek Główny 1; adult/concession 19/16zł; ⊙ 10am-8pm Mon, to 4pm Tue, to 10pm Wed-Sun; ☷ 1, 6, 8, 13, 18) This fascinating attraction beneath the market square consists of an underground route through medieval market stalls and other long-forgotten chambers. The 'Middle Ages meets 21st century' experience is enhanced by holograms and audiovisual wizardry. Buy tickets at an office on the western side of the Cloth Hall (Sukiennice 21), where an electronic board shows tour times and tickets available. The entrance to the tunnels is on the northeastern end of the Cloth Hall.

★**St Mary's Basilica** CHURCH
(Basilica of the Assumption of Our Lady; ☑ 12 422 0737; www.mariacki.com; Plac Mariacki 5, Rynek Główny; adult/concession church 10/5zł, tower 15/10zł; ⊙ 11.30am-6pm Mon-Sat, 2-6pm Sun; ☷ 1, 6, 8, 13, 18) Overlooking Rynek Główny, this striking brick church, best known simply as St Mary's, is dominated by two towers of different heights. The first church here was built in the 1220s and following its destruction during a Tatar raid, construction of the basilica began. Tour the exquisite interior, with its remarkable carved wooden altarpiece, and in summer climb the tower for excellent views. Don't miss the hourly *hejnał* (bugle call) from the taller tower.

👁 **Kazimierz & Podgórze**

Founded by King Kazimierz III Wielki in 1335, Kazimierz was originally an independent town and then became a Jewish district. During WWII, the Germans relocated Jews south across the Vistula River to a walled ghetto in Podgórze. They were exterminated in the nearby Płaszów Concentration Camp, as portrayed in the Steven Spielberg film *Schindler's List*. In addition to the attractions below, many synagogues are still standing and can be visited individually.

★**Schindler's Factory** MUSEUM
(Fabryka Schindlera; ☑ 12 257 0096; www.mhk.pl; ul Lipowa 4; adult/concession 21/16zł, free Mon; ⊙ 10am-4pm Mon, 9am-8pm Tue-Sun; ☷ 3, 9, 19, 24, 50) This impressive interactive museum covers the German occupation of Kraków in WWII. It's housed in the former enamel factory of Oskar Schindler, the Nazi Germany industrialist who famously saved the lives of members of his Jewish labour force during the Holocaust. Well-organised, innovative exhibits tell the moving story of the city from 1939 to 1945.

From the main post office in the Old Town, catch any tram down ul Starowiślna and alight at the first stop over the river at Plac Bohaterów Getta. From here, follow the signs east along ul Kącik, under the railway line to the museum.

★**Galicia Jewish Museum** MUSEUM
(☑ 12 421 6842; www.galiciajewishmuseum.org; ul Dajwór 18; adult/concession 16/11zł; ⊙ 10am-6pm; ☎; ☷ 3, 9, 19, 24, 50) This museum both commemorates Jewish victims of the Holocaust and celebrates the Jewish culture and history of the former Austro-Hungarian region of Galicia. It features an impressive photographic exhibition depicting modern-day remnants of southeastern Poland's once-thriving Jewish community, called *Traces of Memory*, along with video testimony of survivors and regular temporary exhibits. The museum also leads guided tours of the Jewish sites of Kazimierz. Call or email for details.

🛏 **Sleeping**

Kraków is unquestionably Poland's major tourist destination, with prices to match. **Hamilton Suites** (☑ 12 346 4670; www.krakow-apartments.biz; apt 300-600zł; ☎) is one of several companies offering good-value, short-term apartment rentals.

★**Mundo Hostel** HOSTEL €
(☑ 12 422 6113; www.mundohostel.eu; ul Sarego 10; dm 60-65zł, d 170-190zł; @☎; ☷ 6, 8, 10, 13, 18) Attractive, well-maintained hostel in a quiet courtyard location neatly placed between the Old Town and Kazimierz. Each room is decorated for a different country; for example, the Tibet room is decked out with colourful prayer flags. Barbecues take place in summer. There's a bright, fully equipped kitchen for do-it-yourself meals.

★**Wielopole** HOTEL €€
(☑ 12 422 1475; www.wielopole.pl; ul Wielopole 3; s/d 260/360zł; ✳☎; ☷ 3, 10, 19, 24, 52) Wielopole's selection of bright, modern rooms – all of them with spotless bathrooms – is housed in a renovated block with a great courtyard on the eastern edge of the Old Town, within easy walk of Kazimierz. The breakfast spread here is impressive.

**Hotel Eden** HOTEL €€
(☑ 12 430 6565; www.hoteleden.pl; ul Ciemna 15; s/d 240/320zł; ☎; ☷ 3, 9, 19, 24, 50) Located

## A UNESCO-PROTECTED SALT MINE

Some 14km southeast of Kraków, **Wieliczka** (📞12 278 7302; www.kopalnia.pl; ul Daniłowicza 10; adult/concession 84/64zł; ⏱7.30am-7.30pm Apr-Oct, 8am-5pm Nov-Mar) – pronounced vyeh-leech-kah – is famous for its deep salt mine. It's an eerie world of pits and chambers, and everything within its depths has been carved by hand from salt blocks. A section of the mine, some 22 chambers, is open to the public and it's a fascinating trip.

You visit three upper levels of the mine, from 64m to 135m below ground. Some have been made into chapels, with altarpieces and figures, others are adorned with statues and monuments – and there are even underground lakes.

Guided tours take about two hours. Wear comfortable shoes and dress warmly as the temperature in the mine is 14°C. In summer, English-language tours depart every half-hour. During the rest of the year, tours are less frequent.

Minibuses to Wieliczka (3zł) depart Kraków frequently from ul Pawia near the Galeria Krakowska shopping mall next to Kraków Główny train station.

within three meticulously restored 15th-century townhouses, the Eden has comfortable rooms and comes complete with a sauna and the only *mikvah* (traditional Jewish bath) in Kraków. Kosher meals are available on request.

⭐**Hotel Pugetów**　　　BOUTIQUE HOTEL €€€
(📞12 432 4950; www.donimirski.com; ul Starowiślna 15a; s/d 330/460zł; 🅿❄🛜; 🚌1, 3, 19, 24, 52) This charming boutique hotel stands proudly next to the 19th-century neo-Renaissance palace of the same name. It offers just seven rooms with distinctive names (Conrad, Bonaparte) and identities. Think embroidered bathrobes, black-marble baths and a fabulous breakfast room in the basement.

## ✖ Eating

⭐**Glonojad**　　　　　　VEGETARIAN €
(📞12 346 1677; www.glonojad.com; Plac Matejki 2; mains 16-20zł; ⏱8am-10pm; 🛜🍴; 🚌2, 4, 14, 19, 20, 24) Attractive and much-lauded, this vegetarian restaurant has a great view onto Plac Matejki, just north of the Barbican. The diverse menu has a variety of tasty dishes including samosas, curries, potato pancakes, burritos, gnocchi and soups. There's also an all-day breakfast menu, so there's no need to jump out of that hotel bed too early.

⭐**Marchewka z Groszkiem**　　POLISH €€
(📞12 430 0795; www.marchewkazgroszkiem.pl; ul Mostowa 2; mains 11-29.50zł; ⏱9am-10pm; 🛜; 🚌6, 8, 10, 13) Traditional Polish cooking, with hints of influence from neighbouring countries like Ukraine (beer), Hungary (wine) and Lithuania. Excellent potato pancakes and a delicious boiled beef with horseradish sauce highlight the menu. There are a few sidewalk

tables to admire the parade of people down one of Kazimierz' up-and-coming streets.

**Trufla**　　　　　　　　ITALIAN €€
(📞12 422 1641; ul Św Tomasza 2; mains 25-43zł; ⏱9am-11pm Mon-Fri, 10am-11pm Sat & Sun; 🛜; 🚌2, 4, 14, 18, 20, 24) Affordable yet quality Italian food, including steaks, seafood, pasta and risotto – but no pizza. The decor is uncluttered: think hardwood floors and simple, wooden tables. Yet the overall ambience is relaxing. In summer, there's a pretty garden out back (to access the garden, walk through a corridor to the left of the main entrance).

⭐**Miód Malina**　　　　　POLISH €€€
(📞12 430 0411; www.miodmalina.pl; ul Grodzka 40; mains 24-69zł; ⏱noon-11pm; 🛜; 🚌1, 6, 8, 13, 18) The charmingly named 'Honey Raspberry' serves Polish dishes in colourful surrounds. Grab a window seat and order the wild mushrooms in cream, and any of the duck or veal dishes. There's a variety of beef steaks on the menu as well. The grilled sheep's cheese appetiser, served with cranberry jelly, is a regional speciality. Reservations essential.

## 🍷 Drinking & Nightlife

There are hundreds of pubs and bars in Kraków's Old Town, many housed in ancient vaulted cellars. Kazimierz also has a lively bar scene, centred on Plac Nowy.

⭐**Café Bunkier**　　　　　　　　CAFE
(📞12 431 0585; http://en.bunkiercafe.pl; Plac Szczepański 3a; ⏱9am-late; 🛜; 🚌2, 4, 14, 18, 20, 24) The 'Bunker' is a wonderful cafe with a positively enormous glassed-in terrace tacked onto the Bunkier Sztuki (Art Bunker), a cutting-edge gallery northwest of the Rynek. The garden space is heated in winter

**POLAND** KRAKÓW

and seems to always have a buzz. Excellent coffee, non-filtered beers and homemade lemonades, as well as light bites like burgers and salads. Enter from the Planty.

★ **Cheder**                                    CAFE
(☑515 732 226; www.cheder.pl; ul Józefa 36; ◷10am-10pm; ☒3, 9, 19, 24, 50) Unlike most of the other Jewish-themed places in Kazimierz, this one aims to entertain *and* educate. Named after a traditional Hebrew school, the cafe offers access to a decent library in Polish and English, regular readings and films, as well as real Israeli coffee, brewed in a traditional Turkish copper pot with cinnamon and cardamom, and snacks like homemade hummus.

**Mleczarnia**                                  CAFE
(☑12 421 8532; www.mle.pl; ul Meiselsa 20; ◷10am-late; ☒6, 8, 10, 13) Wins the prize for best courtyard cafe – located across the street. Shady trees and blooming roses make this place tops for a sunny-day drink. If it's rainy, never fear, for the cafe is warm and cosy, with crowded bookshelves and portrait-covered walls. Interesting beverages available here include mead and cocoa with cherry vodka. Self-service.

## ☆ Entertainment

★ **Harris Piano Jazz Bar**                     JAZZ
(☑12 421 5741; www.harris.krakow.pl; Rynek Główny 28; ◷3pm-late Mon-Fri, from 1pm Sat & Sun; ☒1, 6, 8, 13, 18) This lively jazz haunt is housed in an atmospheric, intimate cellar space right on the Rynek Główny. Harris hosts jazz and blues bands most nights of the week from around 9.30pm, but try to arrive an hour earlier to get a seat (or book in advance by phone). Wednesday nights see weekly (free) jam sessions.

**Filharmonia Krakowska**              CLASSICAL MUSIC
(Filharmonia im. Karola Szymanowskiego w Krakowie; ☑reservations 12 619 8722, tickets 12 619 8733; www.filharmonia.krakow.pl; ul Zwierzyniecka 1; ◷box office 10am-2pm & 3-7pm Tue-Fri; ☒1, 2, 6) Home to one of Poland's best orchestras. Tickets start at 25zł.

## ⓘ Information

The official tourist information office, **Info-Kraków** (www.infokrakow.pl), maintains branches around town, including at the **Cloth Hall** (☑12 354 2716; www.infokrakow.pl; Cloth Hall, Rynek Główny 1/3; ◷9am-7pm May-Sep, to 5pm Oct-Apr; ☎; ☒1, 6, 8, 13, 18), **Kazimierz** (☑12 354 2728; www.infokrakow.pl; ul Józefa 7; ◷9am-5pm; ☒6, 8, 10, 13), the **Old Town**

(☑12 354 2725; www.infokrakow.pl; ul Św Jana 2; ◷9am-7pm; ☒1, 6, 8, 13, 18) and the **Airport** (☑12 285 5341; www.infokrakow.pl; John Paul II International Airport, Balice; ◷9am-7pm).

## ⓘ Getting There & Away

### AIR

Kraków's **John Paul II International Airport** (KRK; ☑information 12 295 5800; www.krakowairport.pl; Kapitana Mieczysława Medweckiego 1, Balice; ☎) is located in the town of Balice, about 15km west of the centre. A regular train service (8zł, 17 minutes), departing once or twice an hour between 4am and 11.30pm, runs to Kraków Główny station. Taxis to the centre cost about 80zł.

The main Polish carrier LOT (p311) flies to Warsaw and other large cities. Budget operators connect Kraków to cities in Europe.

### BUS

Kraków's modern **bus station** (☑703 403 340; www.mda.malopolska.pl; ul Bosacka 18; ◷information 7am-8pm Mon-Fri, 9am-5pm Sat & Sun; ☒2, 3, 4, 10, 14, 19, 24, 52) is conveniently located next to the main train station, Kraków Główny, on the fringe of the Old Town.

Bus travel is the best way to reach Zakopane (16zł, two hours, hourly). Modern **Polski Bus** (☑emergencies 703 502 504; www.polskibus.com) coaches depart from here to Warsaw (five hours, several daily) and Wrocław (three hours, several daily); check fares and book tickets online.

### TRAIN

Newly remodelled and gleaming **Kraków Główny** (Dworzec Główny; ☑information 703 202 025; www.pkp.pl; Plac Dworcowy; ☒2, 3, 4, 10, 14, 19, 24, 52) train station, on the northeastern outskirts of the Old Town, handles all international trains and most domestic rail services.

Useful domestic destinations include Gdańsk (80zł, eight hours, three daily), Lublin (62zł, four hours, two daily), Poznań (80zł, eight hours, three daily), Toruń (73zł, seven hours, three daily), Warsaw (60zł to 130zł, three hours, at least hourly) and Wrocław (50zł, 5½ hours, hourly).

Popular international connections include Bratislava (7½ hours, one daily), Berlin (10 hours, one daily), Budapest (10½ hours, one daily), Lviv (7½ to 9½ hours, two daily) and Prague (10 hours, one daily).

# Lublin

POP 342,000

Poland's eastern metropolis admittedly lacks the grandeur of Gdańsk or Kraków, but does have an attractive Old Town, with beautiful churches and tiny alleyways. It's a natural jumping-off point for exploring southeast-

## AUSCHWITZ-BIRKENAU

Many visitors pair a trip to Kraków with a visit to the **Auschwitz-Birkenau Museum & Memorial** (Auschwitz-Birkenau Miejsce Pamięci i Muzeum; ☑ guides 33 844 8100; www. auschwitz.org; ul Więźniów Oświęcimia 20; tours 45zł; ☺ 7.30am-7pm Jun-Aug, to 6pm Apr-May & Sep, to 5pm Mar & Oct, 8am-4pm Feb, to 3pm Jan & Nov, to 2pm Dec) **FREE** – or as it's known officially the 'Auschwitz-Birkenau: German Nazi Concentration & Extermination Camp' – in the town of Oświęcim. More than a million Jews and will large numbers of ethnic Poles and Roma were systematically murdered here by occupying Germans during WWII.

Both the main camp at Auschwitz (Auschwitz I) and a larger outlying camp at Birkenau (Auschwitz II), about 2km away, are open to the public and admission is free (though if arriving between 10am and 3pm from May to October, a guided tour is compulsory). A visit is essential to understanding the Holocaust, though the scope and nature of the crimes are horrifying and may not be suitable for children under 14.

The tour begins at the main camp, Auschwitz I, which began life as a Polish military barracks but was co-opted by the Nazi Germans in 1940 as an extermination camp. Here is the infamous gate, displaying the grimly cynical message: 'Arbeit Macht Frei' (Through Work Freedom). Some 13 of 30 surviving prison blocks house museum exhibitions.

From here, the tour moves to Birkenau (Auschwitz II), where most of the killings took place. Massive and purpose-built to be efficient, the camp had more than 300 prison barracks. Here you'll find the remnants of gas chambers and crematoria.

Auschwitz-Birkenau is a workable day trip from Kraków. Most convenient are the approximately hourly buses to Oświęcim (12zł, 1½ hours), departing from the bus station in Kraków. There are also numerous minibuses to Oświęcim (10zł, 1½ hours) from the minibus stands off ul Pawia, next to Galeria Krakowska.

ern Poland. Thousands of students make for a lively restaurant, bar and club scene.

Lublin plays an important role in Polish and Jewish history. It was here in 1569 that the Lublin Union was signed, uniting Poland and Lithuania to form one of the largest and most powerful entities in Europe in its day. For those interested in Jewish heritage, for centuries Lublin served as a centre of European Jewish culture. The Holocaust ended this vibrant community, and one of the most notorious Nazi German extermination camps, Majdanek, lies at Lublin's doorstep.

### ◉ Sights

**Lublin Castle**  MUSEUM
(☑ 81 532 5001; www.zamek-lublin.pl; ul Zamkowa 9; adult/concession museum 6.50/4.50zł, chapel 6.50/4.50zł; ☺10am-6pm Tue-Sun Jun-Aug, 9am-5pm Sep-May) Lublin's royal castle dates from the 12th and 13th centuries, though it's been rebuilt many times over the years. It was here in 1569 that the union with Lithuania was signed. The castle is home to both the **Lublin Museum** and the surviving **Gothic Chapel of the Holy Trinity**, which dates from the 14th century. Each requires a separate entry ticket. The museum's permanent collection features mainly art, folk art and weaponry. The 14th-century chapel is con-

sidered a masterpiece of the Middle Ages, with Russian-Byzantine-inspired frescos. Painted in 1418, only to be later plastered over, they were rediscovered in 1897 and painstakingly restored over a 100-year period. These are possibly the finest examples of medieval wall paintings in the country.

During WWII the occupying German army used the castle as a prison, holding as many as 40,000 inmates. The darkest day of the war here came in July 1944, just ahead of the prison's liberation by the Soviet Red Army, when the Germans executed 300 prisoners on the spot.

**Kraków Gate**  MUSEUM
(Brama Krakowska; ☑81 532 6001; www.muzeum lubelskie.pl; Plac Łokietka 3; adult/concession 5.50/4.50zł; ☺10am-6pm Tue-Sun Jun-Aug, to 5pm Sep-May) The only significant surviving remnant of the fortified walls that once surrounded the Old Town is the 14th-century Gothic-style Kraków Gate. It was conceived during the reign of Kazimierz III Wielki following the Mongol attack in 1341. It received its octagonal Renaissance superstructure in the 16th century, and its Baroque crown in 1782. These days it's home to the **Historical Museum of Lublin** and its small collection of documents and photographs of the town's history.

### Cathedral of St John the Baptist CHURCH

(www.archidiecezjalubelska.pl; Plac Katedralny; ☉ dawn-sunset, treasury 10am-2pm & 3-5pm Tue-Sun) FREE This former Jesuit church dates from the 16th century and is the largest in Lublin. There are many impressive details to behold, including the Baroque trompe l'oeil frescos (the work of Moravian artist Józef Majer) and the 17th-century altar made from a black Lebanese pear tree. The acoustic vestry (so called for its ability to project whispers) and the **treasury** *(skarbiec)*, behind the chapel, also merit attention.

The painting of the *Black Madonna* is said to have shed tears in 1945, making it a source of much reverence for local devotees.

### Majdanek HISTORIC SITE

(Państwowe Muzeum na Majdanku; ☑ 81 710 2833; www.majdanek.eu; Droga Męczenników Majdanka 67; admission free; ☉ 9am-6pm Apr-Oct, to 4pm Nov-Mar, museum closed Mon) FREE Four kilometres southeast of the centre of Lublin is the Nazi German Majdanek extermination camp, where tens of thousands of people, mainly Jews, were murdered during WWII. The Germans went to no effort to conceal Majdanek, as they did at other extermination camps. A 5km walk starts at the visitors centre, passes the foreboding Monument of Fight & Martyrdom, goes through parts of the barracks and finishes at the mausoleum. The camp is accessible by public transport: from the Krakowska Gate, take bus 23.

### ☞ Tours

### Underground Route WALKING

(☑ tour bookings 81 534 6570; Rynek 1; adult/concession 10/8zł; ☉ 10am-4pm Tue-Fri, noon-5pm Sat & Sun) This 280m trail winds its way through connected cellars beneath the Old Town, with historical exhibitions along the way. Entry is from the neoclassical Old Town Hall in the centre of the pleasant Market Sq (Rynek) at approximately two-hourly intervals; check with the tourist office for exact times.

### 🛏 Sleeping

### Hostel Lublin HOSTEL €

(☑ 792 888 632; www.hostellublin.pl; ul Lubartowska 60; dm/r 40/95zł; ☜) The city's first modern hostel is situated within a former apartment building and contains neat, tidy dorms, a basic kitchenette and a cosy lounge. Take trolleybus 156 or 160 north from the Old Town; after you cross busy al Tysiąclecia, exit at the second stop.

### Vanilla Hotel HOTEL €€

(☑ 81 536 6720; www.vanilla-hotel.pl; ul Krakowskie Przedmieście 12; s 265-330zł, d 315-395zł; P @ ☜) The name must be tongue-in-cheek. This beautiful boutique, just off the main pedestrian thoroughfare, is anything but vanilla. The rooms are filled with inspired, even bold, styling: vibrant colours, big headboards behind the beds, and stylish, retro lamps and furniture. There's lots of attention to detail here, which continues into the chic restaurant and coffee bar. Lower prices on weekends.

### Hotel Waksman HOTEL €€

(☑ 81 532 5454; www.waksman.pl; ul Grodzka 19; s/d 210/230zł, apt from 290zł; P @ ☜) Hotel Waksman deserves a blue ribbon for many reasons, not least of which is the atmospheric Old Town location. Each standard room (named 'yellow', 'blue', 'green' or 'red' for its decor) has individual character. The two apartments on top are special; they offer ample space for lounging or working, and views over the Old Town and castle.

### ✕ Eating

### ★ Kardamon INTERNATIONAL €€

(☑ 81 448 0257; www.kardamon.eu; ul Krakowskie Przedmieście 41; mains 24-69zł; ☉ noon-11pm Mon-Sat, to 10pm Sun; ☜) By many accounts, Lublin's best restaurant is this lush, cellar affair on the main street. The menu is a mix of international staples such as grilled pork tenderloin, along with Polish favourites such as duck served in cranberry sauce, and some rarer regional specialities. The 'gooseneck', a regional dish served with liver stuffing and buckwheat, is a particular favourite.

### Mandragora JEWISH €€

(☑ 81 536 2020; www.mandragora.lublin.pl; Rynek 9; mains 20-49zł; ☉ noon-10pm Sun-Thu, to midnight Fri & Sat; ☜) There's good kitsch and there's bad kitsch, and at Mandragora, it's all good. Sure they're going for the *Fiddler on the Roof* effect with the lace tablecloths, knick-knacks and photos of old Lublin, but in the romantic Rynek locale, it works wonderfully. The food is a hearty mix of Polish and Jewish, featuring mains such as goose and duck.

### 🍷 Drinking & Nightlife

### Szklarnia CAFE

(Centrum Kultury w Lublinie; ☑ 81 466 6140; www.ck.lublin.pl; ul Peowiaków 12; ☉ 10am-11pm Mon-Fri, noon-midnight Sat & Sun; ☜) It's not easy

## ZAMOŚĆ: POLAND'S RENAISSANCE HEART

While most Polish cities' attractions centre on their medieval heart, Zamość (zah-moshch) is pure 16th-century Renaissance. It was founded in 1580 by nobleman Jan Zamoyski and designed by an Italian architect. The splendid architecture of Zamość's Old Town escaped serious destruction in WWII and was added to Unesco's World Heritage List in 1992.

The **Rynek Wielki** (Great Market Square; Rynek Wielki) is the heart of Zamość's attractive Old Town. This impressive Italianate Renaissance square (exactly 100m by 100m) is dominated by a lofty, pink town hall and surrounded by colourful, arcaded burghers' houses. The **Museum of Zamość** (Muzeum Zamojskie; ☑ 84 638 6494; www.muzeum-zamojskie.pl; ul Ormiańska 30; adult/concession 10/6zł; ☺ 9am-5pm Tue-Sun) is based in two of the loveliest buildings on the square and houses interesting exhibits, including paintings, folk costumes and a scale model of the 16th-century town.

The city's **synagogue** (☑ 84 639 0054; www.zamosc.fodz.pl; ul Pereca 14; admission 7zł; ☺ 10am-6pm Tue-Sun Mar-Oct, 9am-2pm Nov-Feb) was recently reopened to the public after a long renovation. It was built around 1620 and served as the Jewish community's main house of worship until WWII, when it was shuttered by the Germans. The highlight of the exhibition is a gripping computer presentation on the history of the town's Jewish community, including its roots in Sephardic Judaism.

The helpful **tourist office** (☑ 84 639 2292; www.travel.zamosc.pl; Rynek Wielki 13; ☺ 8am-6pm Mon-Fri, 10am-5pm Sat & Sun May-Sep, 8am-5pm Mon-Fri, 9am-3pm Sat & Sun Oct-Apr) in the town hall has maps, brochures and souvenirs. Zamość makes for an easy day trip from Lublin. Buses and minibuses make the 80km trip (15zł) in around 90 minutes.

---

finding good coffee in Lublin. This sleek cafe in the recently refurbished Lublin Cultural Centre has great coffee as well as a daily selection of cakes. There's live entertainment some nights, and a nice terrace at the back in warm weather.

**Czarna Owca**                                    PUB
(☑ 81 532 4130; ul Narutowicza 9; ☺ noon-midnight Sun-Tue, to 3am Wed-Sat) The 'Black Sheep' is a legendary Lublin watering hole, going strong until the wee morning hours from Wednesday to Saturday. In addition to beers and shots of vodka chasers, it has decent pub food, pizzas and toasts to munch on.

### ❶ Information

**Tourist Information Centre** (LOITiK; ☑ 81 532 4412; www.lublin.eu; ul Jezuicka 1/3; ☺ 9am-7pm Mon-Fri, 10am-7pm Sat & Sun May-Oct, 9am-5pm Mon-Fri, 10am-5pm Sat & Sun Nov-Apr) Extremely helpful English-speaking staff. There are souvenirs for sale and lots of brochures, including handy maps of the most popular walking tours in Lublin. There's also a computer on hand for short-term web-surfing.

### ❶ Getting There & Away

**BUS**

PKS buses run from the **bus station** (☑ 703 402 900; lublin.pks.busportal.pl; ul Hutnicza 1,

cross al Tysiąclecia), opposite the castle. From here, Polski Bus (www.polskibus.com) heads to Warsaw (25zł, three hours, five daily). Private minibuses run to various destinations, including Zamość (15zł, 1½ hours, hourly), from a minibus station north of the bus terminal.

**TRAIN**

The **train station** (Dworzec Kolejowy Lublin Główny; ☑ info 703 202 025; www.pkp.pl; Plac Dworcowy 1) is 1.8km south of the Old Town. Useful direct train connections included to Kraków (62zł, four hours, two daily) and Warsaw (37zł, 2¾ hours, five daily).

# CARPATHIAN MOUNTAINS

The Carpathians (Karpaty) stretch from the southern border with Slovakia into Ukraine, and their wooded hills and snowy mountains are a magnet for hikers, skiers and cyclists. The most popular destination here is the resort of Zakopane.

## Zakopane

POP 27,000

Zakopane, 100km south of Kraków, is Poland's main alpine resort, situated at the foot of the Tatra Mountains. It's a popular jumping-off spot for **trekking and mountain hikes**, as well as **skiing**. The busy high street, ul Krupówki, is a jumble of souvenir shops, bars and restaurants, but away from the centre, the pace slows down. This was an artists' colony in the early 20th century, and the graceful timbered villas from those days – built in what's known as the 'Zakopane style' – are still scattered around town.

## Sights & Activities

### Museum of Zakopane Style
MUSEUM

(Willa Koliba; ☑18 201 3602; www.muzeumtatrzanskie.pl; ul Kościeliska 18; adult/concession 7/5.50zł; ⊙10am-6pm Tue-Sat, 9am-3pm Sun Jul & Aug, 9am-5pm Wed-Sat, 9am-3pm Sun Sep-Jun) Housed in the Willa Koliba, this was the first of several grand wooden villas designed by the noted Polish painter and architect Stanisław Witkiewicz in his 'Zakopane Style' (similar to the Arts and Crafts movement that swept the US and Britain at the turn of the 20th century). The interior has been restored to its original state, complete with highlander furnishings and textiles, all designed for the villa.

### Old Church & Cemetery
CHURCH

(Stary Kościół, Pęksowy Brzyzek National Cemetery; ul Kościeliska; ⊙dawn-dusk) **FREE** This small wooden church and adjoining atmospheric cemetery date from the mid-19th century. The Old Church has charming carved wooden decorations and pews, and the Stations of the Cross painted on glass on the windows. Just behind, the old cemetery is certainly one of the country's most beautiful, with a number of amazing wood-carved headstones, some resembling giant chess pieces. The noted Polish painter and creator of the Zakopane Style, Stanisław Witkiewicz, is buried here beneath a modest wooden grave marker.

### Morskie Oko
LAKE

(☑18 202 3300; www.tpn.pl; park 5zł) The most popular outing near Zakopane is to this emerald-green mountain lake, about 20km southeast of the centre. Buses regularly depart from ul Kościuszki, across from the main bus station, for Polana Palenica (45 minutes), from where a 9km-long road continues uphill to the lake. Cars, bikes and buses are not allowed, so you'll have to walk (about two hours each way). Travel agencies organise day trips.

### Kasprowy Wierch Cable Car
CABLE CAR

(☑18 201 5356; www.pkl.pl; Kuźnice; adult/concession return 63/48zł; ⊙ 7.30am-4pm Jan-Mar, 7.30am-6pm Apr-Jun & Sep-Oct, 7am-9pm Jul & Aug, 9am-4pm Nov-Dec) The cable-car trip from Kuźnice (2km south of Zakopane) to the Mt Kasprowy Wierch summit (1985m) is a classic tourist experience. At the end of the ascent (20 minutes, climbing 936m), you can get off and stand with one foot in Poland and the other in Slovakia. The view from the top is spectacular (clouds permitting). The cable car normally closes for two weeks in May, and won't operate if the snow or wind conditions are dangerous.

## Sleeping

Travel agencies in Zakopane can usually arrange private rooms. Expect a double to cost about 80zł in the high season in the town centre, and about 60zł for somewhere further out.

### Target Hostel
HOSTEL €

(☑730 955 730, 18 207 4596; www.targethostel.pl; ul Sienkiewicza 3b; dm 29-55zł; @ 🛜) This private, well-run hostel is within easy walking distance of the bus station, which is convenient if you're arriving from Kraków. Accommodation is in four- to 10-bed dorms, with the smaller rooms priced slightly higher. Dorms are classic light wood, with wooden floors. There's a common room and collective kitchen, as well as niceties such as free wi-fi and computers to check email.

### Czarny Potok
HOTEL €€

(☑18 202 2760; www.czarnypotok.pl; ul Tetmajera 20; s/d from 270/320zł; P 🛜 🛜 ☲) The 'Black Stream', set upon a pretty brook amid lovely gardens, is a 44-room pension-like hostelry along a quiet street just south of the pedestrian mall. It has a great fitness centre with two saunas.

### Hotel Sabała
HOTEL €€€

(☑18 201 5092; www.sabala.zakopane.pl; ul Krupówki 11; s/d from 300/400zł; ⊜ 🛜 ☲) Built in 1894 but thoroughly up to date, this striking timber hotel has a superb location overlooking the picturesque pedestrian thoroughfare. The hotel offers 51 cosy, attic-style rooms, and there's a sauna, solarium and swimming pool. The restaurant here serves both local specialities and international favourites.

## Eating

### Pstrąg Górski
SEAFOOD €€

(☑512 351 746; www.pstrag-zakopane.pl; ul Krupówki 6a; mains 20-40zł; ⊙10am-10pm; ⊜ 🛜) This fish restaurant, done up in timber-rich traditional style and overlooking a narrow stream, serves some of the freshest trout, salmon and sea fish in town. Trout is priced at 5zł and up per 100g (whole fish), bringing the price of a standard fish dinner to around 30zł, not including sides.

### Karczma Zapiecek          POLISH €€
(☑18 201 5699; www.karczmazapiecek.pl; ul Krupówki 43; mains 17-29zł; ☺10am-11pm) One of the better choices among a group of similar highlander-style restaurants along ul Krupówki, with great food, an old stove and a terrace. Traditional dishes on offer include *haluski* (noodles) with *bryndza* (sheep's cheese) and baked trout.

### ❶ Information

**Tatra National Park Headquarters** (Tatrzański Park Narodowy; ☑18 200 0308; www.tpn.pl; ul Chałubińskiego 42; ☺office 9am-4pm Mon-Fri) The information office of the Tatra National Park is located in a small building near the Rondo Kuźnickie on the southern outskirts of the city. It's a good place for maps, guides and local weather and hiking information.

**Tourist Information Centre** (☑18 201 2211; www.zakopane.pl; ul Kościuszki 17; ☺9am-5pm Mar-Aug, 9am-5pm Mon-Fri Sep-Feb) Small but helpful municipal tourist office just south of the bus station on the walk toward the centre. It has free city maps and sells more-detailed hiking maps.

### ❶ Getting There & Away

Though Zakopane has a small train station, the majority of visitors arrive by bus from Kraków. Coaches make the journey (16zł, 1¾ hours) every 30 to 60 minutes during the day. The leading bus company is **Szwagropol** (☑12 271 3550; www. szwagropol.pl). Buy tickets bound for Kraków at Zakopane **bus station** (PKS; ☑666 396 090; www.zdazakopane.pl; ul Kościuszki 23).

# SILESIA

Silesia (Śląsk in Polish; pronounced *shlonsk*), in the far southwest of the country, is a traditional industrial and mining region with a fascinating mix of landscapes.

## Wrocław

POP 635,000

Everyone loves Wrocław (vrots-wahf) and it's easy to see why. The city's gracious Old Town is a mix of Gothic and Baroque styles, and its large student population ensures a healthy number of restaurants, bars and nightclubs. Wrocław has been traded back and forth between various domains over the centuries, but began life around 1000 AD.

History buffs may know the city better as Breslau, the name it had as part of Germany until the end of WWII. When the city went over to Polish hands after the war, Wrocław was a shell of its former self. Sensitive restoration has returned the historic centre to its former beauty.

### ◉ Sights

The hub of city life is the city's magnificent market square, the **Rynek**.

### ◎ Old Town

★**Old Town Hall**          HISTORIC BUILDING
(Stary Ratusz; Rynek) This grand edifice took almost two centuries (1327–1504) to complete, and work on the 66m-high tower and decoration continued for another century.

The eastern facade reflects three distinct stages of the town hall's development. The segment to the right, with its austere early Gothic features, is the oldest, while the delicate carving in the section to the left shows elements of the early Renaissance style. The central 16th-century section is topped by an ornamented triangular roof adorned with pinnacles.

**Wrocław Dwarves**          PUBLIC ART
(Wrocławskie Krasnale; www.krasnale.pl) See if you can spot the diminutive statue of a resting dwarf at ground level, just to the west of the **Hansel and Gretel houses** (Jaś i Małgosia; ul Odrzańska 39/40) off Wrocław's main square. A few metres away you'll spot firemen dwarves, rushing to put out a blaze. These figures are part of a collection of over 300 scattered through the city. Though whimsical, they're also a reference to the symbol of the Orange Alternative, a communist-era dissident group that used ridicule as a weapon. They're sometimes identified in English as gnomes, as the Polish folkloric character they're based on (the leprechaun-like *krasnoludek*) resembles a cross between a dwarf and a gnome. Buy a 'dwarf map' (6zł) from the tourist office and go dwarf-spotting.

### ◎ Outside the Old Town

★**Panorama of Racławice**          MUSEUM
(Panorama Racławicka; www.panoramaraclawicka. pl; ul Purkyniego 11; adult/concession 30/23zł; ☺9am-5pm mid-Apr–Sep, to 4pm Tue-Sun Oct–mid-Apr) Wrocław's pride and joy is this giant painting of the battle for Polish independence fought at Racławice on 4 April 1794,

POLAND WROCŁAW

between the Polish army led by Tadeusz Kościuszko and Russian troops under General Alexander Tormasov. The Poles won but it was all for naught: months later the nationwide insurrection was crushed by the tsarist army. The canvas measures 15m by 114m, and is wrapped around the internal walls of a rotunda.

Visits are by guided tour, departing every half-hour. You move around the balcony, inspecting each scene in turn, while an audioguide provides recorded commentary. The small rotunda behind the ticket office features a model of the battlefield and the uniforms of forces engaged in the battle.

The painting came into being when, a century after the battle, a group of patriots in Lviv (then the Polish city of Lwów) commissioned the panorama. The two main artists, Jan Styka and Wojciech Kossak, were helped by seven other painters who did the background scenes and details. They completed the monumental canvas in just over nine months, using 750kg of paint.

After WWII the painting was sent to Wrocław, but since it depicted a defeat of the Russians (Poland's then official friend and liberator), the communist authorities were reluctant to put it on display. The pavilion built for the panorama in 1967 sat empty until 1985, when the canvas was shown for the first time in more than four decades.

### National Museum
MUSEUM

(Muzeum Narodowe; ☑ 71 372 5150; www.mnwr. art.pl; Plac Powstańców Warszawy 5; adult/concession 15/10zł; ☉10am-5pm Tue-Sun, to 6pm Sat) A treasure trove of fine art, 200m east of the Panorama of Racławice. Medieval stone sculpture is displayed on the ground floor; exhibits include the Romanesque tympanum from the portal of the Church of St Mary Magdalene, depicting the Assumption of the Virgin Mary, and 14th-century sarcophagi from the Church of SS Vincent and James. There are also collections of Silesian paintings, ceramics, silverware and furnishings from the 16th to 19th centuries.

### Cathedral of St John the Baptist
CHURCH

(Archikatedra Św Jana Chrzciciela; www.katedra.archidiecezja.wroc.pl; Plac Katedralny 18; tower adult/concession 5/4zł; ☉tower 10am-5.30pm Mon-Sat, from 2pm Sun) The centrepiece of Cathedral Island, this three-aisled Gothic basilica was built between 1244 and 1590. Seriously damaged during WWII, it was reconstructed in its previous Gothic form, complete with dragon guttering. The high altar boasts a gold and silver triptych from 1522 attributed to the school of Veit Stoss, and the western portico is a medieval gem. For once you don't need strong legs to climb the 91m-high tower, as there is a lift.

## 🛏 Sleeping

### ★ Hotel Piast
HOTEL €

(☑71 343 0033; www.piastwroclaw.pl; ul Piłsudskiego 98; s/d from 130/180zł; ☜) Known as the Kronprinz (Crown Prince) in German times, this former hostel has recently been upgraded to a neat and tidy two-star hotel. Its fully renovated rooms are clean and light, great value for the price and very handy for the train station. There's a restaurant on the premises, and breakfast costs an additional 20zł.

### Hostel Mleczarnia
HOSTEL €

(☑71 787 7570; www.mleczarniahostel.pl; ul Włodkowica 5; dm from 35zł, r 220zł; ☜) On a quiet road not far from the Rynek, this hostel has bags of charm, having been decorated in a deliberately old-fashioned style within a former residential building. There's a women-only dorm available, along with a kitchen and free laundry facilities. Downstairs is the excellent Mleczarnia cafe-bar.

### Hotel Patio
HOTEL €€

(☑71 3750 400; www.hotelpatio.pl; ul Kiełbaśnicza 24; s/d from 300/340zł; P☀☜) The Patio offers pleasant lodgings a short hop from the main square, within two buildings linked by a covered, sunlit courtyard. Rooms are clean and light, sometimes small but with reasonably high ceilings, and there's a spectacular breakfast spread.

### Hotel Monopol
HOTEL €€€

(☑71 772 3777; www.monopolwroclaw.hotel.com. pl; ul Modrzejewskiej 2; s/d 600/650zł; ☀☜☲) In its heyday the elegant Monopol hosted such luminaries as Pablo Picasso and Marlene Dietrich (along with unsavoury characters such as Adolf Hitler). It's opposite the opera house, 350m south of the Rynek off ul Świdnicka. It boasts restaurants, bars, a cafe, a spa and boutiques, so you won't be short of pampering – though you might soon be short of cash.

## 🍴 Eating

### Bar Wegetariański Vega
VEGETARIAN €

(☑71 344 3934; www.barvega.wroclaw.pl; Rynek 1/2; mains 5.50-10.50zł; ☉8am-7pm Mon-Thu, 8am-9pm Fri, 9am-9pm Sat, 9am-7pm Sun; ☝) Cheap, meat-free cafeteria on two floors in the centre of the Rynek, offering vegetarian and vegan dishes in a light green space.

There's a good choice of soups and crêpes. Set menu options run from 10zł to 22zł.

**Bernard** CZECH, INTERNATIONAL €€
(☑71 344 1054; www.bernard.wroclaw.pl; Rynek 35; mains 32-75zł; ☺10.30am-11pm; ☻) This lively split-level bar-restaurant is inspired by the Czech beer of the same name, and the menu features some Czech dishes such as rabbit and pork knee. There's upmarket comfort food including burgers, steak and fish dishes, as well as plenty of beer. The stylish interior is conducive to a quiet evening or group outing. Breakfast is served from 10.30am to noon.

**Restauracja Jadka** POLISH €€€
(☑71 343 6461; www.jadka.pl; ul Rzeźnicza 24/25; mains 56-86zł; ☺1-11pm) Well-regarded fine-dining option presenting impeccable modern versions of Polish classics such as wild boar in cranberry sauce and pork knuckle, and with silver-service table settings (candles, crystal, linen) in delightful Gothic surrounds. Bookings are recommended, especially at weekends.

## Drinking & Nightlife

★**Vinyl Cafe** BAR
(☑508 260 288; ul Kotlarska 35/36; ☺10am-late; ☻) Hitting the retro button hard, this cool cafe-bar is a jumble of mismatched furniture, old framed photos and stacks of vinyl records. It's a great place to grab a drink, both day and night.

**Mleczarnia** BAR
(☑71 787 7576; www.mle.pl; ul Włodkowica 5; ☺8am-4am; ☻) Hidden away in an area that was once the city's main Jewish neighbourhood, this atmospheric place is stuffed with chipped old wooden tables bearing lace doilies and candlesticks. It turns out good coffee and light meals, including breakfast. At night the cellar opens, adding another moody dimension. There's a beautiful back garden in summer.

**Bezsenność** CLUB
(www.bezsennosclub.com; ul Ruska 51; ☺7pm-late) With its alternative/rock/dance line-up and distressed decor, 'Insomnia' attracts a high-end clientele and is one of the most popular clubs in town. It's located in the Pasaż Niepolda, home to a group of bars, clubs and restaurants, just off ul Ruska.

## ☆ Entertainment

**Filharmonia** CLASSICAL MUSIC
(Philharmonic Hall; ☑tickets 71 715 9700; www. nfm.wroclaw.pl; ul Piłsudskiego 19) Hear classical music at this venue, located 800m southwest of the Rynek.

## ℹ Information

**Intermax** (☑71 794 0573; www.imx.pl; ul Psie Budy 10/11; per hr 4zł; ☺9am-11pm Mon-Sat, from 10am Sun) Internet access. Enter from ul Kazimierza Wielkiego.

**Tourist Office** (☑71 344 3111; www.wroclaw -info.pl; Rynek 14; ☺9am-7pm) Provides advice and assistance to visitors to Wrocław.

## ℹ Getting There & Away

### BUS
The **bus station** (Dworzec Centralny PKS; ☑703 400 444; ul Sucha 1/11) is south of the train station. For most destinations the train is a better choice, though handy Polski Bus services run from here to Warsaw (five hours, hourly) and Prague (five hours, four daily). Book these via www.polskibus.com.

### TRAIN
**Wrocław Main Train Station** (☑32 428 8888; www.pkp.pl; ul Piłsudskiego 105) was opened in 1857 as a lavish architectural confection. It's easily Poland's most attractive railway station and worth visiting even if you're not travelling by train. Sample destinations include Warsaw (150zł, 3¾ hours, seven daily), Kraków (40zł, 3½ hours, eight daily) and Poznań (34zł, 2¾ hours, hourly).

# WIELKOPOLSKA

Wielkopolska (Greater Poland) is the region where Poland came to life in the Middle Ages. As a result of this ancient eminence, its cities and towns are full of historic and cultural attractions. The battles of WWII later caused widespread destruction in the area, though Poznań has resumed its prominent economic role.

# Poznań

POP 546,000

Stroll into Poznań's central market square on any evening and you'll receive an instant introduction to the characteristic energy of Wielkopolska's capital. The city's Old Town district is buzzing at any time of the day, and positively jumping by night.

The city is strongly associated with the formation of the Polish kingdom in the 10th century. From the late 18th century to 1945, Poznań was the German-ruled city of Posen. Much of Poznań, including the main square

POLAND POZNAŃ

(Stary Rynek), was destroyed in fighting in WWII and painstakingly rebuilt in the decades after. These days, Poznań is a vibrant university city. There's a beautiful Old Town, with a number of interesting museums and a range of lively bars, clubs and restaurants.

# ◎ Sights

## ◎ Old Town

### Town Hall HISTORIC BUILDING
(Ratusz; Stary Rynek 1) Poznań's Renaissance town hall, topped with a 61m-high tower, instantly attracts attention. Its graceful form replaced a 13th-century Gothic structure, which burned down in the early 16th century. Every day at noon two metal goats appear through a pair of small doors above the clock and butt their horns together 12 times, in deference to an old legend. These days, the town hall is home to the city's Historical Museum. The building was designed by Italian architect Giovanni Battista Quadro and built from 1550 to 1560; only the tower is a later addition, built in the 1780s after its predecessor collapsed. The crowned eagle on top of the spire, with an impressive wingspan of 2m, adds some Polish symbolism.

Concerning the legend of the goats: apparently two goats intended for a celebratory banquet escaped and ended up clashing horns above the about-to-be-unveiled clock, much to the amusement of the assembled dignitaries. The clockmaker was duly ordered to add the errant animals' images to his piece.

### ★ Historical Museum of Poznań MUSEUM
(Muzeum Historii Miasta Poznania; ☑ 61 8568 000; www.mnp.art.pl; Stary Rynek 1; adult/concession 7/5zł, Sat free; ☉ 11am-5pm Tue-Thu, noon-9pm Fri, 11am-6pm Sat & Sun) Inside the town hall, this museum displays an interesting and well-presented exhibition on the town's history, and the building's original interiors are worth the entry price on their own. The Gothic vaulted cellars are the only remains of the first town hall. They were initially used for trade but later became a jail.

## ◎ Ostrów Tumski

The island of Ostrów Tumski, east of the main square and across the Warta River, is the place where Poznań was founded, and with it the Polish state.

### ★ Poznań Cathedral CHURCH
(Katedra Poznańska; ☑ 61 8529 642; www.katedra. archpoznan.pl; ul Ostrów Tumski 17; crypt adult/ concession 3.50/2.50zł; ☉ 9am-6pm) Ostrów Tumski is dominated by this monumental double-towered cathedral. Basically Gothic with additions from later periods, most notably the Baroque tops of the towers, the cathedral was damaged in 1945 and took 11 years to rebuild. The aisles and the ambulatory are ringed by a dozen chapels containing numerous tombstones. The most famous is the Golden Chapel behind the high altar, which houses the remains of the first two Polish rulers: Mieszko I and Bolesław Chrobry.

The rulers' original burial site was the crypt, accessible from the back of the left-hand aisle. Apart from the fragments of what are thought to have been their tombs, you can see the relics of the first pre-Romanesque cathedral dating from 968 and of the subsequent Romanesque building from the second half of the 11th century, along with dozens of coins tossed in by more recent Polish visitors.

### ★ Porta Posnania
### Interactive Heritage Centre MUSEUM
(Brama Poznania ICHOT; www.bramapoznania.pl; ul Gdańska 2; adult/concession 15/9zł, audioguide 5/3zł; ☉ 9am-6pm Tue-Fri, 10am-7pm Sat & Sun; ⏇) Cutting-edge multimedia museum that opened in 2014, telling the tale of Tumski island's eventful history and the birth of the Polish nation via interactive displays and other technological gadgetry. It's located opposite the island's eastern shore and is linked to the cathedral area by footbridge. The exhibitions are multilingual, but opt for an audioguide to help put everything together. To reach the museum from the city centre, take tram 8 eastward to the Rondo Śródka stop.

# 🛏 Sleeping

### Frolic Goats Hostel HOSTEL €
(☑ 61 852 4411; www.frolicgoatshostel.com; ul Wrocławska 16/6; dm 30-50zł, d 210zł; ⏇) Named after the feisty goats who fight above the town hall clock, this popular hostel is aimed squarely at the international backpacker. The pleasant lounge complements tidy, reasonably uncrowded dorms, there's a washing machine and bike hire is available for 50zł per day. Enter from ul Jaskółcza.

### ★ Hotel Stare Miasto HOTEL €€
(☑ 61 663 6242; www.hotelstaremiasto.pl; ul Rybaki 36; s 229zł, d 269-329zł; P ❄ ⏇) Stylish value-for-money hotel with a tastefully chandeliered foyer and spacious breakfast room. Rooms can be small but are clean and bright with lovely starched white sheets.

Some upper rooms have skylights in place of windows.

### Blow Up Hall 5050
HOTEL €€

(☑61 657 9980; www.blowuphall5050.com; ul Kościuszki 42; r from 450zł; P✳🖀) Wild art hotel housed within the solid ex-brewery walls of the Stary Browar shopping mall, 750m south of the Rynek. Each room has an individual hyper-modern design with colour schemes from dazzling white to gleaming black, with shiny angular furniture and fittings. The restaurant and bar are equally impressive.

## ✗ Eating

### Apetyt
CAFETERIA €

(ul Szkolna 4; mains 4-13zł; ☺9am-8pm Mon-Sat, 11am-10pm Sun; ☑) This late-closing *bar mleczny* (milk bar) enjoys a good central location. The Polish cafeteria food is exactly what you'd expect – cheap serves of unfussy, filling food such as *pierogi* (dumplings) and *zupy* (soups), with *naleśniki* (crêpe) choices galore. Includes several good vegetarian items.

### ★ Drukarnia
INTERNATIONAL €€

(☑61 850 1420; www.poznan-drukarnia.pl; ul Podgórna 6; mains 15-79zł; ☺7am-10pm Mon-Wed, to midnight Thu, to 1am Fri, 11am-1am Sat, 11am-10pm Sun) Some Polish restaurants are finally opening for breakfast, and this sleek eatery with exposed beams above concrete floors is a top early-bird's choice. Choices include a full English breakfast with sausage, bacon, eggs and beans, and a more adventurous pasta with smoked mackerel. Later on there's a menu featuring steaks and burgers, as well as a long wine list.

### Ludwiku do Rondla
JEWISH, POLISH €€

(ul Woźna 2/3; mains 28-40zł; ☺1-10pm) Small, cosy place east of the main square, specialising in Jewish and Polish cooking – particularly where the two intertwine. Menu items are helpfully marked if an item is Polish or Jewish in origin, and include such items as herring in oil (Polish/Jewish) and stuffed meat roulade with buckwheat (Polish). The lunchtime set menu is top value at around 25zł.

## 🍷 Drinking & Nightlife

### ★ Stragan
CAFE

(☑789 233 965; ul Ratajczaka 31; ☺8am-10pm Mon-Fri, 11am-10pm Sat, 11am-8pm Sun; 🖀) Cool, contemporary cafe in which even the most bearded hipster would feel at home. Coffee ranges from Chemex brews to flat whites, complemented by excellent cakes and light meals. Also serves breakfast.

### Chmielnik
BAR

(☑790 333 946; ul Żydowska 27; ☺noon-late) Ideal place to sample the output of the booming Polish craft-beer scene, with over 150 beers in stock. Lounge and sip in the pleasant wood-lined interior or in the ambient beer garden out the back.

### Van Diesel Music Club
CLUB

(☑515 065 459; www.vandiesel.pl; Stary Rynek 88; ☺9pm-5am Fri & Sat) Happening venue on the main square, with DJs varying their offerings between pop, house, R&B, soul and dance. Given the variety, you're sure to find a night that will get you on the dance floor.

## ☆ Entertainment

### Centrum Kultury Zamek
CONCERT VENUE

(Castle Cultural Centre; ☑61 646 5260; www.zamek.poznan.pl; ul Św Marcin 80/82; 🖀) Within the grand neo-Romanesque **Kaiserhaus**, built from 1904 to 1910 for German emperor Wilhelm II, this active cultural hub hosts cinema, art and music events.

## ℹ Information

**City Information Centre** (☑61 852 6156; www.poznan.travel; Stary Rynek 59/60; ☺10am-8pm Mon-Sat, 10am-6pm Sun May-Sep, 10am-5pm Oct-Apr) Located conveniently on the main square.

## ℹ Getting There & Away

### BUS

The **bus station** (Dworzec PKS; ☑703 30 3330; www.pks.poznan.pl; ul Dworcowa 1) is located next to the train station and is part of the Poznań City Centre transport and shopping complex. It's 1.5km southwest of the Old Town and can be reached on foot in 15 minutes, or by tram to stop 'Most Dworcowy'.

**Polski Bus** (www.polskibus.com) runs services to Warsaw (four to 5½ hours, seven daily) and Wrocław (3½ hours, three daily). Buy tickets online.

### TRAIN

Busy **Poznań Main Train Station** (ul Dworcowa 1) is 1.5km southwest of the Old Town and can be reached on foot in 15 minutes, or by tram to stop 'Most Dworcowy'.

Useful domestic train connections include to Gdańsk (60zł, 3¾ hours, eight daily), Kraków (67zł, six hours, hourly), Toruń (26zł, 2½ hours, nine daily), Wrocław (34zł, 2½ hours, hourly) and Warsaw (95zł, three hours, hourly). Poznań is a natural jumping-off spot for Berlin (168zł, 2¾ hours, five daily).

# POMERANIA

Pomerania (Pomorze in Polish) is an attractive region with diverse drawcards, from beautiful beaches to architecturally pleasing cities. The historic port city of Gdańsk is situated at the region's eastern extreme, while the attractive Gothic city of Toruń lies inland.

## Gdańsk

POP 460,000

The Hanseatic port of Gdańsk grew wealthy during the Middle Ages, linking inland cities with seaports around Europe. That wealth is on display in the form of a bustling riverbank, mammoth red-brick churches and lively central streets.

Gdańsk has played an outsized role in history. The creation of the 'Free City of Danzig', at the conclusion of World War I, served as a pretext for Hitler to invade Poland at the start of WWII. The Germans fired the first shots of the war here on 1 September 1939 at the Polish garrison at Westerplatte.

In August 1980, the city became the centre of Poland's anticommunist movement with the establishment of the Solidarity trade union, led by its charismatic leader (and future Polish president), Lech Wałęsa.

## ◉ Sights

Gdańsk's major sights are situated in the **Main Town** (Główne Miasto). Much of what you see, including the dazzling palaces that line the central promenade, **Long St** (ul Długa), was rebuilt from rubble after the bombardment of WWII.

### ◉ Main Town

**Historical Museum of Gdańsk**          MUSEUM
(Town Hall; www.mhmg.pl; Długa 46/47; adult/concession 12/6zł, tower 5zł; ⊙9am-1pm Tue, 10am-4pm Wed, Fri & Sat, to 6pm Thu, from 11am Sun) This museum is located in the historic **town hall**

## Gdańsk

(Długi Targ), which claims Gdańsk's highest tower at 81.5m. The showpiece is the Red Room (Sala Czerwona), done up in Dutch Mannerist style from the end of the 16th century. The 2nd floor houses exhibitions related to Gdańsk's history, including mock-ups of old Gdańsk interiors. From here you can access the tower for great views across the city.

The Red Room's interior is not an imitation but the real deal; it was dismantled in 1942 and hidden outside the city until the end of the bombing. The richly carved fireplace (1593) and the marvellous portal (1596) all attract the eye, but the centre of attention is the ornamented ceiling – 25 paintings dominated by an oval centrepiece entitled *The Glorification of the Unity of Gdańsk with Poland*. Other striking rooms include the Winter Hall with its portraits of Gdańsk's mayors up to the 17th century and the Great Council Chamber with its huge oils of Polish kings.

★ **St Mary's Church**   CHURCH
(www.bazylikamariacka.gdansk.pl; ul Podkramarska 5; adult/concession 4/2zł, tower 6/3zł; ☺ 8.30am-6.30pm Mon-Sat, 11am-noon & 1-5pm Sun May-Sep, slightly shorter hours Oct-Apr) Dominating the heart of the Main Town, St Mary's is often cited as the largest brick church in the world. Some 105m long and 66m wide at the transept, its massive squat tower climbs 78m high into the Gdańsk cityscape. Begun in 1343, St Mary's didn't reach its present proportions until 1502. Don't miss the 15th-century astronomical clock, placed in the northern transept, and the church tower (405 steps above the city).

On first sight, the church looks almost empty, but walk around its 30-odd chapels to discover how many outstanding works of art have been accumulated. In the floor alone, there are about 300 tombstones. In the chapel at the back of the left (northern) aisle is a replica of Memling's *The Last Judgment* – the original is in the National Museum's Department of Early Art. The extraordinary Baroque organ manages enough puff to fill the space with its tones.

The church's elephantine size is arresting and you feel even more antlike when you enter the building. Illuminated with natural light passing through 37 large windows (the biggest is 127 sq metres), the three-naved interior, topped by an intricate Gothic vault, is bright and spacious. It was originally covered with frescos, the sparse remains of which are visible in the far right corner.

The high altar boasts a Gothic polyptych from the 1510s, with the Coronation of the Virgin depicted in its central panel. Large as it is, it's a miniature in this vast space. The same applies to the 4m crucifix high up on the rood beam.

**National Maritime Museum**   MUSEUM
(Narodowe Muzeum Morskie w Gdańsku; ☑ Maritime Cultural Centre 58 329 8700, information 58 301 8611; www.nmm.pl; ul Ołowianka 9-13; all sites adult/concession 18/10zł; ☺ 10am-6pm daily) This is a sprawling exhibition of maritime history and Gdańsk's role through the centuries as a Baltic seaport. Headquarters is the multi-million-euro Maritime Cultural Centre, with a permanent interactive exhibition 'People-Ships-Ports'. Other exhibitions include the MS *Sołdek*, the first vessel to be built at the Gdańsk shipyard in the postwar years, and the Żuraw (Crane; www.nmm.pl; ul Szeroka 67/68; adult/concession 8/5zł; ☺ 10am-6pm daily Jul & Aug, closed Mon and shorter hours Sep-Jun), a 15th-century loading crane that was the biggest in its day. The granaries across the river house more displays, which are highly recommended.

POLAND GDAŃSK

---

## Gdańsk

## ◎ Outside the Centre

★**European Solidarity Centre** MUSEUM
(Europejskie Centrum Solidarności; ☑ 58 772 4112; www.ecs.gda.pl; Plac Solidarności 1; adult/concession 17/13zł; ☉ 10am-8pm Jun-Sep, to 6pm Oct-May) Housed in a mind-bogglingly ugly, oh-so 21st-century hulk of architecture, the exhibition in this unmarked centre (finding the entrance will be your first task) has quickly become one of Gdańsk's unmissables since it opened in 2014. Audioguide clamped to ears, the seven halls examine Poland's postwar fight for freedom, from the strikes of the 1970s to the round-table negotiations of the late 1980s and beyond. The displays are a blend of state-of-the-art multimedia experiences and real artefacts. Allow at least two hours.

## 🛏 Sleeping

**3 City Hostel** HOSTEL €
(☑ 58 354 5454; www.3city-hostel.pl; Targ Drzewny 12/14; dm from 49zł, r 170zł; @ 🎅) Big, modern, colourful hostel near the train station, with high ceilings, pleasant common areas, a kitchen, and a lounge with a view. Breakfast is included, plus there are computers on-hand for internet use. Reception runs round the clock.

**Dom Harcerza** HOSTEL €
(☑ 58 301 3621; www.domharcerza.pl; ul Za Murami 2/10; dm/s/d from 25/60/100zł; 🎅) Though occupying a former cinema, the 75-bed 'Scouts' House' has a decidedly un-Hollywood feel. There's dirt-cheap student-oriented dorm accommodation and rooms for one to three people with and without bathrooms. The simple, snug rooms are nothing fancy, but they're clean and tidy. The location near ul Długa is a winner.

**Kamienica Gotyk** HOTEL €€
(☑ 58 301 8567; www.gotykhouse.eu; ul Mariacka 1; s/d 280/310zł; P 🎅) Wonderfully located at the St Mary's Church end of ul Mariacka, Gdańsk's oldest house is filled by this neat, clean, Gothic-themed guesthouse. The seven rooms have Gothic touches such as broken-arched doorways and hefty drapery, though most are thoroughly modern creations and bathrooms are definitely of the third millennium. Breakfast is served in your room.

★**Hotel Podewils** HOTEL €€€
(☑ 58 300 9560; www.podewils.pl; ul Szafarnia 2; s/d 530/620zł; P 🎅) The view from the Podewils across the river to the Main Town can't be beaten, though the owners probably wish they could take its cheery Baroque facade and move it away from the incongruously soulless riverside development that's sprouted next door. Guestrooms are a confection of elegantly curved timber furniture, classic prints and distinctive wallpaper.

## ✕ Eating

**Bar Mleczny Neptun** CAFETERIA €
(☑ 058 301 4988; www.barneptun.pl; ul Długa 33/34; mains 4-9zł; ☉ 7.30am-7pm Mon-Fri, 10am-6pm Sat & Sun, 1hr later Jul & Aug; 🎅 📶) It's surprising just where some of Poland's communist-era milk bars have survived and this one, right on the tourist drag, is no exception. However, the Neptun is a cut above your run-of-the-mill *bar mleczny*, with potted plants, decorative tiling and free wi-fi. Popular with foreigners on a budget, it even has an English menu of Polish favourites such as *naleśniki* (crêpes) and *gołąbki* (cabbage rolls).

★**Tawerna Mestwin** POLISH €€
(☑ 58 301 7882; ul Straganiarska 20/23; mains 20-40zł; ☉ 11am-10pm Tue-Sun, to 6pm Mon; 🎅) The speciality here is Kashubian regional cooking from the northwest of Poland, and dishes like potato dumplings and stuffed cabbage rolls have a pronounced homemade quality. There's usually a fish soup and fried fish as well. The interior is done out like a traditional cottage and the exposed beams and dark-green walls create a cosy atmosphere.

**Restauracja Pod Łososiem** POLISH €€€
(☑ 58 301 7652; www.podlososiem.com.pl; ul Szeroka 52/54; mains 40-110zł; ☉ noon-11pm; 📶) Founded in 1598 and famous for salmon, this is one of Gdańsk's most highly regarded restaurants. Red leather seats, brass chandeliers and a gathering of gas lamps fill out the rather sober interior, illuminated by the speciality drink – Goldwasser. This gooey, sweet liqueur with flakes of gold was produced in its cellars from the 16th century until WWII.

## 🍷 Drinking & Nightlife

★**Józef K** BAR
(☑ 058 550 4935; ul Piwna 1/2; ☉ 10am-last customer; 🎅) Is it a bar or a junk shop? You decide as you relax with a cocktail or a glass of excellent Polish perry (pear cider) on one of the battered sofas, illuminated by an old theatre spotlight. Downstairs is an open

area where the party kicks off at weekends; upstairs is more intimate with lots of soft seating and well-stocked bookcases.

**Lamus**                                                   BAR
(Lawendowa 8, enter from Straganiarska; ⊘ noon-1am Mon-Fri, to 3am Sat, to midnight Sun) This fun retro-drink halt has a random scattering of 1970s furniture, big-print wallpaper from the same period, and a menu of Polish craft beers, cider and coffee. There's also a spillover bar for the Saturday-night crowd.

**Miasto Aniołów**                                          CLUB
(☑58 768 5831; www.miastoaniolow.com.pl; ul Chmielna 26) The City of Angels covers all the bases – late-night revellers can hit the spacious dance floor, crash in the chill-out area or hang around the atmospheric deck overlooking the Motława River. Nightly DJs play disco and other dance-oriented sounds.

## ☆ Entertainment

**Baltic Philharmonic Hall**               CLASSICAL MUSIC
(☑58 320 6262; www.filharmonia.gda.pl; ul Ołowianka 1) The usual home of chamber music concerts also organises many of the major music festivals throughout the year.

## ❶ Information

**Tourist Office** Train station (☑58 721 3277; www.gdansk4u.pl; ul Podwale Grodzkie 8; ⊘9am-7pm May-Sep, to 5pm Oct-Apr); Main Town (☑58 301 4355; www.gdansk4u.pl; Długi Targ 28/29; ⊘9am-7pm May-Sep, to 5pm Oct-Apr); Airport (☑58 348 13 68; www.gdansk4u.pl; ul Słowackiego 210, Gdańsk Lech Wałęsa Airport; ⊘24hr) Relatively efficient but occasionally visitor-weary info points. The train station branch is hidden in the underpass leading to the city centre.

## ❶ Getting There & Away

### BUS

The **bus station** (PKS Gdańsk; ☑801 055 900; www.pks.gdansk.pl; ul 3 Maja 12) is behind the main train station. PKS buses head to Warsaw (50zł, 5¼ hours, hourly), as do services of Polski Bus (4½ to 5½ hours, seven daily). Book tickets for the latter at www.polskibus.com.

### TRAIN

The city's train station, **Gdańsk Główny** (Gdańsk Główny; www.pkp.pl; ul Podwale Grodzkie 1), is located on the western outskirts of the Old Town. Most long-distance trains actually start or finish at Gdynia, so make sure you get on/off quickly here.

Useful direct train connections include to Toruń (40zł, three hours, nine daily), Poznań

**WORTH A TRIP**

## MALBORK

Magnificent **Malbork Castle** (☑tickets 55 647 0978; www.zamek.malbork.pl; ul Starościńska 1; adult/concession 39.50/29.50zł; ⊘9am-7pm May-Sep, 10am-3pm Oct-Apr) makes a great day trip from Gdańsk. It's the largest Gothic castle in Europe and was once headquarters for the medieval Teutonic Knights. Its sinister form looms over the relatively small town and Nogat River. Trains run regularly from Gdańsk Głowny station (14zł, 45 minutes, twice hourly). Once you get to Malbork station, turn right, cross the highway and follow ul Kościuszki to the castle. Compulsory tours come with an audio tour in English. There are places to eat at the castle and in the town.

(60zł, 3½ hours, eight daily) and Warsaw (60zł to 119zł½, three to six hours, hourly).

## Toruń

POP 205,000

Toruń escaped major damage in WWII and is famous for its well-preserved Gothic architecture, along with the quality of its famous gingerbread. The city is also renowned as the birthplace of Nicolaus Copernicus, who revolutionised the field of astronomy in 1543 by asserting the Earth travelled around the Sun. He's a figure you will not be able to escape – you can even buy gingerbread men in his likeness.

## ◉ Sights

The usual starting point on Toruń's Gothic trail is the **Old Town Market Square** (Rynek Staromiejski), lined with finely restored houses. At the southeast corner, look for the picturesque **Statue of Copernicus**.

**Old Town Hall**                                        MUSEUM
(Ratusz Staromiejski; www.muzeum.torun.pl; Rynek Staromiejski 1; adult/concession museum 12/8zł, tower 12/8zł, combined ticket 19/14zł; ⊘museum 10am-6pm Tue-Sun, tower 10am-8pm May-Sep, shorter hours Oct-Apr) The Old Town Hall dates from the 14th century and hasn't changed much since, though some Renaissance additions lent an ornamental touch to the sober Gothic structure. Today, it houses the main branch of the Toruń Regional Museum

## GREAT MASURIAN LAKES

The northeastern corner of Poland features a beautiful postglacial landscape dominated by thousands of lakes. About 200km of canals connect these bodies of water, making the area a prime destination for canoeists, as well as those who love to hike, fish and mountain bike.

The towns of **Giżycko** and **Mikołajki** make good bases. Both the Giżycko **tourist office** (☑ 87 428 5265; www.gizycko.turystyka.pl; ul Wyzwolenia 2; ☺ 8am-5pm Mon-Fri, 10am-2pm Sat & Sun Mar-May & Sep-Oct, 9am-6pm Mon-Fri, 10am-4pm Sat & Sun Jun-Aug, shorter hours Nov-Feb) and the Mikołajki **tourist office** (☑ 87 421 6850; www.mikolajki.pl; Plac Wolności 7; ☺ 10am-6pm Jun-Aug, 10am-6pm Mon-Sat May & Sep) supply useful maps for sailing and hiking, provide excursion boat schedules, and assist in finding accommodation.

Nature aside, there are some interesting fragments of history in this region. A grim reminder of the past is the **Wolf's Lair** (Wilczy Szaniec; ☑ 89 752 4429; www.wolfsschanze.pl; adult/concession 15/10zł; ☺ 8am-dusk). Located at **Gierłoż**, 8km east of Kętrzyn, this ruined complex was Hitler's wartime headquarters for his invasion of the Soviet Union. In 1944, a group of high-ranking German officers tried to assassinate Hitler here. These dramatic events were reprised in the 2008 Tom Cruise movie *Valkyrie*.

boasting displays of Gothic art (painting and stained glass), a display of local 17th- and 18th-century crafts and a gallery of Polish paintings from 1800 to the present, including a couple of Witkacys and Matejkos. Climb the tower for a fine panoramic view of Toruń's Gothic townscape.

#### Cathedral of SS John the Baptist & John the Evangelist            CHURCH
(www.katedra.diecezja.torun.pl; ul Żeglarska 16; ☺ 9am-5.30pm Mon-Sat, 2-5.30pm Sun) Toruń's mammoth Gothic cathedral was begun around 1260 but only completed at the end of the 15th century. Its massive tower houses Poland's second-largest historic bell, the Tuba Dei (God's Trumpet). On the southern side of the tower, facing the Vistula, is a large 15th-century clock; its original face and single hand are still in working order. Check out the dent above the VIII – it's from a cannonball that struck the clock during the Swedish siege of 1703.

#### Toruń Gingerbread Museum            MUSEUM
(Muzeum Toruńskiego Piernika; www.muzeum.torun.pl; ul Strumykowa 4; adult/concession 12/8zł; ☺ 10am-6pm Tue-Sun May-Sep, to 4pm Oct-Apr) Not to be confused with the commercial **Gingerbread Museum** (Muzeum Piernika; ☑ 56 663 6617; www.muzeumpiernika.pl; ul Rabiańska 9; adult/child15/10zł; ☺ 10am-6pm, tours every hour, on the hour) across town, this branch of the Toruń Regional Museum is housed in a former gingerbread factory and looks at the 600-year-long history of the city's favourite sweet.

## 🛏 Sleeping

#### Toruń Główny Hostel            HOSTEL €
(☑ 606 564 600; www.hosteltg.com; Toruń Główny train station; dm/d 39/70zł; ☜) This 56-bed hostel is housed in the old post office building right on the platform at Toruń's recently renovated main train station. The six- and eight-bed dorms are spacious with suitcase-size lockers and reading lamps; free breakfast is taken in the basement kitchen. There are attractive wall frescos of Toruń's old town and, surprisingly, no train noise to keep you awake at night.

#### ★ Hotel Petite Fleur            HOTEL €€
(☑ 56 621 5100; www.petitefleur.pl; ul Piekary 25; s/d from 180/210zł; ☜) One of the better midrange options in Toruń has understated rooms containing slickly polished timber furnishings and elegant prints, though the singles can be a touch small. The French brick-cellar restaurant is one of Toruń's better hotel dining options and the buffet breakfast is one of the best in the north.

#### Hotel Karczma Spichrz            HOTEL €€
(☑ 56 657 1140; www.spichrz.pl; ul Mostowa 1; s/d 250/310zł; ✻ ☜) Wonderfully situated within a historic waterfront granary, this hotel's 19 rooms are laden with personality, featuring massive exposed beams above characterful timber furniture and contemporary bathrooms. The location by the river is within walking distance of the sights but away from the crowds. Good restaurant next door.

## 🍴 Eating

### Karrotka
VEGETARIAN €

(Łazienna 9; mains 5-12zł; ☺noon-7pm Mon-Sat, to 5pm Sun; 🍴) Enjoy tasty vegetarian dishes under a large wall mural of painted carrots crossed in meat-free defiance at this small vegetarian milk bar.

### Oberża
POLISH €

(☑606 664 756; www.gotujemy.pl; ul Rabiańska 9; mains 8-17zł; ☺11am-10pm Mon-Thu, to 11pm Fri & Sat, to 9pm Sun; 🛜) This large self-service canteen stacks 'em high and sells 'em cheap for a hungry crowd of locals and tourists. Find your very own thatched mini cottage or intimate hideout lost amid stained-glass windows, cartwheels, bridles and other rural knick-knacks of yesteryear to enjoy 11 types of *pierogi* (dumplings), soups, salads and classic Polish mains from a menu tuned to low-cost belly-packing.

### ★ Szeroka 9
INTERNATIONAL €€€

(☑56 622 8424; www.szeroka9.pl; ul Szeroka 9; mains 32-49zł; ☺noon-11pm Mon-Fri, from 10am Sat & Sun; 🖺) Arguably Toruń's top restaurant, it offers a changing menu of seasonal gourmet-style fare with everything from rabbit in apple and cream sauce to house tagliatelle. The dessert to plump for is local gingerbread in plum sauce. The decor is contemporary urban and the staff is friendly and knowledgeable about what's on the plate. Reservations are recommended for dinner.

## 🍷 Drinking & Nightlife

### Cafe Molus
CAFE

(☑56 621 1107; www.cafemolus.pl; Rynek Staromiejski 36; ☺8am-last customer) This stylish cafe fulfils the desires of the sweet-toothed and caffeine-cravers under broken Gothic arches, painted ceilings and some of the chunkiest beamery you've ever seen. The highlight here is the secluded Renaissance-style courtyard out back where you can leave the city behind as you take cake.

### Jan Olbracht
BREWERY

(www.browar-olbracht.pl; ul Szczytna 15; ☺10am-11pm Sun-Thu, to midnight Fri & Sat) Take a seat in an egg-shaped indoor booth or at the street-side mini beer garden to sip some of this microbrewery's unusual beers. These include pils, wheat beer, a special ale and, this being Toruń, gingerbread beer, all brewed in the huge copper vats at the front of the huge building.

## ☆ Entertainment

### Dwór Artusa
CLASSICAL MUSIC

(☑56 655 4929; www.artus.torun.pl; Rynek Staromiejski 6) The Artus Court, one of the most impressive mansions on the main square, is now a major cultural centre and has an auditorium hosting musical events, including concerts and recitals.

## ℹ️ Information

**Tourist Office** (☑56 621 0930; www.torun.pl; Rynek Staromiejski 25; ☺9am-6pm Mon-Fri, to 4pm Sat & Sun; 🛜) Free wi-fi access, heaps of info and professional staff who know their city.

## ℹ️ Getting There & Away

### BUS

The **bus station** (Dworzec Autobusowy Arriva; www.rozklady.com.pl; ul Dąbrowskiego 8-24) is a 10-minute walk north of the Old Town. From here, Polski Bus connects to Warsaw (3½ hours, four daily) and Gdańsk (two hours, five daily); fares vary, so book online at www.polskibus.com. For other places, it's usually better to take the train.

### TRAIN

Toruń's **main train station** (Toruń Główny; www.pkp.pl; Kujawska 1; 🚌22, 27) is located on the opposite side of the Vistula River and linked to the Old Town by bus 22 or 27 (or a 2km walk). Useful direct train connections include those to Gdańsk (45zł, three hours, nine daily), Kraków (65zł, seven hours, three daily), Poznań (26zł, 2½ hours, nine daily) and Warsaw (45zł, 2¾ hours, eight daily).

POLAND TORUŃ

---

### ESSENTIAL FOOD & DRINK

**Barszcz** Famous beetroot soup comes in two varieties: red (made from beetroot) and white (with wheat flour and sausage).

**Bigos** Thick stew with sauerkraut and meat.

**Pierogi** Flour dumplings, usually stuffed with cheese, mushrooms or meat.

**Szarlotka** Apple cake with cream; a Polish classic.

**Wódka** Vodka: try it plain, or ask for *myśliwska* (flavoured with juniper berries).

**Żurek** Hearty, sour rye soup includes sausage and hard-boiled egg.

# SURVIVAL GUIDE

## ℹ️ Directory A–Z

### ACCOMMODATION

➤ Polish accommodation runs the gamut from youth hostels, bungalows and mountain cabins to modest hotels and pensions all the way to up-market boutiques and business-oriented chains.

➤ Youth hostels are divided into 'older-style', where accommodation is offered in basic dorms, and modern hostels, geared toward international backpackers. A dorm bed can cost anything from 40zł to 60zł per person per night.

➤ A handy campsite resource is the website of the **Polish Federation of Camping and Caravanning** (www.pfcc.eu).

➤ Hotel prices vary substantially depending on the day of the week or season. In cities, expect higher rates during the week and weekend discounts. In heavily touristed areas, rates may rise over the weekend.

➤ In big cities like Warsaw, Kraków and Gdańsk, private apartments with washing machines are available for short-term rentals. These can offer an affordable alternative to hotels, and compensate for the lack of laundromats in Poland.

### GAY & LESBIAN TRAVELLERS

➤ Homosexual activity is legal in Poland and overt discrimination is banned, though public attitudes are generally not supportive.

➤ Warsaw and Kraków are the best places to find gay-friendly bars and clubs.

➤ A decent source of online information: www.gayguide.net.

### INTERNET ACCESS

➤ Nearly all hotels and hostels offer internet, usually wi-fi.

---

### COUNTRY FACTS

**Area** 312,679 sq km

**Capital** Warsaw

**Country Code** ☎48

**Currency** Złoty (zł)

**Emergency** Ambulance ☎999, fire ☎998, police ☎997; from mobile phones ☎112

**Language** Polish

**Money** ATMs all over; banks open Monday to Friday

**Population** 38.5 million

**Visas** Not required for citizens of the EU, US, Canada, New Zealand and Australia.

---

---

### SLEEPING PRICE RANGES

Accommodation listings are grouped by price then ordered by preference. Prices listed are for an average double room in high season, with private bathroom and including breakfast.

**€** less than 150zł

**€€** 150–400zł

**€€€** more than 400zł

---

➤ Many cafes, restaurants and bars offer free wi-fi for customers.

➤ Internet cafes are not as abundant as they were, but normally charge around 6zł per hour.

### MONEY

➤ Poland's currency is the złoty (zwo-ti), abbreviated as zł (international currency code PLN). It's divided into 100 groszy (gr).

➤ *Bankomats* (ATMs) accept most international credit cards and are easily found. Private *kantors* (foreign-exchange offices) are also everywhere.

➤ Tipping isn't common in Poland, but feel free to leave 10% extra for waitstaff or taxi drivers if you've had good service.

### OPENING HOURS

**Banks** 9am–4pm Monday to Friday, 9am–1pm Saturday (varies)

**Offices** 9am–5pm Monday to Friday, 9am–1pm Saturday (varies)

**Post Offices** 8am–7pm Monday to Friday, 8am–1pm Saturday (cities)

**Restaurants** 11am–10pm daily

**Shops** 8am–6pm Monday to Friday, 10am–2pm Saturday

### PUBLIC HOLIDAYS

**New Year's Day** 1 January

**Epiphany** 6 January

**Easter Sunday** March or April

**Easter Monday** March or April

**State Holiday** 1 May

**Constitution Day** 3 May

**Pentecost Sunday** Seventh Sunday after Easter

**Corpus Christi** Ninth Thursday after Easter

**Assumption Day** 15 August

**All Saints' Day** 1 November

**Independence Day** 11 November

**Christmas** 25 and 26 December

### TELEPHONE

All Poland phone numbers have nine digits. Landlines are written ☎12 345 6789, while mobile phone numbers are written ☎123 456 789. To call abroad from Poland, dial the international access code (00), then the country code, then the area code (minus any initial zero) and the number. To dial Poland from abroad, dial your country's international access code, then ⏁ 48 (Poland's country code) then the nine-digit local number.

## VISAS

EU citizens do not need visas and can stay indefinitely. Citizens of the USA, Canada, Australia, New Zealand, Israel, Japan and many other countries can stay in Poland for up to 90 days without a visa. Other nationalities should check with their local Polish embassy or at the Polish Ministry of Foreign Affairs website (www.msz.gov.pl).

# ❶ Getting There & Away

### AIR

➡ Warsaw-Frédéric Chopin Airport (p288) is the nation's main international gateway, while other important airports include Kraków, Gdańsk, Poznań and Wrocław.

➡ The national carrier **LOT** (⏁ 22 577 7755; www.lot.com) flies to major European cities and select destinations further afield.

➡ A vast array of budget carriers, including **Ryanair** (www.ryanair.com) and **Wizz Air** (www.wizzair.com), fly into Poland from airports across Europe, including regional airports in Britain and Ireland.

### LAND
#### Border Crossings

➡ As Poland is a member of the EU's Schengen Zone, there are no passport or customs controls if arriving from Germany, the Czech Republic, Slovakia or Lithuania.

➡ Expect border delays if arriving from Ukraine, Belarus or Russia's Kaliningrad province.

#### Bus

➡ International buses head in all directions, including eastward to the Baltic States. From Zakopane, it's easy to hop to Slovakia via bus or minibus.

➡ Several companies operate long-haul coach service. Two reliable operators include **Eurolines Polska** (⏁ 146 571 777; www.eurolines.pl) and Polski Bus (www.polskibus.com).

#### Car & Motorcycle

➡ The minimum legal driving age is 18.

➡ The maximum blood-alcohol limit is 0.02%.

➡ All drivers are required to carry their home driving licence, along with identity card, vehicle registration and liability insurance.

#### Train

There are direct rail services from Warsaw to several surrounding capitals, including Berlin, Prague, Minsk and Moscow. Kraków also has useful international rail connections.

### SEA

Ferry services operated by **Polferries** (⏁ 801 003 171; www.polferries.pl), **Stena Line** (⏁ 58 660 9200; www.stenaline.pl) and **Unity Line** (⏁ 91 359 5600; www.unityline.pl) connect Poland's Baltic coast ports of Gdańsk, Gydnia and Świnoujscie to destinations in Scandinavia.

# ❶ Getting Around

### AIR

LOT flies between Warsaw, Gdańsk, Kraków, Poznań, Wrocław and Lublin.

### BUS

➡ Most buses are operated by the state bus company, PKS. It operates both ordinary buses (marked in black on timetables) and fast buses (marked in red).

➡ Buy tickets at bus terminals or directly from the driver.

➡ Private company Polski Bus offers modern, comfortable long-haul coach service to select large Polish cities and beyond; buy tickets from its website (www.polskibus.com).

### CAR

Major international car-rental companies are represented in larger cities and airports.

### TRAIN

**Polish State Railways** (PKP; ⏁ information 703 202 020; www.pkp.pl) operates trains to nearly every tourist destination; its online timetable is helpful, providing routes, fares and intermediate stations in English.

➡ EIC (Express InterCity) and EC (EuroCity) trains link large cities and offer the best and fastest connections. Reservations are obligatory.

➡ TLK (Tanie Linie Kolejowe) trains tend to be as fast as EC, but are cheaper. Trains are often crowded and no reservations are taken for 2nd class on some trains.

➡ IR (InterRegio) and R (Regio) are cheap and slow local trains.

➡ Buy tickets at ticket machines, station ticket windows or at special PKP passenger-service centres, located in major stations. Also buy online at the Polish State Railways (PKP) website.

# Romania

## Includes ➡

## Best Places to Eat

➡ Lacrimi şi Sfinţi (p317)

➡ Bistro de l'Arte (p320)

➡ Crama Sibiul Vechi (p324)

➡ Roata (p327)

➡ Caruso (p330)

## Best Places to Stay

➡ Little Bucharest Old Town Hostel (p316)

➡ Rembrandt Hotel (p317)

➡ Casa Georgius Krauss (p323)

➡ Youthink Hostel (p326)

## Why Go?

Beautiful and beguiling, Romania's rural landscape remains relatively untouched by the country's urban evolution. It's a land of aesthetically stirring hand-ploughed fields, sheep-instigated traffic jams and lots of homemade plum brandy.

Most visitors focus their attention on Transylvania, with its legacy of fortified Saxon towns like Braşov and Sighişoara, plus tons of eye-catching natural beauty. Similar in character but even more remote, the region of Maramureş offers authentic folkways and villages marked by memorable wooden churches. Across the Carpathians, the Unesco-listed painted monasteries dot southern Bucovina. The Danube Delta has more than 300 species of birds, including many rare varieties, and is an ideal spot for birdwatching.

Energetic cities like Timişoara, Sibiu, Cluj-Napoca and, especially, Bucharest offer culture – both high- and lowbrow – and showcase Romania as a rapidly evolving European country.

## When to Go
### Bucharest

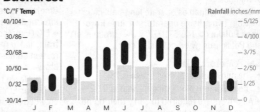

**May** Trees in full blossom; birdwatching in the Danube Delta at its best.

**Jun** Mountain hiking starts in mid-June; castles and museums are open and in high gear.

**Sep** The summer heat is gone, but sunny days are perfect for exploring big cities.

## Romania Highlights

**1 Brașov** (p319) Basing yourself here to ascend castles and mountains (and castles on top of mountains).

**2 Southern Bucovina** (p328) Following the Unesco World Heritage line of painted monasteries.

**3 Sibiu** (p323) Soaking in this beautifully restored Saxon town.

**4 Sighișoara** (p322) Exploring this medieval citadel and birthplace of Dracula.

**5 Danube Delta** (p326) Rowing through the tributaries and the riot of nature.

**6 Bucharest** (p313) Enjoying the museums and cacophonous nightlife of the capital.

# BUCHAREST

📞 021 / POP 1,900,000

Romania's capital gets a bad rap, but in fact it's dynamic, energetic and fun. It's where still-unreconstructed communism meets unbridled capitalism; where the soporific forces of the EU meet the passions of the Balkans. Many travellers give the city just a night or two before heading off to Transylvania, but that's not enough. Budget at least a few days to take in the good museums, stroll the parks and hang out at trendy cafes.

## ☉ Sights

### ⊙ South of the Centre

★**Palace of Parliament**　HISTORIC BUILDING
(Palatul Parlamentului, Casa Poporului; 📞 tour bookings 0733-558 102; http://cic.cdep.ro; B-dul Națiunile Unite; adult/student complete tours 55/28 lei,

# Central Bucharest

N 0 — 200 m
0 — 0.1 miles

Midland Youth Hostel (350m)

**13**

B-dul Gen Magheru

Shift Pub (250m)

Icoanei Garden

Str Pictor Verona

Grigore Antipa Natural History Museum (1.2km); Museum of the Romanian Peasant & Gift Shop (1.5km); Atlassib (1.6km); Seneca Anticafe (2.1km)

**16**

**12**
**18**

Str Pictor Verona

Str Georges Clemenceau

Str Mendeleev

Str Nicolae Golescu

Str Episcopiei

Str George Enescu

B-dul Nicolae Bălcescu

Str Dionisie Lupu

Str Pitar Moș

Vila Arte (500m)

**Romanian Athenaeum 1**

Str Franklin

Str C A Rosetti

**10**

Calea Victoriei

Str Luterană

Str Știrbei Vodă

Piața George Enescu

Str C A Rosetti

Str Boteanu

Str Nicolae Filipescu

Str Tudor Arghezi

**2**

Piața Revoluției

Str D I Dobrescu

**4**

Str Ion Câmpineanu

**17**

Piața Walter Mărăcineanu

Str Ion Câmpineanu

Str Matei Millo

Str Ion Brezoianu

Str E Quinet

**Universitate**

**15**

Str Constantin Mille

University (Piața Universității)

Cișmigiu Garden

B-dul Regina Elisabeta

Str Academiei

Bucharest National Opera House (1.2km)

Str Domnita Anastasia

Str Eforie

Str Ion Ghica

Romanian National Library

Str Colței

Str Lipscani

**14**

Str Lipscani

Str M Vodă

Bucharest Financial Plaza

Str Doamnei

**7**

Str Blănari

Spl Independenței

Str Ilfov

**8**

Str Stavropoleos

Str Lipscani

**6**

Str Hanul cu Tei

Calea Victoriei

**5**

**HISTORIC QUARTER**

**11**

**9**

Palace of Parliament (400m)

Str Poștei

Str Smârdan

Str Șelari

Str Gabroveni

Str Covaci

B-dul I C Brătianu

B-dul Națiunile Unite

Piața Națiunile Unite

Str Franceză

**3**

Great Synagogue (800m)

Dâmbovița River

# Central Bucharest

standard tours 35/18 lei, photography 30 lei; ⊙ 9am-5pm Mar-Oct, to 4pm Nov-Feb; Ⓜ Izvor) The Palace of Parliament is the world's second-largest administrative building (after the Pentagon) and former dictator Nicolae Ceaușescu's most infamous creation. Started in 1984 (and still unfinished), the building has more than 3000 rooms and covers 330,000 sq metres. Entry is by guided tour only (book in advance). Entry to the palace is from B-dul Națiunile Unite on the building's northern side (to find it, face the front of the palace from B-dul Unirii and walk around the building to the right). Bring your passport.

**Great Synagogue** SYNAGOGUE
(📞 0734-708 970; Str Adamache 11; ⊙ 9am-3pm Mon-Thu, to 1pm Fri & Sun; Ⓜ Piața Unirii) FREE This important synagogue dates from the mid-19th century and was established by migrating Polish Jews; entry is free, but a donation (10 lei) is expected. It's hard to find, hidden on three sides by public housing blocks, but worth the effort to see the meticulously restored interior and to take in the main exhibition on Jewish life and the Holocaust in Romania.

---

## ⊙ Historic Centre & Piața Revoluției

Bucharest's Historic Centre (Centrul Istoric), sometimes referred to as the Old Town, lies south of Piața Revoluției. It was the seat of power in the 15th century but today is filled with clubs and bars.

Piața Revoluției saw the heaviest fighting in the overthrow of communism in 1989. Those days are commemorated by the **Rebirth Memorial** (Memorialul Renașterii; Calea Victoriei, Piața Revoluției; ⊙ 24hr; Ⓜ Universitate) in the centre of the square.

**Old Princely Court Church** CHURCH
(Biserica Curtea Veche; Str Franceză; ⊙ 7am-8pm; Ⓜ Piața Unirii) FREE The Old Princely Court Church, built from 1546 to 1559 during the reign of Mircea Ciobanul (Mircea the Shepherd), is considered to be Bucharest's oldest church. The faded 16th-century frescoes next to the altar are originals. The carved stone portal was added in 1715.

**Stavropoleos Church** CHURCH
(📞 021-313 4747; www.stavropoleos.ro; Str Stavropoleos 4; ⊙ 7am-8pm; Ⓜ Piața Unirii) FREE The tiny and lovely Stavropoleos Church, which dates from 1724, perches a bit oddly a block over from some of Bucharest's craziest Old Town carousing. It's one church, though, that will make a lasting impression, with its courtyard filled with tombstones, ornate wooden interior and carved wooden doors.

★ **Romanian Athenaeum** HISTORIC BUILDING
(Ateneul Român; 📞 box office 021-315 6875; www.fge.org.ro; Str Benjamin Franklin 1-3; tickets 20-65 lei; ⊙ box office noon-7pm Tue-Fri, 4-7pm Sat, 10-11am Sun; Ⓜ Universitate, Piața Romană) The exquisite Romanian Athenaeum is the majestic heart of Romania's classical music tradition. Scenes from Romanian history are featured on the interior fresco inside the Big Hall on the 1st floor; the dome is 41m high. A huge appeal dubbed 'Give a Penny for the Athenaeum' saved it from disaster after funds dried up in the late 19th century. Today it's home to the George Enescu Philharmonic Orchestra and normally only open during concerts, but you can often take a peek inside.

## ITINERARIES

### One Week

Spend a day ambling around the capital, then take a train to Braşov – Transylvania's main event – for castles, activities and beer at streetside cafes. Spend a day in Sighişoara's medieval citadel, then catch a train back to Bucharest or on to Budapest.

### Two Weeks

Arrive in Bucharest by plane or Timişoara by train, then head into **Transylvania**, devoting a day or two each to Braşov, Sighişoara and Sibiu. Tour southern **Bucovina**'s painted monasteries, then continue on to **Bucharest**.

**National Art Museum**                   MUSEUM
(Muzeul Naţional de Artă; ☑ information 021-313 3030; www.mnar.arts.ro; Calea Victoriei 49-53; 15 lei; ☉ 11am-7pm Wed-Sun; Ⓜ Universitate) Housed in the 19th-century Royal Palace, this massive, multipart museum – all signed in English – houses two permanent galleries: one for National Art and the other for European Masters. The national gallery is particularly strong on ancient and medieval art, while the European gallery includes some 12,000 pieces and is laid out by nationality.

## ◉ North of the Centre

Luxurious villas and parks line grand Şos Kiseleff, which begins at Piaţa Victoriei. The major landmark is the **Triumphal Arch** (Arcul de Triumf; Piaţa Arcul de Triumf; ☉ closed to the public; Ⓜ Aviatorilor) FREE, which stands halfway up Şos Kiseleff.

**★ Former Ceauşescu Residence**             HISTORIC BUILDING
(Primăverii Palace; ☑ 021-318 0989; www.palatul-primaverii.ro; B-dul Primăverii 50; guided tours in English adult/child 45/30 lei; ☉ 10am-6pm Wed-Sun; Ⓜ Aviatorilor) This restored villa is the former main residence of Nicolae and Elena Ceauşescu, who lived here for around two decades up until the end of 1989. Everything has been returned to its former lustre, including the couple's bedroom and the private apartments of the three Ceauşescu children. Highlights include a cinema in the basement, Elena's opulent private chamber, and the back garden and swimming pool. Reserve a tour in advance by phone or on the website.

**★ Grigore Antipa Natural History Museum**             MUSEUM
(Muzeul de Istorie Naturală Grigore Antipa; ☑ 021-312 8826; www.antipa.ro; Şos Kiseleff 1; adult/student 20/5 lei; ☉ 10am-8pm Wed-Sun; ♿; Ⓜ Piaţa Victoriei) One of the few attractions in Bucharest aimed squarely at kids, this natural history museum has been thoroughly renovated and features modern bells and whistles such as video displays, games and interactive exhibits. Much of it has English signage.

**Museum of the Romanian Peasant**   MUSEUM
(Muzeul Ţăranului Român; ☑ 021-317 9661; www.muzeultaranuluiroman.ro; Şos Kiseleff 3; adult/child 8/2 lei; ☉ 10am-6pm Tue-Sun; Ⓜ Piaţa Victoriei) The collection of peasant bric-a-brac, costumes, icons and partially restored houses makes this one of the most popular museums in the city. There's not much English signage, but insightful little cards in English posted in each room give a flavour of what's on offer. An 18th-century church stands in the back lot, as does a great **gift shop** (www.muzeultaranuluiroman.ro; Şos Kiseleff 3; ☉ 10am-6pm Tue-Sun; Ⓜ Piaţa Victoriei) and restaurant.

## ⌶ Sleeping

Hotels in Bucharest are typically aimed at businesspeople, and prices are higher here than the rest of the country. **Cert Accommodation** (☑ 0720-772 772; www.cert-accommodation.ro; apt 250-500 lei) offers good-value private apartment stays starting at around 200 lei per night.

**★ Little Bucharest Old Town Hostel**                  HOSTEL €
(☑ 0786-329 136; www.littlebucharest.ro; Str Smârdan 15; dm 50-60 lei, r 250 lei; ☕@🛜; Ⓜ Piaţa Unirii) Bucharest's most central hostel, in the middle of the lively Historic Centre, is super clean well-run. Accommodation is over two floors, with dorms ranging from six to 12 beds. Private doubles are also available. The staff is travel friendly and youth oriented, and can advise on sightseeing and fun. Book over the website or by email.

**Midland Youth Hostel**             HOSTEL €
(☑ 021-314 5323; www.themidlandhostel.com; Str Biserica Amzei 22; dm 40-60 lei; ☕❄@🛜; Ⓜ Piaţa Romană) A happening hostel, with an excellent central location not far from popular Piaţa Amzei. Accommodation is in four-, eight- or 12-bed dorms. There's a common kitchen too.

★**Rembrandt Hotel**                    HOTEL €€
(📞021-313 9315; www.rembrandt.ro; Str Smârdan 11; s/d tourist 180/230 lei, standard 260/300 lei, business 350/380 lei; 🖨❄@🛜; Ⓜ Universitate) It's hard to say enough good things about this place. Stylish beyond its three-star rating, this 16-room, Dutch-run hotel faces the landmark National Bank in the Historic Centre. Rooms come in three categories – tourist, standard and business – with the chief difference being size. Book well in advance.

**Vila Arte**                    BOUTIQUE HOTEL €€€
(📞021-210 1035; www.vilaarte.ro; Str Vasile Lascăr 78; s/d 260/320 lei; 🖨❄@🛜; Ⓜ Piața Romană, 🚌5, 21) A renovated villa transformed into an excellent-value boutique hotel stuffed with original art that pushes the envelope on design and colour at this price point. The services are top drawer and the helpful reception makes every guest feel special. The 'Ottoman' room is done in an updated Turkish style, with deep-red spreads and fabrics, and oriental carpets.

## ✖ Eating

★**Caru' cu Bere**                    ROMANIAN €€
(📞021-313 7560; www.carucubere.ro; Str Stavropoleos 3-5; mains 20-45 lei; ⊘8am-midnight Sun-Thu, to 2am Fri & Sat; 🛜; Ⓜ Piața Unirii) Despite a decidedly touristy-leaning atmosphere, with peasant-girl hostesses and sporadic traditional song-and-dance numbers, Bucharest's oldest beer house continues to draw in a strong local crowd. The colourful belle-époque interior and stained-glass windows dazzle, as does the classic Romanian food. Dinner reservations are essential.

**Shift Pub**                    INTERNATIONAL €€
(📞021-211 2272; www.shiftpub.ro; Str General Eremia Grigorescu 17; mains 25-40 lei; ⊘noon-2am; Ⓜ Piața Romană) Great choice for salads and burgers as well as numerous beef and pork dishes, often sporting novel Asian, Middle Eastern or Mexican taste touches. Try to arrive slightly before meal times to grab a coveted table in the tree-covered garden.

**Lente Praporgescu**                    INTERNATIONAL €€
(📞021-310 7424; www.lente.ro; Str Gen Praporgescu 31; mains 25-40 lei; ⊘11.30am-1am; 🛜; Ⓜ Piața Romană) The main branch of three 'Lente' restaurants scattered around the city centre. The recipe for all three is broadly the same: inventive soups and salads, an eclectic design of mismatched chairs and old books, and a relaxed, vaguely alternative vibe. A ter-rific choice for lunch or a casual dinner. The garden terrace offers respite on a hot day.

★**Lacrimi și Sfinți**                    ROMANIAN €€€
(📞0725-558 286; www.lacrimisisfinti.com; Str Șepcari 16; mains 30-50 lei; ⊘12.30pm-2am Tue-Sun, 6pm-2am Mon; 🛜; Ⓜ Piața Unirii) A true destination restaurant in the Historic Centre, Lacrimi și Sfinți takes modern trends such as farm-to-table freshness and organic sourcing and marries them to old-school Romanian recipes. The philosophy extends to the simple, peasant-inspired interior, where the woodwork and decorative elements come from old farmhouses. The result is authentic and food that is satisfying. Book in advance.

## 🍷 Drinking & Nightlife

★**Grădina Verona**                    CAFE
(📞0/32-003 060; www.facebook.com/GradinaVerona; Str Pictor Verona 13-15; ⊘9am-midnight May-Sep; 🛜; Ⓜ Piața Romană) A garden oasis hidden behind the Cărturești bookshop, serving standard-issue but excellent espresso drinks and some of the wackiest iced-tea infusions ever concocted in Romania, such as peony flower, mango and lime (it's not bad).

**M60**                    CAFE
(📞031-410 0010; www.facebook.com/m60cafeamzei/; Str Mendeleev 2; ⊘10am-1am; 🛜; Ⓜ Piața Romană) M60 is a category-buster, transforming through the day from one of the city's pre-eminent morning coffee houses to a handy lunch spot (healthy salads and vegetarian options) and then morphing into a meet-up and drinks bar in the evening. It's been a hit since opening day, as city residents warmed to its clean, minimalist Scandinavian design and living-room feel.

**Origo**                    CAFE
(📞0757-086 689; https://origocoffee.ro; Str Lipscani 9; ⊘7.30am-8pm Mon, to midnight Tue-Fri, 9am-midnight Sat & Sun; 🛜; Ⓜ Piața Unirii) Arguably the best coffee in town and *the* best place to hang out in the morning, grab a table and check your email. Lots of special coffee roasts and an unlimited number of ways to imbibe. There are a dozen pavement tables for relaxing on a sunny day.

**Fire Club**                    BAR
(📞0732-166 604; www.fire.ro; Str Gabroveni 12; ⊘10am-4am Sun-Thu, to 6am Fri & Sat; 🛜; Ⓜ Piața Unirii) A crowded student-oriented bar and rock club that's much less flash and more relaxed than some of the other venues around the Historic Centre.

## ☆ Entertainment

### Control
LIVE MUSIC

(☑0733-927 861; www.control-club.ro; Str Constantin Mille 4; ☉noon-4am; 🛜; Ⓜ Universitate) This is a favourite among club-goers who like alternative, turbo-folk, indie and garage sounds. Hosts both live acts and DJs, depending on the night.

### Green Hours 22
LIVE MUSIC

(☑bar reservations 0751-772 275; www.greenhours.ro; Calea Victoriei 120; ☉9am-4am; Ⓜ Piaţa Romană) This old-school basement jazz club runs a lively programme of jazz and experimental theatre most nights through the week, and hosts an international jazz fest in May/June. There's also a popular bar, bistro and garden terrace. Check the website for the schedule during your trip and book in advance by email.

### Bucharest National Opera House
OPERA

(Opera Naţională Bucureşti; ☑box office 021-310 2661; www.operanb.ro; B-dul Mihail Kogălniceanu 70-72; tickets 10-70 lei; ☉box office 9am-1pm & 3-7pm; Ⓜ Eroilor) The city's premier venue for classical opera and ballet. Buy tickets online or at the venue box office.

## 🛍 Shopping

### ★ Anthony Frost
BOOKS

(☑021-311 5136; www.anthonyfrost.ro; Calea Victoriei 45; ☉10am-8pm Mon-Fri, to 7pm Sat, to 2pm Sun; Ⓜ Universitate) Serious readers will want to make time for arguably the best small English-language bookshop in Eastern Europe. Located in a small passage next to the Creţulescu Church, this shop has a carefully chosen selection of highbrow contemporary fiction and nonfiction.

### Cărtureşti Verona
BOOKS

(☑0728 828 916; www.carturesti.ro; Str Pictor Verona 13-15, cnr B-dul Nicolae Bălcescu; ☉10am-10pm; Ⓜ Piaţa Romană) This bookshop, music store, tearoom and funky backyard garden is a must-visit. Amazing collection of design, art and architecture books, as well as carefully selected CDs and DVDs, including many classic Romanian films with English subtitles. Also sells Lonely Planet guidebooks.

## ℹ Information

You'll find hundreds of bank branches and ATMs in the centre. Banks usually have currency exchange offices, but bring your passport as you'll have to show it to change money.

### Bucharest Tourist Information Center

(☑021-305 5500, ext 1003; http://seebucharest.ro; Piaţa Universităţii; ☉10am-5pm Mon-Fri, to 2pm Sat & Sun; Ⓜ Universitate) Not much information, though the English-speaking staff can field basic questions.

### Central Post Office
(☑021-315 9030; www.posta-romana.ro; Str Matei Millo 10; ☉7.30am-8pm Mon-Fri; Ⓜ Universitate)

### Emergency Clinic Hospital
(☑021-599 2300; www.scub.ro; Calea Floreasca 8; ☉24hr; Ⓜ Ştefan cel Mare) Arguably the city's, and country's, best emergency hospital.

### Seneca Anticafe
(☑0720-331 100; www.senecanticafe.ro; Str Arhitect Ion Mincu 1; per hr 8 lei; ☉9am-10pm; 🛜; 🚌24, 42, 45) Coffee and internet access.

## ℹ Getting There & Away

### AIR

All international and domestic flights use **Henri Coandă International Airport** (OTP, Otopeni; ☑arrivals 021-204 1220, departures 021-204 1210; www.bucharestairports.ro; Şos Bucureşti-Ploieşti; 🚌783), often referred to by its previous name, Otopeni. Henri Coandă is 17km north of Bucharest on the road to Braşov. The airport is a modern facility, with restaurants, newsagents, currency exchange offices and ATMs.

It's also the hub for national carrier **Tarom** (☑call centre 021-204 6464, office 021-316 0220; www.tarom.ro; Spl Independenţei 17, City Centre; ☉9am-5pm Mon-Fri; Ⓜ Piaţa Unirii). Tarom has a comprehensive network of internal flights to major Romanian cities as well as to capitals and big cities around Europe and the Middle East.

### BUS

It's possible to get just about anywhere in the country by bus from Bucharest, but figuring out where your bus or maxitaxi departs from can be tricky. Bucharest has several bus stations and they don't seem to follow any discernible logic. The best bet is to consult the websites www.autogari.ro and www.cdy.ro.

Sample domestic destinations and fares from Bucharest include Braşov (from 35 lei, three hours, hourly), Cluj-Napoca (90 lei, nine hours, six daily), Sibiu (55 lei, 4½ hours, 10 daily) and Tulcea/Danube Delta (45 lei, five hours, 10 daily).

### CAR & MOTORCYCLE

Driving in Bucharest is lunacy and you won't want to do it for more than a few minutes before you stow the car and use the metro. If you're travelling around by car and want to visit Bucharest for the day, park at a metro station on the outskirts and take the metro in.

## TRAIN

**Gara de Nord** (☏ phone reservations 021-9522; www.cfrcalatori.ro; Piaţa Gara de Nord 1; Ⓜ Gara de Nord) is the main station for most national and all international trains. The station is accessible by metro from the centre.

Buy tickets at station ticket windows. A seat reservation is compulsory if you are travelling with an InterRail or Eurail pass.

Check the latest train schedules on either www.cfr.ro or the reliable German site www.bahn.de. Sample fares from Bucharest on fast IC trains include Braşov (50 lei, 2½ hours, several daily), Cluj-Napoca (92 lei, 7½ hours, four daily), Sibiu (85 lei, six hours, two daily), Timişoara (101 lei, nine hours, three daily) and Suceava (90 lei, seven hours, three daily).

## ❶ Getting Around

### TO/FROM THE AIRPORT
### Bus

Express bus 783 leaves every 30 minutes from the airport arrivals hall to various points in the centre, including Piaţa Victoriei and Piaţa Unirii. A single journey on the express bus costs 7 lei.

### Taxi

Order a taxi by touchscreen at the arrivals terminal. Simply choose a company and rate (all are about the same), and you'll get a ticket and number. Pay the driver. A reputable taxi to the centre should cost no more than 50 lei.

### PUBLIC TRANSPORT

Bucharest's public transport system of metro, buses, trams and trolleybuses is operated by the transport authority **RATB** (Regia Autonomă de Transport Bucureşti; ☏ 021-9391; www.ratb.ro). The system runs daily from about 4.30am to approximately 11.30pm.

The ticketing situation differs for street transport (buses, trams and trolleybuses) and for the metro system. To use buses, trams or trolleybuses, you must first purchase an **Activ** card (3.70 lei) from any RATB street kiosk, which you then load with credit that is discharged as you enter the transport vehicles. Trips cost 1.30 lei each.

Metro stations are identified by a large letter 'M'. To use the metro, buy a magnetic-strip ticket available at ticketing machines or cashiers inside station entrances (have small bills handy). Tickets valid for two journeys cost 5 lei. A 10-trip ticket costs 20 lei.

# TRANSYLVANIA

After a century of being name-checked in literature and cinema, the word 'Transylvania' enjoys worldwide recognition. The mere mention conjures a vivid landscape of mountains, castles, spooky moonlight and at least one well-known count with a wicked overbite. Unexplained puncture wounds notwithstanding, Transylvania is all those things and more. A melange of architecture and chic sidewalk cafes punctuate the towns of Braşov, Sighişoara and Sibiu, while the vibrant student town Cluj-Napoca has some vigorous nightlife.

# Braşov

POP 275,000

Gothic spires, medieval gateways, Soviet blocks and a huge Hollywood-style sign: Braşov's skyline is instantly compelling. A number of medieval watchtowers still glower over the town. Between them sparkle baroque buildings and churches, while easy-going cafes line main square Piaţa Sfatului. Visible from here is forested Mt Tâmpa, sporting 'Braşov' in huge white letters.

## ◉ Sights

In addition to the sights below, explore the **Old Town Fortifications** that line the centre on the eastern and western flanks. Many have been restored.

**Black Church**      CHURCH
(Biserica Neagră; ☏ 0268-511 824; www.honterusgemeinde.ro; Curtea Johannes Honterus 2; adult/student/child 9/6/3 lei; ◷ 10am-7pm Tue-Sat & noon-7pm Sun Apr-Oct, 10am-3pm Tue-Sat & noon-3pm Sun Nov-Mar) Romania's largest Gothic church rises triumphantly over Braşov's old town. Built between 1385 and 1477, this German Lutheran church was named for its charred appearance after the town's Great Fire in 1689. Restoration of the church took a century. Today it towers 65m high at its bell tower's tallest point. Organ recitals are held in the church three times a week during July and August, usually at 6pm Tuesday, Thursday and Saturday.

**St Nicholas' Cathedral**      CHURCH
(Biserica Sfântul Nicolae; Piaţa Unirii 1; ◷ 7am-7pm) With forested hills rising behind its prickly Gothic spires, St Nicholas' Cathedral is one of Braşov's most spectacular views. First built in wood in 1392, it was replaced by a Gothic stone church in 1495 and later embellished in Byzantine style. It was once enclosed by military walls; today the site has a small cemetery. Inside are murals of Romania's last king and queen, covered by

plaster to protect them from communist leaders and uncovered in 2004.

### Mt Tâmpa
MOUNTAIN

(Muntele Tâmpa) Rising 940m high and visible around Braşov, Mt Tâmpa is adorned with its very own Hollywood-style sign. Hard as it is to imagine, it was the site of a mass-impaling of 40 noblemen by Vlad Ţepeş. Banish such ghoulish images from your head as you take the cable car (Telecabina; ☑0268-478 657; Aleea Tiberiu Brediceanu; adult one way/return 10/16 lei, child one way/return 6/9 lei; ☺9.30am-5pm Tue-Sun, noon-6pm Mon), or hike (about an hour), to reach a small viewing platform offering stunning views over the city. There's a slightly drab cafe at the top.

## 🏃 Activities

### ⭐Transylvanian Wolf
TOURS

(☑0744-319 708; www.transylvanian.ro; ☺year-round) This family-run nature-tour company, with award-winning Romanian guide Dan Marin at its helm, leads walks on the trail of animals such as wolves, bears and lynx (€40 per person, minimum two people). Adventurous rambles in pure nature are guaranteed, though sightings aren't. Alternatively, sightings are very likely on excursions to a bear hide (€55 per person for two hours; price includes transfers).

## 🛏 Sleeping

### Rolling Stone Hostel
HOSTEL €

(☑0268-513 965; www.rollingstone.ro; Str Piatra Mare 2A; dm/r €10/30; P@🛜) Powered by enthusiastic staff, Rolling Stone has clean dorm rooms that sleep between six and 10. Most rooms have high ceilings and convenient touches like lockers and reading lamps for each bed. Private doubles are comfy, or you can sleep in the wood-beamed attic for a stowaway vibe. Maps and excellent local advice are supplied the moment you step through the door.

### ⭐Bella Muzica
HOTEL €€

(☑0268-477 956; www.bellamuzica.ro; Piaţa Sfatului 19; s/d/apt from 220/270/540 lei; 🌬🛜) A regal feel permeates Bella Muzica, housed within a 400-year-old building, thanks to its tastefully restored wooden beams, exposed brick, high ceilings and occasional antiques. The main square location of this refined hotel is hard to top.

### Casa Reims
B&B €€

(☑0368-467 325; www.casareims.ro; Str Castelului 85; s/d from €48/56; P🌬🛜) Pastels and acid tones mingle beautifully with bare brick and wooden beams at this boutique B&B. Personalised service from the friendly owners adds to the VIP feel, and most rooms have views of Mt Tâmpa.

## 🍴 Eating

### Sergiana
ROMANIAN €€

(☑0268-419 775; www.sergianagrup.ro; Str Mureşenilor 28; mains 25-40 lei; ☺11am-11pm) Steaming soups in hollowed-out loaves of bread, paprika-laced meat stews, and the most generous ratio of cheese and sour cream we've ever seen in a polenta side dish – do not wear your tight jeans for a feast at Sergiana. The subterranean dining hall, lined with brick and wood, is lively and casual – fuelled by ample German beer and loud conversation.

### ⭐Bistro de l'Arte
BISTRO €€

(☑0720-535 566; www.bistrodelarte.ro; Piaţa Enescu 11; mains 15-35 lei; ☺9am-midnight Mon-Sat, noon-midnight Sun; 🛜☑) Tucked down a charming side street, this bohemian joint can be spotted by the bike racks shaped like penny-farthings. There's an almost Parisian feel in Bistro de l'Arte's arty decor and champagne breakfasts (59 lei), though its menu picks the best from France, Italy and beyond: bruschetta, fondue, German-style cream cake, and a suitably hip cocktail list.

## 🍷 Drinking

### Croitoria de Cafea
COFFEE

(☑0770-263 333; Str Iuliu Maniu 17; ☺8am-7pm Mon-Fri, 9.30am-6pm Sat, to 4pm Sun) The best coffee in town can be sipped at this hole-in-the-wall cafe, which has a few wooden stools for you to perch amid bulging bags of beans.

### Festival 39
BAR

(☑0743-339 909; www.festival39.com; Str Republicii 62; ☺7am-midnight) Jazz flows from this vintage-feel watering hole and restaurant, an art-deco dream of stained-glass, high ceilings, wrought-iron finery, candelabra and leather banquettes. As good for clanking together beer glasses as for cradling a hot chocolate over your travel journal.

## ⓘ Information

You'll find numerous ATMs and banks on and around Str Republicii and B-dul Eroilor.

**Central Post Office** (Str Nicolae Iorga 1; ☺8am-7pm Mon-Fri, 9am-1pm Sat) Opposite the Heroes' Cemetery.

# Braşov

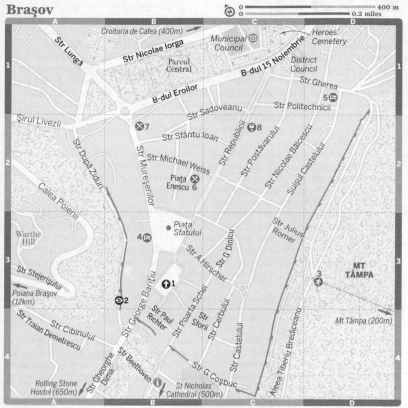

## Braşov

### ⊙ Sights
| | |
|---|---|
| 1 Black Church | B3 |
| 2 Old Town Fortifications | B3 |

### ⊙ Activities, Courses & Tours
| | |
|---|---|
| 3 Mt Tâmpa Cable Car | D3 |

### ⊙ Sleeping
| | |
|---|---|
| 4 Bella Muzica | B3 |
| 5 Casa Reims | D1 |

### ⊗ Eating
| | |
|---|---|
| 6 Bistro de l'Arte | B2 |
| 7 Sergiana | B2 |

### ⊙ Drinking & Nightlife
| | |
|---|---|
| 8 Festival 39 | C2 |

**County Hospital** (Spitalul Judetean; ☎ 0268-135 080; www.hospbv.ro; Calea Bucureşti 25-27; ☉24hr) Hospital with emergency clinic, northeast of the centre.

**Tourist Information Centre** (www.brasovtourism.eu; Str Prundului 1; ☉9am-5pm Mon-Fri) Cordial staff offer maps and local advice. Check www.brasovtravelguide.ro for general info.

## ⓘ Getting There & Around

### BUS

Maxitaxis are the best way to reach places near Braşov, including Bran and Râşnov. The most accessible station is **Bus Station 1** (Autogara 1; ☎ 0268-427 267; www.autogari.ro; B-dul Gării 1), next to the train station.

From 6am to 7.30pm, maxitaxis leave every half-hour for Bucharest (from 35 lei, 2½ to 3½ hours). About 12 daily buses or maxitaxis leave for Sibiu (30 lei, 2½ hours). Three go daily to Sighişoara (30 lei). Less frequent buses reach Cluj-Napoca (65 lei, five to 5½ hours, three daily).

### TRAIN

The **train station** (Gara Braşov; ☎ 0268-410 233; www.cfrcalatori.ro; B-dul Gării 5) is 2km

**WORTH A TRIP**

## BRAN CASTLE & RÂȘNOV FORTRESS

Rising above the town on a rocky promontory, **Bran Castle** (☑0268-237 700; www. bran-castle.com; Str General Traian Moșoiu 24; adult/student/child 35/20/7 lei; ☉9am-6pm Tue-Sun, noon-6pm Mon Apr-Sep, same hours to 4pm Oct-Mar) holds visitors in thrall. Illuminated by the light of a pale moon, the vampire's lair glares down from its rocky bluff. An entire industry has sprouted around describing the pile as 'Dracula's Castle', and at first glance the claims look legit. Regrettably, though, Bran Castle's blood-drinking credentials don't withstand scrutiny. It's unlikely Vlad Țepeș – either 'the Impaler' or 'protector of Wallachia' – ever passed through. Nor did the castle inspire Bram Stoker in writing his iconic Gothic novel *Dracula*.

These seem minor quibbles when you gaze up at the turreted fortress, guarded from the east by the Bucegi Mountains and from the west by Piatra Craiului massif. Meanwhile, the castle's museum pays greater homage to Romanian royals than immortal counts. Ignoring this, a gauntlet of souvenir sellers hawk fang-adorned mugs and Vlad-the-Impaler compact mirrors (really).

Commonly paired with Bran Castle on day trips from Brașov, nearby **Râșnov Fortress** (Cetatea Râșnov; adult/child 12/6 lei; ☉9am-6pm) might just be the more enchanting of the two. The medieval citadel, built by Teutonic Knights to guard against Tatar and Turkish invasion, roosts on a hilltop 19km southwest of Brașov by road. Visitors are free to stroll between sturdy watchtowers, browse medieval-themed souvenir and craft stalls, and admire views of rolling hills from the fortress' highest point. Walk from the village or take the lift.

Bran is a 45-minute bus ride from Brașov, with a stop in Râșnov, and makes an easy day trip.

---

northeast of the centre. Buy tickets at the station. There are ATMs and a left-luggage office.

Brașov is an important train junction and connections are good. Daily domestic train service includes hourly trains to Bucharest (49 lei, three hours), seven daily to Sighișoara (40 lei, 2½ hours), six to Sibiu (45 lei, four hours) and several to Cluj-Napoca (80 lei, seven hours).

# Sighișoara

POP 28,100

So resplendent are Sighișoara's pastel-coloured buildings, stony lanes and medieval towers, you'll rub your eyes in disbelief. Fortified walls encircle Sighișoara's lustrous merchant houses, now harbouring cafes, hotels and craft shops. Lurking behind the gingerbread roofs and turrets of the Unesco-protected old town is the history of Vlad Țepeș, the country's most notorious ruler; he was allegedly born in a house here that is visitable to this day.

## ◉ Sights

### Citadel                                              FORTRESS

Sighișoara's delightful medieval buildings are enclosed within its citadel, a Unesco-listed complex of protective walls and watchtowers. Walking in the citadel is today a tranquil, fairytale-like experience, but these towers were once packed with weapons and emergency supplies, guarding Sighișoara from Turkish attacks (note the upper windows, from which arrows could be fired).

### Clock Tower                                           MUSEUM

(Turnul cu Ceas; Piața Muzeului 1; adult/child 14/3.50 lei; ☉9am-6.30pm Tue-Fri, 10am-5.30pm Sat & Sun) The multicoloured tiled roof of Sighișoara's Clock Tower glitters like the scales of a dragon. The tower was built in the 14th century and expanded 200 years later. It remains the prettiest sight in town, offering a magnificent panorama from the top. The views are as good a reason to visit as the museum inside, a patchy collection of Roman vessels, scythes and tombstones, and a scale model of the fortified town (English-language explanation is variable).

### Casa Vlad Dracul                          HISTORIC BUILDING

(www.casavladdracul.ro; Str Cositorarilor 5; 5 lei; ☉10am-10pm) Vlad Țepeș (aka Dracula) was reputedly born in this house in 1431 and lived here until the age of four. It's now a decent restaurant, but for a small admission fee the staff will show you Vlad's old room (and give you a little scare). Bubble-buster: the building is indeed centuries old, but has been completely rebuilt since Vlad's days.

## 🛏 Sleeping

**Burg Hostel** HOSTEL €
(☏0265-778 489; www.burghostel.ro; Str Bastionu-lui 4-6; dm 45 lei, s/d 90/110 lei, without bathroom 85/100 lei; ⊛⊠) A great budget choice without compromising on charm, Burg Hostel has spacious dorms (with handy touches like plug sockets close to beds). Common areas have chandeliers made from old cartwheels, ceramic lamps, vaulted ceilings and other rustic touches. Staff are friendly and there's a relaxing courtyard cafe. Breakfast isn't included, but you can buy meals from the cafe.

**Pensiunea Legenda** GUESTHOUSE €€
(☏0748-694 368; www.legenda.ro; Str Bastionului 8; r €26-39; ⊛) The owners of this historic guesthouse whisper that Vlad Țepeș once wooed a beautiful young woman within these walls, a myth that will either charm or chill you. All five rooms at this well-run guesthouse have snug beds and occasional vampiric twists like black chandeliers and dungeon-like doors. Breakfast not included.

★**Casa Georgius Krauss** BOUTIQUE HOTEL €€€
(☏0365-730 840; www.casakrauss.com; Str Bastionului 11; r 243-450 lei; P⊛⊛) This dazzling boutique hotel is hived out of an old burgher's house at the northern end of the citadel. The restoration left period details like wood-beamed ceilings, while adding tasteful modern bathrooms and plush-linened beds. The Krauss Room, number 2, has original paintings including a medieval coat of arms, plus a four-poster bed.

## 🍴 Eating

**Central Park** INTERNATIONAL €€
(☏0365-730 006; www.hotelcentralpark.ro; Central Park Hotel, Piața Hermann Oberth 25; mains 25-40 lei; ⊗11am-11pm; ⊛) Even if you're not staying at the Central Park **hotel** (☏0365-730 006; www.hotelcentralpark.ro; Piața Hermann Oberth 25; s/d/ste €77/90/110; P⊛@⊛), plan a meal here. Sighişoara is short on good restaurants and this is one of the best. The food is a mix of Romanian and international dishes, and the carefully selected wine list offers the best domestic labels. Dress up for the lavish dining room or relax on the terrace.

**Casa Vlad Dracul** ROMANIAN €€
(☏0265-771 596; www.casavladdracul.ro; Str Cositorarilor 5; mains 24-35 lei; ⊗11am-11pm; ⊞) The link between Dracula and tomato soups, or medallions with potato and chicken roulade, we'll never quite understand. But the

house where Vlad was born could have been dealt a worse blow than this atmospheric, wood-panelled restaurant. The menu of Romanian, Saxon and grilled specials is dotted with Dracula references. With a little embellishing from you, your kids will love it.

## 🛍 Shopping

★**Arts & Crafts** ARTS & CRAFTS
(www.thespoonman.ro; Str Cositorarilor 5; ⊗10am-6pm) Inside Casa Vlad Dracul, this wondrous handicraft shop is the brainchild of self-styled 'Spoonman' Mark Tudose, who employs traditional woodcarving methods to fashion Transylvanian spoons (each with a local legend behind it), as well as painted-glass icons, clay statues, painted eggs and much more. It's a beautiful place to browse, and your best bet for finding a culturally meaningful souvenir.

## ℹ️ Information

There are numerous ATMs and banks lining Sighişoara's main street, Str 1 Decembrie 1918.
**Tourist Information Centre** (☏0788-115 511; Piața Muzeului 6; ⊗9am-5pm) Cordial, multilingual information service adjoining the Clock Tower, with maps and transport information.

## ℹ️ Getting There & Away

### BUS
Next to the train station on Str Libertăţii, the **bus station** (Autogara Sighişoara; ☏0265-771 260; www.autogari.ro; Str Libertăţii 53) sends buses around the country, including to Braşov (18 to 25 lei, 2½ hours, three daily) and Sibiu (20 lei, 2½ hours, four daily).

### TRAIN
Sighişoara is on a main international line and direct trains connect the town's **train station** (☏0265-771 130; www.cfrcalatori.ro; Str Libertăţii 51) with Braşov (18 to 40 lei, 2½ to 3½ hours, six daily), Bucharest (67 lei, five to 5½ hours, three daily; more via Braşov), Cluj-Napoca (30 to 60 lei, 4½ to six hours, four daily; more via Teius) and Sibiu (13 lei, 2½ to three hours, two daily; more via Mediaş).

# Sibiu
POP 154,890
Sibiu is awash in aristocratic elegance. Noble Saxon history emanates from every art-nouveau façade and gold-embossed church, all parked elegantly around graceful squares. Renowned composers Strauss, Brahms and Liszt all played here during the 19th century,

and Sibiu has stayed at the forefront of Romania's cultural scene. Houses with distinctive eyelid-shaped windows (imagine a benign *Amityville Horror* House) watch a cast of artists and buskers bustling below them. Cafes and bars inhabit brick-walled cellars and luminously decorated attics.

##  Sights

### ★St Mary's Evangelical Church    CHURCH
(Catedrala Evanghelică Sfânta Maria; Piaţa Huet; adult/child 5/2 lei, with tower 8/3 lei; ⊙9am-8pm Mon-Sat, 11.30am-8pm Sun) Sibiu's Gothic centrepiece rises more than 73m over the old town. Inside, marvel at ghoulish stone skeletons, 17th-century tombs and the largest organ in Romania, all framed by a magnificent arched ceiling. Built in stages from the mid-1300s to 1520, the church was planted atop the site of an older 12th-century sanctuary. The four turrets on its tower once signified the right of the town to sentence criminals to death.

### Brukenthal Palace    GALLERY
(European Art Gallery; ☑0269-217 691; www.brukenthalmuseum.ro/europeana; Piaţa Mare 5; adult/student 20/5 lei; ⊙10am-6pm Tue-Sun summer, closed Tue winter) Brukenthal Palace is worth visiting as much for its resplendent period furnishings as for the European art within. Duck beneath the Music Room's chandeliers to admire colourful friezes and 18th-century musical instruments, before sidling among chambers exhibiting 17th-century portraits amid satin chaise longues and cases packed with antique jewellery. Sumptuously curated.

### History Museum    MUSEUM
(Casa Altemberger; www.brukenthalmuseum.ro/istorie; Str Mitropoliei 2; adult/child 20/5 lei; ⊙10am-6pm Tue-Sun Apr-Oct, 10am-6pm Wed-Sun Nov-Mar) This impressive museum begins with re-enactments of cave dwellers squatting in the gloom and dioramas of Dacian life. Out of these shadowy corridors, the museum opens out to illuminating exhibitions about Saxon guilds and local handicrafts (most impressive is the 19th-century glassware from Porumbacu de Sus). There's plenty of homage to Saxon efficiency: you could expect a fine for improperly crafting a copper cake tin.

### ASTRA National Museum Complex    MUSEUM
(Muzeul Civilizaţiei Populare Tradiţionale ASTRA; ☑0269-202 447; www.muzeulastra.ro; Str Pădurea Dumbrava 16-20; adult/child 17/3.50 lei; ⊙8am-8pm May-Sep, 9am-5pm Oct-Apr) Five kilometres from central Sibiu, this is Europe's largest open-air ethnographic museum, where churches, mills and traditional homes number among 400 folk architecture monuments on-site. In summer, ASTRA hosts numerous fairs, dance workshops and musical performances, so it's worthwhile checking the website for events. There's also a nice gift shop and restaurant with creekside bench seats. Get there via bus 13 from Sibiu's train station.

## 🛏 Sleeping

### Welt Kultur    HOSTEL €
(☑0269-700 704; www.weltkultur.ro; Str Nicolea Bălcescu 13; dm 45-53 lei, d from 137 lei; ❄@🤀) Almost too chic to be dubbed a hostel, Welt has elegant wrought-iron bunks in its spotless four-, six- and eight-bed dorms (one is women-only). Meanwhile doubles are plain but easily as comfortable as Sibiu's pricier midranges. The best rooms face the street: they have more light and better views. There are lockers and a friendly chill-out room.

### The Council    BOUTIQUE HOTEL €€
(☑0369-452 524; www.thecouncil.ro; Piaţa Mică 31; s/d/apt from €50/55/109; ❄🤀) Tapping into Sibiu's medieval lifeblood, this opulent hotel occupies a 14th-century hall in the heart of the old town. Individually designed rooms are equipped with desks, security safes and plenty of contemporary polish, but there are aristocratic touches like crimson throws, bare wooden rafters and Turkish-style rugs.

### Am Ring    HOTEL €€
(☑0269-206 499; www.amringhotel.ro; Piaţa Mare 14; s/d/ste 250/290/390 lei; ❄🤀) Centrally located and decorated in a smorgasbord of styles, this is Sibiu's most lavish place to sleep. From the vaulted brick dining room to bedrooms styled with original wooden beams, throne-like chairs and baroque touches like gold candelabra, Am Ring exudes old-world elegance.

## 🍴 Eating

### ★Crama Sibiul Vechi    ROMANIAN €€
(☑0269-210 461; www.sibiulvechi.ro; Str Papiu-Ilarian 3; mains 25-30 lei; ⊙11am-10pm) Hidden in an old wine cellar, this is the most evocative restaurant in Sibiu. Explore Romanian fare such as cheese croquettes, minced meatballs

and peasant's stew with polenta. Show up early, or reserve ahead; it's very popular.

⭐**Kulinarium**　　　ROMANIAN, EUROPEAN €€
(☑0721-506 070; www.kulinarium.ro; Piaţa Mică 12; mains 25-35 lei; ⊘noon-midnight) Fresh, well-presented Italy- and France-leaning cuisine, using seasonal ingredients, graces plates at Kulinarium. The restaurant has an intimate, casual feel, with roughly painted stone walls and dangling modern lampshades. Choose from smoky Austrian sausages, spinach soup with quail eggs, rare-beef salad, trout with polenta or well-executed pasta dishes.

**Weinkeller**　　　ROMANIAN €€
(☑0269-210 319; www.weinkeller.ro; Str Turnului 2; mains 20-30 lei; ⊘noon-midnight) Mixing traditional Romanian mains such as stuffed cabbage leaves with Austro-Hungarian-influenced fare like *Tafelspitz* (boiled beef) and goulash, this romantic wine cellar and restaurant is the best date spot in Sibiu.

## 🍷 Drinking & Nightlife

**Music Pub**　　　BAR
(☑0369-448 326; www.musicpubsibiu.ro; Piaţa Mică 23; ⊘8am-3am Mon-Fri, from 10am Sat & Sun) Skip down the graffitied corridor and rub your eyes in astonishment as a cellar bar and airy verandah opens up. One of the merriest spots in town, Music Pub sparkles with straw lamps and little candles, while '90s dance and rock plays on. There's table service, it's friendly, and there's occasional live music: a sure-fire winning night out.

**Cafe Wien**　　　CAFE
(☑0269-223 223; www.cafewien.ro; Piaţa Huet 4; ⊘10am-2am Mon, 9am-2am Tue-Sun; 🛜) There's no more genteel Viennese tradition than *Kaffee und Kuchen* (coffee and cake), and Cafe Wien has just the right blend of refinement and relaxation to accompany your strudel or Sachertorte (chocolate cake).

## ☆ Entertainment

**State Philharmonic**　　　CLASSICAL MUSIC
(www.filarmonicasibiu.ro; Str Cetăţii 3-5; tickets 16-30 lei; ⊘box office noon-4pm Mon-Fri) Founded in 1949, this has played a key role in maintaining Sibiu's prestige as a main cultural centre of Transylvania. It's the key venue for performances at the annual **opera festival** (www.filarmonicasibiu.ro; ⊘mid-Sep).

## ℹ️ Information

ATMs are located all over the centre.

**Hospital** (☑0269-215 050; www.scjs.ro; Str Izvorului) Has an accident and emergency department.

**Tourist Information Centre** (☑0269-208 913; www.turism.sibiu.ro; Piaţa Mare 2; ⊘9am-8pm Mon-Fri, to 6pm Sat & Sun May-Sep, 9am-5pm Mon-Fri, to 1pm Sat & Sun Oct-Apr) Based at the town hall, staff can offer free maps and plenty of local transport advice.

## ℹ️ Getting There & Around

### BUS

The main **bus station** (Autogara Sibiu; ☑0269-217 757; www.autogari.ro; Piaţa 1 Decembrie 1918) is opposite the train station. Bus and maxitaxi services include Braşov (28 lei, 2½ hours, 12 daily), Bucharest (55 lei, 4½ hours, 10 daily), Cluj-Napoca (35 lei, 3½ hours, several daily) and Timişoara (65 lei, six hours, seven daily).

### TRAIN

There are nine daily direct trains to Braşov (40 lei, three hours), four trains to Bucharest (61 lei, six hours) and two to Timişoara (61 lei, six hours). To get to/from Cluj-Napoca (56 lei, five hours, several daily), you'll usually change at Copşa Mică or Mediaş.

The **train station** (Gara Sibiu; ☑0269-211 139; www.cfrcalatori.ro; Piaţa 1 Decembrie 1918, 6) is 2km east of the centre, about 20 minutes on foot.

# Cluj-Napoca

POP 324,500

Bohemian cafes, music festivals and vigorous nightlife are the soul of Cluj-Napoca, Romania's second-largest city. With increasing flight links to European cities, Cluj is welcoming more and more travellers, who usually shoot off to the Apuseni Mountains, Maramureş or more popular towns in southern Transylvania. But once arrived, first-time visitors inevitably lament their failure to allow enough time in Cluj.

## ◉ Sights

**St Michael's Church**　　　CHURCH
(Biserica Sfantul Mihail; ☑0264-592 089; Piaţa Unirii; ⊘8am-6pm) The showpiece of Piaţa Unirii is 14th- and 15th-century St Michael's, the second-biggest Gothic church in Romania (after Braşov's Black Church). Its neo-Gothic clock tower (1859), 80m high, with original Gothic features – such as the 1444 front portal – can still be admired. In

**WORTH A TRIP**

## DANUBE DELTA

After passing through several countries and absorbing countless lesser waterways, the Danube River empties into the Black Sea in eastern Romania, just south of the Ukrainian border.

The Danube Delta (Delta Dunării), included on Unesco's World Heritage list, is one of Romania's leading attractions. At the port of **Tulcea** (pronounced tool-cha), the river splits into three separate channels: the Chilia, Sulina and Sfântu Gheorghe arms, creating a constantly evolving 4187 sq km wetland of marshes, floating reed islets and sandbars. The region provides sanctuary for 300 species of bird and 160 species of fish. Reed marshes cover 1563 sq km, constituting one of the largest single expanses of reed beds in the world.

The delta is a haven for wildlife lovers, birdwatchers, fishers and anyone wanting to get away from it all. There are beautiful, secluded beaches at both **Sulina** and **Sfântu Gheorghe**, and the fish and seafood, particularly the fish soup, are the best in Romania.

Tulcea is the largest city in the delta and the main entry point for accessing the region. It's got good bus and minibus connections to the rest of the country, and is home to the main passenger ferries.

There is no rail service in the delta and few paved roads, meaning the primary mode of transport is ferry boat. Regularly scheduled ferries, both traditional 'slow' ferries and faster (and more expensive) hydrofoils, leave from Tulcea's main port on select days throughout the week and access major points in the delta.

The helpful staff at the **Tourism Information Centre** (☑ 0240-519 130; www.cnipt tulcea.ro; Str Gării 26; h8am-4pm Mon-Fri) in Tulcea

---

side, soaring rib vaults lift the gaze towards fading frescoes.

### Pharmacy History Collection
MUSEUM
(Piața Unirii 28; adult/child 6/3 lei; ☺10am-4pm Mon-Wed & Fri, noon-6pm Thu) Cluj-Napoca's oldest pharmacy building holds an intriguing collection of medical miscellany. 'Crab eyes' skulls, and powdered mummy are just a few of the cures on display in these antique-filled rooms. The prettiest is the Officina, a polished room with dark filigree swirling around its walls. You'll also learn that the 18th-century recipe for a love potion sounds suspiciously like mulled wine...

It's just past the northeast corner of the square, towards Str Regele Ferdinand I.

### Fabrica de Pensule
ARTS CENTRE
(Paintbrush Factory; ☑ 0727-169 569; www.fabricadepensule.ro; Str Henri Barbusse 59-61; ☺tours 4-8pm Mon-Sat) **FREE** More of a living, breathing creative space than a gallery, Fabrica de Pensule teems with just-made artwork by local and foreign creators who use this former paintbrush factory as a studio. Visits are by free guided tour, and depending on when you visit you'll spy anything from haunting urban photography to surreal Icelandic ceramics. You'll either adore visiting this artistic community in a post-industrial setting,

or be bemused by the work-in-progress art within boxy gallery spaces.

### Parcul Etnografic Romulus Vuia
MUSEUM, PARK
(www.muzeul-etnografic.ro; Aleea Muzeului Etnografic; adult/child 6/3 lei; ☺10am to 6pm summer, 9am to 4pm winter) Traditional architecture from around Romania has been faithfully reassembled at this open-air museum, 5km northwest of central Cluj. Most impressive is the Cizer Church; get the attention of a caretaker to allow you inside to view frescoes covering its wooden interior.

## 🛏 Sleeping

### ★ Youthink Hostel
HOSTEL €
(☑ 0745-202 911; www.youthinkhostel.com; Str Republicii 74; dm/d €15/35; [P ⊗ 🛜] ) A labour-of-love restoration project has transformed a 1920 building, abandoned for a decade, into something between a hostel and an ecotourism retreat. Original wood beams, fireplace and hardwood floors retain the building's early-20th-century splendour, while the seven- and eight-bed dorms are clean and modern. Aptly for such a cheery and eco-conscious hostel, you'll be greeted by friendly dogs and a cat.

★ **Lol & Lola** BOUTIQUE HOTEL €€
(☑ 0264-450 498; www.loletlolahotel.ro; Str Neagră 9; s/d €67/79; P ※ 🛜) This enjoyably zany hotel has a rainbow of individually styled rooms to choose from, with themes ranging from Hollywood, ballet, and a rock 'n' roll room with vinyl and guitars. It's ultra-modern with friendly service.

**Hotel Confort** HOTEL €€
(☑ 0264-598 410; www.hotelconfort.ro; Calea Turzii 48; s/d/ste 200/220/255 lei; P ※ 🛜) Huge rooms with wooden floors and fuzzy rugs are accented with flower arrangements and arty prints at this chic hotel. Four rooms have balconies, and most have big windows and billowy drapes. It's a car-friendly location, a 15-minute walk outside central Cluj. Parking is free but limited; ask ahead. Breakfast is an extra 12 lei.

## ✕ Eating

★ **Roata** ROMANIAN €€
(☑ 0264-592 022; www.restaurant-roata.ro; Str Alexandru Ciurea 6; mains 20-28 lei; ⊘ noon-11pm; 🍴) Transylvanian cuisine just like Granny made it, in an untouristed part of Cluj. Settle in beneath the vine-covered trellis in the outdoor area, and agonise between roasted pork ribs and pike with capers. Or go all out with a 'Transylvanian platter' for two (52 lei), with homemade sausages, meatballs, sheep's cheese, aubergine stew and spare elastic for when your pants snap (we wish).

**Camino** INTERNATIONAL €€
(☑ 0749-200 117; Piața Muzeului 4; mains 20-30 lei; ⊘ 9am-midnight; 🛜) This boho restaurant has a raffish charm, its peeling interior decked in candelabra and threadbare rugs, and outdoor seating spilling into monumental Piața Muzeului. Italian, Spanish and Indian dishes grace the menu. Ideal for solo book-reading over a pressed lemonade or alfresco tapas for two.

**Bricks – (M)eating
Point Restaurant** STEAK €€€
(☑ 0364-730 615; www.bricksrestaurant.ro; Str Horea 2; mains 33-58 lei; ⊘ 11am-11pm; 🛜) Jazz flows right along with the cocktails at this chic steakhouse overhanging the river. Italian pasta dishes, burgers and barbecued meats dominate the menu, alongside a couple of vegetarian options and plump desserts like cottage-cheese pancakes. Lunch specials (15 lei) offer the best value.

## 🍷 Drinking & Nightlife

**Insomnia** BAR, BEER GARDEN
(www.insomniacafe.ro; Str Universității 2; ⊘ 9am-1am Mon-Fri, 11am-1am Sat & Sun) Squeezed into a narrow courtyard, a jaunty beer garden adjoins this zanily decorated bohemian cafe. Insomnia is one of a slew of bars catering to Cluj's arty crowd (which seems to be half the city) within the student quarter.

**Joben Bistro** CAFE
(www.jobenbistro.ro; Str Avram Iancu 29; ⊘ 8am-2am Mon-Thu, noon-2am Fri-Sun; 🛜) This steampunk cafe will lubricate the gears of any traveller with a penchant for Victoriana. Aside from the fantasy decor, with skull designs, taxidermied deer heads and copper pipes on bare brick walls, it's a laid-back place to nurse a lavender-infused lemonade or perhaps the potent 'Drunky Hot Chocolate'.

**Roots** CAFE
(B-dul Eroilor 4; ⊘ 7.30am-11.30pm Mon-Fri, 9am-11.30pm Sat, to 5pm Sun) Competition for Cluj's best brew is stiff, but Roots' silky coffee is the front runner. Staff are as friendly as the flat whites are smooth.

**Irish & Music Pub** BAR
(☑ 0729-947 133; www.irishmusicpub.ro; Str Horea 5; ⊘ 10am-4am Mon-Sat, 6pm-4am Sun) Before you flee from the hackneyed 'Irish pub abroad' theme, know that this subterranean place has plenty of atmosphere resounding from its cavernous brick walls, plus a menu of steak sandwiches and veggie-friendly bar snacks to line your stomach.

## ☆ Entertainment

**National Theatre** THEATRE
(Teatrul Național Lucian Blaga; www.teatrulnationalcluj.ro; Piața Ștefan cel Mare 2-4; tickets from 20 lei) From Molière and Shakespeare through to modern drama, the Romanian-language performances at the National Theatre are the slickest productions in town. Buy tickets at the nearby **box office** (☑ tickets 0264-595 363; Piața Ștefan cel Mare 14; ⊘ 11am-2pm & 3-5pm Tue-Sun & 1 hour before performances).

**Flying Circus** CONCERT VENUE, CLUB
(www.flyingcircus.ro; Str Iuliu Maniu 2; entry before/after 1am 7/10 lei; ⊘ 5pm-dawn) Arrive around midnight to see this student-oriented club begin to swing. Punters come for the music rather than to pose, so check the theme before you rock up: events vary from doom

WORTH A TRIP

## PAINTED MONASTERIES OF SOUTHERN BUCOVINA

The painted monasteries of southern Bucovina are among the greatest artistic monuments of Eastern Europe. In 1993 they were collectively designated a Unesco World Heritage site.

Erected in the 15th and 16th centuries, when Moldavia was threatened by Turkish invaders, the monasteries were surrounded by strong defensive walls. Biblical stories were portrayed on the church walls in colourful pictures so that illiterate worshippers could better understand them.

The most impressive collection of monasteries is located west of Suceava. It includes the Arbore, Humor, Voroneţ and Moldoviţa monasteries.

**Arbore Monastery** (Manastirea Arbore; ☑ 0740-154 213; www.manastireaarbore.ro; Hwy DN2K 732, Arbore; adult/student 5/2 lei, photography 10 lei; ☺ 8am-7pm May-Sep, to 4pm Oct-Apr) (1503), the smallest of the main monasteries, receives a fraction of the visitors the others receive. The smaller scale allows you to study the paintings up close, to appreciate the skills and techniques.

**Humor Monastery** (Mănăstirea Humorului; Gura Humorului; adult/student 5/2 lei, photography 10 lei; ☺ 8am-7pm May-Sep, to 4pm Oct-Apr) (1530), near the town of Gura Humorului, boasts arguably the most impressive interior frescoes.

**Voroneţ Monastery** (Mănăstirea Voroneţ; ☑ 0230-235 323; Str Voroneţ 166, Voroneţ; adult/child 5/2 lei, photography 10 lei; ☺ 8am-7pm May-Sep, to 4pm Oct-Apr), also not far from Gura Humorului, is the only one to have a specific colour associated with it. 'Voroneţ Blue', a vibrant cerulean colour created from lapis lazuli, is prominent in its frescoes. The monastery was built in just three months and three weeks by Ştefan cel Mare following a 1488 victory over the Turks.

**Moldoviţa Monastery** (Mânăstirea Moldoviţa; Vatra Moldoviţei; adult/student 5/2 lei, photography 10 lei; ☺ 8am-7pm May-Sep, to 4pm Oct-Apr) (1532), 35km northwest of the Voroneţ Monastery, occupies a fortified quadrangular enclosure with tower, gates and flowery lawns. The central painted church has been partly restored, and features impressive frescoes from 1537.

The main gateway to the monasteries is **Suceava**, reachable by direct train from both Bucharest (91 lei, seven hours, six daily) and Cluj-Napoca (73 lei, seven hours, four daily).

metal to euphoric drum and bass. There's usually a free shot with the entry fee.

## ℹ Information

There are many banks and ATMs scattered around the centre.

**Tourist Information Office** (☑ 0264-452 244; www.visitcluj.ro; B-dul Eroilor 6; ☺ 8.30am-8pm Mon-Fri, 10am-6pm Sat & Sun) Super-friendly office with free maps, thoughtful trekking advice, and tons of info on transport links, accommodation, events and more.

## ℹ Getting There & Around

### BUS

Domestic and international bus services depart mostly from **Bus Station 2** (Autogara 2, Autogara Beta; ☑ 0264-455 249; www.autogara-beta-cluj.ro; Str Giordano Bruno 1-3). The bus station is 350m northwest of the train station (take the overpass). Popular destinations include Braşov (65 lei, five hours, four daily),

Bucharest (90 lei, nine hours, six daily) and Sibiu (35 lei, four hours, almost hourly).

### TRAIN

Cluj has decent train connections. Sample destinations include five daily trains to Bucharest (87 lei, 10 hours), six to Braşov (75 lei, seven hours) and four to Sighişoara (52 lei, four hours). Change at Teiuş or Mediaş for Sibiu (46 lei, four hours).

The **train station** (www.cfrcalatori.ro; Str Căii Ferate) is 1km north of the centre. Buy tickets at the station or in town at the **Agenţia de Voiaj CFR** (☑ 0264-432 001; Piaţa Mihai Viteazu 20; ☺ 8.30am-8pm Mon-Fri).

# BANAT

Western Romania, with its geographic and cultural ties to neighbouring Hungary and Serbia and its historical links to the Austro-Hungarian Empire, enjoys an ethnic diversity that much of the rest of the country lacks. Timişoara, the regional hub, has a nationwide reputation as a beautiful and lively metropolis, and for a series of 'firsts'. It was the world's first city to adopt electric street lights (in 1884) and, more importantly, the first city to rise up against dictator Nicolae Ceauşescu in 1989.

# Timişoara

POP 319,280

Romania's third-largest city (after Bucharest and Cluj-Napoca) is also one of the country's most attractive urban areas, built around a series of beautifully restored public squares and lavish parks and gardens. The city's charms have been recognised by the EU, which named Timişoara as the European Capital of Culture for 2021. Locally, Timişoara is known as 'Primul Oraş Liber' (The First Free City), for it was here that anti-Ceauşescu protests first exceeded the Securitate's capacity for violent suppression in 1989, eventually sending Ceauşescu and his wife to their deaths.

## Sights

### Piaţa Unirii & Around

Piaţa Unirii is Timişoara's most picturesque square, featuring the imposing sight of the Catholic and Serbian **churches** facing each other.

★**Museum of the 1989 Revolution** MUSEUM
(0256-294 936; www.memorialulrevolutiei.ro; Strada Popa Şapcă 3-5; entry by donation; 8am-4pm Mon-Fri, 10am-2pm Sat) This is an ideal venue to brush up on the December 1989 anticommunist revolution that began here in Timişoara. Displays include documentation, posters and photography from those fateful days, capped by a graphic 20-minute video (not suitable for young children) with English subtitles. Enter from Str Oituz 2.

**Synagogue in the Fortress** SYNAGOGUE
(Sinagoga din Cetate; Str Mărăşeşti 6) Built in 1865 by Viennese architect Ignatz Schuhmann, the synagogue acts as an important keynote in Jewish history – Jews in the Austro-Hungarian Empire were emancipated in 1864, when permission was given to build the synagogue. It was closed at the time of research for a massive renovation, but the fine exterior is worth taking in.

**Timişoara Art Museum** MUSEUM
(Muzeul de Artă Timişoara; 0256-491 592; www.muzeuldeartatm.ro; Piaţa Unirii 1; adult 10 lei, child free; 10am-6pm Tue-Sun) This museum displays a representative sample of paintings and visual arts over the centuries as well as regular, high-quality temporary exhibitions. It's housed in the baroque **Old Prefecture Palace** (built 1754), which is worth a look inside for the graceful interiors alone.

### Piaţa Victoriei & Around

Piaţa Victoriei is a beautifully green pedestrian mall, dotted with fountains and lined on both sides by shops and cafes.

**Orthodox Metropolitan Cathedral** CATHEDRAL
(Catedrala Ortodoxă Mitropolitană; www.mitropolia-banatului.ro; B-dul Regele Ferdinand I; 6am-8pm) The Orthodox cathedral was built between 1936 and 1946. It's unique for its Byzantine-influenced architecture, which recalls the style of the Bucovina monasteries; the floor tiles recall traditional Banat carpets. At 83m, the dome is the highest in Romania.

**Reformed Church** CHURCH
(Biserica Reformată; Str Timotei Cipariu 1) The 1989 revolution began at the Reformed Church, where Father László Tőkés spoke out against Ceauşescu. You can sometimes peek in at the church, and it is usually open during times of worship.

## Sleeping

★**Hostel Costel** HOSTEL €
(0356-262 487; www.hostel-costel.ro; Str Petru Sfetca 1; dm 50-60 lei, d 135 lei; @) This charming 1920s art-nouveau villa is the city's best-run hostel. The vibe is relaxed and congenial. There are three dorm rooms with six to 10 beds and one private double, plus ample chill rooms, a kitchen and a big garden with hammocks for relaxing.

★**Pensiunea Casa Leone** PENSION €€
(0723-329 612, 0256-292 621; www.casaleone.ro; B-dul Eroilor de la Tisa 67; s/d/tr 140/160/225 lei; ) This lovely, very welcoming 10-room *pensiune* offers exceptional service and individually decorated rooms. The surrounding garden is a cool and leafy oasis in summer. To find it, take tram 8 from the train station, alight at Deliblata station and walk one block northeast to B-dul Eroilor. Or phone ahead to arrange transport.

★**Vila La Residenza** HOTEL €€€
(☑0256-401 080; www.laresidenza.ro; Str Independenței 14; s/d/ste €80/92/108; P❄@🛜🏊) 
This converted villa recalls an English man-
or, with a cosy reading room and library off
the lobby and an enormous, well-tended garden in the back with swimming pool. Its 15
rooms are comfort-driven in a similar understated way. A first choice for visiting celebri-
ties and *the* place to stay if price is no object.

## ✗ Eating

★**Casa Bunicii** ROMANIAN €€
(☑0356-100 870; www.casa-bunicii.ro; Str Virgil
Onitiu 3; mains 20-50 lei; ⊙noon-midnight; 🍴)
The names translate to 'Granny's House'
and indeed this casual, family-friendly restaurant specialises in home cooking and regional specialities from the Banat, with an
emphasis on dishes based on *spätzle* (egg
noodles). The duck soup with dumplings (10
lei) and grilled chicken breast served in sour
cherry sauce (20 lei) both come recommended. Folksy surrounds.

★**Caruso** INTERNATIONAL €€€
(☑0256-224 771; www.restaurantcaruso.ro; Str En-
rico Caruso 2; mains 56-115 lei; ⊙noon-midnight)
Probably Timișoara's finest restaurant, Caruso serves superb international and New
Romanian cuisine that puts a 21st-century
spin on old favourites. Foie gras with cocoa? Breast of pigeon with pear mouse? Or
try veal sweetbreads with bacon mash and
morel sauce. Seating on two levels and minimalist decor with lots of photos of the celebrated Italian tenor.

## 🍸 Drinking & Nightlife

**Scârț loc lejer** CAFE
(☑0751-892 340; www.facebook.com/scartlocle-
jer; Str Laszlo Szekely 1; ⊙9am-11pm Mon-Fri, 11am-
11pm Sat, 2-11pm Sun; 🛜) An old villa that's
been retro-fitted into a funky coffee house
called something like the 'Creaky Door', with
old prints on the walls and chill tunes on the
turntable. There are several cosy rooms in
which to read and relax, but our favourite is
the garden out back, with shady nooks and
even hammocks to stretch out on.

**Aethernativ** CAFE
(☑0724-012 364; www.facebook.com/Aethernativ;
Str Mărășești 14; ⊙10am-1am Mon-Fri, noon-1am
Sat, 5pm-1am Sun) This trendy art club, cafe
and bar occupies a courtyard of an old building two blocks west of Piața Unirii and has

eclectic furnishings and an alternative, student vibe. There are no signs to let you know
you're here; simply find the address and push
open the door. Always a fun crowd on hand.

## ☆ Entertainment

**La Căpițe** LIVE MUSIC
(☑0720-400 333; www.lacapite.ro; B-dul Pârvan
Vasile; ⊙10am-1am Mon-Sat, 10am-noon Sun; 🛜)
Shaggy riverside beer garden and alternative hang-out strategically located across the
street from the university, ensuring lively
crowds on warm summer evenings. Most
nights have live music or DJs. The name
translates as 'haystack', and bales of hay
strewn everywhere make for comfy places to
sit and chill.

**National Theatre**
**& Opera House** THEATRE, OPERA
(Teatrul Național și Opera Română; ☑opera 0256-
201 286, theatre 0256-499 908; www.tntimisoara.
com; Str Mărășești 2) The National Theatre
and Opera House features both dramatic
works and classical opera, and is highly regarded. Buy tickets (from around 40 lei) at
the **box office** (☑0256-201 117; www.ort.ro; Str
Mărășești 2; ⊙11am-7pm Tue-Sun) or via email,
but note that most of the dramatic works
will be in Romanian.

## ℹ️ Information

**County Emergency Hospital** (Spitalul Clinic
Județean de Urgență Timișoara; ☑0356-433
111; www.hosptm.ro; B-dul Iosif Bulbuca 10)
Modern hospital, located 2km south of the
centre, with 24-hour emergency service.

**Tourist Information Centre** (Info Centru Tu-
ristic; ☑0256-437 973; www.timisoara-info.ro;
Str Alba Iulia 2; ⊙9am-7pm Mon-Fri, 10am-4pm
Sat May-Sep, 9am-6pm Mon-Fri, 10am-3pm Sat
Oct-Apr) This great tourist office can assist with
accommodation and trains, and provide maps
and regional information on the Banat.

## ℹ️ Getting There & Away

**BUS**
Timișoara lacks a centralised bus station. Buses
and minibuses are privately operated and depart
from several points around the city. Consult the
website www.autogari.ro for departure points.
Sample fares include Arad (15 lei), Cluj-Napoca
(75 lei) and Sibiu (65 lei).

International buses leave from the **East Bus
Station** (Gara de Est; www.autogari.ro). The
main international operators include **Atlassib**
(☑0256-226 486, local office 0757-112 370;
www.atlassib.ro; Calea Stan Vidrighin 12) and

Eurolines (0256-288 132, 0372-766 478; www.eurolines.ro; Str M Kogălniceanu 20). Belgrade-based **Gea Tours** (0316-300 257; www.geatours.rs) offers daily minibus service between Timişoara and Belgrade (one way/return €15/30); book over the website.

### TRAIN

Trains depart from the **Northern Train Station** (Gara Timişoara-Nord; 0256-200 457; www.cfrcalatori.ro; Str Gării 2), though it's actually 'west' of the centre. Daily express trains include services to Bucharest (112 lei, nine hours, two daily), Cluj-Napoca (80 lei, six hours, two daily), Arad (18 lei, one hour, four daily) and Oradea (49 lei, three hours, three daily).

# SURVIVAL GUIDE

## ℹ Directory A–Z

### ACCOMMODATION

Romania has a wide choice of accommodation to suit most budgets. Book summer lodging along the Black Sea coast well in advance. Elsewhere, it's usually not necessary to reserve ahead.

Budget properties include hostels, camping grounds and cheaper guesthouses. Midrange accommodation includes three-star hotels and pensions. Top-end means fancy hotels, corporate chains and boutiques.

### GAY & LESBIAN TRAVELLERS

Public attitudes towards homosexuality remain generally negative. In spite of this, Romania has made significant legal progress in decriminalising homosexual acts and adopting antidiscrimination laws.

➞ Bucharest remains the most tolerant city, though here too open displays of affection between same-sex couples are rare.

➞ The Bucharest-based **Accept Association** (www.acceptromania.ro) promotes rights of gays and lesbians at the national level. Each year in June the group helps to organise the six-day festival **Bucharest Pride** (www.bucharestpride.ro; ☉ Jun), with films, parties, conferences and a parade.

### INTERNET RESOURCES

**Bucharest Life** (www.bucharestlife.net)
**Romania National Tourism Office** (www.romaniatourism.com)
**Bus Timetable** (www.autogari.ro)
**Train Timetable** (www.cfrcalatori.ro)

### MONEY

The currency is the leu (plural: lei). One leu is divided into 100 bani. Banknotes come in denominations of one, five, 10, 50, 100, 200 and 500 lei. Coins come in 50 and 10 bani.

➞ Romania is a member of the European Union, but the euro does not circulate.

➞ ATMs are nearly everywhere and give 24-hour withdrawals in lei on most international bank cards. ATMs require a four-digit PIN.

➞ The best place to exchange money is a bank. You can also change money at a private exchange booth (*casa de schimb*), but be wary of commission charges.

➞ International credit and debit cards are widely accepted in cities. In rural areas, bring cash.

### TELEPHONE

➞ All Romanian numbers have 10 digits, consisting of a 0, plus a city code and number. Mobile phone numbers have a three-digit prefix starting with 7.

➞ Romanian mobiles use the GSM 900/1800 network, the standard throughout Europe as well as in Australia and New Zealand, but not compatible with mobile phones in North America or Japan.

➞ To reduce expensive roaming fees, buy a prepaid local SIM card from one of three main carriers: **Vodafone** (www.vodafone.ro), **Telekom Romania** (www.telekom.ro) and **Orange** (www.orange.ro).

---

**COUNTRY FACTS**

**Area** 237,500 sq km

**Capital** Bucharest

**Country code** 40

**Currency** Romanian leu

**Emergency** 112

**Language** Romanian

**Money** ATMs abundant

**Population** 19.9 million

**Visas** Not required for citizens of the EU, USA, Canada, Australia, New Zealand

---

**SLEEPING PRICE RANGES**

The following price ranges refer to a double room with a bathroom, including breakfast (Bucharest prices tend to be higher).

**€** less than 150 lei

**€€** 150–300 lei

**€€€** more than 300 lei

## ESSENTIAL FOOD & DRINK

Romanian food borrows heavily from its neighbours, including Turkey, Hungary and the Balkans, and is centred on pork and other meats. Farm-fresh, organically raised fruits and vegetables are in abundance, lending flavour and colour to a long list of soups and salads. Condiments typically include sour cream, garlic sauce and grated sheep's cheese.

**Ciorbă** Sour soup that's a mainstay of the Romanian diet.

**Covrigi** Oven-baked pretzels served warm from windows around town.

**Mămăligă** Cornmeal mush, sometimes topped with sour cream or cheese.

**Sarmale** Spiced meat wrapped in cabbage or grape leaves.

**Ţuică** Fiery plum brandy sold in water bottles at roadside rest stops.

➡ Public phones require a magnetic-stripe phonecard bought at post offices and newspaper kiosks. Phonecard rates start at about 10 lei.

### VISAS

Citizens of EU countries do not need visas to visit Romania and can stay indefinitely. Citizens of the USA, Canada, Australia, New Zealand, Israel, Japan and some other countries can stay for up to 90 days without a visa. Other nationalities check with the Romanian **Ministry of Foreign Affairs** (www.mae.ro) before departure.

## ⓘ Getting There & Away

### AIR

Romania has good air connections to Europe and the Middle East. At the time of research there were no direct flights to Romania from North America or Southeast Asia.

### Airports

The majority of international flights to Romania arrive at Bucharest's **Henri Coandă International Airport**. Other international airports:

**Cluj Avram Iancu International Airport** (CLJ; ☑ 0264-307 500, 0264-416 702; www.airport-cluj.ro; Str Traian Vuia 149)

**Sibiu International Airport** (SBZ; ☑ 0269-253 135; www.sibiuairport.ro; Şoseaua Alba Iulia 73)

**Timişoara Traian Vuia International Airport** (TSR; ☑ 0256-386 089; http://aerotim.ro/en; Str Aeroport 2, Ghiroda)

### EATING PRICE RANGES

The following price ranges refer to an average main course.

**€** less than 20 lei

**€€** 20–40 lei

**€€€** more than 40 lei

### LAND

Romania shares a border with five countries: Bulgaria, Hungary, Moldova, Serbia and Ukraine. Most crossings follow international highways or national roads. Romania has two bridge and three car-ferry crossings with Bulgaria over the Danube River. Highway border posts are normally open 24 hours, though some smaller crossings may only be open from 8am to 8pm.

Romania is not a member of the EU's common customs and border area, the Schengen area, so even if you're entering from an EU member state (Bulgaria or Hungary), you'll still have to show a passport or valid EU identity card.

### Bus

Long-haul bus services remain a popular way of travelling from Romania to Western Europe as well as to parts of southeastern Europe and Turkey. Bus travel is comparable in price to train travel, but can be faster and require fewer connections.

Bus services to and from Western Europe are dominated by two companies: **Eurolines** (www.eurolines.ro) and **Atlassib** (☑ 021-222 8971, call centre 080-10 100 100; www.atlassib.ro; Str Gheorghe Duca 4, Bucharest; Ⓜ Gara de Nord). Both maintain vast networks from cities throughout Europe to destinations all around Romania. Check the companies' websites for the latest schedules, prices and departure points.

For sample prices, a one-way ticket from Vienna to Bucharest costs roughly €70. From Paris, the trip is about €100.

### Car & Motorcycle

Romania has decent road and car-ferry connections to neighbouring countries, and entering the country by car or motorcycle will present no unexpected difficulties.

At border crossings, drivers should be prepared to show the vehicle's registration, proof of insurance (a 'green' card) and a valid driver's license.

All foreigners, including EU nationals, are required to show a valid passport (or EU identity card).

## Train

Romania is integrated into the European rail grid, and there are decent connections to Western Europe and neighbouring countries. Nearly all of these arrive at and depart from Bucharest's main station, **Gara de Nord**.

Budapest is the main rail gateway in and out of Romania from Western Europe. There are two daily direct trains between Budapest and Bucharest, with regular onward direct connections from Budapest to Prague, Munich and Vienna.

## ⓘ Getting Around

### AIR

Given the distances and poor state of the roads, flying between cities is a feasible option if time is a primary concern.

➡ The Romanian national carrier **Tarom** (www.tarom.ro) operates a comprehensive network of domestic routes and has a network of ticket offices around the country. The airline flies regularly between Bucharest and Cluj-Napoca, Iaşi, Oradea, Suceava and Timişoara.

➡ The budget carrier **Blue Air** (www.blueair-web.com) has a network of domestic destinations that overlaps with Tarom, but includes Sibiu and Constanţa.

### BUS

A mix of buses and maxitaxis form the backbone of the national transport system. If you understand how the system works, you can move around easily and cheaply, but finding updated information without local help can be tough. The website www.autogari.ro is a helpful online timetable.

### CAR & MOTORCYCLE

Roads are generally crowded and in poor condition. The country has only a few stretches of motorway *(autostrada)*, meaning most of your travel will be along two-lane national highways *(DN, drum naţional)* or secondary roads *(DJ, drum judeţean)*. These pass through every village en route and are choked with cars and trucks, and even occasionally horse carts and tractors pulling hay racks. When calculating arrival times, figure on covering about 50km per hour.

Western-style petrol stations are plentiful, but be sure to fill up before heading on long trips through the mountains or in remote areas. A litre of unleaded 95 octane costs about 5 lei.

### Road Rules

Motorists are required to buy and display a sticker, called a **rovinieta** (www.roviniete.ro), purchased on the border, at petrol stations or online. A vignette valid for one week costs 15 lei.

Other traffic rules:

**Speed limits** 50km/h in town; 90km/h on national roads; 130km/h on expressways

**Minimum driving age** 18

**Blood-alcohol limit** 0.00%

**Seat belts** compulsory

**Headlights** on day and night

### LOCAL TRANSPORT

Romanian cities have good public-transport systems comprised of buses, trams, trolleybuses and, in some cases, maxitaxis. Bucharest is the only city with an underground metro. The method for accessing the systems is broadly similar. Purchase bus or tram tickets at newsagents or street kiosks marked *bilete* or *casă de bilete* before boarding, and validate the ticket once onboard. For maxitaxis, you usually buy a ticket directly from the driver. Tickets generally cost from 1 to 3 lei per ride.

### Taxis

Taxis are cheap, reliable and a useful supplement to the public-transport systems. Drivers are required by law to post their rates on car doors or windscreens. The going rate varies from city to city but ranges from 1.39 to 1.79 lei per kilometre. Any driver posting a higher fare is likely looking to rip off unsuspecting passengers.

### TRAIN

Trains are slow but reliable for getting around Romania. The extensive network covers much of the country, including most of the main tourist sights and key destinations. The national rail system is run by **Căile Ferate Române** (CFR; www.cfrcalatori.ro); the website has a handy online timetable (*mersul trenurilor*). Buy tickets at train-station windows, specialised **Agenţia de Voiaj CFR** ticket offices, private travel agencies or online at www.cfrcalatori.ro.

# Russia

## Best Places to Eat

➜ Lavka-Lavka (p342)
➜ Delicatessen (p342)
➜ Duo Gastrobar (p351)
➜ Clean Plates Society (p352)

## Best Places to Stay

➜ Hotel Metropol (p342)
➜ Blues Hotel (p341)
➜ Soul Kitchen Hostel (p351)
➜ Rachmaninov Antique Hotel (p351)

## Why Go?

Could there be a more iconic image of Eastern Europe than the awe-inspiring architectural ensemble of Moscow's Red Square? The brash, exciting and oil-rich capital of Russia (Россия) is a must on any trip to the region.

St Petersburg, on the Baltic coast, is another stunner. The former imperial capital is still Russia's most beautiful and alluring city, with its grand Italianate mansions, wending canals and enormous Neva River. Also make time for Suzdal to get a glimpse of old Russia with its golden cupolas and fortress-like monasteries. Emulating the tourist-friendly nature of its Baltic neighbours is little Kaliningrad, wedged between Poland and Lithuania on the Baltic Sea. It's a fascinating destination, combining all the best elements of its enormous mother.

Visa red tape deters many travellers from visiting – don't let it keep you from experiencing the incredible things to see and do in the European part of the world's largest country.

## When to Go
### Moscow

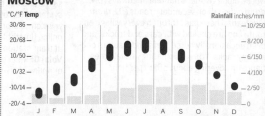

**May** Big military parades and a public holiday mark the end of WWII.

**Jun–Jul** Party during St Petersburg's White Nights, and bask on the beaches of Kaliningrad.

**Dec–Jan** Snow makes Moscow and St Petersburg look magical, while hotel rates drop.

# Russia

**❶ Moscow** (p336) Being awe-inspired by the massive scale and riches of Russia's brash, energetic capital.

**❷ St Petersburg** (p347) Taking a walking, bike or boat tour of a glorious Italianate slice of Old Europe incongruously placed in Russia.

**❸ State Hermitage Museum** (p351) Ogling the seemingly endless collection of masterpieces in St Petersburg's unrivalled museum.

**❹ Petrodvorets** and **Tsarskoe Selo** (p353) Taking a day trip out of St Petersburg to see the imperial country estates in these spectacular sights.

**❺ Suzdal** (p346) Crisscrossing this beautiful town by bicycle or on foot, listening to the music of church bells and nightingales.

**❻ Kaliningrad** (p354) Exploring this historic city, once part of the Prussian empire, and home to the pristine beaches of the Kurshskaya Kosa National Park.

# Moscow     Москва

📞 495 & 499 / POP 12.2 MILLION

Huge and prone to architectural gigantism, full of energy, both positive and dark, refined and tasteless at the same time, Moscow is overwhelming in every way. After the major spruce-up it has undergone in recent years, the mind-bogglingly eclectic Russian capital may look like hipster-ridden parts of Brooklyn at one point and a thoroughly glossed-over version of North Korea at another.

The sturdy stone walls of the Kremlin, the apex of Russian political power and once the centre of the Orthodox Church, occupy the city's founding site on the northern bank of the Moscow River. Remains of the Soviet state, such as Lenin's Tomb, are nearby in Red Square and elsewhere in the city, which radiates from the Kremlin in a series of ring roads.

## ◉ Sights

### ◉ The Kremlin

Covering Borovitsky Hill on the north bank of the Moscow River, the **Kremlin** (Кремль; 📞 495-695 4146; www.kreml.ru; R500; ⊘ 10am-5pm Fri-Wed, ticket office 9.30am-4.30pm Fri-Wed; Ⓜ Aleksandrovsky Sad) is enclosed by high walls 2.25km long, with Red Square outside the east wall. The best views of the complex are from Sofiyskaya nab across the river.

Before entering the Kremlin, deposit bags at the **left-luggage office** (⊘ 9am-6.30pm Fri-Wed), beneath the Kutafya Tower. The main ticket office is in the Alexandrovsky Garden. The entrance ticket covers admission to all five church-museums, and the Patriarch's Palace. It does not include the Armoury, the Diamond Fund Exhibition or special exhibits, which are priced separately.

From the Kutafya Tower, walk up the ramp and pass through the Kremlin walls beneath the **Trinity Gate Tower** (Троицкая башня). The lane to the right (south) passes the 17th-century **Poteshny Palace** (Потешный дворец), where Stalin lived. The horribly out of place glass-and-concrete **State Kremlin Palace** (Государственный кремлёвский дворец; 📞 495 620 7846; www.kremlinpalace.org/en) houses a concert and ballet auditorium, where many Western pop stars play when they are in Moscow.

Photography is not permitted inside the Armoury or any of the buildings on Sobornaya pl (Cathedral Sq).

### ★ Armoury     MUSEUM

(Оружейная палата; R700; ⊘ 10am, noon, 2.30pm & 4.30pm Fri-Wed; Ⓜ Aleksandrovsky Sad) The Armoury dates back to 1511, when it was founded under Vasily III to manufacture and store weapons, imperial arms and regalia for the royal court. Later it also produced jewellery, icon frames and embroidery. To this day, the Armoury still contains plenty of treasures for ogling, and remains a highlight of any visit to the Kremlin. If possible, buy your time-specific ticket to the Armoury when you buy your ticket to the Kremlin.

---

## ITINERARIES

### One Week

In **Moscow**, touring the Kremlin and Red Square will take up one day, viewing the spectacular collections at the Tretyakov, New Tretyakov and Pushkin art museums another. On day three stretch your legs in the revamped Gorky Park.

Take the night train to **Veliky Novgorod** and spend a day exploring its ancient kremlin and churches. The rest of the week is reserved for splendid **St Petersburg**. Wander up Nevsky pr, see Dvortsovaya pl, and spend a half-day at the Hermitage. Tour the canals and the mighty Neva River by boat. Visit Peter & Paul Fortress, the Church of the Saviour on Spilled Blood and the wonderful Russian Museum.

### Two Weeks

With two extra days in Moscow, sweat it out in the luxurious Sanduny Baths or do a metro tour. In St Petersburg, spend more time in the Hermitage and other museums, and tack on an excursion to **Petrodvorets** or **Tsarskoe Selo**. Then fly to **Kaliningrad**. Admire the capital's reconstructed Gothic Cathedral and wander along the river to the excellent Museum of the World Ocean. Enjoy either the old Prussian charm of the spa town of **Svetlogorsk** or the sand dunes and forests of the **Kurshskaya Kosa National Park**.

⭐ **Red Square** HISTORIC SITE

(Красная площадь; Krasnaya pl; Ⓜ Ploshchad Revolyutsii) Immediately outside the Kremlin's northeastern wall is the celebrated Red Square, the 400m by 150m area of cobblestones that is at the very heart of Moscow. Commanding the square from the southern end is **St Basil's Cathedral** (Покровский собор, Храм Василия Блаженного; www.saint-basil.ru; adult/student R350/100; ⊘ticket office 11am-4.30pm; Ⓜ Ploshchad Revolyutsii). This panorama never fails to send the heart aflutter, especially at night.

⭐ **Lenin's Mausoleum** MEMORIAL

(Мавзолей Ленина; www.lenin.ru; ⊘10am-1pm Tue-Thu & Sat; Ⓜ Ploshchad Revolyutsii) **FREE** Although Vladimir Ilych requested that he be buried beside his mum in St Petersburg, he still lies in state at the foot of the Kremlin wall, receiving visitors who come to pay their respects. Line up at the western corner of the square (near the entrance to Alexander Garden) to see the embalmed leader, who has been here since 1924. Note that photography is not allowed and stern guards ensure that all visitors remain respectful and silent.

**State History Museum** MUSEUM

(Государственный исторический музей; www.shm.ru; Krasnaya pl 1; adult/student R350/100, audioguide R300; ⊘ticket office 10am-5pm Wed & Fri-Mon, 11am-8pm Thu; Ⓜ Okhotny Ryad) At the northern end of Red Square, the State History Museum has an enormous collection covering the whole Russian empire from the time of the Stone Age. The building, dating from the late 19th century, is itself an attraction – each room is in the style of a different period or region, some with highly decorated walls echoing old Russian churches.

## ◉ South of the Moscow River

⭐ **State Tretyakov Gallery Main Branch** GALLERY

(Главный отдел Государственной Третьяковской галереи; www.tretyakovgallery.ru; Lavrushinsky per 10; R400; ⊘10am-6pm Tue, Wed & Sun, to 9pm Thu, Fri & Sat, last tickets 1hr before closing; Ⓜ Tretyakovskaya) The exotic boyar castle on a little lane in Zamoskvorechie contains the main branch of the State Tretyakov Gallery, housing the world's best collection of Russian icons and an outstanding collection of other pre-revolutionary Russian art. Show up early to beat the queues.

---

**THE BANYA**

Taking a traditional Russian *banya* is a must. These wet saunas are a social hub and a fantastic experience for any visitor to Russia. Leave your inhibitions at home and be prepared for a beating with birch twigs (far more pleasant than it sounds). Ask at your accommodation for the nearest public *banya*. In Moscow, try the luxurious **Sanduny Baths** (☑495-782 1808; www.sanduny.ru; Neglinnaya ul 14; R1600-2500; ⊘8am-10pm Wed-Mon, Second Male Top Class 10am-midnight Tue-Fri, 8am-10pm Sat & Sun; Ⓜ Kuznetsky Most) and in St Petersburg the traditional **Mytninskiye Bani** (Мытнинские бани; www.mybanya.spb.ru; ul Mytninskaya 17-19; per hr R200-300; ⊘8am-10pm Fri-Tue; Ⓜ Ploshchad Vosstaniya).

---

⭐ **Gorky Park** PARK

(Парк Горького; ⊘24hr; 🛜 🎡; Ⓜ Oktyabrskaya) **FREE** Moscow's main escape from the city within the city is not your conventional expanse of nature preserved deep inside an urban jungle. It is not a fun fair either, though it used to be one. Its official name says it all – Maxim Gorky's Central Park of Culture & Leisure. That's exactly what it provides: culture and leisure in all shapes and forms. Designed by avant-garde architect Konstantin Melnikov as a piece of communist utopia in the 1920s, these days it showcases the enlightened transformation Moscow has undergone in the recent past.

**New Tretyakov Gallery** GALLERY

(Новая Третьяковская галерея; www.tretyakovgallery.ru; ul Krymsky val 10; R400; ⊘10am-6pm Tue, Wed & Sun, to 9pm Thu-Sat, last tickets 1hr before closing; Ⓜ Park Kultury) The premier venue for 20th-century Russian art is this branch of the State Tretyakov Gallery, better known as the New Tretyakov. This place has much more than the typical socialist realist images of muscle-bound men wielding scythes and busty women milking cows (although there's that, too). The exhibits showcase avant-garde artists such as Malevich, Kandinsky, Chagall, Goncharova and Popova.

**Art Muzeon & Krymskaya Naberezhnaya** PUBLIC ART

(ul Krymsky val 10; Ⓜ Park Kultury) **FREE** Now fully revamped and merged with the wonderfully reconstructed Krymskaya

# Central Moscow

1 km
0.5 miles

Winzavod 10
ArtPlay 2
Bolshoy Polyarskaya per

Izmaylovsky Market (7.7km)

Elokhovsky Hotel (750m)
Novaya Basmannaya ul
Park im Baumana

ul Zemlyanoy val

Kursky Vokzal
Chkalovskaya
Kazenny per

Ryazansky per
Novoryazanskaya ul
Kazansky Vokzal
Komsomolskaya pl
Komsomolskaya
Yaroslavsky Vokzal
Leningradsky Vokzal

Kalanchevskaya ul
Bolshaya Spasskaya ul
Dokuchaev per
Skryazhny per
ul Masha Poryvaevoy

Orlikov per
Kalanchevskaya ul
Krasnye Vorota
Pl Krasnye Vorota
Bolshoy Kharitonyevsky per

(Garden Ring)
ul Chaplygina
Pokrovsky bul
Lyapin per
Yauzsky bul
ul Pokrovka
pl Pokrovskie Vorota

KITAY-GOROD
Podkolokolny per
ul Solyanka
Kolpachny per

Bolshoy Balkansky per
Grokholsky per
pr Akademika Sakharova
Sadovaya-Spasskaya ul

Chistye Prudy 48
43
Chistoprudny bul
Potapovsky per
Armyansky per

pr Mira
ul Sretenka
Rozhdestvensky bul
Sretensky Bulvar
Turgenevskaya pl
Myasnitskaya ul
ul Malaya Lubyanka
ul Bolshaya Lubyanka

Lubyansky proezd
Staraya pl
Slavyanskaya pl
Kitay-Gorod
ul Varvarka
31
Lubyanka
Novaya pl

ul Giliyarovskogo
Sukharevskaya pl
ul Durova
ul Shchepkina
Troitskaya ul
Samotechnaya pl
pr Olimpiysky
Delegatskaya ul

Sadovaya-Sukharevskaya ul
Trubnaya ul
Pechatnikov per
Pushkarev per
Posledny per
Kuznetsky Most

Tsvetnoy Bulvar
Bolshoy Kiselny per
Zvonarsky per
Kostyansky per

Tsvetnoy bul
Trubnaya
ul Neglinnaya
34
Ploshchad Revolyutsii
Teatralny proezd
Teatralnaya pl

Bolshoy Karetny per
32
37
Sadovaya-Samotechnaya ul
42
40
49
30
ul Petrovka
ul Kuznetsky most
ul Bolshaya Dmitrovka

Kremlin (See Kremlin)
Vetoshny per
Saviour Gate Tower
Left-Luggage Office

Petrovsky bul
Strastnoy bul
Petrovka
41
Hermitage Gardens
ul Karetny Ryad
Uspensky per
Chekhovskaya

Manezhnaya pl
Okhotny Ryad
38
Gazetny per
Aleksandrovsky Sad

Dolgorukovskaya ul
ul Malaya Dmitrovka
Tverskaya
36
39
Pushkinskaya
Tverskaya pl
Maly Gnezdnikovsky per

Biblioteka imeni Lenina
Bolshoy Kislovsky per
29

46
33
Pushkinskaya
Bolshaya Bronnaya ul
Tverskoy bul
Nikitsky bul
Bolshaya Nikitskaya ul
pl Nikitskie Vorota
Vozdvizhenka ul

MAYAKOVSKAYA
Triumfalnaya pl
Mayakovskaya
Oruzheyny per
50
47
Sadovaya-Triumfalnaya
Bolshaya Sadovaya ul
Tverskaya-Yamskaya ul
1-ya Tverskaya-Yamskaya ul

ul Krasina
ul Spiridonovka
Granatny per
Malaya Bronnaya ul
Malaya Nikitskaya ul
Bolshaya Nikitskaya ul

European Medical Centre
Patriarch's Pond
ul Novy Arbat
Skatertny per
Khlebny per
Povarskaya ul

Belorusskaya
Belorussky Vokzal
1-ya Tverskaya-Yamskaya ul
1-ya Brestskaya ul
ul Fadeeva
ul Vasilievskaya
ul Juliusa Fučíka
Tishinskaya pl

Bolshaya Gruzinskaya ul
Zoologicheskaya ul
Bolshaya Sadovaya ul
Sadovaya-Kudrinskaya ul
Kudrinskaya pl
Novinsky bul
Barrikadnaya
Trubnikovsky per
Spasopeskovsky per

Sixteen Tons (900m)
Rassison River Cruises (950m)

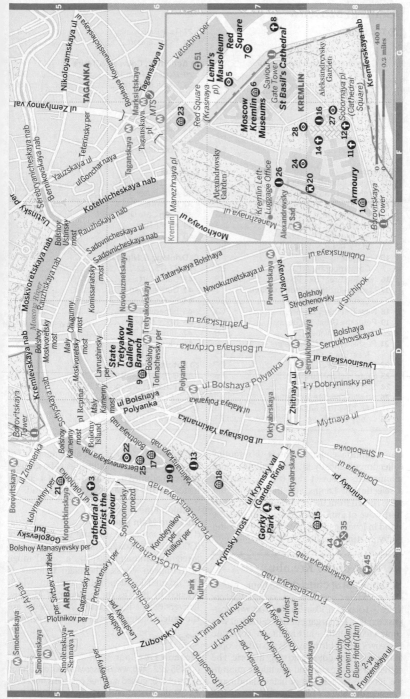

# Central Moscow

Naberezhnaya embankment is this motley collection of (mostly kitschy) sculpture and monuments to Soviet idols (Stalin, Sverdlov, a selection of Lenins and Brezhnevs) that were ripped from their pedestals in the post-1991 wave of anti-Soviet feeling. All of these stand in lovely gardens with boardwalks and many inviting benches.

## ◎ West of the Kremlin

★ **Cathedral of Christ the Saviour** CHURCH
(Храм Христа Спасителя; www.xxc.ru; ul Volkhonka 15; ⊙1-5pm Mon, 10am-5pm Tue-Sun; ⓜKropotkinskaya) **FREE** This gargantuan cathedral was completed in 1997 – just in time to celebrate Moscow's 850th birthday. It is amazingly opulent, garishly grandiose and truly historic. The cathedral's sheer size and splendour guarantee its role as a love-it-or-hate-it landmark. Considering Stalin's plan for this site (a Pal-

ace of Soviets topped with a 100m statue of Lenin), Muscovites should at least be grateful they can admire the shiny domes of a church instead of the shiny dome of Ilyich's head.

**Pushkin Fine Arts Museum Main Building** MUSEUM
(Главное здание; ul Volkhonka 12; adult/student R300/150; ⓜKropotkinskaya) Moscow's premier foreign-art museum displays a broad range of European works. The main building is the original location of the museum, which opened in 1912 as the museum of Moscow University. The highlights of the museum are the Dutch masterpieces from the 17th century.

## ☞ Tours

**Moscow Free Tour** WALKING
(☎495-222 3466; www.moscowfreetour.com; Nikolskaya ul 4/5; guided walk free, paid tours from €35) Every day these enthusiastic ladies offer an

informative, inspired two-hour guided walk around Red Square and Kitay Gorod – and it's completely free. It's so good, that (they think) you'll sign up for one of their excellent paid tours, covering the Kremlin, the Arbat and the Metro, or more thematic tours, such as communist Moscow or mystical Moscow.

### Radisson River Cruises — BOATING

(www.radisson-cruise.ru; 2½hr cruise R750; ⓜ Kievskaya) The Radisson operates big river boats that cart 140 people up and down the Moscow River from the dock in front of the hotel and from the dock in Gorky Park. In summer, there are five or six daily departures from each location (check the website for times). Boats are enclosed (and equipped with ice cutters), so the cruises run year-round, albeit less frequently in winter.

## 🛏 Sleeping

### Godzillas Hostel — HOSTEL €

(☏ 495-699 4223; www.godzillashostel.com; Bolshoy Karetny per 6; dm from R750, s/d R2500/2800; ❄ @ ☎; ⓜ Tsvetnoy Bulvar) Tried and true, Godzillas is Moscow's best-known hostel, with dozens of beds spread out over four floors. The rooms come in various sizes, but they are all spacious and light-filled and painted in different colours. To cater to the many guests, there are bathroom facilities on each floor, three kitchens and a big living room with satellite TV.

### Comrade Hostel — HOSTEL €

(☏ 499-709 8760; www.comradehostel.com; ul Maroseyka 11; dm/s/d R650/2200/2700; ❄ @ ☎; ⓜ Kitay-Gorod) It's hard to find this tiny place – go into the courtyard and look for entrance No 3, where you might spot a computer-printed sign in the 3rd-floor window. Inside is a great welcoming atmosphere, although the place is usually packed. Ten to 12 beds are squeezed into the dorm rooms, plus there are mattresses on the floor if need be.

### ★ Blues Hotel — BOUTIQUE HOTEL €€

(☏ 495-961 1161; www.blues-hotel.ru; ul Dovatora 8; r from R4600; ❄ ❄ ☎; ⓜ Sportivnaya) The location is not exactly central, but is not a disadvantage. It is steps from the red-line metro (five stops to Red Square) and a few blocks from Novodevichy, with several worthwhile restaurants in the vicinity. Considering that, this friendly, affordable boutique hotel is a gem, offering stylish, spotless rooms with king-size beds and flat-screen TVs.

### Elokhovsky Hotel — HOTEL €€

(Отель Елоховский; ☏ 495-632 2300; www.elo-hotel.ru; ul Spartakovskaya 24; s/d R4500/5300;

---

### SOBORNAYA PLOSHCHAD

On the northern side of Sobornaya pl, with five golden helmet domes and four semicircular gables facing the square, is the **Assumption Cathedral** (Успенский собор), built between 1475 and 1479. As the focal church of prerevolutionary Russia, it's the burial place of most heads of the Russian Orthodox Church from the 1320s to 1700. The iconostasis dates from 1652, but its lowest level contains some older icons, including the Virgin of Vladimir (Vladimirskaya Bogomater), an early-15th-century Rublyov-school copy of Russia's most revered image, the Vladimir Icon of the Mother of God (Ikona Vladimirskoy Bogomateri).

The delicate little single-domed church beside the west door of the Assumption Cathedral is the **Church of the Deposition of the Robe** (Церковь Ризоположения), built between 1484 and 1486 by masons from Pskov.

With its two golden domes rising above the eastern side of Sobornaya pl, the 16th-century **Ivan the Great Bell Tower** (Колокольня Ивана Великого; R250) is the Kremlin's tallest structure. Beside the bell tower stands the **Tsar Bell** (Царь-колокол), a 202-tonne monster that cracked before it ever rang. North of the bell tower is the mammoth **Tsar Cannon** (Царь-пушка), cast in 1586 but never shot.

The 1508 **Archangel Cathedral** (Архангельский собор), at the square's southeastern corner, was for centuries the coronation, wedding and burial church of tsars. The tombs of all of Russia's rulers from the 1320s to the 1690s are here bar one (Boris Godunov, who was buried at Sergiev Posad).

Finally, the **Annunciation Cathedral** (Благовещенский собор), at the southwest corner of Sobornaya pl and dating from 1489, contains the celebrated icons of master painter Theophanes the Greek. He probably painted the six icons at the right-hand end of the diesis row, the biggest of the six tiers of the iconostasis. Archangel Michael (the third icon from the left on the diesis row) and the adjacent St Peter are ascribed to Russian master Andrei Rublyov.

✹ ☎; Ⓜ Baumanskaya) Admittedly not very central and occupying the top floor of a shopping arcade, this hotel is nevertheless about the best value for money you can find in Moscow. Room themes are based on the world's major cities, and are painted in soothing, homey colours. The coffee machine in the lobby is available 24 hours. Baumanskaya metro and Yelokhovsky Cathedral are a stone's throw away.

### ★ Hotel de Paris BOUTIQUE HOTEL €€

(☏ 495-777 0052; www.hotel-deparis.ru; Bolshaya Bronnaya ul 23, bldg 3; s/d from R6400/6800; ℙ✹☎; Ⓜ Pushkinskaya) Steps from the madness of Tverskaya, this is a delightfully stylish hotel tucked into a quiet courtyard off the Boulevard Ring. Situated on the lower floors, the rooms do not get much natural light, but they feature king-size beds, jacuzzi tubs and elegant design. Service is consistently friendly. Prices drop by 40% on weekends, offering terrific value.

### ★ Hotel Metropol HISTORIC HOTEL €€€

(☏ 499-501 7800; www.metropol-moscow.ru; Teatralny proezd 1/4; r from R15,500; ✹✹@✹; Ⓜ Teatralnaya) Nothing short of an art nouveau masterpiece, the 1907 Metropol brings an artistic, historic touch to every nook and cranny, from the spectacular exterior to the grand lobby to the individually decorated (but small) rooms. The breakfast buffet (R2000) is ridiculously priced, but it's served under the restaurant's gorgeous stained-glass ceiling.

## ✕ Eating

### Danilovsky Market MARKET €€

(www.danrinok.ru; Mytnaya ul 74; mains R400-600; ⊙8am-8pm; Ⓜ Tulskaya) A showcase of the ongoing gentrification of Moscow, this giant So-

viet-era farmers market is now largely about deli food cooked and served in a myriad of little eateries, including such gems as a Dagestani dumpling shop and a Vietnamese pho soup kitchen. The market itself looks very orderly, if a tiny bit artificial, with uniformed vendors and thoughtfully designed premises.

### ★ Delicatessen INTERNATIONAL €€

(Деликатесы; www.newdeli.ru; Savodvaya-Karetnaya ul 20; mains R500-800; ⊙noon-midnight Tue-Sun; ☎@; Ⓜ Tsvetnoy Bulvar) The affable (and chatty) owners of this place travel the world and experiment with the menu a lot, turning burgers, pizzas and pasta into artfully constructed objects of modern culinary art. The other source of joy is a cabinet filled with bottles of ripening fruity liquors, which may destroy your budget if consumed uncontrollably (a pointless warning, we know).

### ★ Khachapuri GEORGIAN €€

(☏ 8-985-764 3118; www.hacha.ru; Bolshoy Gnezdnikovsky per 10; mains R400-600; ⊝☎@; Ⓜ Pushkinskaya) Unassuming, affordable and appetising, this urban cafe exemplifies what people love about Georgian culture: the warm hospitality and the freshly baked *khachapuri* (cheese bread). Aside from seven types of delicious *khachapuri,* there's also an array of soups, shashlyki (kebabs), *khinkali* (dumplings) and other Georgian favourites.

### Gran Cafe Dr Zhivago RUSSIAN €€

(☏ 499-922 0100; www.drzhivago.ru; ul Mokhovaya 15/1; mains R540-1200; ⊙24hr; Ⓜ Okhotny Ryad) An excellent breakfast choice before visiting the Kremlin, this round-the-clock place mixes Soviet nostalgia with a great deal of mischievous irony in both design and food. The chef has upgraded the menu of a standard pioneer camp's canteen to near haute cuisine level, with masterfully cooked porridge, pancakes, *vareniki* (dumplings) and cottage-cheese pies.

### ★ Lavka-Lavka INTERNATIONAL €€

(Лавка-Лавка; ☏ 8-903-115 5033; www.restoran. lavkalavka.com; ul Petrovka 21 str 2; mains R500-950; ⊙noon-midnight Tue-Thu & Sun, to 1am Fri & Sat; ♿; Ⓜ Teatralnaya) ✔ Welcome to the Russian Portlandia – all the food here is organic and hails from little farms where you may rest assured all the lambs and chickens lived a very happy life before being served to you on a plate. Irony aside, this is a great place to sample local food cooked in a funky improvisational style.

## METRO TOUR

For just R40 you can spend the day touring Moscow's magnificent metro stations. Many of the stations are marble-faced, frescoed, gilded works of art. Among our favourites are **Komsomolskaya**, a huge stuccoed hall, its ceiling covered with mosaics depicting military heroes; **Novokuznetskaya**, featuring military bas-reliefs done in sober khaki, and colourful ceiling mosaics depicting pictures of the happy life; and **Mayakovskaya**, Grand Prize winner at the 1939 World's Fair in New York.

★ **Café Pushkin** RUSSIAN €€€

(Кафе Пушкинь; ☑ 495-739 0033; www.ca-fe-pushkin.ru; Tverskoy bul 26a; business lunch from R620, mains R800-1800; ⊘ 24hr; ⊟ 🛜 🖥; Ⓜ Pushkinskaya) The tsarina of *haute-russe* dining, with an exquisite blend of Russian and French cuisines – service and food are done to perfection. The lovely 19th-century building has a different atmosphere on each floor, including a richly decorated library and a pleasant rooftop cafe.

## 🍷 Drinking

★ **32.05** CAFE

(☑ 905-703 3205; www.veranda3205.ru; ul Karetny Ryad 3; ⊘ 11am-3am; Ⓜ Pushkinskaya) The biggest drinking/eating establishment in Hermitage Gardens, this verandah positioned at the back of the main building looks a bit like a greenhouse. In summer, tables (and patrons) spill out into the park, making it one of the city's best places for outdoor drinking. With its long bar and joyful atmosphere, the place also heaves in winter.

**Cafe Mart** CAFE

(Кафе Март; www.cafemart.ru; ul Petrovka 25; meals R800-1200; ⊘ 11am-midnight Sun-Wed, 11am-6am Thu-Sat, jazz concert 9pm Thu; 📶; Ⓜ Chekhovskaya) It looks like another cellar bar, but if you walk all the way through the underground maze you'll find yourself in the huge overground 'orangerie' hall with mosaic-covered walls, warm lighting and possibly a jazz concert. When the weather is fine, Mart spills into the sculpture-filled courtyard of the adjacent Moscow Museum of Contemporary Art.

★ **Noor / Electro** BAR

(☑ 8-903-136 7686; www.noorbar.com; ul Tverskaya 23/12; ⊘ 8pm-3am Mon-Wed, to 6am Thu-Sun; Ⓜ Pushkinskaya) There is little to say about this misleadingly unassuming bar, apart from the fact that everything in it is close to perfection. It has it all – prime location, convivial atmosphere, eclectic DJ music, friendly bartenders and superb drinks. Though declared 'the best' by various magazines on several occasions, it doesn't feel like they care.

**Time-Out Bar** COCKTAIL BAR

(www.timeoutbar.ru; 12th fl, Bolshaya Sadovaya ul 5; ⊘ noon-2am Sun-Thu, noon-6am Fri & Sat; Ⓜ Mayakovskaya) On the upper floors of the throwback Pekin Hotel, this trendy bar is nothing but 'now'. That includes the bartenders sporting plaid and their delicious concoctions, especially created for different times of day. The

---

### CAFES, CLUBS & ANTI-CAFES

There's a hazy distinction between cafe, bar and nightclub in Russia's cities, with many places serving all three functions. As such, we list them all in one place.

Top clubs have strict *feis kontrol* (face control); beat it by arriving early before the bouncers are posted, or by speaking English, as being a foreigner helps.

Currently popular are 'anti-cafes': 'creative spaces' where you pay by the minute and enjoy coffee, snacks and access to everything from wi-fi to computer games and musical instruments. They are great places to meet locals.

---

decor is pretty impressive – particularly the spectacular city skyline. Perfect place for sundowners (or sun-ups, if you last that long).

**Ukuleleshnaya** BAR

(Укулелешная; ☑ 495-642 5726; www.uku-uku.ru; ul Pokrovka 17 str 1; ⊘ noon-midnight Sun-Thu, to 4am Fri & Sat; Ⓜ Chistye Prudy) In its new location, this is now more of a bar than a musical instrument shop, although ukuleles still adorn the walls, prompting an occasional jam session. Craft beer prevails on the drinks list, but Ukuleleshnaya also serves experimental cocktails of its own invention. Live concerts happen regularly and resident Pomeranian Spitz Berseny (cute dog) presides over the resulting madness.

**Coffee Bean** CAFE

(www.coffeebean.ru; ul Pokrovka 21; ⊘ 8am-11pm; Ⓜ Chislye Prudy) Winds of change brought US national Jerry Ruditser to Moscow in the early 1990s on a mission to create the nation's first coffee chain, in which he succeeded long before Starbucks found Russia on the map. Some argue it's still the best coffee served in the capital. That might be disputed, but on the friendliness front Coffee Bean is unbeatable.

## ☆ Entertainment

To find out what's on, see the entertainment section in Thursday's *Moscow Times*. Most theatres, including the Bolshoi, are closed between late June and early September.

★ **Bolshoi Theatre** BALLET, OPERA

(Большой театр; ☑ 495-455 5555; www.bolshoi.ru; Teatralnaya pl 1; tickets R100-12,000; ⊘ closed Jul & Aug; Ⓜ Teatralnaya) An evening at the Bolshoi

## MOSCOW'S WHITE-HOT ART SCENE

Revamped old industrial buildings and other spaces in Moscow are where you'll find gems of Russia's super-creative contemporary art scene. Apart from the following recommended spots, also see www.artguide.ru.

**Garage Museum of Contemporary Art** (☑ 495-645 0520; www.garagemca.org; ul Krymsky val 9/32; adult/student R400/200; 11am-10pm; Ⓜ Oktyabrskaya) Having moved into a permanent Gorky Park location, a Soviet-era building renovated by the visionary Dutch architect Rem Koolhaas, Garage hosts exciting exhibitions by top artists.

**Vinzavod** (Винзавод; www.winzavod.ru; 4 Syromyatnichesky per 1; Ⓜ Chkalovskaya) FREE A former wine factory has morphed into this postindustrial complex of prestigious galleries, shops, a cinema and trendy cafe. Nearby, another converted industrial space, the **Artplay** (☑ 495-620 0882; www.artplay.ru; Nizhny Syromyatnichesky per 10; ☺ noon-8pm Tue-Sun; Ⓜ Chkalovskaya) FREE ,is home to firms specialising in urban planning and architectural design, as well as furniture showrooms and antique stores.

**Proekt_Fabrika** (www.proektfabrika.ru; 18 Perevedenovsky per; ☺ 10am-8pm Tue-Sun; Ⓜ Baumanskaya) FREE A still-functioning paper factory is the location for this nonprofit set of gallery and performance spaces enlivened by arty graffiti and creative-industry offices.

**Red October** (Завод Красный Октябрь; Bersenevskaya nab; Ⓜ Kropotkinskaya) FREE The red-brick buildings of this former chocolate factory now host the **Lumiere Brothers Photography Centre** (www.lumiere.ru; Bolotnaya nab 3, bldg 1; R200-430; ☺ noon-9pm Tue-Fri, to 10pm Sat & Sun) plus other galleries, cool bars and restaurants. In an adjacent building the **Strelka Institute for Media, Architecture and Design** (www.strelkainstitute.ru; bldg 5a, Bersenevskaya nab 14/5; Ⓜ Novokuznetskaya) is worth checking out for its events, bookshop and bar. Also, look out for **GES-2**, a new large contemporary art space that was due to open in an old power station in 2017.

is still one of Moscow's most romantic and entertaining options for a night on the town. The glittering six-tier auditorium has an electric atmosphere, evoking over 240 years of premier music and dance. Both the ballet and opera companies perform a range of Russian and foreign works here. After the collapse of the Soviet Union, the Bolshoi was marred by politics, scandal and frequent turnover. Yet the show must go on – and it will.

**Tchaikovsky Concert Hall**     CLASSICAL MUSIC
(Концертный зал имени Чайковского; ☑ 495-232 0400; www.meloman.ru; Triumfalnaya pl 4/31; tickets R300-3000; ☺ closed Jul & Aug; Ⓜ Mayakovskaya) Home to the famous Moscow State Philharmonic (Moskovskaya Filharmonia), the capital's oldest symphony orchestra, Tchaikovsky Concert Hall was established in 1921. It's a huge auditorium, with seating for 1600 people. This is where you can expect to hear the Russian classics such as Stravinsky, Rachmaninov and Shostakovich, as well as other European favourites. Look out for special children's concerts.

**Sixteen Tons**     LIVE MUSIC
(Шестнадцать тонн; ☑ 495-253 1550; www.16tons.ru; ul Presnensky val 6; cover R600-1200;

☺ 11am-6am; 🖥; Ⓜ Ulitsa 1905 Goda) Downstairs, the brassy English pub-restaurant has an excellent house-brewed bitter. Upstairs, the club gets some of the best Russian bands that play in Moscow and an occasional first-rate or semi-obscure Western visitor. Show times are subject to change so check the website for details.

## 🛍 Shopping

Ul Arbat has always been a tourist attraction and is littered with souvenir shops and stalls.

**GUM**     MALL
(ГУМ; www.gum.ru; Krasnaya pl 3; ☺ 10am-10pm; Ⓜ Ploshchad Revolyutsii) The elaborate 240m facade on the northeastern side of Red Square, GUM is a bright, bustling shopping mall with hundreds of fancy stores and restaurants. With a skylight roof and three-level arcades, the spectacular interior was a revolutionary design when it was built in the 1890s, replacing the Upper Trading Rows that previously occupied this site.

**Izmaylovsky Market**     MARKET
(www.kremlin-izmailovo.com; Izmaylovskoye shosse 73; ☺ 10am-8pm; Ⓜ Partizanskaya) Never mind the kitschy faux 'tsar's palace' it surrounds,

Izmaylovsky flea market is the ultimate place to shop for *matryoshki* (nesting dolls), military uniforms, icons, Soviet badges and some real antiques. Huge and diverse, it is almost a theme park, including shops, cafes and a couple of not terribly exciting museums.

Serious antiquarians occupy the 2nd floor of the wooden trade row surrounding the palace, but for really good stuff you need to come here at an ungodly hour on Saturday morning and compete with pros from Moscow galleries. Keep in mind that Russia bans the export of any item older than 100 years.

## ⓘ Information

Wireless access is ubiquitous and almost always free.

**36.6** A chain of 24-hour pharmacies with many branches all around the city.

**European Medical Centre** (☑ 495-933 6655; www.emcmos.ru; Spirodonevsky per 5; ⊘24hr; Ⓜ Mayakovskaya) Offers 24-hour emergency service, consultations and a full range of medical specialists.

**Main Post Office** (Myasnitskaya ul 26; ⊘24hr; Ⓜ Chistye Prudy)

**Moscow Times** Best locally published English-language newspaper, widely distributed free of charge.

**Unifest Travel** (☑ 495-234 6555; www.unifest.ru; Komsomolsky pr 16/2 str 3-4; ⊘9am-7pm Mon-Fri, visa department 10am-6pm Mon-Fri) On-the-ball travel company offers rail and air tickets, visa support and more.

## ⓘ Getting Around

### TO/FROM THE AIRPORT

All three Moscow airports (Domodedovo, Sheremetyevo or Vnukovo) are accessible by the convenient **Aeroexpress Train** (☑ 8-800 700 3377; www.aeroexpress.ru; R420; ⊘6am-midnight) from the city centre; reduced rates are available for online purchase.

Alternatively, order an official airport taxi from the dispatcher's desk in the terminal (R2000 to R2200 to the city centre). If you can order a taxi by phone or with a mobile phone app (you'll need a Russian SIM card and some knowledge of the language) it will be about 50% cheaper. Consider asking fellow Russian travellers on your plane – someone should be able to help if you ask nicely.

### PUBLIC TRANSPORT

The **Moscow Metro** (www.mosmetro.ru) is by far the easiest, quickest and cheapest way of getting around the city. Stations are marked outside by 'M' signs. Magnetic tickets (R55) are sold at ticket booths. Save time by buying unlimited travel tickets (one day R210, three days R400, seven days R800) or multiple-ride tickets (five rides for R160, 20 rides for R720).

The ticket is a contactless smart card, which you must tap on the reader before going through the turnstile.

Buses, trolleybuses and trams are useful along a few radial or cross-town routes that the metro misses, and are necessary for reaching sights away from the city centre. Same tickets as in the metro apply and you can buy them from the driver. Boarding is only through the first door, where you need to apply the magnetic card at a turnstile.

### TAXI

Taxi cabs are affordable, but not that easy for casual visitors to Moscow to use as you can't really flag down an official metered taxi in the street. These days, most people use mobile phone apps (such as Uber, Gett and Yandex Taxi) to order a cab.

You can also order an official taxi by phone or book it online, or ask a Russian-speaker to do this for you. **Taxi Tsel** (☑ 495-204 2244; www.taxicel.ru) is a reliable company, but operators don't speak English.

# Golden Ring
## Золотое Кольцо

The Golden Ring is textbook Russia: onion-shaped domes, kremlins and gingerbread cottages with cherry orchards. It is a string of the country's oldest towns that formed the core of eastern Kyivan Rus. Too engrossed in fratricide, they failed to register the rise of Moscow, which elbowed them out of active politics. Largely untouched by Soviet industrialisation, places like Suzdal now attract flocks of Russian tourists in search of the lost idyll. The complete circular route, described in the Lonely Planet guide to Russia, requires about a week to be completed. But several gems can be seen on one- or two-day trips from Moscow.

## Vladimir   Владимир

Vladimir may look like another Soviet Gotham City, until you pass the medieval Golden Gate and stop by the cluster of exquisite churches and cathedrals, some of the oldest in Russia. Hiding behind them is an abrupt bluff with spectacular views of the Oka Valley. Prince Andrei Bogolyubsky chose Vladimir as his capital in 1157 after a stint in the Holy Land where he befriended European crusader kings, such as Friedrich Barbarossa. They sent him their best architects, who designed the town's landmarks, fusing Western and Kyivan traditions. The main jewel, **Assumption Cathedral** (Успенский собор; ☑4922-325 201; www.vladmuseum.ru; pl Sobornaya; R100; ☺ services 7am-8pm, visitors 1pm-4.45pm Tue-Sun), features frescoes by Russia's most prominent icon painter, Andrei Rublyov. Vladimir flourished for less than a century under Andrei's successor, Vsevolod III, until a series of devastating Tatar-Mongol raids led to its decline and dependence on Moscow. The last, a 1408 siege, is vividly if gruesomely reenacted in Andrei Tarkovsky's film *Andrei Rublyov*. Vsevolod's legacy is the exquisite **Cathedral of St Dmitry** (Дмитриевский собор; www.vladmuseum.ru; Bolshaya Moskovskaya ul 60; R80; ☺10am-5pm Wed-Mon Apr-Oct, to 4pm Nov-Mar), its exterior covered in an amazing profusion of images carved in limestone.

Most people don't overnight in Vladimir, preferring the charming Suzdal 35km away. But if you need to, head to **Voznesenskaya Sloboda** (Вознесенская слобода; ☑4922-325 494; www.vsloboda.ru; ul Voznesenskaya 14b; d R4800; P☀🛜), a mansion dramatically set on the high bank of the Oka and featuring a decent restaurant. For lunch or dinner, check out **Piteyny Dom Kuptsa Andreyeva** (☑4922-232 6545; www.andreevbeer.com/dom; Bolshaya Moskovskaya ul 16; mains R350-600; ☺11am-midnight; 🛜📶) that serves traditional Russian fare, like *shchi* cabbage soup and *bliny* pancakes, as well as home-brewed beer.

## ⓘ Getting There & Away

Vladimir is on the main Trans-Siberian line between Moscow and Nizhny Novgorod and the parallel highway. There are four train services a day from Moscow, with modern Strizh and slightly less comfortable Lastochka trains (R900 to R1100, 1¾ hours). Buses for Suzdal (R87, one hour, half-hourly) depart from the bus station, located across the square from the train station.

## Suzdal · Суздаль

The Golden Ring comes with a diamond and that's Suzdal. If you have only one place to visit near Moscow, come here – even though everyone else will do the same. In 1864, local merchants failed to coerce the government into building the Trans-Siberian Railway through their town. Instead it went through Vladimir, 35km away. As a result, Suzdal was bypassed not only by trains, but by the 20th century altogether. This is why the place remains largely the same as ages ago – its cute wooden cottages mingling with golden cupolas that reflect in the river, which meanders through gentle hills and meadows.

A grandfather of its Moscow namesake, Suzdal's **Kremlin** (Кремль; joint ticket excluding Nativity cathedral adult/child R250/100; ☺10am-6pm Wed-Mon) was the seat of Prince Yury Dolgoruky, who founded both Suzdal and the Russian capital, a rather unimportant outpost in his times. An even more grandiose sight is the **Saviour Monastery of St Euthymius** (Спасо-Евфимиев мужской монастырь; ☑49231-20 746; adult/student R400/200; ☺10am-6pm Tue-Sun), which harks back to the times of Ivan the Terrible.

Suzdal has plenty of accommodation, from quaint two- or three-room guesthouses to vast holiday resorts. One of the latter, **Pushkarskaya Sloboda** (Пушкарская слобода; ☑49231-23 303; www.pushkarka.ru; ul Lenina 45; hotel d from R3750, village d from R5400; ☀🛜📶), is arguably the most reliable and centrally located option for a short stay. Equally reliable, the unpretentious **Kharchevnya** (Харчевня; ☑49231-20 722; ul Lenina 73; R200-400), serves traditional Russian staples.

## ⓘ Getting There & Away

The bus station is 2km east of the centre on Vasilievskaya ul. Some long-distance buses pass the central square on the way. A train/bus combination via Vladimir is by far the best way of getting from Moscow. Buses run every 45 minutes to/from Vladimir (R87, one hour) and there is a daily bus to Moscow (R500, five hours).

## Sergiev Posad · Сергиев Посад

Blue and golden cupolas offset by snow-white walls – this colour scheme lies at the heart of the Russian perception of divinity and Sergiev Posad's **Trinity Monastery of St Sergiy** (Troitse-Sergieva Lavra; ☑496-544 5356; www.stsl.ru; ☺5am-9pm) FREE is a textbook example. It doesn't get any holier than here in Russia, for the place was founded in 1340 by the country's most revered saint, St Sergius of Radonezh. Since the 14th century, pilgrims have been journeying to this place to pay homage to him.

Although the Bolsheviks closed the monastery, it was reopened following WWII as a museum, residence of the patriarch and a working monastery. The patriarch and the church's administrative centre moved to the Danilovsky Monastery in Moscow in 1988, but Sergiev Posad remains one of the most important spiritual sites in Russia.

Sergiev Posad is an easy day trip from Moscow and that's how most people visit it.

## ⓘ Getting There & Away

Considering horrendous traffic jams on the approaches to Moscow, train is a much better way of getting to Sergiev Posad from the capital. The fastest option is the express commuter train that departs from Moscow's Yaroslavsky vokzal (R210, one hour, six daily). Bus 388 to Sergiev Posad from Moscow's VDNKh metro station departs hourly from 7am to 10pm (R206).

# St Petersburg
## Санкт Петербург

📋 812 / POP 4.9 MILLION

Affectionately known as Piter to locals, St Petersburg is a visual delight. The Neva River and surrounding canals reflect unbroken facades of handsome 18th- and 19th-century buildings that house a spellbinding collection of cultural storehouses, culminating in the incomparable Hermitage. Home to many of Russia's greatest creative talents (Pushkin, Dostoevsky, Tchaikovsky), Piter still inspires a contemporary generation of Russians, making it a liberal, hedonistic and exciting place to visit.

The city covers many islands, some real, some created through the construction of canals. The central street is Nevsky pr, which extends some 4km from the Alexander Nevsky Monastery to the Hermitage.

## ◉ Sights

**Dvortsovaya Ploshchad**     HISTORIC SITE
(Palace Sq) The monumental **Dvortsovaya pl** is one of the most impressive and historic spaces in the city. Stand well back to admire the palace and the central 47.5m **Alexander Column**, named after Alexander I and commemorating the 1812 victory over Napoleon. It has stood here, held in place by gravity alone, since 1834. It was in this square that tsarist troops fired on peaceful protestors in 1905 (on a day now known as Bloody Sunday), sparking the revolution of that year. At least once a year, in summer, the square is used for free outdoor concerts; the Rolling Stones and Roger Waters have played here.

**★ Russian Museum**     MUSEUM
(Русский музей; 📋 812-595 4248; www.rusmuseum.ru; Inzhenernaya ul 4; adult/student R450/200, 4-palace ticket adult/student R600/300; ◷ 10am-6pm Mon, Wed & Fri-Sun, 1-9pm Thu; Ⓜ Nevsky

Prospekt) The handsome Mikhailovsky Palace is home to the country's biggest collection of Russian art. After the Hermitage you may feel you have had your fill of art, but try your utmost to make some time for this gem of a museum. There's also a lovely garden behind the palace.

**★ Church of the Saviour on the Spilled Blood**     CHURCH
(Церковь Спаса на Крови; www.cathedral.ru; Konyushennaya pl; adult/student R250/150; ◷ 10.30am-6pm Thu-Tue; Ⓜ Nevsky Prospekt) This five-domed dazzler is St Petersburg's most elaborate church with a classic Russian Orthodox exterior, and an interior decorated with some 7000 sq metres of mosaics. Officially called the Church of the Resurrection of Christ, its far more striking colloquial name references the assassination attempt on Tsar Alexander II here in 1881.

**★ St Isaac's Cathedral**     MUSEUM
(Isaakievsky Sobor; www.cathedral.ru; Isaakievskaya pl; cathedral adult/student R250/150, colonnade R150; ◷ cathedral 10.30am-6pm Thu-Tue, colonnade 10.30am-10.30pm May-Oct, to 6pm Nov-Apr, 3rd Wed of month closed; Ⓜ Admiralteyskaya) The golden dome of St Isaac's Cathedral dominates the St Petersburg skyline. Its obscenely lavish interior is open as a museum, although services are held in the cathedral on major religious holidays. Most people bypass the museum to climb the 262 steps to the *kolonnada* (colonnade) around the drum of the dome, providing superb city views.

**★ Peter & Paul Fortress**     FORTRESS
(Петропавловская крепость; www.spbmuseum.ru; grounds free, Peter & Paul Cathedral adult/child R450/250, combined ticket for 5 exhibitions R600/350; ◷ grounds 8.30am-8pm, exhibitions 11am-6pm Mon & Thu-Sun, 10am-5pm Tue; Ⓜ Gorkovskaya) Housing a cathedral where the Romanovs are buried, a former prison and various exhibitions, this large defensive fortress on Zayachy Island is the kernel from which St Petersburg grew into the city it is today. History buffs will love it and everyone will swoon at the panoramic views from atop the fortress walls, at the foot of which lies a sandy riverside beach, a prime spot for sunbathing.

**★ Kunstkamera**     MUSEUM
(Кунсткамера; www.kunstkamera.ru; Tamozhenny per; adult/child R250/50; ◷ 11am-6pm Tue-Sun; Ⓜ Admiralteyskaya) Also known as the Museum of Ethnology and Anthropology, the

# Central St Petersburg

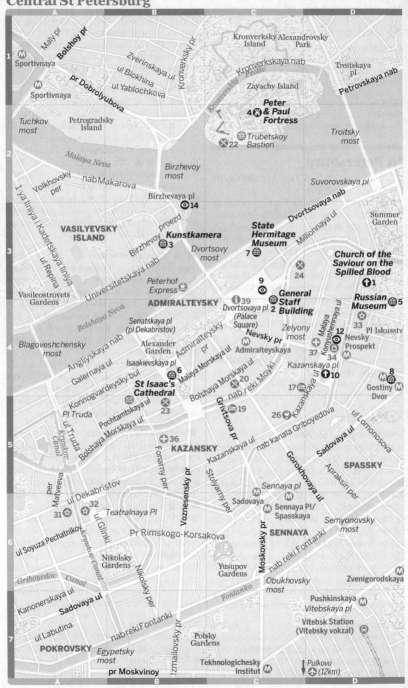

A | B | C | D

Maly pr
Bolshoy pr
Sportivnaya
Sportivnaya
pr Dobrolyubova
Zverinskaya ul
ul Blokhina
ul Yablochkova
Kronverkskiy pr

Kronverksky Alexandrovsky
Island Park
Kronverkskaya nab
Proliv
Zayachy Island
Troitskaya
pl
Petrovskaya nab

Peter
4 & Paul
Fortress

Tuchkov
most
Petrogradsky
Island

Troitsky
most

Trubetskoy
22 Bastion

Malaya Neva
Volkhovsky
per
nabMakarova
Birzhevoy
most
Suvorovskaya pl

Birzhevaya pl
14

1-ya liniya i Kadetskaya liniya
ul Repina

VASILYEVSKY
ISLAND

Birzhevoy proezd
Kunstkamera
3
Dvortsovy
most

State
Hermitage
Museum
7

Dvortsovaya nab
Millionnaya ul

Summer
Garden

Church of the
Saviour on the
Spilled Blood
1

Vasileostrovets
Gardens

Universitetskaya nab

Peterhof
Express

ADMIRALTEYSKY

Dvortsovaya pl
(Palace
Square)

9
24

General
Staff
Building
2

39
i

Russian
Museum
5

33
Pl Iskusstv

Bolshaya Neva
Blagoveshchensky
most

Senatskaya pl
(pl Dekabristov)

Angliyskaya nab
Galernaya ul

Alexander
Garden

Isaakievskaya pl

St Isaac's
Cathedral
6

Admiralteysky
pr

Nevsky pr
Admiralteyskaya

Zelyony
most

Malaya Konyushennaya ul

12
Nevsky
Prospekt
37 34

Kazanskaya pl
10

8
Gostiny
Dvor

17

26

Kazanskaya ul

Pl Truda

Konnogvardeysky bul

Pochtamtskaya ul
Bolshaya Morskaya ul

Malaya Morskaya ul
Bolshaya Morskaya ul
20
nab reki Moyki
19

23

ul Truda
Kryukov Canal
per Matveeva

36

Fonarny per

Voznesensky pr

Stolyarny per

KAZANSKY
Kazanskaya ul

nab kanala Griboyedova

Gorokhovaya ul

Sadovaya ul

Lomonosova
SPASSKY
Apraksin per

31 32
ul Dekabristov
ul Glinki

Teatralnaya Pl

Pr Rimskogo-Korsakova

Sennaya pl
Sadovaya
Sennaya Pl/
Spasskaya
SENNAYA

Semyonovsky
most

ul Soyuza Pechatnikov
Nikolsky
Gardens

Nikolsky per

Yusupov
Gardens

Moskovsky pr
nab reki Fontanki

Zvenigorodskaya

Griboyedov Canal
Kanonerskaya ul
Sadovaya ul

Kryukov Canal

Fontanka
Obukhovsky
most

Pushkinskaya
Vitebskaya pl

Vitebsk Station
(Vitebsky vokzal)

ul Labutina

POKROVSKY

Egypetsky
most

pr Moskvinoy

Izmailovsky pr

Polsky
Gardens

nabreki Fontanki

Tekhnologichesky
Institut

Pulkovo
(12km)

A | B | C | D

# Central St Petersburg

Kunstkamera is the city's first museum and was founded in 1714 by Peter himself. It is famous largely for its ghoulish collection of monstrosities, preserved 'freaks', two-headed mutant foetuses, deformed animals and odd body parts, all collected by Peter with the aim of educating the notoriously superstitious Russian people. While most rush to see these sad specimens, there are also very interesting exhibitions on native peoples from around the world.

**Strelka**          LANDMARK

Among the oldest parts of Vasilyevsky Island, this eastern tip is where Peter the Great wanted his new city's administrative and intellectual centre to be. In fact, the Strelka became the focus of St Petersburg's maritime trade, symbolised by the colonnaded Customs House (now the Pushkin House). The two Rostral Columns, archetypal St Petersburg landmarks, are studded with ships' prows and four seated sculptures representing four of Russia's great rivers: the Neva, the Volga, the Dnieper and the Volkhov.

★ **General Staff Building**          MUSEUM

(Здание Главного штаба; www.hermitagemuseum.org; Dvortsovaya pl 6-8; R300; incl main State Hermitage & other buildings R600; ⊙10.30am-6pm Tue, Thu, Sat & Sun, to 9pm Wed & Fri; ⊠Admiralteyskaya) The east wing of this magnificent building, wrapping around the south of Dvortsovaya pl and designed by Carlo Rossi in the 1820s, marries restored interiors with contemporary architecture to create a series of galleries displaying the Hermitage's amazing collection of Impressionist and post-Impressionist works. Contemporary art is here, too, often in temporary exhibitions by major artists.

🏃 **Activities**

Especially during White Nights, cycling is a brilliant and economical way to get around St Petersburg's spread-out sights, restaurants and bars. Off main drags like Nevsky pr (where you can ride on the sidewalk), St Petersburg's backstreets are quiet and sublime.

## 🛏 Sleeping

High season is May to September, with some hotels increasing their rates even further in June and July. You can get great deals in the low season, when hotel prices drop 30% on average.

### ★ Soul Kitchen Hostel HOSTEL €
(☎ 8-965-816 3470; www.soulkitchenhostel.com; nab reki Moyki 62/2, apt 9, Sennaya; dm/d from R985/2700; ❂ @ ☎; Ⓜ Admiralteyskaya) Soul Kitchen blends boho hipness and boutique-hotel comfort, scoring perfect 10s in many key categories: private rooms (chic), dorm beds (double-wide with privacy-protecting curtains), common areas (vast), kitchen (vast *and* beautiful) and bathrooms (downright inviting). There is also bike hire, table football, free Macs to use, free international phone calls and stunning Moyka River views from a communal balcony.

### ★ Baby Lemonade Hostel HOSTEL €
(☎ 812-570 7943; Inzhenernaya ul 7; dm/d with shared bathroom from R500/1700, d from R2200; @ ☎; Ⓜ Gostiny Dvor) The owner of Baby Lemonade is crazy about the 1960s and it shows in the pop-art, psychedelic design of this friendly, fun hostel with two pleasant, large dorms and a great kitchen and living room. However, it's worth splashing out for the boutique-hotel-worthy private rooms that are in a separate flat with great rooftop views.

### ★ Rachmaninov Antique Hotel BOUTIQUE HOTEL €€
(☎ 812-327 7466; www.hotelrachmaninov.com; Kazanskaya ul 5; s/d from R3100/4200; @ ☎; Ⓜ Nevsky Prospekt) The long-established Rachmaninov still feels like a secret place for those in the know. Perfectly located and run by friendly staff, it's pleasantly old world with hardwood floors and attractive Russian furnishings, particularly in the breakfast salon, which has a grand piano.

### ★ Rossi Hotel BOUTIQUE HOTEL €€€
(☎ 812-635 6333; www.rossihotels.com; nab reki Fontanki 55; d/ste from R6700/15,500; ❄ @ ☎; Ⓜ Gostiny Dvor) Occupying a beautifully restored building on one of St Petersburg's prettiest squares, the Rossi's 53 rooms are all designed differently, but their brightness and moulded ceilings are uniform. Antique beds, super-sleek bathrooms, exposed brick walls and lots of cool designer touches create a great blend of old and new.

##  Eating

### ★ Duo Gastrobar FUSION €
(☎ 812-994 5443; www.duobar.ru; ul Kirochnaya 8A; mains R350-500; ⊙ 1pm-midnight; ❂; Ⓜ Chernyshevskaya) This light-bathed place, done out

RUSSIA ST PETERSBURG

---

## STATE HERMITAGE MUSEUM

Mainly set in the magnificent Winter Palace and adjoining buildings, the **Hermitage** (Государственный Эрмитаж; www.hermitagemuseum.org; Dvortsovaya pl 2; joint ticket R600; ⊙ 10.30am-6pm Tue, Thu, Sat & Sun, to 9pm Wed & Fri; Ⓜ Admiralteyskaya) fully lives up to its sterling reputation. You can be absorbed by its treasures for days and still come out wanting more.

The enormous collection (over three million items, only a fraction of which are on display in around 360 rooms) almost amounts to a comprehensive history of Western European art. Viewing it demands a little planning, so choose the areas you'd like to concentrate on before you arrive.The museum consists of five connected buildings. From west to east they are:

**Winter Palace** Designed by Bartolomeo Rastrelli, its opulent state rooms, Great Church, Pavilion Hall and Treasure Rooms shouldn't be missed.

**Small Hermitage and Old Hermitage** Both were built for Catherine the Great, partly to house the art collection started by Peter the Great, which she significantly expanded. Here you'll find works by Rembrandt, Da Vinci and Caravaggio.

**New Hermitage** Built for Nicholas II, to hold the still-growing art collection. The Old and New Hermitages are sometimes grouped together and labelled the Large Hermitage.

**State Hermitage Theatre** Built in the 1780s by the Giacomo Quarenghi. Concerts and ballets are still performed here.

## RUSSIA'S MOST FAMOUS STREET

Walking **Nevsky Prospekt** is an essential St Petersburg experience. Highlights along it incude the **Kazan Cathedral** (Казанский собор; http://kazansky-spb.ru; Kazanskaya pl 2; ⊙8.30am-7.30pm; Ⓜ Nevsky Prospekt) `FREE`, with its curved arms reaching out towards the avenue.

Opposite is the **Singer Building** (Nevsky pr 28; Ⓜ Nevsky Prospekt), a Style Moderne (art deco) beauty restored to all its splendour when it was the headquarters of the sewing-machine company; inside is the bookshop **Dom Knigi** (www.spbdk.ru; Nevsky pr 28; ⊙9am-1am; Ⓜ Nevsky Prospekt) and **Café Singer** (Nevsky pr 28; ⊙9am-11pm; 🛜; Ⓜ Nevsky Prospekt), serving good food and drinks with a great view over the street.

Further along are the covered arcades of Rastrelli's historic **Bolshoy Gostiny Dvor** (Большой Гостиный Двор; http://bgd.ru; Nevsky pr 35; ⊙10am-10pm; Ⓜ Gostiny Dvor) department store, while on the corner of Sadovaya ul is the Style Moderne classic **Kupetz Eliseevs** (http://kupetzeliseevs.ru; Nevsky pr 56; ⊙10am-10pm; 🛜; Ⓜ Gostiny Dvor) reincarnated as a luxury grocery and cafe.

An enormous **statue of Catherine the Great** stands at the centre of **Ploshchad Ostrovskogo** (Площадь Островского; Ⓜ Gostiny Dvor), commonly referred to as the Catherine Gardens; at the southern end of the gardens is **Alexandrinsky Theatre** (☑812-710 4103; www.alexandrinsky.ru; pl Ostrovskogo 2; Ⓜ Gostiny Dvor), where Chekhov's *The Seagull* premiered (to tepid reviews) in 1896.

---

in wood and gorgeous glass lampshades, has really helped put this otherwise quiet area on the culinary map. Its short fusion menu excels, featuring such unlikely delights as passionfruit and gorgonzola mousse and salmon with quinoa and mascarpone. There are also more conventional choices such as risottos, pastas and salads.

★**Clean Plates Society**　INTERNATIONAL €
(Общество чистых тарелок; www.cleanplates-cafe.com; Gorokhovaya ul 13; mains R350-500; ⊙11am-1am; 🛜📶; Ⓜ Admiralteyskaya) Burgers, curry, borsch and burritos all get a look-in on this stylish and relaxed restaurant's menu. The horseshoe bar and the inventive cocktail and drinks list are its prime attractions. The name derives from a short story by Vladimir Bonch-Bruyevich about Lenin's visit to a kindergarten.

★**Yat**　RUSSIAN €€
(Ять; ☑812-957 0023; www.eatinyat.com; nab reki Moyki 16; mains R370-750; ⊙11am-11pm; 🛜📶; Ⓜ Admiralteyskaya) Perfectly placed for eating near the Hermitage, this country-cottage-style restaurant has a very appealing menu of traditional dishes, presented with aplomb. The *shchi* (cabbage-based soup) is excellent, and there is also a tempting range of flavoured vodkas. There's a fab kids area with pet rabbits for them to feed.

★**Teplo**　MODERN EUROPEAN €€
(☑812-570 1974; www.v-teple.ru; Bolshaya Morskaya ul 45; mains R280-840; ⊙9am-midnight; 🍽🛜📶📶; Ⓜ Admiralteyskaya) This much-feted, eclectic and original restaurant has got it all just right. The venue itself is a lot of fun to nose around, with multiple small rooms, nooks and crannies. Service is friendly and fast (when it's not too busy) and the peppy, inventive Italian-leaning menu has something for everyone. Reservations are usually required, so call ahead.

**Koryushka**　RUSSIAN, GEORGIAN €€
(Корюшка; ☑812-640 1616; www.ginza.ru/spb/restaurant/korushka; Petropavlovskaya krepost 3, Zayachy Island; mains R550-1300; ⊙noon-midnight; 🛜📶📶; Ⓜ Gorkovskaya) Lightly battered and fried smelt *(koryushka)* is a St Petersburg speciality every April, but you can eat the small fish year-round at this relaxed, sophisticated restaurant beside the Peter and Paul Fortress. There are plenty of other very appealing Georgian dishes on the menu to supplement the stunning views across the Neva.

## 🍷 Drinking

★**Borodabar**　COCKTAIL BAR
(☑8-911-923 8940; Kazanskaya ul 11; ⊙5pm-2am Sun-Thu, to 4am Fri & Sat; 🛜; Ⓜ Nevsky Prospekt) Boroda means beard in Russian, and sure enough you'll see plenty of facial hair and

tattoos in this hipster cocktail hang-out. Never mind, as the mixologists really know their stuff – we can particularly recommend their smoked old fashioned, which is infused with tobacco smoke, and their colourful (and potent) range of shots.

### Bekitser
BAR

(Бекицер; ☑ 812-926 4342; www.facebook.com/bktzr; ul Rubinshteyna 41; ☺ noon-6am; Ⓜ Dostuyevskaya) Always crowded and spilling out into the street, this Israel-themed bar cum falafel shop has instantly become the flagship of St Peterburg's main bar row – ul Rubinshteyna. Not kosher, and open on Saturdays, the place lures hip and joyful people with its trademark Shabad Sholom cocktail, Israeli Shiraz and the best falafel wraps this side of the Baltic Sea.

### Dead Poets Bar
COCKTAIL BAR

(☑ 812-449 4656; www.deadpoetsbar.com; ul Zhukovskogo 12; ☺ 2pm-2am Sun-Thu, to 8am Fri & Sat; ☎; Ⓜ Mayakovskaya) This very cool place has a sophisticated drinks menu and an almost unbelievable range of spirits stacked along the long bar and served up by a committed staff of mixologists. It's more of a quiet place, with low lighting, a jazz soundtrack and plenty of space to sit down.

### ★ Union Bar & Grill
BAR

(www.facebook.com/barunion; Liteyny pr 55; ☺ 6pm-6am; ☎; Ⓜ Mayakovskaya) The Union is a glamorous and fun place, characterised by one enormous long wooden bar, low lighting and a New York feel. It's all rather adult, with a serious cocktail list and designer beers on tap. It's crazy at the weekends, but quiet during the week, and always draws a cool twenty- and thirty-something crowd.

### Warszawa
BAR

(ul Kazanskaya 11; ☺ 10am-2am Sun-Thu, to 4am Fri & Sat; Ⓜ Nevsky Prospekt) Russian urbanites have always harboured a special admiration for the quaint provincialism of Eastern Europe, hence this smallish bar with old-fashioned wallpaper, vintage furniture and portraits of 20th-century Polish film stars. Polish beer is on tap and cocktails are based on liquors you may have never heard of. Good for deep, vodka-infused philosophical conversations.

### Dyuni
BAR

(Дюны; www.facebook.com/dunes.on.ligovsky; Ligovsky pr 50; ☺ 4pm-midnight Sun-Thu, to 6am Fri & Sat; ☎; Ⓜ Ploshchad Vosstaniya) What looks like a small suburban house sits rather incongruously here amid repurposed warehouses in this vast courtyard. There's a cosy indoor bar and a sand-covered outside area with table

---

WORTH A TRIP

## PETERHOF & TSARSKOE SELO

Several palace estates around St Petersburg, country retreats for the tsars, are now among the most spectacular sights in Russia.

**Peterhof** (Петергоф; also known as Petrodvorets), 29km west of the city and built for Peter the Great, is best visited for its **Grand Cascade** (☺ 11am-5pm Mon-Fri, to 6pm Sat & Sun May-early Oct) and Water Avenue, a symphony of over 140 fountains and canals located in the **Lower Park** (Нижний парк; www.peterhofmuseum.ru; adult/student May-Oct R700/350, Nov-Apr free; ☺ 9am-7pm). There are several additional palaces, villas and parks here, each of which charges its own hefty admission price.

**Tsarskoe Selo** (Царское Село), 25km south of the city in the town of Pushkin, is home to the baroque **Catherine Palace** (Екатерининский дворец; www.tzar.ru; Sadovaya ul 7; adult/student R1000/290, audioguide R150; ☺ 10am-4.45pm Wed-Sun), expertly restored following its near destruction in WWII. From May to September individual visits to Catherine's Palace are limited to noon to 2pm and 4pm to 5pm, other times being reserved for tour groups.

Buses and *marshrutky* (fixed-route minibuses) to Petrodvorets (R55, 30 minutes) run frequently from outside metro stations Avtovo and Leninsky Prospekt. From May to September, the **Peterhof Express** (www.peterhof-express.com; single/return adult R750/1300, student R500/900; ☺ 10am-6pm) hydrofoil leaves from jetties behind the Hermitage and the Admiralty.

The easiest way to get to Tsarskoe Selo is by *marshrutka* (R35) from Moskovskaya metro station.

**WORTH A TRIP**

## KALININGRAD REGION

Sandwiched by Poland and Lithuania, the Kaliningrad Region is a Russian exclave that's intimately attached to the Motherland yet also a world apart. In this 'Little Russia' – only 15,100 sq km with a population of 941,873 – you'll also find beautiful countryside, charming old Prussian seaside resorts and splendid beaches. Citizens of Japan and many European countries can visit Kaliningrad on a 72-hour visa.

The capital, **Kaliningrad** (Калининград; formerly Königsberg), was once a Middle European architectural gem equal to Prague or Kraków. Precious little of this built heritage remains but there are attractive residential suburbs and remnants of the city's old fortifications that evoke the Prussian past. The most impressive building is the Gothic **Kaliningrad Cathedral** (Кафедральный собор Кёнигсберга; ☎ 4012-631 705; www.sobor-kaliningrad.ru; Kant Island; adult/student R200/100, photos R50, concerts from R150; ⏱ 10am-6pm Mon-Thu, to 7pm Fri-Sun), founded in 1333 and restored after almost being destroyed during WWII. West of the cathedral along the river also make time for the fascinating **Museum of the World Ocean** (Музей Мирового Океана; www.world-ocean.ru; nab Petra Velikogo 1; adult/student R300/150, individual vessels adult/student R150/100; ⏱ 10am-6pm Wed-Mon).

The best places to stay are the budget **Oh, my Kant** (☎ 4012-390 278; www.ohmykant.ru; ul Yablonevaya Alleya 34; dm from R300, d from R1200; 🛜), with local born German philosopher Immannuel Kant in the name, and the midrange **Skipper Hotel** (Гостиница Шкиперская; ☎ 4012-307 237; www.skipperhotel.ru; r from R4300; ❄ 🛜) in the attractive, slightly kitsch Fish Village riverside development. There are plenty of good places to eat and drink including **Fish Club** (Рыбный клуб; ul Oktyabrskaya 4a; mains R500-1500; ⏱ noon-midnight), **Zarya** (Заря; ☎ 4012-300 388; pr Mira 43; mains R200-540; ⏱ 10am-3am; 🛜) and the hip apartment-cum-cafe **Kvartira** (Apartment; ☎ 4012-216 736; www.vk.com/kvartira_koloskova13; ul Serzhanta Koloskova 13; 🛜).

It's easy to access the region's other key sights on day trips from Kaliningrad, but if you did want to spend time away from the city, base yourself in the seaside resort of **Svetlogorsk** (Светлого́рск), which is only a few hours' drive down the Baltic coast from the pine forests and Sahara-style dunes of the **Kurshskaya Kosa National Park** (Национальный парк Куршская коса; www.park-kosa.ru; admission per person/car R40/300), a Unesco World Heritage site.

football and ping pong, which keeps the cool kids happy all night in the summer months. To find it, simply continue in a straight line from the courtyard entrance.

## ☆ Entertainment

From July to mid-September the big theatres like the Mariinsky and the Mikhailovsky close but plenty of performances are still staged. Check the *St Petersburg Times* for comprehensive listings.

**Mariinsky Theatre**   BALLET, OPERA
(Мариинский театр; ☎ 812-326 4141; www.mariinsky.ru; Teatralnaya pl 1; tickets R1000-6000; Ⓜ Sadovaya) St Petersburg's most spectacular venue for ballet and opera, the Mariinsky Theatre is an attraction in its own right. Tickets can be bought online or in person, but they should be bought in advance during the summer months. The magnificent interior is the epitome of imperial grandeur, and any evening here will be an impressive experience.

**Mariinsky II**   THEATRE
(Мариинский II; ☎ 812-326 4141; www.mariinsky.ru; ul Dekabristov 34; tickets R300-6000; ⏱ ticket office 11am-7pm; Ⓜ Sadovaya) Finally opening its doors in 2013 after more than a decade of construction, legal wrangles, scandal and rumour, the Mariinsky II is a showpiece for St Petersburg's most famous ballet and opera company. It is one of the most technically advanced music venues in the world, with superb sightlines and acoustics from all of its 2000 seats.

**Mikhailovsky Opera & Ballet Theatre**   BALLET, OPERA
(☎ 812-595 4305; www.mikhailovsky.ru; pl Iskusstv 1; tickets R300-4000; Ⓜ Nevsky Prospekt) While not quite as grand as the Mariinsky, this illustrious stage still delivers the Russian ballet or operatic experience, complete with multi-tiered theatre, frescoed ceiling and elaborate concerts. Pl Iskusstv (Arts Sq) is a lovely setting

for this respected venue, which is home to the State Academic Opera & Ballet Company.

## ⓘ Information

Free wi-fi access is common across the city.

**American Medical Clinic** (☑ 812-740 2090; www.amclinic.ru; nab reki Moyki 78; ⊘ 24hr; Ⓜ Admiralteyskaya) One of the city's largest private clinics.

**Apteka Petrofarm** (Nevsky pr 22; ⊘ 24hr) An excellent, all-night pharmacy.

**Main Post Office** (Pochtamtskaya ul 9; ⊘ 24hr; Ⓜ Admiralteyskaya) Worth visiting for its elegant Style Moderne interior.

**Ost-West Kontaktservice** (☑ 812-327 3416; www.ostwest.com; Nevsky pr 100; ⊘ 10am-6pm Mon-Fri; Ⓜ Ploshchad Vosstaniya) Can find you an apartment to rent and organise tours and tickets.

**St Petersburg Times** (www.sptimes.ru) Published every Tuesday and Friday, when it has an indispensable listings and arts review section.

**Tourist Information Bureau** (☑ 812-310 2822; http://eng.ispb.info; Sadovaya ul 14/52; ⊘ 10am-7pm Mon-Fri, noon-6pm Sat; Ⓜ Gostiny Dvor) There are also branches outside the **Hermitage** (Dvortsovaya pl; ⊘ 10am-7pm; Ⓜ Admiralteyskaya) and **Pulkovo airport** (⊘ 9am-8pm Mon-Fri).

## ⓘ Getting Around

### TO/FROM THE AIRPORT

From St Petersburg's superb new airport, an official taxi to the centre should cost between R900 and R1400, or you can take bus 39 (35 minutes) or 39A (20 minutes) to Moskovskaya metro station for R30, then take the metro from Moskovskaya (Line 2) all over the city for R35.

### PUBLIC TRANSPORT

The metro is usually the quickest way around the city. *Zhetony* (tokens) and credit-loaded cards can be bought from booths in the stations (R45). Multiride cards are also available (R355 for 10 trips, R680 for 20 trips).

Buses, trolleybuses and *marshrutky* (fixed-route minibuses fare R34) often get you closer to the sights and are especially handy to cover long distances along main avenues like Nevsky pr.

### TAXI

Taxi apps, such as Uber, Gett and Yandex Taxi, are all the rage in St Petersburg and they've brought down the prices while improving the service a great deal. You need a Russian SIM card to use them. Otherwise, the best way to get a taxi is to order it by phone. **Taxi Millon** (☑ 812-600 0000; www.6-000-000.ru) has English-speaking operators.

# SURVIVAL GUIDE

## ⓘ Directory A–Z

### ACCOMMODATION

The devaluation of the rouble in 2014 has suddenly made hotels in Russia considerably more affordable, with prices similar to those in Central Europe. The hotel scene has improved a great deal over recent years in terms of quality and diversity of choice – from youth hostels and B&Bs to Western chains and boutique hotels.

There has been a boom in budget-friendly hostels in both Moscow and St Petersburg, and if you're on a budget you'll want to consider these – even if you typically don't 'do' hostels, most offer a few private rooms.

### Apartment Rental

Booking an apartment is a good way to save money on accommodation, especially for small groups. They typically cost around R4300 to R8600 per night. The following agencies can make bookings in Moscow and/or St Petersburg.

**Enjoy Moscow** (www.enjoymoscow.com; per night from US$155; ☎)

**HOFA** (www.hofa.ru; apt from per night €44; ☎)

**Moscow Suites** (www.moscowsuites.ru; studio per night from US$199; ☎)

**Ost-West Kontaktservice** (p355)

### BUSINESS HOURS

Restaurants and bars often stay open later than their stated hours if the establishment is full. In fact, many simply say that they work *do poslednogo klienta* (until the last customer leaves).

Note that most museums close their ticket offices one hour (in some cases 30 minutes) before the official closing time.

**Banks** 9am–6pm Monday to Friday, some open 9am–5pm Saturday

**Bars** noon–midnight, to 5am Friday and Saturday

**Restaurants** noon–midnight

**Shops** 10am–8pm

---

### SLEEPING PRICE RANGES

The following price ranges are for high season and include private bathroom unless otherwise stated. Prices exclude breakfast unless otherwise stated.

**€** less than R1500 (less than R3000 in Moscow & St Petersburg)

**€€** R1500–R4000 (R3000–R8000 in Moscow & St Petersburg)

**€€€** more than R4000 (more than R8000 in Moscow & St Petersburg)

## INTERNET RESOURCES

**Afisha** (www.afisha.ru) Extensive restaurant, bar, museum and event listings for all major cities; in Russian only.

**Lonely Planet** (www.lonelyplanet.com/russia) Destination information, hotel bookings, traveller forum and more.

**Moscow Expat Site** (www.expat.ru) Mine expat knowledge of Russia.

**Way to Russia** (www.waytorussia.net) Comprehensive online travel guide.

## MONEY

The Russian currency is the rouble, written as 'рубль' and abbreviated as 'руб' or 'р'. Roubles are divided into 100 almost worthless *kopeyki* (kopecks). Coins come in amounts of R1, R2, R5 and R10 roubles, with banknotes in values of R10, R50, R100, R200, R500, R1000, R2000 and R5000.

ATMs that accept all major credit and debit cards are everywhere, and most restaurants, shops and hotels in major cities gladly accept plastic. Visa and MasterCard are the most widespread card types, while American Express can be problematic in some hotels and shops. You can exchange dollars and euros (and some other currencies) at most banks; when they're closed, try the exchange counters at top-end hotels. You may need your passport. Note that crumpled or old banknotes are often refused.

## POST

The Russian post service is **Pochta Rossia** (www.russianpost.ru). The main offices are open from 8am to 8pm or 9pm Monday to Friday, with shorter hours on Saturday and Sunday. To send a postcard or letter up to 20g anywhere in the world by air costs R37.

---

### COUNTRY FACTS

**Area** 17,098,242 sq km

**Capital** Moscow

**Country Code** ☑7

**Currency** Rouble (R)

**Emergency** Stationary/mobile phone –ambulance ☑03/103, fire ☑01/101, police ☑02/102

**Language** Russian

**Money** Plenty of ATMs, most accepting foreign cards

**Population** 143.8 million

**Visas** Required by all – apply at least a month in advance of your trip

---

## PUBLIC HOLIDAYS

Many businesses are closed from 1 to 7 January. Russia's main public holidays:

**New Year's Day** 1 January

**Russian Orthodox Christmas Day** 7 January

**Defender of the Fatherland Day** 23 February

**International Women's Day** 8 March

**International Labour Day/Spring Festival** 1 May

**Victory Day** 9 May

**Russian Independence Day** 12 June

**Unity Day** 4 November

## SAFE TRAVEL

Travellers have nothing to fear from Russia's 'mafia' – the increasingly respectable gangster classes are not interested in such small fry. However, petty theft and pickpockets are prevalent in both Moscow and St Petersburg, so be vigilant with your belongings.

Some police officers can be bothersome, especially to dark-skinned or foreign-looking people. Other members of the police force target tourists, though reports of tourists being hassled about their documents and registration have declined. Still, you should always carry a photocopy of your passport, visa and registration stamp. If you are stopped for any reason – legitimate or illegitimate – you will surely be hassled if you don't have these.

Sadly, racism is a problem in Russia, though the number of hate attacks against people of Central Asian, Mideastern and African appearance has declined considerably in recent years. Exercise extra caution, but don't succumb to paranoia, if you are dark-skinned. Try not to venture into dodgy outlying areas of large cities on your own. Avoid domestic football (soccer) games unless accompanied by Russian friends. Security standards at major international fixtures are high, so don't be worried about attending the World Cup in 2018.

## TELEPHONE

The international code for Russia is ☑7. The international access code from landline phones in Russia is ☑8, followed by ☑10 after the second tone, followed by the country code.

The four main mobile phone companies, all with prepaid and 4G internet options, are **Beeline**, **Megafon** (www.megafon.ru), **Tele 2** (www.tele2.ru) and **MTS** (www.mts.ru). Company offices are everywhere. It costs almost nothing to purchase a SIM card, but bring your passport.

Internal roaming that still existed in Russia at the time of writing was due to be abolished by the end of 2017. But you may still have to pay more for calling from one Russian region to another, if this long overdue decision is for some reason postponed.

## VISAS

Everyone needs a visa to visit Russia. For most travellers a tourist visa (single- or double-entry, valid for a maximum of 30 days) will be sufficient. If you plan to stay longer than a month, you can apply for a business visa or – if you are a US citizen – a three-year multi-entry visa.

Applying for a visa is undeniably a headache, but the process is actually quite straightforward. There are three stages: invitation, application and registration.

### Invitation

To obtain a visa, everyone needs an invitation also known as 'visa support'. Hotels and hostels will usually issue anyone staying with them an invitation voucher free or for a small fee (typically around €20 to €30). If you are not staying in a hotel or hostel, you will need to buy an invitation – this can be done through most travel agents or via specialist visa agencies, also for around €20.

### Application

Invitation voucher in hand, you can then apply for a visa. Wherever in the world you are applying you can start by entering details in the online form of the Consular Department of the Russian Ministry of Foreign Affairs (https://visa.kdmid.ru/PetitionChoice.aspx).

Take care in answering the questions accurately on this form, including listing all the countries you have visited in the last 10 years and the dates of the visits – stamps in your passport will be checked against this information and if there are anomalies you will likely have to restart the process. Keep a note of the unique identity number provided for your submitted form – if you have to make changes later, you will need this to access it without having to fill in the form from scratch again.

Russian embassies in the UK and US have contracted separate agencies to process the submission of visa applications; these companies use online interfaces that direct the relevant information into the standard visa application form. In the UK, the agency is **VFS. Global** (http://ru.vfsglobal.co.uk) with offices in London and Edinburgh; in the US it's **Invisa Logistic Services** (http://ils-usa.com) with offices in Washington, DC, New York, San Francisco, Houston and Seattle.

Consular offices apply different fees and slightly different application rules country by country. Avoid potential hassles by checking well in advance what these rules might be. Among the things that you will need:
➺ a printout of the invitation/visa support document
➺ a passport-sized photograph for the application form
➺ if you're self-employed, bank statements for the previous three months showing you have sufficient funds to cover your time in Russia

---

> **EATING PRICE RANGES**
>
> The following price ranges refer to a standard main course.
>
> **€** less than R300 (less than R500 in Moscow & St Petersburg)
>
> **€€** R300–R800 (R500–R1000 in Moscow & St Petersburg)
>
> **€€€** more than R800 (more than R1000 in Moscow & St Petersburg)

➺ details of your travel insurance.

The charge for the visa will depend on the type of visa applied for and how quickly you need it.

We highly recommend applying for your visa in your home country rather than on the road.

### Registration

Every visitor to Russia must have their visa registered *within seven days of arrival*, excluding weekends and public holidays. Registration is handled by your accommodating party. If staying in a homestay or rental apartment, you'll either need to make arrangements with the landlord or a friend to register you through the post office. See http://waytorussia.net/RussianVisa/Registration.html for how this can be done.

Once registered, you'll receive a registration slip. Keep this safe – that's the document that any police who stop you will ask to see. You do not need to register more than once unless you stay in additional cities for more than seven days, in which case you'll need additional registration slips.

### 72-Hour Visa-Free Travel

To qualify for this visa for St Petersburg, you need to enter and exit the city on a cruise or ferry such as that offered by **St Peter Line** (☑ 812-386 1147; www.stpeterline.com). For Kaliningrad, make arrangements in advance with locally based tour agencies.

### Immigration Form

Immigration forms are produced electronically by passport control at airports. Take good care of your half of the completed form as you'll need it for registration and could face problems while travelling in Russia – and certainly will on leaving – if you can't produce it.

## ⓘ Getting There & Away

### AIR

International flights land and take off from Moscow's three airports – **Domodedovo** (Домодедово; ☑ 495-933 6666; www.domodedovo.ru), **Sheremetyevo** (Шереметьево; ☑ 495-578 6565; www.svo.aero) and **Vnukovo**

## ESSENTIAL FOOD & DRINK

Russia's rich black soil provides an abundance of grains and vegetables used in a wonderful range of breads, salads, appetisers and soups. Its waterways yield a unique range of fish and, as with any cold-climate country, there's a great love of fat-loaded dishes – Russia is no place to go on a diet!

**Soups** For example, the lemony, meat *solyanka* or the hearty fish *ukha*.

**Bliny** (pancakes) Served with *ikra* (caviar) or *tvorog* (cottage cheese).

**Salads** A wide variety usually slathered in mayonnaise, including the chopped potato Olivier.

**Pelmeni** (dumplings) Stuffed with meat and eaten with sour cream and vinegar.

**Central Asian dishes** Try *plov* (Uzbek pilaf), shashlyk (kebab) or *lagman* (noodles).

**Vodka** The quintessential Russian tipple.

**Kvas** A refreshing, beer-like drink, or the red berry juice mix *mors*.

(Внуково; ☑ 495-937 5555; www.vnukovo. ru) – and St Petersburg's **Pulkovo** (LED; ☑ 812-337 3822; www.pulkovoairport.ru) airport. International flights to Kaliningrad's **Khrabrovo** (☑ 4012-610 620; www.kgd.aero) airport are rarer.

### LAND

Russia has excellent train and bus connections with the rest of Europe. However, many routes connecting St Petersburg and Moscow with points west – including Kaliningrad – go through Belarus, for which you'll need a transit visa. Buses are the best way to get from St Petersburg to Tallinn. St Petersburg to Helsinki can be done by bus or train.

Adjoining 13 countries, the Russian Federation has a huge number of border crossings. From Eastern Europe you are most likely to enter from Finland near Vyborg; from Estonia at Narva; from Latvia at Rēzekne; from Belarus at Krasnoye or Ezjaryshcha; and from Ukraine at Chernihiv. You can enter Kaliningrad from Lithuania and Poland at any of seven border posts, but visa-free arrangements are limited to the two checkpoints on the Polish border.

### SEA

Between early April and late September, international passenger ferries connect Stockholm and Tallinn with St Petersburg's **Morskoy Vokzal** (Морской вокзал; pl Morskoy Slavy 1).

## ⓘ Getting Around

Getting around Russia is a breeze thanks to a splendid train network and a packed schedule of flights between all major and minor towns and cities. In the summer months many rivers and lakes are navigable and have cruises and ferry operations. For hops between towns, there are buses, most often *marshrutky* (fixed-route minibuses).

### AIR

Safety paranoia associated with Russian airlines is largely a thing of the past. The prime concern these days is the petty nastiness of budget carriers and problems associated with it – delays, cancellations and torturously insufficient legroom.

Major Russian airlines, including Aeroflot (www.aeroflot.com), Rossiya (www.rossiya-airlines.com), S7 Airlines (www.s7.ru), Ural Airlines (www.uralairlines.com), UTAir (www.utair.ru) and the new budget airline Pobeda (wwww.pobeda.aero), have online booking, with the usual discounts for advance purchases. Otherwise, it's no problem buying a ticket at ubiquitous *aviakassa* (ticket offices), which may be able to tell you about flights that you can't easily find out about online overseas. Online agencies specialising in Russian air tickets with English interfaces include **Anywayanyday** (☑ 8-800 775 7753; www.anywayanyday.com), www.onetwotrip.ru and www.tickets.ru. Skyscanner.ru is a great aggregator that compares prices on different sites.

Whenever you book airline tickets in Russia you'll need to show your passport and visa. Tickets can also be purchased at the airport right up to the departure of the flight and sometimes even if the city centre office says that the plane is full. Return fares are usually double the one-way fares.

Most internal flights in Moscow use either Domodedovo or Vnukovo airports; if you're connecting to Moscow's Sheremetyevo international airport, allow a few hours to cross town (at least three hours if you need to go by taxi, rather than train and metro). Small town airports offer facilities similar to the average bus shelter.

## BUS

Long-distance buses tend to complement rather than compete with the rail network. They generally serve areas with no railway or routes on which trains are slow, infrequent or overloaded.

Most cities have an intercity bus station (автовокзал; *avtovokzal*). Tickets are sold at the station or on the bus. Fares are normally listed on the timetable and posted on a wall.

*Marshrutky* (a Russian diminutive form of *marshrutnoye taksi*, meaning a fixed-route taxi) are minibuses that are sometimes quicker than larger buses and rarely cost much more.

## CAR & MOTORCYCLE

Bearing in mind erratic road quality, lack of adequate signposting and fine-seeking highway police officers, driving in Russia can be a challenge. But if you've a sense of humour, patience and a decent vehicle, it's an adventurous way to go. That said, both road quality and driving culture have improved a great deal in the last decade, so driving has become much more pleasant than previously.

You can bring your own vehicle into Russia, but expect delays, bureaucracy and the attention of the roundly hated GIBDD (traffic police), who take particular delight in stopping foreign cars for document checks.

To enter Russia with a vehicle you will need a valid International Driving Permit as well as the insurance and ownership documents for your car.

As you don't really need a car to get around big cities, hiring a car comes into its own for making trips out of town where public transport may not be so good. All the major agencies have offices in Moscow and St Petersburg.

Driving is on the right-hand side, and at an intersection traffic coming from the right generally (but not always) has the right of way. The maximum legal blood-alcohol content is 0.03%, a rule that is strictly enforced.

## TAXI

Normal yellow taxis, which one could hail in the street and which used meters, disappeared after the fall of communism. The taxi situation was a pain until a few years ago, when Uber and its competitors, such as Gett and Yandex Taxi, made cabs much more affordable and easy to use.

Elsewhere, taxis are ordered by phone, which is usually advertised on branded cabs, so you can find one by simply standing still and watching the traffic for five minutes. But English-speaking operators are rare.

It's less common these days, but it's still possible to flag down a taxi, or just a random driver whose owner needs some extra cash, in the street. Check with locals to determine the average taxi fare in that city at the time of your visit; taxi prices around the country vary widely.

## TRAIN

Russia's extensive train network is efficiently run by **Russian Railways** (РЖД; ☎8-800 775 0000; www.rzd.ru). High-speed trains connect Moscow with St Petersburg in the west and Nizny Novgorod (via Vladimir) in the east. Slower sleeper trains service other long-distance lines around the country.

There are a number of options on where to buy, including online from RZD. Bookings open 45 days before the date of departure. You'd be wise to buy well in advance over the busy summer months and holiday periods such as New Year and early May, when securing berths at short notice on certain trains can be difficult.

For long-distance trains, unless otherwise specified we quote 2nd-class sleeper *(kupe)* fares. Expect 1st-class (SV) fares to be double this, and 3rd class *(platskartny)* to be about 40% less. Children under five travel free if they share a berth with an adult; otherwise, children under 10 pay a reduced fare for their own berth.

You'll need your passport (or a photocopy) to buy tickets. You can buy tickets for others if you bring their passports or photocopies. Queues can be very long and move with interminable slowness. At train ticket offices ('*Zh/D kassa*', short for '*zheleznodorozhnaya kassa*'), which are all over most cities, you can pay a surcharge of around R200 and avoid the queues. Alternatively, most travel agencies will organise the reservation and delivery of train tickets for a substantial mark-up.

*Prigorodny* (suburban) or short-distance trains – also known as *elektrichky* – do not require advance booking: you can buy your ticket at the *prigorodny poezd kassa* (suburban train ticket offices) at train stations.

# Serbia

## Best Places to Eat

➜ Lorenzo & Kakalamba (p366)

➜ Radost Fina Kuhinjica (p366)

➜ Fish i Zeleniš (p372)

➜ Čarda Aqua Doria (p372)

## Best Places to Stay

➜ Yugodom (p365)

➜ Narrator (p372)

➜ Varad Inn (p372)

➜ Hostelche (p363)

## Why Go?

Warm, welcoming and a hell of a lot of fun – everything you never heard about Serbia (Србија) is true. Exuding a feisty mix of élan and *inat* (Serbian trait of rebellious defiance), this country doesn't do 'mild': Belgrade is one of the world's wildest party destinations, Novi Sad hosts the rocking EXIT festival, and even its hospitality is emphatic – expect to be greeted with *rakija* (fruit brandy) and a hearty three-kiss hello.

While political correctness is as commonplace as a non-smoking bar, Serbia is nevertheless a cultural crucible: the art nouveau town of Subotica revels in its proximity to Hungary, bohemian Niš echoes to the clip-clop of Roma horse carts, and minaret-studded Novi Pazar nudges some of the most sacred sites in Serbian Orthodoxy. For something truly wild, head to the stunningly scenic Tara, Djerdap and Fruška Gora National Parks.

Forget what you think you know: come and say *zdravo* (hello)...or better yet, *živeli* (cheers)!

## When to Go
### Belgrade

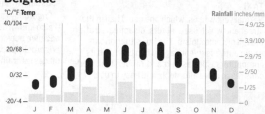

**Apr** Watch winter melt away with a scenic ride on the nostalgic Šargan 8 railway.

**Jul & Aug** Rock out at Novi Sad's EXIT, go wild at Guča and get jazzy at Nišville.

**Dec–Mar** Head to Tara National Park and Zlatibor for alpine adventure.

# Serbia Highlights

**1 Kalemegdan Citadel**
(p362) Soaking up Belgrade's bloody, bawdy history at this formidable fortress.

**2 EXIT Festival** (p372) Joining thousands of party people for beats and bacchanalia in Novi Sad.

**3 Tara National Park** (p369) Hiking, biking or paddling

around this scenic slice of Serbia. Watch out for bears!

**4 Mokra Gora** (p373) Escaping reality in the village of Drvengrad and on a whimsical Šargan 8 train ride.

**5 Guča Festival** (p360) Steeling your eardrums (and liver) at this frenetic music festival.

**6 Fruška Gora National Park**
(p371) Rambling the ranges of this gentle region studded with ancient monasteries and ancestral vineyards.

**7 Niš** (p373) Getting a Balkan-flavoured taste of old Rome at the birthplace of Constantine the Great.

# BELGRADE БЕОГРАД

☑ 011 / POP 1.6 MILLION

Outspoken, adventurous, proud and audacious: Belgrade is by no means a 'pretty' capital, but its gritty exuberance makes it one of the most happening cities in Europe. While it hurtles towards a brighter future, its chaotic past unfolds before your eyes: socialist blocks are squeezed between art nouveau masterpieces, and remnants of the Habsburg legacy contrast with Ottoman relics.

It's here where the Sava River meets the Danube, contemplative parkland nudges hectic urban sprawl, and old-world culture gives way to new-world nightlife.

Grandiose coffee houses and smoky dives all find their rightful place along Knez Mihailova, a lively pedestrian boulevard flanked by historical buildings all the way to the ancient Kalemegdan Citadel, crown of the city. The old riverside Savamala quarter has gone from ruin to resurrection, and is the city's creative headquarters. Deeper in Belgrade's bowels are museums guarding the cultural, religious and military heritage of the country. 'Belgrade' literally translates as 'White City', but Serbia's colourful capital is red hot.

## ◉ Sights & Activities

### ★ Kalemegdan Citadel  FORTRESS
(Kalemegdanska tvrđava; www.beogradskatvrdjava.co.rs) FREE Some 115 battles have been fought over imposing, impressive Kalemegdan; the citadel was destroyed more than 40 times throughout the centuries. Fortifications began in Celtic times, and the Romans extended it onto the flood plains during the settlement of 'Singidunum', Belgrade's Roman name. Much of what stands today is the product of 18th-century Austro-Hungarian and Turkish reconstructions. The fort's bloody history, discernible despite today's plethora of jolly cafes and funfairs, only makes Kalemegdan all the more fascinating. Kalemegdan is littered with museums, monuments and absorbing architecture. Must-sees include the **Military Museum** (www.muzej.mod.gov.rs; adult/child 150/70DIN; ⊘10am-5pm Tue-Sun), **Gunpowder Magazine** (200DIN; ⊘11am-7pm), **Nebojša Tower** (200DIN; ⊘11am-7pm Wed-Sun) and the creepy, mysterious **Roman Well** (120DIN; ⊘11am-7pm).

### ★ Museum of Yugoslav History  MUSEUM
(www.mij.rs; Botićeva 6; incl Maršal Tito's Grave 400DIN; ⊘10am-8pm Tue-Sun May-Oct, to 6pm Nov-Apr) This must-visit museum houses an invaluable collection of more than 200,000 artefacts representing the fascinating, tumultuous history of Yugoslavia. Photographs, artworks, historical documents, films, weapons, priceless treasure; it's all here. It can be a lot to take in; English-speaking guides are available if booked in advance via email, or you can join a free tour on weekends (11am and noon).

**Tito's Mausoleum** is also on the museum grounds; admission is included in the ticket price.

Take trolleybus 40 or 41 at the south end of Parliament on Kneza Miloša. It's the second stop after turning into Bul Mira: ask the driver to let you out at Kuća Cveća.

### Zepter Museum  GALLERY
(☑ 011 328 3339; www.zeptermuseum.rs/; Knez Mihailova 42; 200DIN; ⊘10am-8pm Tue, Wed, Fri & Sun, noon-10pm Thu & Sat) This impressive collection of works by contemporary Serbian artists became Serbia's first private museum in 2010, but remains somewhat hidden even though it's housed in a magnificent 1920s building in the heart of pedestrianised Knez Mihailova. The interior's eclectic design is a perfect backdrop to the broad range of styles on display. The permanent collection is a great introduction to the main trends in Serbian art from the second half of the 20th century. The museum also hosts temporary exhibitions and other events.

### ★ Nikola Tesla Museum  MUSEUM
(www.nikolateslamuseum.org; Krunska 51; admission incl guided tour in English 500DIN; ⊘10am-6pm Tue-Sun) Meet the man on the 100DIN note at

---

## ITINERARIES

### One Week
Revel in three days of cultural and culinary exploration in **Belgrade**, allowing for at least one night of hitting the capital's legendary nightspots. Carry on to **Novi Sad** for trips to the vineyards and monasteries of **Fruška Gora National Park** and **Sremski Karlovci**.

### Two Weeks
Follow the above itinerary, then head north for the art nouveau architecture of **Subotica**, before either slicing southwest to **Tara National Park** en route to traditional Serbian villages, or southeast via **Djerdap National Park** to lively **Niš**.

## BELGRADE'S HISTORIC 'HOODS

**Skadarska** or 'Skadarlija' is Belgrade's Montmartre. This cobblestoned strip east of Trg Republike was the bohemian heartland at the turn of the 20th century; local artistes and dapper types still gather in its legion of cute restaurants and cafes.

**Savamala**, cool-Belgrade's destination du jour, stretches along the Sava down ul Karad-jordjeva. Constructed in the 1830s for Belgrade's smart set, the neighbourhood now hous-es cultural centres, ramshackle, photogenic architecture, nightspots and a buzzing vibe.

**Dorćol**, an Ottoman-era multicultural marketplace, is now dotted with mega-hip side-walk cafes, boutiques and cocktail bars.

**Zemun**, 6km northwest of central Belgrade, was the most southerly point of the Austro-Hungarian Empire when the Turks ruled Belgrade. These days it's known for its fish res-taurants and quaint, non-urban ambience.

one of Belgrade's best museums, where you can release your inner nerd with some won-drously sci-fi-ish interactive elements. Tesla's ashes are kept here in a glowing, golden orb: debate has been raging for years between the museum (and its secular supporters) and the church as to whether the remains should be moved to Sveti Sava Temple.

### Royal Compound
PALACE
(☑ 011 2635 622; www.royalfamily.org; Bul Kneza Aleksandra Karađorđevića, Dedinje; 450DIN; ⊙ 11am & 2pm Sat & Sun Apr-Oct) The Royal and White Palaces (1929 and 1937, respectively) were residences of King Peter II and used by the communist regime after WWII; today, they're home to the descendants of the Karađorđević dynasty. The white marble Royal Palace's most impressive rooms include the fres-co-covered Entrance Hall and the baroque Blue Drawing Room. The classicist White Pal-ace houses a notable art collection and a vast basement (with a wine cellar, billiards room and cinema) featuring scenes from Serbian national mythology. Bookings essential.

### Sveti Sava Temple
CHURCH
(www.hramsvetogsave.com; Svetog Save; ⊙ 7am-7pm) **FREE** Sveti Sava is the Balkans' biggest (and the world's second-biggest) Orthodox church, a fact made entirely obvious when looking at the city skyline from a distance or standing under its dome. The church is built on the site where the Turks apparently burnt relics of St Sava. Work on the interior (fre-quently interrupted by wars) continues today.

### Ada Ciganlija
BEACH
(www.adaciganlija.rs) In summertime, join the hordes of sea-starved locals (up to 250,000 a day) for sun and fun at this artificial island on the Sava. Cool down with a swim, kayak

or windsurf after a leap from the 55m bungee tower. Take bus 52 or 53 from Zeleni Venac.

### National Museum
MUSEUM
(Narodni Muzej; www.narodnimuzej.rs; Trg Republike 1a; adult/child 200/100DIN; ⊙ 10am-5pm Tue-Wed & Fri, noon-8pm Thu & Sat, 10am-2pm Sun) Trg Republike (Republic Sq), a meeting point and outdoor exhibition space, is home to the National Museum. Lack of funding for reno-vations has kept it mostly shuttered for more than 10 years, though some exhibitions are occasionally open to the public. Some of its collections are available for viewing in other museums around town, including the **His-torical Museum of Serbia** (Istorijski Muzej Sr-bije; www.imus.org.rs; Trg Nikole Pašića 11; 200DIN; ⊙ noon-8pm Tue-Sun) and the **Gallery of the Natural History Museum** (www.nhmbeo.rs; Kalemegdan Citadel; adult/child 100/80DIN; ⊙ 10am-9pm Tue-Sun summer, to 5pm winter).

### Yugotour
DRIVING
(☑ 066 900 8386; http://yugotour.com/; per per-son €45; ⊙ from 11am daily) Yugotour is a mini road trip through the history of Yugoslavia and the life of its president Tito. Belgrade's communist years are brought to life in the icon of Yugo-nostalgia: a Yugo car! Tours are led by young locals happy to share their own perceptions of Yugoslavia; they take in the communist-era architecture of New Bel-grade, the Museum of Yugoslav History and Tito's mausoleum, among other locations.

## 🛏 Sleeping

### ★ Hostelche
HOSTEL €
(☑ 011 263 7793; www.hostelchehostel.com; Kral-ja Petra 8; dm from €10, private r from €25; ❄ 🐠 ) A bend-over-backwards staff, homey at-mosphere, free walking tours and a super

# Central Belgrade

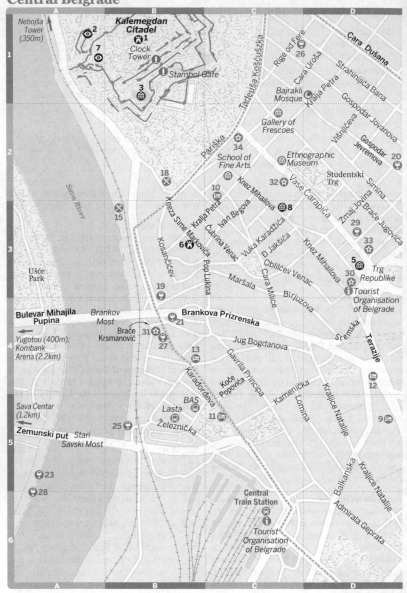

location make this award-winner popular for all the right reasons. There is also a branch in **Smederevo** (☑064 984 3861; www.hostelchehostel.com/SD; Beogradski put 88, Smederevo; dm/r from €6/20).

★**Hostel Bongo**  HOSTEL €
(☑011 268 5515; www.hostelbongo.com; ul Terazije 36; dm/d from €20/34; ❋ ☎) Guests at the modern, brightly painted Bongo can take their pick: plunge into the tonne of attractions, bars and restaurants nearby, or hide from it all in

brilliant B&B is all early 1900s charm out the front, nouveau-Savamala graffiti-murals out the back. As hip as you'd expect from its location in Belgrade's coolest quarter, the digs here are furnished with a mix of period furniture and the work of up-and-coming Belgrade designers. It's close to the city's main sights, and there are tonnes of happening bars and restaurants within staggering distance.

### Hotel Bristol
HISTORIC HOTEL €€
(☑ 011 262 2128; www.vudedinje.mod.gov.rs; Karađorđeva 50, Savamala; s 2947-3467DIN, d/tr 4624/6561DIN, day rate d 1728DIN; ☎) If slick service and shiny spaces are your bag, don't even think about dropping yours here. But if you revel in retro ramshackelry, this Savamala icon is for you. The delightfully unrenovated hotel hosts an eclectic crowd here for the cheap (drab) rooms, in-the-thick-of-it location and a surprisingly good restaurant. The bar is a great spot for drinks with eccentric locals. Built in 1912 and run by an army agency, the Bristol was once a haven for the rich and famous, including the Rockefeller and British royal families. Day rates (10am to 6pm) available.

### ★ Yugodom
GUESTHOUSE €€€
(☑ 065 984 6366; www.yugodom.com; Strahinjica Bana 80; r €80; ✳) This remarkable, evocative guesthouse offers more than a comfortable and stylish place to sleep; it's also a vessel for time travel. Billed as a 'stayover museum', Yugodom (*dom* means 'house' in Serbian) is decked out with gorgeous art and furnishings from the Tito era (though you'll find all the mod cons and self-catering facilities you need disguised among the retro trappings).

The location is as impeccable as the surrounds; smack in the middle of Dorćol and across the road from Bajloni farmers market.

### ★ Hotel Moskva
HISTORIC HOTEL €€€
(Hotel Moscow; ☑ 011 364 2069; www.hotelmoskva.rs; Terazije 20; s/d/ste from €129/139/210; ✳☎) Art nouveau icon and proud symbol of the best of Belgrade, the Moskva has been wowing guests – including Albert Einstein, Indira Gandhi and Alfred Hitchcock – since 1906. Laden with ye olde glamour, this is the place to write your memoirs at a big old desk.

## ✕ Eating

### ★ To Je To
BALKAN €
(bul Despota Stefana 21; mains 220-800DIN; ☺8am-midnight) 'To je to' means 'that's it', and in this case, they're talking about meat.

the hostel's sweet garden terrace. Fantastic staff with oodles of hostelling experience.

### ★ Savamala Bed & Breakfast
B&B €€
(☑ 011 406 0264; www.savamalahotel.rs; Kraljevića Marka 6, Savamala; s/d from €38/50; ✳☎) This

# Central Belgrade

Piles of the stuff, grilled in all its juicy glory, make up the menu here in the forms of Sarajevo-style *ćevapi* (spicy skinless sausages), turkey kebab, sweetbreads and more. It serves homemade *sarma* (stuffed cabbage rolls) on the weekends. Cheap, scrumptious and highly recommended by locals.

★**Radost Fina Kuhinjica**    VEGETARIAN €€
(☑060 603 0023; www.facebook.com/Radost-FinaKuhinjica; Pariska 3; mains 420-1240DIN; ⊙2pm-midnight Tue-Sat,1-9pm Sun; 🖉) Barbecue-obsessed Serbia isn't the easiest place for vegetarians, but thanks to this cheery eatery, you'll never have to settle for eating garnish and chips again. Its ever-changing menu features curries, veg burgers, innovative pastas and meat substitutes galore, some of which are vegan. The healthy cupcakes are a delight.

**Dva Jelena**    SERBIAN €€
(Two Deer; ☑011 723 4885; www.dvajelena.rs; Skadarska 32; mains 620-1650DIN; ⊙11am-1am) A local icon, Dva Jelena has been dishing up hearty fare for over 180 years. Rustic, homespun and with the obligatory violin serenades, it ticks all the Skadarlija boxes.

★**Little Bay**    EUROPEAN €€
(www.littlebay.rs; Dositejeva 9a; mains 595-1390DIN; ⊙11am-1am) Little wonder locals and visitors have long been singing the praises of this gem: it's one of the most interesting dining experiences in Belgrade. Tuck yourself into a private opera box and let any of the meaty treats melt in your mouth as a live opera singer does wonderful things to your ears. It does a traditional English roast lunch (795DIN) on Sundays.

★**Lorenzo & Kakalamba**    INTERNATIONAL €€€
(☑011 329 5351; www.lk.rs; Cvijićeva 110; mains 900-1950DIN; ⊙noon-midnight) Covered from floor to ceiling in a riot of out-there artworks and marvellous miscellany, and staffed (and frequented) by peculiar characters, to step inside here is to fall down the rabbit-hole to Wonderland. The food is as much of a masterpiece as the interior, with an extensive menu split between Italian (the handmade pastas are to die for) and southern Serbian cuisines; the starters alone are worth a trip.

★**Ambar**    BALKAN €€€
(☑011 328 6637; www.ambarrestaurant.com; Beton Hala; mains 510-3300DIN; ⊙10am-2am) Traditional Balkan cuisine has been given a contemporary spin at this chic spot; even the *pljeskavica* (hamburger) gets the five-star treatment. Service is helpful and attentive; put your meal choices in the hands of the staff and you won't be disappointed. Ambar is one of many upmarket restaurants in Beton Hala, a once-derelict concrete warehouse overlooking the Sava.

# Drinking & Nightlife

## Bars

### ⭐Blaznavac
BAR

(www.facebook.com/blaznavac; Kneginje Ljubice 18, Dorćol; ⊘9am-1am) Part cafe, part bar, part wonderfully wacko gallery, this pocket-sized place is one of the city's best spots for pre-drink drinks. Plastered in murals and quirky collectables, it's used as an exhibition space for young Belgrade artists; it also hosts live music and spoken-word events. Blaznavac's appeal isn't limited to night-time jams and cocktails; it also makes a mean coffee, and is a great spot for a snack.

### ⭐Kafana Pavle Korčagin
TAVERNA

(☏011 240 1980; www.kafanapavlekorcagin.rs; Ćirila i Metodija 2a; ⊘7.30am-1am Mon-Fri, 10am-1am Sat, 11am-11.30pm Sun) Raise a glass to Tito at this frantic, festive *kafana* (tavern). Lined with communist memorabilia and packed to the rafters with revellers and grinning accordionists, this table-thumping throwback fills up nightly; reserve a table via the website.

### Dvorištance
BAR

(www.facebook.com/klub.dvoristance; Cetinjska 15; ⊘9am-midnight Sun-Thu, to 1am Fri & Sat) Whimsical little Dvorištance is a rainbow-bright cafe by day, absolute ripper of a bar/performance space by night. It regularly hosts live gigs and alternative/indie DJ parties.

### Rakia Bar
BAR

(www.rakiabar.com; Dobračina 5, Dorćol; ⊘9am-midnight Sun-Thu, to 1am Fri & Sat) An ideal spot for *rakija* rookies to get their first taste of the spirit of Serbia. English-speaking staff will gently guide you through the extensive drinks menu, but beware: this stuff is strong.

### Miners Pub
PUB

(www.miners-pub.com; Rige od Fere 16, Dorćol; ⊘2pm-midnight Sun-Thu, to 1am Fri-Sun) With a huge assortment of craft beers, cool art on the walls, rock'n'roll on the stereo and a pinball machine, this little place is a gem of a hang-out. Happy hour daily (2pm to 7pm).

## Nightclubs

Belgrade has a reputation as one of the world's top party cities, with a wild club scene limited only by imagination and hours in the day. Many clubs move to river barges in summertime.

### ⭐Kenozoik
CLUB

(www.facebook.com/kenozoik.beograd; Cetinjska 15; ⊘8pm-2am winter) Housed within an abandoned brewery, Kenozoik is Cetinjska 15's cool-culture HQ, with live music, diverse DJ sets, movie screenings and art exhibitions drawing a more alternative crowd than the flashier Belgrade beats. You've got to be 23 and up to enter.

Kenozoik is a winter club; come summer, it moves the party to the **Favela** (www.facebook.com/favela.beograd; Ušće bb; ⊘6pm-late summer) river barge.

### Drugstore
CLUB

(www.facebook.com/drugstore.beograd; Bul Despota Stefana 115; ⊘11pm-late Fri & Sat) This cavernous space – formerly a slaughterhouse – can hold up to 1000 people, and its wild popularity means that it often does. Playing techno, underground house and genre-defying tunes to an avant-garde crowd, Drugstore's industrial-arty vibe is an intriguing blend of Belgrade and Berlin.

---

## ESSENTIAL FOOD & DRINK

Serbia is famous for grilled meats; regional cuisines range from spicy Hungarian goulash in Vojvodina to Turkish kebabs in Novi Pazar. Vegetarians should try asking for *posna hrana* ('meatless food'); this is also suitable for vegans.

**Kajmak** Along the lines of a salty clotted cream, this dairy delight is lashed on to everything from bread to burgers.

**Ćevapčići** The ubiquitous skinless sausage and *pljeskavica* (spicy hamburger) make it very easy to be a carnivore in Serbia.

**Burek** Flaky meat, cheese or vegetable pie eaten with yoghurt.

**Karađorđeva šnicla** Similar to chicken Kiev, but with veal or pork and lashings of *kajmak* and tartar.

**Rakija** Distilled spirit most commonly made from plums. Treat with caution: this ain't your grandpa's brandy.

**Plastic**  CLUB
(www.klubplastic.rs; cnr Dalmatinska & Takovska;
⊙10pm-6am Wed-Sat Oct-May) A perennial
favourite among electro-heads and booty
shakers, this slick venue is frequented by
top local and international DJs. The more
intimate Mint Club is within Plastic.

### River Barges

Belgrade is famous for its Sava and Danube river-barge clubs, known collectively as
*splavovi*. Most are open only in summer.

The Sava boasts a 1.5km strip of *splavovi*
on its west bank: these are the true wild-
and-crazy party boats. Walk over Brankov
Most or catch tram 7, 9 or 11 from the city.

Adjacent to Hotel Jugoslavija in Novi Belgrade, the 1km strip of Danube barges are
a bit more sophisticated; many are restaurants that get their dancing shoes on later in
the evening. Take bus 704 or 706 from Zeleni
Venac and get out by Hotel Jugoslavija.

★**Povetarac**  RIVER BARGE
(Brodarska bb, Sava River; ⊙11pm-late) This rust-
ing cargo ship attracts a fun indie crowd
for its eclectic playlist, cheap drinks and
exceedingly welcoming atmosphere. Open
year-round (8pm to late winter).

★**Blek Panters**  RIVER BARGE
(Crni Panteri; Ada Ciganlija bb; ⊙8pm-late Wed-
Mon) If wild, reeling Balkan music floats your
boat, make your way to this legendary *splav*

for an unforgettable night of dancing and
drinking. Run by the Roma band that gives
the club its name, this is one of Belgrade's
most famous nightspots. The party gets into
full swing about midnight. Open year-round.

**Freestyler**  RIVER BARGE
(www.freestyler.rs; Brodarska bb, Sava River;
⊙midnight-6am) Freestyler has been a symbol
of *splav* saturnalia for years, not least for its
infamous foam parties.

## ☆ Entertainment

For concert and theatre tickets, go to **Bilet
Servis** (☑0900 110 011; www.eventim.rs; Trg Republike 5; ⊙10am-8pm Mon-Fri, noon-8pm Sat).
Large venues for visiting acts include **Sava
Centar** (☑011 220 6060; www.savacentar.net; Mi-
lentija Popovića 9; ⊙box office 10am-8pm Mon-Fri,
to 3pm Sat) and **Kombank Arena** (☑011 220
2222; www.kombankarena.rs; Bul Arsenija Čarnoje-
vića 58; ⊙box office 10am-8pm Mon-Fri, to 3pm Sat).

**Mikser House**  CULTURAL CENTRE
(www.house.mikser.rs; Žorža Klemansoa, IMK Building; ⊙noon-midnight) Innovative, outré and
hip as hell, Mikser House is Belgrade's creative hub. Located in an industrial-chic complex in Dorćol, it has a shop, artistic work-
spaces, a cafe and galleries showcasing the
talents of local designers; come nighttime,
it morphs into a bar, restaurant and music
venue hosting live acts and DJs from Serbia
and around the world.

---

### THE SAVAMALA SCENE

The once-derelict, now-dapper Savamala creative district is Belgrade's hip HQ, with bars,
clubs and cultural centres that morph into achingly cool music/dance venues come
sundown. Dress codes and attitudes are far more relaxed here than in other parts of the
city; music-wise, indie, electro, rock and '90s disco are the go. Don't let the bedraggled
buildings fool you; there's magic going down inside. Some happening haunts:

**KC Grad** (www.gradbeograd.eu; Braće Krsmanović 4, Savamala; ⊙noon-midnight Mon-Thu, to
2am Fri & Sat, 2pm-midnight Sun) This wonderful warehouse space promotes local creativity with workshops, exhibitions, a restaurant and nightly avant-garde music events.

**Brankow** (www.facebook.com/brankow; Crnogorska 12, Savamala; ⊙11.30pm-5am winter) This
uber-urbane winter club inside one of the pillars of Brankov Most (bridge) attracts a trendy
crowd for its miscellany of music and sophisticated surrounds. In summer, the party moves
to **Lasta** (www.facebook.com/LastaGradskiSplav; Hercegovačka bb, Savamalski kej; ⊙11pm-5am
Thu-Sat, 6pm-3am Sun) – Belgrade's first city-side *splav* (river-barge nightclubs).

**Bašta** (www.jazzbasta.com; Karadjordjeva 43, Savamala; ⊙5pm-1am Mon-Thu, noon-2am
Fri-Sun) Hidden in an old building with a whimsical courtyard, creative cocktails and frequent live jazz, Bašta is so very Savamala.

**Mladost i Ludost** (www.mladost-ludost.com; Karadjordjeva 44, Savamala; ⊙9pm-6am)
These two bars are within the same building; punters hepped up on old-school DJ tunes
criss-cross between them at their leisure.

## GO WILD: TARA & DJERDAP NATIONAL PARKS

Serbia's cities offer fun, festivals and possibly the nattiest nightlife in Europe. But if you need a breather from bacchanalia, two spectacular national parks offer fresh-air fun in droves.

The sprawling **Djerdap National Park** (636 sq km) is home to one of Serbia's 'seven wonders', the awe-inspiring **Iron Gates gorge** (*Djerdapska klisura*). Its formidable cliffs – some of which soar over 500m – dip and dive for 100km along the Danube to form a natural border with Romania. Though the Iron Gates presented a rugged barrier to trade and travel – hence the name – the hulking **Golubac Fortress** (Tvrđava Golubački Grad), ancient settlement of **Lepenski Vir** (www.lepenski-vir.org; adult/child 400/250DIN; ⊘9am-8pm) and **Tabula Traiana** (a water-level plaque commemorating an AD 103 Roman bridge across the Danube) are testimony to old-time tenacity.

With 220 sq km of forested slopes, dramatic ravines, jewel-like waterways and rewarding views, **Tara National Park** is scenic Serbia at its best. Pressed up against – and affording gorgeous glimpses into – Bosnia and Herzegovina, this western wonderland attracts both adventurers eager for escapism and exploration. The park's main attraction is the vertigo-inducing **Drina River canyon**, the third-largest of its kind in the world. The gloriously green river of the same name slices through its cliffs, offering prime panoramas and ripper rafting; Tara's two artificial lakes – **Perućac** and **Zaovine** – are ideal for calm-water kayaking.

**National Theatre** THEATRE
(☑011 262 0946; www.narodnopozoriste.rs; Trg Republike; ⊘box office 11am-3pm & 5pm-performance time) This glorious 1869 building hosts operas, dramas and ballets during autumn, winter and spring.

**Bitef Art Cafe** LIVE MUSIC
(www.bitefartcafe.rs; Mitropolita Petra 8; ⊘9am-4am) There's something for everyone at this delightful hotchpotch of a cafe-club. Funk, soul and jazz get a good airing, as do rock, world music and classical. In summer, Bitef moves its stage to Kalemegdan Fortress.

**Cultural Centre of Belgrade** ARTS CENTRE
(Kulturni Centar Beograda, KCB; www.kcb.org.rs; Trg Republike 5) The KCB hosts a miscellany of alternative events, including art-house film screenings, exhibitions, experimental music concerts and various hip happenings.

**Madlenianum**
**Opera & Theatre** OPERA, THEATRE
(☑011 316 2797; www.operatheatremadlenianum.com; Glavna 32, Zemun) The first private opera house in southeastern Europe hosts regular musicals, plays, ballets and – of course – operas. Be sure to book ahead, as this intimate venue (maximum capacity 524) often sells out.

**Kolarac University Concert Hall** LIVE MUSIC
(☑011 2630 550; www.kolarac.rs; Studentski Trg 5; ⊘box office 10am-2.30pm & 3-8.30pm Mon-Fri,

10am-2pm Sat, plus 6-8pm for weekend concerts) The hall is home to the Belgrade Philharmonica; other classical music performances are also held here. A gallery, bookshop and cinema are also on-site.

**Yugoslav Cinematheque** CINEMA
(☑011 3286 723; www.kinoteka.org.rs; Uzun Mirkova 1; ⊘hours vary) The Yugoslav Cinematheque's impressive and recently renovated building across from the Ethnographic Museum screens everything from the classics of world cinema to art-house productions and cult Yugoslav-era movies. There are also regular screenings in its other building in Kosovska street. Check the website for the current program.

## ❶ Information

### TOURIST INFORMATION

**Tourist Organisation of Belgrade (**www.tob.rs) has locations at **Trg Republike 5** (☑011 263 5622; Trg Republike 5; ⊘9am-9pm Mon-Sat, 10am-3pm Sun), the **train station** (☑011 361 2732; Train Station; ⊘7am-8pm Mon-Fri, 7am-2.30pm Sat & Sun) and **Nikola Tesla Airport**. You will find helpful folk with a raft of brochures, city maps and all the info you could need.

### WEBSITES

**Belgrade Cat** (www.belgradecat.com)
**Belgrade My Way** (www.belgrademyway.com)
**Lonely Planet** (www.lonelyplanet.com/serbia/belgrade)

## ⓘ Getting There & Away

### BUS

Belgrade has two adjacent bus stations, near the eastern banks of the Sava River: **BAS** (Central Bus Station; ☑ 011 263 6299; www.bas. rs; Železnička 4) and **Lasta** (☑ 011 334 8555, freecall 0800 334 334; www.lasta.rs; Železnička 2). Buses run from both to international and Serbian destinations. Sample daily routes include Belgrade to Sarajevo (2585DIN, eight hours, three daily), Ljubljana (4300DIN, 7½ hours, two daily), Priština (3075DIN, seven hours, six daily) and Vienna (4430DIN, nine hours, two daily); frequent domestic services include Subotica (800DIN, three hours), Novi Sad (570DIN, one hour), Niš (1240DIN, three hours) and Novi Pazar (1470DIN, three hours).

### CAR & MOTORCYCLE

There are many rental car offices at Nikola Tesla Airport, including **Budget** (☑ 011 228 6361; www.budget.rs; ☺ 6am-11pm), **Avis** (☑ 011 209 7062; www.avis.com; ☺ 7am-11pm Mon-Fri, 8am-10pm Sat & Sun) and **Avaco** (☑ 011 243 3797; www.avaco.rs; ☺ 9am-9am). See www. beg.aero/en for a full list of agencies.

### TRAIN

The **central train station** (Savski Trg 2) has an information office on Platform 1, tourist information office, **exchange bureau** (☺ 6am-10pm) and **sales counter** (Savski Trg 2; ☺ 24hr).

Frequent trains go to Novi Sad (288DIN, 1½ hours, hourly), Subotica (560DIN, three hours, at least five daily) and Niš (784DIN, four hours, at least five daily). International destinations include Bar (2954DIN, 11½ hours, two daily), Budapest (1846DIN, eight hours, four daily) and Zagreb (2338DIN, seven hours, two daily). See www.serbianrailways.com for updated timetables and fares.

## ⓘ Getting Around

### TO/FROM THE AIRPORT

**Nikola Tesla Airport** (☑ 011 209 4444; www. beg.aero) is 18km from Belgrade. Local bus 72 (89DIN to 150DIN, half-hourly, 4.50am to midnight from airport, 4am to 11.40pm from town) connects the airport with Zeleni Venac; the cheapest tickets must be purchased from news stands. A minibus also runs between the airport and the central Slavija Sq (300DIN, 5am to 3.50am from the airport, 4.20am to 3.20am from the square).

Don't get swallowed up by the airport taxi shark pit. Head to the taxi information desk (near baggage claim area); they'll give you a taxi receipt with the name of your destination and the fare price. A taxi from the airport to Knez Mihailova should be around 1800DIN.

### CAR & MOTORCYCLE

Parking in Belgrade is regulated by three parking zones – red (one hour, 56DIN), yellow (two hours, 48DIN per hour) and green (three hours, 41DIN per hour). Tickets must be bought from kiosks or via SMS (in Serbian).

### PUBLIC TRANSPORT

Trams and trolleybuses ply limited routes but buses chug all over town. Rechargeable BusPlus cards can be bought and topped up (89DIN per ticket) at kiosks across the city; they're 150DIN if you buy from the driver.

Tram 2 connects Kalemegdan Citadel with Trg Slavija, bus stations and the central train station.

Zemun is a 45-minute walk from central Belgrade (across Brankov Most, along Nikole Tesle and the Kej Oslobođenja waterside walkway). Alternatively, take bus 15 or 84 from Zeleni Venac market, or bus 83 or 78 from the main train station.

### TAXI

Move away from obvious taxi traps and flag down a distinctly labelled cruising cab, or get a local to call you one. Flagfall is 170DIN; reputable cabs should charge about 70DIN per kilometre. Make absolutely sure the meter is turned on.

# VOJVODINA  ВОЈВОДИНА

Home to more than 25 ethnic groups, six languages and the best of Hungarian and Serbian traditions, Vojvodina's pancake plains mask a diversity unheard of in the rest of the country. Affable capital Novi Sad hosts the eclectic EXIT festival – the largest in southeast Europe – while the hilly region of Fruška Gora keeps the noise down in hushed monasteries and ancestral vineyards. Charming Subotica, 10km from Hungary, is an oasis of art nouveau delights. Compact and well linked by good roads, the region's tranquil nature, mellow villages and unhurried vibe make Vojvodina an ideal slow-travel destination.

# Novi Sad  Нови Сад

☑ 021 / POP 250,440

As convivial as a *rakija* toast – and at times just as carousing – Novi Sad is a chipper town with all the spoils and none of the stress of the big smoke. Locals sprawl in pretty parks and outdoor cafes, and laneway bars on pedestrian thoroughfare, Zmaj Jovina, which stretches from the town square (Trg Slobode) to Dunavska street, pack out nightly.

## SREM DISTRICT

Nicknamed 'the jewel of Serbia', **Fruška Gora** is an 80km stretch of rolling hills where cloistered life has endured since monasteries were built between the 15th and 18th centuries to safeguard Serbian culture and religion from the Turks. Of the 35 original monasteries, 16 remain, and they're open to visitors. Fruška Gora is also famous for its small but select wineries; grapes were first planted here in AD 3 by the Roman Emperor Probus.

The park is an easy 11km drive (20 to 30 minutes) from Novi Sad. If you're relying on public transport, catch a bus in Novi Sad bound for Irig (175DIN, 40 minutes) and ask to be let out at the **Novo Hopovo Monastery** (Irig; ☺9am-5pm). From here, walk or catch local buses to other points such as Vrdnik and Iriški Venac.

At the edge of Fruška Gora on the banks of the Danube is the photogenic village of **Sremski Karlovci**. It's lined with stunning structures like the **St Nicholas Orthodox cathedral** (1758–62), the working **Karlovci Orthodox Theological Seminary** (1794) – the second of its kind in the world – and the magnificent **Four Lions fountain**; the round yellow **Chapel of Peace** at the southern end of town is where the Turks and Austrians signed the 1699 Peace Treaty. Sremski Karlovci is also at the heart of a famed wine region and hosts a **grape harvesting festival** in late September. Visit the **Museum of Beekeeping & Wine Cellar** (✉021 881 071; www.muzejzivanovic.com; Mitropolita Stratimirovića 86) to try famous *bermet* wine, or drop in at any of the family-owned cellars around town. Take frequent buses 60, 61 or 62 from Novi Sad (145DIN, 30 minutes) and visit the tourist organisation just off the main square.

**Sremska Mitrovica**, in the western corner of Srem, was once Sirmium, one of the Roman Empire's four capitals and, at its peak, one of the largest cities in the world. You can visit what remains of old Rome at the **Sirmium Imperial Palace Complex** (✉022 621 568; www.carskapalata.rs; Pivarska 2, Sremska Mitrovica; adult/child 150/100DIN; ☺9am-5pm), a 50km drive from Sremski Karlovci.

Novi Sad is 2019's European Youth Capital, and in 2021 it will become the first non-EU city to spend a year with the prestigious title of European Capital of Culture.

## ◉ Sights

### ★ Petrovaradin Citadel  FORTRESS

(Tvrdjava) Towering over the river on a 40m-high volcanic slab, this mighty citadel is aptly nicknamed 'Gibraltar on the Danube'. Constructed with slave labour between 1692 and 1780, its dungeons have held notable prisoners including Karađorđe (leader of the first uprising against the Turks and founder of a royal dynasty) and Tito. Have a good gawk at the iconic clock tower: the size of the minute and hour hands are reversed so far-flung fisherfolk can tell the time.

Within the citadel walls, a **museum** (Muzej Grada Novog Sada; ✉021 6433 145; www.museumns.rs; 150DIN; ☺9am-5pm Tue-Sun) offers insight into the site's history. The museum can also arrange tours (in English; 500DIN per person) of Petrovaradin's 16km of creepy, but cool, unlit underground tunnels known locally as *katakombe*. While their official use was for military purposes, rumours abound

of mysterious treasure troves, tunnel-dwelling reptiles and still-roaming ghosts.

Petrovaradin hosts Novi Sad's wildly popular EXIT Festival each July.

### ★ Gallery of Matica Srpska  MUSEUM

(www.galerijamaticesrpske.rs; Trg Galerija 1; 100DIN; ☺10am-6pm Tue-Thu & Sat, noon-8pm Fri) First established in Pest (part of modern Budapest) in 1826 and moved to Novi Sad in 1864, this is one of Serbia's most important and long-standing cultural institutions. It's not a mere gallery, but rather a national treasure, with three floors covering priceless Serbian artworks from the 18th, 19th and 20th centuries in styles ranging from Byzantine to the baroque, with countless icons, portraits, landscapes and early graphic art (and more) in between.

### Museum of Vojvodina  MUSEUM

(Muzej Vojvodine; www.muzejvojvodine.org.rs; Dunavska 35-7; 200DIN; free Sun; ☺9am-7pm Tue-Fri, 10am-6pm Sat & Sun) This museum houses historical, archaeological and ethnological exhibits. Building 35 covers Vojvodinian history from Palaeolithic times to the late 19th century. Building 37 takes the story to 1945 with a harrowing emphasis on WWI and WWII.

**Štrand** BEACH

(50DIN) One of Europe's best by-the-Danube beaches, this 700m-long stretch morphs into a city of its own come summertime, with bars, stalls and all manner of recreational diversions attracting thousands of sun- and fun-seekers from across the globe. It's also the ultimate Novi Sad party venue, hosting everything from local punk gigs to EXIT raves.

It's also great for kids (watch them by the water: the currents here are strong), with playgrounds, trampolines and dozens of ice-cream and fast-food stalls.

## ★ Festivals & Events

The Petrovaradin Citadel is stormed by thousands of revellers each July during the epic **EXIT Festival** (www.exitfest.org; ⊙ Jul). The first festival in 2000 lasted 100 days and galvanised a generation of young Serbs against the Milošević regime. The festival has been attended by the likes of Chemical Brothers, Gogol Bordello and Patti Smith...and an annual tally of about 200,000 merrymakers.

## ⌂ Sleeping

★**Varad Inn** HOSTEL €

(☑ 021 431 400; www.varadinn.com; Štrosmajerova 16, Petrovaradin; dm €10-13, r €30; ❋ ☎) Sitting in the shadow of Petrovaradin Fortress, this excellent budget option is housed in a gorgeous yellow baroque-style building constructed in 1714. Completely renovated but making beautiful use of salvaged historical bits and bobs, the Varad Inn (get it?) has beautiful feel-at-home rooms (all with their own bathrooms, lockers and towels), a lovely garden cafe and communal kitchen.

★**Narrator** APARTMENT €€

(☑ 060 6767 886; www.en.narator.rs; Dunavska 17; apt from €30; ❋ ☎) The super-central designer digs at Narrator do indeed tell a story; eight of them, in fact, one for every themed, individually decorated apartment. With names like 'The Chambermaid from Eden', 'The Bookworm' and 'Captain Honeymoon', each room's tale unfolds via a series of exquisite, original naive-style portraits scattered across the walls. All apartments are self-contained.

★**Hotel Veliki** HOTEL €€

(☑ 021 4723 840; www.hotelvelikinovisad.com; Nikole Pašića 24; s/d €34/50, apt from €69; P ❋ ☎) Sitting atop an absolutely stupendous Vojvodinian restaurant of the same name, the Veliki ('Big') lives up to its name: some of the rooms are truly huge. Staff are delightful, and the location, around the corner from Zmaj Jovina, is top-notch. Bonus: free breakfast downstairs!

## ✗ Eating

★**Fish i Zeleniš** MEDITERRANEAN €€

(Fish and Greens; ☑ 021 452 000; www.fishizelenis.com; Skerlićeva 2; mains 690-1740DIN; ⊙ noon-midnight; ☑) This bright, snug little nook serves up the finest vegetarian/pescatarian meals in northern Serbia (don't fret, meat lovers – there's plenty here for you, too). Organic, locally sourced ingredients? Ambient? Ineffably delicious? Tick, tick, tick. A three-minute walk from Zmaj Jovina.

**Alla Lanterna** ITALIAN €€

(www.allalanterna.rs; Dunavska 27; pizzas from 600DIN, mains 500-1400DIN; ⊙ 8am-midnight) Come for the toothsome pastas, pizzas and Italian-influenced mains, stay for the jaw-dropping decor; thousands of polished pebbles and tiles have been meticulously arranged into psychedelic swirling patterns that run from the vaulted ceiling to the polished floorboards.

★**Čarda Aqua Doria** SEAFOOD €€€

(☑ 021 6430 949; www.carda.rs; Petrovaradin Fortress; mains 560-1700DIN; ⊙ 8am-midnight) All

---

### MADNESS, MADE IN SERBIA

On the surface, the **Dragačevo Trumpet Assembly** (an annual gathering of brass musicians) sounds harmless; nerdily endearing even. But band camp this ain't: it *is*, however, the most boisterous music festival in all of Europe, if not the world.

Known simply as 'Guča', after the western Serbian village that has hosted it each August since 1961, the four-day debauch is hedonism at its most rambunctious: tens of thousands of beer-and-brass-addled visitors dance wild *kola* (fast-paced circle dances) through the streets, gorging on spit-meat and slapping dinar on the sweaty foreheads of the (mostly Roma) *trubači* performers. See www.guca.rs for information on accommodation and transport.

## ZLATIBOR

Zlatibor is a romantic region of gentle mountains, traditions and hospitality. It's also a popular skiing destination. Quirky adventures await in the village of **Mokra Gora**. There's the mini-village of **Drvengrad** (Küstendorf; www.mecavnik.info; Mećavnik hill, Mokra Gora; adult/child 250/100DIN; ⊙7am-7pm), built by Serbian director Emir Kusturica for his film *Life is a Miracle*, offering surreal fun and prime panoramas. And there's the joy of a 2½-hour journey on the **Šargan 8 railway** (☑Mon-Fri 031 510 288, Sat-Sun 031 800 003; www.serbianrailways.com; Mokra Gora; adult/child 600/300DIN; ⊙daily Apr-Oct, by appointment Nov-Mar) tourist train and its disorienting twists, turns and tunnels (all 22 of them).

Reach these sights via bus from Užice or through **Zlatibor Tours** (☑031 845 957; zlatibortours@gmail.com; Tržni centar, bus station; ⊙8am-10pm).

aboard for romance, river views and rich fish dishes! Bobbing in the shadow of Petrovaradin Fortress, this beautiful barge restaurant is popular with locals looking to splurge on exquisitely prepared *čorba* (fish stew), smoked fish and other Danube delights. Impeccable service, top-notch *rakija* (fruit brandy), sublime views and live *tamburaši* (musicians playing mandolin-like instruments) make meals here utterly memorable.

## 🍷 Drinking & Nightlife

**Laze Telečkog** (pedestrian side street running off Zmaj Jovina) is lined with bars to suit every whim. The ramshackle **Chinese Quarter** (Kineska Četvrt; Bul Despota Stefana) houses Novi Sad's alternative-scene clubs and secret saloons.

★**Martha's Pub**                                    BAR
(Laze Telečkog 3; ⊙8am-3am) One of the best in a street of top bars, Martha's is a small, smoky and stupendously sociable den famous for its divine *medovuču* (honey brandy). Crowbar yourself inside, or get there early to nab a table outside to watch the party people of Laze Telečkog romp by.

**The Quarter**                                    CLUB
(www.facebook.com/ClubQuarter; Bul Despota Stefana 5, Chinese Quarter; ⊙hours vary) Hosting regular exhibitions, live music gigs and all manner of avant-garde performances, the Quarter is also a top spot for a drink and hanging out with the offbeat locals that the Chinese Quarter attracts. Pop next door to **Fabrika**, the neighbourhood's arty-crew HQ.

**Culture Exchange**                                    CAFE
(www.facebook.com/cultureexchangeserbia; Jovana Subotića 21; ⊙9am-11pm; 🛜) Run by well-travelled volunteers, Culture Exchange offers coffees, cakes and pretty much everything else you can imagine: free bike repairs, Serbian

language classes, live music gigs, film screenings and art exhibitions. It's also a top spot for pre-big-night-out drinks. There's nowhere quite like it in town (or indeed, Serbia!).

## ℹ Information

**Novi Sad Greeters** (☑021 530 231; www.novisadgreeters.rs)

**Tourist Information Centre** (www.novisad.travel/en; Jevrejska 10; ⊙9am-5pm Mon-Fri, 10am-3pm Sat)

## ℹ Getting There & Away

The **bus station** (Bul Jaše Tomića; ⊙information counter 6am-11pm) has regular departures to Belgrade (570DIN, one hour, every 10 minutes) and Subotica (600DIN, 1½ hours), plus services to Užice (1230DIN, five hours) and Zlatibor (1330DIN, six hours).

From the station, four stops on bus 4 will take you to the town centre: nip down the underpass and you'll see Trg Slobode on emerging.

Frequent trains leave the **train station** (Bul Jaše Tomića 4), next door to the bus station, for Belgrade (288DIN, 1½ hours) and Subotica (384DIN, 1½ hours). At least four trains go daily to Budapest (1479DIN, 6½ hours).

# SOUTH SERBIA

## Niš                                    Ниш
☑018 / POP 183,000

Serbia's third-largest metropolis is a lively city of curious contrasts, where Roma in horse-drawn carriages trot alongside new cars, and posh cocktails are sipped in antiquated alleyways. Niš was settled in pre-Roman times and flourished during the time of local-boy-made-good Emperor Constantine (AD 280–337).

SERBIA NIŠ

## ◉ Sights

### Niš Fortress
FORTRESS

(Niška tvrđava; Jadranska; ☉24hr) Though its current incarnation was built by the Turks in the 18th century, there have been forts on this site since ancient Roman times. Today, it's a sprawling recreational area with restaurants, cafes, market stalls and ample space for moseying. It hosts the **Nišville International Jazz Festival** (www.nisville.com; ☉Aug) each August and **Nišomnia** (www.facebook.com/festivalnisomnia; ☉Sep), featuring rock and electro acts, in September. The city's main pedestrian boulevard, Obrenovićeva, stretches before the citadel.

### Ćele Kula
MONUMENT

(Tower of Skulls; Bul Zoran Đinđić; 150DIN; ☉9am-7pm Tue-Fri, to 5pm Sat & Sun) With Serbian defeat imminent at the 1809 Battle of Čegar, the Duke of Resava kamikazed towards the Turkish defences, firing at their gunpowder stores, killing himself, 4000 of his men and 10,000 Turks. The Turks triumphed regardless, and to deter future acts of rebellion, they beheaded, scalped and embedded the skulls of the dead Serbs in this tower. Only 58 of the initial 952 skulls remain. Contrary to Turkish intention, the tower serves as proud testament to Serbian resistance.

Get there on any bus marked 'Niška Banja' from the stop opposite the abandoned Ambassador Hotel: ask to be let out at Ćele Kula.

### Medijana
RUINS

(Bul Cara Konstantina; 150DIN; ☉10am-6pm Tue-Fri, to 3pm Sat & Sun) **FREE** Medijana is what remains of Constantine the Great's luxurious 4th-century Roman palace. The recently unveiled 1000 sq metres of gorgeous mosaics are the highlight here; they were hidden from public view until protective renovations were completed in 2016. Digging has revealed a palace, a forum, a church and an expansive grain-storage area. There's not much in the way of signage, but knowledgeable staff are on hand to talk visitors through the complex. Medijana is a short walk from Ćele Kula.

### Red Cross Concentration Camp
MUSEUM

(Crveni Krst; Bul 12 Februar; 150DIN; ☉9am-4pm Tue-Fri, 10am-3pm Sat & Sun) One of the best-preserved Nazi camps in Europe, the deceptively named Red Cross held about 30,000 Serbs, Roma, Jews and Partisans during the German occupation of Serbia (1941–45). Harrowing displays tell their stories, and those of the prisoners who attempted to flee in the biggest-ever breakout from a concentration camp. The English-speaking staff are happy to provide translations and explain the exhibits in depth. The camp is a short walk north of the Niš bus station.

## 🛏 Sleeping

### Aurora Hostel
HOSTEL €

(☏018 214 642; www.aurorahostel.rs; Dr Petra Vučinića 16; dm/r from 790/1190DIN; ❄🛜) Set within a 19th-century former Turkish consulate, Aurora offers charm and comfort by the ladle-load. Though the building has been renovated, its wood-heavy interiors and hospitable host are redolent of a more gentle era. Rooms are spic, and there's a good communal kitchen and a lovely garden area.

### ★ArtLoft Hotel
BOUTIQUE HOTEL €€

(☏018 305 800; www.artloft.rs; Oblačića Rada 8; s/d/ste from €42/55/66; ❄🛜) Central and chic, this designer hotel takes its name literally, with original murals and paintings by local artists dominating every room. The modern feel extends to the professional staff, who take service to the next level by offering friendly assistance, advice and little touches including complimentary fruit and drinks. It's a short stroll from here to Trg Republike and Kopitareva.

## ✖ Eating & Drinking

The cobblestoned Kopitareva (Tinkers' Alley) is full of eating and drinking options.

### ★Hamam
BALKAN €€

(Niš Fortress; mains 520-2400DIN; ☉8am-midnight) This former Turkish bathhouse once provided respite for weary travellers from Istanbul; today, it welcomes visitors from all over with lashings of Ottoman-influenced treats. The menu is chock-a-block with spicy meats, hearty stews and perennial Balkan classics; its location by the fortress gate makes it a good spot for just a drink and a spot of people-watching as well.

---

**EATING PRICE RANGES**

The following price categories are based on the cost of a main course:

**€** less than 600DIN

**€€** 600DIN–1000DIN

**€€€** more than 1000DIN

**Saloon Tvrdjava** BAR

(Niš Fortress; ⊙10am-late) As dark and dingy as any self-respecting rock-and-roll bar should be, this fortress bar packs out regularly, especially on nights when there's live music. Escape the crowds (and cigarette smoke) by making a beeline for the beer garden.

## ℹ Information

**Tourist Organisation of Niš** (☑ 018 250 222; www.visitnis.com; Tvrđava; ⊙7.30am-7pm Mon-Fri, 9am-1pm Sat) Helpful info within the citadel gates. There's another branch at Vožda Karađorđa 7 in the city centre.

## ℹ Getting There & Away

Behind Niš Fortress, the **bus station** (Bul 12 Februar) has frequent services to Belgrade (1240DIN, three hours) and Brus (720DIN, 1½ hours) for Kopaonik, and three daily to Novi Pazar (1200DIN, four hours).

From the **train station** (Dimitrija Tucovića), there are seven trains to Belgrade (784DIN, 4½ hours) and two to Sofia (730DIN, five hours).

**Niš Constantine The Great Airport** (www.nis-airport.com) is 4km from downtown Niš, serving destinations including Germany, Italy, Slovakia and the Netherlands. Get here on bus 34.

# SURVIVAL GUIDE

## ℹ Directory A–Z

### MONEY

Serbia retains the dinar (DIN); though accommodation prices are often quoted in euro, you must pay in dinar.

### VISAS

Tourist visas for stays of less than 90 days aren't required by citizens of EU countries, most other European countries, Australia, New Zealand, Canada and the USA. Officially, all visitors must register with the police. Hotels and hostels will do this for you but if you're camping or staying in a private home, you are expected to register within 24 hours of arrival. Unofficially? This is rarely enforced, but being unable to produce

---

### SLEEPING PRICE RANGES

The following price categories are based on the cost of a high-season double room:

€ less than 3000DIN

€€ 3000DIN–7000DIN

€€€ more than 7000DIN

---

registration documents upon leaving Serbia could result in a fine.

## ℹ Getting There & Away

### AIR

Belgrade's **Nikola Tesla Beograd Airport** (p370) handles most international flights. Serbia's national carrier is Air Serbia (www.airserbia.com).

### LAND

Because Serbia does not acknowledge crossing points into Kosovo as international border crossings, it may not be possible to enter Serbia from Kosovo unless you first entered Kosovo from Serbia. Driving Serbian-plated cars into Kosovo isn't advised, and is often not permitted by rental agencies or insurers.

Drivers need International Driving Permits. If you're in your own car, you'll need your vehicle registration, ownership documents and locally valid insurance (such as European Green Card vehicle insurance). Otherwise, border insurance costs about €150 for a car, €95 for a motorbike; www.registracija-vozila.rs has updated price lists.

Bus services to both Western Europe and Turkey are well developed.

International rail connections leaving Serbia originate in Belgrade. For more information, visit **Serbian Railways** (www.serbianrailways.com).

## ℹ Getting Around

Bus services are extensive, though outside major hubs connections can be sporadic. Reservations are only worthwhile for international buses and during festivals.

Serbian Railways serves Novi Sad, Subotica, Užice and Niš from Belgrade.

Bicycle paths are improving in larger cities.

# Slovakia

## Best Places to Eat

➜ Vino & Tapas (p385)
➜ Modrá Hviezda (p382)
➜ Republika Východu (p392)
➜ Med Malina (p392)

## Best Places to Stay

➜ Hotel Marrol's (p381)
➜ Hotel Bankov (p392)
➜ Penzión Sabato (p385)
➜ Grand Hotel Kempinski (p387)

## Why Go?

Right in the heart of Europe, Slovakia is a land of castles and mountains, occasionally interrupted by concrete sprawl. More than two decades after Czechoslovakia's break-up, Slovakia has emerged as a self-assured, independent nation. Capital city Bratislava draws the most visitors, thanks to its excellent nightlife, resplendent old town and sheer ease of access from around Europe. Beyond Bratislava are countless gingerbread-style villages, a clear sign that modern Slovakia still reveres its folk traditions.

Slovakia shines brightest for lovers of the outdoors. The High Tatras are heavenly for walking or winter sports, and national parks like Slovenský Raj sparkle with waterfalls. Castles worthy of a Disney princess perch on hills, and quaint churches speckle the less-discovered east around friendly second city Košice. Within a long weekend in this small country, you can hike or ski epic mountains, blink in astonishment at socialist-era oddities and clink glasses in cellar restaurants.

## When to Go
### Bratislava

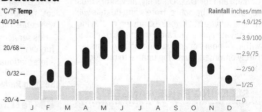

**Jun & Jul** Cultural festivals amp up, and all hiking trails are open.

**Sep & Oct** Fewer crowds but clement walking weather, plus festivals galore.

**Late Dec–Feb** Christmas markets twinkle in Bratislava, skiers flock to Poprad and High Tatras.

# BRATISLAVA

📓 02 / POP 5.45 MILLION

Bratislava doesn't provoke admiring swoons; it intrigues. In the midst of Slovakia's capital, a flying saucer hovers above forest-fringed riverbanks. Its castle presides over a pastel-hued old town, but a concrete jungle looms behind. Despite the march of modernism, Bratislava is green. It banks the Danube River, by the Austrian border, and its hilly parks are threaded with hiking and biking trails. The Male Karpaty (Small Carpathians) roll north, with vineyards in their lowlands.

No wonder Bratislava feels like a frenetic mix of wild and urban, classic and contemporary: it became capital of newly independent Slovakia only in 1993. Bratislava preserved spires and squares from its 18th-century heyday, but now socialist-era monuments (and an eyebrow-raising cast of statues) have joined the party. Speaking of which, Bratislava's nightlife is crowd-pleasing whether you prefer beer halls, rooftop cocktails or stag-party mayhem. In a city this exciting, who needs postcard pretty?

## History

First inhabited by Slavs during the 6th century, the earliest mention of Bratislava and its castle was in AD 907. By the 12th century Bratislava (then called Poszony in Hungarian or Pressburg in German) was a large city in greater Hungary. King Matthias Corvinus founded a university here, Academia Istropolitana. Many of the imposing baroque palaces you see date to the reign of Austro-Hungarian empress Maria Theresa (1740–80), when the city flourished. From the 16th-century Turkish occupation of Budapest to the mid-1800s, the Hungarian parliament met locally and monarchs were crowned in St Martin's Cathedral.

'Bratislava' was officially born as the second city of a Czechoslovakian state after WWI and became capital of the new nation of Slovakia in 1993.

## ◉ Sights

### ★ Bratislava Castle                    CASTLE
(www.snm.sk; grounds free, museum adult/student €7/4; ⊙ grounds 9am-9pm, museum 10am-6pm Tue-Sun) Square, a brilliant shade of white and flanked by four stocky towers, bold Bratislava Castle looks as though it has been transplanted straight from a children's picturebook. The fortification's history dates to the 9th century, though today's incarnation is a 1960s rebuild in Renaissance style; the castle had lain in ruins after a fire in 1811. Exhibitions feature a picture gallery, model reconstruction of the castle and Middle Ages history.

### Hlavné Námestie                    SQUARE
The nucleus for Bratislava's history, annual festivals and cheerful cafe culture is Hlavné nám (Main Sq). **Roland Fountain** (Hlavné nám), at the square's heart, is thought to have been built in 1572 as a public water supply. Flanking the northeast side of the square is the 14th-century **Old Town Hall** (www.muzeum.bratislava.sk; Primaciálne nám 3; adult/child €6/3; ⊙ 10am-5pm Tue-Fri, 11am-6pm Sat & Sun), home to the Municipal Museum.

### ★ St Martin's Cathedral                    CHURCH
(Dóm sv Martina; http://dom.fara.sk; cnr Kapitulská & Staromestská; ⊙ 9-11.30am & 1-6pm Mon-Sat, 1.30-4pm Sun May-Sep, until 4pm Mon-Sat Oct-Apr) The crown at the top of St Martin's Cathedral is 300kg of real gold. By comparison, its interior is rather modest, though 19 royal coronations have been held within its 14th-century walls.

---

## ITINERARIES

### Three Days
Spend three days in Bratislava. It's enough to enjoy the main sights – Bratislava Castle, Hlavné nám, Soviet oddities – and take excursions to **Devín Castle** and **Danublana Meulensteen Art Museum**.

### One Week
After three days in Bratislava and its surrounds, venture east to **Starý Smokovec** for two glorious days of hiking. Press on to dramatic **Spiš Castle**, then spend a final day or two in culture-packed **Košice**.

# Slovakia Highlights

**1 Bratislava** (p377)
Strolling from hilltop castles to sci-fi monuments en route to your next cafe or beer stop.

**2 High Tatras** (p386)
Thundering down ski slopes,

or hiking between huts, in this extraordinary mountainscape.

**3 Slovenský Raj National Park** (p390) Clinging to ladders and being splashed by

waterfalls along treks through this dramatic reserve.

**4 Spiš Castle** (p390)
Strutting along the ramparts of a 13th-century castle.

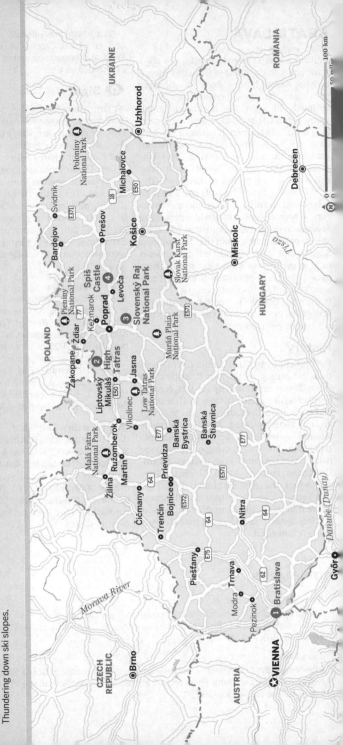

## Museum of Jewish Culture
MUSEUM

(www.snm.sk; Židovská 17; adult/child €7/2; ☺11am-5pm Sun-Fri) This enriching museum unveils the lives of Bratislava's once-thriving Jewish community through photographs and objects from daily life, with a focus on the impressive Jewish architecture lost both during and after WWII. Most moving are the oil paintings of death marches, created by Jewish survivors of the war, and timelines of the community's destruction by the Nazis.

## Blue Church
CHURCH

(Kostol Svätej Alžbety; Bezručova 2) The early-20th-century Church of St Elizabeth, known as the Blue Church, unites 50 shades of blue into an art nouveau delight. From the outside you can admire its powder-blue clock tower, glinting sapphire-tinged ceramic roof and columns that look rolled in icing. During the erratic and infrequent opening hours, you can see baby-blue pews and gold decoration.

## 🏃 Activities

### Bratislava Bike Point
CYCLING

(✆0944 103 432; www.bratislavabikepoint.com; bike rental per hr/day €6/15; ☺10am-6pm mid-Apr–Sep) Hire a bike from this summer rental outfit beneath the UFO (Most SNP). You can also book an Iron Curtain–themed three-hour bike tour (from €29).

## ☞ Tours

### ★ Authentic Slovakia
CULTURAL

(✆0908 308 234; www.authenticslovakia.com; per person per 2/4hr tour from €22/32) Always with ribald humour and an eye for the dark side, Authentic Slovakia leads you into Bratislava's seamy history and wacky architecture (usually aboard a retro Škoda car). Want to see 'Bratislava's Beverly Hills', Brutalist cityscapes or drink your way around Devín Castle? You're in safe hands.

## 🎉 Festivals & Events

### Fjúžn
CULTURAL

(Festival of Minorities; www.fjuzn.sk; ☺Apr) Concerts, debates and food festivals form the varied program of this annual celebration of Slovak minorities and their cultures.

### Bratislava Music Festival
MUSIC

(www.bhsfestival.sk; ☺Oct/Nov) One of Slovakia's most important music festivals; international classical music performances take place from October or November.

---

### SOCIALIST BRATISLAVA

Slovakia's stint under socialism left its mark in bizarre and monumental ways. It's impossible to miss futuristic flying saucer bridge **Most SNP** (New Bridge; www.u-f-o.sk; Viedenská cesta; observation deck adult/child €7.40/3.95; ☺10am-11pm). Another strange silhouette is the **Slovak Radio Building** (Slovenský rozhlas; ul Mýtna), designed in the shape of an inverted pyramid. Meanwhile the **Petržalka** neighbourhood gained notoriety as a concrete jungle, though it's an increasingly pleasant area to live.

---

### Christmas Markets
CHRISTMAS MARKET

(☺Nov-Dec) From late November, Hlavné and Hviezdoslavovo nám fill with food and drink, crafts for sale and festive performances. Towards the end you can buy a tree or live carp for Christmas dinner (locals keep them in the bath, but we don't recommend it).

## 🛏 Sleeping

Getting a short-term rental flat in the old town is a great way to stay central without paying hotel prices, plus you can self-cater. Managed by a friendly, family team, **Apartments Bratislava** (✆0918 397 924; www.apartmentsbratislava.com; apt €55-69; 🛜) has 12 modern properties in the old-town centre and near the Blue Church.

### Hostel Possonium
HOSTEL €

(✆02-2072 0007; www.possonium.sk; Šancová 20; dm €9-20, d €40-70; 🛜) A friendly traveller bolthole just five minutes' walk from the train station, Possonium has an underground and outdoor bar, as well as well-tended dorm rooms and essentials like a shared kitchen and washing machine. Modern, smooth-running and worth booking in advance. Rates vary by season.

### Penzión Portus
GUESTHOUSE €

(✆0911 978 026; www.portus.sk; Paulínyho 10; d/tr/q incl breakfast from €40/60/80; 🛜) Resisting the encroaching embassies and modern buildings, rose-pink Portus somehow retains its old-timey vibe. Simple rooms roost above a restaurant, in a hard-to-beat location less than 100m south of Hviezdoslavovo nám.

# Central Bratislava

Hostel Possonium (850m)

Slovak Radio Building (500m)

Moyzesova

Tolstého

Sládkovičova

Štefánikova

Grassalkovich Palace (Presidential Palace)

Nám 1 mája

Palisády

Hodžovo nám

Mýtna

Tatra centrum

Vysoká

Panenská

16

Konventná

Crowne Plaza

Drevená

11

Obchodná

Kozia

Zochova

Pilárikova ulica

Staromestská

Hurbanovo nám

Poštová

Nám SNP

Monument of the Slovak National Uprising

Svoradova

Zámocká

Skalná

Kapucínska

Michael's Gate & Tower

Zámočnícka

Františkánska

Nám SNP

23

20

Nedbalova

Baštová

Uršulínska

Klariská

12

Michalská

Biela

Klobučnícka

Tourist Information Centre

Farská

Františkánske nám

Primaciálne nám

6

Laurinská

Kapitulská

Sedlárska

Venturská

Prepoštská

Klobučnícka

4

8

Radničná

7

Židovská

Staromestská

Úzka

Zelená

Hlavné nám

17

Rybárska brána

1

Bratislava Castle

Panská

Gorkého

21

Jesenského

Eugena Suchoň nám

2

Rudnayovo nám

St Martin's Cathedral

Hviezdoslavovo nám

Palackého

14

Žámocké schody

Mostová

22

Medená

Nový Most Bus Stop

Rybné nám

13

10

Paulínyho

Nám L Štúra

Židovská

Nábr arm gen L Svobodu

Rázusovo nábr

Twin City Liner

Propeller Terminal

5

Danube River

Bratislava Bike Point (150m)

SLOVAKIA BRATISLAVA

**Hotel Arcus**      GUESTHOUSE €€
(☏ 02-5557 2522; www.hotelarcus.sk; Moskovská 5; s €54-66, d €80-100, tr €109-127, all incl breakfast; P ？) There is a relaxing ambience at this place, tucked away on a residential street. Room sizes vary, but all have a good amount of space, and there's a garden out the back to relax in. Most rooms are doubles but one family room can sleep up to four.

**★ Hotel Marrol's**      BOUTIQUE HOTEL €€€
(☏ 02-5778 4600; www.hotelmarrols.sk; Tobrucká 4; d incl breakfast from €138; P ？ ✉) Even travellers with aristocratic tastes will raise an approving eyebrow at the art deco furnishings, elegant Jasmine spa (treatments by arrangement) and exemplary service at Marrol's. Rooms are plush, in soft shades of ivory and gold, or you can linger by the fireplace in the lobby bar.

# Eating

Hviezdoslavovo nám and Laurinská are well-touristed, but have plenty of choice. Set-lunch menus usually offer the best value.

### ★ Modrá Hviezda
SLOVAK €

(☑0948 703 070; www.modrahviezda.sk; ul Be-blavého 14; mains €9-20; ⊙11am-11pm) The 'Blue Star' specialises in rich, regally executed Slovak dishes: rabbit in red wine, baked trout, and mangalica pork (from woolly pigs) on a silky purée of chestnuts. Seasonal ingredients inform the changing menu, and the brick-lined cellar space, twinkling with candlelight, feels equal parts romantic and rustic. A must-eat.

### Funki Punki
CRÊPES €

(www.funkipunki.sk; Klariská 12; mains €5; ⊙10am-10pm Mon-Fri, noon-10pm Sun; ☑🖉🖾) Dig in to sweet or savoury crêpes at this bohemian spot with schoolroom seating and pretty murals. Pancakes are stuffed with classic Slovak flavours like bacon and *bryndza* cheese, plenty of veggie options, and tempting sweet chestnut and kiwi, and you can choose the type of batter (including gluten-free buckwheat). Wash it down with a homemade lemonade and drift off to the ethereal soundtrack.

### Štúr
CAFE €

(www.sturcafe.sk; Štúrova 8; snacks €4-7; ⊙8.30am-10pm Mon-Fri, 9am-10pm Sat, 9am-9pm Sun; ☎🖉🖾) Wonderful coffee, gateaus from coconut sponge to caramel cheesecake, and soups served in a comforting, bookish *kaviareň* (cafe or coffee shop). It's named for Ľudovít Štúr, pioneer of the Slovak literary language.

### Bratislavský Meštiansky Pivovar
SLOVAK €€

(☑0944 512 265; www.mestianskypivovar.sk; Drevená 8; mains €7-22; ⊙11am-midnight Mon-Thu & Sat, to 1am Fri, 11am-11pm Sun; ☎🖾) Continuing Bratislava's 600-year-old brewing tradition, Meštiansky Pivovar offers local and German beers to accompany its menu of Central European stomach liners (sometimes infusing it into the dishes). Within the elegantly vaulted beer hall, choose from trout with bacon, beer and onion goulash, strudels, and moreish snacks from cheese plates to crackling pork.

### Lemon Tree
THAI, MODERN EUROPEAN €€€

(☑0948 109 400; www.lemontree.sk; Hviezdoslavovo nám 7; mains €10-20; ⊙11am-midnight Mon-Fri, from noon Sat & Sun; 🖉🖾) If panang curry

duck followed by poppyseed cake sounds like a match made in heaven, head to this top-end Thai and European restaurant. Thai dishes like green papaya salad and pad thai are beautifully executed, while European flavours like pheasant soup and poached rabbit are just as much of a tastebud adventure.

#  Drinking & Nightlife

From mid-April to October, sidewalk cafe tables sprout all over the pedestrian old town. Hviezdoslavovo nám has good options. Admission prices for Bratislava's clubs are usually low (free to €5).

### Slovak Pub
PUB

(www.slovakpub.sk; Obchodná 62; ⊙10am-midnight Tue-Thu & Sat, to 2am Fri, noon-11pm Sun, 10am-11pm Mon; ☎) Touristy but difficult to resist, Slovak Pub serves every national dish you can think of (mains €3.50 to €11) in a big, wood-walled tavern. Before you get beer goggles, you might even learn something about Slovak culture from wall decorations like knightly regalia, antlers and embroidered folk costumes.

### Cork
WINE BAR

(www.cork.sk; Panská 4; ⊙5pm-midnight Sun-Thu, to 2am Fri & Sat) Lost your taste for beer after too many hoppy nights in Bratislava? This intimate wood-lined wine cellar, with bottles displayed floor to ceiling, offers pan-European wines as a sophisticated alternative.

### Nu Spirit Bar
BAR

(www.nuspirit.sk; Medená 16; ⊙5pm-3am Mon-Sat, to 1am Sun) Deservedly popular cellar bar with regular live music as underground as its location: jazz, reggae, electronica, soul.

### Apollon Club
GAY & LESBIAN

(www.gdisco.sk; Panenská 24; ⊙8pm-3am Tue & Thu, to 5am Wed, Fri & Sat) Slovakia's oldest gay club, friendly Apollon has themed nights from disco to karaoke and 'beach parties'.

# ☆ Entertainment

Check **Kam do Mesta** (www.kamdomesta.sk/bratislavsky-kraj) for the latest.

### Slovak National Theatre
THEATRE

(Slovenské Národné Divadlo; SND; ☑02-2047 2299; www.snd.sk; Hviezdoslavovo nám) The national theatre company stages quality operas (Slavic and international), ballets and dramas in two venues: the gilt decoration of the landmark **Historic SND** (☑box office 02-2049 4290; www.snd.sk; Hviezdoslavovo nám, booking office cnr

Jesenského & Komenského; tickets €4-20; ⊘ box-office 8am-7pm Mon-Fri, 9am-noon & 2-7pm Sat & Sun, plus 1hr before performances) is a show in itself; the modern **New SND** (☑ 02-2047 2111; www.snd.sk; Pribinova 17) has a cafe and guaranteed English-speaking reservation line.

**Slovak Philharmonic** THEATRE
(www.filharmonia.sk; Eugena Suchoň nám; tickets €5-20; ⊘ 9am-2pm Mon, 1-6pm Tue-Fri & before performances) Neo-baroque Reduta Palace houses the Slovak Philharmonic. Tickets can be reserved online.

**Dunaj** PERFORMING ARTS
(www.kcdunaj.sk; Nedbalova 3; ⊘ noon-1am Mon-Wed, to 3am Thu, to 4am Fri, 4pm-4am Sat, 4pm-midnight Sun; 🎤) Cultural centre hosting some of Slovakia's most interesting drama and music performances, as well as comedy, club nights, visual arts and the odd literary evening. Something is on almost nightly, plus there is a terrace bar with panoramic old-town views.

# 🛍 Shopping

Find craft and jewellery stores around Hlavné nám, as well as souvenir booths (fancy a brassiere-themed 'Bra-tislava' T-shirt?). Artisan galleries and antique shops inhabit alleyways off old-town streets.

**Úľuv** ARTS & CRAFTS
(Centre for Folk Art Production; www.uluv.sk; Námestie SNP 12; ⊘ 10.30am-6pm Mon-Fri, to 2pm Sat) Shops in Bratislava's old town overflow with mass-produced souvenirs, so Úľuv's handcrafted folk art is a breath of fresh air. This branch of Slovakia's handicraft cooperative is a delightful place to rummage for pottery jugs, framed pieces of lace, and sheep-shaped money banks, painted by hand.

At the time of research, Úľuv's **main branch** (www.uluv.sk; Obchodná 64; ⊘ 10.30am-6pm Mon-Fri, to 2pm Sat) in Bratislava was being renovated but was expected to reopen in the near future.

# ℹ Information

Most cafes have wi-fi access; Hlavné nám and Hviezdoslavovo nám are free wi-fi zones. Bratislava's old town has banks and ATMs, especially along Poštova. The train and bus stations, and airport, have ATMs/exchange booths.

**Main Police Station** (☑ 0961 01 1111, emergency 112, emergency 158; Hrobákova 44) Main police station for foreigners, in Petržalka, about 3.5km south of Most SNP.

**Main Post Office** (Nám SNP 34-35; ⊘ 7am-8pm Mon-Fri, to 6pm Sat) In a beautiful building.

**Poliklinika Ruzinov** (☑ 02-4827 9111; www.ruzinovskapoliklinika.sk; Ružinovská 10) Hospital with emergency services and 24-hour pharmacy, 3km east of the old town.

**Tatra Banka** (Dunajská 4; ⊘ 8am-6pm Mon-Fri) English-speaking staff.

**Tourist Information Centre** (☑ 02-5441 9410; http://visit.bratislava.sk; Klobučnícka 2; ⊘ 9am-7pm Apr-Oct, to 6pm Nov-Mar) Helpful and multilingual official tourist office. Brochures galore, including a small Bratislava guide and maps.

# ℹ Getting There & Away

Bratislava is the main hub for trains, buses and the few planes that head in and out of the country.

## AIR

Keep in mind that Vienna's much busier international airport is only 60km west.

**Bratislava Airport** (BTS; ☑ 02-3303 3353; www.bts.aero; Ivanská cesta) A 15km drive northeast of central Bratislava. Direct flights to Dubai, Germany, Greece, Ireland, Italy, Russia, Spain, UK cities and more.

## BOAT

From April to October, plying the Danube is a cruisey way to get between Bratislava and Vienna.

**Twin City Liner** (☑ 0903 610 716; www.twincityliner.com; Propeller Terminal, Rázusovo nábr) Up to four boats daily to Vienna (one way €20 to €35, 1½ hours). You can also book through the office of **Flora Tours** (☑ 02-5443 5803; www.floratour.sk; Kúpelná 6; ⊘ 9am-5pm Mon-Fri).

## BUS

Direct destinations include cities throughout Slovakia and Europe, but the train is usually comparably priced and more convenient. The **Bratislava bus station** (Mlynské nivy; 🚏 Autobusová stanica, AS) is 1km east of the old town; locals call it 'Mlynské Nivy' (the street name). For schedules, see cp.atlas.sk.

**Eurolines** (☑ Bratislava office 02-5556 2195; www.eurolines.sk; Bratislava bus station, Mlynské Nivy) Contact for most international buses with services to Budapest (€12, three to 3¾ hours, two daily) and Vienna (€5, 1¼ hours, four daily). Less-frequent long-distance services operate to Paris (€75, 18¾ hours) and Venice (€55, 10 hours).

**Slovak Lines** (☑ 02-5542 2734; www.slovaklines.sk; Bratislava bus station, Mlynské Nivy; ⊘ ticket sales 6.30am-6.30pm) Services throughout the country as well as daily buses to Vienna (€5, 1¼ hours, half-hourly), Budapest (€12, three to 3¾ hours, five daily), Prague

**WORTH A TRIP**

## THE VILLAGE TIME FORGOT

The tiny mountain hamlet of **Vlkolínec** (www.vlkolinec.sk; adult/child €2/1; ⊙9am-6pm Mon-Fri, to 7pm Sat & Sun) has an otherworldly atmosphere, somewhere between medieval Europe and a Hobbit village. Vlkolínec, 80km west of Poprad, earned its Unesco listing thanks to 45 traditional buildings. Cottages are painted shades from peach to powder blue, there's an 18th-century timber bell tower, neoclassical Catholic chapel, and dozens of woodcarved sculptures representing village life and folklore.

Vlkolínec opens its doors to visitors but it remains a functioning village (population 19), so don't wander into gardens or photograph through windows.

(€14, 4¼ hours, eight daily) and even occasional services to Clermont-Ferrand in France (€92, 25½ hours).

### TRAIN

Rail is the main way to get around Slovakia and to neighbouring countries. Intercity (IC) and Eurocity (EC) trains are quickest. *Rýclik* (R; 'fast' trains) take slightly longer, but run more frequently and cost less. For schedules see cp.atlas.sk.

Domestic trains run to Poprad (€15, 4½ hours, 12 daily, some with changes) and Košice (€19, 5½ hours, eight daily, more with changes).

International trains run to Vienna (return €17.50; includes Vienna city transport, one hour, hourly), Prague (from €15, 4¼ hours, six daily) and Budapest (from €15, 2¾ hours, six daily).

**Main Train Station** (Hlavná Stanica; www.slovakrail.sk; Franza Liszta nám)

## 🛈 Getting Around

### TO/FROM THE AIRPORT

➡ City bus 61 links Bratislava Airport with the main train station (20 minutes).

➡ Standing taxis (over)charge to town, some as much as an eye-watering €25; ask the price before you get in.

➡ Buses (€5 to €7.50, one hour, 14 daily) connect Vienna International Airport to Bratislava Airport (also stopping at Most SNP); find timetables on www.flixbus.com.

### CAR

Numerous international car-hire companies such as Hertz and Sixt have offices at Bratislava Airport.

**Abrix** (⊡0905 405 405; www.abrix.sk; Pestovateľská 1; ⊙8am-6pm Mon-Fri) Rates around €18 to €25 per day for short hires and as low as €16 for 20 days or more.

### PUBLIC TRANSPORT

Bratislava has an extensive tram, bus and trolleybus network; though the old town is small, so you won't often need it. **Dopravný Podnik Bratislava** (DPB; www.dpb.sk) is the public transport company; you'll find a route map online. Check www.imhd.zoznam.sk for city-wide schedules.

Tickets cost €0.70/0.90/1.20 for 15/30/60 minutes. Buy at machines next to stops and news stands, and always validate on board (or risk a legally enforceable €50 to €70 fine). Passes start at €3.50/8 for 24/72 hours.

**Bus 93** Main train station to Hodžovo nám then Petržalka train station.

**Trolleybus 207** Hodžovo nám to Bratislava Castle.

**Trolleybus 210** Bratislava bus station to main train station.

### TAXI

Standing cabs compulsorily overcharge foreigners; an around-town trip should never cost above €10. To save money ask someone to help you order a taxi (not all operators speak English). Uber operates in Bratislava.

**AA Euro Taxi** (⊡0903 807 022, in Slovakia 02-16 022; www.aataxieuro.sk; minimum fare €3.89, per km €1.45)

# Around Bratislava

If you don't manage at least a half-day trip out of the city, you're doing Bratislava wrong. **Devín Castle** (www.muzeum.bratislava.sk; adult/child €4/2; ⊙10am-6pm Tue-Fri, to 7pm Sat & Sun May-Sep, to 5pm Tue-Sun Apr-Oct), 9km west, has stood since the 9th century. The castle's name originates from the Slavic *deva* (girl), and its Maiden Watchtower has acquired various legends of tragic young ladies across its long history. Wave at Austria, just across the river from the castle. Bus 29 links Devín with Bratislava's Nový Most bus stop, under Most SNP.

Some 15km south of Bratislava is **Danubiana Meulensteen Art Museum** (www.danubiana.sk; Via Danubia, Čunovo; adult/child €10/5; ⊙11am-7pm Tue-Sun May-Sep, 10am-6pm Tue-Sun Oct-Apr), innovatively designed on a spit of land jutting into the Danube. Boat trips run from the city centre on weekends from May to October (return tickets are adult/child €12/8, including the gallery ticket; see www.lod.sk for details). Otherwise take bus 90 (€1.20) from Nový Most bus stop to Čunovo and walk from the terminus (2.5km).

# TATRAS MOUNTAINS

## Poprad

📱 052 / POP 55,000 / ELEV 672M

Gateway to the High Tatras, Poprad is the place to mug up on hiking or skiing information before you head into the wilds. Mountain trails, forests and gorges lie in its surrounds: by road, hike hub Starý Smokovec is 14km north, tranquil lake spot Štrbské Pleso 26km west and Hrabušice (for Slovenský Raj National Park) 15km south.

### ⊙ Sights & Activities

**Spišská Sobota**                             AREA
Renaissance-style merchant houses dating as far back as the 15th century line Spišská Sobota town square, 2km north of Poprad's modern centre, Sv Egídia nám. A 13th-century church and baroque column are planted in the centre, and placards around the square detail each building's links to Hungarian kings and nobles. A worthy ramble.

**Adventoura**                    ADVENTURE SPORTS
(📱 0903 641 549; www.adventoura.eu) Dog sledding, walking and adventure holidays, ski packages...this energetic outfit can arrange the works. Day rates for private trips around the Tatras and its surroundings begin at around €30 per person. Book at least four weeks ahead of your trip, particularly in the busy summer and winter seasons.

**Aqua City**                                   SPA
(📱 052-785 1111; www.aquacity.sk; Športová 1397; day pass adult/child €22/19, 3hr pass adult/child €19/16; ⊙8am-9pm; 🖈) 🪷 Poprad's thermal water park not only has saunas, pools and Mayan-themed outdoor water slides (summer only), it's something of an eco pioneer in Central Europe. Its heat and electricity derive from geothermal and solar sources; knowing this will give you an additional glow as you soak in 30°C to 35°C pools. Book ahead for Thai massage and other treatments.

### 🛏 Sleeping & Eating

**⭐ Penzión Sabato**                         B&B €€
(📱 052-776 9580; www.sabato.sk; Sobotské nám 6; r incl breakfast €60-90; 🅿🛜) Within this peach-coloured mansion, dating to 1730, find eight romantic rooms with billowy drapes, wood-beamed ceilings and handsome Renaissance-era furniture. Each one is different (they're priced by size) and five have fireplaces.

### FOLK CULTURE FRENZY

Soak up the best Slovak folk culture at **Východná Folk Festival** (www.festivalvychodna.sk/en; Východná; ⊙late Jun/early Jul), an extravaganza of music, dance, craft workshops and mountain cuisine. The annual event is one of the largest of its kind in Slovakia, assembling as many as 1400 performers. Expect oversized musical instruments, choirs, wood-chopping, loom demonstrations and more accordions than you've ever seen assembled in one place. Východná is 32km west of Poprad.

**⭐ Vino & Tapas**            INTERNATIONAL €€€
(📱 0918 969 101; Sobotské nám 38; mains €13-15; ⊙5-11pm Tue-Sat) Truffled eggs, delicate ravioli, flower-strewn desserts...Vino & Tapas offers an exceptional dining experience in an atmospheric, brick-walled restaurant. Opt for a set menu with amuse-bouche (€39) to savour the best stuff. Phone ahead as it's rightly popular.

### ⓘ Information

**City Information Centre** (📱 052-16 186; www.visitpoprad.sk; Svätého Egídia nám 86; ⊙8am-8pm Mon-Fri, 9am-1pm Sat year-round, plus 2-5pm Sun Jun-Sep) Helpful, multilingual visitors centre; also sells stamps.

### ⓘ Getting There & Away

#### AIR

**Poprad-Tatry International Airport** (📱 052-776 3875; www.airport-poprad.sk; Na Letisko 100), 4km west of town, has links to London, Moscow, Riga, Kyiv and Antalya. There is no public transport to the airport from Poprad town. **Taxis** (📱 052-772 3623) cost about €4.

#### BUS

Buses serve Levoča (€1.70, 45 minutes, almost hourly), Bardejov (€4.50, 2½ hours, seven daily, more via Prešov) and Zakopane in Poland (€5.50, two hours, two to four daily mid-June to mid-October).

#### CAR

Rates from €22 per day are offered by well-established **Car Rental Poprad** (📱 0903 639 179; http://carrental-poprad.com; Nálepkova 11, Batizovce; ⊙8am-6pm Mon-Fri, to 2pm Sat, other times by arrangement).

## TRAIN

Poprad is accessible by direct train from Bratislava (€15, 4¾ hours, seven daily) and Košice (€5.30, 1¼ to two hours, at least hourly). Buses also reach Poprad from Košice (€6.90, 2½ hours, five daily), with more services via Prešov.

# HIGH TATRAS

☑ 052

The High Tatras (Vysoké Tatry), the tallest range in the Carpathian Mountains, tower over most of Eastern Europe. Some 25 peaks measure above 2500m, but the massif is only 25km wide and 78km long, with pristine snowfields, ultramarine mountain lakes, thundering waterfalls, undulating pine forests and shimmering alpine meadows.

The highest trails are closed because of snow from November to mid-June. June and July can be especially rainy; July and August are the warmest (and most crowded) months.

## 👁 Sights & Activities

The High Tatras hiking routes are colour-coded, and distances for hikes in Slovak national parks are officially given in hours rather than kilometres. Pick up one of numerous maps and hiking guides from bookshops and information offices.

Many hiking routes criss-cross, or form part of, the 65km-long **Tatranská Magistrála**. This mighty trail starts at the base of the Western (Západné) Tatras, but mostly runs beneath the peaks (between 1300m and 1800m) of the High Tatras, with mountain hut stop-offs and cable-car/ski-lift access.

## 👁 Smokovec Resort Towns

If you're looking for an easy access point to half-day hikes, head to **Hrebienok** (1280m), which is connected by funicular railway to Starý Smokovec. East and west from here, the red Tatranská Magistrála Trail transects the southern slopes of the High Tatras for 65km start to finish. Bilíkova Chata (p387), a log-cabin lodge and restaurant, is a short walk from the funicular railway terminus. Heading west, you can hike along the base of Slavkovsky štít to lakeside **Sliezsky dom** hotel (red, two hours), then down a small connector trail to the yellow-marked trail back to Starý Smokovec (four hours total). An easy and well-signposted northbound walk-

---

### ℹ HIKING SAFETY

Park regulations require you to keep to trails and refrain from picking flowers. Be aware that many trails are rocky and uneven, and watch for sudden thunderstorms on ridges where there's no protection. Consider engaging a guide from the **Mountain Guide Society** (☑ 0905 428 170; www.tatraguide.sk; Starý Smokovec 38; ☺ noon-6pm Mon-Fri, to 6pm Sat & Sun, closed weekends Oct-May), whose experts know the range as well as their own knuckles (day rates from €175).

Slovakia's **Mountain Rescue Service** (Horská záchranná služba; ☑ 052-787 7711, emergency 18 300; www.hzs.sk) lists avalanche warnings and weather conditions on its website; be aware that rescue services are not free.

---

ing trail (green) leads from Bilíkova Chata to **Studený potok** waterfalls (Vodopády Studeného Potoka), taking about 30 minutes; 30 additional minutes brings you up to **Zamkovského chata** hut.

This is also a good base for more adventurous trekkers: mountain climbers scale to the top of **Slavkovský štít** (2452m) via the blue trail from Starý Smokovec (eight to nine hours return). To ascend the peaks without marked hiking trails (Gerlachovský štít included), you must hire a guide. Contact the Mountain Guide Society (p386): rates for these experienced mountain guides vary according to the length and difficulty of a hike (or ice climb), starting at €175.

## 👁 Tatranská Lomnica & Around

While in the Tatras, you shouldn't miss the precipitous **Lomnický štít Ascent** (www. vt.sk; return adult/child €46/30; ☺ 8.30am-5.30pm Jul & Aug, to 3.30pm Sep-Jun) (bought as a single ticket). Gondolas rise from Lomnica to **Štart**, where you can change cable cars up to the skiing zone and lake of **Skalnaté pleso**. Another cable car climbs an additional 855m to **Lomnický štít**, a perilous 2634m at its summit. There is a high price tag for these majestic views, though this doesn't deter visitors (arrive early, as tickets sell out on sunny days). Timed tickets allow 50 minutes at the summit, enough to take photos, walk the observation platforms, and grab a drink or snack before returning.

Alternatively, at Skalnaté pleso you can change to a **quadlift** (one way adult/child €19/14, 9am to 4pm) towards **Lomnické sedlo**, a 2190m saddle below the peak of Lomnický štít.

## 👁 Štrbské Pleso & Around

Condo and hotel development continue unabated in the village but the namesake clear-blue glacial lake (*pleso*) remains beautiful. Hire **row boats** (per 40min/1hr €15/25; ⊙10am-6pm May-Sep) outside Grand Hotel Kempinski and bob across Slovakia's most postcard-perfect waters.

## 🛏 Sleeping

Wild camping isn't permitted, but there is a camping ground near Tatranská Lomnica. For the quintessential Slovak mountain experience, you can't beat hiking from one *chata* (mountain hut; anything from a shack to a chalet) to the next, high up among the peaks. Food (optional meal service or restaurant) is always available. Beds fill up, so book ahead.

## 🛏 Smokovec Resort Towns

The main road running through Nový Smokovec to Horný Smokovec is lined with places to stay, ranging from no-frills pensions to spa hotels. Starý Smokovec is most convenient (and popular); it's quieter in the towns on either side. Book far in advance for July and August, and for ski season.

**Bilíkova Chata**  HUT €
(📞0949 579 777; www.bilikovachata.sk; Hrebienok 14; r from €46, without bathroom €28, apt from €80; 🛜) A 300m walk from Hrebienok funicular station, this log cabin is basic but its lofty location compensates (1225m), planting you in the heart of hiking trails. There's a restaurant (open 7am to 8pm) serving filling Slovak fare, and there are big low-season discounts.

**Villa Siesta**  SPA HOTEL €€
(📞052-478 0931; www.villasiesta.com; Nový Smokovec 88; s/d/ste €54/81/103; 🅿🛜) This contemporary mountain villa is a romantic choice, with 18 airy rooms and a spa featuring a silky hot tub and sauna. The restaurant serves light, seasonally driven Slovak cuisine.

**Grand Hotel Starý Smokovec**  HOTEL €€
(📞044-290 1339; www.grandhotel.sk; Starý Smokovec 38; d incl breakfast from €77; 🅿🛜🏊) Starý Smokovec's *grande dame* is this 1904 man-

sion with a mountain backdrop. Staff are eager to please, and the rooms retain art deco stylings (the chic deluxe rooms, from €97, are worth a splurge). The pool and wellness area is leafy and warm-hued, and treatments start from a reasonable €15.

## 🛏 Tatranská Lomnica & Around

Look for private rooms (*privat* or *zimmer frei*), from €15 per person, on the back streets south and east of the train station.

**Zamkovského Chata**  HUT €
(📞0905 554 471, 052-442 2636; www.zamka.sk; per person €19; ⊙year-round) Atmospheric wood chalet at 1475m above sea level, with 23 bunk beds and a restaurant with steaming soups and traditional dumplings. A great hike stop midway between Skalnaté Pleso and Hrebienok (it's an hour's hike from the latter). Breakfast is €5 and half board is a reasonable €13.

**Grandhotel Praha**  HOTEL €€
(📞044-290 1338; www.ghpraha.sk; Tatranská Lomnica; d/ste incl breakfast from €81/131; 🅿🛜🏊) Stepping into this 1905 art nouveau hotel, the indignities of ski-lift queues and mud-spattered hikes melt away. The marble staircase and sparkling chandeliers set the tone. The ample rooms are similarly lavish, with gilt-edged mirrors and burnished wallpaper, and the spa is fragrant with mountain herbs, oils and healing salt lamps.

## 🛏 Štrbské Pleso & Around

⭐ **Grand Hotel Kempinski**  HOTEL €€€
(📞052-326 2222; www.kempinski.com/hightatras; Kupelna 6, Štrbské Pleso; d €180-210, ste from €320; 🅿❄@🛜🏊) Everything you'd expect from this sumptuous hotel chain, with the bonus of dreamy lake views, the Kempinski is Štrbské Pleso's best address. Elegantly furnished rooms have balconies that lean towards lake and spruce forest. Every luxury is here, from a heated indoor pool with chandeliers and mountain views, to the dining room where waiters whisk quinoa risotto and grilled tiger prawns to the tables.

## 🍴 Eating

The resort towns are close enough that it's easy to sleep in one and eat in another. There's at least one grocery store per town.

## ⓘ MULTIRESORT SKI PASSES

Ski areas in Štrbské Pleso, Starý Smokovec and Tatranská Lomnica have joined forces to offer multi-resort lift passes (adult one-/six-day €35/167, child one-/six-day €25/116). They're cheaper outside the late-December to mid-March rush, though snow conditions will be more of a gamble. Small savings are available if you buy online (www. gopass.sk).

## ✗ Smokovec Resort Towns

### Reštaurácia Svišť
SLOVAK €€

(☎0918 195 811; www.kupelens.sk; Nový Smokovec 30; mains €5-17; ⊙11am-10pm) Stuffed pancakes, stuffed chicken breasts, stuffed diners. The food in this log-lined haunt will have you full to bursting; fortunately, its traditional decor is worth lingering in while you recover.

### Pizzeria La Montanara
ITALIAN €€

(Starý Smokovec 22; mains €5-12; ⊙11am-10pm) Pizza, lasagne, tiramisu: the holy trinity of carb-loading satisfies many a hiker at this simple Italian joint. It's above a grocery store at the east end of town.

## ✗ Štrbské Pleso & Around

### ★Koliba Patria
SLOVAK €€

(http://hotelpatria.sk; eastern lakeshore, Štrbské Pleso; mains €8-18; ⊙11.30am-10.30pm) On a pretty lakeshore perch with an outdoor terrace, wood-lined Koliba Patria exceeds expectations with refined (though comforting) takes on Slovak shepherd cuisine. Chilled strawberry soup, chicken salads and hulking portions of smoky pork allow for anything from light refreshment to a pre-hike feast.

## 🍷 Drinking & Nightlife

### Humno Tatry
BAR

(www.humnotatry.sk; Tatranská Lomnica; ⊙11am-11pm Thu, noon-4am Fri & Sat, noon-11pm Sun, closed Mon-Wed) Roll straight from the cable-car station base into this club, diner and cocktail bar, where the sound of clunking ski boots is as loud as the soundtrack within. It's an enormous, wood-beamed temple to après-ski that gets wild at weekends.

### U Vlka
CAFE

(www.kaviarenacajovnauvlka.sk; Cesta Slobody 4d, Starý Smokovec; ⊙9am-9pm) Near Sport 2000 and La Montanara, 'The Wolf' is a ramshackle, hippie-chic hang-out with coffee, snacks and a huge range of teas. Film and cultural events take place in summer; keep an eye on the posters outside.

## ⓘ Information

All three main resort towns have ATMs on the main street.

### EMERGENCY

**Mountain Rescue Service** (☎052-442 2820, emergency 18 300; www.hzs.sk; Starý Smokovec 23) The website has mountain weather forecasts, while avalanche warnings can be checked on www.laviny.sk.

### TOURIST INFORMATION

**High Tatras Tourist Trade Association** (www. tatryinfo.sk) Lists chalets and other hiking accommodation options, and gives an overview of the region.

**T-Ski Travel** (☎052-442 3201; www.slovakia travel.sk; Starý Smokovec 46; ⊙9am-4pm Mon-Thu, to 5pm Fri-Sun) Books lodgings, arranges ski and snowboard instruction, runs mountain-biking programs, and rents wintersports gear.

**Tatras Information Office** (Tatranská informačná kancelária; ☎052-442 3440; www. tatry.sk; Starý Smokovec 23; ⊙8am-6pm Jan-Mar, to 4pm Apr-Dec) Starý Smokovec information office, with helpful English-speaking staff and vast quantities of brochures.

**Tatry.sk** (www.tatry.sk) Official website of Tatra towns, with thorough information on accommodation, outdoor activities and transport.

## ⓘ Getting There & Around

To reach the Tatras by public transport, switch in Poprad. From the main train station there, a narrow-gauge electric train runs up to Starý Smokovec, then makes numerous stops in the resort towns along the main road; buses go to smaller, downhill villages as well. Either way, to get between Štrbské Pleso and Tatranská Lomnica, change in Starý Smokovec. Check schedules at cp.atlas.sk.

### BUS

The main bus routes from Poprad include to Starý Smokovec (€0.90, 20 minutes, hourly), Tatranská Lomnica (€1.30, 30 minutes, hourly), Štrbské Pleso (€1.70, one hour, four daily) and Ždiar (€2, one hour, seven daily, or change in Kežmarok).

## TRAIN

Electric trains (TEŽ) run more or less hourly. Buy individual TEŽ tickets at stations and block tickets at tourist offices. Validate all on board. Bringing bikes on board costs €1.50, large luggage costs €1, but skis and snowboards incur no charge.

Regular trains run from Poprad up to Starý Smokovec (€1.50, 25 minutes). From here reach Tatranská Lomnica (€1,15 minutes) and Štrbské Pleso (€1.50, 40 minutes).

# EAST SLOVAKIA

Welcome to Slovakia's untrammelled east. Freethinking Košice, Slovakia's second-largest city, is the prime reason to visit, with waterfall-kissed Slovenský Raj National Park close behind. Combine these with architectural gems like Levoča and Bardejov, and you have one unforgettable road trip.

## Levoča

☑ 053 / POP 14,800

Levoča's Unesco-listed centre packs centuries of history between its high medieval walls. A Gothic church and fine town hall compete for attention in the main square, Majstra Pavla nám, which is hemmed by burgher mansions with gabled roofs. Presiding over it all is the celestial apparition of the Church of Mariánska Hora, on a hilltop 2km north of town. Take a day trip from Poprad, or stop en route to Spiš Castle, and see what all the fuss is about.

### ◉ Sights

**Majstra Pavla Nám** SQUARE
Gothic and Renaissance eye candy abound on Levoča's main square, including the **Historic Town Hall** (☑ 053-451 2449; Majstra Pavla nám 2; adult/child €4/2; ⊘ 9am-5pm) and private **Thurzov House**, at No 7, with a characteristically frenetic Spiš Renaissance roofline and turn-of-the-20th-century window decorations.

**Church of Mariánska Hora** CHURCH
(☑ 053-451 2347; http://rkc.levoca.sk; Bazilika Panny Márie; ⊘ hours vary, services 2.30pm Sun summer; P) Glowing beatifically from a hill 2km north of Levoča, the Church of Mariánska Hora is Slovakia's most famous Catholic pilgrimage site. For hundreds of years on the first Sunday in July, worshippers from around the country have filed towards this church. You can drive up to the church, or it's a 30-minute hike from town. Just as heavenly as the church itself are the views of Levoča, nestled in the meadowlands beneath.

### ⌂ Sleeping & Eating

**Hotel U Leva** HOTEL €
(☑ 053-450 2311; www.uleva.sk; Majstra Pavla nám 25; s/d/ste incl breakfast €33/43/89; P ⊛) Cutting a dapper silhouette in the main square, Levoča's best hotel is spread across two pyramid-roofed buildings. Rooms are painted in warming sunset shades, with rustic accents in the form of wooden beams. Each room is unique, and most suites have a kitchenette. Book ahead for disability-accessible hotel rooms.

U Leva's fine restaurant (mains €6 to €12) muddles Mediterranean flavours among time-honoured Slovak recipes (like chicken stuffed with cheese and pesto, and broccoli soup with almonds).

### ⓘ Information

Everything you're likely to need, banks and post office included, is on the main square.
**Tourist Information Office** (☑ 053-451 3763; http://eng.levoca.sk; Majstra Pavla nám 58; ⊘ 9am-noon & 12.30-5pm)

### ⓘ Getting There & Away

Levoča is on the main E50 motorway between Poprad (25km) and Košice (90km).

**BUS**
The **bus station** (Železničný riadok 31) is 1km by foot from the main square. Direct services reach Košice (€5, two hours, four daily), Poprad (€2, 45 minutes, every one to two hours), Spišská Nová Ves (€0.90 to €2, up to one hour, half-hourly) and Spišské Podhradie (€1, 30 minutes, one to two per hour).

## Spišské Podhradie

☑ 053 / POP 4000

Spišské Podhradie snoozes contentedly between two Unesco World Heritage sites. Rising above the village is Spiš Castle, the former stomping ground of medieval watchmen and Renaissance nobles. This spellbinding ruin is perched on a rocky ridge, surrounded by verdant meadows, and is likely Slovakia's most-photographed sight. While the castle is unquestionably the main draw, it's worth lingering to see 'Slovakia's Vatican', a Gothic ecclesiastical settlement west of the village.

## ◉ Sights

### ★ Spiš Castle CASTLE

(Spišský hrad; adult/student/child €6/4/3; ⊗9am-6pm May-Sep, to 4pm Apr & Oct, 10am-4pm Nov, closed Dec-Mar) Crowning a travertine hill above Spišské Podhradie village, this vast castle is one of Slovakia's most impressive medieval fortifications. Spiš Castle spreads over 4 hectares, making it one of the largest in Central Europe. Its bulwarks and thick defensive walls date to the 12th century (at the latest), and once housed Hungarian royals and nobles. Highlights are views from the 22m-high tower, and a museum of medieval history within the former palace.

### Spiš Chapter CATHEDRAL

(Spišská kapitula; Levočská cesta) On the west side of Spišské Podhradie is still-active Spiš Chapter, a 13th-century Catholic complex fondly referred to as 'Slovakia's Vatican'. Encircled by a 16th-century wall, its pièce de résistance is St Martin's Cathedral (1273), towering above a huddle of Gothic houses. If you're travelling by bus from Levoča, get off 1km before Spišské Podhradie, at Kapitula.

## ⌂ Sleeping & Eating

This is best experienced as a day trip from the High Tatras or Košice.

### Penzión Podzámok GUESTHOUSE €

(⌨053-454 1755; www.penzionpodzamok.sk; Podzámková 28; s/d from €18/27; P🅿🛜🐾) Simple but snug rooms within a homely (though slightly worn) guesthouse. Ceramics and wall-mounted antlers give a farmhouse feel to the attached restaurant, and the view of Spiš Castle from the yard is spectacular. The pool is open in summer. Breakfast is €4.

### Spišsky Salaš SLOVAK €

(⌨053-454 1202; http://spisskysalas.sk; Levočská cesta 11; mains from €4; ⊗10am-9pm; 🅿👶) An almost mandatory refuelling stop before or after Spiš Castle, this folksy dining room (complete with cow bells) hurries plates of *pirohy* (dumplings), lamb stew and barbecued meat to its wooden tables. There is ample outdoor dining space, overlooking a big play area for kids. Informal, with occasionally chaotic service, but satisfying nonetheless.

Spišsky Salaš is 1km northwest of Spiš Chapter, on a hill overlooking the E50 Hwy towards Levoča.

## ❶ Getting There & Away

Spišské Podhradie is 15km east of Levoča and 78km northwest of Košice.

### BUS

Buses connect with Levoča (€1, 20 to 30 minutes, regular), Poprad (€2.35, one hour, one to two hourly) and Košice (€4.30, 1½ hours, four daily, more via Prešov or Levoča).

### TRAIN

Spišské Podhradie is connected by bus to Spišské Vlachy (€0.90, 15 minutes, 10 daily), which has direct rail links west to Spišská Nová Ves (for Slovenský Raj) and east to Košice.

# Slovenský Raj & Around

📋053
You don't simply visit Slovenský Raj National Park. It's more accurate to say that you clamber, scramble and get thoroughly drenched in this dynamic landscape of caves, canyons and waterfalls. Hikers in 'Slovak Paradise' climb ladders over gushing cascades, trek to ruined monasteries and shiver within an ice cave – and that's just on day one.

The park is hugged by the Low Tatras and the Slovak Ore Mountains, with deep gorges sliced by the Hornád River. The nearest major town is Spišská Nová Ves, 23km southeast of Poprad. Closer to the action are the park's three major trailhead villages, each with food and accommodation options: most popular is Podlesok, outside Hrabušice (a 16km drive southeast of Poprad); pretty and low-key Čingov is 5km west of Spišská Nová Ves; and lakeside Dedinky fringes the park's southern edge.

## ◉ Sights & Activities

Before hiking, pick up VKÚ's 1:25,000 Slovenský Raj hiking map (No 4) or 1:50,000 regional map (No 124). Cycling trails crisscross the park, and swimmers can take a dip in Dedinky. During winter, ski at small resorts like Gugel, which has 5km of pistes and 35km of cross-country trails.

### ★ Slovenský Raj National Park PARK

(www.slovenskyraj.sk; Jul & Aug €1.50, Sep-Jun free) In Slovenský Raj, rocky plateaus, hills and primeval forests are interlaced with thrashing streams and waterfalls. This is some of the most thrilling hiking terrain in Slovakia, and not for the timid: treks usually involve scaling metal ladders or balancing on footbridges over cascades. Aside from the exhilaration of being lashed with crystal water, the rewards are breathtakingly green views. Trails are challenging but well-marked, and multilingual staff at the information centres offer excellent advice.

### Dobšinská Ice Cave
CAVE

(Dobšinská ľadová jaskyňa; www.ssj.sk; adult/child €8/4; ⊙ 9am-4pm Tue-Sun by hourly tour late May-Sep, closed Oct–mid-May) More than 110,000 cubic metres of ice are packed into the gleaming walls of this Unesco-listed ice cave, near the southern edge of Slovenský Raj National Park. Frosty stalagmites and chambers where tendrils of ice sparkle from the ceiling create an otherworldly atmosphere. The departure point is a half-hour walk from the car park, so arrive in good time ahead of guided tours (on the hour).

## 🛏 Sleeping & Eating

Camping grounds and budget guesthouses are good value in these parts, and most are fabulous for families. Many lodgings have restaurants, and there are several eateries and a small grocery store in Podlesok. Spišská Nová Ves has several large supermarkets.

### Autocamping Podlesok
CAMPGROUND €

(☑ 053-429 9165; www.podlesok.sk; per adult/child/tent €4/2.50/3, hut from €50; P 🗟) The office at this well-located camping ground provides substantial trail info. Pitch a tent or choose from fairly up-to-date two to 12-bed huts and cottages with bathrooms. Book huts well in advance.

### ★ Relax Farma Mariánka
GUESTHOUSE €

(☑ 0905 714 583; www.relaxfarmamarianka.sk; Betlanovce 83; d/tr from €28/38; P 🗟 👶) 🖉 The hospitable owners of this big, well-kept eight-room pension can advise you about outdoor activities. Relax in the hot tub, meet the pigs or enjoy Janka's scrumptious organic cooking (breakfast €4). Family-friendly perks include games rooms, a communal kitchen and a sauna (for exhausted parents). From Hrabušice, it's just past the Podlesok turn-off where the road kinks sharp right.

### Reštaurácia Rumanka
SLOVAK €

(☑ 0907 289 262; www.podlesok.com; Podlesok; mains €5-8) Enormously popular Rumanka serves enough varieties of halušky (dumplings) to satisfy ravenous hikers, as well as crispy fried pirohy (stuffed with mushrooms or meat), pork chops, and sheep's cheese in handy takeaway portions (from €0.95).

## ℹ Information

Outside Spišská Nová Ves, guesthouses and camping grounds are an excellent source of information. The park info centre is only open in July and August. Get cash before you arrive in the park; there is an ATM and exchange at Spišská Nová Ves train station.

**Mountain Rescue Service** (☑ 053-429 7902, emergency 183 00; http://his.hzs.sk) For emergencies in the park.

**National Park Information Centre** (www.npslovenskyraj.sk; Hlavná, Hrabušice; ⊙ 7.30am-3pm Mon-Fri, 9.30am-4.30pm Sat & Sun Jul & Aug, closed Sep-Jun) Friendly staff can advise on activities and hiking trails.

## ℹ Getting There & Around

During low season especially, you may consider hiring a car in Košice; connections to the park can be a chore. You'll have to transfer at least once, usually in Spišská Nová Ves.

### BUS

Buses are most frequent in July and August, and services thin out on weekends. Carefully check schedules at cp.atlas.sk.

Buses run from Slovenský Raj's transport hub of Spišská Nová Ves to Poprad (€1.70, 45 minutes, at least hourly Monday to Friday and every one to two hours Saturday and Sunday), sometimes with a change in Spišský Štvrtok. Other buses run from Spišská Nová Ves to Levoča (€0.90 to €2, 30 minutes, hourly) and Čingov (€0.60, 15 minutes, four daily), and there are bus connections to Hrabušice (for Podlesok; €1.10, 30 minutes, six daily) and Dedinky (€2.60, 80 minutes, four daily or change in Poprad).

### TRAIN

Trains run from Spišská Nová Ves to Poprad (€1.55, 20 minutes, at least hourly) and Košice (€4, one hour, every one to two hours).

# Košice

☑ 055 / POP 242,000

Equal parts pretty and gritty, Košice lures you with its dazzling historic core but holds your interest with free-spirited nightlife. The pride of Eastern Slovakia's largest city is Hlavná, the central square with the country's largest concentration of historic monuments. Since its tenure as European Capital of Culture 2013, Košice has grown increasingly confident. The cultural scene continues to bloom in unconventional ways: offbeat bars, Soviet city tours and vegan dining share the limelight with well-established draws like the showstopping Gothic cathedral, philharmonic orchestra and, yes, ice hockey.

## ◉ Sights & Activities

### ★ Cathedral of St Elizabeth CHURCH
(Dóm Sv Alžbety; Hlavné nám; tower adult/child €1.50/1; ⏰1-4pm Mon, 9.30am-4.30pm Tue-Sat) This 14th-century cathedral dominates the main square, resplendent with elaborate tracery, prickly turrets and colourful roof tiles. One of Europe's easternmost Gothic cathedrals, 60m-long St Elizabeth is the largest in the country. Ascend the narrow, circular stone steps up the church's 59m-tall tower for city views.

### Hlavné Nám SQUARE
Much of Košice's finery is assembled along Hlavná, a long plaza lined with floral gardens, and flanked with cafes on either side. Stroll past the central musical fountain to hear its hourly chimes, across from the 1899 State Theatre (Štátne divadlo Košice; ☎055-245 2269; Hlavné nám 58). Look for the turn-of-the-20th-century, art nouveau Hotel Slávia at No 63. The 1779 Shire Hall (Župný Dom; Hlavné nám 27), crowned with a coat of arms, is today home to the East Slovak Gallery (☎055-681 7511; www.vsg.sk; Hlavná 27; adult/child full admission €5/3, special exhibitions €2/1; ⏰10am-6pm Tue-Sun).

### Hrnčiarska HISTORIC SITE
(Ulička Remesiel; Hrnčiarska) FREE Arts and crafts workshops line quaint Hrnčiarska, such as herbalists, potters and purveyors of precious stones, whose methods haven't changed in 200 years. Some buildings along this cobbled lane have traditional crafts demonstrations, others house arty coffee shops.

### ★ Authentic Košice CULTURAL
(☎0908 808 848, 0905 848 750; http://authentic kosice.com; per person 2hr tour €23-35, 4hr tour €32-49) Let locals lead you to Košice's less discovered corners. These witty and intriguing tours take in Soviet landmarks, concrete housing estates, factories, breweries and sites of intrigue, usually in a retro Czechoslovak car like a Škoda. Nostalgic snacks are included. Prices depend on group size.

## 🛏 Sleeping

### Košice Hostel HOSTEL €
(☎055-633 5192, 0907 933 462; www.kosice hostel.sk; Jesenského 20; dm €11-13, s/d €22/28; P@🛜) This well-run hostel has clean, airy dorm rooms, a couch-filled common room, shared kitchen and backpacker essentials, like lockers and 24-hour reception.

### ★ Hotel Bankov HISTORIC HOTEL €€
(☎ext 4 055-632 4522; www.hotelbankov.sk; Dolný Bankov 2; s/d incl breakfast from €59/74; P✳🛜✴) Effortlessly uniting 19th-century elegance with modern luxuries, Slovakia's oldest hotel (1869) lies 4km northwest of central Košice in a verdant location. Rooms ooze old-world charm (beams, period furniture), and there's an excellent restaurant serving upmarket European fare (pork with figs, oyster mushroom risotto). The wellness centre has an elemental feel, thanks to saunas and treatment chambers lined in stone and wood.

## 🍴 Eating

### ★ Republika Východu INTERNATIONAL, CAFE €
(www.republikavychodu.sk; Hlavná 31; mains €5-8; ⏰8am-11pm Mon-Thu, to midnight Fri & Sat, to 10pm Sun; 🛜🍴♿) Proudly proclaiming independence from Western Slovakia and indeed anywhere else, Republika Východu (Republic of the East) tempts you with coffees, cakes, health-boosting quinoa salads, avocado on toast and zesty smoothies. The cafe is lined with bookshelves, there's a children's game area, and friendly service welcomes regulars and tourists alike.

### Med Malina POLISH, SLOVAK €€
(☎055-622 0397; www.medmalina.sk; Hlavná 81; mains €6-14; ⏰11am-11pm Mon-Sat, to 10pm Sun; 🍴) Dumplings with sheep's cheese, duck with potato pancakes, and *bigos* (cabbage and mushroom stew, flavoured with sausage meat): a medley of Polish and Slovak specialities are served with cheer in a simple but homely setting. Worth reserving on weekends.

### Karczma Mlyn SLOVAK €€
(☎055-622 0547; www.karczmamlyn.sk; Hlavná 86; mains €7-10; ⏰11am-11pm Mon-Thu, to midnight Fri & Sat, 11.30am-10pm Sun; 🛜) Like dining inside the prettiest of barns, sheepskin rugs and cartwheels surround you, while you settle in on a tree-trunk stool for Goral (mountain) cuisine: plates of buckwheat dumplings with curd cheese, pork steaks and raw cakes. Traditional live music on Friday nights.

SLOVAKIA KOŠICE

#  Drinking & Entertainment

Nightlife options range from sidewalk cafes and boho wine bars along the main square to beer halls and nightclubs. Browse entertainment listings on www.kamdomesta.sk/kosice.

### Retro Cult Club                    CLUB
(http://retro.cultclub.sk; Kováčska 49; ⊙9pm-2am Mon-Sat, sometimes to 4am) Dance and drink under neon lights and sparkling disco balls at this cocktail bar and club, whose events roam from local DJs to student nights.

### Jazz Club                         CLUB
(www.jazzclub-ke.sk; Kováčska 39; ⊙bar 11.30am-midnight Mon-Fri, 6pm-midnight Sat & Sun, club 9am-4am Tue & Wed-Sat) Part cafe-bar, part nightclub, Jazz Club has something to suit most revellers. It's an appealing mix of medieval-style arches, steampunk brass and wood decor and bright lights. A youthful crowd totters along to student nights and dance parties, or you can stick to the charismatic bar and terrace.

### State Philharmonic Košice   CLASSICAL MUSIC
(Štátna filharmónia Košice, House of the Arts; ☑ ticket office 055-622 0763; www.sfk.sk; Moyzesova 66; ⊙2-4pm Mon, to 5pm Tue-Thu, plus 1hr before concerts) Jazz, choral and orchestral music fill this concert hall on evenings around the year. Check the events calendar online, or time your Košice trip for the **Spring Music Festival** (www.filharmonia.sk; ⊙mid-Apr) to enjoy a wealth of musical performances.

## ℹ Information

Most hotels, cafes and restaurants have free wi-fi. Lots of banks with ATMs are scattered around Hlavné nám.

**City Information Centre** (☑ 055-625 8888; www.visitkosice.eu; Hlavná 59; ⊙10am-6pm Mon-Fri, to 3pm Sat & Sun) Offers excellent local advice, and can arrange accommodation, themed city tours (including Jewish history) and more.

**Ľudová Banka** (Mlynská 29)

**Nemocnica Košice-Šaca** (☑ 055-723 4111; www.nemocnicasaca.sk; Lúčna 9, Košice-Šaca) Private healthcare, 12km southwest of central Košice.

**Police Station** (☑158; Pribinova 6)

## ℹ Getting There & Away

Check bus and train schedules at www.cp.atlas.sk.

### AIR
**Košice International Airport** (KSC; www.airportkosice.sk; Košice-Barca) is 7km southwest of the city centre by road; bus 23 connects them hourly.

### BUS
Buses reach Levoča (€5, two hours, 12 to 14 daily), with many routes requiring a change in Prešov. For Poprad, you'll usually need to switch buses in Prešov or Zvolen. Book ahead for Ukraine-bound buses through **Eurobus** (☑ 055-680 7306; www.eurobus.sk; Staničné nám 9); services reach Uzhhorod (€7, three hours, twice daily). Getting to Poland is easier from Poprad.

### CAR
Several international car-hire companies such as Avis and Eurocar have representatives at the airport.
**Buchbinder** (☑ 055-683 2397, 0911 582 200; www.buchbinder.sk; Košice International Airport; ⊙8am-4.30pm Mon-Fri)

### TRAIN
Trains from Košice run to Bratislava (€19, five to seven hours, every 1½ hours), Poprad in the High Tatras (€5, 1¼ to two hours, hourly) and Spišská Nová Ves for Slovenský Raj (€3 to €4, one hour, hourly). There are also trains over the border to Miskolc, Hungary (€7, 1½ hours, one to two daily) continuing to Budapest (€15, 3½ hours).

## ℹ Getting Around

The old town is small and walkable. Transport tickets (30-/60-minute ticket €0.60/0.70) cover most buses and trams; buy them at news stands and machines and validate as soon as you board. Bus 23 runs between the airport and train station; buy tickets on board for €1.

# SURVIVAL GUIDE

## ℹ Directory A–Z

### ACCOMMODATION
Advance booking is advisable in July and August, and in mountain areas during ski season (mid-December through to mid-March). Bratislava has the country's best choice of accommodation, including excellent hostels, though centrally located hotel hargains are hard to find; check out **Bratislava Hotels** (www.bratislavahotels.com). Outside the capital, you'll find plenty of reasonable *penzióny* (guesthouses). Breakfast is usually available (often included) at all lodgings and wi-fi is near ubiquitous. Many lodgings offer nonsmoking rooms. Parking is only a problem in Bratislava.

## COUNTRY FACTS

**Area** 49,035 sq km

**Capital** Bratislava

**Country Code** ☑ 00421

**Currency** euro (€)

**Emergency** ☑ 112 (general), ☑ 150 (fire), ☑ 155 (ambulance), ☑ 158 (police)

**Language** Slovak

**Money** ATMs widely available in cities

**Population** 5.45 million

**Visas** Not required for most visitors staying less than 90 days

### INTERNET ACCESS

Wi-fi is widely available at lodgings and cafes across the country; so much so that internet cafes are becoming scarce. For the laptopless, some hotels (especially four-stars) have computers guests can use.

### MONEY

➡ In January 2009 Slovakia's legal tender became the euro. Previously, it was the Slovak crown, or Slovenská koruna (Sk).

➡ Slovaks don't tip consistently, but rounding off the bill or leaving an extra 10% is becoming increasingly common (and is often expected of foreign tourists).

### POST

For outgoing mail, bank on five working days to reach other parts of Europe and seven for the US/Australia. Post offices are found across Slovakia, including the main post office (p383) in Bratislava.

### TELEPHONE

Landline numbers can have either seven or eight digits. Mobile phone numbers (10 digits) are often used for businesses; they start with 09. When dialling from abroad, you need to drop the zero from both city area codes and mobile phone numbers. Purchase local and international phonecards at newsagents. Dial ☑ 00 to call out of Slovakia.

#### Mobile Phones

Slovakia has very good network coverage and you only need to bring a passport to buy a local SIM card. Major providers include Orange, T-Mobile and O2.

### TOURIST INFORMATION

**Association of Information Centres of Slovakia** (AICES; ☑ 044-551 4541; www.aices.sk) Runs an extensive network of city information centres.

**Slovak Tourist Board** (http://slovakia.travel/en) The country's overarching tourist resource is online.

### VISAS

For a full list of visa requirements, see www.mzv.sk (under 'Consular Info').

➡ No visa is required for EU citizens.

➡ Visitors from Australia, New Zealand, Canada, Japan and the US do not need a visa for up to 90 days.

➡ Visas are required for South African nationals, among others. For the full list see www.slovak-republic.org/visa-embassies.

## ⓘ Getting There & Away

Bratislava and Košice are the country's main entry and exit points by air, road and rail. Poprad is in distant third place. Entering Slovakia from the EU is a breeze. Lengthy customs checks make arriving from Ukraine more tedious.

Bratislava has the most international flights, and well-connected Vienna International Airport is just 60km away. By train from Bratislava, Budapest (2¾ hours) and Prague (4¼ hours) are easily reachable, as is Vienna (one hour). Buses connect to Uzhhorod in Ukraine (three hours) from Košice.

### AIR

Bratislava Airport (p383), 9km northeast of the city centre, has direct flights to Dubai, Ireland, Italy, Germany, Greece, Russia, Spain, UK cities and more. Dedicated buses run between Bratislava and **Vienna International Airport** (VIE; ☑ 01-700 722 233; www.viennaairport.com; ☎) in Austria, the nearest big international air hub. A few international routes reach Košice and Poprad.

#### Airports

**Bratislava Airport** (p383)

**Košice International Airport** (p393)

**Poprad-Tatry International Airport** (p385)

#### Airlines

**Austrian Airlines** (www.austrian.com) Connects Košice with Vienna.

**Czech Airlines** (www.csa.cz) Flies between Košice, Bratislava and Prague.

**LOT** (www.lot.com) Flies between Warsaw and Košice.

### SLEEPING PRICE RANGES

The following price ranges refer to a double room with bathroom.

**€** less than €60

**€€** €60–€130

**€€€** more than €130

**Ryanair** (www.ryanair.com) Connects Bratislava with numerous destinations across the UK and Italy, coastal Spain, Dublin, Paris and Brussels.

**Wizz Air** (http://wizzair.com) Connects Košice to a few UK airports, and Poprad to London Luton.

### LAND

Border posts between Slovakia and fellow EU Schengen member states – Czech Republic, Hungary, Poland and Austria – are almost nonexistent. Checks at the Ukrainian border are much more stringent, as you will be entering the EU. By bus or car, expect at least one to two hours' wait.

### Bus

Local buses connect Poprad with Poland during the summer season. Eurolines (p383) and Košice-based Eurobus (p393) handle international routes across Europe from Bratislava and heading east to Ukraine from Košice.

### Car & Motorcycle

Private vehicle requirements for driving in Slovakia are vehicle registration papers, proof of third-party liability insurance and a nationality sticker. Vehicles must carry a first-aid kit, reflective jacket and warning triangle, and a toll sticker for highways.

### Train

See www.cp.atlas.sk for domestic and international train schedules. Direct trains connect Bratislava to Austria, the Czech Republic, Poland, Hungary and Russia; from Košice, trains connect to the Czech Republic, Poland, Ukraine and Russia.

### RIVER

Danube riverboats offer an alternative way to get between Bratislava and Vienna.

## ⓘ Getting Around

### AIR

Czech Airlines (www.csa.cz) offers the only domestic air service, between Bratislava and Košice.

### BICYCLE

Roads can be narrow and potholed, and in towns cobblestones and tram tracks can prove dangerous for bike riders. Bike rental outfits aren't very common. Charges apply for bringing bikes aboard trains.

---

### EATING PRICE RANGES

The following price ranges refer to a main course.

**€** less than €7

**€€** €7–€12

**€€€** more than €12

---

## ESSENTIAL FOOD & DRINK

**Sheep's cheese** Sample *bryndza* (tangy, soft and spreadable) and *oštiepok* (salty and chewy), or sip *žinčina*, a traditional sheep's-whey drink (like sour milk).

**Soups** Slurp *vývar* (chicken/beef broth served with *sližiky*, thin pasta strips, or liver dumplings) or *kapustnica* (thick sauerkraut and meat soup, often with ham or mushrooms).

**Dumplings** Varieties include *halušky* (mini-dumplings in cabbage or *bryndza* sauce topped with bacon) or *pirohy* (pocket-shaped dumplings stuffed with *bryndza* or smoked meat).

**Fruity firewater** Liquor made from berries and pitted fruits, such as *borovička* (from juniper) and *slivovica* (from plums).

### BUS

Read timetables carefully; different schedules apply for weekends and holidays. Find up-to-date schedules online at cp.atlas.sk.

### CAR & MOTORCYCLE

➜ Driving with a blood alcohol level above zero is an offence. If fined for a traffic offence, ask for a receipt.

➜ Toll stickers are required on *all* green-signed motorways. Buy at petrol stations or border crossings (per 10 days/month €10/14). Rental cars usually have them.

➜ City streetside parking restrictions are eagerly enforced. In some places you can pay by SMS (Slovak SIM cards only).

➜ Headlights stay on permanently and drivers must respect pedestrian priority at crossings.

➜ Winter tyres or snow chains are compulsory in some snowy destinations.

➜ Car hire is easily available in Bratislava, Košice and Poprad.

### LOCAL TRANSPORT

Towns all have efficient bus systems; most villages have surprisingly good services. Bratislava and Košice have trams and trolleybuses; the High Tatras also has an efficient electric railway.

➜ Public transport generally operates from 5am to 10.30pm (4.30am to 11pm in Bratislava).

➜ City transport tickets are good for all local buses, trams and trolleybuses. Buy at news stands and validate on board or risk serious fines.

# Slovenia

## Why Go?

It's a pint-sized place, with a surface area of just over 20,000 sq km, and two million people. But 'good things come in small packages', and never was that old chestnut more appropriate than in describing Slovenia. The country has everything – from beaches, snowcapped mountains, hills awash in grape vines and wide plains blanketed in sunflowers to Gothic churches, baroque palaces and art-nouveau buildings. Its incredible mixture of climates brings warm Mediterranean breezes up to the foothills of the Alps, where it can snow in summer.

The capital, Ljubljana, is a culturally rich city that values liveability and sustainability over unfettered growth. This sensitivity towards the environment also extends to rural and lesser-developed parts of the country.

## Best Places to Eat

➡ Druga Violina (p399)

➡ Prince of Orange (p399)

➡ Cantina Klet (p410)

➡ Restaurant Proteus (p408)

➡ Štrud'l (p406)

## Best Places to Stay

➡ Hostel Vrba (p399)

➡ Adora Hotel (p399)

➡ Rustic House 13 (p406)

➡ Old Parish House (p404)

➡ Hostel Soča Rocks (p407)

## When to Go
### Ljubljana

**Apr–Jun** A great time to be in the lowlands and the flower-carpeted valleys of the Julian Alps.

**Sep** This is the month made for everything – still warm enough to swim and tailor-made for hiking.

**Dec–Mar** Everyone (and their grandma) dons their skis in this winter-sport-mad country.

## Slovenia Highlights

**❶ Ljubljana Castle** (p398) Enjoying a 'flight' on the funicular up to this spectacular hilltop castle.

**❷ National & University Library** (p398) Considering the genius of architect Jože Plečnik at Ljubljana's historic library.

**❸ Lake Bled** (p403) Gazing at the natural perfection of this crystal green lake.

**❹ Škocjan Caves** (p408) Gawking in awe at the 100m-high walls of this incredible cave system.

**❺ Mt Triglav** (p407) Climbing to the top of the country's tallest mountain.

**❻ Piran** (p409) Getting lost wandering the narrow Venetian alleyways of this seaside town.

# LJUBLJANA

♪ 01 / POP 278,800

Slovenia's capital and largest city also happens to be one of Europe's most liveable capitals. Car traffic is restricted in the centre, leaving the leafy banks of the emerald-green Ljubljanica River, which flows through the city's heart, free for pedestrians and cyclists. In summer, cafes set up terrace seating along the river, lending the feel of a perpet-

ual street party. Slovenia's master of early-Modern, minimalist design, Jože Plečnik, graced Ljubljana with beautiful bridges and buildings. The museums, hotels and restaurants are among the best in the country.

## ☉ Sights

The easiest way to see Ljubljana is on foot. The oldest part of town, with the most important historical buildings and sights (including

Ljubljana Castle), lies on the right (east) bank of the Ljubljanica River. Center, which has the lion's share of the city's museums and galleries, is on the left (west) side of the river.

### ★ Ljubljana Castle                    CASTLE
(Ljubljanski Grad; ☏ 01-306 42 93; www.ljubljanskigrad.si; Grajska Planota 1; adult/child incl funicular & castle attractions €10/7, castle attractions only €7.50/5.20; ⊙ castle 9am-11pm Jun-Sep, to 9pm Apr, May & Oct, 10am-8pm Jan-Mar & Nov, to 10pm Dec) Crowning a 375m-high hill east of the Old Town, the castle is an architectural mishmash, but most of it dates to the early 16th century when it was largely rebuilt after a devastating earthquake. It's free to ramble around the castle grounds, but you'll have to pay to enter the Watchtower, the Chapel of St George, to see the worthwhile Exhibition on Slovenian History, visit the new Puppet Theatre and take the Time Machine tour.

### ★ National & University Library        ARCHITECTURE
(Narodna in Univerzitetna Knjižnica (NUK); ☏ 01-200 11 10; www.nuk.uni-lj.si; Turjaška ulica 1; ⊙ 8am-8pm Mon-Fri, 9am-2pm Sat) This library is Jože Plečnik's masterpiece, completed in 1941. To appreciate this great man's philosophy, enter through the main door (note the horse-head doorknobs) on Turjaška ulica – you'll find yourself in near darkness, entombed in black marble. As you ascend the steps, you'll emerge into a colonnade suffused with light – the light of knowledge, according to the architect's plans.

### ★ Central Market                       MARKET
(Centralna Tržnica; Vodnikov trg; ⊙ open-air market 6am-6pm Mon-Fri, 6am-4pm Sat summer, 6am-4pm Mon-Sat winter) Central Market is Ljubljana's larder and worth a trip both to stock up on provisions or just have a good snoop (and sniff) around. Go first to the vast open-air market (Tržnica na Prostem) just across the Triple Bridge to the southeast of Prešernov trg on Vodnikov trg. Here you'll find a daily farmers market (except Sunday). In the next neighbouring square – Pogačarjev trg – there are always stalls selling everything from foraged wild mushrooms and forest berries to honey and homemade cheeses.

### City Museum of Ljubljana              MUSEUM
(Mestni Muzej Ljubljana; ☏ 01-241 25 00; www.mgml.si; Gosposka ulica 15; adult/child €4/2.50, special exhibits €6/4; ⊙ 10am-6pm Tue, Wed & Fri-Sun, to 9pm Thu) The excellent city museum established in 1935 focuses on Ljubljana's history, culture and politics via imaginative multimedia and interactive displays. The reconstructed street that once linked the eastern gates of the Roman colony of Emona (today's Ljubljana) to the Ljubljanica River and the collection of well-preserved classical artefacts in the basement treasury are worth a visit in themselves. So too are the models of buildings that the celebrated architect Jože Plečnik never got around to erecting.

### National Museum of Slovenia           MUSEUM
(Narodni Muzej Slovenije; ☏ 01-241 44 00; www.nms.si; Prešernova cesta 20; adult/student €6/4, with National Museum of Slovenia Metelkova or Slovenian Museum of Natural History €8.50/6, 1st Sun of month free; ⊙ 10am-6pm Fri-Wed, to 8pm Thu) Housed in a building dating from 1888, highlights at this museum include a highly embossed Vače situla, a Celtic pail from the late 6th century BC unearthed in a town east of Ljubljana, and a Stone Age bone flute discovered near Cerkno in western Slovenia in 1995. There are also examples of Roman glass and jewellery found in 6th-century Slavic graves as well as a huge glass-enclosed Roman lapidarium outside to the north.

---

## SLOVENIA ITINERARIES

### Three Days
Spend a couple of days in **Ljubljana**, then head north to unwind in romantic **Bled** or **Bohinj** beside idyllic mountain lakes. Alternatively, head south to visit the caves at **Škocjan** or **Postojna**.

### One Week
A full week will allow you to see the country's top highlights. After two days in the capital, head for Bled and Bohinj. Depending on the season, take a bus or drive over the hair-raising **Vršič Pass** into the valley of the vivid-blue **Soča River** and take part in some adventure sports in **Bovec**. Continue south to the caves at Škocjan and Postojna and then to the sparkling Venetian port of **Piran** on the Adriatic.

# 🛏 Sleeping

Accommodation prices in Ljubljana are the highest in the country. **Ljubljana Tourist Information Centre (TIC)** (www.visitljubljana.com) maintains a list of hotels and sleeping options, including private rooms (single/double/triple from €30/50/75). A few are in the centre, but most require a bus trip.

### ⭐ Hostel Vrba HOSTEL €
(☎064 133 555; www.hostelvrba.si; Gradaška ulica 10; dm €13-22, d €40; @🖙) Probably our favourite new budget accommodation in Ljubljana, this nine-room hostel on the Gradiščica Canal is just opposite the bars and restaurants of delightful Trnovo. There are three doubles, dorms with four to eight beds, hardwood floors and always a warm welcome. Free bikes, too, in summer.

### ⭐ Hostel Tresor HOSTEL €€
(☎01-200 90 60; www.hostel-tresor.si; Čopova ulica 38; dm €15-24, s/d €40/70; ❄@🖙) This new 28-room hostel in the heart of Center is housed in a Secessionist-style former bank, and the money theme continues right into rooms named after currencies and financial aphorisms on the walls. Dorms have between four and 12 beds but are spacious. The communal areas (we love the atrium) are stunning; breakfast is in the vaults.

### ⭐ Adora Hotel HOTEL €€
(☎082 057 240; www.adorahotel.si; Rožna ulica 7; s €85-125, d €170-250, apt €85-155; P❄@🖙) This small hotel below Gornji trg is a welcome addition to accommodation in the Old Town. The 10 rooms are small but fully equipped, with lovely hardwood floors and tasteful furnishings. The lovely breakfast room looks out onto a small garden, bikes are free for guests' use and the staff are overwhelmingly friendly and helpful.

### ⭐ Vander Urbani Resort BOUTIQUE HOTEL €€€
(☎01-200 90 00; www.vanderhotel.com; Krojaška ulica 6; r €120-207; ❄@🖙🏊) This stunning new boutique hotel in the heart of Ljubljana's Old Town was formed from four 17th-century buildings. But history stops there, for this hostelry – with 16 rooms over three floors – is as modern as tomorrow. Designed by the trendsetting Sadar Vuga architectural firm, the rooms are not huge but each is unique and makes use of natural materials.

### ⭐ Antiq Palace Hotel & Spa BOUTIQUE HOTEL €€€
(☎083 896 700, 040 638 163; www.antiqpalace.com; Gosposka ulica 10; s/d €180/210; ❄@🖙) The city's most luxurious sleeping option, the Antiq Palace occupies a 16th-century townhouse, about a block from the river. Accommodation is in 21 individually designed rooms and suites, some stretching to 250 sq metres in size and with jacuzzi. Many retain their original features (hardwood floors, floor-to-ceiling windows) and are furnished in an eclectic manner with quirky rococo touches.

# 🍴 Eating

Ljubljana has Slovenia's best selection of restaurants; even the more expensive restaurants usually offer an excellent value three-course *dnevno kosilo* (set lunch) for under €10.

### ⭐ Prince of Orange ITALIAN €
(☎083 802 447; Komenskega ulica 30; dishes €4.50-9; ⊗7.30am-9.30pm Mon-Fri) This true find – a bright and airy cafe just above Trubarjeva cesta – serves outstanding shop-made soups and bruschetta. Ask for some of the farmer's goat cheese and about the link between the cafe and England's King William III (the pub sign on the wall is a clue).

### ⭐ Druga Violina SLOVENIAN €
(☎082 052 506; Stari trg 21; mains €4.50-10; ⊗8am-midnight) Just opposite the Academy of Music, the 'Second Fiddle' is an extremely pleasant and affordable place for a meal in the Old Town. There are lots of very Slovenian dishes like *ajdova kaša z jurčki* (buckwheat groats with ceps) and *obara* (a thick stew of chicken and vegetables) on the menu. It's a social enterprise designed to help those with disabilities.

### ⭐ Taverna Tatjana SEAFOOD €€
(☎01-421 00 87; www.taverna-tatjana.si; Gornji trg 38; mains €9-25; ⊗5pm-midnight Mon-Sat) This charming little tavern bordering Old Town specialises in fish and seafood (though there's beef and foal on the menu too). Housed in several vaulted rooms of an atmospheric old townhouse with wooden ceiling beams, the fish is fresher than a spring shower. Go for something you wouldn't normally find elsewhere like *brodet* (Croatian fish stew with polenta) or cuttlefish black risotto.

# Ljubljana

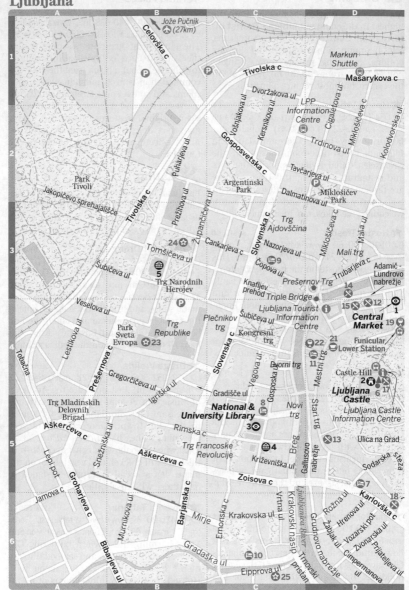

**SLOVENIA** LJUBLJANA

★**Strelec**　　　　　　SLOVENIAN €€€
(Archer; ☎031 687 648; www.kaval-group.si/
strelec.asp; Grajska Planota 1; mains €12-28;
⊗noon-10pm Mon-Sat) This is haute cuisine
from on high – Ljubljana Castle's Archer's
Tower, no less – with a menu that traces the
city's history chosen by ethnologist Janez
Bogataj and prepared by Igor Jagodic, recognised as one of the top chefs in Slovenia.
Tasting menus are priced from €32 to €77
for between three and nine courses.

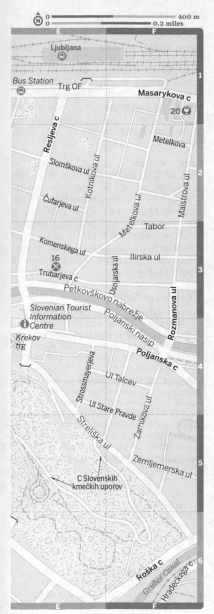

## 🍷 Drinking & Nightlife

Ljubljana offers a dizzying array of drinking options, whether your tipple is beer, wine and spirits, or tea and coffee.

### ★ Pritličje
CAFE

(Ground Floor; ☎040 204 693; www.pritlicje.si; Mestni trg 2; ☯9am-1am Sun-Wed, to 3am Thu-Sat) Ultra-inclusive cultural centre 'Ground Floor' offers something for everyone: cafe, bar, live music, cultural centre and comic-book shop, and is one of the very few LGBT-friendly places in town. Events are scheduled almost nightly and the location next to the Town Hall, with good views across Mestni trg, couldn't be more perfect.

### ★ Slovenska Hiša
COCKTAIL BAR

(Slovenian House; ☎083 899 811; www.slovenska-hisa.si; Cankarjevo nabrežje 13; ☯8am-1am Sun-

## Self-Catering

**Covered Market**
MARKET €

(Pokrita Tržnica; Dolničarjeva ulica; ☯7am-4pm Mon-Fri, 7am-2pm Sat) The covered part of central market sells meats and cheeses.

Thu, to 3am Fri & Sat) Our favourite new boozer along the river is so cute it's almost twee. Sourcing only Slovenian products makes the cocktails that much more inventive (gin – yes, tonic – no), meat and cheese plates (€4 to €7) are worthy blotter, and should you want cigarettes, you must buy from a Kompas 'Duty-Free Shop', as they're not made in Slovenia.

★ **Klub Daktari**                                  BAR
(📞 059 055 538; www.daktari.si; Krekov trg 7; ⊗ 8am-1am Mon-Sat, 9am-midnight Sun) This rabbit warren of a watering hole at the foot of the funicular to Ljubljana Castle is so chilled there's practically frost on the windows. The decor is retro-distressed, with shelves full of old books and a player piano in the corner. More of a cultural centre than club, Daktari hosts live music sets and an eclectic mix of other cultural events.

## ☆ Entertainment

Buy tickets for shows and events at the venue's box office, online through **Eventim** (📞 430 24 05; http://www.eventim.si/en/), or at the Ljubljana Tourist Information Centre. Expect to pay €10 to €20 for tickets to live acts.

★ **Sax Pub**                                        JAZZ
(📞 040 168 804; www.saxhostelljubljana.com/sax-pub.html; Eiprova ulica 7; ⊗ 8am-1am Mon-Fri, 9am-1am Sat & Sun) More than a quarter-century in Trnovo and decorated with colourful murals and graffiti outside, the tiny and convivial Sax has live jazz as well as blues,

folk and hip-hop at 8pm on Thursday year-round. Canned stuff rules at other times.

**Opera Ballet Ljubljana**                        OPERA
(📞 01-241 59 00, box office 01-241 59 59; www.opera.si; Župančičeva ulica 1; ⊗ box office 10am-1pm & 2-6pm Mon-Fri, 10am-1pm Sat, 1hr before performance) Home to the Slovenian National Opera and Ballet companies, this historic neo-Renaissance theatre has been restored to its former glory in recent years. Enter from Cankarjeva cesta.

**Cankarjev Dom**                        CLASSICAL MUSIC
(📞 01-241 71 00, box office 01-241 72 99; www.cd-cc.si; Prešernova cesta 10; ⊗ box office 11am-1pm & 3-8pm Mon-Fri, 11am-1pm Sat, 1hr before performance) Ljubljana's premier cultural and conference centre has two large auditoriums (the Gallus Hall is said to have perfect acoustics) and a dozen smaller performance spaces offering a remarkable smorgasbord of performance arts.

## ❶ Information

There are ATMs at every turn, including several outside the main Ljubljana Tourist Information Centre office. At the train station you'll find a **bureau de change** (📞 01-432 10 14; ⊗ 8am-8pm) changing cash for no commission, but not travellers cheques.

**Ljubljana Tourist Information Centre** (TIC; 📞 01-306 12 15; www.visitljubljana.com; Adamič-Lundrovo nabrežje 2; ⊗ 8am-9pm Jun-Sep, to 7pm Oct-May) Knowledgeable and enthusiastic staff dispense information, maps and useful literature and help with accommodation. Maintains an excellent website.

**Slovenian Tourist Information Centre** (STIC; 📞 01-306 45 76; www.slovenia.info; Krekov trg 10; ⊗ 8am-9pm Jun-Sep, 8am-7pm Mon-Fri, 9am-5pm Sat & Sun Oct-May) Good source of information for the rest of Slovenia, with internet and bicycle rental also available.

## ❶ Getting There & Away

### BUS

Buses to destinations both within Slovenia and abroad leave from the **bus station** (Avtobusna Postaja Ljubljana; 📞 01-234 46 00; www.ap-ljubljana.si; Trg Osvobodilne Fronte 4; ⊗ 5am-10.30pm Mon-Fri, to 10pm Sat, 5.30am-10.30pm Sun) in front of the train station. Next to the ticket windows are multilingual information phones and a touch-screen computer. Frequent buses serve Bohinj (€8.70, two hours, 91km, hourly) via Bled (€6.30, 1¼ hours, 57km), Piran (€12, 2½ hours, 140km, up to seven daily) and Postojna (€6, one hour, 53km, half-hourly).

---

### METELKOVA MESTO

For a scruffy alternative to trendy clubs, head for **Metelkova Mesto** (Metelkova Town; www.metelkovamesto.org; Masarykova cesta 24), an ex-army garrison taken over by squatters in the 1990s and converted into a free-living commune. In this two-courtyard block, a dozen idiosyncratic venues hide behind brightly tagged doorways, coming to life generally after midnight daily in summer and on Friday and Saturday the rest of the year. While it's certainly not for the genteel and the quality of the acts and performances varies with the night, there's usually a little of something for everyone.

## TRAIN

Domestic and international trains arrive at and depart from central Ljubljana's **train station** (Železniška Postaja; ☑ 01-291 33 32; www.slo-zeleznice.si; Trg Osvobodilne Fronte 6; ☺ 5am-10pm), where you'll find a separate information centre on the way to the platforms. Buy domestic tickets from windows No 1 to 8 and international ones from either window No 9 or the information centre. Useful domestic destinations include Bled (€6.60, one hour, half-hourly) and Divača (€5.80, one hour, several daily).

## ℹ Getting Around

### TO/FROM THE AIRPORT

The cheapest way to Ljubljana's **Jože Pučnik Airport** (Aerodrom Ljubljana; ☑ 04-206 19 81; www.lju-airport.si/eng; Zgornji Brnik 130a, Brnik) is by public bus (€4.10, 45 minutes, 27km) from stop No 28 at the bus station. These run at 5.20am and hourly from 6.10am to 8.10pm Monday to Friday; at the weekend there's a bus at 6.10am and then one every two hours from 9.10am to 7.10pm. Buy tickets from the driver.

Two airport-shuttle services that get consistently good reviews are **GoOpti** (☑ 01-320 45 30; www.goopti.com) and **Markun Shuttle** (☑ 051 321 414, 041 041 792 865; www.prevozi-markun.com), which will transfer you from Brnik to central Ljubljana for €9 in half an hour. Book by phone or online.

A taxi from the airport to Ljubljana will cost €35 to €45.

### BICYCLE

Ljubljana is a pleasure for cyclists, and there are bike lanes and special traffic lights.

**Ljubljana Bike** (☑ 01-306 45 76; www.visitljubljana.si; Krekov trg 10; per 2hr/day €2/8; ☺ 8am-7pm Mon-Fri, 9am-5pm Sat & Sun Apr, May & Oct, 8am-9pm Jun-Sep) rents two-wheelers in two-hour or full-day increments from April through October from the **Slovenia Tourist Information Centre**. For short rides, you can hire bicycles as needed from 32 **Bicike(lj)** (☑ 080 23 34; www.bicikelj.si; subscription weekly/yearly €1/3 plus hourly rate; ☺ 24hr) stations with 300 bikes located around the city. To rent a bike requires pre-registration and subscription over the company website plus a valid credit or debit card.

### PUBLIC TRANSPORT

Ljubljana's city buses, many running on methane, operate every five to 15 minutes from 5am (6am on Sunday) to around 10.30pm. There are also a half-dozen night buses. A flat fare of €1.20 (good for 90 minutes of unlimited travel, including transfers) is paid with a stored-value magnetic **Urbana** (☑ 01-474 08 00; www.jhl.si/en/single-city-card-urbana) card, which can be purchased at news stands, tourist offices and the **LPP Information Centre** (☑ 01-430 51 74; www.lpp.si/en; Slovenska cesta 56; ☺ 7am-7pm Mon-Fri) for €2; credit can then be added (€1 to €50). **Kavalir** (☑ 031 666 331, 031 666 332; ☺ 8am-8pm) is an LPP-run transport service that will pick you up and drop you off anywhere in the pedestrianised Old Town free of charge. All you have to do is call (and wait – there are only three golf cart-like vehicles available April to October and just one the rest of the year).

# JULIAN ALPS

The Julian Alps – named in honour of Caesar himself – form Slovenia's dramatic northwest frontier with Italy. Triglav National Park, established in 1924, includes almost all of the Alps lying within Slovenia, including triple-peaked Mt Triglav, at 2864m Slovenia's highest mountain. Along with an abundance of fauna and flora, the area offers a wide range of adventure sports.

# Bled

☑ 04 / POP 5120

Yes, it's every bit as lovely in real life. With its emerald-green lake, picture-postcard church on an islet, a medieval castle clinging to a rocky cliff and some of the highest peaks of the Julian Alps and the Karavanke as backdrops, Bled is Slovenia's most popular resort, drawing everyone from honeymooners lured by the over-the-top romantic setting to backpackers, who come for the hiking, biking, water sports and canyoning possibilities.

## ◉ Sights

### ★ Lake Bled                                             LAKE

(Blejsko jezero) Bled's greatest attraction is its exquisite blue-green lake, measuring just 2km by 1.4km. The lake is lovely to behold from almost any vantage point, and makes a beautiful backdrop for the 6km walk along the shore. Mild thermal springs warm the water to a swimmable 26°C (79°F) from June through August. The lake is naturally the focus of the entire town: you can rent boats, go diving or simply snap countless photos.

### ★ Bled Island                                          ISLAND

(Blejski Otok; www.blejskiotok.si) Tiny, tear-shaped Bled Island beckons from the shore. There's the **Church of the Assumption** and a small **museum**, but the real thrill is the ride out by *pletna* (gondola). The *pletna* will set you down on the south side at the monumental **South Staircase** (Južno Stopnišče), built in 1655. The staircase comprises 99 steps – a local tradition is for the husband to carry his new bride up them.

⭐**Bled Castle**                                    CASTLE
(Blejski Grad; ☑04-572 97 82; www.blejski-grad.si; Grajska cesta 25; adult/child €10/5; ◉8am-9pm mid-Jun–mid-Sep, to 8pm Apr–mid-Jun & mid-Sep–Oct, to 6pm Nov-Mar) Perched atop a steep cliff more than 100m above the lake, Bled Castle is how most people imagine a medieval fortress to be, with towers, ramparts, moats and a terrace offering magnificent views. The castle houses a **museum collection** that traces the lake's history from earliest times to the development of Bled as a resort in the 19th century.

⭐**Vintgar Gorge**                              PARK
(Soteska Vintgar; ☑031 344 053; www.vintgar.si; adult/child €5/2.50; ◉8am-7pm late Apr-Oct) One of the easiest and most satisfying half-day trips from Bled is to Vintgar Gorge, some 4km to the northwest of Bled village. The highlight is a 1600m wooden walkway through the gorge, built in 1893 and continually rebuilt since. It criss-crosses the swirling Radovna River four times over rapids, waterfalls and pools before reaching 16m-high Šum Waterfall.

## 🏃 Activities

Several local outfits organise a wide range of outdoor activities in and around Bled, including trekking, mountaineering, rock climbing, ski touring, cross-country skiing, mountain biking, rafting, kayaking, canyoning, caving, horse riding and paragliding.

⭐**3glav Adventures**          ADVENTURE SPORTS
(☑041 683 184; www.3glav.com; Ljubljanska cesta 1; ◉9am-noon & 4-7pm mid-Apr–Sep) The number-one adventure-sport specialists in Bled for warm-weather activities. 3glav Adventures' most popular trip is the Emerald River Adventure (from €80), an 11-hour hiking and swimming foray into Triglav National Park and along the Soča River that covers a huge sightseeing loop of the region (from Bled over the Vršič Pass and down the Soča Valley, with optional rafting trip).

## 🛏 Sleeping & Eating

Bled has a wide range of accommodation – from Slovenia's original hostel to a five-star hotel in a villa that was once Tito's summer retreat. Private rooms and apartments are offered by dozens of homes in the area. Both Kompas and the TIC have lists, with prices for singles ranging from €16 to €33 and doubles €24 to €50.

⭐**Jazz Hostel & Apartments**         HOSTEL, GUESTHOUSE €
(☑040 634 555; www.jazzbled.com; Prešernova cesta 68; dm €35, d without/with bathroom €50/60, apt d/q €80/85; 🅿♨@🛜) If you don't mind being a little way (a short walk) from the action, this is a first-class budget choice. Guests rave about Jazz, mainly thanks to Jani, the superbly friendly owner who runs a sparkling, well-kitted-out complex. There are dorms (bunk-free, and with underbed storage) and colourful en suite rooms, plus family-sized apartments with full kitchen.

⭐**Old Parish House**          GUESTHOUSE €€
(☑045 741 203; www.blejskiotok.si/hotel; Riklijeva cesta 22; s/d from €45/98; 🅿🛜) In a privileged position, the Old Parish House (Stari Farovž) belonging to the Parish Church of St Martin has been newly transformed into a simple, welcoming guesthouse, with timber beams, hardwood floors and neutral, minimalist style. Pros include car parking, lake views and waking to church bells.

⭐**Garden Village Bled**          RESORT €€€
(☑083 899 220; www.gardenvillagebled.com; Cesta Gorenjskega odreda 16; pier tent €110, treehouse €290, glamping tent €340; ◉Apr-Oct; 🅿♨@🛜🐾) Garden Village embraces and executes the eco-resort concept with aplomb, taking glamping to a whole new level and delivering lashings of wow factor. Accommodation ranges from small two-person tents on piers over a trout-filled stream (shared bathroom), to family-sized treehouses and large safari-style tents. Plus there are beautiful grounds, a natural swimming pool and an organic restaurant. Superb.

⭐**Finefood – Penzion Berc**          SLOVENIAN €€€
(☑04-574 18 38; www.penzion-berc.si; Želješka cesta 15; mains €16-30; ◉5-11pm late Apr-late Oct) In a magical garden setting, Penzion Berc sets up a summertime restaurant, with local produce served fresh from its open kitchen. Try sea bass with asparagus soufflé, homemade pasta with fresh black truffle, deer entrecôte or Black Angus steak. Finefood's reputation for high-class flavour and atmosphere is growing: book ahead.

## ESSENTIAL FOOD & DRINK

Little Slovenia boasts an incredibly diverse cuisine, with as many as two dozen different regional styles of cooking. Here are some highlights:

**Brinjevec** A strong brandy made from fermented juniper berries.

**Gibanica** Layer cake stuffed with nuts, cheese and apple.

**Jota** Hearty bean-and-cabbage soup.

**Postrv** Trout, particularly from the Soča River, is a real treat.

**Potica** A nut roll eaten at teatime or as a dessert.

**Prekmurska gibanica** A rich concoction of pastry filled with poppy seeds, walnuts, apples and cheese and topped with cream.

**Pršut** Air-dried, thinly sliced ham from the Karst region.

**Štruklji** Scrumptious dumplings made with curd cheese and served either savoury as a main course or sweet as a dessert.

**Wine** Distinctively Slovenian tipples include peppery red Teran from the Karst region and Malvazija, a straw-colour white from the coast.

**Žganci** The Slovenian stodge of choice – groats made from barley or corn but usually *ajda* (buckwheat).

**Žlikrofi** Ravioli-like parcels filled with cheese, bacon and chives.

★ **Castle Restaurant** SLOVENIAN €€€
(☑ 04-620 34 44; www.jezersek.si/en/bled-castle-restaurant; Grajska cesta 61; mains €15-30; ☺11am-10pm) It's hard to fault the superb location of the castle's restaurant, with a terrace and views straight from a postcard. What a relief the food is as good as it is: black risotto with octopus, lake trout fillet, veal fillet with tarragon dumplings. Book in advance to score a table with a view – note: with a reservation, you don't pay to enter the castle.

## ℹ Information

**Tourist Information Centre** (☑ 04-574 11 22; www.bled.si; Cesta Svoboda 10; ☺8am-9pm Mon-Sat, 9am-5pm Sun Jul & Aug, reduced hours Sep-Jun) Occupies a small office behind the Casino at Cesta Svobode 10; sells maps and souvenirs, rents bikes and has internet access. It's open year-round: until at least 6pm Monday to Friday, to 3pm Sunday.

## ℹ Getting There & Around

### BUS

Bled is well connected by bus; the **bus station** (Cesta Svobode 4) is a hub of activity at the lake's northeast. Popular services include Lake Bohinj (€3.60, 37 minutes, 29km, up to 12 daily) and Ljubljana (€6.30, 80 to 90 minutes, 57km, up to 15 daily).

### TRAIN

Bled has two train stations, though neither is close to the centre. Mainline trains to/from Ljubljana (€5.08 to €6.88, 40 minutes to one hour, 51km, up to 20 daily) and Austria use Lesce-Bled station, 4km to the east of town. Trains to/from Bohinjska Bistrica (€1.85, 20 minutes, 18km, seven daily), from where you can catch a bus to Lake Bohinj, use the smaller Bled Jezero station, 2km west of central Bled.

## Bohinj

☑ 04 / POP 5300

Many visitors to Slovenia say they've never seen a more beautiful lake than Bled...that is, until they've seen Lake Bohinj, just 26km to the southwest. We'll refrain from weighing in on the Bled versus Bohinj debate other than to say we see their point. Admittedly, Bohinj lacks Bled's glamour, but it's less crowded and in many ways more authentic. People come primarily to chill out or to swim in the crystal-clear, blue-green water, with leisurely cycling and walking trails to occupy them.

## ◉ Sights & Activities

Mt Triglav is visible from Bohinj and there are activities galore – from kayaking and mountain biking to trekking up Triglav via one of the southern approaches.

★ **Church of St John the Baptist** CHURCH
(Cerkev Sv Janeza Krstnika; Ribčev Laz; ⊙ 10am-4pm Jul & Aug, group bookings only May & Sep) This postcard-worthy church, at the head of the lake and right by the stone bridge, is what every medieval church should be: small, surrounded by natural beauty, and full of exquisite frescoes. The nave is Romanesque, but the Gothic presbytery dates from about 1440. Many walls and ceilings are covered with 15th- and 16th-century frescoes.

★ **Savica Waterfall** WATERFALL
(Slap Savica; Ukanc; adult/child €3/1.50; ⊙ 8am-8pm Jul & Aug, 9am-7pm Apr-Jun, 9am-5pm Sep-Nov) The magnificent Savica Waterfall, which cuts deep into a gorge 78m below, is 4km from Ukanc and can be reached by a walking path from there in 1½ to two hours. By car, you can continue past Ukanc via a sealed road to a car park beside the Savica restaurant, from where it's a 20-minute walk up more than 500 steps and over rapids and streams to the falls. Wear decent shoes for the slippery path.

**Alpinsport** ADVENTURE SPORTS
(⊘ 04-572 34 86, 041 596 079; www.alpinsport.si; Ribčev Laz 53; ⊙ 9am-noon & 3-7pm) Rents equipment: canoes, kayaks, SUPs and bikes in summer, skis and snowboards in winter. It also operates guided rafting and canyoning trips. Its base is opposite Hotel Jezero in Ribčev Laz.

## 🛏 Sleeping & Eating

The TICs can arrange accommodation: private rooms (€14 to €20 per person), plus apartments and holiday houses. Apartments for two/six in summer start at €48/116. The website www.bohinj.si has more details.

★ **Camp Zlatorog** CAMPGROUND €
(⊘ 059 923 648; www.camp-bohinj.si; Ukanc 5; per person €10-15; ⊙ May-Sep; P 🛜) This tree-filled campground can accommodate up to 750 guests and sits photogenically on the lake's southwestern corner, 5km from Ribčev Laz. Prices vary according to site location, with the most expensive (and desirable) sites right on the lake. Facilities are very good – including restaurant, laundry and water-sport rentals, and the tourist boat docks here. Tents can be hired.

★ **Rustic House 13** PENSION €€
(Hiša 13; ⊘ 031 466 707; www.studor13.si; Studor 13; d/q €70/110; P 🛜) Cosy and rustic down to the last detail (from the wooden balcony to the garden area), Rustic House gives you a delightful taste of village life. It's owned by an Australian-Slovenian couple and houses two super suites that each sleep up to four. There's a shared kitchen and lounge – admire Andy's photos of the surrounds (he also offers photography tours).

★ **Vila Park** BOUTIQUE HOTEL €€€
(⊘ 04-572 3300; www.vila-park.si; Ukanc 129; d €100-120; P 🛜) Vila Park creates a great first impression, with sunloungers set in expansive riverside grounds, and balconies overflowing with flowers. The interior is equally impressive, with eight elegant rooms plus a handsome lounge and dining area. Note: it's a kid-free zone.

★ **Štrud'l** SLOVENIAN €
(⊘ 041 541 877; www.strudl.si; Triglavska cesta 23; mains €6-12; ⊙ 8am-9pm Sun-Thu, to 10pm Fri & Sat) This modern take on traditional farmhouse cooking is a must for foodies keen to sample local specialities. Overlook the incongruous location in the centre of Bohinjska Bistrica, and enjoy dishes like *ričet s klobaso* (barley porridge with sausage and beans).

**Gostišče Erlah** SLOVENIAN €€
(⊘ 04-572 33 09; www.erlah.com; Ukanc 67; mains €8-18; ⊙ 11am-9pm Sun-Fri, to 10pm Sat) Local trout is king at this relaxed eatery, and it comes perfectly prepared: smoked, grilled or *en brochette* (skewered). There's a rustic, timber-lined terrace, and families will be happy with the kids' playground right next door. Rooms are also available.

## ℹ Information

**Tourist Information Centre Ribčev Laz** (TIC; ⊘ 04-574 60 10; www.bohinj-info.com; Ribčev Laz 48; ⊙ 8am-8pm Mon-Sat, 8am-6pm Sun Jul & Aug, 9am-5pm Mon-Sat, 9am-3pm Sun Nov & Dec, 8am-6pm Mon-Sat, 9am-3pm Sun Jan-Jun & Sep & Oct)

**TNP Center Bohinj** (⊘ 04-578 0245; www.tnp.si; Stara Fužina 37-38; ⊙ 10am-6pm late Apr-Jun & Sep–mid-Oct, 9am-7pm Jul-Aug, 10am-3pm mid-Oct–late Apr, closed 1 Nov) A brand-new national park info centre about 1km north of the Church of St John the Baptist, full of exhibits, maps and books. There's a summer program of free events that includes talks, walks and stargazing. You can also arrange a trekking guide here, or a guide for an ascent of Mt Triglav.

## ℹ Getting There & Away

**BUS**
Buses run regularly from Ljubljana (€8.30, two hours, 86km, hourly). Around 12 buses daily go from Bled (€3.60, 40 minutes) to Bohinj Jezero (via Bohinjska Bistrica) and return.

## TRAIN

A half-dozen daily trains make the run to Bohinjska Bistrica from Ljubljana (€7.17, two hours, 74km), though this route requires a change in Jesenice. There are also frequent trains between Bled's small Bled Jezero station (€1.85, 20 minutes, 18km, seven daily) and Bohinjska Bistrica.

# SOČA VALLEY

The Soča Valley region (Posočje) stretches from Triglav National Park to Nova Gorica, including the outdoor activity centres of Bovec and Kobarid. Threading through it is the magically aquamarine Soča River. Most people come here for the rafting, hiking and skiing though there are plenty of historical sights and locations, particularly relating to WWI, when millions of troops fought on the mountainous battlefront here.

## Bovec

🗾 05 / POP 1593

Soča Valley's de facto capital, Bovec offers plenty for adventure-sports enthusiasts. With the Julian Alps above, the Soča River below and **Triglav National Park** all around, you could spend a week here rafting, hiking, kayaking, mountain biking and, in winter, skiing, without ever doing the same thing twice.

### 🏃 Activities

You'll find everything you need on the compact village square, Trg Golobarskih Žrtev, including a half-dozen adrenaline-raising adventure-sports companies. Among the best are **Aktivni Planet** (🗾040 639 433; http://aktivniplanet.si; Trg Golobarskih Žrtev 19)

---

**THE GREAT OUTDOORS**

Slovenes have a strong attachment to nature, and most lead active, outdoor lives from an early age. As a result, the choice of activities and range of facilities on offer are endless. From skiing and climbing to canyoning and cycling, Slovenia has it all and it's always affordable. The major centres are Bovec, Lake Bled and Lake Bohinj. The Slovenian Tourist Board publishes specialist brochures on skiing, hiking, cycling, golfing and horse riding as well as top spas and heath resorts.

---

and **Soča Rafting** (🗾05-389 62 00, 041 724 472; www.socarafting.si; Trg Golobarskih Žrtev 14).

**Rafting, kayaking** and **canoeing** on the beautiful Soča River are major draws. The season lasts from April to October. Rafting trips on the Soča over a distance of around 8km (1½ hours) cost €35 to €40; longer trips may be possible when water levels are high. Prices include guiding, transport to/from the river, a neoprene suit, boots, life jacket, helmet and paddle. Wear a swimsuit; bring a towel.

A canyoning trip, in which you descend through gorges and jump over falls near the Soča attached to a rope, costs around €45.

### 🛏 Sleeping & Eating

The TIC has dozens of private rooms and apartments (from €20) on its lists.

★**Hostel Soča Rocks**          HOSTEL €
(🗾041 317 777; http://hostelsocarocks.com; Mala Vas 120; dm €13-15, d €34-40; P@🛜) This welcome new arrival sleeps 68 and is a new breed of hostel: colourful, spotlessly clean and social, with a bar that never seems to quit. Dorms sleep maximum six; there are also a few doubles (all bathrooms shared). Cheap meals are served (including summertime barbecue dinners), and a full activity menu is offered: the hostel is affiliated with Aktivni Planet.

★**Dobra Vila**          BOUTIQUE HOTEL €€€
(🗾05-389 64 00; www.dobra-vila-bovec.si; Mala Vas 112; d €120-165; P✳@🛜) This stunning 10-room boutique hotel is housed in an erstwhile telephone-exchange building dating from 1932. Peppered with art deco flourishes, interesting artefacts and objets d'art, it has its own library and wine cellar, and a fabulous restaurant with a winter garden and outdoor terrace.

**Martinov Hram**          SLOVENIAN €€
(🗾05-388 62 14; www.martinov-hram.si; mains €8-18; ⏱10am-10pm Tue-Fri, to midnight Sat & Sun) This traditional restaurant gets mixed reviews, but on a good day you'll enjoy well-prepared local specialities including venison, Soča trout and mushroom dishes. The best place to enjoy them is from the street-front terrace, under the grapevines.

### ℹ Information

**Tourist Information Centre** (TIC; 🗾05-384 19 19; www.bovec.si; Trg Golobarskih Žrtev 22; ⏱8am-8pm Jul & Aug, 9am-7pm Jun & Sep, 9am-6pm May, shorter hours Oct-Apr) The TIC is open year-round. Winter hours will depend on the reopening of the local ski centre – expect long hours when the ski season is in full swing.

## ℹ️ Getting There & Away

There are a couple of daily buses to Ljubljana (€13.60, 3¾ hours, 151km) via Kobarid and Idrija. From late June to August a service to Kranjska Gora (€6.70, 1¾ hours, 46km) via the Vršič Pass departs several times a day, continuing on to Ljubljana.

# KARST & COAST

Slovenia's short coast (47km) is an area for both recreation and history; the town of Piran, famed for its Venetian Gothic architecture and picturesque narrow streets, is among the main drawcards here. En route from Ljubljana or the Soča Valley, you'll cross the Karst, a huge limestone plateau and a land of olives, ruby-red Teran wine, *pršut* (air-dried ham), old stone churches and deep subterranean caves, including those at Postojna and Škocjan.

## Postojna & Škocjan Caves

📞 05 / POP 9366

As much of a draw as the mountains and the sea in Slovenia are two world-class but very different cave systems in the Karst area.

## 👁️ Sights

### ★ Postojna Cave                                    CAVE

(Postojnska Jama; 📞 05-700 01 00; www.postojnska-jama.eu; Jamska cesta 30; adult/child €23.90/14.30, with Predjama Castle €31.90/19.10; ⏰ tours hourly 9am-5pm or 6pm Jul & Aug, 9am-5pm May, Jun & Sep, 10am, noon or 3pm Nov-Mar, 10am-noon & 2-4pm Apr & Oct) The jaw-dropping Postojna Cave system, a series of caverns, halls and passages some 24km long and two million years old, was hollowed out by the Pivka River, which enters a subterranean tunnel near the cave's entrance.

Visitors get to see 5km of the cave on 1½-hour tours; 3.2km of this is covered by a cool electric train. Postojna Cave has a constant temperature of 8°C to 10°C with a humidity of 95%, so a warm jacket and decent shoes are advised.

### ★ Škocjan Caves                                    CAVE

(Škocjanske Jame; 📞 05-708 21 00; www.park-skocjanske-jame.si; Škocjan 2; cave tour adult/child €16/7.50; ⏰ tours hourly 10am-5pm Jun-Sep, 10am, 1pm & 3.30pm Apr, May & Oct, 10am & 1pm Mon-Sat, 10am, 1pm & 3pm Sun Nov-Mar) Touring the huge, spectacular subterranean chambers of the 6km-long Škocjan Caves is a must. This remarkable cave system was carved out by the Reka River, which enters a gorge below the village of Škocjan and eventually flows into the Dead Lake, a sump at the end of the cave where it disappears. It surfaces again as the Timavo River at Duino in Italy, 34km northwest, before emptying into the Gulf of Trieste. Dress warmly and wear good walking shoes.

## 🛏️ Sleeping & Eating

### ★ Youth Hostel Proteus Postojna      HOSTEL €

(📞 05-850 10 20; www.proteus.sgls.si; Tržaška cesta 36; dm/d/s €15/17/23; 🅿️ @ 🛜) Don't be fooled by the institutional exterior – inside, this place is a riot of colour. It's surrounded by parkland and is a fun, chilled-out space, with three-bed rooms (shared bathrooms), kitchen and laundry access, and bike rental. The year-round hostel shares the building with student accommodation, so facilities are good. It's about 500m southwest of Titov trg.

### ★ Lipizzaner Lodge              GUESTHOUSE €€

(📞 040 378 037; www.lipizzanerlodge.com; Landol 17; s/d/q from €55/80/100; 🅿️🛜) In a relaxing rural setting 9km northwest of Postojna Cave, a Welsh-Finnish couple have established this very hospitable, affordable guesthouse. They offer seven well-equipped rooms (including family-sized, and a self-catering apartment); great-value evening meals on request (€14); and brilliant local knowledge (check out their comprehensive website for an idea). Forest walks (including to Predjama in 40 minutes) plus bike rental.

### ★ Restaurant Proteus              SLOVENIAN €€

(📞 081 610 300; Titov trg 1; mains €12-20; ⏰ 8am-10pm) The fanciest place in town: inside is modern and white, with booths fringed by curtains, while the terrace overlooking the main square is a fine vantage point. Accomplished cooking showcases fine regional produce – house specialities include venison goulash and steak with Teran (red wine) sauce. It's hard to go past the four-course Chef's Slovenian Menu (€35) for value and local flavour.

### Information

**Tourist Information Centre Postojna** (TIC; 📞 064 179 972; tic.postojna.info@gmail.com; Tržaška cesta; ⏰ 9am-9pm Jul & Aug, to 6pm Jun & Sep, shorter hours Oct, Nov, Apr & May, closed Jan-Mar) A smart new pavilion

## PREDJAMA CASTLE

Nine kilometres from Postojna is **Predjama Castle** (☑ 05-700 01 00; www.postojnska-jama.eu; Predjama 1; adult/child €11.90/7.10, with Postojna Cave €23.90/19.10; ☺ 9am-7pm Jul & Aug, to 6pm May, Jun & Sep, 10am-5pm Apr & Oct, 10am-4pm Nov-Mar), one of the world's most dramatic castles. It teaches a clear lesson: if you want to build an impregnable fortification, put it in the gaping mouth of a cavern halfway up a 123m cliff. Its four storeys were built piecemeal over the years from 1202, but most of what you see today is from the 16th century. It looks simply unconquerable.

An audioguide (available in 15 languages) details the site's highlights and history. The castle holds great features for kids of any age – holes in the ceiling of the entrance tower for pouring boiling oil on intruders, a very dank dungeon, a 16th-century chest full of treasure (unearthed in the cellar in 1991), and an eyrie-like hiding place at the top called Erazem's Nook, named for Erazem (Erasmus) Lueger, a 15th-century robber-baron who, like Robin Hood, stole from the rich to give to the poor.

The cave below the castle is part of the 14km Predjama cave system. It's open to visitors from May to September (closed in winter so as not to disturb its colony of bats). Tours need to be booked at least three days in advance; caving tours range in price from €24 to €80.

has been built in the town's west, on the road into town (by the supermarket Mercator). It's ideal for motorists, not so good for those on public transport, so there is a small info area inside the library at Trg Padlih Borcev 5, not far southwest of Titov trg.

### ❶ Getting There & Away

Buses from Ljubljana en route to Piran stop in Postojna (€6, one hour, 54km, hourly) and Divača (€7.90, 1½ hours, 82km, seven daily). Postojna is on the main train line linking Ljubljana (€5.80, one hour, 67km) with Sežana and Trieste via Divača. In July and August there is a free shuttle bus from the train station to Postojna Cave.

## Piran

☑ 05 / POP 3975

Picturesque Piran (Pirano in Italian), sitting pretty at the tip of a narrow peninsula, is everyone's favourite town on the Slovenian coast. Its Old Town – one of the best-preserved historical towns anywhere on the Adriatic – is a gem of Venetian Gothic architecture, but it can be a mob scene at the height of summer. In quieter times, it's hard not to fall instantly in love with the atmospheric winding alleyways, the sunsets and the seafood restaurants.

### ◉ Sights

★ **Cathedral of St George**  CATHEDRAL
(Župnijska Cerkev Sv Jurija; www.zupnija-piran.si; Adamičeva ulica 2) A cobbled street leads from behind the Venetian House to Piran's hilltop cathedral, baptistery and bell tower. The

cathedral was built in baroque style in the early 17th century, on the site of an earlier church from 1344.

The cathedral's doors are usually open and a metal grille allows you to see some of the richly ornate and newly restored interior, but full access is via the **Parish Museum of St George** (☑ 05-673 34 40; Adamičeva ulica 2; adult/child €1.50/0.75; ☺ 10am-4pm Wed-Mon), which includes the church's treasury and catacombs.

★ **Bell Tower**  TOWER
(Zvonik; Adamičeva ulica; €1; ☺ 10am-8pm summer) The Cathedral of St George's freestanding, 46.5m bell tower, built in 1609, was clearly modelled on the campanile of San Marco in Venice and provides a fabulous backdrop to many a town photo. Its 147 rickety stairs can be climbed for superb views of the town and harbour. Next to it, the octagonal 17th-century **baptistery** *(krstilnica)* contains altars and paintings. It is now sometimes used as an exhibition space. To the east is a 200m-long stretch of the 15th-century **town wall**.

★ **Sergej Mašera Maritime Museum**  MUSEUM
(☑ 05-671 00 40; www.pomorskimuzej.si; Cankarjevo nabrežje 3; adult/child €3.50/2.10; ☺ 9am-noon & 5-9pm Tue-Sun Jul & Aug, 9am-5pm Tue-Sun Sep-Jun) Located in the 19th-century **Gabrielli Palace** on the waterfront, this museum's focus is the sea, with plenty of salty-dog stories relating to Slovenian seafaring. In the archaeological section, the 2000-year-old Roman amphorae beneath the glass floor are impressive. The antique model ships

upstairs are very fine; other rooms are filled with old figureheads and weapons, including some lethal-looking blunderbusses. The folk paintings are offerings placed by sailors on the altar of the pilgrimage church at Strunjan for protection against shipwreck.

## 🛏 Sleeping & Eating

Prices are higher in Piran than elsewhere on the coast, and it's not a good idea to arrive without a booking in summer. If you need to find a private room, start at the Maona Tourist Agency or **Turist Biro** (📞05-673 25 09; www.turistbiro-ag.si; Tomažičeva ulica 3; ⊙9am-1pm & 4-7pm Mon-Sat, 10am-1pm Sun).

### ★PachaMama                   GUESTHOUSE, APARTMENT €€
(📞059 183 495; www.pachamama.si; Trubarjeva 8; per person €30-35; ❈🛜) Built by travellers for travellers, this excellent new guesthouse ('PachaMama Pleasant Stay') sits just off Tartinijev trg and offers 12 simple, fresh rooms, decorated with timber and lots of travel photography. Cool private bathrooms and a 'secret garden' add appeal. There are also a handful of studios and family-sized apartments under the PachaMama umbrella, dotted around town and of an equally high standard.

### ★Max Piran                                   B&B €€
(📞041 692 928, 05-673 34 36; www.maxpiran. com; Ulica IX Korpusa 26; d €65-70; ❈🛜) Piran's most romantic accommodation has just six handsome, compact rooms, each bearing a woman's name rather than a number, in a delightful, coral-coloured, 18th-century townhouse. It's just down from the Cathedral of St George, and excellent value.

### ★Cantina Klet                            SEAFOOD €
(Trg 1 Maja 10; mains €5-9; ⊙10am-11pm) This small wine bar sits pretty under a grapevine canopy on Trg 1 Maja. You order drinks from the bar (cheap local wine from the barrel or well-priced beers), but we especially love the self-service window (labelled 'Fritolin pri Cantini') where you order from a small blackboard menu of fishy dishes, like fish fillet with polenta, fried calamari or fish tortilla.

## ℹ Information

**Tourist Information Centre** (TIC; 📞05-673 44 40; www.portoroz.si; Tartinijev trg 2; ⊙9am-10pm Jul & Aug, to 7pm May, to 5pm Sep-Apr & Jun) In the impressive Municipal Hall.

## ℹ Getting There & Away

### BUS
At least three buses a day make the run to/from Ljubljana (€12, three hours, 140km via Divača and Postojna). One bus a day heads to Trieste (€5.90, 1½ hours, 43km) in Italy. One bus a day heads south for Croatian Istria from late June to September, stopping at the coastal towns of Umag, Poreč and Rovinj (€9, 2¾ hours).

# SURVIVAL GUIDE

## ℹ Directory A–Z

### MONEY
The official currency is the euro. Exchanging cash is simple at banks, major post offices, travel agencies and a *menjalnica* (bureau de change), although many don't accept travellers cheques. Major credit and debit cards are accepted almost everywhere, and ATMs are ubiquitous.

### TELEPHONE
Slovenia uses GSM 900, which is compatible with the rest of Europe and Australia but not with the North American GSM 1900 or the Japanese system.

### TOURIST INFORMATION
The **Slovenian Tourist Board** (Slovenska Turistična Organizacija, STO; 📞01-589 85 50; www. slovenia.info; Dimičeva 13), based in Ljubljana, is the umbrella organisation for tourist promotion in Slovenia, and produces a number of excellent brochures, pamphlets and booklets in English. In addition, the organisation oversees dozens of tourist information centres (TICs) across the country.

---

### COUNTRY FACTS

**Area** 20,273 sq km

**Capital** Ljubljana

**Country code** 📞386

**Currency** euro (€)

**Emergency** Ambulance 📞112, fire 📞112, police 📞113

**Language** Slovene

**Money** ATMs are everywhere; banks open Monday to Friday and (rarely) Saturday morning

**Population** 2.06 million

**Visas** Not required for citizens of the EU, Australia, USA, Canada or New Zealand

# ⓘ Getting There & Away

## AIR

Slovenia's main international airport is Jože Pučnik Airport, located 27km north of Ljubljana. In the arrivals hall there's a **Slovenia Tourist Information Centre desk** (STIC; www.visitljubljana.si; Jože Pučnik Airport; ⊗ 8am-7pm Mon-Fri, 9am-5pm Sat & Sun Oct-May, 8am-9pm Jun-Sep), travel agencies and an ATM.

**Adria Airways** (☑ 04-259 45 82, 01-369 10 10; www.adria-airways.com), the Slovenian flag-carrier, serves more than 20 European destinations on regularly scheduled flights. Budget carriers include **EasyJet** (☑ 04-206 16 77; www.easyjet. com) and **Wizz Air** (☑ in UK 44-330 977 0444; www.wizzair.com).

## LAND
### Bus

International bus destinations from Ljubljana include Serbia, Germany, Croatia, Bosnia & Hercegovina, Macedonia, Italy and Scandinavia. You can also catch buses to Italy and Croatia from coastal towns, including Piran.

### Train

It is possible to travel to Italy, Austria, Germany, Croatia and Hungary by train; Ljubljana is the main hub, although you can hop on international trains in certain other cities. International train travel can be expensive. It is sometimes cheaper to travel as far as you can on domestic routes before crossing borders.

### Sea

Piran sends catamarans to Trieste daily and to Venice at least twice a week in season.

# ⓘ Getting Around

## BICYCLE

Cycling is a popular way of getting around. Bikes can be transported for €3.50 in the baggage compartments of some IC and regional trains. Larger buses can also carry bikes as luggage. Most towns and cities have dedicated bicycle lanes and traffic lights.

---

### EATING PRICE RANGES

The following price ranges refer to a two-course, sit-down meal, including a drink, for one person. Many restaurants also offer an excellent-value set menu of two or even three courses at lunch.

**€** less than €15

**€€** €16–€30

**€€€** more than €31

---

### SLEEPING PRICE RANGES

The following price ranges refer to a double room with en suite toilet and bath or shower, and include tax and breakfast.

**€** less than €50

**€€** €51–€100

**€€€** more than €100

---

## BUS

You can buy your ticket at the *avtobusna postaja* (bus station) or simply pay the driver as you board. In Ljubljana you should book your seat (€1.50/3.70 domestic/international) a day in advance if you're travelling on Friday, or to destinations in the mountains or on the coast on a public holiday. A range of bus companies serve the country, but prices are uniform: €3.10/5.60/9.20/16.80 for 25/50/100/200km of travel.

## CAR & MOTORCYCLE

Roads in Slovenia are generally good. Tolls are no longer paid separately on the motorways. Instead, cars must display a *vinjeta* (road-toll sticker) on the windscreen. It costs €15/30/110 for a week/month/year for cars and €7.50/30/55 for motorbikes and is available at petrol stations, post offices and certain news stands and tourist information centres. Failure to display a sticker risks a fine of up to €300.

Renting a car in Slovenia allows access to cheaper out-of-centre hotels and farm or village homestays. Rentals from international firms such as Avis, Budget, Europcar and Hertz vary in price; expect to pay from €38/200 per day/week, including unlimited mileage, taxes and required insurance. Some smaller agencies have more competitive rates; booking on the internet is always cheaper.

Dial ☑ 1987 for roadside assistance.

## TRAIN

Much of the country is accessible by rail, run by the national operator, **Slovenian Railways** (Slovenske Železnice, SŽ; ☑ 01-291 33 32; www. slo-zeleznice.si). The website has an easy-to-use timetable.

Figure on travelling at about 65km/h except on the fastest InterCity Slovenia (ICS) express trains that run at an average speed of 90km/h.

Purchase your ticket at the *železniška postaja* (train station) itself; buying it from the conductor on the train costs an additional €3.60. An invalid ticket or fare dodging earns a €40 fine.

# Ukraine

## Best Places to Eat

➡ Trapezna Idey (p421)

➡ Arbequina (p418)

➡ Dim Lehend (p421)

➡ Baczewski (p421)

➡ Kanapa (p418)

## Best Places to Stay

➡ Sunflower B&B (p418)

➡ Villa Stanislavsky (p420)

➡ Leopolis Hotel (p420)

➡ Dream House Hostel (p413)

## Why Go?

Shaped like a broken heart, with the Dnipro River dividing it into two, this Slavic hinterland is a vast swath of sage-flavoured steppe filled with sunflowers and wild poppies. Blessed with a near-ideal climate and the richest soil in Europe, it's one huge garden of a country where flowers are blossoming, fruit are ripening and farmers markets sing hymns of abundance.

If only its history were as idyllic. Just over two decades into a very troubled independence, Ukraine (Україна) is dogged by a conflict with neighbouring Russia that has left Crimea and a small chunk of its eastern territory off limits to most travellers. But the country's main attractions, including eclectic and rebellious Kyiv, architecturally rich Lviv and flamboyant Odesa, are well away from the conflict zone. A long stretch of the Black Sea coast invites beach fun, while the Carpathians draw skiers in winter and cyclists in summer.

## When to Go
### Kyiv

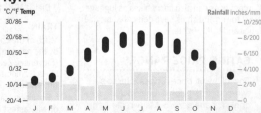

**Jan** Party on New Year's Eve then repent at an Orthodox Christmas service a week later.

**May** A great time to visit Kyiv when its countless horse chestnut trees are in blossom.

**Aug** Sip Ukraine's best coffee in one of Lviv's many outdoor cafes.

# Kyiv Київ

♪ 044 / POP 2.9 MILLION

Sometimes chaotic central Asia, other times quaint central Europe, Kyiv (many agree) is the former USSR's most pleasant metropolis. A pretty spot amid the wooded hills hemming the wide River Dnipro, this eclectic capital has preserved the legacy of its former possessors, from Viking chieftains to post-Soviet dictators. Despite its starring role in the 2014 Maidan Revolution which toppled the last of those rulers, only the very centre around Maidan Nezalezhnosti bears any scars, the rest of the city being untouched by the tumultuous events that have put the geopolitical spotlight firmly on Ukraine.

## ◉ Sights

★ **Kyevo-Pecherska Lavra** MONASTERY
(Києво-печерська лавра | Caves Monastery; ♪044-406 6375; kplavra.kiev.ua; vul Lavrska 9; grounds 20uah, caves & exhibitions adult/child 60/30uah; ⊙8am-7pm Apr-Oct, 9am-6pm Nov-Mar; Ⓜ Arsenalna) Tourists and Orthodox pilgrims alike flock to the Lavra. Set on 28 hectares of grassy hills above the Dnipro River, the monastery's cluster of gold-domed churches is a feast for the eyes, the hoard of Scythian gold rivals that of the Hermitage in St Petersburg, and the underground labyrinths lined with mummified monks are exotic and intriguing. That's from a tourist's perspective, but for pilgrims this is simply the holiest ground in three East Slavic countries – Ukraine, Russia and Belarus.

**Andriyivsky Uzviz** HISTORIC SITE
(Ⓜ Kontraktova pl) According to legend, a man walked up the hill here, erected a cross and prophesied: 'A great city will stand on this spot'. That man was the Apostle Andrew, hence the name of Kyiv's quaintest thoroughfare, a steep cobbled street that winds its way up from Kontraktova pl to vul Volodymyrska, with a vaguely Monparnasse feel. Its highlight is the stunning gold and blue **St Andrew's Church** (Andriyivsky uzviz; ⊙10am-6pm; Ⓜ Kontraktova pl) FREE, a five-domed, cross-shaped baroque masterpiece that celebrates the apostle legend.

★ **St Sophia's Cathedral** CHURCH
(n.sophiakievska.org; pl Sofiyska; grounds/cathedral/bell tower 20/60/30uah; ⊙grounds 9am-7pm, cathedral 10am-6pm Thu-Tue, to 5pm Wed; Ⓜ Maydan Nezalezhnosti) The interior is the most astounding aspect of Kyiv's oldest standing church. Many of the mosaics and frescoes are original, dating back to 1017–31, when the cathedral was built to celebrate Prince Yaroslav's victory in protecting Kyiv from the Pechenegs (tribal raiders). While equally attractive, the building's gold domes and 76m-tall wedding-cake bell tower are 18th-century baroque additions.

★ **Maidan Nezalezhnosti** SQUARE
(майдан Незалежності | Independence Sq; Ⓜ Maydan Nezalezhnosti) Independent Ukraine has a short history, and pretty much all of it was written here. Popularly known as Maidan, the square was the site of pro-independence protests in the 1990s and Orange Revolution in 2004. But all of that was eclipsed by the Revolution of Dignity in the winter of 2013-14, when the square was transformed into an urban guerrilla camp besieged by government forces. Makeshift memorials to fallen revolutionaries on vul Instytutska serve as a sombre reminder.

## 🛏 Sleeping

**Dream House Hostel** HOSTEL €
(♪095 703 2979; www.dream-family.com; Andriyivsky uzviz 2D; dm/d from 170/650uah, d with bathroom from 820uah; ❋ @ 🛜; Ⓜ Kontraktova pl) Kyiv's most happening hostel is this gleaming

---

### ITINERARIES

#### Two Days

A couple of days are just enough to 'do' Kyiv, starting at its stellar attraction, the Kyevo-Pecherska Lavra (aka the Caves Monastery). Follow this with a hike up artsy Andriyivsky uzviz for a taste of prewar Ukraine, before plunging into the beeswax-perfumed Byzantine interior of Unesco-listed St Sophia's Cathedral.

#### Five Days

Having seen the sights in Kyiv, hop aboard a slow night train to Lviv, Ukraine's most central European city complete with bean-scented coffee houses, Gothic and baroque churches, and quaintly rattling trams.

# Ukraine Highlights

**1 Kyevo-Pecherska Lavra** (p413) Inspecting Kyiv's collection of mummified monks by candlelight.

**2 Andriyivsky Uzviz** (p413) Making an ascent of Kyiv's most atmospheric street.

**3 Lviv** (p419) Doing a spot of cobble-surfing in the historical centre packed with churches, museums and eccentric restaurants.

**4 Lychakiv Cemetery** (p419) Exploring Lviv's final resting place of Ukraine's great and good.

# Central Kyiv

500 m
0.25 miles

Dnipro River

Mezhyhirya Estate (30km)

Dniprovsky Park

Park Miský Sad

Park Petrivska aleya

Naberezhne shose

Park Askoldova Mohyla

pl Evropeiska

vul Naberezhno-Khreshchatytska

PODIL

vul Hryhoriya Skovorody

vul Illynska

vul Voloska

Kontraktova pl

vul Bratska

vul Sahaydachnoho

pl Poshtova

Volodymyrsky uzviz

Poshtova pl

Zhyvopysna aleya

12

Maydan Nezalezhnosti

vul Mykhailivska

13

15

vul Mala Zhytomyrska

prov Tarasa Shevchenka

vul Sofiyska

vul Spaska

Kontraktova pl

vul Pokrovska

vul Prytytsko My...

vul Khoreviy

Provulok Khoreviy

6 10

vul Borychiv Tik

Volodymyrska Hirka Park

14

4

9

5

7

pl Mykhaylivska

11

vul Irynynska

vul Volodymyrska

vul Kostyantynivska

vul Kyrylivska

vul Lukyanivska

vul Verkhniy Val

Andriyivsky Uzviz

3

vul Vozdvyzhenska

VERKHNIY GOROD

vul Kozhumyatska

8

St Sophia's Cathedral

2

pl Sofiyska

vul Striletska

vul Reytarska

vul YaroslavivVal

Peyzazhna aleya

vul Lvivska

vul Velyka Zhytomyrska

vul Petrivska

vul Kudryavska

vul Voznesensky uzviz

vul Observatorna

prov Chekhovsky

vul Olesya Honchara

vul Kudryavska

vul Hlybochytska

vul Sichovykh Striltsiv

17

vul Mykoly Pymonenka

vul Yuriya Kotsyubynskoho

vul Gogolivska

vul Turgenivska

Bulvar-Kudryavska

vul Pottavska

vul Dmytrivska

vul Zolotoustivska

vul Pavlivska

vul Lukyanivska

Lukyanivska

pl Lukyanivska

vul Hlybochytska

vul Vyacheslava Chornovola

vul Vyacheslava Chornovola

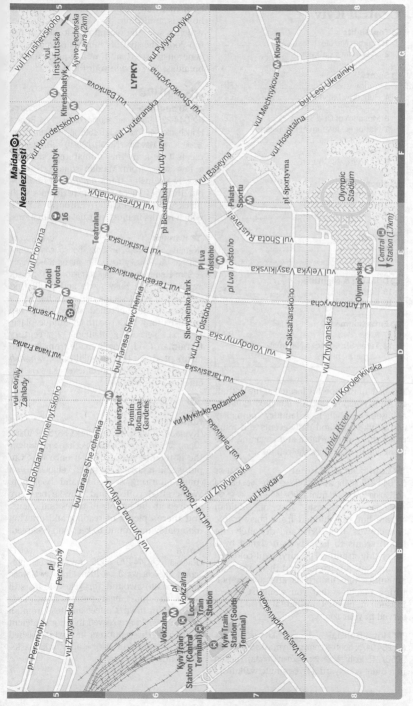

## Central Kyiv

100-bed affair superbly located at the bottom of Andriyivsky uzviz. An attached cafe-bar, a basement kitchen, a laundry room, key cards, bike hire, and daily events and tours make this a comfortable and engaging base from which to explore the capital.

★ **Sunflower B&B Hotel**  B&B €€
(☑044 279 3846; www.sunflowerhotel.kiev.ua; vul Kostyolna 9/41; s/d from 1200/1450uah; ❄@🛜; Ⓜ Maidan Nezalezhnosti) Just off Maidan square but well hidden from noisy traffic and crowds, this B&B (and definitely not hotel) seems to have been designed by a super-tidy granny. The airy, light-coloured rooms have a retro feel and there are extra amenities like umbrellas and a shoe-polishing machine that you wouldn't expect in such a place. Continental breakfast is served in your room.

★ **Hotel Bontiak**  BOUTIQUE HOTEL €€€
(☑284 0475; bontiak.com; vul Irynynska 5; s/d from 2050/2450uah; ❄@🛜; Ⓜ Zoloti Vorota) Tucked in a quiet courtyard a five-minute walk from both main city squares, this cosy boutique hotel is built into Kyiv's hilly landscape, which is why the reception is located at the top floor. The stylishly minimalist rooms are generously sized and well equipped, and breakfast is served in your room.

## 🍴 Eating

★ **Arbequina**  SPANISH, SEAFOOD €€
(☑044-223 9618; arbequina.com.ua; vul Borysa Hrinchenka 4; mains 120-160uah; ⊗9am-11pm; 🛜🅟; Ⓜ Maidan Nezalezhnosti) Barcelona meets Odesa in this miniature restaurant a few steps from Maidan square. Food is mostly Spanish – think *paella* and *fideua* – but the chef successfully experiments with Black Sea fish and Eastern European staples, which results in most unusual combinations.

★ **Kanapa**  UKRAINIAN €€
(Канапа; ☑044-425 4548; borisov.com.ua/uk/kanapa; Andriyivsky uzviz 19; mains 80-400uah; ⊗9am-11pm; 🛜🅟; Ⓜ Kontraktova pl) Sneak away from the busy uzviz and you'll find yourself in what seems like a treehouse – a wooden terrace perched above the dense green canopy underneath. A unique place, Kanapa serves gentrified, 21st-century Ukrainian food, largely made from its own farm's produce. Traditional it is not: *borshch* is made of nettle and chicken Kiev is not chicken but pheasant.

## 🍷 Drinking

**Kupidon**  PUB
(Купідон | Cupid; vul Pushkinska 1-3/5; ⊗10am-10pm; 🛜; Ⓜ Khreshchatyk) Perhaps no longer the hotbed of nationalism it once was, Cupid is still a great Lviv-styled cellar *knaypa* (pub), abutting a secondhand bookshop. Well-crafted coffees and Lvivske beer are enjoyed at the jumble of tables and chairs, and there's plenty of reading and drawing material lying around to keep you occupied.

**Kaffa**  COFFEE
(Каффа; ☑044-270 6505; www.kaffa.ua; prov Tarasa Shevchenka 3; ⊗10am-10pm; Ⓜ Maidan Nezalezhnosti) Around for years, Kaffa still serves the most heart-pumping, rich-tasting brew in town. Coffees and teas from all over the world are served in a pot sufficient for two or three punters in a whitewashed African-inspired interior – all ethnic masks, beads and leather.

## ⭐ Entertainment

**Atlas**                                    CONCERT VENUE
(Атлас; ☑ 067 155 2255; facebook.com/Atlas37/;
vul Sichovikh Striltsiv 37-41; Ⓜ Lukyanivska) This
industrial-style multistorey venue, complete
with roof terrace, caters to all musical tastes
from techno to heavy metal with a sprin-
kling of theatre and poetry readings. The
best of the best in Ukrainian and foreign
music gravitate here these days.

**Taras Shevchenko**
**National Opera Theatre**                          OPERA
(☑ 044-235 2606; www.opera.com.ua; vul Volodymyrska 50; Ⓜ Zoloti Vorota) Performances at
this lavish theatre (opened 1901) are grandiose affairs, but tickets are cheap. True
disciples of Ukrainian culture should not
miss a performance of *Zaporozhets za
Dunaem* (Zaporizhzhyans Beyond the Danube), a sort of operatic, purely Ukrainian
version of *Fiddler on the Roof*.

## ⓘ Information

Almost every cafe and restaurant offers free wi-fi
and there are hotspots throughout the city centre.

## ⓘ Getting There & Away

### AIR

Most international flights use Boryspil International Airport, 35km east of the city. Some
domestic airlines and Wizzair use **Zhulyany
airport** (☑ 044 585 7254; www.airport.kiev.ua),
7km southwest of the centre. There's at least
one flight a day to all regional capitals and international flights serve many European cities.

Plane tickets are sold at **Kiy Avia** (www.ki-
yavia.com; pr Peremohy 2; ⊙ 8am-9pm Mon-Fri,
8am-8pm Sat, 9am-6pm Sun; Ⓜ Vokzalna).

### BUS

A couple of overnight coaches (eight hours,
250uah) make the Lviv run from the **Central Bus
Station** (Tsentralny Avtovokzal; pl Moskovska 3).

### TRAIN

Kyiv's **train station** (☑ 044 503 7005; pl
Vokzalna 2; Ⓢ Vokzalna) handles domestic ser-
vices as well as international trains to Moscow,
Warsaw, Berlin, Chişinău and Bucharest.

The quickest way to Lviv is on the Intercity+
express (330uah, five hours, one daily), which
leaves early evening. Cheaper overnight passenger trains and a few daytime services (165uah to
250uah, eight to 10 hours) are more popular.

Buy tickets at the station or the **advance train
ticket office** (bul Tarasa Shevchenka 38/40;
⊙ 7am-9pm; Ⓢ Universytet).

---

**WORTH A TRIP**

### MEZHYHIRYA

Kyiv's newest tourist attraction is
Mezhyhirya, the estate that once belonged to ex-president and wannabe
Ukrainian dictator, Viktor Yanukovych, famously ousted in the Maidan Revolution
of 2014. A wander through the opulent
mansion and grounds costing millions of
dollars to create gives visitors an idea of
just how corrupt the Yanukovych regime
had become. Mezhyhirya lies 30km
north of Kyiv. Take the metro to the
terminus at Heroyiv Dnipra from where
buses shuttle visitors to the estate.

## ⓘ Getting Around

### TO/FROM THE AIRPORT

A taxi to the city centre costs around 400uah.

SkyBus (63uah, one hour) departs round the
clock from behind the train station's South Terminal every 20 to 40 minutes.

Trolleybus 22 runs to Zhulyany airport from
Shulyavska metro station.

### PUBLIC TRANSPORT

Kyiv's metro runs between around 6am and
midnight. Plastic tokens (*zhetony*; 4uah) are sold
at windows and dispensers at stations.

Buy tickets (3uah) for buses, trolleybuses,
trams and *marshrutky* (fixed-route minibuses)
from the driver or conductor.

---

# Lviv                                              Львів

☑ 032 / POP 729,800

If you've done time in any other Ukrainian
region, Lviv will come as a shock. Mysterious
and architecturally lovely, this Unesco World
Heritage–listed city is the country's least Soviet and exudes the same central European
charm as pre-tourism Prague or Kraków once
did. Its quaint cobbles, aromatic coffee houses and rattling trams feel a continent away
from the war-torn badlands of Ukraine's east.
It's also a place where the candle of Ukrainian national identity burns brightest.

## ⊙ Sights

⭐ **Lychakiv Cemetery**                          CEMETERY
(Личаківське кладовище; ☑ 032 275 5415;
www.lviv-lychakiv.ukrain.travel; vul Pekarska; adult/
student 25/15uah; ⊙ 9am-6pm Oct-Mar, to 9pm
Apr-Sep) Don't leave town until you've seen

this amazing cemetery, only a short ride on tram 7 from the centre. This is the Père Lachaise of Eastern Europe, with the same sort of overgrown grounds and Gothic aura as the famous Parisian necropolis (but containing less-well-known people). Laid out in the late 18th century, it's packed full of western Ukraine's great and good. Pride of place goes to the grave of revered nationalist poet Ivan Franko.

### Ploshcha Rynok                              SQUARE

FREE Lviv was declared a Unesco World Heritage site in 1998, and this old market square lies at its heart. The square was progressively rebuilt after a major fire in the early 16th century destroyed the original. The 19th-century **Ratusha** (Town Hall; city-adm.lviv.ua/; pl Rynok 1; ◷9am-6pm Mon-Thu, to 5pm Fri) stands in the middle of the plaza, with fountains featuring Greek gods at each of its corners. Vista junkies can climb the 65m-high neo-Renaissance **tower** (pl Rynok 1; 10uah; ◷9am-9pm Apr-Oct, to 6pm Nov-Mar). The ticket booth is on the 4th floor.

### Latin Cathedral                          CATHEDRAL

(pl Katedralna 1; ◷7.30am-7pm, closed 2-3pm Mon-Fri) With various chunks dating from between 1370 and 1480, this working cathedral is one of Lviv's most impressive churches. The exterior is most definitely Gothic, while the heavily gilded interior, one of the city's highlights, has a more baroque feel, with colourfully wreathed pillars hoisting frescoed vaulting and mysterious side chapels glowing in candlelit half-light. Services are in four languages, including English.

## 🛏 Sleeping

### ★Old City Hostel                          HOSTEL €

(☎032 294 9644; www.oldcityhostel.lviv.ua; vul Beryndy 3; dm/d from 170/500uah; @🛜) Occupying two floors of an elegantly fading tenement just steps from pl Rynok, this expertly run hostel with period features and views of the Shevchenko statue from the wraparound balcony has long since established itself as the city's best. Fluff-free dorms hold four to 16 beds, shower queues are unheard of, sturdy lockers keep your stuff safe and there's a well-equipped kitchen.

### ★Villa Stanislavsky              BOUTIQUE HOTEL €€

(☎032-275 2505; villastanislavskyi.com.ua/; vul Henerala Tarnavskoho 75; r from 1215uah; 🅿✳) This hilltop villa stands amid the splendid decay of what used to be a posh fin de siècle residential neighbourhood, 20 minutes on foot from the centre. The dark, polished wood of the stairs and furniture and the placid surroundings provide much-needed respite from the old town's hustle and bustle. A dedicated chess room is the cherry on the sundae.

### ★Leopolis Hotel                          HOTEL €€€

(☎032-295 9500; www.leopolishotel.com; vul Teatralna 16; s/d from 3100/3500uah; 🌀✳@🛜) One of the historical centre's finest places to catch some Zs. Every guest room in this 18th-century edifice is different, but all have a well-stocked minibar, elegant furniture and an Italian-marble bathroom with underfloor heating. Wheelchair-friendly facilities, a new spa/fitness area in the cellars and a pretty decent brasserie are extras you won't find anywhere else.

## CHORNOBYL

The world's most unlikely tourist attraction, and one of dark tourism's most sinister day's out, a tour of Chornobyl will be the most thought-provoking nine hours you'll spend in Ukraine – few fail to be stirred, scared and/or angered by the apocalyptic site of the world's worst nuclear accident. Chornobyl is located 110km north of Kyiv city centre as the crow flies, around two hours' drive. You can only realistically visit as part of a guided tour from Kyiv and you need to book around 10 days in advance to give the authorities time to run security checks. Different people react in different ways to the tour. Whether it be the sight of reactor No 4, or the plight of the 'liquidators', the nonchalance of the Soviet authorities or the tragedy of the model Soviet town of Pripyat that leaves the biggest impression, you're likely to be in a pensive mood by the end of the tour. Expect to pay $150 to $500 per person, depending on the number of people in your party and which tour company you choose.

## ODESA (ОДЕСА)

Ukraine's window on the Black Sea, lively Odesa is a vibrant, Russian-speaking city that attracts surprising numbers of foreign visitors.

With Crimea off limits Odesa these days is packed with Ukrainian holidaymakers. Apart from the **sandy beaches**, the first place many head to is the seafront **Potemkin Steps** (Потьомкінські сходи), star of the most famous scene in the Soviet-era film *Battleship Potemkin*. In the city centre you'll find the **Museum of Western & Eastern Art** (Музей західного та східного мистецтва; www.oweamuseum.odessa.ua; vul Pushkinska 9; adult/child & student 50/30uah; ☺10.30am-6pm Thu-Tue) occupying a beautifully renovated mid-19th-century palace. Top attraction here is Caravaggio's painting *The Taking of Christ*, famously stolen in 2008 in Ukraine's biggest art heist. Now safely recovered, it's undergoing restoration. Odesa's main commercial street, pedestrian **vul Derybasivska** (Дерибасівська вулиця), is jam-packed with restaurants, bars and, in the summer high season, tourists.

Bus is by far the quickest way to travel from Kyiv (330uah to 430uah, six to seven hours, five daily). For Lviv train is better (260uah, 12 hours, four daily).

## ✗ Eating

### ★ Baczewski
EASTERN EUROPEAN €€
(Ресторація Бачевських; ☎032-224 4444; kumpelgroup.com; Shevska 8; mains 60-200; ☺8am-midnight) Here's how you compress your Lviv cultural studies into one evening out. Start with Jewish *forschmak* (herring pâté), eased down by Ukrainian *nalivki* (digestives) and followed by Hungarian fish soup. Proceed to Polish *pierogi* (dumplings) and finish with Viennese *Sachertorte* with Turkish coffee. An essential Lviv experience. Be sure to reserve a table for dinner at this mega-popular place.

### ★ Trapezna Idey
UKRAINIAN €€
(Трапезна ідей; ☎032-254 6155; idem.org.ua; mains 50-100uah; ☺11am-11pm; 🛈) An unmarked door behind the paper-aeroplane monument leads into the bowels of a Bernardine monastery, where this lovely local-intelligentsia fave is hiding, together with a modern art gallery called the Museum of Ideas. People flock here for the hearty *bohrach* (a Ukrainian version of goulash) and *banosh* (Carpathian polenta with salty cottage cheese).

### Dim Lehend
UKRAINIAN €€
(Дім легенд; vul Staroyevreyska 48; mains 55-140uah; ☺11am-2am; 🛈) Dedicated to the city of Lviv, there's nothing dim about the 'House of Legends'. The five floors contain a library stuffed with Lviv-themed volumes, a room showing live webcam footage of Lviv's underground river, rooms dedicated to lions and cobblestones, and another featuring the city in sounds. The menu is limited to Ukrainian staples. Excellent desserts are a bonus.

## 🍷 Drinking

### Dzyga
CAFE
(Дзига; www.dzyga.com.ua; vul Virmenska 35; ☺10am-midnight; 📶) This cafe–art gallery in the shadow of the Dominican Cathedral has a relaxed vibe. It's particularly popular with bohemian, alternative types but seems to attract pretty much everyone, really. The summertime outdoor seating is gathered around the city's Monument to the Smile. If it's full, there are other attractive options nearby on postcard-pretty vul Virmenska.

### Lvivska Kopalnya Kavy
CAFE
(pl Rynok 10; ☺8am-midnight Mon-Thu, to 2am Fri-Sun; 📶) Lviv is Ukraine's undisputed coffee capital, and the 'Lviv Coffee Mine' is where the stratum of arabica is excavated by local colliers from deep beneath pl Rynok. You can tour the mine or just sample the heart-pumping end product at tables as dark as the brews inside, or out in the courtyard beneath old timber balconies.

## ℹ Information

**Tourist Information Centre** (☎032-254 6079; www.touristinfo.lviv.ua; pl Rynok 1, Ratusha; ☺10am-8pm Mon-Fri, to 7pm Sat, to 6pm Sun May-Sep, shorter hours Oct-Apr) Ukraine's best tourist information centre. Branches at the airport (☎067 673 9194; ☺10am-8pm Mon-Fri, to 7pm Sat, to 6pm Sun May-Sep, shorter hours Oct-Apr) and the train station (☎032-226 2005; Ticket Hall; ☺10am-8pm Mon-Fri, to 7pm Sat, to 6pm Sun May-Sep, shorter hours Oct-Apr).

## ESSENTIAL FOOD & DRINK

'Borshch and bread – that's our food.' With this national saying, Ukrainians admit that theirs is a cuisine of comfort, full of hearty, mild dishes designed for fierce winters rather than one of gastronomic zing. Here are some of the Ukrainian staples you are certain to find on restaurant menus:

**Borshch** The national soup made with beetroot, pork fat and herbs.

**Salo** Basically raw pig fat, cut into slices and eaten with bread.

**Varenyky** Pasta pockets filled with everything from mashed potato to sour cherries.

**Kasha** Buckwheat swimming in milk and served for breakfast.

**Vodka** Also known as horilka, it accompanies every celebration and get-together – in copious amounts.

## ❶ Getting There & Away

### AIR

Lviv's new **Danylo Halytskyi International Airport** (☑ 032-229 8112; www.lwo.aero; vul Lyubinska 168) stands 7km west of the city centre. UIA operates flights to Borispil airport in Kyiv (1½ hours, two daily). Dniproavia flies to Kyiv's Zhulyany airport as well as to Ivano-Frankivsk, Dnipro, Kharkiv and Odesa. Book through **Kiy Avia** (☑ 032-255 3263; www.kiyavia.com; vul Hnatyuka 24; ☉ 8am-8pm Mon-Fri, 9am-5pm Sat, 10am-3pm Sun).

Lviv attracts a good number of international flights. There are currently services to/from Vienna, İstanbul, Munich, Warsaw and Madrid.

### BUS

Take trolleybus 25 to the **main bus station** (Holovny Avtovokzal; ☑ 032-263 2497; vul Stryska 109) 8km south of the centre.

There are overnight services to Kyiv (275uah, nine hours, five daily).

### TRAIN

The quickest way to Kyiv is on the Intercity+ express (360uah, five hours, one daily) departing early morning. There are also cheaper overnight and daytime passenger trains (165uah to 250uah, eight to 10 hours).

Buy tickets from the station or city centre **train ticket office** (Залізничні Квіткові Каси; vul Hnatyuka 20; ☉ 8am-2pm & 3-8pm Mon-Sat, to 6pm Sun).

## ❶ Getting Around

From the train station, take tram 1, 6 or 9 to the centre. Trolleybus 9 goes to/from the university to the airport. Bus 48 also runs to the airport from pr Shevchenka.

# SURVIVAL GUIDE

## ❶ Directory A–Z

### ACCOMMODATION

Ukraine has hundreds of hostels with Lviv and Kyiv boasting tens each. There's also a bewildering array of hotel and room types from Soviet-era budget crash pads to 'six-star' overpriced luxury. Everything in between can be hit and miss, and there are no national standards to follow.

Booking ahead isn't normally essential except around New Year. Accommodation is the single biggest expense in Ukraine, but with the virtual collapse of the hryvnya rooms are very affordable.

### BUSINESS HOURS

**Banks** 9am–5pm

**Restaurants** 11am–11pm

**Shops** 9am–6pm, to 8pm or 9pm in cities

**Sights** 9am–5pm or 6pm, closed at least one day a week

### CUSTOMS REGULATIONS

You are allowed to bring in up to US$10,000, 1L of spirits, 2L of wine, 5L of beer, 200 cigarettes or 250g of tobacco, and food up to the value of €50.

### INTERNET ACCESS

Most hotels offer free wi-fi and free hotspots are much more common than in much of Western Europe. Many restaurants and cafes have wi-fi. Internet cafes are not as common as they once were.

### INTERNET RESOURCES

**Lonely Planet** (www.lonelyplanet.com/ukraine) Info, hotel bookings, traveller forum and more.

**Ukraine.com** (www.ukraine.com) Gateway site with news and lots of background info.

**Ukraine Encyclopaedia** (www.encyclopediao-fukraine.com) One of the largest sources of info on Ukraine.

## MONEY

US dollars, the euro and Russian roubles are the easiest currencies to exchange. Ukraine remains primarily a cash economy.
➡ Coins: one, five, 10, 25 and 50 kopecks and one hryvnia.
➡ Notes: one, two, five, 10, 20, 50, 100, 200 and 500 hryvnya.
➡ Hryvnya are virtually impossible to buy pre-departure.
➡ ATMs are common.

## POST

The national postal service is run by **Ukrposhta** (www.ukrposhta.com).
➡ Sending a postcard or a letter of up to 20g costs 4.30uah to anywhere outside Ukraine.
➡ Mail takes about a week or less to reach Europe, and two to three weeks to the USA or Australia.

## PUBLIC HOLIDAYS

Currently the main public holidays in Ukraine are the following:
**New Year's Day** 1 January
**Orthodox Christmas** 7 January
**International Women's Day** 8 March
**Orthodox Easter (Paskha)** April/May
**Labour Day** 1–2 May
**Victory Day (1945)** 9 May
**Constitution Day** 28 June
**Independence Day (1991)** 24 August
**Defender of Ukraine Day** 14 October

## SAFE TRAVEL

Despite the recent conflict, Western Ukraine and Kyiv remain safe. Donetsk, Luhansk and Crimea are off limits to foreigners and care should be taken when visiting other Russian-speaking cities in the east and south.

## TELEPHONE

All numbers in Ukraine start with 0 and there are no pre-dialling codes.

---

### SLEEPING PRICE RANGES

The following price indicators apply for a high-season double room:

**€** less than 400uah
**€€** 400uah–800uah
**€€€** more than 800uah

---

### COUNTRY FACTS

**Area** 603,628 sq km

**Capital** Kyiv

**Country Code** ☎ 380

**Currency** Hryvnya (uah)

**Emergency** ☎ 112

**Language** Ukrainian, Russian

**Money** ATMs common; credit cards widely accepted.

**Population** 44.6 million

**Visas** Not required for EU, UK, US and Canadian citizens for stays of up to 90 days.

---

Ukraine's country code is ☎ 0038. To call Kyiv from overseas, dial ☎ 00 38 044 and the subscriber number.

To call internationally from Ukraine, dial ☎ 0, wait for a second tone, then dial 0 again, followed by the country code, city code and number.

European GSM phones work in Ukraine. Local SIM cards work out much cheaper if making several calls.

## VISAS

Tourist visas for stays of less than 90 days aren't required by citizens of the EU/EEA, Canada, the USA and Japan. Australians and New Zealanders still need a visa.

## ❶ Getting There & Away

The majority of visitors to Ukraine fly – generally to Kyiv. Flights, tours and rail tickets can be booked online through Lonely Planet (www.lonelyplanet.com/bookings).

### AIR

Only a couple of low-cost airlines fly to Ukraine.

Most international flights use Kyiv's main airport, **Boryspil International Airport** (☎ 044 393 4371; www.kbp.aero). **Lviv International Airport** (LWO; ☎ 032-229 8112; www.lwo.aero) also has a few international connections.

Ukraine International Airlines (www.flyuia.com) is Ukraine's flag carrier.

### LAND

Ukraine is well linked to its neighbours. Kyiv is connected by bus or train to Minsk, Warsaw and Budapest, as well as other Eastern European capitals. Lviv is the biggest city servicing the Polish border – it's possible to take a budget flight to Poland then cross the border to Lviv by bus or train.

## EATING PRICE RANGES

The following price indicators are for a main meal:

€ less than 50uah

€€ 50uah–150uah

€€€ more than 150uah

### Bus

Buses are slower, less frequent and less comfortable than trains for long-distance travel.

### Car & Motorcycle

To bring your own vehicle into the country, you'll need your original registration papers and a 'Green Card' International Motor Insurance Certificate.

## ⓘ Getting Around

### AIR

Flying is an expensive way of getting around. Overnight train is cheaper and more reliable.

**Kiy Avia** (www.kiyavia.com) has branches across the country.

### BUS

Buses and minibuses serve every city and small town, but are best for short trips (three hours or less). Tickets resembling shop-till receipts are sold at bus stations up to departure.

### LOCAL TRANSPORT

Trolleybus, tram, bus and metro run in Kyiv. A ticket for one ride by bus, tram or trolleybus costs 2uah to 5uah. There are no return, transfer, timed or day tickets available. Tickets must be punched on board (or ripped by the conductor).

Metro barriers take plastic tokens (*zhetony*), sold at counters inside stations.

### TRAIN

For long journeys, overnight train is best. **Ukrainian Railways** (www.uz.gov.ua) features timetables and an online booking facility.

All trains have assigned places. Carriage (*vahon*) and bunk (*mesto*) numbers are printed on tickets.

# Survival Guide

# Directory A–Z

## Accommodation

### Price Ranges
Rates often drop outside high season by as much as 50%. Price categories are broken down differently for individual countries.

### Reservations
➡ Reserving online or by phone is generally a good idea in high season.

➡ Hostels and cheap hotels fill up very quickly, especially in popular backpacker destinations such as Prague, Budapest and Kraków.

➡ Tourist offices, where they exist, may be able to make reservations on your behalf (some charge a small fee for this service). Bear in mind that the level of English spoken, and the quality of tourist-office services, varies enormously across Eastern Europe.

➡ In rural, less-touristed areas, email enquiries in English may not even receive a response; it's often better to ask a local to call ahead if you have your sights set on a remote guesthouse.

### Seasons
➡ High season is usually in July and August (with a winter peak season in ski areas like the Tatras, typically December to March).

➡ Rates usually drop outside the high season, sometimes by as much as 50%.

➡ In mountainous areas, some hotels close during October and November (months that typically suit neither hikers nor skiers). Accommodation in beach destinations (like the Croatian and Black Sea coasts) may hibernate all winter.

➡ In business-oriented hotels in cities, rooms are most expensive from Monday to Friday and cheaper over the weekend.

### Camping
Eastern Europe's numerous camping grounds are generally inexpensive and family-friendly places to stay. They are best suited to beach holidays or travellers with cars, as they tend to be far from city attractions (though most are accessible by public transport).

Many camping grounds in Eastern Europe rent small on-site cabins, bungalows or caravans for double or triple the regular camping fee; bungalows fill quickly for July and August. Generally, camping grounds charge per tent, plus an extra fee per person (as well as per car, per pet and other fees).

The standard of camping grounds in Eastern Europe varies from country to country. They're unreliable in Romania, crowded in Slovenia and Hungary (especially on Lake Balaton), and variable in the Czech Republic, Poland, Slovakia and Bulgaria. Some countries, including Moldova and Belarus, have very few official camping grounds, but you can usually find somewhere to pitch your tent. Croatia's coast has nudist camping grounds galore (signposted FKK, the German acronym for naturist), which enjoy secluded locations.

➡ Camping grounds may be open from April to October, May to September, or perhaps only June to August, depending on location and demand.

➡ A few private camping grounds are open year-round.

➡ Camping in the wild is usually illegal; ask local people about the situation before you pitch your tent on a beach or an open field.

➡ In Eastern Europe you are sometimes allowed to build a campfire; ask first.

---

**BOOK YOUR STAY ONLINE**

For more accommodation reviews by Lonely Planet authors, check out http://lonelyplanet.com/hotels/. You'll find independent reviews, as well as recommendations on the best places to stay. Best of all, you can book online.

## Farmhouses

Variously described as 'farm tourism' and 'village tourism', farm lodgings and eco-minded homestays are a well developed concept in several Eastern European countries, including Estonia, Hungary, Latvia, Lithuania, Slovakia and Slovenia. It's like staying in a private room or pension, except that the participating farms are in picturesque rural areas and may have activities nearby such as horse riding, kayaking, skiing and cycling.

See World Wide Opportunities on Organic Farms (www.wwoof.net) for information about working on organic farms in exchange for room and board.

## Guesthouses & Pensions

Small private guesthouses (or 'pensions') are common in parts of Eastern Europe. Priced somewhere between hotels and private rooms, they typically have fewer than a dozen rooms and usually have a small restaurant or bar on the premises. You'll often get much more personal service at a pension than you would at a hotel, though there's a bit less privacy and it's a less polished operation (don't expect speedy wi-fi or 24-hour reception). Call ahead to check prices and reserve – someone will usually speak some halting English, German or Russian.

## Homestays, Private Rooms & Couchsurfing

Homestays can offer glimpses of local life that you might not enjoy at a hotel or hostel, though their quality and professionalism varies hugely.

➡ In most Eastern European countries, travel agencies can arrange accommodation in private rooms in local homes. In Hungary you can get a private room almost anywhere, but in other countries only the main tourist centres have them. Some rooms are like mini-apartments, with cooking facilities and private bathrooms for the sole use of guests.

➡ Prices are low but there's often a 30% to 50% surcharge if you stay fewer than three nights. In Hungary, the Czech Republic and Croatia, higher taxation has added to the cost of a private room, but it's still good value and cheaper than a hotel.

➡ People may approach you at train or bus stations in Eastern Europe offering a private room or a hostel bed. If you're interested, insist that they point to the homestay's location on a map, and negotiate a clear price. Obviously, if you are staying with strangers, you don't leave your money, credit cards, passport or other essential valuables behind when you go out.

➡ Any house, cottage or farmhouse with *Zimmer Frei* (German), сниму комнату (Russian), *sobe* (Slovak) or *szoba kiadó* (Hungarian) displayed outside is advertising the availability of private rooms; knock on the door and ask if any are available. However, in countries such as Russia or Belarus where visa registration is necessary, you may have to pay a travel agency to register your visa with a hotel.

➡ Online hospitality clubs, linking travellers with global residents who'll let you occupy their couch or spare room for free – and sometimes show you around town – include Couchsurfing (www.couchsurfing.com), Global Freeloaders (www.globalfreeloaders.com), Hospitality Club (www.hospitalityclub.org) and 5W (www.womenwelcomewomen.uk). Check the rules of each organisation.

➡ If you're staying for free with friends or strangers, make sure you bring some small gifts for your hosts – it's a deeply ingrained cultural tradition throughout the region. Flowers, chocolates or nicely packaged biscuits or cakes will work.

➡ Always let friends and family know where you're staying and carry your mobile phone with you. Solo travellers should be especially careful in homestay situations – as well as following general safety rules, if you get weird vibes from your host on arrival, back out politely rather than risk staying on.

## Hostels

Hostels offer about the cheapest roof over your head in Eastern Europe and you don't have to be young to take advantage of them. Many hostels are part of the national Youth Hostel Association (YHA), which is affiliated with the Hostelling International (HI; www.hihostels.com) umbrella organisation.

➡ Hostels vary widely in character and quality. A number of privately run hostels in Prague, Budapest, Moscow and St Petersburg are serious party venues, while many Hungarian hostels outside Budapest are student dormitories that open to travellers for six or seven weeks in summer only.

➡ Hostels affiliated with HI can be found in most Eastern European countries. A hostel card is seldom required, but you sometimes get a small discount if you have one.

➡ At a hostel, you get a bed for the night plus use of communal facilities; there's often a kitchen where you can prepare your own meals. You may be required to have a bed sheet or a sleeping bag; if you don't have one, you can usually hire one for a small fee.

➡ Many hostels accept reservations by phone or email, but not always during peak periods (though they might hold a bed for you for a couple of hours if you call from the train or bus station). You can also book beds through national hostel offices.

## Hotels

At the bottom end of the scale, cheap hotels may be no more expensive than private rooms or guesthouses, while at the other extreme you'll find beautifully designed boutique hotels and five-star hotels with price tags to match.

➡ Solo travellers in Eastern Europe may pay over the odds, as you are generally charged by the room and not by the number of people in it.

➡ The cheapest rooms have a washbasin but no bathroom, which means you'll have to go down the corridor to use the toilet and shower.

➡ Breakfast may be included in the price of a room, or it may be extra.

## Rental Accommodation

In larger cities, renting an apartment is an excellent option. These are often better value than a hotel (and some are a steal for their size), and you can self-cater and be far more independent, but quality varies. Agencies operate independently and sometimes quasi-legally, so you may have no recourse if you have a disagreement. When dealing with agencies you've found online, never send money in advance unless you're sure they're genuine.

## University Accommodation

Some universities rent out space in student halls in July and August. This is quite popular in the Baltic countries, Croatia, the Czech Republic, Hungary, Macedonia, Poland, Slovakia and Slovenia.

➡ Accommodation will sometimes be in single rooms (but is more commonly in doubles or triples) and will come with shared bathrooms. Basic

cooking facilities may be available.

➡ Enquire at the college or university, at student-information services or at local tourist offices.

# Children

Travelling with your children in Eastern Europe will be a treat and a challenge.

➡ Children will usually be adored and welcomed into cafes, restaurants and hotels.

➡ Depending on the country, children don't always blend seamlessly into evening dining and drinking scenes (as in Western Europe, where it's not unusual for children to sit in high chairs while mum or dad sips wine).

➡ Eastern Europe offers plenty of attractions for young travellers, from kid-friendly museums to parks and zoos.

➡ Pizza and American-style food (burgers, fries) are popular in numerous countries so fussy palates can usually be catered for with ease.

For inspiration and tips on family travel, pick up a copy of Lonely Planet's *Travel with Children* guide.

## Practicalities

➡ In Eastern Europe most car-rental firms have children's safety seats for hire at a small cost, but it is essential that you book them in advance.

➡ High chairs and cots are standard in many restaurants and hotels, but numbers are limited.

➡ The choice of baby food, infant formulas, soy and cows' milk, disposable nappies and other essentials is often as great in Eastern European supermarkets as it is back home.

➡ Discretion is advised when breastfeeding; unfortunately it remains taboo in some public places.

➡ Nappy-changing facilities aren't reliably common in public toilets (and certainly not reliably clean).

➡ Child care is considered a high-end service, but may be available at some of the swankier hotels.

# Discount Cards

## Camping Card International

The Camping Card International (CCI; www.campingcardinternational.com) is an ID that can be used when checking into a camping ground. Many camping grounds offer a small discount if you sign in with one and it includes third-party insurance.

## Hostel Cards

Hostels may charge you less if you have a **Hostelling International** (HI; www.hihostels.com) card. Some hostels will issue one on the spot or after a few days' stay, though this might cost a bit more than getting it at home.

## Rail Passes

The RailPlus card, available to buy at many international ticket outlets, entitles the holder to train-fare reductions of 25% on standard tickets for conventional international trains. It can be used on many Eastern European cross-border routes, and is sold at many international ticket offices.

If you plan to visit more than a few countries, or one or two countries in depth, you might also save money with a rail pass.

## Senior Cards

Many attractions offer reduced-price admission for people over 60 or 65. EU residents, especially, are eligible for discounts in many EU countries; make sure you bring proof of age.

Senior Travel Expert (http://seniortravelexpert.com) is a useful resource with tips on senior discounts.

## Student, Youth & Teacher Cards

The International Student Identity Card (ISIC; www.isic.org) is available for students, offering thousands of worldwide discounts on transport, museum entry, youth hostels and even some restaurants. Similar discounts are available with ISIC's under-30s and teacher cards. Apply for a card online or via issuing offices, which include STA Travel (www.statravel.com).

For under-26s, there's also the European Youth Card (www.euro26.org). Several countries have raised the age limit for this card to 30.

## Electricity

Plugs in Eastern Europe are the standard round two-pin variety, sometimes called the europlug.

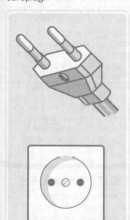

**Type C
220V/50Hz**

## Health
### Before You Go

There are no mandatory vaccinations for entering Eastern Europe, but some are recommended. Most vaccines don't produce immunity until two weeks after they're given. Visit your doc-

tor at least a month before departure to ensure you are up to date with routinely recommended vaccines, and in good time to make arrangements for any travel-related health needs. The vaccinations you are most likely to need are the following:

**MMR** (measles, mumps and rubella)

**Hepatitis A and B**

**Diphtheria**

**Tetanus**

**Rabies Pre-Exposure Vaccine** if you plan on spending a lot of time in remote places or in the company of animals. You will still need to seek post-exposure treatment if exposed to the virus.

**Tick-Borne Encephalitis** if hiking in wild areas is a significant part of your plans

### Availability & Cost of Health Care

In most countries, good basic health care is readily available and pharmacists can give valuable advice and sell over-the-counter medication for minor illnesses. They can also advise when more specialised help is required and point you in the right direction.

For major hospitals with English-speaking staff, capital cities are your best bet. But large hospitals can be found in numerous towns.

By Western European or North American standards, health care is often cheap. It tends to be more expensive in EU member states than in non-EU member states. In most non-EU states you'll probably want to attend a private clinic for anything serious. Comprehensive health insurance is essential, as costs accumulate rapidly in private clinics. The standard of dental care is usually good, and some countries (like Serbia and Poland) even attract dental tourism.

The availability and standard of health care in Belarus isn't high; if at all possible, head overland to Poland or Lithuania. Ukraine's healthcare system is also poor by Western European standards.

Medical care is not always readily available outside major cities, but embassies, consulates and five-star

### EUROPEAN HEALTH INSURANCE CARD

Citizens of EU countries and Switzerland, Iceland, Norway and Liechtenstein should acquire a European Health Insurance Card (EHIC), entitling them to free or reduced-cost emergency healthcare in EU countries. Transporting you back to your home country, in the event of illness, is not covered so a robust travel-insurance policy is still strongly recommended. Every EU individual needs their own card. In the UK, you can apply online (www.ehic.org.uk/Internet/startApplication.do).

The EHIC does not cover private health care, so make sure you are treated by a state health care provider. In EU countries where state-provided healthcare isn't free, you will need to pay yourself and fill in a treatment form; keep the form to claim any refunds. In general, you can claim back around 70% of the standard treatment cost.

hotels can usually recommend doctors or clinics. In some cases, medical supplies required in hospital may need to be bought from a pharmacy and nursing care may be limited. In some rural areas (Ukraine, Russia and Romania in particular), there can be a risk of hepatitis B and HIV transmission from poorly sterilised medical equipment.

## Water

Not everywhere in Eastern Europe has safe tap water. In some countries (like Slovenia) it's almost always drinkable; in others (like Ukraine) it never is. Seek local advice and err towards bottled water, which is readily available. Even where tap water is safe, you'll see locals opting for bottled water (especially in cities where it has an unpleasant taste). Alternatively, use water-purification tablets or a filter.

Do not drink water from rivers or lakes, as it may contain bacteria or viruses that can cause diarrhoea or vomiting. Exceptions are hiking areas where drinkable water sources are clearly marked. Brushing your teeth with tap water is unlikely to lead to problems, but use bottled water if you want to be very cautious.

## Insurance

A travel-insurance policy to cover theft, loss and medical problems is always a good idea. The policies written by STA Travel and other student-travel organisations are usually good value.

➜ Some insurance policies will specifically exclude 'dangerous activities', which can include scuba diving, motorcycling and even hiking. Winter-sports and car-rental cover is sometimes limited, so check the fine print.

➜ Some policies even exclude certain countries.

➜ Check that your policy covers ambulances and an emergency flight home.

➜ You may prefer a policy that pays doctors or hospitals directly rather than reimbursing your claims after the fact.

➜ Some policies ask you to call back (reverse charges) to a centre in your home country, where an immediate assessment of your problem is made.

➜ If you have to file a claim, make sure you gather and keep all documentation (like police or hospital reports). Worldwide travel insurance is available at www.lonelyplanet.com/travel-insurance. You can buy, extend and claim online at any time – even if you're already on the road.

## Internet Access

With few exceptions, any decent-sized town in Eastern Europe has internet access in some shape or form. In general, the internet cafe is a thing of the past as wi-fi has become ubiquitous. Laptops and smartphones can easily connect in many cafes, bars, libraries, hotels, hostels and some public places. Some countries, like Romania and Russia, pride themselves on their wi-fi speed (and it may put to shame your connection back home). In others, like Belarus, you might find certain websites inaccessible, thanks to legislation allowing surveillance and selective blocking of the web. Connections in rural areas (especially mountainous ones) are likely to be slow.

In large towns, 'internet cafes' might be little more than a poky room full of teenagers playing online games. Hostels and hotels with a computer terminal are a better bet, and it's practically universal for lodgings to have wi-fi (if not always in the rooms). A few still charge for this service (five-star international chains are the worst offenders), but nearly all boutique, midrange and budget hotels are likely to offer it for free.

## Legal Matters

➜ Cigarette-smoking bans in bars, restaurants and other public places are increasingly common across the region, so ask before lighting up.

➜ Drinking alcohol in public can attract big fines in a number of countries.

➜ Drugs are available in the region, but they aren't legal. Getting caught with drugs can lead to long prison sentences, particularly in countries such as Russia, Albania and Belarus.

➜ Protesting can attract severe penalties in countries like Russia and Belarus. In these same countries, journalists are advised not to advertise their profession.

➜ If arrested, most countries will honour your right to a translator and allow you to contact your embassy; do so at the first opportunity.

➜ The presumption of innocence applies across EU countries (that is, the burden of proof is on the prosecutor to prove you committed a crime). In theory it also applies in countries such as Belarus and Russia, though there has been criticism of how this rule has been applied and signs that the law may change.

## LGBT Travellers

Consensual homosexual sex is legal across Eastern Europe, but the general population isn't always open-minded.

➜ The Czech Republic and Slovenia have the best reputation for acceptance of LGBT people (and Prague has a thriving gay scene).

➜ You are unlikely to raise any eyebrows by sharing a double room with your same-sex partner in towns and cities, but rural areas might be a different story.

➜ In many countries, overt displays of affection between members of the same sex are likely to attract negative attention.

➜ LGBT travellers should be particularly cautious in Belarus, Hungary, Russia and Romania.

➜ Most countries have online forums and gay advocacy groups.

➜ Many capitals have small, lively gay scenes, and annual pride parades, though some of these have attracted (sometimes violent) counter-demonstrations.

➜ Outside large towns, the internet is the only realistic way to make contact with other gay people.

# Money

Journeys around Eastern Europe require you to flit between the kuna, złoty, leu, lev, lek and other currencies. The euro is used in Estonia, Latvia, Lithuania, Kosovo, Montenegro, Slovakia and Slovenia; it remains the easiest currency to change throughout the region. The convertibility of almost all Eastern European currencies makes them a stable and reliable way to carry cash. The days when hoteliers would slash rates if you paid in US dollars are long gone.

Many other countries in Eastern Europe are hoping to adopt the euro in the future, though economic turbulence has tempered enthusiasm in many quarters. That said, it's often possible to pay for services such as hotels and tours in euro in countries where it's not the currency: Albania, Belarus, Moldova and Russia are all very euro friendly, for example.

## ATMs

Nearly all Eastern European countries have plenty of ATMs in their capitals and sizeable towns. Check the specific situation in your destination before setting out from the big city – and never rely entirely on being able to find an ATM.

➜ Cash or debit cards can be used throughout Eastern Europe at ATMs linked to international networks.

➜ Before leaving home, check your bank's fees for using an ATM abroad. The exchange rate may be better than that offered for travellers cheques or cash exchanges.

➜ If you choose to rely on plastic, go for two different cards – one to be used as backup in the case of loss, or more commonly, if a bank does not accept one card.

➜ A combination of cards and cash is the best approach.

## Cash

➜ The two most favoured foreign currencies throughout Eastern Europe are the euro and the US dollar.

➜ Although it's not difficult to exchange other major world currencies in big cities, you are at the mercy of the exchange office and its rates.

➜ Local currency is almost always preferred, and usually the only kind accepted within a country. But some non-euro countries may accept (even prefer) payment in euros, such as Bosnia & Hercegovina and Moldova.

➜ In some places banks will not change or accept damaged banknotes. This is especially true in the former Soviet Union, so bring clean and newish notes from home, whenever possible, and keep your local currency pristine.

## Credit Cards

➜ Credit cards are commonly accepted. You'll be able to use them at upmarket restaurants, shops, hotels, car-rental firms, travel agencies and many petrol stations.

➜ It's no guarantee that small restaurants and guesthouses will take cards, even if you booked online and secured your reservation by card. Ask ahead or bring back-up cash.

➜ Bear in mind that if you use a credit card for purchases, exchange rates may have changed by the time your bill is processed, which can work out to your advantage or disadvantage.

➜ Companies such as Amex have offices in most countries in Eastern Europe and, because they treat you as a customer of the company rather than of the bank that issued the card, they can often replace a lost card within a couple of working days.

➜ Credit cards such as Visa and MasterCard are more widely accepted because they tend to charge merchants lower commissions.

## Moneychangers

Don't exchange your hard-earned cash without first shopping around for a decent rate. If you happen to be in a tourist area, you will be offered crappy rates everywhere; for example around the Charles Bridge in Prague. Leave for a less touristy neighbourhood if you can.

Border crossings, airports and train stations are typically places where rates aren't great, but many people change money here out of necessity. Never change money on the street.

## Tipping

Tipping practices vary from country to country. You can't go wrong if you add 10% onto your bill at a restaurant.

**Hotels** Porters in upmarket hotels will appreciate a couple of euros.

**Restaurants** In fashionable venues, waiting staff will expect a tip; in rural locations you might astonish your server. Some restaurant servers may 'tip themselves' by withholding change.

**Taxi drivers** In many destinations they may round up the fare.

## Travellers Cheques

It's become more difficult to find places that cash travellers cheques. In parts of Eastern Europe only a few banks handle them, and the process can be bureaucratic and costly.

That said, some travellers consider a few cheques to be a good back-up. If they're stolen you can claim a refund, provided you have a separate record of cheque numbers.

Amex and Thomas Cook are reliable brands, while cheques in US dollars, euros or British pounds are the easiest to cash. When changing them ask about fees and commissions as well as the exchange rate.

## Opening Hours

Opening hours vary; we've listed the most common hours. Saturday and Sunday are official days off, though most shops and cafes open daily. During hot summer months, some enterprises shut in the early afternoon, reopening at 3pm or 4pm and working into the evening.

**Banks and offices** 9am–5pm Monday to Friday (sometimes with an hour or two off for lunch); may open Saturday morning

**Museums** 10am–5pm Tuesday to Sunday; shorter hours October to April

**Restaurants** 10am–10pm

**Shops** 9am or 10am–7pm or later; hours limited in winter

## Photography & Video

➡ Photographing military installations, even casually, is never a good idea. In Belarus and Russia, you may have serious explaining to do.

➡ Ask permission before taking close-up photos of people.

➡ Museums often demand you buy permission to photograph or video displays.

➡ Digital memory, film and camera equipment is available everywhere in Eastern Europe, though you'll have a better selection in larger towns.

➡ Lonely Planet's Guide to Travel Photography covers all aspects of technique and etiquette.

## Post

The efficiency and cost of the postal systems in Eastern Europe vary enormously. EU countries are likely to be faster, more reliable and more expensive than non-EU states.

➡ Service from Belarus, Moldova, Montenegro, Russia and Ukraine is slow, but mail usually reaches its destination eventually. For added assurance and speed, most of these countries offer an express service.

➡ To send a parcel from Eastern Europe you usually have to take it unwrapped to a main post office; parcels weighing more than 2kg often must be taken to a special customs post office. Post-office staff will usually wrap the parcels for you. They may ask to see your passport and note the number on the form; if you don't have a return address within the country put the address of your hotel.

➡ If you desperately need something posted to you, do your research – find a friend of a friend who could receive the mail at their address, or ask nicely at a hotel you plan to stay at. You can have mail sent to you at Amex offices if you have an Amex card or its travellers cheques.

## Public Holidays

This list isn't exhaustive across countries, which may also have public holidays for national days, saints' days, International Women's Day and other celebrations. Dates for Orthodox Christmas and Easter are different to those of their Catholic and Protestant counterparts (though Easter sometimes falls on the same date by both calendars).

**New Year's Day** 1 January

**Orthodox Christmas Day** 7 January

**Catholic Easter** Country-dependent, dates vary

**Orthodox Easter** Country-dependent, dates vary

**May Day/International Labour Day** 1 May

**Christmas Day** 25 December

## Safe Travel

Eastern Europe is as safe – or unsafe – as any other part of the developed world. Stay aware of your surroundings, and you'll probably be fine.

➡ You're most vulnerable to crime aboard transport, from crowded buses to overnight trains; keep valuables close.

➡ You're likely to encounter beggars, some may follow you. Not engaging is the best way to deflect interest.

➡ Taxi and currency-exchange scams are the likeliest pitfalls. Insist on taxi meters; only change money at legitimate outlets.

➡ Locals might regale you with tales of muggings and kidnappings, often involving scapegoats like Roma, Romanians and Albanians. Many stories are exaggerated.

### Corruption

➡ Low-level corruption is disappearing fast and is now rare for travellers to encounter. Do not pay bribes to people in official positions, such as police, border guards, train conductors and ticket inspectors.

➡ Be aware, however, that these systems still exist in Belarus, Moldova (and Transdniestr) and Russia. If corrupt cops want to hold you up because some obscure stamp is missing from your documentation or on another pretext, just let them and consider the experience an integral part of your trip. Insisting on calling your embassy is a good move; officers are likely to receive grief if their superiors learn they are harassing tourists.

➡ If you're taken to the police station for questioning, in most cases the senior officers will eventually let you go (assuming, of course, you haven't committed a crime).

→ If you do have to pay a fine or supplementary charge, insist on a proper receipt before turning over any money. In all of this, try to maintain your cool, as any threats from you will only make matters worse.

## Landmines

Parts of Albania, Bosnia & Hercegovina, Croatia and Kosovo still have landmines in remote areas. Touristed areas and national parks have been prioritised for landmine clearance, but in some places the process is ongoing. Ask locally for the latest information, and pay careful attention to advice about hiking trails (or better yet, hire a local guide). Always stick to established roads and paths in regions where mines are still a problem.

## Scams

→ Taxi scams vary from claiming the meter is broken to deliberately misquoting the currency (you assumed the price was quoted in Bulgarian lei? He's now claiming it's euro). Get cabs from taxi ranks, avoid hawkers at airports, and keep your luggage beside you, so they can't hold it hostage.

→ Double-receipt scams are increasingly common. You are presented with the bill for the service you bought (meal or taxi ride) along with an unrelated bill. The scammer will claim this is a service, parking or other charge. Examine receipts carefully. A local intermediary is best for resolving these matters if they escalate.

→ Fraudulent shopkeepers have been known to make several charge-slip imprints with your credit card when you're not looking and then simply copy your signature from the authorised slip.

→ There have been reports of people making duplicates of credit- or debit-card information with high-tech machines. If your card leaves your sight for longer than you think necessary, consider

cancelling it. Be alert to rigged cash machines (wiggle the card slot or keypad).

→ Currency-exchange scams are less prevalent than they once were. Anyone who approaches you offering suspiciously good exchange rates (uncommon these days) is an outright thief.

## Theft

Definitely a problem in Eastern Europe; the threat comes from both local thieves and fellow travellers. The most important things to guard are your passport, other documents, tickets and money.

→ Consider using a money-belt beneath your shirt or an inner zip-up pocket to keep your valuables secure and out of sight.

→ Train-station lockers or luggage-storage counters are useful to store your luggage (not valuables), but be suspicious of non–staff members who offer to help you operate your locker.

→ A small daypack is more secure than a camera or shoulder bag, but don't keep valuables in the outside pockets. Loop the strap around your leg while seated at bars or cafes.

→ Pickpockets are most active in dense crowds, especially in busy train stations and on public transport during peak hours.

→ Don't leave valuables lying around your hotel room. Use your own padlock for hostel lockers.

→ Parked cars containing luggage or other bags are prime targets for petty criminals; cars with foreign number plates and/or rental-agency stickers attract particular attention. While driving in cities, beware of snatch thieves when you pull up at the lights – keep doors locked and windows rolled up.

→ In the case of theft or loss, always report the incident to the police and ask for a statement; otherwise your

travel insurance company won't pay up.

## Racially Motivated Violence

Many countries in Eastern Europe have thriving neo-Nazi movements, which tend to target local Roma populations and in some cases, non-Caucasian travellers. Countries such as Poland, Slovakia and Slovenia are racially homogeneous. While stares are likely, it's unlikely that travellers will encounter any violence while in Eastern Europe. However, Russian neo-Nazis have been known to seek out fights with nonwhite people on Hitler's birthday (20 April); St Petersburg in particular has seen an extraordinary amount of violence against ethnic minorities – and not only on this date.

# Telephone Services

Telephone services in Eastern Europe are generally excellent. The mobile phone is king across the region and post office telephone centres are being phased out. Overall you can expect a good level of mobile coverage, though in remote areas you will have trouble getting a signal.

## Mobile Phones

→ Mobile phones operate on the GSM standard. If you have roaming, your phone will usually switch automatically over to a local network. This can be expensive if you use the phone a great deal (or rely on data), but is useful for ad hoc and emergency use.

→ If you plan to spend more than a week or so in any one country, consider buying a SIM card to slip into your phone. Check with your provider at home that your handset has been unlocked.

→ SIM cards can cost as little as €5 and can be topped up with cards available at supermarkets, kiosks, newsagents and mobile-phone dealers. With a smartphone, you can use a local SIM card for data as well.

➡ When buying a SIM card, come equipped with your passport (and in countries like Belarus and Russia, any registration paperwork).

### Phone Codes

➡ To call abroad from a landline you dial the international access code for the country you are calling from (most commonly 00 in Eastern Europe, but 8-10 in Belarus and Russia).

➡ From a mobile phone simply dial + followed by the country code, the city code and the local number.

➡ To make a domestic call to another city in the same country, you generally need to dial the area code (with the initial zero) and the number; however, in some countries the area code is an integral part of the phone number and must be dialled every time – even if you're just calling next door.

### Phonecards

Local telephone cards are available from post offices, telephone centres, newsstands or retail outlets. In any given country, there's a wide range of local and international phonecards available. For local calls you're usually better off with a local phonecard.

## Time

➡ Eastern Europe spans three time zones: Central European Time (GMT+1), Eastern European Time (GMT+2) and Further-Eastern European Time, or 'Moscow Time' (GMT+3). At noon in New York, it's 6pm in Warsaw, 7pm in Sofia and 8pm in Moscow.

➡ All countries except Russia employ daylight savings. Clocks are put forward an hour at the start of daylight savings, usually on the last Sunday in March. They are set back one hour on the last Sunday in October.

## Toilets

➡ The vast majority of toilets you use will be modern, sit-down, flushing toilets.

➡ In a few countries, including Albania, Belarus, Moldova, Russia and Ukraine, you can expect to find squat toilets at transport stations and some sights (usually poorly maintained). They are rare in restaurants or hotels.

➡ You'll need to pay a small fee to use most public toilets in Eastern Europe. There may be an extra fee for toilet paper.

➡ Using hotel or restaurant facilities is nearly always free and one way to ensure you'll be using a clean bathroom.

## Tourist Information

Countries that have successfully realised their potential as holiday destinations have a network of excellent tourist information centres (TICs). However, there are still many countries that appear to take little interest in developing their tourism offering.

➡ Countries in the latter category are Belarus, Ukraine and Moldova. Much of Russia is similarly badly organised, though there are TICs in St Petersburg.

➡ Among the best prepared are Croatia, the Czech Republic, Hungary, Poland, Slovakia and Slovenia, many of which have tourist offices abroad as well as throughout the country.

## Travellers with Disabilities

Depending on the destination, Eastern Europe is generally challenging for travellers with disabilities. While individual museums and hotels are slowly being brought up to Western European standards of accessibility, provision isn't reliable. Away from the beaten track, facilities are almost nonexistent and transport presents a challenge.

➡ In general, wheelchair-accessible rooms are available only at top-end hotels (and are limited, so be sure to book in advance).

➡ Rental cars and taxis may be accessible, but public transport rarely is.

➡ Many major museums and sites have some form of disabled access. It's best to call ahead or ask locally when it comes to castles and other ancient sites.

---

### GOVERNMENT TRAVEL ADVICE

The following government websites offer travel advisories and information on current areas to avoid.

**Australian Department of Foreign Affairs** (www.smarttraveller.gov.au)

**British Foreign and Commonwealth Office** (www.gov.uk/foreign-travel-advice)

**Canadian Department of Foreign Affairs** (www.dfait-maeci.gc.ca)

**Japan Ministry of Foreign Affairs** (www.anzen.mofa.go.jp)

**New Zealand Ministry of Foreign Affairs** (www.safetravel.govt.nz)

**US State Department** (www.travel.state.gov)

→ If you have a physical disability, get in touch with your national support organisation (preferably the travel officer if there is one) and ask about the countries you plan to visit. The organisations often have libraries devoted to travel, including access guides, and staff can put you in touch with travel agencies who specialise in tours for disabled people. Download Lonely Planet's free *Accessible Travel* guide from http://lptravel.to/AccessibleTravel.

## Visas

EU, US, Canadian, Australian and New Zealand passport holders don't require a visa for most Eastern European countries, but a few countries do require visas.

Belarus and Russia require nearly all nationalities to obtain visas, but citizens of 80 countries can now visit Belarus visa-free for up to five days, if arriving by air. Aussie and Kiwi travellers also need visas to enter Ukraine.

If you do need to get a visa, note it has an expiration date and you'll be refused entry after that period has elapsed. Consulates sometimes issue visas on the spot, although some levy a 50% to 100% surcharge for 'express service'. If there's a choice, get a visa in advance – they're often cheaper in your home country and this can save on bureaucratic procedure.

Decide in advance if you want a tourist or transit visa; transit visas, usually valid for just 48 or 72 hours, are often cheaper and issued faster, but it's usually not possible to extend a transit visa or change it into a tourist visa.

### Registration

Some countries require visitors to register with the local authorities within 48 hours of arrival, supposedly so they know where you are staying.

→ If you're staying at a hotel or other official accommodation, the administration will take care of registration for you.

→ If you're staying with friends, relatives or in a private room, you're supposed to register with the police yourself. In some cases, this is a formality that is never enforced, so you can skip it. In other cases (such as Russia), you can be fined if you do not go through the motions.

→ Obtaining registration through the proper channels is a major hassle, often requiring fluent language skills, a pile of documents and several hours of negotiation. You are better off paying a local travel agency for the registration instead of trying to do it yourself.

## Women Travellers

Women travellers will generally find Eastern Europe safe and welcoming, whether you're in company or on your own. Macho attitudes prevail in some areas, so you can expect some condescension dressed as courtesy (asking about your husband, or unsolicited help parking your car).

It is not unusual for women to be propositioned by strangers on the street, which can be annoying and sometimes threatening. As a rule, the further east you go, the more exotic foreigners will seem; attention is rarely dangerous and is easily deflected with a shake of the head and a firm 'no'. Remember that in some of the Balkans (Albania and Bulgaria) a nod of the head means no, not yes! Use the local language if you can, but English usually works fine.

In Muslim countries, women travelling solo will certainly be of interest or curiosity to both local men and women. In Albania and Bosnia & Hercegovina, women may feel self-conscious in bars and cafes outside larger

cities, which are usually populated only by men. (The same gender imbalance may also apply at cafes in rural parts of non-Muslim countries.) Unmarried men rarely have contact with women outside their family unit and so may shower travelling women with too much attention. (In such areas, women travelling with a male companion will often experience the opposite and may need to pinch themselves as a reminder that yes, they actually exist.)

## Work

EU citizens have free rein to work in many countries in the region. However, with unemployment still a problem in many areas, Eastern European countries aren't always keen on handing out jobs to foreigners.

If you're not an EU citizen, the paperwork involved in arranging a work permit can be almost impossible, especially for temporary work. That doesn't prevent enterprising travellers from topping up their funds occasionally – and they don't always have to do this illegally. If you do find a temporary job in Eastern Europe, though, the pay is likely to be low. Do it for the experience, not to earn your fortune.

→ Teaching English is the easiest way to make some extra cash, but the market is saturated in places such as Prague and Budapest. You'll probably be more successful in less popular places such as Sofia and Bucharest.

→ If you play an instrument or have other artistic talents, you could try working the streets. Some countries may require municipal permits for this sort of thing, so talk to other street artists before you start.

→ *Work Your Way Around the World* by Susan Griffith gives good, practical advice on a wide range of issues.

# Transport

## GETTING THERE & AWAY

### Entering Eastern Europe

It's never been easier (or cheaper) to reach Eastern Europe, especially from major Western European cities. The region has long been easily accessible by rail and bus, with hubs like Prague particularly well-connected. There's an enormous range of routes by air, thanks to budget carriers like easyJet and Wizz Air, with budget flights (particularly from the UK) reaching airports from the Czech Republic to Ukraine.

Flights, cars and tours can be booked online at lonelyplanet.com/bookings.

### Air

Thanks to the budget-airline boom, there is an abundant choice of destinations in Eastern Europe to which you can fly direct. Some routes are seasonal (coming to life only in summer or for the ski season) while popular destinations – Prague, Budapest, Kraków and Moscow – are well served by year-round flights. Book up to three months in advance if possible, but low prices are often available at short notice (outside high summer).

### Airports

Moscow (Russia), Prague (Czech Republic), Budapest (Hungary) and Warsaw (Poland) are the region's best-connected air hubs. They all have transatlantic flights as well as plenty of flights from Western Europe; they are also well served by budget airlines. Other smaller hubs are St Petersburg (Russia), Rīga (Latvia), Cluj-Napoca and Timişoara (Romania), Zagreb (Croatia), Kyiv (Ukraine) and Bratislava (Slovakia), all of which have daily flights to many major European cities. Most of the small hubs also have budget-airline connections, though these tend to be less frequent further east.

### Land

Apart from standard border queues, document checks and the occasional search, reaching Eastern Europe overland is fairly straightforward. Many travellers arrive in this way, into major rail and bus stations such as Belgrade, Budapest, Prague and Moscow. These hubs are well connected to numerous major cities in Western Europe.

Depending on the countries and borders involved, the relative efficiency of train and bus links can vary greatly (along with border waiting times); it's worth doing some research about the best mode of transport from your departure country.

---

### CLIMATE CHANGE & TRAVEL

Every form of transport that relies on carbon-based fuel generates $CO_2$, the main cause of human-induced climate change. Modern travel is dependent on aeroplanes, which might use less fuel per kilometre per person than most cars but travel much greater distances. The altitude at which aircraft emit gases (including $CO_2$) and particles also contributes to their climate change impact. Many websites offer 'carbon calculators' that allow people to estimate the carbon emissions generated by their journey and, for those who wish to do so, to offset the impact of the greenhouse gases emitted with contributions to portfolios of climate-friendly initiatives throughout the world. Lonely Planet offsets the carbon footprint of all staff and author travel.

## Bus

Buses are a useful fallback if there are no trains or flights to your destination, and in some areas they may be quicker and more reliable than trains. As a means for travelling from Western Europe they are also cheap. Journeys between Schengen countries will be uninterrupted; otherwise there may be border passport checks on or off the bus.

**Ecolines** (http://ecolines.net/en) Runs buses between Eastern and Western Europe.

**Eurolines** (www.eurolines.com) Has a vast network with member companies in many Eastern European countries and offers innumerable routes across the continent.

## Car & Motorcycle

Travelling by car or motorcycle into Eastern Europe gives travellers an immense amount of freedom and is generally worry-free. But keep in mind that some insurance packages, especially those covering rental cars, do not include all European countries. Be sure to ask the agency to insure the car in all the countries where you plan to travel. It's outright forbidden to take rental cars into certain countries; always double-check with your provider.

Since 2016, citizens of third countries are not permitted to use highway crossings between Russia and Belarus.

Some countries require the purchase of a *vignette*, a road-tax sticker displayed on the windscreen, whatever the journey length on their roads. *Vignettes* can be bought, along with fuel, at almost all major road border points.

## Train

There are numerous routes into the region by train. Major railway hubs are Prague (Czech Republic), Budapest (Hungary), Bucharest (Romania), Belgrade (Serbia) and Moscow (Russia). Alba-

nia has no international train services.

From Asia, the Trans-Siberian, Trans-Mongolian and Trans-Manchurian Railways connect Moscow to the Russian Far East, China, North Korea and Mongolia. Long-distance trains from Moscow reach central Asian cities such as Tashkent (Uzbekistan), Bishkek (Kyrgyzstan) and Almaty (Kazakhstan). Overnight trains also connect Belgrade, Budapest and Sofia (Bulgaria) with İstanbul (Turkey). At the time of writing, rail routes between İstanbul and Bucharest required a change by bus.

Depending on the countries, expect some degree of checks when crossing the border. They usually involve guards boarding a train to view travel tickets, visas (bought separately and in advance) and passports, and perform checks for stowaways in train compartments. In some places (like the Russia–China border) there may be a long wait for bogie exchange, which is needed where rail-track gauges differ between countries.

Seat 61 (www.seat61. com) is an indispensable resource to start planning long-distance train travel into Eastern Europe.

## Sea

Boats from several companies connect Italy with Croatia, Slovenia, Montenegro and Albania; there are also services between Corfu (Greece) and Albania. Timetables vary greatly by season so check well ahead.

Ferries also ply the Gulf of Finland and Baltic Sea, connecting Helsinki (Finland) and Stockholm (Sweden) with Tallinn (Estonia), St Petersburg (Russia) and Rīga (Latvia). In Poland, Gdańsk and Gdynia are linked to Sweden, and Świnoujście (near Szczecin) to Denmark. Klaipėda (Lithuania) is served by ferries from Germany.

# GETTING AROUND

## Air

Major Eastern European cities are connected by a full schedule of regular flights within the region. Budget-airline prices are competitive with trains and sometimes with buses.

Many countries offer domestic flights, although there is rarely a need to fly internally unless you are in a particular rush. Russia is the exception; flying from either Moscow or St Petersburg to Kaliningrad saves you the trouble of getting a double-entry Russian visa, which you would need if travelling to Kaliningrad overland (which crosses the border and gives your visa an exit stamp).

## Bicycle

Eastern Europe is compact enough for exciting cross-border biking routes, and mountainous enough to thrill even seasoned cyclists. Easy areas to cycle include Bulgaria's Black Sea coast, flat Estonia, Hungary and Poland. Cycling culture is slow to catch on in several countries, though Slovakia and Romania have small but growing bike scenes. Cycling is a tough mode of transport to explore certain countries, such as Albania.

**European Cyclists' Federation** (www.ecf.com) Advocates bike-friendly policies and offers advice.

**EuroVelo** (www.eurovelo.com) Details long-distance bike routes across the continent, including many in Eastern Europe.

## Hire

Except in a few of the more visited regions, it can be difficult to hire bikes. The most reliable spots are often camping grounds and

## CROSSING BORDERS

The Schengen Agreement, which allows for passport-free travel within a large chunk of Europe, includes the Czech Republic, Estonia, Hungary, Latvia, Lithuania, Poland, Slovakia and Slovenia. Prospective Schengen area members include Bulgaria, Croatia and Romania – for up-to-date details see www.schengenvisainfo.com.

### Russia–Belarus Border

There is effectively no border between Russia and Belarus, though visas for both countries are a legal requirement for travellers. However most nationals don't need a Belarus visa if visiting Belarus for five days or less and arriving by air. You'll still need a Russian visa if you're travelling onward to Russia.

Hotels in both countries won't take you without a visa, if required, and if your visa-less documents are checked on the street, you will be deported. In 2016, Russia announced that highway crossings between Russia and Belarus can't be used by citizens of third countries.

If you do not receive a migration card when entering Russia, contact your embassy immediately upon arrival. If you do not receive an entry stamp, go to the local OVIR (Visa and Registration) office in Russia – but bring a full supply of patience.

If you plan to travel from Belarus into Russia, ensure you have a valid visa for Russia as well. This will be stamped by Belarusian control on entry to Belarus and, under the terms of the Russian–Belarusian 'one state' agreement, is valid as an entry stamp for Russia. Keep your immigration card from Belarus and use it when you leave Russia, as they are valid in both countries.

### Russia–Ukraine Border

Following the annexation of Crimea in 2014, scores of border posts between Russia and Ukraine were closed at the time of writing. It was still possible to cross in both directions by vehicle or train, with the exception of rebel-held zones in southeastern Ukraine and Crimea. Crossing into rebel-held zones or Crimea from the Russian side is a criminal offence under Ukrainian law. To enter Crimea from Ukraine, you need special permission from the Ukrainian authorities and you must return by the same route.

resort hotels during summer months, or hostels in major cities.

## Transporting a Bicycle

When flying with your own bike, it's best to take it apart and pack the pieces in a bike bag or box. Some airlines will simply tag a bike as check-in luggage, others will refuse to handle them unbagged; check ahead.

Bikes can usually be transported on trains as luggage, subject to a fairly small supplementary fee. If it's possible, book tickets in advance. Alternatively you can look into sending your bike on to your desired destination on a cargo train.

## Tours

Plenty of specialist companies offer organised cycling tours of Eastern Europe. They generally plan the itinerary, organise accommodation and transport luggage, making life a lot simpler for cyclists.

**Experience Plus** (www.experienceplus.com) Runs tours throughout the region, including Croatian islands, the Carpathian Mountains and Slovenia's lakes.

**Top Bicycle** (www.topbicycle.com) This Czech company offers cycling tours of the Czech Republic, Hungary, Poland and Slovakia, as well as more extensive tours around the region.

**Velo Touring** (www.velo-touring.hu) Based in Budapest, this company offers tours of Hungary, as

well as bike rentals for those who want to go it alone.

## Boat

Eastern Europe's rivers, canals, lakes and seas provide rich opportunities for boat travel, although in almost all cases these are very much pleasure cruises rather than particularly practical ways to get around. Boat travel is usually far more expensive than the equivalent bus or train journey, but that's not necessarily the point.

## Bus

Buses are a viable alternative to the rail network in most Eastern European countries (and a better option than trains in Albania and Bulgaria). Generally they tend to complement the rail system rather than duplicate it, though in some countries – notably Hungary, the Czech Republic and Slovakia – you'll almost always have a choice between the two options.

➡ Buses tend to be best for shorter hops, getting around cities and reaching remote rural villages. They are often the only option in mountainous regions.

➡ In general, buses are slightly cheaper and slower than trains. The ticketing system varies in each country, but advance reservations are rarely necessary. On long-distance buses you can often pay upon boarding, although it's safest to buy your ticket in advance at the station.

➡ The only company covering the majority of the region is Eurolines (www. eurolines.com).

## Car & Motorcycle

Travelling with your own vehicle allows you increased flexibility and the option to get off the beaten track. However, cars can be inconvenient in city centres when you have to negotiate strange one-way systems or find somewhere to park in the narrow streets of old towns.

It is definitely not recommended to drive a rental car from Serbia into Kosovo, and vice versa.

### Driving Licence & Documentation

➡ Always double-check which type of licence is required in your chosen destination before departure.

➡ An EU driving licence may be used throughout most of Eastern Europe, as may North American and Australian ones. If you want to be extra cautious – or if you have any other type of licence – you should obtain an International Driving Permit (IDP).

➡ Proof of ownership of a private vehicle should always be carried when driving in Eastern Europe.

➡ If you bring your car into Eastern Europe and it has significant body damage from a previous accident, point this out to customs upon arrival in the country and have it noted somewhere. Damaged vehicles may only be allowed to leave the country with police permission.

### Fuel & Spare Parts

Fuel prices vary considerably from country to country.

➡ Belarus and Russia have the cheapest fuel, followed by Moldova and Ukraine.

➡ At more than double the price, Eastern Europe's most expensive countries for fuel are Albania, Croatia, Slovakia and Slovenia.

➡ Unleaded petrol of 95 or 98 octane is widely available throughout the region and it's a bit cheaper than super (premium grade). Diesel is usually slightly cheaper.

➡ Fuel is readily available across Eastern Europe, but always fill your tank before driving into mountainous or otherwise-remote areas.

➡ Spare parts are widely available from garages and dealerships around the region, although this is less the case in Belarus, Moldova and Ukraine, and of course in more rural areas.

### Hire

➡ The big international companies will give you reliable service and a good standard of vehicle. Prebooked rates are generally lower than walk-in rates at rental offices.

➡ Local companies will usually offer lower prices than the multinationals, but it's best to use ones with good reputations – try asking at your hotel.

➡ Bear in mind that many companies will not allow you to take cars into certain countries. Russia, Belarus, Moldova and Kosovo all regularly feature on forbidden lists – check in advance with the car-hire company you're planning to use.

➡ Remember that even if your hire company allows the vehicle to be taken into that country, your travel-insurance policy may not cover you in that country.

### Insurance

Third-party motor insurance is compulsory throughout the EU. For non-EU countries make sure you check the requirements with your insurer. For more information contact the Association of British Insurers (www.abi.org.uk).

➡ Get your insurer to issue a green card (which may cost extra), an internationally recognised proof of insurance, and check that it lists all the countries you intend to visit. Find details on www.cobx.org.

➡ If the green card doesn't list one of the countries you're visiting and your insurer cannot (or will not) add it, you will have to take out separate third-party cover at the border of the country in question (where available).

➡ The European Accident Statement is available from your insurance company and allows each party at an accident to record information for insurance purposes. The Association of British Insurers has more details. Never sign an accident statement you cannot understand – insist on a translation and sign only if it's acceptable.

➡ Taking out a European breakdown-assistance policy, such as those offered by the AA (www.theaa.com)

and RAC (www.rac.co.uk), is a good investment.

→ Non-Europeans might find it cheaper to arrange for international coverage with their own national motoring organisation before leaving home. Ask about reciprocal services offered by affiliated organisations around Europe.

## Road Rules

Motoring organisations can supply members with country-by-country information on motoring regulations, or they may produce motoring guidebooks for general sale.

Standard international road signs are used in Eastern Europe. When driving in the region, keep the following rules in mind:

→ Drive on the right-hand side of the road and overtake on the left.

→ Seatbelts are mandatory for the driver and all passengers.

→ Motorcyclists (and passengers) must wear a helmet.

→ Children under 12 and intoxicated passengers are not allowed to sit in the front seat in most countries.

→ Speed limits are posted, but do research on the country's speed limits and driving norms before you head out.

→ Drink-driving is a serious offence – most Eastern European countries have a 0% blood-alcohol concentration (BAC) limit.

→ Some countries require headlights to be switched on low beam at all times; rental cars may be set up to do so automatically.

→ Trams have priority at crossroads and when they are turning right. Don't pass a tram that's stopping to let off passengers until everyone is out and the doors have closed again, and never block a tram route.

→ It's usually illegal to stop or park at the top of slopes, in front of pedestrian crossings, at bus or tram stops, on bridges or at level crossings.

→ Traffic police usually administer fines on the spot; always ask for a receipt (if they refuse, it may be a scam).

→ Almost everywhere in Europe it is compulsory to carry a red warning triangle, which you must use when parking on a highway in an emergency. If you don't use the triangle and another vehicle hits you from behind, you will be held responsible.

→ A first-aid kit, fire extinguisher and reflective vest are also required in most Eastern European countries.

## Road Hazards

Driving in Eastern Europe can be much more dangerous than in Western Europe. In the event of any accident, notify the police and your insurer.

→ Theft from vehicles is a problem in many areas and foreign or rental cars make an attractive target. Never leave valuables in your car.

→ In rural areas you may encounter horse-drawn vehicles, cyclists, domestic animals and kamikaze pedestrians.

→ The quality of country roads varies immensely. Don't trust your satnav over local advice, or you may end up on a gravelled, pot-holed road only suited to 4WDs.

→ Driving at night can be particularly hazardous in rural areas where roads are narrow and poorly lit.

→ Winter tyres may be necessary in snow-clad mountainous areas; ask your rental outfit.

## Hitching

Hitching is never entirely safe in any country and we don't recommend it. Travellers who hitch should understand they are taking a small but potentially serious risk.

Public transport remains relatively cheap in Eastern Europe, so hitching is more for the adventure than for the transport, except in some rural areas poorly served by public transport. In some countries, drivers will expect the equivalent of a bus fare, and a few may ask for fuel money.

If you want to give it a try, remember the following key points:

→ Solo travellers expose themselves to the greatest risk when hitching. Hitching in pairs is safer.

→ Don't hitch from city centres; take public transport to suburban exit routes.

→ Make a clearly written cardboard sign indicating your intended destination, remembering to use the local name for the town or city (Praha not Prague, Warszawa not Warsaw).

→ Don't let your luggage be put in the boot, only sit next to a door you can open, and unless you've been holding up a sign, ask drivers where they are going before you say where you're going.

→ Always let someone know where you're going before heading off.

## Local Transport

Eastern European cities generally have good public transport. There are excellent metro networks in Moscow and St Petersburg (Russia), Warsaw (Poland), Prague (Czech Republic), Kyiv (Ukraine), Minsk (Belarus), Budapest (Hungary), Bucharest (Romania) and Sofia (Bulgaria).

Throughout the region, you'll also come across shared minibuses (*marshrutka* in the former Soviet Union, *furgon* in the Balkans) used as both inter- and intra-city transport. It's the most likely way you'll travel between mountain towns in Albania, for example.

Trolleybuses are another phenomenon of Eastern Europe. Although slow, they are environmentally friendly (being powered by electricity) and can be found throughout the former Soviet Union.

Trams are also popular, though they vary greatly in speed and modernity. Those in Russia are often borderline antiques, while Prague's fleet of sleek trams have electronic destination displays and automated announcements.

# Train

Trains are the most atmospheric way to make long overland journeys in Eastern Europe, though in some countries they are slower and less reliable than buses. All major cities are on the rail network and it's perfectly feasible for train travel to be your only form of intercity transport. In general, trains run efficiently.

➡ If you're travelling overnight (which is often the case when you're going between countries), you'll get a bed reservation included in the price of your ticket, although you may have to pay a few euros extra for the bedding once on board.

➡ Each carriage is administered by a steward, who will look after your ticket and – crucially, if you arrive during the small hours – make sure that you get off at the correct stop.

➡ Each carriage has a toilet and washbasin at either end – the state of cleanliness varies. Be aware that toilets may be closed while the train is at a station and for a good 30 minutes before you arrive in a big city.

➡ Overnight trains have the benefit of saving you a night's accommodation, and they are a great way to meet locals.

## Reservations

It's always advisable to buy a ticket in advance. Seat reservations are recommended (where applicable), but are only necessary if the timetable specifies one is required. On busy routes and during the summer, always try to reserve a seat several days in advance.

➡ You can book most routes in the region from any main station in Eastern Europe.

➡ In some countries, especially when buying tickets for long-distance routes, you may be asked to show your passport.

➡ For peace of mind, you may prefer to book tickets via travel agencies before you leave home, although this will be more expensive than booking on arrival.

## Resources

If you plan to travel extensively by train, the following resources are useful planning tools:

**Deutsche Bahn** (www.bahn.com) A useful resource for timetables (and some fares) for trains across Eastern Europe; the website is available in many languages, including English.

**European Rail Timetable** (www.europeanrailtimetable.co.uk) Buy complete listings of train schedules, updated monthly, that indicate where supplements apply or where reservations are necessary.

**Voyages SNCF** (http://uk.voyages-sncf.com/en) Provides information on fares and schedules for trains across Europe.

## Safety

Trains, while generally safe, can attract petty criminals.

➡ Carry your valuables on you at all times – keep your cash, wallet and passport on you, even when visiting the bathroom.

➡ If you are sharing a compartment with others, you'll have to decide whether or not you trust them. It's always best to keep your essential documents on you.

➡ At night, make sure your door is locked from the inside. Stow your valuables in secure pockets or a money belt, or hide them in your luggage under the bed (which usually can't be accessed when someone is lying down).

➡ If you have a compartment to yourself, you can ask the steward to lock it while you go to the dining car or go for a wander outside when the train is stopped. However, be aware that most criminals strike when they can easily disembark from the train and on rare occasions stewards are complicit.

➡ In the former Soviet Union, opinions vary on open-plan 3rd-class accommodation – with so many people observing the carriage's goings-on it can be argued these are actually safer than 2nd- and 1st-class compartments.

## Train Classes

The system of train classes in Eastern Europe is similar to that in Western Europe. Short trips, or longer ones that don't involve sleeping on the train, are usually seated like a normal train – benches (on suburban trains) or aeroplane-style seats (on smarter intercity services).

There are generally three classes of sleeping accommodation on trains – each country has a different name for what are broadly 3rd, 2nd and 1st class. First-class tickets cost one-third more, or even double the price, of 2nd-class tickets.

**Third class** Generally consists of six berths in each compartment and is the cheapest option; not ideal if you like your privacy. In the former Soviet Union, 3rd class is called *platskartny* and does not have compartments; instead, there's just one open-plan carriage with beds everywhere. Third class is not widely available.

**Second class** Known as *kupe* in the former Soviet Union, 2nd class has four berths in a closed compartment; it's the option most used by travellers. If there are two of you, you will share your accommodation with two others. However, if there are three of you, you may have the compartment to yourselves.

**First class** SV or *myagky* in the former Soviet Union is a treat, although generally you are paying for space rather than decor. Here you'll find two berths in a compartment plus, possibly, other amenities such as TV or meals.

## Train Passes

Passes are available online or through most travel agents. Not all countries in Eastern Europe are covered by rail passes, but they can be worthwhile if you are concentrating your travels on a particular part of the region, and if you're planning on extensive travel by rail. Always do the maths before committing to a pass: purchasing separate advance tickets for a few journeys may be cheaper. Check out the excellent summary of available passes, and their pros and cons, at Man In Seat 61 (www.seat61.com/Railpass-and-Eurail-pass-guide.htm)

Keep in mind that all passes offer discounted 'youth' prices for travellers who are under 28 years of age on the first day of travel. Some passes allow an accompanying child to travel for free. Discounted fares are available if you are travelling in a group of two to five people (although you must always travel together).

In the USA and Australia, you can buy passes through Rail Europe (www.raileurope. com and www.raileurope. com.au); in Australia you can also use Rail Plus (www.rail-plus.com.au) or International Rail (www.internationalrail. com.au).

### BALKAN FLEXIPASS

The Balkan Flexipass covers Bosnia & Hercegovina, Bulgaria, Greece, Macedonia, Montenegro, Romania, Serbia and Turkey, and includes some ferries to Corfu and Italy. It is not available to anyone who is a resident of the countries included in the pass. It's valid for 1st-class travel only.

### EURAIL GLOBAL

The famous Eurail Pass (www.eurail.com) allows the greatest flexibility for 'overseas' visitors only – if you are a resident of Europe, check out the InterRail Pass. The Eurail Global pass allows unlimited travel in up to 28 countries, including Croatia, the Czech Republic, Hungary, Romania and Slovenia. The pass is valid for a set number of consecutive days or a set number of days within a period of time.

### EURAIL SELECT

Again, only non-European residents can purchase this pass, which covers travel in two to four neighbouring countries, which you choose from the 26 available. Your Eastern European options include Bulgaria, Croatia, the Czech Republic, Hungary, Montenegro, Poland, Romania, Serbia, Slovakia and Slovenia. Note that Serbia and Montenegro count as one country for Eurail pass purposes, as do Croatia and Slovenia.

### INTERRAIL GLOBAL

These passes are available to European residents (proof of residency is required), including residents of Turkey. Terms and conditions vary slightly from country to country, but the InterRail pass is not valid for travel within your country of residence. For complete information, go online to InterRail (www.interrail.eu).

InterRail Global allows unlimited travel in 30 European countries, including Bosnia & Hercegovina, Bulgaria, Croatia, the Czech Republic, Hungary, Macedonia, Montenegro, Poland, Romania, Serbia, Slovakia and Slovenia.

### INTERRAIL & EURAIL COUNTRY PASSES

If you are intending to travel extensively within any one country, you might consider purchasing a Country Pass – InterRail (www.interrail.eu) if you are an EU resident, Eurail (www.eurail.com) if not. The Eurail Country Pass is available for Bulgaria, Croatia, the Czech Republic, Hungary, Poland, Romania, Slovakia and Slovenia. The InterRail Country Pass is available for all of those countries, plus Macedonia and Serbia. The passes and prices vary for each country, so check out the websites for more information. You'll need to travel extensively to recoup your money, but the passes will save you the time and hassle of buying individual tickets that don't require reservations. Some of these countries also offer national rail passes.

# Language

This chapter offers basic vocabulary to help you get around Eastern Europe. Read our coloured pronunciation guides as if they were English and you'll be understood. The stressed syllables are indicated with italics.

Some phrases in this chapter have both polite and informal forms (indicated by the abbreviations 'pol' and 'inf' respectively). The abbreviations 'm' and 'f' indicate masculine and feminine gender respectively.

## ALBANIAN

In Albanian – also understood in Kosovo – ew is pronounced as 'ee' with rounded lips, uh as the 'a' in 'ago', dh as the 'th' in 'that', dz as the 'ds' in 'adds', and zh as the 's' in 'pleasure'. Also, ll and rr are pronounced stronger than when they are written as single letters.

## Basics

| | | |
|---|---|---|
| Hello. | Tungjatjeta. | toon·dya·tye·ta |
| Goodbye. | Mirupafshim. | mee·roo·paf·sheem |
| Excuse me. | Më falni. | muh fal·nee |
| Sorry. | Më vjen keq. | muh vyen kech |
| Please. | Ju lutem. | yoo loo·tem |
| Thank you. | Faleminderit. | fa·le·meen·de·reet |
| Yes. | Po. | po |
| No. | Jo. | yo |

**What's your name?**
Si quheni?                  see choo·he·nee

**My name is ...**
Unë quhem ...               oo·nuh choo·hem ...

**Do you speak English?**
A flisni anglisht?          a flees·nee ang·leesht

**I don't understand.**
Unë nuk kuptoj.             oo·nuh nook koop·toy

## Accommodation

| | | |
|---|---|---|
| campsite | vend kampimi | vend kam·pee·mee |
| guesthouse | bujtinë | booy·tee·nuh |

| | | |
|---|---|---|
| hotel | hotel | ho·tel |
| youth hostel | fjetore për të rinj | fye·to·re puhr tuh reeny |

**Do you have a single/double room?**
A keni një dhomë teke/dopjo?    a ke·nee nyuh dho·muh te·ke/dop·yo

**How much is it per night/person?**
Sa kushton për një natë/njeri?    sa koosh·ton puhr nyuh na·tuh/nye·ree

## Eating & Drinking

**Is there a vegetarian restaurant near here?**
A ka ndonjë restorant vegjetarian këtu afër?    a ka ndo·nyuh res·to·rant ve·dye·ta·ree·an kuh·too a·fuhr

**What would you recommend?**
Çfarë më rekomandoni?    chfa·ruh muh re·ko·man·do·nee

**I'd like the bill/menu, please.**
Më sillni faturën/ menunë, ju lutem.    muh seell·nee fa·too·ruhn/ mc·noo·nuh yoo loo·tem

| | | |
|---|---|---|
| I'll have ... | Dua ... | doo·a ... |
| Cheers! | Gëzuar! | guh·zoo·ar |

## Emergencies

| | | |
|---|---|---|
| Help! | Ndihmë! | ndeeh·muh |
| Go away! | Ik! | eek |

| Numbers – Albanian | | |
|---|---|---|
| 1 | një | nyuh |
| 2 | dy | dew |
| 3 | tre | tre |
| 4 | katër | ka·tuhr |
| 5 | pesë | pe·suh |
| 6 | gjashtë | dyash·tuh |
| 7 | shtatë | shta·tuh |
| 8 | tetë | te·tuh |
| 9 | nëntë | nuhn·tuh |
| 10 | dhjetë | dhye·tuh |

**Call the doctor/police!**
*Thirrni doktorin/*
*policinë!*
*theerr·nee dok·to·reen/*
*po·lee·tsee·nuh*

**I'm lost.**
*Kam humbur rrugën.*
kam *hoom*·boor *rroo*·guhn

**I'm ill.**
*Jam i/e sëmurë. (m/f)*
yam ee/e suh·*moo*·ruh

**Where are the toilets?**
*Ku janë banjat?*
koo *ya*·nuh *ba*·nyat

## Shopping & Services

**I'm looking for ...**
*Po kërkoj për ...*
po kuhr·*koy* puhr ...

**How much is it?**
*Sa kushton?*
sa koosh·*ton*

**That's too expensive.**
*Është shumë*
*shtrenjtë.*
uhsh·tuh *shoo*·muh
*shtreny*·tuh

| | | |
|---|---|---|
| **market** | *treg* | treg |
| **post office** | *posta* | *pos*·ta |
| **tourist office** | *zyrë* | *zew*·ra |
| | *turistike* | too·rees·*tee*·ke |

## Transport

| | | |
|---|---|---|
| **boat** | *anija* | a·*nee*·ya |
| **bus** | *autobusi* | a·oo·to·*boo*·see |
| **plane** | *aeroplani* | a·e·ro·*pla*·nee |
| **train** | *treni* | *tre*·nee |
| **One ... ticket (to Shkodër), please.** | *Një biletë ... (për në Shkodër), ju lutem.* | nyuh bee·*le*·tuh ... (puhr nuh *shko*·duhr) yoo *loo*·tem |
| one-way | *për vajtje* | puhr *vai*·tye |
| return | *kthimi* | *kthee*·mee |

# BULGARIAN
In Bulgarian, vowels in unstressed syllables are generally pronounced shorter and weaker than they are in stressed syllables. Note that uh is pronounced as the 'a' in 'ago' and zh as the 's' in 'pleasure'.

## Basics

| | | |
|---|---|---|
| **Hello.** | Здравейте. | zdra·*vey*·te |
| **Goodbye.** | Довиждане. | do·*veezh*·da·ne |
| **Excuse me.** | Извинете. | iz·vee·*ne*·te |
| **Sorry.** | Съжалявам. | suh·zhal·*ya*·vam |
| **Please.** | Моля. | *mol*·ya |
| **Thank you.** | Благодаря. | bla·go·dar·*ya* |

### Numbers – Bulgarian

| | | |
|---|---|---|
| 1 | един | ed·*een* |
| 2 | два | dva |
| 3 | три | tree |
| 4 | четири | *che*·tee·ree |
| 5 | пет | pet |
| 6 | шест | shest |
| 7 | седем | *se*·dem |
| 8 | осем | *o*·sem |
| 9 | девет | *de*·vet |
| 10 | десет | *de*·set |

| | | |
|---|---|---|
| **Yes.** | Да. | da |
| **No.** | Не. | ne |

**What's your name?**
Как се казвате/
казваш? (pol/inf)
kak se *kaz*·va·te/
*kaz*·vash

**My name is ...**
Казвам се ...
*kaz*·vam se ...

**Do you speak English?**
Говорите ли
английски?
go·*vo*·ree·te lee
ang·*lees*·kee

**I don't understand.**
Не разбирам.
ne raz·*bee*·ram

## Accommodation

| | | |
|---|---|---|
| **campsite** | къмпинг | *kuhm*·peeng |
| **guesthouse** | пансион | pan·see·*on* |
| **hotel** | хотел | ho·*tel* |
| **youth hostel** | общежитие | ob·shte·*zhee*·tee·ye |

| | | |
|---|---|---|
| **Do you have a ... room?** | Имате ли стая с ...? | ee·*ma*·te lee *sta*·ya s ... |
| single | едно легло | ed·*no* leg·*lo* |
| double | едно голямо легло | ed·*no* go·*lya*·mo leg·*lo* |

**How much is it per night/person?**
Колко е на вечер/
човек?
*kol*·ko e na ve·*cher*/
cho·*vek*

## Eating & Drinking

**Do you have vegetarian food?**
Имате ли
вегетерианска
храна?
ee·*ma*·te lee
ve·ge·te·ree·*an*·ska
hra·*na*

**What would you recommend?**
Какво ще
kak·*vo* shte

препоръчате? | pre·po·*ruh*·cha·te

**I'd like the bill/menu, please.**
Дайте ми сметката/ | *dai*·te mee *smet*·ka·ta/
менюто, моля. | men·*yoo*·to *mol*·ya

**I'll have ...** | Ще взема ... | shte *vze*·ma ...
**Cheers!** | Наздраве! | na·*zdra*·ve

## Emergencies

**Help!** | Помощ! | po·mosht
**Go away!** | Махайте се! | *ma*·hai·te se

**Call the doctor/police!**
Повикайте лекар/ | po·*vee*·kai·te le·kar/
полицията! | po·*lee*·tsee·ya·ta
**I'm lost.**
Загубих се. | za·*goo*·beeh se
**I'm ill.**
Болен/Болна | bo·len/*bol*·na
съм. (m/f) | suhm
**Where are the toilets?**
Къде има тоалетни? | kuh·*de* ee·ma to·a·*let*·nee

## Shopping & Services

**I'm looking for ...**
Търся ... | *tuhr*·sya ...
**How much is it?**
Колко струва? | *kol*·ko *stroo*·va
**That's too expensive.**
Скъпо е. | *skuh*·po e

**bank** | банка | *ban*·ka
**post office** | поща | *po*·shta
**tourist office** | бюро за | *byoo*·ro za
| туристическа | too·*ree*·stee·
| информация | ches·ka een·for·
| | ma·tsee·ya

## Transport

**boat** | корабът | ko·*ra*·buht
**bus** | автобусът | av·to·*boo*·suht
**plane** | самолетът | sa·mo·*le*·tuht
**train** | влакът | *vla*·kuht

**One ... ticket** | Един билет | e·*deen* bee·*let*
**(to Varna),** | ... (за Варна), | ... (za *var*·na)
**please.** | моля. | *mol*·ya
  **one-way** | в едната | v ed·*na*·ta
  | посока | po·*so*·ka
  **return** | за отиване | za o·*tee*·va·ne
  | и връщане | ee *vruhsh*·
  | | ta·ne

# CROATIAN & SERBIAN

Croatian and Serbian are very similar and mutually intelligible. Using them, you will also be fully understood in Bosnia & Hercegovina, and Montenegro, and in parts of Kosovo.

In this section, significant differences between Croatian and Serbian are indicated with (C) and (S) respectively. Note that r is rolled and that zh is pronounced as the 's' in 'pleasure'.

## Basics

**Hello.** | Zdravo. | *zdra*·vo
**Goodbye.** | Zbogom. | *zbo*·gom
**Excuse me.** | Oprostite. | o·*pro*·sti·te
**Sorry.** | Žao mi je. | *zha*·o mi ye
**Please.** | Molim. | *mo*·lim
**Thank you.** | Hvala. | *hva*·la
**Yes.** | Da. | da
**No.** | Ne. | ne

**What's your name?**
*Kako se zovete/* | *ka*·ko se zo·ve·te/
*zoveš?* (pol/inf) | zo·vesh
**My name is ...**
*Zovem se ...* | zo·vem se ...
**Do you speak English?**
*Govorite/Govoriš li* | go·vo·ri·te/go·vo·rish
*engleski?* (pol/inf) | li *en*·gle·ski
**I don't understand.**
*Ja ne razumijem.* | ya ne ra·*zu*·mi·yem

## Accommodation

**campsite** | *kamp* | kamp
**guesthouse** | *privatni* | pri·*vat*·ni
| *smještaj* | *smyesh*·tai
**hotel** | *hotel* | *ho*·tel
**youth** | *prenoćište* | pre·no·*chish*·te
**hostel** | *za mladež* | za *mla*·dezh

**Do you have a single/double room?**
*Imate li jednokrevetnu/* | i·ma·te li yed·no·kre·vet·nu/
*dvokrevetnu sobu?* | dvo·kre·vet·nu *so*·bu
**How much is it per night/person?**
*Koliko stoji po* | ko·*li*·ko *sto*·yi po
*noći/osobi?* | *no*·chi/o·so·bi

## Eating & Drinking

**What would you recommend?**
*Što biste preporučili?* | shto *bi*·ste pre·po·*ru*·chi·li
**Do you have vegetarian food?**

| | | |
|---|---|---|
| Da li imate vegetarijanski obrok? | | da li i·ma·te ve·ge·ta·ri·yan·ski o·brok |

**I'd like the bill/menu, please.**

| | | |
|---|---|---|
| Mogu li dobiti račun/ jelovnik, molim? | | mo·gu li do·bi·ti ra·chun/ ye·lov·nik mo·lim |

| I'll have ... | Želim ... | zhe·lim ... |
|---|---|---|
| Cheers! | Živjeli! | zhi·vye·li |

## Emergencies

| Help! | Upomoć! | u·po·moch |
|---|---|---|
| Go away! | Maknite se! | mak·ni·te se |

| Call the ...! | Zovite ...! | zo·vi·te ... |
|---|---|---|
| doctor | liječnika (C) lekara (S) | li·yech·ni·ka le·ka·ra |
| police | policiju | po·li·tsi·yu |

**I'm lost.**

| | | |
|---|---|---|
| Izgubio/Izgubila sam se. (m/f) | | iz·gu·bi·o/iz·gu·bi·la sam se |

**I'm ill.**

| | | |
|---|---|---|
| Ja sam bolestan/ bolesna. (m/f) | | ya sam bo·le·stan/ bo·le·sna |

**Where are the toilets?**

| | | |
|---|---|---|
| Gdje se nalaze zahodi/toaleti? (C/S) | | gdye se na·la·ze za·ho·di/to·a·le·ti |

## Shopping & Services

**I'm looking for ...**

| Tražim ... | tra·zhim ... |
|---|---|

**How much is it?**

| | | |
|---|---|---|
| Koliko stoji/ košta? (C/S) | | ko·li·ko sto·yi/ kosh·ta |

**That's too expensive.**

| To je preskupo. | to ye pre·sku·po |
|---|---|

| bank | | |
|---|---|---|
| banka | | ban·ka |

### Numbers – Croatian & Serbian

| 1 | jedan | ye·dan |
|---|---|---|
| 2 | dva | dva |
| 3 | tri | tri |
| 4 | četiri | che·ti·ri |
| 5 | pet | pet |
| 6 | šest | shest |
| 7 | sedam | se·dam |
| 8 | osam | o·sam |
| 9 | devet | de·vet |
| 10 | deset | de·set |

| post office | poštanski ured | po·shtan·skee oo·red |
|---|---|---|
| tourist office | turistička agencija | tu·ris·tich·ka a·gen·tsi·ya |

## Transport

| boat | brod | brod |
|---|---|---|
| bus | autobus | a·u·to·bus |
| plane | zrakoplov (C) avion (S) | zra·ko·plov a·vi·on |
| train | vlak/voz (C/S) | vlak/voz |

| One ... ticket (to Sarajevo), please. | Jednu ... kartu (do Sarajeva), molim. | yed·nu ... kar·tu (do sa·ra·ye·va) mo·lim |
|---|---|---|
| one-way | jedno- smjernu | yed·no- smyer·nu |
| return | povratnu | po·vrat·nu |

## CZECH

An accent mark over a vowel in written Czech indicates it's pronounced as a long sound. Note that air is pronounced as in 'hair', aw as in 'law', oh as the 'o' in 'note', ow as in 'how', uh as the 'a' in 'ago', kh as the 'ch' in the Scottish *loch*, and zh as the 's' in 'pleasure'. Also, r is rolled in Czech and the apostrophe ( ' ) indicates a slight y sound.

## Basics

| Hello. | Ahoj. | uh·hoy |
|---|---|---|
| Goodbye. | Na shledanou. | nuh·skhle· duh·noh |
| Excuse me. | Promiňte. | pro·min'·te |
| Sorry. | Promiňte. | pro·min'·te |
| Please. | Prosím. | pro·seem |
| Thank you. | Děkuji. | dye·ku·yi |
| Yes. | Ano. | uh·no |
| No. | Ne. | ne |

**What's your name?**

| | | |
|---|---|---|
| Jak se jmenujete/ jmenuješ? (pol/inf) | | yuhk se yme·nu·ye·te/ yme·nu·yesh |

**My name is ...**

| Jmenuji se ... | yme·nu·yi se ... |
|---|---|

**Do you speak English?**

| Mluvíte anglicky? | mlu·vee·te uhn·glits·ki |
|---|---|

**I don't understand.**

| Nerozumím. | ne·ro·zu·meem |
|---|---|

| Numbers – Czech | | |
|---|---|---|
| 1 | jeden | ye·den |
| 2 | dva | dvuh |
| 3 | tři | trzhi |
| 4 | čtyři | chti·rzhi |
| 5 | pět | pyet |
| 6 | šest | shest |
| 7 | sedm | se·dm |
| 8 | osm | o·sm |
| 9 | devět | de·vyet |
| 10 | deset | de·set |

## Accommodation

| campsite | tábořiště | ta·bo·rzhish·tye |
|---|---|---|
| guesthouse | penzion | pen·zi·on |
| hotel | hotel | ho·tel |
| youth hostel | mládežnická ubytovna | mla·dezh·nyits·ka u·bi·tov·nuh |

**Do you have a ... room?**
*Máte jednolůžkový/* ma·te yed·no·loozh·ko·vee
*dvoulůžkový pokoj?* dvoh·loozh·ko·vee po·koy

| How much is it per ...? | Kolik to stojí ...? | ko·lik to sto·yee ... |
|---|---|---|
| night | na noc | nuh nots |
| person | za osobu | zuh o·so·bu |

## Eating & Drinking

**What would you recommend?**
*Co byste doporučil/* tso bis·te do·po·ru·chil/
*doporučila? (m/f)* do·po·ru·chi·luh

**Do you have vegetarian food?**
*Máte vegetariánská* ma·te ve·ge·tuh·ri·ans·ka
*jídla?* yeed·luh

**I'd like the bill/menu, please.**
*Chtěl/Chtěla bych* khtyel/khtye·luh bikh
*účet/jídelníček,* oo·chet/yee·del·nyee·chek
*prosím. (m/f)* ... pro·seem

| I'll have ... | Dám si ... | dam si ... |
|---|---|---|
| Cheers! | Na zdraví! | nuh zdruh·vee |

## Emergencies

| Help! | Pomoc! | po·mots |
|---|---|---|
| Go away! | Běžte pryč! | byezh·te prich |

**Call the doctor/police!**
*Zavolejte lékaře/* zuh·vo·ley·te lair·kuh·rzhe/
*policii!* po·li·tsi·yi

**I'm lost.**
*Zabloudil/* zuh·bloh·dyil/
*Zabloudila jsem. (m/f)* zuh·bloh·dyi·luh ysem

**I'm ill.**
*Jsem nemocný/* ysem ne·mots·nee/
*nemocná. (m/f)* ne·mots·na

**Where are the toilets?**
*Kde jsou toalety?* gde ysoh to·uh·le·ti

## Shopping & Services

**I'm looking for ...**
*Hledám ...* hle·dam ...

**How much is it?**
*Kolik to stojí?* ko·lik to sto·yee

**That's too expensive.**
*To je moc drahé.* to ye mots druh·hair

| bank | banka | buhn·kuh |
|---|---|---|
| post office | pošta | posh·tuh |
| tourist office | turistická informační kancelář | tu·ris·tits·ka in·for·muhch·nyee kuhn·tse·larzh |

## Transport

| bus | autobus | ow·to·bus |
|---|---|---|
| plane | letadlo | le·tuhd·lo |
| train | vlak | vluhk |

| One ... ticket to (Telč), please. | ... jízdenku do (Telče), prosím. | ... yeez·den·ku do (tel·che) pro·seem |
|---|---|---|
| one-way | Jedno-směrnou | yed·no-smyer·noh |
| return | Zpáteční | zpa·tech·nyee |

# ESTONIAN

Double vowels in written Estonian indicate they are pronounced as long sounds. Note that air is pronounced as in 'hair', aw as in 'law', ea as in 'ear', eu as the 'u' in 'nurse', ew as 'ee' with rounded lips, oh as the 'o' in 'note', ow as in 'how', uh as the 'a' in 'ago', kh as in the Scottish loch, and zh as the 's' in 'pleasure'.

## Basics

| Hello. | Tere. | te·re |
|---|---|---|
| Goodbye. | Nägemist. | nair·ge·mist |
| Excuse me. | Vabandage. (pol) | va·ban·da·ge |
| | Vabanda. (inf) | va·ban·da |
| Sorry. | Vabandust. | va·ban·dust |

| | | |
|---|---|---|
| Please. | Palun. | pa·lun |
| Thank you. | Tänan. | tair·nan |
| Yes. | Jaa. | yaa |
| No. | Ei. | ay |

**What's your name?**
Mis on teie nimi?     mis on tay·e ni·mi

**My name is ...**
Minu nimi on ...     mi·nu ni·mi on ...

**Do you speak English?**
Kas te räägite     kas te rair·git·te
inglise keelt?     ing·kli·se keylt

**I don't understand.**
Ma ei saa aru.     ma ay saa a·ru

## Eating & Drinking

**What would you recommend?**
Mida te soovitate?     mi·da te saw·vit·tat·te

**Do you have vegetarian food?**
Kas teil on taimetoitu?     kas tayl on tai·met·toyt·tu

**I'd like the bill/menu, please.**
Ma sooviksin     ma saw·vik·sin
arvet/menüüd, palun.     ar·vet/me·newt pa·lun

| I'll have a ... | Ma tahaksin ... | ma ta·hak·sin ... |
|---|---|---|
| Cheers! | Terviseks! | tair·vi·seks |

## Emergencies

| Help! | Appi! | ap·pi |
|---|---|---|
| Go away! | Minge ära! | ming·ke air·ra |

**Call the doctor/police!**
Kutsuge arst/     ku·tsu·ge arst/
politsei!     po·li·tsay

**I'm lost.**
Ma olen ära eksinud.     ma o·len air·ra ek·si·nud

**Where are the toilets?**
Kus on WC?     kus on ve·se

### Numbers – Estonian

| | | |
|---|---|---|
| 1 | üks | ewks |
| 2 | kaks | kaks |
| 3 | kolm | kolm |
| 4 | neli | ne·li |
| 5 | viis | vees |
| 6 | kuus | koos |
| 7 | seitse | say·tse |
| 8 | kaheksa | ka·hek·sa |
| 9 | üheksa | ew·hek·sa |
| 10 | kümme | kewm·me |

## Shopping & Services

**I'm looking for ...**
Ma otsin ...     ma o·tsin

**How much is it?**
Kui palju see maksab?     ku·i pal·yu sey mak·sab

**That's too expensive.**
See on liiga kallis.     sey on lee·ga kal·lis

| bank | pank | pank |
|---|---|---|
| market | turg | turg |
| post office | postkontor | post·kont·tor |

## Transport

| boat | laev | laiv |
|---|---|---|
| bus | buss | bus |
| plane | lennuk | len·nuk |
| train | rong | rongk |

| One ... ticket (to Pärnu), please. | Üks ... pilet (Pärnusse), palun. | ewks ... pi·let (pair·nus·se) pa·lun |
|---|---|---|
| one-way | ühe otsa | ew·he o·tsa |
| return | edasi-tagasi | e·da·si·ta·ga·si |

# HUNGARIAN

A symbol over a vowel in written Hungarian indicates it's pronounced as a long sound. Double consonants should be drawn out a little longer than in English. Note also that aw is pronounced as in 'law', eu as the 'u' in 'nurse', ew as 'ee' with rounded lips, and zh as the 's' in 'pleasure'. Finally, keep in mind that r is rolled in Hungarian and that the apostrophe ( ' ) indicates a slight y sound.

## Basics

| Hello. | Szervusz. (sg) | ser·vus |
|---|---|---|
| | Szervusztok. (pl) | ser·vus·tawk |
| Goodbye. | Viszlát. | vis·lat |
| Excuse me. | Elnézést kérek. | el·ney·zeysht key·rek |
| Sorry. | Sajnálom. | shoy·na·lawm |
| Please. | Kérem. (pol) | key·rem |
| | Kérlek. (inf) | keyr·lek |
| Thank you. | Köszönöm. | keu·seu·neum |
| Yes. | Igen. | i·gen |
| No. | Nem. | nem |

**What's your name?**
*Mi a neve/*          mi o *ne*·ve/
*neved?* (pol/inf)    *ne*·ved

**My name is ...**
*A nevem ...*         o *ne*·vem ...

**Do you speak English?**
*Beszél/Beszélsz*     be·seyl/be·seyls
*angolul?* (pol/inf)  on·gaw·lul

**I don't understand.**
*Nem értem.*          nem eyr·tem

## Accommodation

| | | |
|---|---|---|
| **campsite** | *kemping* | kem·ping |
| **guesthouse** | *panzió* | pon·zi·âw |
| **hotel** | *szálloda* | sal·law·do |
| **youth hostel** | *ifjúsági* | if·yū·sha·gi |
| | *szálló* | sal·lâw |

**Do you have a single/double room?**
*Van Önnek kiadó egy*    von *eun*·nek ki·o·dâw ed'
*egyágyas/duplaágyas*    ej·a·dyosh/dup·lo·a·dyosh
*szobája?*               saw·ba·yo

**How much is it per night/person?**
*Mennyibe kerül egy*    men'·nyi·be ke·rewl ej
*éjszakára/főre?*        ey·so·ka·ro/fēū·re

## Eating & Drinking

**What would you recommend?**
*Mit ajánlana?*         mit o·yan·lo·no

**Do you have vegetarian food?**
*Vannak Önöknél*        von·nok eu·neuk·neyl
*vegetáriánus ételek?*  ve·ge·ta·ri·a·nush ey·te·lek

**I'll have ...**
*... kérek.*            ... key·rek

**Cheers! (to one person)**
*Egészségedre!*         e·geys·shey·ged·re

**Cheers! (to more than one person)**
*Egészségetekre!*       e·geys·shey·ge·tek·re

**I'd like the ...**   *... szeretném.*   ... se·ret·neym
  **bill**     *A számlát*    o sam·lat
  **menu**     *Az étlapot*   oz eyt·lo·pawt

## Emergencies

| | | |
|---|---|---|
| **Help!** | *Segítség!* | she·geet·sheyg |
| **Go away!** | *Menjen innen!* | men·yen in·nen |

**Call the doctor!**
*Hívjon orvost!*       heev·yawn awr·vawsht

**Call the police!**
*Hívja a*             heev·yo o
*rendőrséget!*         rend·ēūr·shey·get

---

| 1 | *egy* | ej |
|---|---|---|
| 2 | *kettő* | ket·tēū |
| 3 | *három* | ha·rawm |
| 4 | *négy* | neyj |
| 5 | *öt* | eut |
| 6 | *hat* | hot |
| 7 | *hét* | heyt |
| 8 | *nyolc* | nyawlts |
| 9 | *kilenc* | ki·lents |
| 10 | *tíz* | teez |

**I'm lost.**
*Eltévedtem.*          el·tey·ved·tem

**I'm ill.**
*Rosszul vagyok.*      raws·sul vo·dyawk

**Where are the toilets?**
*Hol a vécé?*          hawl o vey·tsey

## Shopping & Services

**I'm looking for ...**
*Keresem a ...*        ke·re·shem o ...

**How much is it?**
*Mennyibe kerül?*      men'·nyi·be ke·rewl

**That's too expensive.**
*Ez túl drága.*        ez tūl dra·go

| | | |
|---|---|---|
| **market** | *piac* | pi·ots |
| **post office** | *postahivatal* | pawsh·to·hi·vo·tol |
| **tourist office** | *turistairoda* | tu·rish·to·i·raw·do |

## Transport

| | | |
|---|---|---|
| **bus** | *busz* | bus |
| **plane** | *repülőgép* | re·pew·lēū·geyp |
| **train** | *vonat* | vaw·not |
| **One ... ticket** | *Egy ... jegy* | ej ... yej |
| **to (Eger),** | *(Eger)be.* | (e·ger)·be |
| **please.** | | |
|   **one-way** | *csak oda* | chok aw·do |
|   **return** | *oda-vissza* | aw·do·vis·so |

## LATVIAN

A line over a vowel in written Latvian indicates it's pronounced as a long sound. Note that air is pronounced as in 'hair', aw as in 'law', ea as in 'ear', ow as in 'how', wa as in 'water', dz as the 'ds' in 'adds', and zh as the 's' in 'pleasure'. The apostrophe ( ' ) indicates a slight y sound.

## Basics

| Hello. | Sveiks. | svayks |
|--------|---------|--------|
| Goodbye. | Atā. | a·taa |
| Excuse me. | Atvainojiet. | at·vai·nwa·yeat |
| Sorry. | Piedodiet. | pea·dwa·deat |
| Please. | Lūdzu. | loo·dzu |
| Thank you. | Paldies. | pal·deas |
| Yes. | Jā. | yaa |
| No. | Nē. | nair |

**What's your name?**
Kā Jūs sauc? — kaa yoos sowts

**My name is ...**
Mani sauc ... — ma·ni sowts ...

**Do you speak English?**
Vai Jūs runājat angliski? — vai yoos ru·naa·yat ang·li·ski

**I don't understand.**
Es nesaprotu. — es ne·sa·prwa·tu

## Eating & Drinking

**What would you recommend?**
Ko Jūs iesakat? — kwa yoos ea·sa·kat

**Do you have vegetarian food?**
Vai Jums ir veģetārie ēdieni? — vai yums ir ve·dye·taa·rea air·dea·ni

**I'd like the bill/menu, please.**
Es vēlos rēķinu/ ēdienkarti, lūdzu. — es vair·lwas rair·tyi·nu/ air·dean·kar·ti loo·dzu

**I'll have a ...**
Man lūdzu vienu ... — man loo·dzu vea·nu ...

**Cheers!**
Priekā! — prea·kaa

## Emergencies

| Help! | Palīgā! | pa·lee·gaa |
|-------|---------|-----------|
| Go away! | Ej prom! | ay prwam |

**Call the doctor/police!**
Zvani ārstam/policijai! — zva·ni aar·stam/po·li·tsi·yai

**I'm lost.**
Esmu apmaldījies. — es·mu ap·mal·dee·yeas

**Where are the toilets?**
Kur ir tualetes? — kur ir tu·a·le·tes

## Shopping & Services

**I'm looking for ...**
Es meklēju ... — es mek·lair·yu ...

**How much is it?**
Cik maksā? — tsik mak·saa

### Numbers – Latvian

| 1 | viens | veans |
|---|-------|-------|
| 2 | divi | di·vi |
| 3 | trīs | trees |
| 4 | četri | che·tri |
| 5 | pieci | pea·tsi |
| 6 | seši | se·shi |
| 7 | septiņi | sep·ti·nyi |
| 8 | astoņi | as·twa·nyi |
| 9 | deviņi | de·vi·nyi |
| 10 | desmit | des·mit |

**That's too expensive.**
Tas ir par dārgu. — tas ir par daar·gu

| bank | banka | ban·ka |
|------|-------|--------|
| market | tirgus | tir·gus |
| post office | pasts | pasts |

## Transport

| boat | laiva | lai·va |
|------|-------|--------|
| bus | autobus | ow·to·bus |
| plane | lidmašīna | lid·ma·shee·na |
| train | vilciens | vil·tseans |

| One ... ticket (to Jūrmala), please. | Vienu ... biļeti (uz Jūrmalu), lūdzu. | vea·nu ... bi·lye·ti (uz yoor·ma·lu) loo·dzu |
|-----|-----|-----|
| one-way | vienvirziena | vean·vir·zea·na |
| return | turp-atpakaļ | turp·at·pa·kal' |

# LITHUANIAN

Symbols on vowels in written Lithuanian indicate they are pronounced as long sounds. Note that aw is pronounced as in 'law', ea as in 'ear', ow as in 'how', wa as in 'water', dz as the 'ds' in 'adds', and zh as the 's' in 'pleasure'.

## Basics

| Hello. | Sveiki. | svay·ki |
|--------|---------|---------|
| Goodbye. | Viso gero. | vi·so ge·ro |
| Excuse me. | Atleiskite. | at·lays·ki·te |
| Sorry. | Atsiprašau. | at·si·pra·show |
| Please. | Prašau. | pra·show |
| Thank you. | Ačiū. | aa·choo |
| Yes. | Taip. | taip |
| No. | Ne. | ne |

**What's your name?**
Koks jūsų vardas?  kawks yoo·soo var·das

**My name is ...**
Mano vardas ...  ma·no var·das ...

**Do you speak English?**
Ar kalbate angliškai?  ar kal·ba·te aang·lish·kai

**I don't understand.**
Aš nesuprantu.  ash ne·su·pran·tu

## Eating & Drinking

**What would you recommend?**
Ką jūs rekomenduo-  kaa yoos re·ko·men·dwo·
tumėte?  tu·mey·te

**Do you have vegetarian food?**
Ar turite vegetariško  ar tu·ri·te ve·ge·taa·rish·ko
maisto?  mais·to

**I'd like the bill/menu, please.**
Aš norėčiau  ash no·rey·chyow
sąskaitos/meniu  saas·kai·taws/me·nyu

**I'll have a ...**
Aš užsisakysiu ...  ash uzh·si·sa·kee·syu ...

**Cheers!**
Į sveikatą!  ee svay·kaa·taa

## Emergencies

**Help!**  Padėkit!  pa·dey·kit
**Go away!**  Eikit iš čia!  ay·kit ish chya

**Call the doctor/police!**
Iškvieskit gydytoją/  ish·kveas·kit gee·dee·to·ya/
policiją!  po·li·tsi·ya
**I'm lost.**
Aš pasiklydau.  ash pa·si·klee·dow
**Where are the toilets?**
Kur yra tualetai?  kur ee·ra tu·a·le·tai

### Numbers – Lithuanian

| | | |
|---|---|---|
| 1 | vienas | vea·nas |
| 2 | du | du |
| 3 | trys | trees |
| 4 | keturi | ke·tu·rl |
| 5 | penki | pen·ki |
| 6 | šeši | she·shi |
| 7 | septyni | sep·tee·ni |
| 8 | aštuoni | ash·twa·ni |
| 9 | devyni | de·vee·ni |
| 10 | dešimt | de·shimt |

## Shopping & Services

**I'm looking for ...**
Aš ieškau ...  ash eash·kow ...

**How much is it?**
Kiek kainuoja?  keak kain·wo·ya

**That's too expensive.**
Per brangu.  per bran·gu

| | | |
|---|---|---|
| bank | bankas | baan·kas |
| market | turgus | tur·gus |
| post office | paštas | paash·tas |

## Transport

| | | |
|---|---|---|
| boat | laivas | lai·vas |
| bus | autobusas | ow·to·bu·sas |
| plane | lėktuvas | leyk·tu·vas |
| train | traukinys | trow·ki·nees |

| | | |
|---|---|---|
| One ... ticket (to Kaunas), please. | Vieną bilietą ... (Į Kauną), prašau. | vea·naa bi·lye·taa ... (ee kow·naa) pra·show |
| one-way | Į vieną pusę | ee vea·naa pu·sey |
| return | Į abi puses | ee a·bi pu·ses |

# MACEDONIAN

Note that dz is pronounced as the 'ds' in 'adds', r is rolled, and zh as the 's' in 'pleasure'.

## Basics

| | | |
|---|---|---|
| **Hello.** | Здраво. | zdra·vo |
| **Goodbye.** | До гледање. | do gle·da·nye |
| **Excuse me.** | Извинете. | iz·vi·ne·te |
| **Sorry.** | Простете. | pros·te·te |
| **Please.** | Молам. | mo·lam |
| **Thank you.** | Благодарам. | bla·go·da·ram |
| **Yes.** | Да. | da |
| **No.** | Не. | ne |

**What's your name?**
Како се викате/  ka·ko se vi·ka·te/
викаш? (pol/inf)  vi·kash

**My name is ...**
Јас се викам ...  yas se vi·kam ...

**Do you speak English?**
Зборувате ли  zbo·ru·va·te li
англиски?  an·glis·ki

**I don't understand.**
Јас не разбирам.  yas ne raz·bi·ram

LANGUAGE POLISH

## Accommodation

| campsite | камп | kamp |
| guesthouse | приватно сместување | pri·vat·no smes·tu·va·nye |
| hotel | хотел | ho·tel |
| youth hostel | младинско преноќиште | mla·din·sko pre·no·kyish·te |

**Do you have a single/double room?**
Дали имате еднокреветна/ двокреветна соба? — da·li i·ma·te ed·no·kre·vet·na/ dvo·kre·vet·na so·ba

**How much is it per night/person?**
Која е цената за ноќ/еден? — ko·ya e tse·na·ta za noky/e·den

## Eating & Drinking

**What would you recommend?**
Што препорачувате вие? — shto pre·po·ra·chu·va·te vi·e

**Do you have vegetarian food?**
Дали имате вегетаријанска храна? — da·li i·ma·te ve·ge·ta·ri·yan·ska hra·na

**I'd like the bill/menu, please.**
Ве молам сметката/ мени. — ve mo·lam smet·ka·ta/ me·ni

**I'll have ...**
Јас ќе земам ... — yas kye ze·mam ...

**Cheers!**
На здравје! — na zdrav·ye

## Emergencies

| Help! | Помош! | po·mosh |
| Go away! | Одете си! | o·de·te si |

**Call the doctor/police!**
Викнете лекар/ полиција! — vik·ne·te le·kar/ po·li·tsi·ya

### Numbers – Macedonian

| 1 | еден | e·den |
| 2 | два | dva |
| 3 | три | tri |
| 4 | четири | che·ti·ri |
| 5 | пет | pet |
| 6 | шест | shest |
| 7 | седум | se·dum |
| 8 | осум | o·sum |
| 9 | девет | de·vet |
| 10 | десет | de·set |

**I'm lost.**
Се загубив. — se za·gu·biv

**I'm ill.**
Јас сум болен/ болна. (m/f) — yas sum bo·len/ bol·na

**Where are the toilets?**
Каде се тоалетите? — ka·de se to·a·le·ti·te

## Shopping & Services

**I'm looking for ...**
Барам ... — ba·ram ...

**How much is it?**
Колку чини тоа? — kol·ku chi·ni to·a

**That's too expensive.**
Тоа е многу скапо. — to·a e mno·gu ska·po

| market | пазар | pa·zar |
| post office | пошта | posh·ta |
| tourist office | туристичко биро | tu·ris·tich·ko·to bi·ro |

## Transport

| boat | брод | brod |
| bus | автобус | av·to·bus |
| plane | авион | a·vi·on |
| train | воз | voz |

**One ... ticket (to Ohrid), please.**
Еден ... (за Охрид), ве молам. — e·den ... (za oh·rid) ve mo·lam

| one-way | билет во еден правец | bi·let vo e·den pra·vets |
| return | повратен билет | pov·ra·ten bi·let |

# POLISH

Polish vowels are generally pronounced short. Nasal vowels are pronounced as though you're trying to force the air through your nose, and are indicated with n or m following the vowel. Note that ow is pronounced as in 'how', kh as the 'ch' in the Scottish *loch*, and zh as the 's' in 'pleasure'. Also, r is rolled in Polish and the apostrophe ( ' ) indicates a slight y sound.

## Basics

| Hello. | *Cześć.* | cheshch |
| Goodbye. | *Do widzenia.* | do vee·dze·nya |
| Excuse me. | *Przepraszam.* | pshe·pra·sham |
| Sorry. | *Przepraszam.* | pshe·pra·sham |
| Please. | *Proszę.* | pro·she |

| Thank you. | *Dziękuję.* | jyen·*koo*·ye |
|---|---|---|
| Yes. | *Tak.* | tak |
| No. | *Nie.* | nye |

### What's your name?

| *Jak się pan/pani* | yak shye pan/*pa*·nee |
|---|---|
| *nazywa?* (m/f pol) | na·*zi*·va |
| *Jakie się nazywasz?* (inf) | yak shye na·*zi*·vash |

### My name is ...

| *Nazywam się ...* | na·*zi*·vam shye ... |
|---|---|

### Do you speak English?

| *Czy pan/pani mówi* | chi pan/*pa*·nee *moo*·vee |
|---|---|
| *po angielsku?* (m/f) | po an·*gyel*·skoo |

### I don't understand.

| *Nie rozumiem.* | nye ro·*zoo*·myem |
|---|---|

## Accommodation

| campsite | *kamping* | *kam*·peeng |
|---|---|---|
| guesthouse | *pokoje* | po·*ko*·ye |
| | *gościnne* | gosh·*chee*·ne |
| hotel | *hotel* | *ho*·tel |
| youth hostel | *schronisko* | skhro·*nees*·ko |
| | *młodzieżowe* | mwo·jye·*zho*·ve |

| Do you have | *Czy jest* | chi yest |
|---|---|---|
| a ... room? | *pokój ...?* | po·kooy ... |
| single | *jedno-* | yed·no· |
| | *osobowy* | o·so·*bo*·vi |
| double | *z podwójnym* | z pod·*vooy*·nim |
| | *łóżkiem* | *woozh*·kyem |

### How much is it per night/person?

| *Ile kosztuje* | ee·le kosh·*too*·ye |
|---|---|
| *za noc/osobę?* | za nots/*o*·so·be |

## Eating & Drinking

### What would you recommend?

| *Co by pan polecił?* (m) | tso bi pan po·*le*·cheew |
|---|---|
| *Co by pani poleciła?* (f) | tso bi *pa*·nee po·*le*·chee·wa |

### Do you have vegetarian food?

| *Czy jest żywność* | chi yest zhiv·noshch |
|---|---|
| *wegetariańska?* | ve·ge·tar·*yan*'·ska |

### I'd like the ..., please.

| *Proszę o rachunek/* | pro·she o ra·*khoo*·nek/ |
|---|---|
| *jadłospis.* | ya·*dwo*·spees |

| I'll have ... | *Proszę ...* | pro·she ... |
|---|---|---|
| Cheers! | *Na zdrowie!* | na *zdro*·vye |

### Numbers – Polish

| 1 | *jeden* | ye·den |
|---|---|---|
| 2 | *dwa* | dva |
| 3 | *trzy* | tshi |
| 4 | *cztery* | chte·ri |
| 5 | *pięć* | pyench |
| 6 | *sześć* | sheshch |
| 7 | *siedem* | shye·dem |
| 8 | *osiem* | o·shyem |
| 9 | *dziewięć* | jye·vyench |
| 10 | *dziesięć* | jye·shench |

## Emergencies

| Help! | *Na pomoc!* | na po·mots |
|---|---|---|
| Go away! | *Odejdź!* | o·deyj |

### Call the doctor/police!

| *Zadzwoń po lekarza/* | zad·zvon' po le·*ka*·zha/ |
|---|---|
| *policję!* | po·*lee*·tsye |

### I'm lost.

| *Zgubiłem/* | zgoo·*bee*·wem/ |
|---|---|
| *Zgubiłam się.* (m/f) | zgoo·*bee*·wam shye |

### I'm ill.

| *Jestem chory/a.* (m/f) | yes·tem *kho*·ri/a |
|---|---|

### Where are the toilets?

| *Gdzie są toalety?* | gjye som to·a·*le*·ti |
|---|---|

## Shopping & Services

### I'm looking for ...

| *Szukam ...* | shoo·kam |
|---|---|

### How much is it?

| *Ile to kosztuje?* | ee·le to kosh·*too*·ye |
|---|---|

### That's too expensive.

| *To jest za drogie.* | to yest za *dro*·gye |
|---|---|

| market | *targ* | tark |
|---|---|---|
| post office | *urząd* | oo·zhond |
| | *pocztowy* | poch·*to*·vi |
| tourist office | *biuro* | *byoo*·ro |
| | *turystyczne* | too·ris·*tich*·ne |

## Transport

| boat | *łódź* | wooj |
|---|---|---|
| bus | *autobus* | ow·*to*·boos |
| plane | *samolot* | sa·*mo*·lot |
| train | *pociąg* | po·chonk |

| One ... ticket (to Katowice), please. | Proszę bilet ... (do Katowic). | pro·she bee·let ... (do ka·to·veets) |
|---|---|---|
| one-way | w jedną stronę | v yed·nom stro·ne |
| return | powrotny | po·vro·tni |

# ROMANIAN

Note that ew is pronounced as 'ee' with rounded lips, oh as the 'o' in 'note', ow as in 'how', uh as the 'a' in 'ago', and zh as the 's' in 'pleasure'. The apostrophe ( ' ) indicates a very short, unstressed i (almost silent).

## Basics

| Hello. | Bună ziua. | boo·nuh zee·wa |
|---|---|---|
| Goodbye. | La revedere. | la re·ve·de·re |
| Excuse me. | Scuzaţi-mă. | skoo·za·tsee·muh |
| Sorry. | Îmi pare rău. | ewm' pa·re ruh·oo |
| Please. | Vă rog. | vuh rog |
| Thank you. | Mulţumesc. | mool·tsoo·mesk |
| Yes. | Da. | da |
| No. | Nu. | noo |

**What's your name?**
Cum vă numiţi? — koom vuh noo·meets'

**My name is ...**
Numele meu este ... — noo·me·le me·oo yes·te ...

**Do you speak English?**
Vorbiţi engleza? — vor·beets' en·gle·za

**I don't understand.**
Eu nu înţeleg. — ye·oo noo ewn·tse·leg

## Accommodation

| campsite | teren de camping | te·ren de kem·peeng |
|---|---|---|
| guesthouse | pensiune | pen·syoo·ne |
| hotel | hotel | ho·tel |

| Numbers – Romanian | | |
|---|---|---|
| 1 | unu | oo·noo |
| 2 | doi | doy |
| 3 | trei | trey |
| 4 | patru | pa·troo |
| 5 | cinci | cheench' |
| 6 | şase | sha·se |
| 7 | şapte | shap·te |
| 8 | opt | opt |
| 9 | nouă | no·wuh |
| 10 | zece | ze·che |

| youth hostel | hostel | hos·tel |
|---|---|---|
| Do you have a ... room? | Aveţi o cameră ...? | a·vets' o ka·me·ruh ... |
| single | de o persoană | de o per·so·a·nuh |
| double | dublă | doo·bluh |
| How much is it per ...? | Cît costă ...? | kewt kos·tuh ... |
| night | pe noapte | pe no·ap·te |
| person | de persoană | de per·so·a·nuh |

## Eating & Drinking

**What would you recommend?**
Ce recomandaţi? — che re·ko·man·dats'

**Do you have vegetarian food?**
Aveţi mâncare vegetariană? — a·ve·tsi mewn·ka·re ve·je·ta·rya·nuh

| I'll have ... | Aş dori ... | ash do·ree ... |
|---|---|---|
| Cheers! | Noroc! | no·rok |

| I'd like the ..., please. | Vă rog, aş dori ... | vuh rog ash do·ree ... |
|---|---|---|
| bill | nota de plată | no·ta de pla·tuh |
| menu | meniul | me·nee·ool |

## Emergencies

| Help! | Ajutor! | a·zhoo·tor |
|---|---|---|
| Go away! | Pleacă! | ple·a·kuh |

| Call the ...! | Chemaţi ...! | ke·mats' ... |
|---|---|---|
| doctor | un doctor | oon dok·tor |
| police | poliţia | po·lee·tsya |

**I'm lost.**
M-am rătăcit. — mam ruh·tuh·cheet

**I'm ill.**
Mă simt rău. — muh seemt ruh·oo

**Where are the toilets?**
Unde este o toaletă? — oon·de yes·te o to·a·le·tuh

## Shopping & Services

**I'm looking for ...**
Caut ... — kowt ...

**How much is it?**
Cât costă? — kewt kos·tuh

**That's too expensive.**
*E prea scump.* — ye pre·*a* skoomp

| | | |
|---|---|---|
| **market** | *piaţă* | pya·tsuh |
| **post office** | *poşta* | posh·ta |
| **tourist office** | *biroul de informaţii Iuristice* | bee·ro·ool de een·for·*ma*·tsee too·*rees*·tee·che |

## Transport

| | | |
|---|---|---|
| **boat** | *vapor* | va·*por* |
| **bus** | *autobuz* | ow·to·*booz* |
| **plane** | *avion* | a·*vyon* |
| **train** | *tren* | *tren* |

| | | |
|---|---|---|
| **One ... ticket (to Cluj), please.** | *Un bilet ... (până la Cluj),vă rog.* | oon bee·*let* ... (pew·ruh la kloozh) vuh rog |
| one-way | *dus* | doos |
| return | *dus-întors* | doos ewn·*tors* |

# RUSSIAN

In Russian – also widely used in Belarus – the kh is pronounced as the 'ch' in the Scottish *loch* and zh as the 's' in 'pleasure'. Also, r is rolled in Russian and the apostrophe ( ' ) indicates a slight y sound.

## Basics

| | | |
|---|---|---|
| **Hello.** | Здравствуйте. | *zdrast*·vuyl·ye |
| **Goodbye.** | До свидания. | da svee·*dan*·ya |
| **Excuse me./ Sorry.** | Извините, пожалуйста. | eez·vee·*neet*·ye pa·*zhal*·sta |
| **Please.** | Пожалуйста. | pa·*zhal*·sta |
| **Thank you.** | Спасибо | spa·*see*·ba |
| **Yes.** | Да. | da |
| **No.** | Нет. | nyet |

**What's your name?**
Как вас зовут? — kak vaz za·*vut*

**My name is ...**
Мсня зовут ... — meen·*ya* za·*vut* ...

**Do you speak English?**
Вы говорите по-английски? — vi ga·va·*reet*·ye pa·an·*glee*·skee

**I don't understand.**
Я не понимаю. — ya nye pa·nee·*ma*·yu

## Accommodation

| | | |
|---|---|---|
| **campsite** | кемпинг | *kyem*·peeng |
| **guesthouse** | пансионат | pan·see·a·*nat* |

### Numbers – Russian

| 1 | один | a·*deen* |
|---|---|---|
| 2 | два | dva |
| 3 | три | tree |
| 4 | четыре | chee·*ti*·ree |
| 5 | пять | pyat' |
| 6 | шесть | shest' |
| 7 | семь | syem' |
| 8 | восемь | *vo*·seem' |
| 9 | девять | *dye*·veet' |
| 10 | десять | *dye*·seet' |

| | | |
|---|---|---|
| **hotel** | гостиница | ga·*stee*·neet·sa |
| **youth hostel** | общежитие | ap·shee·*zhi*·tee·ye |

| | | |
|---|---|---|
| **Do you have a ... room?** | У вас есть ...? | u vas yest' ... |
| single | одноместный номер | ad·nam·*yes*·ni *no*·meer |
| double | номер с двуспальней кроватью | *no*·meer z dvu·*spaln*·yey kra·*vat*·yu |

| | | |
|---|---|---|
| **How much is it ...?** | Сколько стоит за ...? | *skol*'·ka *sto*·eet za ... |
| for two people | двоих | dva·*eekh* |
| per night | ночь | noch' |

## Eating & Drinking

**What would you recommend?**
Что вы рекомендуете? — shto vi ree·ka·meen·*du* cet yo

**Do you have vegetarian food?**
У вас есть вегетарианские блюда? — u vas yest' vi·gi·ta·ri·*an*·ski·ye *blyu*·da

**I'd like the bill/menu, please.**
Я бы хотел/хотела счёт/меню. (m/f) — ya bi khat·*yel*/khat·ye·la shot/meen·*yu*

| | | |
|---|---|---|
| **I'll have ...** | ..., пожалуйста. | ... pa·*zhal*·sta |
| **Cheers!** | За здоровье! | za zda·*rov*·ye |

## Emergencies

| | | |
|---|---|---|
| **Help!** | Помогите! | pa·ma·*gee*·tye |
| **Go away!** | Идите отсюда! | ee·*deet*·ye at·*syu*·da |

**Call the doctor/police!**

| | | |
|---|---|---|
| Вызовите врача/ милицию! | *vi*·za·veet·ye vra·*cha*/mee·*leet*·si·yu | |
| **I'm lost.** | | |
| Я потерялся/ потерялась. (m/f) | ya pa·teer·*yal*·sa/ pa·teer·*ya*·las' | |
| **I'm ill.** | | |
| Я болею. | ya bal·*ye*·yu | |
| **Where are the toilets?** | | |
| Где здесь туалет? | gdye zdyes' tu·al·*yet* | |

## Shopping & Services

| | | |
|---|---|---|
| **I'd like ...** | | |
| Я бы хотел/ хотела ... (m/f) | ya bi khat·*yel*/ khat·ye·la ... | |
| **How much is it?** | | |
| Сколько стоит? | *skol'*·ka *sto*·eet | |
| **That's too expensive.** | | |
| Это очень дорого. | e·ta o·*cheen'* *do*·ra·ga | |

| | | |
|---|---|---|
| **bank** | банк | bank |
| **market** | рынок | *ri*·nak |
| **post office** | почта | *poch*·ta |
| **tourist office** | туристическое бюро | tu·rees·*tee*· chee·ska·ye byu·*ro* |

## Transport

| | | |
|---|---|---|
| **boat** | параход | pa·ra·*khot* |
| **bus** | автобус | af·*to*·bus |
| **plane** | самолёт | sa·mal·*yot* |
| **train** | поезд | po·*yeest* |

| | | |
|---|---|---|
| **One ... ticket (to Novgorod), please.** | Билет ... (на Новгород). | beel·*yet* ... (na *nov*·ga·rat) |
| one-way | в один конец | v a·*deen* kan·*yets* |
| return | в оба конца | v o·ba kant·sa |

# SLOVAK

An accent mark over a vowel in written Slovak indicates it's pronounced as a long sound. Note that air is pronounced as in 'hair', aw as in 'law', oh as the 'o' in 'note', ow as in 'how', uh as the 'a' in 'ago', dz as the 'ds' in 'adds', kh as the 'ch' in the Scottish loch, and zh as the 's' in 'pleasure'. The apostrophe ( ' ) indicates a slight y sound.

## Basics

| | | |
|---|---|---|
| **Hello.** | *Dobrý deň.* | do·bree dyen' |
| **Goodbye.** | *Do videnia.* | do *vi*·dye·ni·yuh |
| **Excuse me.** | *Prepáčte.* | pre·pach·tye |
| **Sorry.** | *Prepáčte.* | pre·pach·tye |
| **Please.** | *Prosím.* | pro·seem |
| **Thank you.** | *Ďakujem* | dyuh·ku·yem |
| **Yes.** | *Áno.* | a·no |
| **No.** | *Nie.* | ni·ye |

| | | |
|---|---|---|
| **What's your name?** | | |
| *Ako sa voláte?* | uh·ko suh vo·la·tye | |
| **My name is ...** | | |
| *Volám sa ...* | vo·lam suh ... | |
| **Do you speak English?** | | |
| *Hovoríte po anglicky?* | ho·vo·ree·tye po uhng·lits·ki | |
| **I don't understand.** | | |
| *Nerozumiem.* | nye·ro·zu·myem | |

## Accommodation

| | | |
|---|---|---|
| **campsite** | *táborisko* | ta·bo·ris·ko |
| **guesthouse** | *penzión* | pen·zi·awn |
| **hotel** | *hotel* | ho·tel |
| **youth hostel** | *nocľaháreň pre mládež* | nots·lyuh·ha·ren' pre mla·dyezh |

| | | |
|---|---|---|
| **Do you have a single room?** | | |
| *Máte jedno- posteľovú izbu?* | ma·tye yed·no- pos·tye·lyo·voo iz·bu | |
| **Do you have a double room?** | | |
| *Máte izbu s manželskou posteľou?* | ma·tye iz·bu s muhn·zhels·koh pos·tye·lyoh | |
| **How much is it per ...?** | | |
| *Koľko to stojí na noc/osobu?* | kol'·ko to sto·yee nuh nots/o·so·bu | |

## Eating & Drinking

| | | |
|---|---|---|
| **What would you recommend?** | | |
| *Čo by ste mi odporučili?* | cho bi stye mi od·po·ru·chi·li | |
| **Do you have vegetarian food?** | | |
| *Máte vegetariánske jedlá?* | ma·tye ve·ge·tuh·ri·yan·ske yed·la | |

| | | |
|---|---|---|
| **I'll have ...** | *Dám si ...* | dam si ... |
| **Cheers!** | *Nazdravie!* | nuhz·druh·vi·ye |
| **I'd like the ..., please.** | *Prosím si ...* | pro·seem si ... |
| bill | *účet* | oo·chet |

### Numbers – Slovak

| 1 | jeden | ye·den |
|---|-------|--------|
| 2 | dva | dvuh |
| 3 | tri | tri |
| 4 | štyri | shti·ri |
| 5 | päť | pet' |
| 6 | šesť | shest' |
| 7 | sedem | se·dyem |
| 8 | osem | o·sem |
| 9 | deväť | dye·vet' |
| 10 | desať | dye·suht' |

| menu | jedálny lístok | ye·dal·ni lees·tok |
|------|----------------|--------------------|

## Emergencies

| Help! | Pomoc! | po·mots |
|-------|--------|---------|
| Go away! | Choďte preč! | khod'·tye prech |

| Call ...! | Zavolajte ...! | zuh·vo·lai·tye ... |
|-----------|----------------|--------------------|
| a doctor | lekára | le·ka·ruh |
| the police | políciu | po·lee·tsi·yu |

**I'm lost.**
Stratil/Stratila
som sa. (m/f) — struh·tyil/struh·tyi·luh som suh

**I'm ill.**
Som chorý/
chorá. (m/f) — som kho·ree/ kho·ra

**Where are the toilets?**
Kde sú tu záchody? — kdye soo tu za·kho·di

## Shopping & Services

**I'm looking for ...**
Hľadám ... — hlyuh·dam ...

**How much is it?**
Koľko to stojí? — kol'·ko to sto·yee

**That's too expensive.**
To je príliš drahé. — to ye pree·lish druh·hair

| market | trh | trh |
|--------|-----|-----|
| post office | pošta | posh·tuh |
| tourist office | turistická kancelária | tu·ris·tits·ka kuhn·tse·la·ri·yuh |

## Transport

| bus | autobus | ow·to·bus |
|-----|---------|-----------|
| plane | lietadlo | li·ye·tuhd·lo |

| train | vlak | vluhk |
|-------|------|-------|

| One ... ticket (to Poprad), please. | Jeden ... lístok (do Popradu), prosím. | ye·den ... lees·tok (do pop·ruh·du) pro·seem |
|---|---|---|
| one-way | jedno- smerný | yed·no- smer·nee |
| return | spiatočný | spyuh·toch·nee |

# SLOVENE

Note that uh is pronounced as the 'a' in 'ago', oh as the 'o' in 'note', ow as in 'how', zh as the 's' in 'pleasure', r is rolled, and the apostrophe ( ' ) indicates a slight y sound.

## Basics

| Hello. | Zdravo. | zdra·vo |
|--------|---------|---------|
| Goodbye. | Na svidenje. | na svee·den·ye |
| Excuse me. | Dovolite. | do·vo·lee·te |
| Sorry. | Oprostite. | op·ros·tee·te |
| Please. | Prosim. | pro·seem |
| Thank you. | Hvala. | hva·la |
| Yes. | Da. | da |
| No. | Ne. | ne |

**What's your name?**
Kako vam/ti
je ime? (pol/inf) — ka·ko vam/tee ye ee·me

**My name is ...**
Ime mi je ... — ee·me mee ye ...

**Do you speak English?**
Ali govorite
angleško? — a·lee go·vo·ree·te ang·lesh·ko

**I don't understand.**
Ne razumem. — ne ra·zoo·mem

## Accommodation

| campsite | kamp | kamp |
|----------|------|------|
| guesthouse | gostišče | gos·teesh·che |
| hotel | hotel | ho·tel |
| youth hostel | mladinski hotel | mla·deen·skee ho·tel |

**Do you have a single/double room?**
Ali imate
enoposteljno/
dvoposteljno sobo? — a·lee ee·ma·te e·no·pos·tel'·no/ dvo·pos·tel'·no so·bo

**How much is it per night/person?**
Koliko stane na
noč/osebo? — ko·lee·ko sta·ne na noch/o·se·bo

## Eating & Drinking

**What would you recommend?**
*Kaj priporočate?*    kai pree·po·ro·cha·te

**Do you have vegetarian food?**
*Ali imate*    a·lee ee·ma·te
*vegetarijansko hrano?*    ve·ge·ta·ree·yan·sko hra·no

| | | |
|---|---|---|
| **I'll have ...** | *Jaz bom ...* | yaz bom ... |
| **Cheers!** | *Na zdravje!* | na zdrav·ye |

| | | |
|---|---|---|
| **I'd like the ...,** | *Želim ...,* | zhe·leem ... |
| **please.** | *prosim.* | pro·seem |
| bill | *račun* | ra·choon |
| menu | *jedilni list* | ye·deel·nee leest |

## Emergencies

**Help!**    *Na pomoč!*    na po·moch
**Go away!**    *Pojdite stran!*    poy·dee·te stran

**Call the doctor/police!**
*Pokličite zdravnika/*    pok·lee·chee·te zdrav·nee·ka
*policijo!*    po·lee·tsee·yo

**I'm lost.**
*Izgubil/*    eez·goo·beew/
*Izgubila sem se.* (m/f)    eez·goo·bee·la sem se

**I'm ill.**
*Bolan/Bolna sem.* (m/f)    bo·lan/boh·na sem

**Where are the toilets?**
*Kje je stranišče?*    kye ye stra·neesh·che

## Shopping & Services

**I'm looking for ...**
*Iščem ...*    eesh·chem ...

**How much is this?**
*Koliko stane?*    ko·lee·ko sta·ne

**That's too expensive.**
*To je predrago.*    to ye pre·dra·go

| | | |
|---|---|---|
| market | *tržnica* | tuhrzh·nee·tsa |

### WANT MORE?

For in-depth language information and handy phrases, check out Lonely Planet's *Eastern Europe Phrasebook*. You'll find it at **shop.lonelyplanet.com**, or you can buy Lonely Planet's iPhone phrasebooks at the Apple App Store.

## Numbers – Slovene

| | | |
|---|---|---|
| 1 | *en* | en |
| 2 | *dva* | dva |
| 3 | *trije* | tree·ye |
| 4 | *štirje* | shtee·rye |
| 5 | *pet* | pet |
| 6 | *šest* | shest |
| 7 | *sedem* | se·dem |
| 8 | *osem* | o·sem |
| 9 | *devet* | de·vet |
| 10 | *deset* | de·set |

| | | |
|---|---|---|
| **post office** | *pošta* | posh·taw |
| **tourist office** | *turistični urad* | too·rees·teech·nee oo·rad |

## Transport

| | | |
|---|---|---|
| **boat** | *ladja* | lad·ya |
| **bus** | *avtobus* | av·to·boos |
| **plane** | *letalo* | le·ta·lo |
| **train** | *vlak* | vlak |

| | | |
|---|---|---|
| **One ... ticket to (Koper), please.** | *... vozovnico do (Kopra), prosim.* | ... vo·zov·nee·tso do (ko·pra) pro·seem |
| one-way | *Enosmerno* | e·no·smer·no |
| return | *Povratno* | pov·rat·no |

# UKRAINIAN

Vowels in unstressed syllables are generally pronounced shorter and weaker than they are in stressed syllables. Note that kh is pronounced as the 'ch' in the Scottish *loch* and zh as the 's' in 'pleasure'. The apostrophe ( ' ) indicates a slight y sound.

## Basics

| | | |
|---|---|---|
| **Hello.** | Добрий день. | do·bry den' |
| **Goodbye.** | До побачення. | do po·ba·chen·nya |
| **Excuse me.** | Вибачте. | vy·bach·te |
| **Sorry.** | Перепрошую. | pe·re·pro·shu·yu |
| **Please.** | Прошу. | pro·shu |
| **Thank you.** | Дякую. | dya·ku·yu |
| **Yes.** | Так. | tak |
| **No.** | Ні. | ni |

**What's your name?**

Як вас звати? | yak vas zva·ty

**My name is ...**
Мене звати … | me·*ne* zva·ti …

**Do you speak English?**
Ви розмовляєте | vy roz·mow·*lya*·ye·te
англійською | an·*hliys'*·ko·yu
мовою? | *mo*·vo·yu

**I don't understand.**
Я не розумію. | ya ne ro·zu·*mi*·yu

## Accommodation

| | | |
|---|---|---|
| **campsite** | кемпінг | *kem*·pinh |
| **double room** | номер на двох | *no*·mer na dvokh |
| **hotel** | готель | ho·*tel'* |
| **single room** | номер на одного | *no*·mer na o·dno·ho |
| **youth hostel** | молодіжний гуртожиток | mo·lo·*dizh*·ni hur·*to*·zhi·tok |

**Do you have any rooms available?**
У вас є вільні номери? | u vas ye *vil'*·ni no·me·*ri*

**How much is it per night/person?**
Скільки коштує | *skil'*·ky ko·shtu·ye
номер за ніч/особу? | *no*·mer za nich/o·so·bu

## Eating & Drinking

**What do you recommend?**
Що Ви порадите? | shcho vy po·*ra*·dy·te

**I'm a vegetarian.**
Я вегетаріанець/ | ya ve·he·ta·ri·a·nets'/
вегетаріанка. (m/f) | ve·he·ta·ri·*an*·ka

| | | |
|---|---|---|
| **Cheers!** | Будьмо! | *bud'*·mo |
| **I'd like ...** | Я візьму … | ya viz'·*mu* … |
| **bill** | рахунок | ra·*khu*·nok |
| **menu** | меню | me·*nyu* |

## Emergencies

**Help!**
Допоможіть! | do·po·mo·*zhit'*

**Go away!**
Іди/Ідіть звідси! (pol/inf) | i·*di*/i·*dit'* zvid·si

**Call the doctor/police!**
Викличте лікаря/ | *vi*·klich·te *li*·ka·rya/
міліцію! | mi·*li*·tsi·yu

**I'm lost.**
Я заблукав/ | ya za·blu·*kaw*/
заблукала. (m/f) | za·blu·*ka*·la

## Numbers – Ukrainian

| 1 | один | o·*din* |
|---|---|---|
| 2 | два | dva |
| 3 | три | tri |
| 4 | чотири | cho·*ti*·ri |
| 5 | п'ять | pyat' |
| 6 | шість | shist' |
| 7 | сім | sim |
| 8 | вісім | *vi*·sim |
| 9 | дев'ять | de·vyat' |
| 10 | десять | de·syat' |

**I'm ill.**
Мені погано. | me·*ni* po·*ha*·no

**Where's the toilet?**
Де туалети? | de tu·a·le·ti

## Shopping & Services

**I'd like to buy ...**
Я б хотів/хотіла | ya b kho·*tiw*/kho·*ti*·la
купити … (m/f) | ku·*pi*·ti …

**How much is this?**
Скільки це він/вона | *skil'*·ki tse vin/vo·*na*
коштує? (m/f) | ko·shtu·ye?

**That's too expensive.**
Це надто дорого. | tse *nad*·to *do*·ro·ho

| | | |
|---|---|---|
| **ATM** | банкомат | ban·ko·*mat* |
| **market** | ринок | *ri*·nok |
| **post office** | пошта | *po*·shta |
| **tourist office** | туристичне бюро | tu·ri·*stich*·ne byu·*ro* |

## Transport

**I want to go to ...**
Мені треба їхати | me·*ni* tre·ba yi·kha·ti
до … | do …

| | | |
|---|---|---|
| **bus** | автобус | aw·*to*·bus |
| **one-way ticket** | квиток в один бік | kvi·*tok* v o·*din* bik |
| **plane** | літак | li·*tak* |
| **return ticket** | зворотний квиток | zvo·*ro*·tni kvi·*tok* |
| **train** | поїзд | *po*·yizd |

# Behind the Scenes

## SEND US YOUR FEEDBACK

We love to hear from travellers – your comments keep us on our toes and help make our books better. Our well-travelled team reads every word on what you loved or loathed about this book. Although we cannot reply individually to your submissions, we always guarantee that your feedback goes straight to the appropriate authors, in time for the next edition. Each person who sends us information is thanked in the next edition – the most useful submissions are rewarded with a selection of digital PDF chapters.

Visit **lonelyplanet.com/contact** to submit your updates and suggestions or to ask for help. Our award-winning website also features inspirational travel stories, news and discussions.

Note: We may edit, reproduce and incorporate your comments in Lonely Planet products such as guidebooks, websites and digital products, so let us know if you don't want your comments reproduced or your name acknowledged. For a copy of our privacy policy visit lonelyplanet.com/privacy.

## OUR READERS

**Many thanks to the travellers who used the last edition and wrote to us with helpful hints, useful advice and interesting anecdotes:** Julie Cowan, Peter Stumvoll, Ramadan Besim, Sandra Buchanan, Simone Mollard

## WRITER THANKS

### Greg Bloom

Big thanks to pop for tagging along and lending anecdotes, insight and much bar research. To Callie, who couldn't wait until after my deadline to arrive: you were so worth the sleepless nights. To her mama, Windi, T.Y. for keeping it together while I was away. To Callie's sister, Anna, thanks always for keeping me sane.  On the road, thanks to Nikolai (Minsk) and Leonid (Chişinău), and to Mike T and Fabian M, respectively, for setting me up with them.

### Mark Elliott

Countless kind Bosnians (and Hercegovinians, too) offered more help than I have space to acknowledge. Enormous thanks to the great philosophers at Savat, to Kate Hunt for so much emotion, Wangdi for the space and sustenance, and to Harriet Einsiedel, Izzy and Shashka for the amazing coincidences. Love and endless gratitude beyond words to my unbeatable family.

### Anita Isalska

My research in Slovakia was hugely enriched by the people I met on the road. I'm especially thankful for the tips and insights from Slavo Stankovič, Marek Leskovjanský, Erik Ševčík, Jiri Sikora, the incredibly helpful tourist office teams in Bratislava, Žilina and Martin, and pretty much everyone in friendly Košice. Big hugs to Normal Matt for being an invaluable write-up morale-booster.

### Tom Masters

Many thanks to Valmir, Emin, Esra, Granit, Shemsi and Lorik in Pristina, to Shpendi, Joard, Mateo, Renato and Rita in Tirana, and to dozens of hostel owners around both countries who supplied such helpful information, especially to Walter in Gjirokastra, Catherine in Valbona, Roza in Shkodra, and the crews at Driza's House in Prizren, Tirana Backpacker's Hostel in Tirana and Hostel Saraç in Peja. Special thanks also to Jimmy in Theth for being a good Samaritan when I had car trouble!

### Lorna Parkes

A huge thank you to the friendly people of Macedonia who helped guide me through bad signposting, lost trail markers, GPS black holes and the basics of Cyrillic. Your warmth and good nature is a testament to your country. Equal thanks go to my husband, Rob, without whom I would not have been able to do this job, both mentally and physically, and my beautiful son, Austin, who patiently waited for my return.

### Leonid Ragozin

Huge thanks to Olexiy Skrypnik, Serhiy Savchuk and Yevhen Stepanenko for helping me to explore Lviv. Another jumbo plane of gratitude goes to Lena Lebedinskaya, Ruslan Popkov and their wonderful friends in Odesa. Finally, thank you, Masha Makeeva, for enduring my long absences.

### Tamara Sheward

Every time I go to Serbia, the *hvala* list gets outrageously longer; if I keep this up, I'll be trying to cram 7.13 million names into this tiny space. To whittle down the numbers somewhat, I'll offer my undying gratitude to the Lučić and Eremić families, Srdjan (the lifesaver) and Gordana, the NS Kitchen Collective, the wonderful folks of Šekspirova, and Brana Vladisavljevic at LP. My Dušan and Masha, may 10000 *trubači* bands forever toot in your honour: *poljupci zauvek!*

## ACKNOWLEDGEMENTS

Climate map data adapted from Peel MC, Finlayson BL & McMahon TA (2007) 'Updated World Map of the Köppen-Geiger Climate Classification', *Hydrology and Earth System Sciences*, 11, 163344.

Cover photograph: Fresco, Rila Monastery, Bulgaria. Walter Bibikow / AWL ©

BEHIND THE SCENES

## THIS BOOK

This 14th edition of Lonely Planet's *Eastern Europe* guidebook was curated by Mark Baker, Greg Bloom, Peter Dragicevich, Marc Di Duca, Anita Isalska, Tom Masters, Hugh McNaughton, Lorna Parkes, Leonid Ragozin, Tim Richards, Simon Richmond, Tamara Sheward and Anna Tyler. This guidebook was produced by the following:

**Destination Editors** Gemma Graham, Lauren Keith, Anna Tyler, Branislava Vladisavljevic
**Product Editors** Anne Mason, Jenna Myers

**Senior Cartographer** Mark Griffiths
**Book Designer** Mazzy Prinsep
**Assisting Editors** Janet Austin, Sarah Bailey, Michelle Bennett, Kate Chapman, Katie Connolly, Melanie Dankel, Bruce Evans, Sam Forge, Carly Hall, Trent Holden, Kate James, Amy Karafin, Kellie Langdon, Jodie Martire, Anne Mulvaney, Rosie Nicholson, Lauren O'Connell, Kristin Odijk, Charlotte Orr, Monique Perrin, Sarah Reid, Gabbi Stefanos, Saralinda Turner, Fionnuala Twomey

**Assisting Cartographer** Valentina Kremenchutskaya
**Cover Researcher** Naomi Parker
**Thanks to** Cheree Broughton, Jennifer Carey, David Carroll, Kate Chapman, Neill Coen, Daniel Corbett, Joel Cotterell, Shona Gray, Jane Grisman, Andi Jones, Ivan Kovanovic, Borbála Molnár-Ellis, Catherine Naghten, Claire Naylor, Karyn Noble, Bridget Nurre Jennions,, Martine Power, Rachel Rawling, Kirsten Rawlings, Kathryn Rowan, Ellie Simpson, Tony Wheeler, Dora Whitaker

# Index

NOTES

# Map Legend

## Sights

- Beach
- Bird Sanctuary
- Buddhist
- Castle/Palace
- Christian
- Confucian
- Hindu
- Islamic
- Jain
- Jewish
- Monument
- Museum/Gallery/Historic Building
- Ruin
- Shinto
- Sikh
- Taoist
- Winery/Vineyard
- Zoo/Wildlife Sanctuary
- Other Sight

## Activities, Courses & Tours

- Bodysurfing
- Diving
- Canoeing/Kayaking
- Course/Tour
- Sento Hot Baths/Onsen
- Skiing
- Snorkelling
- Surfing
- Swimming/Pool
- Walking
- Windsurfing
- Other Activity

## Sleeping

- Sleeping
- Camping

## Eating

- Eating

## Drinking & Nightlife

- Drinking & Nightlife
- Cafe

## Entertainment

- Entertainment

## Shopping

- Shopping

## Information

- Bank
- Embassy/Consulate
- Hospital/Medical
- Internet
- Police
- Post Office
- Telephone
- Toilet
- Tourist Information
- Other Information

## Geographic

- Beach
- Gate
- Hut/Shelter
- Lighthouse
- Lookout
- Mountain/Volcano
- Oasis
- Park
- Pass
- Picnic Area
- Waterfall

## Population

- Capital (National)
- Capital (State/Province)
- City/Large Town
- Town/Village

## Transport

- Airport
- Border crossing
- Bus
- Cable car/Funicular
- Cycling
- Ferry
- Metro station
- Monorail
- Parking
- Petrol station
- S-Bahn/Subway station
- Taxi
- T-bane/Tunnelbana station
- Train station/Railway
- Tram
- Tube station
- U-Bahn/Underground station
- Other Transport

*Note: Not all symbols displayed above appear on the maps in this book*

## Routes

- Tollway
- Freeway
- Primary
- Secondary
- Tertiary
- Lane
- Unsealed road
- Road under construction
- Plaza/Mall
- Steps
- Tunnel
- Pedestrian overpass
- Walking Tour
- Walking Tour detour
- Path/Walking Trail

## Boundaries

- International
- State/Province
- Disputed
- Regional/Suburb
- Marine Park
- Cliff
- Wall

## Hydrography

- River, Creek
- Intermittent River
- Canal
- Water
- Dry/Salt/Intermittent Lake
- Reef

## Areas

- Airport/Runway
- Beach/Desert
- Cemetery (Christian)
- Cemetery (Other)
- Glacier
- Mudflat
- Park/Forest
- Sight (Building)
- Sportsground
- Swamp/Mangrove

### Tim Richards

Poland Tim is a travel writer whose work has appeared in a variety of newspapers, magazines and websites. He also researches and writes guidebooks for Lonely Planet. Tim lived in Egypt for two years, and Poland for a year, while teaching English as a foreign language in the mid-1990s. Nowadays he lives in the city centre of Melbourne, Australia, with his wife, Narrelle Harris.

### Simon Richmond

Journalist and photographer Simon Richmond has specialised as a travel writer since the early 1990s and first worked for Lonely Planet in 1999 on their Central Asia guide. He's long since stopped counting the number of guidebooks he's researched and written for the company, but countries covered including Australia, China, India, Iran, Japan, Korea, Malaysia, Mongolia, Myanmar (Burma), Russia, Singapore, South Africa and Turkey. For Lonely Planet's website he's penned features on topics from the world's best swimming pools to the joys of Urban Sketching - follow him on Instagram to see some of his photos and sketches. Simon contributed to the Plan and Survival Guide chapters

### Tamara Sheward

Montenegro & Serbia After years of freelance travel writing, rock'n'roll journalism and insalubrious authordom, Tamara leapt at the chance to join the Lonely Planet ranks in 2009. Since then, she's worked on guides to an incongruous jumble of countries including Montenegro, Australia, Serbia, Russia, the Samoas, Bulgaria and Fiji. She's written a miscellany of travel articles for the BBC, *The Independent*, *Sydney Morning Herald* et al; she's also fronted the camera as a documentary presenter for Lonely Planet TV, Nat Geo and Al-Jazeera. Tamara's based in far northern Australia, but you're more likely to find her roaming elsewhere, tattered notebook in one hand, the world's best-travelled toddler in the other.

## Contributing Writers & Researchers

**Carolyn Bain** (Iceland & Slovenia)
**Steve Fallon** (Hungary, Slovenia & Romania)
**Anna Kaminksi** (Hungary)
**Anja Mutić** (Croatia)
**Andy Symington** (Estonia, Latvia & Lithuania)
**Neil Wilson** (Czech Republic)

### Mark Elliott

Bosnia & Hercegovina Having already lived and worked on five continents, Mark started writing travel guides in the pre-Internet dark ages. His first work, *Asia Overland*, was a ludicrously over-ambitious opus covering a whole continent and designed to aid impecunious English teachers make the trip home to Europe from Japan with a minimal budget. It was one of the first guides to help backpackers across the then-new states of the former USSR. Elliott has since written, or co-written, around 60 other travel books, while acting as a travel consultant, occasional tour leader, video presenter, interviewer and blues harmonicist.

### Anita Isalska

Bulgaria, Hungary, Romania & Slovakia Anita is a travel journalist, editor and copywriter whose work for Lonely Planet has taken her from Greek beach towns to Malaysian jungles, and plenty of places in between. After several merry years as an in-house editor and writer – with a few of them in Lonely Planet's London office – Anita now works freelance between the UK, Australia and any Balkan guesthouse with a good wi-fi connection. Anita writes about travel, food and culture for a host of websites and magazines. Read her stuff on www.anita-isalska.com.

### Tom Masters

Albania & Kosovo Dreaming since he could walk of going to the most obscure places on earth, Tom has always had a taste for the unknown. This has led to a writing career that has taken him all over the world, including North Korea, the Arctic, Congo and Siberia. Despite a brief spell living in the English countryside, Tom has always called London, Paris and Berlin home. He currently lives in Berlin and can be found online at www.tommasters.net.

### Hugh McNaughtan

Lithuania A former English lecturer, Hugh swapped grant applications for visa applications, and turned his love of travel intro a full-time thing. A longtime castle tragic with an abiding love of Britain's Celtic extremities, he jumped at the chance to explore Wales, from the Cambrian Mountains to the tip of Anglesey. He's never happier than when on the road with his two daughters. Except perhaps on the cricket field....

### Lorna Parkes

Macedonia Londoner by birth, Melburnian by palate and ex-Lonely Planet staffer in both cities, Lorna has spent more than 10 years exploring the globe in search of the perfect meal, the friendliest B&B, the best-value travel experience, and the most spectacular lookout point – both for her own pleasure and other people's. She's discovered she writes best on planes, and has contributed to numerous Lonely Planet books and magazines. Wineries and the tropics (not at the same time!) are her go-to happy places. Follow her @Lorna_Explorer.

### Leonid Ragozin

Latvia, Russia & Ukraine Leonid studied beach dynamics at the Moscow State University, but for want of decent beaches in Russia, he switched to journalism and spent 12 years voyaging through different parts of the BBC, with a break for a four-year stint as a foreign correspondent for the Russian *Newsweek*. Leonid is currently a freelance journalist focusing largely on the conflict between Russia and Ukraine (both his Lonely Planet destinations), which prompted him to leave Moscow and find a new home in Rīga.

# OUR STORY

A beat-up old car, a few dollars in the pocket and a sense of adventure. In 1972 that's all Tony and Maureen Wheeler needed for the trip of a lifetime – across Europe and Asia overland to Australia. It took several months, and at the end – broke but inspired – they sat at their kitchen table writing and stapling together their first travel guide, *Across Asia on the Cheap*. Within a week they'd sold 1500 copies. Lonely Planet was born.

Today, Lonely Planet has offices in Franklin, London, Melbourne, Oakland, Dublin, Beijing and Delhi, with more than 600 staff and writers. We share Tony's belief that 'a great guidebook should do three things: inform, educate and amuse'.

# OUR WRITERS

### Mark Baker

Bulgaria, Czech Republic, Romania & Slovenia  Mark is a freelance travel writer with a penchant for offbeat stories and forgotten places. He's originally from the United States, but now makes his home in the Czech capital, Prague. He writes mainly on Eastern and Central Europe for Lonely Planet as well as other leading travel publishers, but finds real satisfaction in digging up stories in places that are too remote or quirky for the guides. Prior to becoming an author, he worked as a journalist for *The Economist*, Bloomberg News and Radio Free Europe, among other organisations. Instagram: @markbakerprague Twitter: @markbakerprague

### Greg Bloom

Belarus & Moldova  Greg is a freelance writer, tour operator and travel planner based out of Siem Reap, Cambodia, and Manila, Philippines. Greg began his writing career in the late '90s in Ukraine, working as a journalist and later editor-in-chief of the *Kyiv Post*, an English-language weekly. As a freelance travel writer, he has contributed to some 35 Lonely Planet titles, mostly in Eastern Europe and Asia. In addition to writing, he now organises adventure trips in Cambodia and Palawan (Philippines) through his tour company, Bearcat Travel.

### Marc Di Duca

Croatia, Poland & Ukraine  A travel author for the last decade, Marc has worked for Lonely Planet in Siberia, Slovakia, Bavaria, England, Ukraine, Austria, Poland, Croatia, Portugal, Madeira and on the Trans-Siberian Railway, as well as writing and updating tens of other guides for other publishers. When not on the road, Marc lives between Sandwich, Kent and Mariánské Lázně in the Czech Republic with his wife and two sons.

### Peter Dragicevich

Croatia & Estonia  After a successful career in niche newspaper and magazine publishing, both in his native New Zealand and in Australia, Peter finally gave into Kiwi wanderlust, giving up staff jobs to chase his diverse roots around much of Europe. Over the last decade he's written literally dozens of guidebooks for Lonely Planet on an oddly disparate collection of countries, all of which he's come to love. He once again calls Auckland, New Zealand his home – although his current nomadic existence means he's often elsewhere.

**by Lonely Planet Global Limited**

October 2017
57 145 8
t 2017  Photographs © as indicated 2017
4 3 2 1